WHAT PREDICTS DIVORCE?
The Relationship Between
Marital Processes and Marital Outcomes

WHAT PREDICTS DIVORCE?
The Relationship Between Marital Processes and Marital Outcomes

John Mordechai Gottman
University of Washington

LEA LAWRENCE ERLBAUM ASSOCIATES, PUBLISHERS
1994   Hillsdale, New Jersey   Hove and London

12/2000

Lawrence Erlbaum Associates, Inc., Publishers
365 Broadway
Hillsdale, New Jersey 07642

 # 27896807

A AK - 2981

Library of Congress Cataloging in Publication Data

Gottman, John Mordechai.
    What predicts divorce? : the relationship between marital
processes and marital outcomes / John Mordechai Gottman.
        p. cm.
    Includes bibliographical references and index.
    ISBN 0-8058-1285-7 (cloth) ISBN 0-8058-1402-7 (paper)   **55.00**
    1. Marriage — Psychological aspects. 2. Married people —
Psychology. 3. Divorce — Psychological aspects. I. Title.
    HQ734.G7137   1993
    306.81 — dc20   93-12547
                                                          CIP

Books published by Lawrence Erlbaum Associates are printed
on acid-free paper, and their bindings are chosen for strength
and durability.

Printed in the United States of America
10 9 8 7 6 5

Dedicated to

the true wife of my spirit,
Julie Schwartz Gottman

And For

all women and men
who seek love and a home

Contents

Preface

When I was a young clinical psychology intern at the University of Colorado Medical Center, I did some supervised therapy with married couples. I found it to be fast-paced, exciting, and dynamic. I had no real idea of what I was doing, but I thought that perhaps I had some intuition in this area. I recall that I made one suggestion to a supervisor that we video-tape a couple attempting to resolve an issue unrelated to their marital problems so that we could better assess their strengths and weaknesses. My supervisor thought this was not a good idea and would not permit it, but I resolved to try this idea once I was a professor doing my own unsupervised therapy. As a beginning assistant professor, once I had my first case I suggested the idea to a couple who was unable to resolve their own conflicts. I told the couple that I had never done this before, but they were quite willing to try it. I made three tapes of them, two in my new laboratory. One tape was a videotape of them working on a standard group decision-making task called the NASA moon shot problem. The task was to decide by consensus how to rank order a set of items for their survival value for a life and death trip on the moon to a rendezvous point with the Mother ship. The second tape was a discussion of a major issue in their marriage. The third tape also was a discussion of this issue I asked them to have at home, with no one else present.

I was amazed by these tapes. The couple was a superb team when they worked on the Moon shot problem. They had a lot of fun; they laughed, were affectionate, and were cooperative. They got very high scores on the problem and their group processes were admirable. However, once they began working on their own marital problems, the picture changed. They pouted, sulked, and whined, and became stubborn, angry, hurt, and bitter. At home things were even worse.

They replayed the same scenario with one modification. They repeatedly cycled over the same issues each time, and just when it looked like they were about to reach a solution, one of them seemed to sabotage the process; finally, the tape ended with them in despair and exhaustion. I listened to and watched these tapes over and over again, and then I listened to and watched them with the couple. I asked them to tell me what they were thinking and feeling at certain moments that I thought were critical moments or moments that were puzzling to me.

That was 20 years ago. I puzzled about what to look for in these interactions. I had my own ideas, but being a young scholar I decided that others before me must have investigated these things thoroughly already. So I went to the Indiana University library and looked up the word "marriage" in the card catalogue, took the elevator up to the right section of the stacks, and sat down on the floor to have a look at the books and journals. I was surprised that we had not read this literature in graduate school, but it was a sociological literature and we were psychologists. Marriage was not considered a proper subject for psychologists to study then (only this year has the American Psychological Association begun publishing a journal on Family Psychology). I was amazed at how much research had been done on the subject already. The research was fascinating, but none of it was very useful for helping me look at my tapes. After a few weeks of reading, I realized with delight that I was sailing in uncharted waters.

I searched out the literature on allied disciplines, nonverbal behavior, social psychology, behavior exchange theory, group process research, observational research in classrooms and families, and so on. Several students joined me at this time, two of whom were persistent and very gifted—Howard Markman and Cliff Notarius. Over a period of several years, we developed an observational coding system—the Couples Interaction Scoring System. I had lunch with a postdoc, Bill Mead, and I described an idea for having couples continuously tell me what they were thinking and feeling as they interacted. He suggested that I build an apparatus for couples to do this. In the wonderful Indiana University psychology shop, Gus Abbott and John Waltke built the first "talk table" entirely out of surplus materials they had on hand. Then we began recruiting couples for our first study.

In those early years, I followed a research methodology broadly outlined by my thesis advisor at the University of Wisconsin, Richard McFall. McFall suggested that clinical researchers be ethologists like Von Frisch who studied bees. These researchers should observe the variability in natural behavior objectively. McFall suggested that the trick lay in defining the situations to be studied and finding "competent populations" similar to the clinical populations of interest. Much of this methodology remained to be worked out. That was easy in the area of marriage. In fact, much of the measurement work for defining couples that were satisfied or dissatisfied with their marriages already had been done.

I wrote my first research grant and it was funded. It turned out to be a grant I have had renewed continuously for the past 20 years. When we got our first results, we were amazed that the results actually were statistically significant. It was even more amazing that the results were replicated in Mary Ellen Rubin's masters thesis, and the group means on this study with an entirely different population were the same as those of the first study, often up to the second decimal place. It was an exciting time. An extraordinarily creative and productive research group in Oregon, including Gerald Patterson, Marion Forgatch, Hyman Hops, Robert Weiss, John Vincent, Gary Birchler, and Gayla Margolin, was working on the same problem. At the University of North Carolina, a young man named Neil Jacobson also began working energetically on the problem.

My students and I also were working on the methodological problems of detecting sequencings in observations of interactions using Markov matrix methods when, in 1974, Harold Raush came to Indiana University and I was selected to be his host. I picked him up at the airport and talked to him for a little while before taking him to his hotel. He had a copy of his forthcoming book with him. He graciously let me borrow it, and we scheduled a breakfast the next morning before his afternoon talk. I stayed up all night and read the book cover to cover. I was electrified with excitement. Raush not only had thought of analyzing the sequences of interaction in couples discussions, but he actually had done it. The next morning we had a wonderful talk. We walked all over campus talking about his groundbreaking research and thinking about the processes of communication. My students met him and also were fascinated by his work. Later he agreed to let us listen to his research tapes and to recode them with our new observational system. Mary Ellen Rubin's dissertation emerged from this effort, a direct result of applying McFall's ideas and our new observational system to the Raush project.

Soon after this, Jim Sackett, a former professor of mine at the University of Wisconsin, invited me to a large conference he held on observational research at Lake Wilderness in Washington. Sackett already had written two papers (as yet unpublished) on his new approach to sequential analysis, called "lag sequential analysis," one much less unwieldy and considerably more flexible for exploration than the information theory approach Raush had used. Sackett paired me and Roger Bakeman as roommates during this conference, which was to begin a rewarding lifelong association. I remember being very excited by this conference. Everyone had to write their papers before the conference and distribute them, and they actually did this. I took an Amtrak train from Chicago to Seattle and rented a sleeper. During the long, beautiful ride across this magnificent country, I read every one of the papers, about 800 pages of manuscripts. I returned from Lake Wilderness realizing that Sackett had made a major breakthrough in sequential analysis, and that I could apply his methods to my data. I realized that I also could apply my knowledge of time-series analysis to the problem of detecting patterns in interaction. All of this worked very well.

This led to my first monograph on marriage, called *Marital Interaction: Experimental Investigations*. The book generated considerable interest. Among the interested people was Caas Schapp, a young researcher from Holland who wrote a wonderful monograph attempting to replicate many of my results. Also, a group of very talented researchers from the Max Planck Institute began working in the area. Dirk Revenstorf and Kurt Hahlweg began applying their considerable talents to the problems of analyzing patterns in marital interaction.

After publishing this book, I sent a copy to Paul Ekman, who wrote back and said that he liked the book very much, but that it was a shame that I did not know very much about emotion. This began a long series of very long letters. Eventually I accepted his invitation to visit his lab and to bring some videotapes of couples along with me. I sat between Ekman and Wallace Friesen as they watched my tapes and examined them at key points in slow motion. This had to be done with a deft motion of two hands swiveling the reels of tapes across the video heads. They pointed out the facial expressions of contempt, anger and sadness. I did not see any of these fleeting expressions. With great excitement, I had to admit that I really knew nothing about observing emotion in faces, and I left committed to learning their new Facial Action Coding System (FACS).

I learned to use the FACS, and it opened up a new world in seeing emotion. However, as I tried to apply the FACS to my tapes, I realized that I would have to design a more global and less detailed system that captured emotional information from channels other than the face, voice, language, body, and context. From this effort, I designed the first draft of the Specific Affect Coding System (SPAFF) and the Rapid Couples Interaction Scoring System (RCISS).

My colleague and best friend, Bob Levenson, and I began talking about a collaborative research project focusing on all channels of emotion within an interactional context. We would collect the same standard videotapes that I always had collected, but synchronize this with physiological measures. Instead of the talk table, we also decided to use a rating dial that he had employed in his lab to have couples rate their own emotions while watching the videotape. We collected video and physiological data while they watched the tape and made the ratings. It was great designing this study with Bob, because the only hypothesis we had was one generated by Kaplan, Burch, and Bloom (1964), in which they found physiological linkage between people only when they disliked one another. This was in contrast to the therapy literature, which had used synchronous physiological reactions between patient and therapist as an index of empathy. We decided to collect the data base and then see what hypotheses emerged later. The initial data turned out to be quite astounding. Physiological linkage accounted for enormous portions of the variance in marital satisfaction, in the same way Kaplan et al. (1964) had expected. Change in marital satisfaction, as yet unstudied, could be accounted for by a kind of heightened and diffuse physiological arousal. Behavior, physiology, and the perception of behavior all were related, and related to longitudinal change in marriages.

So began the major research collaboration of my life. It has been a most productive and pleasurable association. It also has been highly influential on the rest of my own work, leading me to a social psychophysiological approach. This book is one of many products of the first decade and a half of this research collaboration with Levenson. Levenson read early drafts of this book, and all his comments have been incorporated. Due mostly to my work on the typology of marriage and his burgeoning research on emotion, he preferred not to be a co-author on this book. As sad as I was not to work with Levenson on this book, it has left me entirely free to give the book my own peculiar stamp, which invariably is tinged with speculations from biology, mathematics, and physics. It also has left me free to make my own mistakes, and to spin out my own attempt at a grand theory. Nonetheless, none of this work would have been possible without Levenson.

I need to acknowledge the assistance and influence of several other people. I have been fortunate to have the assistance and insights of good coders, among them Mary Lynn Fletcher, Gwendolyn Mettetal, Mary Verdier, and, most recently, Kim McCoy, Carol Hooven, Colleen Conroy, Colleen Seto, and David McIntyre. Kim Buehlman made a major contribution to this research by designing the Oral History Coding System (see chapter 15). Regina Rushe made a major contribution with her SPAFF-list methodology when couples are interviewed about their most positively and most negatively rated moments (see chapter 15). Lynn Fainsilber Katz has been a companion and colleague throughout the transition to a social psychophysiology lab, and the DUO86 study would not have occurred without her able guidance. We had to complete this study at the University of Illinois prior to moving to the University of Washington in September 1986.

I need to acknowledge the contributions of my students. Howard Markman, Clifford Notarius, Lowell Krokoff, Lynn Fainsilber Katz, and Regina Rushe have made major contributions to the evolution of my work. Following the inspiration of that brilliant interviewer, Studs Terkel, Lowell Krokoff, and I designed the first draft of the Oral History Interview in 1980, and then Lowell spent a year building the interview with a talented interviewer, Linda Bruene. In 1980, Lowell and I also designed most of the questionnaires used in this research, including those that I later found formed the Distance and Isolation cascade. The Family Research Consortium and the Emotion Consortium have been influential in my thinking, especially the continuing work and thought of Paul Ekman, Mavis Hetherington, and Gerald Patterson.

This work is high tech and I am not, so the work of many engineers has been essential for my research. I already have mentioned Gus Abbott and John Waltke at Indiana University. Eddie Lane designed the video portion of my lab at the University of Illinois, and he and James Long set up my lab at the University of Washington. Long designed the computer-assisted coding stations and their software; the stations were assembled by Al Ross. Levenson agreed to build my first psychophysiology lab at the University of Illinois, and he let me have a copy of his computer program. It is his computer program, called "DUO," that forms the basis of the physiological data and its synchronization with the video time code. The work on the new PC-based psychophysiology lab was conducted at the Instrument Development Lab of the Child Development and Mental Retardation Center (CDMRC), under the direction of Dr. William Moritz. He was ably assisted by Al Ross and Tim Myers. I designed the logic of this new system, and Kathryn Swanson did all the computer programming using ASYST. Ross designed the video portion of my apartment and fixed labs at CDMRC, and designed and built our Affect Wheels for online SPAFF coding. Al Ross has been an extremely able inventor and colleague, amazing for his enthusiasm and his ability to take a crude idea and turn it into a reality. Dr. Michael Guralnick, director of the CDMRC, made space and resources available for the construction of my laboratory, and has been an enormously encouraging colleague and friend. Anup Kumar Roy, Duane Steidinger, and Gary Swift at Illinois, and Kathryn Swanson at Washington were programmers in my lab who greatly assisted our work. Don Goldstein helped with the analysis of the RCISS data. Esther Williams and I wrote our time-series programs under the guidance of mathematician James Ringland. I also want to acknowledge the teaching and guidance I received in time-series analysis from Professor Robert

Bohrer and James Ringland at the University of Illinois during my year as a faculty scholar studying in a second discipline in the mathematics department.

My two colleagues and postdocs, Sybil Carrere and Lauren Bush, helped with the apartment lab, the selection of equipment, the design of computer algorithms, and with the many technical problems we have had to work out in making a transition from DUO to our new program, DUET.

I wish to acknowledge the training I received in psychophysiology from Dr. John Cacioppo's NSF summer training program. It was excellent. I also wish to acknowledge the informal tutoring in psychophysiology I received from Levenson, and from the walks, talks, and readings that Steven Porges was kind enough to provide when we were colleagues at Illinois.

Discussions with my wife, Julie Schwartz Gottman, who is a clinical psychologist, have been very influential; she is an insightful psychologist and a keen observer. This book is dedicated to her, not only for her insights into martial interaction, but also because it is delightful to be married to her.

I want to thank my very talented, loyal, and energetic secretary, Sharon Fentiman, for her assistance and support. She is a gifted artist and a very organized person, and I always am amazed that she has decided to work with me and put up with an organizationally impaired person.

This work would not have been possible without the continuing support of research grants from the National Institute of Mental Health (particularly grants MH42484, MH47083, MH42722), and Research Career Development awards and a Research Scientist Award I have held since 1979 (MHK00257). The MacArthur Foundation paid for some of the construction costs of my apartment and fixed labs at the CDMRC.

I also want to thank my good friend and colleague Gerald Patterson who sat in his leather chair in the early morning hours (after studying calculus) and patiently read my manuscript. His very long and wonderful letter transformed the copy-editing process into a wonderful dialogue with a close comrade in science. With each chapter I was able to consider Gerry's reaction, to contemplate anew the ideas in it, how I approached the science, and think about the art of communication instead of just worrying about references, grammar, and figures. I thank him so much for all the time and effort he put into this labor.

Finally, I sincerely want to thank the hundreds of couples who participated in this research. They trusted us with the most intimate details of their lives, and theirs is really the major contribution toward this effort. They and not the researchers are the experts on marriage. It was our job to listen and to try to understand them. They did the living. They had the passions, the travails, and the insights that have guided us. What they graciously donated to the research effort was the most private and sacred places in their lives. If any good comes of all this work, theirs will have to be recognized as the bravest and most important contribution of all.

John Mordechai Gottman

I

Two are better than one;
Because they have a good reward for their labor.
For if they fall, the one will lift up his fellow,
But woe to him that is alone when he falls,
for he has not another to help him up.
And if two lie together then they have warmth,
but how can one be warm alone?
And if one prevail against him,
two shall withstand him.

(From Ecclesiastes, I: 9-12)

II

Who can find a good wife?
Her worth exceeds that of rubies.
The heart of her husband trusts in her
And nothing shall be lack.
She renders him good and not evil
All the days of her life.
She opens her hand to the needy
And extends her hand to the poor.
She is robed in strength and dignity
And cheerfully faces whatever may come.
She opens her mouth with wisdom,
her tongue is guided by kindness.
She tends to the affairs of her household
And eats not the bread of idleness.
Her husband too, and he praises her:
"Many women have done superbly,
But you surpass them all."

(From the "Eishet Chayil,"
Prayer said traditionally by the husband
to his wife on the eve of the Sabbath)

1

Introduction

The dissolution of marriages has serious consequences. The basic facts on divorce are reviewed in this chapter. The basic task of my research effort is to predict and understand the longitudinal course of marriages. In my laboratory, I now can tell from a brief interview with a couple about the history of their marriage, from a few questionnaires they fill out, and from three brief 15-minute samples of videotape what the eventual fate of a sample of marriages is likely to be. This chapter introduces my basic paradigm for studying marriages. This paradigm consists of eight components. From my videotapes, I code (a) problem solving; (b) affect; (c) power; (d) cross-situational responses (pervasiveness of discord and rebound); (e) the following sequences: start up, continuance, positive reciprocity. During the interaction, I also measure a couple's (f) physiological responses. From questionnaires, I assess the construct of (g) distance and isolation. From coding the tapes of an interview, I assess (h) how the couple views its past history. In this chapter, I discuss why I think that observation of behavior is the cornerstone of this research effort. I also note that it is not at all obvious what to observe, and that early researchers were somewhat befuddled by the huge array of possibilities. However, the early data on marriages led researchers to recognize the importance of problem solving, affect, and power. Most recently, the study of affect has become more precise, and we now are reliably measuring specific affects and patterns of affect expression. To illustrate these, two examples, contempt and defensiveness, are described.

1.1. MARRIAGE AND DIVORCE: THE FACTS

Marriage is perhaps the most commonplace of human social relationships. The interaction of married couples is an everyday occurrence. It is always underfoot, available for observation in every restaurant and shopping mall and other public and private settings. Yet despite its ubiquity, it generally is ignored.

1

The fact remains that the workings of marriage are, for the most part, quite unknown. This is unfortunate, because the current statistics for the survival of marriages are quite grim. Today, separation and divorce are common phenomena. Separation appears to be a trustworthy road to divorce, rather than reconciliation. When couples separate, about 75% of these separations end in divorce (Bloom, Hodges, Caldwell, Systra, & Cedrone, 1977). Current estimates are that the divorce rate in the United States is somewhere between 50% (Cherlin, 1981) and a startling 67% (Martin & Bumpass, 1989). The divorce rate for second marriages is projected to be 10% higher than for first marriages (Glick, 1984). Figure 1.1 strongly suggests that the trend is increasing.

Separation and divorce have strong negative consequences for the mental and physical health of both spouses. These negative effects include increased risk for psychopathology; increased rates of automobile accidents including fatalities; and increased incidence of physical illness, suicide, violence, homicide, and mortality from diseases (Bloom, Asher, & White, 1978; Burman & Margolin, 1992).

Marital disruption may not be related merely to these negative life events, but actually may be among the most powerful predictors of them. In Holmes and Rahe's (1967) scale of stressful life events, marital disruption weighs heavily among the major stresses in discriminating

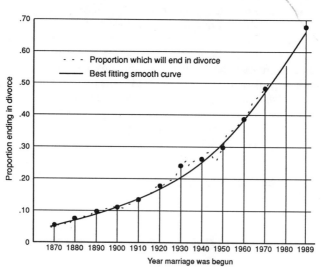

FIG. 1.1. Curve of my current best estimates of the probability that a marriage will end in divorce, plotted over time. The figure up to 1970 is taken from Cherlin (1981); the 1989 point is from Martin and Bumpass (1989). The curve up to 1970 was fit by an exponential in which the probability is expressed as $P = \exp(-a + bt - ct^2)$, where $a = 2.901$, $b = .02272$, and $c = .00002222$; the multiple R^2 of the fit is .993 (Cherlin, 1981).

those who become ill from those who do not. There is even evidence from one large sample, a 9-year epidemiological prospective study on the predictors of dying or staying alive, that the stability of marriage was the best predictor, even controlling for factors such as initial health and health habits (Berkman & Breslow, 1983; Berkman & Syme, 1979). In this study, 4,725 people in Alameda County, California, were studied at two time points separated by 9 years. The presence or absence of four types of social ties (i.e., marriage, friendship, church membership, and informal groups) were associated with the likelihood of a person staying alive in the 9-year period. Marriage and friendship were the stronger predictors of staying alive; marriage had the strongest buffering effect for men, whereas friendship had the strongest buffering effect for women. The effect was stronger as people aged, and the differences were significant when statistically controlled for self-reports of health at Time 1, socioeconomic status, health practices (e.g., smoking, drinking, obesity, exercise), and the use of preventive health services.

Researchers now have some ideas about what the mechanism may be for these powerful health effects of marital disruption. Recent evidence has suggested that the quality of the marital relationship is correlated with in vitro measures of immune functioning. Kiecolt-Glaser et al. (1987, 1988) found that lower marital quality was related to a suppressed immune system. Poorer marital quality was related to poorer cellular immunity. Using dose-response curves with two mitogens, PHA and ConA, they showed there was a significant difference in blastogenic response between low and high marital quality subgroups for all mitogen concentrations of PHA and for the higher mitogen concentrations of ConA. There was also reduced immune response assessed with Epstein-Barr virus antibody titers.

The dissolution of marital relationships also is known to be a more powerful stressor than marital unhappiness, and it also is related to greater suppression in immune functioning. In the Kiecolt-Glaser et al. studies (1987, 1988), recently separated or divorced women were compared with married women. The separated/divorced women had reduced immune response. This reduced response was assessed as significantly higher EBV VCA titers, significantly lower percentages of natural killer (NK) cells, and lower percentages of T-lymphocytes than the married women. There also were differences in the blastogenesis data between the two groups for PHA and the higher doses of ConA. Furthermore, although the two groups differed on self-report psychological variables, they did not differ markedly on other variables assessing sleeplessness, nutrition, or weight loss. Relationships undergoing separation that differed in the emotional conflict surrounding the separation also could be discriminated using the in vitro immune measures. Separated or divorced women who were still high in attachment to their husbands had lower lymphocyte proliferation to ConA and PHA than similar women who were less attached. Attachment was assessed by self-reports of preoccupation and disbelief about the separation or divorce.

To summarize, there appear to be effects linking negative health outcomes and immune functioning with variables that describe the quality and status of people's closest relationships (see also O'Leary, 1990).

Also, there is now convincing evidence to suggest that marital distress, conflict, and disruption are associated with a wide range of deleterious effects on children, including depression, withdrawal, poor social competence, health problems, poor academic performance, and a variety of conduct-related difficulties (Cowan & Cowan, 1987, 1990; Cowan, Cowan, Heming, & Miller, 1991; Easterbrooks, 1987; Emery, 1982, 1988; Emery & O'Leary, 1982; Forehand, Brody, Long, Slotkin, & Fauber, 1986; Gottman & Katz, 1989; Hetherington, 1988; Hetherington & Clingempeel, 1992; Hetherington, Cox, & Cox, 1978, 1982; Howes & Markman, 1989; Katz & Gottman, 1991a, 1991b; Peterson & Zill, 1986; Porter & O'Leary, 1980; Rutter, 1971; Shaw & Emery, 1987; Whitehead, 1979). Furthermore, it is believed that currently 38% of all White children and 75% of all Black children will experience the divorce of their parents before the age of 16, and spend an average of 5 years in single-parent homes. Although remarriage rates are declining slowly, single parenting tends to be a temporary transition point because 72% of women and 80% of men remarry. Unfortunately, as I have noted, the fate of these second marriages appears to be even worse than the fate of the first marriages. As a consequence, 1 out of every 10 children will experience two divorces of the custodial parent before turning 16 (Hetherington & Clingempeel, 1992). Two thirds of the children who experience a divorce by age 12 already experience it by age 6, and infants are more likely to experience a divorce than preschoolers.

There is evidence from two U.S. national probability samples that adults who experienced divorce as children are under considerably more stress than those who did not (Glenn & Kramer, 1985; Kulka & Weingarten, 1979). These adults report less satisfaction with family and friends, greater anxiety, that bad things happen to them more frequently, and that they find it more difficult to cope with life's stresses in general. There is also evidence for a reasonably reliable phenomenon of the intergenerational transmission of divorce, but the effect is not large (Pope & Mueller, 1979). This relationship is not found in every study. In

Kelly and Conley's (1987) 35-year prospective study, these relationships were not statistically significant (although the trend was there).[1]

The effects on children are likely to be even more subtle and powerful than has been imagined previously. Lindner, Hagan, and Brown (1992) reported that children in nondivorced families are socially and scholastically more competent and have fewer behavior problems than children in either divorced or remarried families. I am currently investigating the effects of marital patterns that are predictive of divorce on young children over time, even if the parents stay together. The evidence suggests that the major deleterious effect of these marital interaction patterns is on young children's ability to regulate their own emotions, their ability to self-soothe, and their ability to focus attention. The negative effects wreak their major damage on children's achievement in the early years of school and on children's ability to control their negative emotions (particularly aggression) with other children. There is strong evidence that shows that children of both genders from homes where their parents are unhappily married have greater heart rate physiological reactivity to expressing emotions (Shortt, Bush, McCabe, Gottman, & Katz, in press) and produce greater quantities of stress-related hormones (Gottman & Katz, 1989) than children from homes where the parents are happily married. These results are consistent with a prospective study by Block, Block, and Gjerde (1986). Children in this longitudinal study were assessed at ages 3, 4, 7, and 14. After a time, some of the parents divorced. These investigators then looked back to see if the children of the families that eventually divorced were different from the children of other families, even before the divorce occurred. They found that undercontrolled behavior was observed for boys as many as 11 years prior to the divorce. This is consistent with the notion that family processes that are predictive of divorce also may be deleterious to children before the divorce occurs.

Yet researchers still do not understand how marriages may be patterned in some way that spells their eventual destruction. In a decade review paper, White (1990) said the following about what is known currently of the processes that determine divorce:

> In their 1980 Decade in Review paper on the causes of divorce, Price-Bonham and Balswick (1980) conclude, "Whereas there are substantial

---

[1]The reader should note that these intergenerational relationships are not discussed in the published version of the Kelly and Conley (1987) article, but I happen to have a prepublication manuscript, which contained far more statistical analyses than the published version (which failed even to present t tests). Fortunately, the Kelly and Conley data are also archived by the Murray Center of Radcliffe University and are available to the general research community.

empirical bases for the relationship between demographic variables and divorce, the interpersonal literature is limited primarily to a theoretical and speculative format" (p. 962). The same tendency exists today. Although we have made substantial progress in the last decade, we still know comparatively little about how divorce is related to relationship quality, family structure, or social–psychological factors. (p. 907)

The research agenda is relatively clear. What researchers need to know is whether there are specific trajectories toward marital dissolution or marital stability that are related systematically to qualities of the marriage. Furthermore, they need to have this knowledge from prospective longitudinal studies, rather than retrospective accounts of failed marriages (e.g., Vaughn, 1990), because reconstructions of the past are notoriously unreliable. Critical in this research agenda are two goals: (a) good prediction of which couples will be on which trajectory, and (b) a highly specific empirically based theory of the marital processes associated with dissolution. This book presents research directed to both of these goals.

These facts do not imply that every ailing marriage should stay intact. This is clearly not the case. If the effects on children are considered, the evidence suggests that the stresses of divorce are preferable to continued marital conflict (Emery, 1988; Hetherington et al., 1978, 1982). Nonetheless, given the toll that a dissolving marriage takes, it would be helpful to therapists to have an intervention program that can make divorce less likely, should that be a couple's goal. This intervention program should be informed by prospective research on marital dissolution and stability.

1.2. THE FIRST QUESTION IS WHAT TO OBSERVE

In my laboratory, I now can tell from a brief interview with a couple about the history of their marriage, and from a few questionnaires they fill out and a brief 45-minute sample of videotape what the eventual fate of a particular sample of marriages is likely to be. For example, if I were to collect only our standard Oral History interview of a marriage, I now can predict, from just six variables coded from this interview, with 94% accuracy which marriages are headed for divorce. A few caveats are in order: Although this level of accuracy is encouraging, it needs to be replicated and extended in subsequent research, and it is quite likely that prediction will vary considerably across replication attempts.

Even if the accuracy I have discovered in prediction holds across studies, this does not suggest a mechanism for marital dissolution. For this reason, I set out initially, by design, to supplement my interview data with questionnaire, observational, and physiological data. Put simply, accuracy of prediction does not mean that I understand the processes involved in the maintenance or deterioration of a marriage. I was fortunate that the other data collected turned out to give a fairly clear picture that I could shape into a story, and from there into a theory. This theory, at this stage in my work, must remain highly speculative. This is all correlational research, and I cannot disentangle cause from effect definitively. I only can generate models of causal connection that are consistent with the data, but I never can be sure of causality without direct experimentation.

What is the basic news in this research program to date? The way the spouses talk about how their day went, or the way they attempt to have an enjoyable conversation all provide clues that tell what kind of marriage they have; what they prefer, value, and protect in their relationship; and where their strengths and vulnerabilities lie. All the data, taken together from multiple methods, help tell this story.

The general public's impression of the social sciences is that they are really not like the other sciences. They are "softer," and perhaps there may not even be any real phenomena in the social sciences. If any area of the social sciences is most subject to this view, it is the study of marriages and families. Marriage counselors are the objects of many cartoons and derisive humor. In my opinion, some of this has been well deserved until recently. However, in the past two decades, new methods have been developed for doing very specific kinds of therapy with couples and families (with clearly stated, measurable assumptions), for observing and interviewing couples and families, and for applying modern mathematical and statistical analysis to the data. The effect has been that researchers have found considerable order and stability in their answers to old questions about family and marriage, clearly specifiable phenomena have been uncovered, and they are about to begin a new stage of empirically grounded theory construction.

Researchers have learned that a multimethod approach is critical in the definition of constructs. Despite the importance of all the different methods employed, in my view observational data have a special place for two reasons. First, I believe, based on my experience, that couples generally have very little awareness of the patterns of interaction that have become routine in their marriage. It is a bit like our lack of awareness of how we all behave on elevators, until we were told by sociologist Erving Goffman. Once Goffman told us about elevator behavior, we all recognized ourselves in his descriptions. Second, observational data are needed to provide a backdrop for data about the couples' perception of the marriage. One can then say, "Okay, so he sees things in this way, now what does he actually do?" Without the observational data, one might make the potentially faulty assumption that perceptions are veridical.

Can one really get good and true data in the admittedly artificial climate of a psychology laboratory in which cameras are aimed at people and physiological sensors are attached to their bodies? The answer is yes. However, I have learned (Gottman, 1979) that how couples behave in laboratories with cameras pointed at them is not the same as how they would behave at home without an observer present. The cameras and laboratory staff affect couples' interactions. However, I also know precisely how they are affected. They are a lot nicer to each other when strangers are present than they are when they are at home alone, and they engage in far shorter chains of negativity. I have discovered that the differences that actually exist between happily married and unhappily married couples are greatly underestimated in the lab. I believe that the differences researchers tend to observe between groups of couples in the lab are smaller and more modest than those that would be observed at home if researchers could be invisible and unobtrusive observers. This is good. It means that I am not in danger of overstating my case based on couples' behavior in the lab; on the contrary, I am understating my case.

The other frequently asked question about this research is how representative are these findings of the population at large? Many people tell me that they never would volunteer for this research, therefore the research could not be about their marriage. It turns out that this is mostly not true (Krokoff, 1987; Krokoff, Gottman, & Roy, 1988). In general, for every couple like the one who said it would not participate, there is a couple very much like it that would. I found that when I obtained a representative sample of couples in a midwestern U.S. community (beginning with a large survey that used random digit telephone calls), the data were quite similar to the results obtained from volunteers. The only population I had trouble recruiting in my volunteer samples were elderly couples.

Subsequent to this representative sample study conducted by Krokoff, we (R. Levenson, L. Carstenson, and I) found some new ways to obtain a sample of elderly couples (using volunteers) so that the sample was, in most respects, similar to the demographics of the community, in this case the San Francisco Bay area. Our results are consistent with previous research with younger, volunteer couples. Furthermore, many of the results that have been obtained in observational research on marriage have been replicated in other countries (e.g., Australia, England, Germany, Holland, and Spain).

Social scientists initially had difficulty knowing what to look for in a marital interaction. Early attempts at description turned out to be woefully inadequate. We have come a long way. In my laboratories, I now can tell an enormous amount from just 45 minutes of videotape of a married couple interacting. Nonetheless, observation is a method that remains poorly developed to this day, even among social scientists. There is no final observational system for understanding marital inter- action. Instead, each observational system highlights one facet of a many-sided diamond; each system, by itself, represents only a carica- ture of the richness that is there.

When one begins observing couples in one's research, it becomes an organic process, one that does not really end, but is refined continually. To understand this process of continually redesigning observational systems, I can think of the program notes that accompany a simple Bach piano invention for two hands. The program notes tell about the basic themes, how they change as the invention progresses, and how they are changed from one hand to the other. How wonderful it would be to perform such a complex analysis of marital interaction. Unfortunately, we scientists are a bit like uninformed critics trying to write these program notes. So we build up our knowledge of pattern and sequence by experience of marital interaction across many studies. We start with primitive observational categories. We try to detect small sequences, which are like two-note patterns. Next, we train our observers in the subsequent study to look for these patterns. Then we detect organiza- tion among the two-note patterns, and the process continues to the four-note patterns, and so on. Hopefully, over time and a series of studies, we learn that we can observe complex patterns directly if we train our observers correctly. I have been engaged in this process of designing and revising observational systems to study marital interac- tion for the past 20 years.

One of my goals in this book is to share my enjoyment of observa- tional method. To begin this, I turn to a much admired character in fiction to discuss the importance of being a good observer.

1.3. SHERLOCK HOLMES: THE GREAT OBSERVER

Shakespeare suggested that all the world is a stage; if that were true, observing couples would be easy. People would work at revealing their character and they would display their role actively in the unfolding drama. Hamlet would wait in the airport for his luggage and deliver his famous speech lamenting the hollowness of life on this planet and his lack of delight in both man and woman. One would then have little trouble inferring his inner state. But in everyday life, these soliloquies and other dramatic episodes are nonexistent, or perhaps private and rare, and most human behavior is far more subtle than it is on the stage.

Shakespeare intended the stage to portray life as it is, as one may recall from Hamlet's directions to the actors. Hamlet said:

> Speak the speech, I pray you, as I pronounced it to you, trippingly on the tongue: but if you mouth it, as many of your players do, I had as lief the town-crier spoke my lines. Nor do not saw the air too much with your hand, thus; but use all gently: for in the very torrent, tempest, and, as I must say, the whirlwind of passion, you must acquire and beget a temperance that may give it smoothness. . . . Be not too tame neither, but let your own discretion be your tutor: suit the action to the word, the word to the action; with this special observance, that you o'erstep not the modesty of nature: for anything so overdone is from the purpose of playing, whose end, both at the first and now, was and is, to hold, as 'twere, the mirror up to nature; to show virtue her own feature, scorn her own image, and from the very age of the body of the time his form and pressure. (p. 120)

Yet, in an important way, the world is a stage. As author Kurt Vonnegut suggested, we all know very well that we are the central character, playing, even when alone, to some unseen audience that appreciates our actions, playing to what Vonnegut called the "Great Eye in the Sky." We turn to the Great Eye and replay the latest scene in which our feelings were hurt, only this time it is a retake and we are the victors, ready with the immediate devastating comeback that leaves our opponents cringing in humiliation and the secret audience howling with laughter.

In this Great Play, we observe all the others, the minor characters in our play, with great interest. We scan them carefully, waiting for them to reveal their roles, to perform in the subplots through which we live. In the Great Play, we are the director, and the director is the ultimate interpreter of human nature. Observing people is second nature. It is something we do when we wait in an airport, when we are in a meeting, when we are alone at home, or when we read the newspaper and try to understand the motives and psychology of a mass murderer.

Although observing people is a very human and frequent activity, most people probably have not considered that it is possible to fine tune their abilities. That is precisely the task that confronted early researchers in the 1970s, who turned toward a description of how married couples interact.

Perhaps the greatest observer of people was Sherlock Holmes. Recall a Sherlock Holmes story called, "A Study in Scarlet," which describes Dr. Watson's first meeting with Sherlock Holmes. In this story, Holmes reveals a small bit of the methods he uses to astound others with his ability to watch and analyze people. He alludes to his methods, but he never spells them out exactly.

Watson has just returned from the war in Afghanistan, impoverished financially, depressed, and aimless, when he runs into an old friend named Stamford at the Criterion Bar. Stamford tells Watson that he knows someone who might be interested in a roommate, and together they ascend the dark creaky steps leading to Holmes' laboratory. Holmes is immersed in an experiment, surrounded by bubbling test tubes and Bunsen burners. As they enter, Holmes proclaims, "Egad, I found it! A reagent for hemoglobin and nothing else!" Looking up Holmes sees Stamford and a stranger, and Stamford introduces them, "Dr. Watson, Mr. Sherlock Holmes."

Holmes looks at Watson and says, "How are you?" and then quickly adds, "You have been in Afghanistan, I perceive." "How on earth did you know that?" asks Watson, amazed, and Holmes replies, "Never mind," chuckling to himself.

One morning at breakfast, after the two men have been living together and Watson has been observing his new roommate's habits for a few weeks, Watson notices a magazine opened to an article called, "The Book of Life." He does not realize that Holmes is the author of the article and he reads,

> From a drop of water," said the writer, "a logician could infer the possibility of an Atlantic or a Niagara without having seen or heard of one or the other. So all life is a great chain, the nature of which is known whenever we are shown a single link of it. Like all other arts, the Science of Deduction and Analysis is one which can only be acquired by long and patient study, nor is life long enough to allow any mortal to attain the highest possible perfection in it. Before turning to these moral and mental aspects of the matter which present the greatest difficulties, let the inquirer begin by mastering more elementary problems. Let him, on meeting a fellow mortal, learn at a glance to distinguish the history of the man, and the trade or profession to which he belongs. Puerile as such an exercise may seem, it sharpens the faculties of observation, and teaches one where to look and what to look for. By a man's fingernails, by his coat-sleeve, by his boots, by his trouser-knees, by the callosities of his forefinger and thumb, by his expressions, by his shirt cuffs—by each of these things a man's calling is plainly revealed. That all united should fail to enlighten the competent inquirer in any case is almost inconceivable. (p. 13)

Watson is unimpressed. He says, "What ineffable twaddle. I never read such rubbish in my life." Holmes appears then and announces that he is the author. He says, "Observation with me is second nature. You appeared to be surprised when I told you, on our first meeting, that you had come from Afghanistan." "You were told, no doubt," says Watson, but Holmes responds:

Nothing of the sort. I *knew* you came from Afghanistan. From long habit the train of thoughts ran so swiftly through my mind that I arrived at the conclusion without being conscious of intermediate steps. There were such steps, however. The train of reasonings ran, "Here is a gentleman of a medical type, but with the air of a military man. Clearly an Army doctor, then. He has just come from the tropics, for his face is dark, and that is not the natural tone of his skin, for his wrists are fair. He has undergone hardship and sickness, as his haggard face says clearly. His left arm has been injured. He holds it in a stiff and unnatural manner. Where in the tropics could an English Army doctor have seen such hardship and got his arm wounded? Clearly in Afghanistan." I then remarked that you came from Afghanistan, and you were astonished. (p. 24)

Holmes tells us that his powers are not magical—that they can be learned through patient study. As Holmes often said to Watson, "You saw but you did not observe."

1.4. OBSERVING COUPLES

If most people, including social scientists, were asked to tell what to look for in a brief marital interaction, I think many would be at a loss. Indeed, this was precisely the state of affairs about 30 years ago when two investigators, Soskin and John (1963), built a 3-pound audio radio transmitter with a foot-long antenna that projected from the upper lid of a back pack and gave it to a vacationing married couple so that they could record their conversations. The sound was transmitted to a radio tower at the resort. The unit could be disconnected when the couple wanted privacy. They offered the couple a free vacation at the resort if they would agree to have their every word monitored by the two researchers.

The following are some brief excerpts from the conversations of this couple, which summarize the dilemma of the two investigators. There is an excerpt from the conversations of Jock (J), the husband, and Roz (R), the wife, while they were rowing. As the excerpt shows, the conversation seems quite natural, although there are some references to the equipment. I reproduce this rather long excerpt without comment. As you read it, you might think about how you would divide the interaction into categories that you think are important.

J: Come on! Yo-ho, heave ho. You do the rowing.
R: Nuts to that idea. You're the big, strong man. Mmmm!
J: Yeah, but I have a handicap.
R: Yeah, you have a handicap in your head.

J: (to attendant) Can we take out a boat? (They get a boat from the attendant.)

R: Whoops! Don't get wet. You row for a while and then I'll row. Okay?

J: All right. It's awkward rowing with the transmitter on.

R: Go on. Want me to take it while you're rowing?

J: No, it's okay.

R: Bet you don't know how.

J: Oh, yes I do. I guess I just . . .

R: Here, let me change.

J: I'll just have to set this thing out here.

R: Let me take it.

J: Okay. It's really a clear lake isn't it?

R: It's wonderful. Look, there's a big moth. I wish I had my book with me, then I could tell what kind it was.

J: (handing transmitter to R) Here, put it on.

R: Like this? I wouldn't want my speech distorted, since I usually have so much to say. . . .

J: Aren't *those* cabins nice?

R: Yes, those are the ones we were supposed to be in. I keep telling you.

J: These there? Look how dark the water is down there.

R: You tip this boat over with me in it, and I'll be very upset. Uh, uh, huh, huh, huh, huh.

J: I just felt the . . .

R: (laughs) Jock, I just made a joke. . . . Have you no sense of humor?

J: Look how . . .

R: Why are we going way out in the middle. I'll get sunburned.

J: What's the difference whether you're in the middle or not?

R: You get more reflection in the middle.

J: (scoffs) Oh!

R: Jock, I know!

J: How do you know?

R: I can see! You put on your sun-speks before you get a headache, huh?

J: No.

R: No? Okay. Wanna take your shoes off?

J: No.

R: (taunting in a singing way) Ah, Jock's gonna be sore tomorrow because he insists on showing off. (Jock apparently responds by rocking the boat.) No! Now cut that out! You'll ruin this fifty-thousand dollar equipment.

J: Oh, look. Boy, these are nice oars.

R: You're a good rower, honey.

Soskin and John (1963) tape-recorded the conversations and typed out what the couple said verbatim. They were faced with many days of taped conversation and verbatim transcripts like the one you just read. Like the pioneers they were, they plunged forward enthusiastically, creating many observational systems for categorizing the interaction. The surprising thing was that they became quite discouraged and disappointed once their analyses were completed.

1.5. THE DISAPPOINTMENTS OF SOSKIN AND JOHN'S (1963) OBSERVATIONS

I go into some detail about the analyses Soskin and John undertook to get some idea of the vast array of possibilities of what to observe in a couple's conversation.

Soskin and John (1963) identified many methods of analysis from the excerpts of conversation they collected for several days. For example, they computed such variables as the total talking time and the distribution of utterance durations. They categorized each statement made in a number of ways, and made up exotic new names for their categories. For example, they distinguished some statements as Informational ("That's a Modigliani") and others as Relational messages ("Oh, I like that") or Expressive statements ("Ouch!"). They also had some fairly exotic categories, such as "Excogitative" statements ("Hmm-m-m, what have I done wrong here?"), "Signones" (messages that report the speaker's present physical or psychological state such as "I'm cold"), "Metrones" (appraising and valuing statements, such as "What a fool I've been"), "Regones" (regulative statements that are designed to influence the partner's behavior, such as "Why don't you do it right now?"), and "Structones" (informational statements, such as "I weigh 181 pounds").

Their attempts at description were quite elaborate. For example, in what they called their "dynamic" analysis, they described the message according to "state," "locus-direction," and "bond." The state contains affective information in a six-interval scale (a state of joy, glee, high pleasure; a state of satisfaction, contentment, liking; a state of ambivalence, mild apprehension; a state of dislike, frustration, disappointment; a state of pain, anger, fear, grief; or a state of neutrality); locus-direction (nine subcategories were scored in terms of its primary effect; e.g., wants, wishes, and self-praise were one subcategory); "bonds" indexed the degree of intimacy the speaker was willing to tolerate in the relationship.

When investigators go to great lengths to invent new categories and a new language for the categories, it is a sure sign that they think they are on to something hot. However, at the end of all this analysis, based on their laborious coding and analysis of these conversations, what really seemed to surprise Soskin and John was just how dull their conclusions were.

For example, the main conclusion of what they called their Ecological Analysis was how little time Jock spent alone. In what they called the Structural Analysis, they noted a great deal of variability in Jock's talking time across different episode types, such as breakfast and planning with the wife. They noted that the longer utterances were predominantly structones (i.e., factual information exchange). They concluded that Jock is a highly gregarious individual. They wrote:

> In the structural analysis it develops that he is also very garrulous under some circumstances though less so in others. Over a relatively large sample of situations he speaks about as much as his co-participant. On the other hand, given an appropriate audience he appears quite ready to take the initiative and to claim considerably more than his share of talking time. (pp. 261–262)

They finally decided that this kind of conclusion was unlikely to lead to profound insights into the structure of conversation or marriage. Part of their surprise lay in the realization that, rather than being separate components, emotion and the structure of interaction were connected intricately in everyday marital interaction. For example, in the functional analysis, 1,850 messages were analyzed. They were surprised that a very small proportion of these messages involved exchanging information. Nearly two thirds of the messages were classified as what they called "relation-changing" (i.e., affective messages).

They were struck by the gender differences in the interaction with respect to emotional expression. They found that Roz produced a significantly higher proportion of emotion-venting messages than her husband in both the cabin and in the rowing incident. They wrote: "In the former (cabin) the expressive messages were predominantly in the form of happy outbursts, frequent singing, etc. In the latter (rowing), as the reader will recall, they were mostly expressions of apprehension and annoyance" (p. 264).

To summarize, Soskin and John (1963) found that expressed emotion, or affect, was central to the interaction, and they noted a possible gender difference in this couple with respect to affect. They also concluded that Roz produced significantly more emotion-venting messages in private than she did in public situations, whereas Jock's output was relatively low throughout.

Intuitively, Soskin and John knew that they should describe something about two aspects of the marital interaction: the structure of the interaction and the affective component of the interaction. For Roz and Jock, they tried to capture these two aspects of the marital interaction with their observational coding systems.

They found their dynamic analyses to be most interesting. However, they were puzzled that their codes and analytic methods did not capture the interaction as well as they could by summarizing the action in plain, nonpsychologized English. For example, they summarized one episode as follows:

> Roz had just come out of the shower and was dressing while Jock, who was already dressed and in something of a dour mood, sat in the living room working on his lanyard. In a rather short period of time he pointedly contradicted a casual remark of hers; then he tried to implicate her in a series of errors he had made in his lanyard; and next he refused to help her find a lost lipstick while at the same time criticizing her for her appearance without it. In this sequence Roz, who at first was almost childishly gay and ebullient in the shower, parried his contradiction with an artful display of one-upmanship by subtly exhibiting her superior knowledge of a facet of French history. Next, in the face of continuing criticism she defended herself against his accusation and finally she solicited his help in finding the lipstick and sought his approval for her general appearance. (p. 268)

Using this kind of anecdotal account, Soskin and John obtained a very clear description of the thoughts, feelings, and action of a short segment of interaction. But they felt that their codes failed to capture all this subtlety. They wrote, in reflection:

> The very subtle shifts and variations in the way in which these two people attempted to modify each other's states sequentially throughout this episode obliged us to question whether summaries of very long segments of a record reflect the actual sequential dynamics of the behavior in a given episode. (p. 268)

1.6. WHAT SOSKIN AND JOHN THOUGHT WAS MISSING IN THEIR ANALYSES

After they completed their data analyses, it was clear that there were two dimensions that Soskin and John intuitively thought were important, namely, affect and power. However, they were disillusioned with their ability to get at these two dimensions. For example, at one point in their chapter, they wrote:

As with locus-direction shift, the assessment of affective state changes met with only marginal success. (p. 270) [N]either the locus-direction scoring nor the affective state scoring adequately conveys Jock's practice of scattering a series of mildly provocative messages throughout an episode as, for example, his persistence in the rowing episode in urging Roz to row farther out into the lake despite her growing apprehensiveness. (p. 272)

Soskin and John found Jock's blend of provocation, annoyance, teasing, and mild contempt was a surprising aspect of his behavior while on vacation. They did not have a code for this kind of blend that invoked both negativity and power (or dominance), a blend I code in my laboratory as *belligerence*. Put simply, the investigators intuitively knew what was going on that was important in the interaction, but their measurement and analytic methods prevented them from getting at their intuitions. Their intuitions fell in between the cracks delineated by their codes. Theirs was a fascinating dilemma in the history of coding marital interaction.

1.7. RECENT PROGRESS IN OBSERVING COUPLES

The major point I want to make is that knowing what to observe in marital interaction is not at all obvious or trivial. A lot of smart people researching this area went down a lot of dead ends before they finally figured out what the important things were. However, once one knows what to look for, it is easy to detect it. Then, in hindsight, it all may appear obvious; it may even be tinged with the nostalgia of recognition. Once the obvious is pointed out, the reaction is often something like "Of course!" mixed with "Why didn't I think of that?" Fortunately, as the reader will see, all the results in predicting marital dissolution hang together fairly well, and tell a good story. There are really only a few major things to remember.

I have suggested that the first question of an observational approach is what to observe when watching a married couple interact. Since Soskin and John's (1963) work, about 30 years have passed. What has our progress been?

1.7.1. Brief Recent History of Observing Emotion and Marital Interaction

The systematic observational study of marriage began in the 1970s. Researchers now have experience with several observational systems that have taught a lot about marital interaction. A great deal of the results of this early research led me to recognize the importance of emotion in marital interaction. Coinciding with this realization of the importance of emotion, in the late 1970s Ekman and Friesen's (1978) studies on how to read emotion in the human face culminated in two observational systems: the Facial Action Coding System (FACS) and the Emotion Facial Action Coding System (EMFACS). These were the first anatomically based observational systems for describing how the facial muscles move, and what these movements may mean in terms of expressed emotion.

In the FACS, all movements are described in terms of a set of action units that simply describe the contraction of a set of facial muscle groups. Describing a particular face with a set of numbers was a great breakthrough in research on emotion. Before the FACS, investigators tried to describe facial movement with everyday words such as *frowns, smirks, grimaces,* and *smiles.* There were two problems with this approach. First, there simply are not enough words in the English language to describe the over 2,000 facial configurations possible with over 40 facial muscle groups. Second, the words and phrases that do exist often contain some kind of hidden value judgment about the facial expression, which has no place in a purely descriptive scientific account. For example, there is a kind of smile that raises the lip corners (a contraction of the muscle called zygomaticus major) but does not involve the muscles around the eyes (a contraction of the muscles called orbicularis oculi). In this facial expression, the mouth muscles are involved but the eye muscles are not. There may be no crinkling of the eye corners in this kind of smile. For example, it is much simpler, direct, and more precise to describe this face as a "12 without 6" (that is how it is said in FACS) than to say that this smile is somehow insincere, phony, or unfelt. It remains for research to uncover the circumstances in which this kind of smile occurs to put this sort of interpretation on this smile. It turns out that this kind of smile is indeed usually an unfelt or false smile. But validation research is necessary to decide that this is true. In my laboratories, everyone must speak FACS. It is a precondition to learning my other observational systems.

So far I have mentioned two areas of marital interaction—affect and power. However, as is seen in chapter 2, the area that has received the most attention in marital interaction is neither affect nor power. Rather, it is how the couple resolves disagreements, a set of social acts known collectively as problem solving. As is seen, this focus historically has come from several sources, including sociological studies of marriage. One source was behaviorally oriented marital therapy, which came primarily from the idea that marital discord could be resolved by appropriate social learning. Hence, in the field of observational research on marriage, investigators have focused primarily on three aspects of marital interaction: problem solving, affect, and power.

As a field of scientific research, we have done the best job on problem solving. Recently, we began to describe affect as it occurs in a social interaction in a manner more sophisticated than saying that the affect is positive, negative, or neutral. In a few laboratories, it can be said reliably that the affect is a particular emotion, such as anger, instead of simply describing it as negative. As a field, we have done the worst job in the area of observing power and influence, although most researchers still think that this is a vital area.

1.8. COLLECTING A MULTIMETHOD DATABASE FOR STUDYING COUPLES

It is clear that for some time to come we will be in a phase of scientific research that is fundamentally descriptive. The challenge in this phase of research is to tell a good story about the phenomena of interest. Hopefully, interesting theories will emerge from this good story. The phenomena of interest to me involve the prediction of change over time in marriages.

In this book, when I report research results I restrict myself to eight areas. The first is problem solving. I have employed three different observational systems to measure problem solving.

1.8.1. Problem Solving

The three observational systems I use are the Marital Interaction Coding System (MICS; Weiss & Summers, 1983), the Couples Interaction Scoring System (CISS; Markman & Notarius, 1987), and the Rapid Couples Interaction Scoring System (RCISS; Krokoff, Gottman, & Hass, 1989). The MICS was developed by a group of researchers in Oregon (see chapter 3 for a brief history). I and my students Clifford Notarius and Howard Markman designed the CISS. More recently, I designed the RCISS (Krokoff et al., 1989). My latest creation, the RCISS, assesses problem solving a bit more rapidly than the CISS. I have used all three systems in various studies.

Within the problem-solving area, there are many possible problem-solving skills and deficits that are important in differentiating happily married from unhappily married couples. I review the literature on these skills in chapter 3. I also outline the major issues that remain unresolved in thinking about these questions, and attempt to resolve some of these issues.

1.8.2. Affect

To observe affect I used two systems: the Emotion Facial Action Coding System (EMFACS; Ekman & Friesen, 1978), which describes specific visible facial muscle contractions on the face that are presumed to be related to emotion on the basis of other research; and the Specific Affect Coding System (SPAFF), which I developed. The SPAFF was designed to measure emotional expression using channels in addition to the face (language, voice, context, etc.). Embedded in the assessment of affect are many important aspects of marital interaction, some of which relate to social skills. In the area of positive affect, these include such things as how affectionate the couple is, how much interest they demonstrate to one another, their ability to laugh together, and their responsiveness to each other's positivity. In the area of negative affect, there is a wide array of potentially important affects and affective patterns. These affects include anger, sadness, fear, contempt, and disgust. Affective patterns include complaint, blaming, criticism, whining, defensiveness, belligerence, and domineering.

1.8.3. Physiology

Since 1979, in collaboration with Levenson, I have collected physiological data from husbands and wives as they interact, synchronized with the video time code. These peripheral physiological measures are interbeat interval, or heart period (which is the time between R-waves of the electrocardiogram; the heart rate is 60,000/heart period), the amplitude of blood in the finger, the time it takes blood to get from the heart to the finger, palmar skin conductance, and gross motor movement. More recently, I added the peripheral autonomic measures of ear pulse, ear pulse transit time, and respiration. In some studies, I assayed stress-related hormones in urine and blood, and, most recently, in Seattle, in collaboration with H. Ochs, I assayed blood for in-vitro and in-vivo measures of immune response.

1.8.4. Power

In this book, I describe only one index of power, which is attempts by spouses to influence one another during problem solving. My student, R. Rushe, is developing an observational system designed specifically to examine the ways in which spouses try to influence and control one another.

1.8.5. Cross-Situational Responses

In addition to the conflict discussion, we often employ a nonproblem-solving conversation, in which couples meet at the end of a day, after having been apart for at least 8 hours, and talk about the events of their day. The events-of-the-day conversation comes first. I think it can be useful to provide an index of the background amount of marital conflict before anything else happens in the laboratory. Hostility in talking about how one's day went may be very revealing, and it happens quite often. I use the SPAFF codes during the events-of-the-day conversation to assess the pervasiveness of discord. The very last discussion the couple has in the laboratory is a pleasant topic conversation. I use this conversation to assess the couple's ability to rebound from the previous conflict resolution discussion to the immediately following positive conversation.

1.8.6. Sequences

I also discuss three selected sequences of positive, negative, and neutral affect. I call these sequences startup, continuance, or negative reciprocity (Gottman, 1979; Patterson 1982); and positive reciprocity (Gottman, 1979). The first two sequences, startup and continuance, describe the likelihood that a couple will get into a negative affective state from a previously neutral one, and the likelihood that it will stay in the negative state once it enters it. This sequence of continuance also has been called negative reciprocity. The third sequence, positive reciprocity, describes the likelihood that the couple will stay in a positive state once it enters it.

1.8.7. Distance and Isolation

Using several questionnaires, I describe a perceptual process of increasing distance and isolation in marriages, which accompanies the behavioral differences that predict marital dissolution, and that also, by themselves, predict dissolution. At Time 1, I collected a set of five questionnaires from subjects. These questionnaires were constructed in my laboratory (most were designed in collaboration with L. Krokoff). These questionnaires tap a process of increasing distance and isolation. The assumption was that the underlying variable driving this increased distance and isolation was a concept called *flooding*, which means being surprised, overwhelmed, and disorganized by your partner's expressions of negative emotions. The five questionnaires are as follows: (a) Flooded by Partner's Negative Affect is a scale that assesses the extent to

which spouse A feels that spouse B's negative emotions arise unexpectedly, and are overwhelming and disorganizing to spouse A, alphas =
.82 and .73, for the husband and wife, respectively (ESCAL); (b)
Problems Are Severe is a scale computed from the Couple's Problem
Inventory (Gottman, Markman, & Notarius, 1977), based on a subjective
estimate of the severity of a set of issues in the marriage, alphas = .79
and .75, for the husband and wife, respectively (PROB); (c) Best to Work
Problems out Alone, Not with Spouse is a scale that assesses the extent
to which a person thinks that it is better to avoid problems or to work
them out alone, rather than with the spouse, alphas = .88 and .76, for
the husband and wife, respectively (PHIL); (d) Parallel Lives is a scale
that assesses the extent to which husband and wife have arranged their
lives so that they do not interact very much and do not do things
together (sample item: "My partner and I live pretty separate lives"),
alphas = .95 and .95, for husband and wife, respectively (PARALLEL);
and (e) Loneliness (sample item: "Sometimes I feel so lonely it hurts"),
alphas = .79 and .82, for husband and wife, respectively (LONELY). To
review, the theoretical idea behind the design of these measures was
that they would tap the increasing distance and isolation that might
accompany marital dissolution, and that being flooded by one's partner's negative affect would drive this increased distance and isolation.

1.8.8. How Couples View Their History:
The Oral History Interview

It would be useful for clinical work to have an interview that could tap
processes that were predictive of marital dissolution. Such an interview
would make these processes readily observable to the clinician. I have
developed such an interview. In 1986, I used an interview developed in
my laboratory with L. Krokoff, called The Oral History Interview. The
Oral History Interview is modeled after the interview methods of
sociologist/reporter Studs Terkel. It is a semistructured interview in
which the interviewer asks a set of open-ended questions. The interviewer asks about the history of the couple's relationship—how they
met, how they courted and married, bad times, how they got over these
bad times, what the good times were, and what they are today. The
interviewer also asks about the couple's philosophy of marriage: The
couple is asked to select a good and a bad marriage they know of and to
talk about the differences. They also describe their parents' marriages
and how they compare to their own. I have used the interview as the
first thing couples do in my projects, to build rapport with the couple.
Most couples love doing the Oral History Interview. I also have used it

as the last thing couples do, to allow couples to leave the laboratory in a good mood.

Recently, K. Buehlman developed a behavioral coding system based on couples' responses in this interview. Her coding system assessed several dimensions of marriage. In particular, she recently selected six variables that she thought would be interesting theoretically and predictive of marital dissolution. She noticed that the husband's behavior during this interview showed a striking degree of variation across couples. Hence, she decided that the husband's data would provide the best predictors of the longitudinal fate of the marriage. She coded three positive variables: (a) Husband We-ness, the amount of "we-ness" expressed by the husband in the recollections and philosophies; part of this construct is the use of "we-sentences" rather than "I-sentences," so this construct taps how unified the husband feels with his wife; (b) Husband Expansiveness, how "expansive" the husband was during the interview, as opposed to constricted; an expansive husband elaborated with detailed recollections and philosophy about the marriage; (c) Husband Fondness for His Wife was a simple affective dimension of the degree of affection and pride the husband expressed toward his wife (an opposite example is the husband who cannot think of anything that first attracted him to his wife). She also coded three negative variables: (d) Chaos, a rating given to the spouses about the extent to which they seem to feel out of control of their lives, buffeted by events outside their control (e.g., they got married because she was suddenly pregnant, and this kind of thing seems to characterize their lives); and (e and f) Husband and Wife Disappointment in Their Marriage, which was judged as having expectations of their marriage that are not met. The overall agreement across coders on these dimensions was quite high, about 80%.

1.9. INTEGRATION OF MEASUREMENT INTO A THEORY

The problem with this measurement is coming up with a parsimonious story to tell about these couples and what happens to their marriages over time. The story also needs to illuminate fundamental issues about marriage.

My research has been guided by a fairly simple approach that comes from adopting a social psychophysiological methodology. In this book, I call this approach "balance theory." Because physiological systems in the body often are regulated around some set point (which may be functional or dysfunctional in the long run), there is a natural metaphor for organizing physiological processes in some kind of equation of balance, and then asking questions of how such equations are or are not adaptive. In attempting to find the interfaces between behavior, cognition, and physiology, it also is natural to search for analogous balances in cognition and behavior. This approach is largely successful in understanding the longitudinal course of marriages. In chapter 15, I present a theory (and some preliminary evidence to test it) that attempts to integrate behavior, cognition, and physiology using my multimethod descriptive approach.

APPENDIX 1

The Two Most Corrosive Negative Marital Behaviors— Contempt/Disgust and Defensiveness

In this appendix, I provide more detail on a few affects and affective sequences. This appendix is a brief introduction to a few of the codes in the observational systems. It is a sampler of two kinds of behaviors. I do this here so that the reader can get some idea of what the observational systems are like. As is seen later in this book, there are four kinds of negative marital behaviors that are the most corrosive to the stability of the marriage over time. Two of these are contempt/disgust and defensiveness.

A.1.1. Contempt/Disgust

Contempt or disgust are easy to identify in speech. Disgust typically is communicated by sounding fed up, sickened, and repulsed (i.e., "I've had enough," "I'm not going to swallow any more," or "I'm going to throw up"). In disgust, the speaker is expressing the hidden message of nausea.

Contempt is also easy to identify in speech. It involves any insult, mockery, or sarcasm or derision, of the other person. It includes disapproval, judgment, derision, disdain, exasperation, mockery, put downs, or communicating that the other person is absurd or incompetent. Three types of contempt are hostile humor, mockery, or sarcasm. In this form of contempt, there may be derision, a put down, or cold hate. There is often a definite sense of distance, coldness, and detachment in this category of behavior.

Although these behaviors are often quite easy to detect, they also can have subtle expressions that are harder for a casual observer to detect without adequate training. For example, it may not be so obvious how to read faces to detect disgust and contempt. Disgust is a little easier than contempt. In the face, disgust is communicated by two possible action units. The first is Action Unit 9 (AU9), the nose wrinkle. The second disgust indicator is created by raising the upper lip, a result of Action Unit 10. For contempt, the most reliable indicator turns out to be the result of Action Unit 14, the dimpler muscle. Another possible contempt indicator is the eye roll. Some of these facial expressions are illustrated in Fig. 1.2.

These more subtle facial expressions of disgust and contempt are quite powerful. For example, I have preliminary evidence that people have strong physiological responses to their partner's facial expressions of contempt (Hummel, 1991). The husband's facial expressions of contempt are an excellent predictor of physical illness reported by the wife 4 years later. The wife's facial expressions of disgust at Time 1 are correlated 0.51 ($p < .001$) with the amount of months the couple will be separated in the next 4 years.

A.1.2. Defensiveness

Defensiveness is some attempt to ward off or protect one's self from perceived attack. There may be a denial of responsibility for the problem, a counterblame, or a whine. One excellent indicator of defensiveness has to do with the response to what I call "Negative Mindreading." A mindreading statement was our initial name (in the CISS) for any attribution of motives, feelings, or behaviors to the partner (e.g., "You don't care about how we live," "You never clean up," "You always embarrass me at parties," "You get tense in situations like that one," "You have to spend whatever we save," etc.). Often, mindreading statements are accompanied by "You always" or "You never" phrases. Mindreading is very common in marital interaction, and it is not necessarily negative in its effects. Gottman (1979) found that what was important was the affect with which the mindreading was accompanied. If the affect was negative, it appeared to the listener to be blaming and accusing. The typical response was disagreement and elaboration. For example, "You always get tense in those situations," accompanied by a blaming tone of voice, would tend to receive a response such as "I don't always get tense in those situations. It's just when you don't back me up."

If the same statement were delivered with neutral or positive affect, it would tend to get an entirely different response. It is viewed by the listener as a sensitive probe about feelings. For example, "You always get tense in those situations," accompanied by an affectionate or empathetic tone of voice, would tend to receive a response such as "I know I do. I do get tense in those situations. Maybe I could try to relax

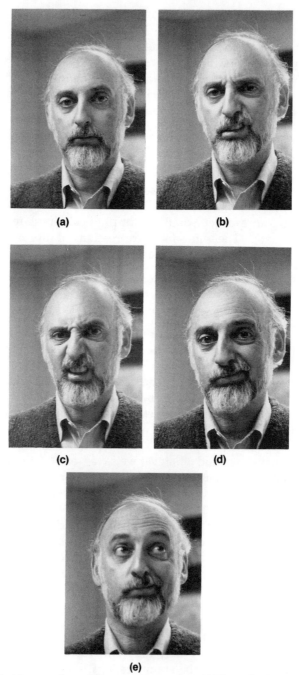

FIG. 1.2. Facial expressions of disgust and contempt. (a) The author's neutral face; (b) (U-AU 10); (c) disgust expression due to unilateral upper lip raise (U-AU10) and nose wrinkle (AU9); (d) contempt expression due to unilateral dimpler (AU14); (e) Contempt expression due to unilateral dimpler (AU14) plus an eye roll.

more." Couples do not tend to ask direct questions about feelings the way therapists do. Instead, they mindread with neutral or positive affect.

The typical defensive statement is self-protective and avoidant of blame and responsibility. The defender appears to feel picked on unfairly and victimized. A common form that this may take nonverbally is whining. Although whining is a common behavior among children, many would be surprised to learn that it is also a common behavior among married couples.

A.1.2.1. Whining

Whining is not really an emotion. It is a well-defined behavior that is quite common in marital interaction, and I am studying it separately until I know where to put it in my specific affects list. Whining is heard as a high-pitched, fluid fluctuation of the voice, generally with one syllable stressed toward the end of the sentence. It reflects dissatisfaction in a very childish way. It often is characterized by a "thin edge" to the voice and an irritating nasal quality.

I have noticed that whining almost always has an innocent victim posture behind it. It is as if the whiner is saying, "It's not fair. Why are you picking on me? I didn't do anything wrong. I'm good." It is possible to hear this plaintive, "Oh poor me" message behind the whine. Sylvan Tomkins thought that whining is very close to crying, and probably akin to sadness. However, for now I reserve judgment and code it separately. There are several types of whining:

Type I: Demand. "I told you to see a *doc*tor."
Type II: Complaint. "You never take me *any*where."
Type III: Direct expression of feeling like an innocent victim. "I feel I'm ganged up on, I don't have a friend in the world." Here whining is purely in the words and not in the voice.
Type IV: Defensive whining. This can be either abrasive or nonabrasive. It includes indignation, self-righteousness; it is distinguished from offensive anger largely by content.

As these descriptions suggest, whining can be detected in the content of the words, not just in the voice tone.

2

What Makes Some Marriages Magical and Some Miserable? Raising the Questions

In this chapter, I discuss an important book in the history of research on marital interaction by Raush, Barry, Hertel, and Swain (1974). In this book, the idea of studying sequences of marital interaction was developed, and the notion of Adaptive Probabilism was defined. This view introduced some simple mathematics that diverged sharply from General Systems theory in its definitions of communication. The essay by Raush et al. (1974) on conflict escalation, symbolic conflict, and conflict avoidance also is reviewed and discussed in this chapter.

2.1. THE SCIENTIFIC OBSERVATION OF COUPLES

Once one places one's bet at the Great Research Roulette Wheel, and decide what to measure, one is ready to ask the oldest and most basic question about marriage, which is why some marriages appear to work as if by magic, whereas others are muddles of pure misery. Observational researchers have made a great deal of progress on this question in the past 20 years, and a great deal about the solution to this fundamental mystery is now known. I summarize these results in chapter 3. Before I can begin to address this first question, I need to talk about some theory and methodology about how I now look at streams of observational data that come from observing a married couple interact.

2.2. RAUSH, BARRY, HERTEL, AND SWAIN (1974)

I mentioned in the preface that in 1974, Raush, Barry, Hertel, and Swain published an important book entitled *Communication, Conflict, and Marriage*. The Raush et al. work proposed the observational longitudinal study of marriages in naturalistic settings. They followed newlyweds

28

from pregnancy through the birth of their first child. This is known to be a period of major transition in marriages, and theirs was the first study of the transition to parenthood. For some time, I have wanted to pay homage to this important book. It raised some very important questions and used some new methods to address old problems in the study of marriage. When I was a beginning professor at Indiana University, Harold Raush came to speak and I was selected to be his host. He had the first advance copy of his book. I prevailed on him to let me borrow that copy, stayed up all night to read it, and had breakfast with him the next morning. That day we spent hours walking around the campus discussing his book. It was an event that changed my life; the book has directed my own thinking about marriage.

In their book, Raush et al. raised two critical questions. The first question was why, in some marriages, minor conflicts "escalate far beyond their apparent triviality" (p. 2). This question by Raush et al. was also more broadly about what makes conflict constructive or destructive in marriages. Raush et al. (1974) gave the example of a couple arguing about which television show to watch. They were impressed that many couples got quite involved with the role-play improvisations. One wife became extremely upset and said, "Damn it, you always watch what you want to see. You're always drinking beer and watching football. Nothing else seems important to you, especially my wishes." The seemingly small discussion of which TV show to watch had led her to escalate and to express her complete exasperation with her partner and their marriage. The second question raised by Raush et al. (1974) was whether the avoidance of conflict in marriage was functional or dysfunctional. These two questions are very important in this book.

The book was also important from a methodological standpoint. The authors said that marriages and families should be studied as systems. Although this was not a new idea in the 1970s, what *was* new was that the book proceeded to suggest how this could be done mathematically using Information Theory (Shannon & Weaver, 1949) for the study of sequential patterns of interaction. They noted that the mathematics of Information Theory change how interaction should be thought of, and they suggested that the mathematics implied a new approach. Hence, instead of this systems concept remaining a vague metaphor, or a mathematical procedure for analyzing data, Raush et al. realized that it represented a whole new way of thinking. They called this approach *adaptive probabilism*.

2.3. WHAT IS ADAPTIVE PROBABILISM?

It was the intention of Raush et al. to introduce the idea of stochastic models to researchers. Stochastic models are uniquely designed for thinking in terms of systems rather than individual behavior. Stochastic models refer to the conceptualization of behavior sequences in terms of probabilities and the reduction of uncertainty in predicting patterns of interaction (for a systematic development of these concepts and their mathematics, see Bakeman & Gottman, 1986; Gottman & Roy, 1990).

In fact, Gregory Bateson and the original General Systems theorists in the 1950s were influenced strongly by MIT mathematician Norbert Wiener. Although he may not be very well known to the average American, Wiener was an eminent mathematician; he had a profound influence in our time. He changed the way we think about systems. He was the man who coined the terms *cybernetics* and *feedback* (with Julian Bigelow). He developed his ideas in a cloak and dagger World War II project, in which the goal was to design an anti-aircraft gun that could anticipate where its target would be. He knew that this would be a significant advance over shooting up flak into the sky and hoping that planes would bump into the flak. In this project, Wiener began considering systems that involved feedback mechanisms. Wiener's student, Claude Shannon, later developed Information Theory, which is the theory that Raush et al. (1974) applied to their work. Wiener tried to influence Bateson, but unfortunately Bateson lacked the mathematical sophistication to understand and apply Wiener and Shannon's ideas.

However, Raush already had been applying these methods to the study of aggressive behavior in boys. Raush also influenced an eminent family researcher, Gerald Patterson (personal communication, 1993). Raush knew that these mathematical models, using Information Theory, would add a great deal of conceptual clarity to a field whose concepts remained at the level of metaphor. I briefly sketch how Raush et al. developed these ideas.

First, a distinction was made by Raush et al. between determinism and probabilism. They wrote:

> Marriage may allow for a variety of alternative modes of dealing with conflict, each of which is associated with a probability of occurrence. At any given moment there is some doubt or uncertainty about which of these alternatives will occur. For example, let us say that in general the likelihood that Bob will insult Sue is very low; but if Sue mocks his mother, Bob insults her more often than not. Sue, however, only mocks his mother when she gets very angry in an argument—which does not happen often. Thus, a heated argument raises the likelihood of Sue's mocking Bob's mother, which in turn increases the likelihood of his insulting Sue. But these are probabilities, not certainties. In the heat of argument Sue does not always mock Bob's mother, nor does he always insult her when she does. (pp. 9–10)

These probabilistic laws, they suggested, were a different way of thinking about family interactions than the usual deterministic strategies that family theorists were proposing.

One could discover laws of interaction that were probabilistic statements about interaction sequences. The laws could be greatly modifiable by family development, they suggested, and these developmental transformations were suitable objects for scientific study. For example, a threat in a marriage usually results in a counterthreat; however, when a threat is made by a pregnant wife in a very happy marriage, the husband is more likely to concede than to counterthreaten. This might be an example of how laws get transformed developmentally. In fact, this example turned out to be close to their actual results.

What Raush meant by these probabilistic laws was an analysis quite detailed and specific, an analysis that recently has come to be called microanalysis. However, Raush et al. (1974) also spoke of these probabilistic laws of interaction at a meta-level. In fact, they suggested that it is the nature of well-functioning interactional systems to proceed by a kind of "probabilistic playfulness," a kind of flexibility for inventing new patterns of interaction. They speculated that these probabilistic modes may become dysfunctional in circumstances in which there is a premium on efficiency rather than flexibility. Thus, one supposedly could identify circumstances in which specific patterns of interaction could be evaluated in terms of their adaptive character with respect to some identifiable contraints. I develop this latent idea of flexibility versus constriction of alternatives as characteristic of dysfunctional relationships in the chapters to come. What Raush did not specify was how this flexibility or rigidity operated to make a marriage functional or dysfunctional. I show how this works when I introduce the notion of negative affect as an absorbing state.

2.4. WHAT IS COMMMUNICATION?

Raush et al. (1974) began extending the ideas of adaptive probabilism to a precise definition of communication itself. They began by stating the fundamental assumption: "If what I do has no effect whatsoever on you, then I have not communicated with you. Communication occurs when what I do affects you in some way"(p. 19). This view was in direct contrast with General Systems theorists, who postulated that all behavior has communicative value, leaving the notion of communication undefined in scientific terms (Watzlawick, Beavin, & Jackson, 1967).

2.4.1. Communication Defined

Raush et al. suggested that communication has to do with structure in time, that is, with temporal form, in which consequent acts are more predictable than they ordinarily would be if we did not know the antecedent acts. The definition is essential to Shannon's Information Theory (Shannon & Weaver, 1949), and involves the reduction of uncertainty. The central idea is that knowledge of the antecedent act in a stream of behavior reduces uncertainty in prediction of the consequent act if communication has occurred. Thus, Information Theory gives the researcher a precise method for determining characteristic patterns of behavior from an observed stream of behavior. In this sense, one can equate communication with constraint. The stream of behavior has patterns in it if there are these constrained probabilistic pathways. Furthermore, and even more exciting, these pathways can be discovered empirically.

2.4.2. Mathematics of Adaptive Probabilism

Actually, the mathematics of adaptive probabilism are not very complicated. I present them here without equations so that they are more accessible to a general audience. Raush et al. (1974) presented an interesting example in the form of a matrix of probabilities from antecedent to consequent acts. Technically, this matrix is called a "Markov Matrix of Transition Probabilities" (Gottman & Roy, 1990). Table 2.1 is an example of such a Markov matrix.

The way to read Table 2.1 is by examining it row by row. Look at the first row, which can be read "Wife's antecedent act is nice." This means that the wife's preceding behavior was to be nice. If the wife's antecedent act is nice, then the estimated probability that her husband will subsequently be nice is .90 (i.e., he will be nice 90% of the time after she has just been nice), whereas 10% of the time he will be nasty after she has been nice. Then read the second row. In the second row, the estimated probability that he will be nice after she has just been nasty is

TABLE 2.1
Example of a Markov Matrix

	Husband's Consequent Act	
Wife's Antecedent Act	Nice	Nasty
Nice	90	10
Nasty	10	90

10%, and the estimated probability that he will reciprocate her nastiness with nastiness of his own is 90%.

Now I discuss this way of examining marital interaction to see why it can add a dimension to my analysis of interaction that I think has profound implications. This dimension is seen in the concept of *absorbing states*.

2.5. ABSORBING STATES

An interesting thing that Raush et al. (1974) did not point out about their example of a transition matrix is that it consists of what are called two absorbing states. An absorbing state is one that is difficult to exit once it is entered. It is analogous to falling down a well that may be a bit too deep to jump out of on your own. This is true for this couple for both nice and nasty behavior. There is only a 10% chance of leaving each state once it is entered. This kind of matrix is precisely what different laboratories have discovered since the work by Raush et al. (1974) as characteristic of the structure of the interaction of unhappily married couples. Later in this book, I talk further about this constriction of alternative behaviors (particularly repair mechanisms) in the marital interaction of unhappily married couples.

2.6. NO COMMUNICATION, OR NO INFLUENCE, IS POSSIBLE WITH THIS SCHEME

Unlike the early General Systems theorists who postulated that "one cannot not communicate" (Watzlawick et al., 1967), the mathematical ideas by Raush et al. (1974) allow for the possibility of no communication in a marital interaction. Compare the earlier matrix (Table 2.1) to the matrix in Table 2.2, in which there is no communication. What would no communication look like in terms of these numbers? The answer is that

TABLE 2.2
No Communication Matrix

Wife's Antecedent Act	Husband's Consequent Act	
	Nice	Nasty
Nice	50	50
Nasty	50	50

no communication occurs when the consequent act is independent of the antecedent. Table 2.2 is an example of no communication.

No matter what the wife's antecedent act has been, the behavior of the husband is the same, because the two rows are symmetrical. This means that his subsequent behavior is not predictable by knowledge of her antecedent behavior. In other words, his subsequent behavior is independent of her antecedent behavior. In the mathematics of Information Theory, this would be stated as there is no reduction of uncertainty in the husband's behavior by knowledge of the wife's immediately prior behavior. Hence, there is no communication, or no influence, in this direction (from wife to husband). Consider another example (Table 2.3):

In this case, once again, the rows are symmetrical, so once again the situation is uniform with respect to the wife's antecedent behavior. Once again, there has been no communication. The difference in this matrix from the preceding one is that in this matrix the husband's nastiness is an absorbing state (it is hard to exit once entered). No matter what his wife does, there is a 90% chance he will subsequently be nasty.

2.6.1. Defining Power Using Information Theory

In the view of Raush et al. (1974), communication is, therefore, equivalent to the existence of temporal form, or temporal patterning in the data stream. There are a lot of possibilities introduced by this way of thinking. For example, it is possible that one can have an asymmetry between husband and wife, in which the wife's behavior is quite predictable from the husband's prior behavior, but not the other way around. Communication (or influence) then flows only in one direction. Gottman (1979) later suggested that the existence of such an asymmetry would be a good way to operationalize the notion of power. The idea is that if it is easier to predict the wife's behavior from the antecedent behavior of the husband, than conversely, then the husband would be considered more powerful than the wife. Gottman (1979) found that this kind of asymmetry (with the husband having the greater power) was more characteristic of dissatisfied than satisfied marriages.

TABLE 2.3
No Communication–Absorbing State Matrix

Wife's Antecedent Act	Husband's Consequent Act	
	Nice	Nasty
Nice	10	90
Nasty	10	90

2.7. THE NATURE OF CONFLICT ESCALATION

The essay by Raush et al. defined conflict in a relationship as the existence of any overt or covert psychological antagonism, and claimed that no relationship is free of conflict. Furthermore, they suggested that no relationship is without ambivalence. The only question is whether the conflict is functional or dysfunctional. They referred to the writing of Coser (1964), who argued that conflict will make a group more cohesive if the conflict can be resolved by appealing to basic principles in which the group believes. However, Coser (1956) suggested if the conflict raises issues about these basic principles, the conflict will be divisive. In a similar way, Raush et al. (1974) suggested that if any conflict winds up being a challenge to the basic beliefs of the marriage, then conflict will be dysfunctional.

2.8. IS SYMBOLIC CONFLICT DYSFUNCTIONAL?

We have all known couples whose interactions consist of a lot of bickering about very trivial matters. We have also probably experienced arguments that have a great deal of emotional energy invested in them and were in fact about some matter like how to load a dishwasher, how the house should be tidied, or how liver is best prepared. Most investigators have been convinced that such issues that escalate out of control have to be about something else other than the seemingly trivial issue being discussed. Gottman, Notarius, Gonso, and Markman (1976) called this other issue a *hidden agenda*. Raush's thinking about this question had to do with the idea that something about the arguments about the liver, the dishwasher, and so on actually were symbols of something else, and that the conflict was symbolic conflict. The couple was not really arguing about how to load the dishwasher, rather they were arguing about a much deeper issue, such as autonomy, caring, respect, and so on. The actual argument was a symbol of something much deeper.

They then suggested that Boulding's (1962) notion of symbolic conflict is the key toward an understanding of how conflict can become destructive. The power to generate escalating conflict, they suggested, is related to the central value of the symbolic image to the person. For example, they wrote:

> Take the value of manliness as an example. Suppose that for Bob Smith manliness, with concomitant ideas of behavior that is dominant, strong, aggressive, potent, unromantic, hard, and the like, is at the core of a self

image that includes a definition of women as submissive, weak, emotional, soft, an so forth. Assume that for Bob this image is very concentrated—it is a central value around which other values are integrated. If Sue were to fail to play her assigned role vis-à-vis Bob, he would be severely threatened; conflict would be inevitable, and it is very likely that such conflict would be severe and disruptive to their relationship. (Gottman et al., 1976, p. 32)

Raush et al. (1974) believed that the presence of a lot of conflict and the escalation of conflict from the seemingly trivial to a heated emotional discussion was dysfunctional. This book states that they were wrong. In studying different types of couples, I believe that things are not quite as simple as Raush et al. suggested. There are couples whose marriages are quite functional, but who engage in arguments quite frequently and who may seem to an outsider to bicker and quarrel. These couples are quite emotionally expressive of both positive and negative effects. What matters in determining the eventual fate of the marriage is the balance of positivity and negativity. Even an essay by a team of brilliant researchers can be wrong, and this points out the importance of quantitative study of these reasonable hypotheses.

There is a great deal of wisdom in the speculations of Raush et al. (1974). The part of their thinking that will prove most useful is not the presence of quarreling, but the presence of defensiveness, hostility, and withdrawal. Thus, the idea that the conflict is threatening and touches on core issues in the relationship is more in line with my findings of what is harmful in a marriage than the presence of high levels of emotionality during quarrels.

I now return to the essay by Raush et al. about symbolic conflict. By drawing on the work of Deutsch (1969), Raush et al. expanded on the notion of symbolic conflict. They suggested that threat leads to increased reliance on threat, coercion, and deception, which are, in turn, reciprocated. They wrote that threat leads to defensiveness and excessive tension, which leads to "the closed mind." Thus, they suggested that perceived threat, or defensiveness, and the resultant closed-mindedness is the result of symbolic conflict. However, they thought that constructive conflict resembles creative thinking.

2.8.1. The Contexts of Conflict

The essay by Raush et al. on conflict continued with suggestions that various factors contextualize conflicts. For example, they suggested that some issues are "hot," whereas others are "cool," and that some times are better than others for raising conflicts. They also suggested that there are core issues in a marriage, and that one of these is separateness and connectedness. However, they speculated that core themes may vary with development. Thus, themes of conflict are contextualized by different stages of the family's life cycle; for example, the issue of connectedness–separateness is likely to be particularly important to newlyweds. With the birth of a child, new issues will arise.

2.8.2. The Male–Female Context

Raush et al. (1974) were very interested in gender differences in marriages. They wrote: "As to modes of handling conflict, there is the lore of masculine rages and feminine tears, of male rationality and female emotionalism" (p. 37). In this book, I have a few things to say about gender differences in marriages (see chapter 12).

2.9. DESTRUCTIVE CONFLICT ENGAGEMENT STYLES

Their essay continued (with no data presented) to map out destructive engagement strategies. They suggested that inflexibility is characteristic of these interactions. They gave the example of long deterministic (rather than probabilistic) chains of disagreement that seem childlike ("Yes, you will," followed by "No, I won't," followed by "Yes, you will," etc.). This is a major theme of their book.

The idea is that *dysfunctional marital interaction consists of inflexibility and a constriction of alternatives*. I build on this idea in chapter 3. They suggested that these inflexible conflicts are characterized by thought patterns associated with anxiety, related to core issues of trust, autonomy, power, and love. They wrote, "some couples give the impression that almost any interpersonal disagreement is capable of impinging on these schemata" (p. 105). It is unclear how Raush et al. (1974) arrived at these conclusions.

3

Terman's Question: What Makes for Marital Happiness? The View From Observational Methods

A great deal of conceptual clarity was introduced into the study of marriage by the direct observation of marital interaction and by the notions of adaptive probabilism. One of the major points I wish to make in this book is that it was not at all obvious what to study in marital interaction, or even what to consider positive and negative. For example, are interruptions, disagreements, anger expressions, and not looking at the speaker positive or negative? These things have to be determined empirically.

The essay by Raush et al. (1974) was a predecessor of a great deal of subsequent research. In this chapter, I review research on Terman's question of what discriminates satisfied from dissatisfied marriages and suggest some caveats and general conclusions. I also explore the implications of greater negative affect reciprocity in dissatisfied compared with satisfied marriages. I take from the research one general conclusion about the failure of repair mechanisms when negative affect becomes an absorbing state.

For the most part, the systematic observation of marital interaction is relatively new. It began less than 20 years ago. However, research on marriage is more than 50 years old. What was the early research like?

3.1. EARLY RESEARCH ON MARRIAGE

Research on marriage began in the 1930s, and the methods used were entirely interviews and questionnaires. It was a remarkably productive period of research. The amazing thing about this early research was well stated by the first published book on marriage by Terman and his associates (1938). Terman noted that there was a "chaos of opinion" about marriage. In short, everyone had a theory and none of these

38

theories had been put to any sort of scientific test. Terman and his colleagues (1938) did just that. Others followed, with Burgess and Cottrell (1939) studying engaged couples longitudinally, Locke (1951) studying divorced people (a first in the 1950s), and so on.

Many of the ideas of these early researchers turned out to be false. For example, they thought that couples that were more happily married would have sex more often. However, there turned out to be no relationship between the frequency of sexual activity and marital satisfaction.

One of the reasons observational methods were not used very much by these early researchers is that the scientific study of marriage was essentially the exclusive province of sociologists until about 1973, when psychologists began employing observational methods to systematically study marital interaction. Although there are some exceptions, sociologists typically rely on surveys, interviews, questionnaires, and other archival data. The sociological tradition, initiated by Terman, Buttenweiser, Ferguson, Johnson, and Wilson (1938), had never employed observational techniques, choosing rather to utilize subjects' self-reports.

On the other hand, the psychologists who studied marriage were interested primarily in developing behavioral approaches to marital therapy. Their behavioral tradition made it natural for them to be suspicious of self-report data, and to rely instead on observing behavior directly.

This should not be taken to imply that self-report data are of little value in the study of marriage. On the contrary. If properly used, they can be quite valuable, and we need to think of their role. A major contribution of the sociological work was the development of a number of respectable self-report measures of marital satisfaction. These measures work very well, despite the fact that they have their problems, and researchers correctly periodically criticize them and try to design better measures of marital quality. Although this is an important goal, there may be limitations in what one can learn about marriage from couples simply by asking them questions.

When one first examines these marital satisfaction measures (e.g., Locke & Wallace, 1959), it is easy to think that they would be subject to all sorts of bias. However, the opposite seems to be true; these measures have been demonstrated to have fairly high levels of construct, discriminant, concurrent, and predictive validity. Terman et al. (1938) even used inventive techniques such as asking friends of the couple about their friends' marriage and found high convergence between the couple's self-report and their friends' reports. As the number of different measures proliferated, and as high levels of intermeasure correlations were found (usually in the range of .80 to .90), there were calls for the use of a common terminology for all marital questionnaires (see Burgess, Locke, & Thomes, 1971a).

High correlations among self-report measures still remain the rule; for example, a newer scale of marital satisfaction by Spanier (1976) correlates very highly with the Locke–Wallace and other scales of marital satisfaction. No doubt one source of these high correlations is the similarity of items that are found on the different scales (Spanier actually rewrote, incorporated, and added to the Locke–Wallace items). But beyond this, it seems that unhappy couples will endorse almost any negative item, and happy couples will endorse almost any positive item about their marriage. The assessment of marital satisfaction by self-report methods is, for the most part, a global judgment about the marriage as a whole. The negative and positive halo effects in this global judgment are being studied now by attribution theorists of marriage (e.g., see Fincham, Bradbury, & Scott, 1990). Hence, if a study includes couples with a wide enough range of marital satisfaction levels, high correlations can be expected across different measure of marital satisfaction.

Still, there are severe limitations to these self-report measures of marital satisfaction. As I have stated already, it is my view that observational measures must supplement self-report measures, and, indeed, should be granted a very special place in the study of marriage. Why? As I noted, I think that, for the most part, people are unaware of the detailed patterns of interaction in their marriages. Also, they tend to be biased to construct a consistent (often self-justified) account of their marriages (e.g., see Weiss & Heyman, 1990). Many psychologists have studied this process of positive distortion in happy marriages and negative distortion in unhappy marriages. Therefore, there are severe limitations to what people can tell you about what they do in their marriages. Therefore, I believe that self-report measures need to be supplemented with observation.

Although these early marital sociologists rarely directly studied couples engaged in the process of making decisions and reaching agreements, an emergent theme in their research was the self-reported importance of consensual processes in marriage. In questionnaires, those items that asked couples about the extent to which they were able to agree about various aspects of marriage were related to marital satisfaction. For example, researchers would find that a demographic variable such as income might be unrelated to marital satisfaction, but agreement between husband and wife about the perception of the adequacy of their income would be related to marital satisfaction.

Despite all of the scientific problems of using self-report measures to explain other self-report measures (known as the common method variance problem) that plague this kind of questionnaire-based research, these results provide some clues as to where to find behavioral differences between satisfied and dissatisfied marriages. Because items that required spousal consensus were related most strongly to marital satisfaction, it was suggested that the first place to look for differences in observable behavior would be when couples were attempting to reach consensus and agreement. Thus, when psychologists began to study marriage, processes of conflict resolution came in for careful scrutiny.

In the review that follows, I refer to two groups of couples—satisfied and dissatisfied couples. This distinction is a generic term that refers to other distinctions made in the literature, such as clinic and nonclinic couples (couples in marital therapy vs. a nontherapy sample), and distressed and nondistressed couples (distressed couples usually refers to therapy couples that are unhappily married as measured by marital satisfaction measures). Generally, results from all these various and other definitions tend to converge (Gottman, 1979).

3.2. RELUCTANCE TO USE OBSERVATION IN STUDYING MARRIAGES

It is my opinion that there is a reluctance to use observational methods for studying marriages. There are many reasons for this reluctance. Some of them have historical roots in the area of personality research. Early observational research on marriage followed closely on the heels of an extremely influential book by Mischel (1968) entitled *Personality and Assessment*. In this book, Mischel reviewed research on personality and suggested that personality theory had come far short of predicting and understanding behavior. He concluded that correlations were quite low on the whole, that the field was plagued with common method variance (mostly self-reports predicting self-reports), and that the best predictors of future behavior were past behavior in similar situations.

This book was a great stimulus to many researchers. It encouraged a new look at personality measurement, validity, and reliability (Wiggins, 1973). It stimulated new kinds of research in personality. However, in my view, it also created the pessimistic view that research in interpersonal psychology would have very little payoff. In general, these thoughts ran as follows: If it would take, say, 50 variables to describe the individual personality, it would take at least $50 \times 50 = 2,500$ variables to describe two people who are interacting. The admonition was implicit: Do not study relationships until you understand the individual. At the time, this seemed like quite a sensible admonition.

Could this view have been wrong? In hindsight, much of the order that exists in notions of consistency in individual personality may exist at the interpersonal level. In fact, Patterson's (1982) analysis of the great consistency across time and situations in aggression was that it should be rethought in interpersonal terms as the aggressive boy's recasting people in his social world to play out dramatic coercive scenes shaped in his family.

If it turns out that a great deal of order exists at an interpersonal level of analysis and not in the study of the individual personality, is this really so amazing? Consider Von Frisch's (1953) studies of the behavior of bees. Von Frisch discovered the famous "dance of the bees," in which a bee that has found a nectar-rich field of flowers returns to the hive and does a complex dance that tells the other bees how to fly with respect to the sun and how far to fly. The strange dance of the bee can only be understood by realizing that the bee's dance is communication. Had Von Frisch taken a solitary bee into the laboratory and placed it on a table, he would have concluded that bees are motivated only to bat their heads repeatedly against glass windows until they drop dead. The order he discovered in studying bees came from going directly to the hive and the fields of flowers that are the business of the hive. Are we *homo sapiens* less social than bees? Maybe not. Hence, modern social psychology, when it brings an individual into a laboratory room, must then become imaginative about how to create a social situation out of this isolated individual. This choice of paradigm often is made in the interests of experimental control of particular social processes, and then it may have great merit, but it has little to recommend it if the goal is to understand interpersonal relationships.

There is a second reason that researchers are reluctant to engage in the process of observing couples. It is simply very costly and frustrating to do observational research. It takes lots of time and experience to develop a good coding system for marital interaction, and even then it takes lots of time to obtain actual numbers from tapes of the interaction. Reliability of measurement is a continual issue in an observational study, and one continually must deal with problems of definition of categories, interobserver reliability, drift, and decay (Reid, 1970). It is much easier to hand out a questionnaire.

Also, observational measures are often somewhat atheoretical. They usually are designed to exhaustively describe all the behaviors that can be observed in a particular situation. This is very different from a questionnaire, which is designed to measure a specific set of constructs, such as egalitarianism in the marriage, paranoid ideation in each partner, and so on. Once one has collected observational data in a study, it is often quite unclear what one has measured. For this reason, a purely descriptive, hypothesis-generating phase of research is required to validate the observational measures. This added phase of research often is skipped by researchers who use observational methods. If it is not skipped, it adds a lot of time to any research program. Although they are often a richer source of hypotheses than questionnaire data, and more satisfying to the truly voyeuristic researcher, observational data also require much more psychometric work to know what one actually has measured. It is also the case that underlying the selection of categories for any observational system is a set of assumptions and some rudimentary theory about what behaviors are important to look for. For example, the Marital Interaction Coding System (MICS) emerged from behavioral marital therapy in which it was important to pinpoint the marital issue; as such, for example, vague statements of the problem were considered negative, whereas specific statements were considered positive.

Furthermore, observational approaches to the study of families were tried in the 1960s and failed miserably. The story of this failure is very dramatic. First, a few maverick psychologists, psychiatrists, and anthropologists in the 1950s observed a strange pattern of interaction between adult schizophrenics and their mothers when they visited them in the hospital. The mothers would greet their children with warmth and then stiff coldness, all packaged in one embrace. The idea these researchers had was called the "double bind" theory of schizophrenia. It maintained that the mother sent a mixed message to her child and that this message put the child in a "double bind," meaning that he or she was damned if he or she responded to one part of the message and damned if he or she responded to the other (contradictory) part of the message. They thought that the resulting double bind created the emotional withdrawal we have come to associate with schizophrenia.

In 1964, a new journal called *Family Process* was formed. It was dedicated to research on possible family origins of mental disorders. A lot of this work was observational, because the theories focused on communication. Unfortunately, this early quantitative observational research was very weak. Not a single hypothesis of these theorists, who called themselves "General Systems theorists," received clear support from actual research, except for the finding that the communication of families with a schizophrenic member was more confusing than that of normal families. This state of affairs was hardly much encouragement to others to do observational research on families.

However, in the early 1970s, several laboratories began to use direct observation to study marital interaction. These laboratories were motivated by the idea that marriages could be helped with a behavioral approach that essentially taught couples new social skills for resolving conflict. Because I came from a behavioral perspective, observation was second nature. In addition to my laboratory, a group of researchers in Oregon (Gerry Patterson, Marion Forgatch, Hyman Hops, Robert Weiss, and their students John Vincent and Gayla Margolin) had committed themselves to observational research on families that had conduct-problem children (e.g., children who are disobedient and throw temper tantrums). They found that these children's parents were getting divorced at a high rate. They decided to do what they hoped would be a brief detour to design an intervention for marriages in distress. They confidently pushed forward and naturally employed observational methods to help distressed couples resolve their conflicts. In this way, in a classic article Weiss, Hops, and Patterson published in 1973, observational research on marriage was born.

3.3. THE OBSERVATION OF CONFLICTUAL MARITAL INTERACTION

The major research question in the early observational studies of marriage was the same question posed by Terman, namely, how are satisfied and dissatisfied marriages fundamentally different? Terman was a psychologist who was well known for his studies of geniuses, but in his marital research he used primarily sociological methods. There were serious problems in the way this question was pursued, but the fact that systematic observation was employed at all turned out to be a major contribution of psychologists in the historical development of marriage research. In almost every case, this observational research began by sampling couples' ability to resolve conflict.

3.4. WHAT WERE THE FIRST CONCLUSIONS ABOUT THE TERMAN QUESTION?

There was an exciting period in the 1970s in which articles were published about what was different about the conflict resolution behavior of distressed couples compared with happily married couples. The apparent consistency of these early results across laboratories and the apparent simplicity of the findings was exciting. This consistency seemed to hold, despite different methods of recruiting and sampling couples, different tasks, and different observational coding systems. What was this apparent remarkable consistency that marital researchers discovered by observing conflictual marital interaction? They allegedly discovered that the interaction of unhappily married couples was more negative and less positive than that of happily married couples. Before reviewing this early research, consider a question.

3.5. ARE THESE CONCLUSIONS ACTUALLY TRIVIAL?

A prominent marital researcher, who will remain anonymous, recently said that observational research in marriage had produced trivial results. He concluded that the results were logically circular. He contended that researchers had taken unhappily and happily married couples and asked them to argue; they discovered that unhappily married couples were more negative and less positive during conflict than happily married couples. He contended this was an obvious result. Furthermore, he noted, this was essentially what they were asking couples to tell them on the marital satisfaction self-report measures. All this, if it were worth anything, was simply a testimony to the usefulness of self-report data, he said. Why bother, he suggested, with costly, time-consuming observations when they yield such obvious and uninteresting fruit? This criticism must be taken quite seriously, but first another question must be asked.

3.6. ARE THESE CONCLUSIONS ACTUALLY TRUE?

These two results are so intuitively appealing that they may seem like they are obtained easily. However, it is not obvious that they are true in general. I examine the alleged conclusions by reviewing the research with one of the first (and most important) observational systems of conflictual marital interaction, the Marital Interaction Coding System, (MICS; pronounced MIX). Although sometimes it has been used for other types of conversations (Birchler, Weiss, & Vincent, 1975), this observational coding system is designed specifically for use with conflict-resolution discussions. It includes codes such as problem description, positive solution, negative solution, agrees, and disagrees. It also includes codes that describe the listener's behavior (attention and engagement or disengagement).

3.6.1. A Careful Examination of the Conclusions

There have been two major reviews to date of research on the question of which marital interaction patterns are related to marital satisfaction

(Schaap, 1982; Weiss & Summers, 1983). Weiss and Summers restricted themselves to 45 studies (35 published, 10 unpublished) that employed at least some version of the Marital Interaction Coding System. The MICS arose from a behavioral approach to marital therapy, in which the goal was to improve couples' problem-solving abilities. It is a hybrid mixture of codes that tap both selected negative, selected positive, selected verbal and nonverbal behaviors, and the problem-solving skills the therapists were trying to teach their clients.

Of all the studies that Weiss and Summers (1983) reviewed, only 12 studies examined behavioral differences between satisfied (or nondistressed) and dissatisfied (or distressed) couples. Of these 12, one (Schaap, 1982) actually employed the content codes of the MICS and the affect codes of a second system, the Couples Interaction Scoring System (CISS; Gottman, Notarius, & Markman, 1977). I delay discussing the Schaap (1982) study because of its special importance.

Of the remaining 11 studies reviewed by Weiss and Summers (1983), 10 collapsed all the 32 MICS codes into some form of an overall positive or an overall negative category, at times discriminating between verbal and nonverbal behaviors, and at times not. One serious problem interpreting the results of these studies is that the rules for combining codes varied inconsistently across studies. For example, Baucom (1982) did not include disagreement and interruption in his negative super-code, but Birchler et al. (1975) did. Cohen and Christensen (1980) used a variety of coding schemes that included disagreement but not inter-ruption, although they had an undefined code called negative response. Harrell and Guerney (1976) included interruption but not disagreement. Some articles employed unique forms of the MICS and failed to specify which subcodes were employed in the assessment of negativity (e.g., Burger & Jacobson, 1979). Hence, attempts at a meaningful review of the literature with the MICS must be hampered by the lack of a precise definition of what is positive and what is negative in a marital conflict interaction.

Still, one can ask whether the results of these MICS studies found any consistency, despite this lack of uniformity in definition. In general, these studies concluded that negative interaction was more character-istic and that positive interaction was less characteristic of dissatisfied than satisfied couples.

However, a caveat remains. Many studies did not employ a neutral category, therefore the positive and negative supercategories were often highly linearly dependent. Without a neutral category, it is impossible to know if the general conclusion is due to less positive or more negative behavior on the part of the unhappily married couple. Margolin and Wampold (1981) shed some light on this question. They had a a neutral category and broke down each supercategory into specific MICS codes. Surprisingly, they did not find differences between satisfied and dissatisfied couples on either negative verbal or nonverbal behaviors in their analyses. However, there was a significant univariate test for a negative listener disengagement code called not tracking.

However, Margolin and Wampold (1981, 1982) found differences in neutral and positive interaction. Satisfied couples exceeded dissatisfied couples in problem-solving statements, verbal positive, and nonverbal positive multivariate analyses. Subcodes in which satisfied couples exceeded dissatisfied were problem solution, agree, assent, physical positive, and smile/laugh. In the neutral supercategory, satisfied couples interrupted one another more (suggesting that interruption should not be grouped with a global negative code automatically), issued more commands (suggesting that commands should not be grouped with a global negative code automatically), and more problem description. Thus, in marital interaction it is not clear that unhappily married couples are more negative than happily married couples when they attempt to resolve conflict.

Another MICS study that analyzed specific codes (Haynes, Follingstad, & Sullivan, 1979) found somewhat mixed results with respect to differences in positivity and negativity. Their six satisfied couples were more likely to show positive physical contact, less likely to criticize their partners, less likely to interrupt, and less likely to disagree than their seven dissatisfied couples. Although interesting, this picture is not consistent with Margolin and Wampold's (1981) results. Also, Haynes et al. (1979) were surprised that dissatisfied couples were more likely to maintain eye contact and more likely to agree than satisfied couples.

Therefore, at the level of specificity of individual MICS codes, we are presented with an unclear picture of the differences between satisfied and dissatisfied couples. There is clearly something there in a discrimination between satisfied and dissatisfied couples, but the conclusions that seemed so obvious and trivial do not seem to hold very consistently. Thus, we need to be skeptical of quick generalizations and simplistic conclusions about what the answer is to the basic Terman question.

What is one to make of these results? Clearly, a healthy skepticism needs to be applied to the global a priori analyses of the MICS categories. Many categories are not necessarily negative, such as interrupts, disagrees, and commands. This means that one does not understand how these codes function. In short, what many of these MICS studies tried to do was skip the necessary descriptive phase of observational research, which helps one know precisely what is being measured with the observational coding scheme. So, before one decides that the two hypotheses are obvious and trivial, one finds that they are actually somewhat elusive results.

Perhaps greater understanding of how individual or grouped MICS codes function within an interaction stream may be obtained by employing sequential analyses of the kind that Raush et al. (1974) recommended. Fortunately, two studies with the MICS actually did this kind of analysis.

3.7. SEQUENTIAL ANALYSES WITH THE MICS

Of the studies that used the MICS to code marital interaction, two employed sequential analyses (Margolin & Wampold, 1981; Revenstorf, Vogel, Wegener, Halweg, & Schindler, 1980). Again, they each defined negativity in their own way. What were the results?

3.7.1. Margolin and Wampold (1981)

Margolin and Wampold (1981) reported the results of interaction with 39 couples (combined from two studies conducted in Eugene, Oregon, and Santa Barbara, California). Codes were collapsed into three global categories: positive (problem solving, verbal, and nonverbal positive), negative (verbal and nonverbal negative), and neutral. For positive reciprocity, they found that: "whereas both groups evidenced positive reciprocity through Lag 2, this pattern appears to continue even into Lag 3 for distressed couples" (p. 559). Thus, reciprocating positive acts was more likely for distressed than for nondistressed couples.

Margolin and Wampold's results on negative reciprocity were as follows: "The data suggest that distressed couples demonstrate negative reciprocity through Lag 2, whereas nondistressed couples do not demonstrate it to any significant extent" (p. 559).

Margolin and Wampold also defined a sequence called "negative reactivity," in which a positive response to a negative antecedent is less likely than a positive response in general (i.e., that there is a suppression of positivity following a negative antecedent in distressed couples). They found this for all four lags for distressed coupes, but they found no evidence for this suppression of positivity by negativity for any lag for nondistressed couples.

3.7.2. Revenstorf et al. (1980)

Revenstorf et al. (1980), studying 20 German couples, collapsed the MICS categories into six rather than three summary codes. These codes were positive reaction, negative reaction, problem solution, problem description, neutral reaction, and filler. Interrupts, disagrees, negative solution, and commands were considered negative. They employed both lag sequential analyses that allowed them to examine sequences out for four lags, as well as multivariate information theory that Raush et al. (1974) had employed. From the multivariate information analysis, Revenstorf et al. (1980) concluded:

> In problem discussions distressed couples respond differently from non-distressed couples. . . . In particular [distressed couples] are more negative and less positive following positive (+) and negative (−) reactions. At the same time they are more negative and more positive, that is more emotional, following problem descriptions (P) of the spouse. Above all distressed couples are more negative and less positive in general that non-distressed couples. (p. 103)

They also found 17 sequences that differentiated the two groups. There is some inconsistency in the group differences for sequences with similar names (e.g., reconciliation), thus I summarize only their clearest results. For what might be called constructive interaction sequences, they found that nondistressed couples engaged in more validation sequences (problem description followed by positivity) and positive reciprocity sequences (positive followed by positive). On the destructive side, they found that distressed couples engaged in more devaluation sequences (negative follows positive), negative continuance sequences ("fighting on" or "fighting back" in three-chain sequences), and negative startup sequences ("yes-butting," meaning that somewhere in the four-chain sequence, negative follows positive) than nondistressed couples.

After an analysis of the sequences following a problem description, they concluded:

> It appears as if the distressed couples would interact like non-distressed— had they only higher positive response rates following a problem description of the spouse. And vice versa. The non-distressed would react equally detrimentally as the distressed—were they to respond more negatively to problem description of their spouse. The way they handle problems [problem description statements] seems to be the critical issue—not the sheer number of problems stated. (p. 107)

Revenstorf et al. (1980) also continued their sequential analyses for five lags and found that these reciprocity differences held across lags. They wrote:

In summary, different patterns of response tendencies emerge for distressed and non-distressed couples. After a positive statement the partner continues to reciprocate it positively in non-distressed, whereas no immediate response is likely in distressed couples. After a negative statement no immediate response is most likely in non-distressed, whereas in distressed couples both partners continue to reciprocate negatively. A problem description finally is repeatedly followed by a positive response in non-distressed. In distressed couples, negative statements follow repeatedly. (p. 109)

Revenstorf et al. (1980) then described four types of sequences. The first type of sequence is continued negativity ("distancing"). This sequence measures the extent to which negativity becomes an absorbing state. The second sequence type was positive reciprocity ("attraction"). This sequence measures the extent to which positivity becomes an absorbing state. The third sequence consisted of alternating problem descriptions and negativity ("problem escalation"). The fourth type of sequence consists of validation sequences, sequences of alternating problem descriptions, and positive responses to it ("problem acceptance"). Their results are graphed in Fig. 3.1. The remarkably creative display of the data in these graphs paints a fascinating picture. In most of the graphs (e.g., for positive reciprocity), the differences between the groups are not very great. However, the evidence is very clear that negativity represents an absorbing state for distressed couples, but not for nondistressed couples. By Lag 2, nondistressed couples begin to escape from the negativity, but distressed couples cannot escape.

These graphs provide dramatic information of group differences reflected in sequential patterning of MICS codes. However, I would like to see more detail. For example, the group difference is reflected dramatically in the sequence type Revenstorf et al. (1980) called problem escalation. It is difficult to know exactly what this sequence is. I expected it to be a sequence of problem description followed by defensiveness (excuse, deny responsibility), but because the negativity code includes so many types of negativity, this remains unclear. To illustrate this lack of specificity, their example of the two-chain sequence (problem description followed by negative) is an example of what I would code as a contempt response: "A: I'm helpless with the car, it wouldn't start this morning. B: You don't even know how to use the choke" (p. 105).

3.7.3. Summary of Sequential Results with the MICS

What is consistent across these two studies is that dissatisfied or distressed couples appear to engage in long chains of reciprocated

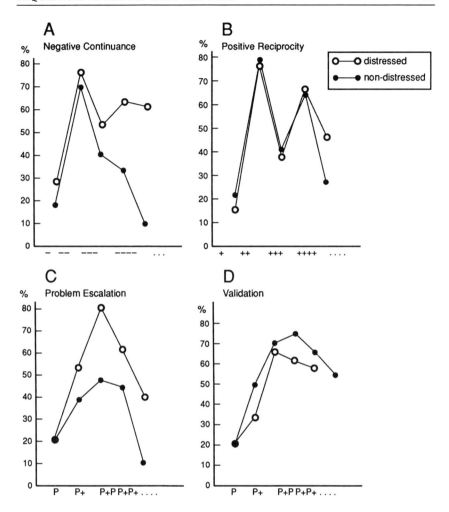

FIG. 3.1. Sequential analyses of interaction data for distressed couples and nondistressed couples as a function of lag. Adapted from "Escalation Phenomena in Interaction Sequences: An Empirical Comparison of Distressed and Nondistressed Couples" by D. Revenstorf, B. Vogel, R. Wegener, K. Hahlweg, and L. Schindler, 1980, Behavior Analysis and Modification, 2. Adapted by permission.

negativity. Is it possible that, despite the lack of a consistent definition of *negativity,* the reciprocation of negative codes is a more consistent characteristic of unhappily married couples than is the sheer amount of negativity? In support of such a notion, Gottman (1980) reported that negative affect reciprocity was more consistent for both satisfied and dissatisfied couples across interaction tasks than the amount of negativity or positivity. Is there support of these results in other studies that may have employed different observational coding system of conflictual marital interaction?

3.8. WORK WITH OTHER OBSERVATIONAL CODING SYSTEMS

I now review the sequential analytic research that has employed specific codes with systems other than the MICS. This restricts me to the work of six laboratories: Raush's, Gottman's, Schapp's (Holland), Ting-Toomey's, the Max Planck group in Munich (e.g., Revenstorf, Hahlweg, Schindler, & Vogel, 1984), and Fitzpatrick's.

3.8.1. Raush et al. (1974): Major Findings

The Raush group used two kinds of improvised conflict scenes—those that induced high conflict and those that induced low conflict. In these improvisations, one coach worked with the husband and the other with the wife (also see Gottman, 1979, for results with a set of empirically derived improvisations, and reanalysis of the Raush et al., 1974, data with a precise coding system). They tried to set the stage for a conflict and tried to make it real to both husband and wife, and then asked them to get together and resolve the conflict as they normally would resolve a real conflict between them. The major findings of the Raush study (1974) specific to the Terman question follow.

Briefly, their analyses proceeded by identifying (on the basis of interviews and questionnaires) a small number (six) of discordant couples and a small number (seven) harmonious couples. Their sample consisted of 46 couples, therefore they had 33 remaining couples. Some of their analyses compared harmonious couples to the group of 33 couples, and some compared discordant couples to the group of 33 couples. Their findings regarding marital quality and marital interaction were quite complex. I summarize only the major results. In general, they found that negative reciprocity (or continuance) was characteristic of lower levels of marital quality. This result was qualified by separate analyses of each of the improvised scenes (given in a fixed order). In the first and issue-oriented scenes (TV and anniversary), the discordant wives were very coercive and very likely to reciprocate negative messages. The discordant husbands were not very negative in these scenes. However, in the later and distance–closeness scenes, the discordant husbands were more coercive and attacking than their wives and more attacking and coercive than other husbands. There was a confrontation and relentless reciprocity of negative messages in the discordant couples.

Raush et al. (1974) provided a footnote not based on quantitative analysis of their data. The harmonious sample (of six couples), they suggested, actually was composed of two types of couples. They described one group as conflict avoiders and the other as sensitive and responsive couples that resolve conflicts easily. Conflict did not escalate in either group (i.e., there was not a great deal of reciprocity of negative messages in either group). They speculated a great deal about the conflict-avoiding couples, and were never quite sure whether conflict avoidance was functional or not. This book has a lot to say about conflict-avoiding couples.

3.8.2. Gottman (1979)

3.8.2.1. The Scope of the Book

The Gottman (1979) book summarized nine studies of marital interaction conducted at Indiana University from 1972 to 1976, primarily with Notarius and Markman. The book introduced the Couples Interaction Scoring System (CISS) and new approaches to sequential and time-series analysis of interactional data. The CISS was designed to disentangle dimensions of substantive behavior from dimensions of affect; these dimensions were confounded by the MICS. The CISS also differed from the MICS in its use of two separate groups of observers: One group coded the content of behaviors (e.g., problem description, agree, disagree), and another independent group of observers coded affect as either positive, negative, or neutral. In this scheme, a code like disagree could be delivered in three different ways, depending on its affect.

In several studies, the CISS was employed to differentiate satisfied couples from dissatisfied couples. Raush made his audiotapes available to my laboratory for recoding and reanalysis for comparisons with my own data. Using the CISS, the book reported the results of a study that recoded and reanalyzed data from the Raush et al. (1974) study on the differences between their discordant and harmonious groups. New improvisations then were developed empirically and employed in a dissertation by Rubin (1976). This study made it possible to examine couples' differences in interaction on various specific issues, including a nonconflict issue called the fun deck.

The book included studies with a device called the talk table, which operationalized couples' perceptions of the positivity of the intent of messages they sent and the impact of messages they received from their partners. This was an operationalization of behavior exchange theory (Thibaut & Kelley, 1959) as a perceptual theory.

The book also used Goldfried and D'Zurilla's (1969) approach to individual social competence assessment to demonstrate that there were social skill deficits in individuals, even when they were not interacting with their partners, but merely imagining this interaction. With this approach, I could vary the antecedent message and code the consequent systematically. In a subsequent controlled study, Gottman and Porterfield (1981) showed that these deficits have to do with the unhappily married husband, but only in decoding his own wife's nonverbal messages, not another person's wife. Noller (1980) independently replicated these results with Australian couples. Gottman and Porterfield (1981) proposed that this particular deficit might have to do with male withdrawal from marital conflict. I return to this theme later in this book (chapter 12).

There were three therapy intervention studies reported in the Gottman (1979) book, and a summary of Markman's dissertation predicting longitudinal change in relationship satisfaction among couples planning to marry.

3.8.2.2. Specific Methods and Results

A general conclusion of the studies in the Gottman (1979) book was that the nonverbal affect codes differentiated happily from unhappily married couples better than the verbal codes.

Specific nonsequential results were:

1. In computing agreement to disagreement ratios, satisfied couples had ratios greater than dissatisfied couples. For satisfied couples, the ratio was 3.17 for wives and 1.94 for husbands; for dissatisfied couples, the ratio was .64 for wives and .85 for husbands.
2. Nonverbal codes were better discriminators between dissatisfied couples and satisfied couples than the verbal codes, including agreement and disagreement.
3. Satisfied couples and dissatisfied couples did not differ on the proportion of positive affect, but satisfied couples were more neutral and less negative than dissatisfied couples.
4. Satisfied couples were less sarcastic than dissatisfied couples.
5. The groups did not differ on the frequency with which they expressed feelings, but dissatisfied couples were more likely to express feelings with accompanying negative affect than satisfied couples.

6. Couples did not directly ask their partners about their feelings; instead they mindread (attribute thoughts, feelings, and behaviors to their partner).
7. Satisfied couples and dissatisfied couples did not differ on the frequency of mindreading. However, mindreading with negative affect, which functions sequentially as a criticism, was more common in dissatisfied couples than in satisfied couples.
8. Disagreement was not more common among dissatisfied couples than satisfied couples, but dissatisfied couples were more likely to disagree with accompanying negative affect.
9. In the use of an important repair mechanism, dissatisfied couples and satisfied couples did not differ in the frequency of metacommunication. However, dissatisfied couples were more likely to metacommuniacte with negative affect, which was reciprocated in long chains of useless metacommunication with negative affect; that is, the negative affect and disagreement predominated. In satisfied couples, metacommunication was used more frequently, but in short chains that resulted in agreement. In other words, the repair mechanism worked in satisfied couples' interactions. (p. 108)

3.8.2.3. Three Phases of Marital Conflict

Using lag-sequential analyses, the interactions of couples were divided into three phases: an agenda-building phase, an arguing phase, and a negotiation phase. The task of the agenda-building phase appears to be to air the issues. The task of the arguing phase is to find areas of common ground, to persuade one another, and to argue for one's own point of view. This arguing phase is usually quite hot emotionally, and it is here that one sees codes and sequences designed to repair the interaction, such as metacommunication and feeling probe messages. Finally, there is a negotiation phase whose goal is to come to a mutually satisfying resolution of the issue. Within each phase, specific sequences were found to discriminate satisfied from dissatisfied couples. Also, nonsequential frequencies of specific codes discriminated.

3.8.2.4. Validation

There were some substantive results reported from these analyses that suggest the pervasive role of various forms of agreement, validation, and acceptance in the interaction of satisfied couples. In general, I can suggest that in the agenda-building phase of the conflict discussion, satisfied couples followed descriptions of an issue with verbal or nonverbal signals that suggested agreement with the feelings being expressed. This is not to say that the partners agreed with their spouses' point of view, but rather that it made sense to feel that way. The listeners tended to track and give the usual backchannels that the MICS system calls attends and assents. These can be as direct as occasional vocalizations ("Mmm-hmmm," "Oh," "Yeah," "I see," "Yup," "OK," etc.) or as indirect as a gaze toward the speaker, head nodding, and responsive facial movements. On the other hand, dissatisfied couples tended to respond to an expression of feelings about a problem with disagreement or a crosscomplaint. The interspersed agreement was far less likely to be there.

3.8.2.5. Repair

In the disagreement phase, two repair processes among satisfied couples were important. One was the feeling probe, and the other was metacommunication. Couples did not tend to discuss or ask about feelings directly. Instead, they used what the CISS called mindreading, an attribution of feelings, motives, or past behaviors to the partner. An example of this is that instead of asking a husband about how he feels about going to dinner at her mother's house, the wife says, "You always get tense at my mother's." Stems of "you always" or "you never" were found to be common in mindreading. The feeling probe was a sequence of neutral affect mindreading followed by agreement and elaboration by the partner. For example: wife: "You always get tense at my mother's" (neutral affect); husband: "Yeah I do, and I think it's because she criticizes the way I discipline Jason." If the mindreading were to have been delivered with negative affect, the sequence most common in dissatisfied couples, the response would be disagreement and elaboration. For example: wife: "You always get tense at my mother's" (neutral affect); husband: "I don't always get tense at your mothers, but when I do I think it's because she criticizes the way I discipline Jason. And you never stand up for me." The latter response is far more self-protective and defensive than the first.

Metacommunication was identified by the classic double-bind article by Bateson, Jackson, Haley, and Weakland (1956). It is a communication about communication, and, as such, it may qualify or change communication. A simple example is the statement, "You're interrupting me." I found that metacommunication was equally likely for both satisfied and dissatisfied couples. However, satisfied couples used it often, with neutral affect, in short chains that ended with agreement. For example: husband: "You're interrupting me"; wife: "Sorry. What were you saying?" In dissatisfied couples, the metacommunication was delivered with negative affect, and the chains were longer and led to countermetacommunication. For example: husband: "You're interrupting me"; wife: "Maybe I wouldn't have to if I could get a word in edgewise"; husband: "Oh, now I talk too much"; wife: "You don't give me a chance to tell you how I feel." The metacommunication could not function as a repair mechanism, because the negative affect from the interaction transferred to what was supposed to be a repair mechanism. It may be in this sense that negative affect reciprocity constricts the social processes available to a couple in the course of trying to resolve an area of disagreement (i.e., the meaning of the negative affective absorbing state). Gottman (1979) explored the anatomy of this constriction in examining the linkages between the affective behavior of the listener and the subsequent behavior of that person when he or she became a speaker. These were called editing sequences, and women performed this function in satisfied marriages. In dissatisfied marriages, women were far less likely to edit. Men performed an editing function only in satisfied marriages and in low-conflict situations.

3.8.2.6. Negotiation

A similar differentiation involving agreement was found in the negotiation stages of the discussion. Satisfied couples were more likely to enter into negotiation sequences, whereas counterproposals were more characteristic of the interaction of dissatisfied couples.

3.8.2.7. Point Graphs

The book also classified couples by interactional deficits and strengths using a graphical transformation of the CISS categorical data into point graph. Point graphs were plots of a cumulative sum of positive minus negative points earned by speaker and listener at each turn at speech. The cumulated point graphs were good discriminators between happily and unhappily married couples. Positive slopes characterized the happily married couples, and flat or negative slopes characterized the unhappily married couples (Fig. 3.2). Using time-series analyses of the noncumulated curves, it was possible to find some support for the hypothesis that husband dominance patterning was more characteristic of dissatisfied marriages. Dominance was defined specifically as asymmetry in predictability in the point graphs. For example, if one could predict the wife's data better from the husband's than conversely, then the husband was said to be dominant in that interaction.

3.8.2.8. Summary

Several findings emerged from the observational studies reported by Gottman (1979). The first is that there was greater negative affect in the

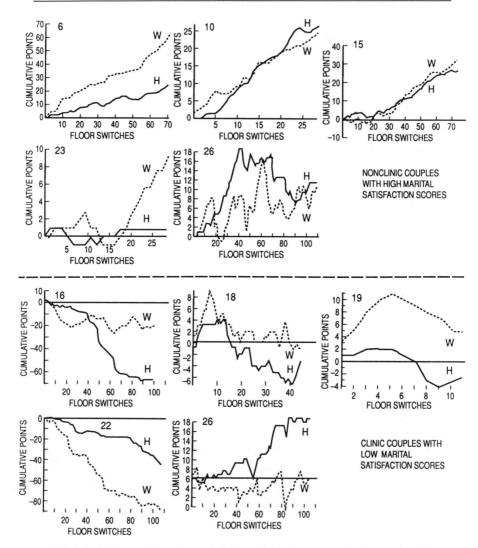

FIG. 3.2. Point graphs of cumulated positive minus negative interaction for distressed and nondistressed couples. From *Marital Interaction: Experimental Investigations* by J. M. Gottman, 1979, New York: Academic Press. Copyright 1979 by Academic Press. Reprinted by permission.

interaction of dissatisfied couples compared with satisfied couples, even when affect was coded separately from content and when a neutral affect code was employed. Second, there was greater negative affect reciprocity in the interactions of dissatisfied couples compared with satisfied couples. Third, there was evidence of negative affect turning normal social processes available to satisfied couples into a negative affect absorbing state for dissatisfied couples. It was as if they had no way of escaping this state once it was entered. All roads led to this particular Rome.

3.8.3. Schaap (1982)

An ambitious dissertation by Schaap (1982) with Dutch couples sought to test the generality of both the studies that had employed the MICS and the observational studies and some of the analyses reported in Gottman (1979). Schaap employed the content codes of the MICS and the affect codes of the CISS in his analyses. He also computed the point graphs presented in Gottman (1979), but did no time-series analysis of the data. He did not divide the conversation into thirds, but he had two interactional tasks. The first he called a habituation phase, in which the couple discussed its courtship and early marriage. Schaap had three groups of couples, but I review only the differences between the groups he called distressed and nondistressed.

Schaap (1982) divided his results into frequency and sequential. In the habituation phase, he found that dissatisfied couples laughed less often and used command and disagree codes more often than satisfied couples. During the conflict discussion, dissatisfied couples showed less humor, laughter, agreement, approval, assent, and compliance. Dissatisfied couples also showed less negative solution (saying what they want to see less of in the marriage); issued more commands, disagreements, and criticisms; and made more excuses and put downs (verbal contempt). Agreement to disagreement ratios also discriminated the groups. Schaap's ratios of agreement to disagreement were higher than those reported in Gottman (1979) for both satisfied and dissatisfied couples.

3.8.3.1. Affect Code Frequencies

Schaap (1982) found no significant differences between satisfied and dissatisfied couples on neutral codes, but his nondistressed couples were more positive and his distressed couples were more negative than those reported in Gottman (1979). This may be due, in part, to the fact that he asked couples to resolve *two* major issues in their discussion rather than one as in Gottman. These instructions may have generated more conflict in distressed couples. Schaap (1982) also found that wives delivered more codes with negative affect, whereas husbands delivered more codes with positive affect, a finding he noted was reminiscent of the gender differences reported by Raush et al. (1974).

3.8.3.2. Listener Withdrawal

Schaap (1982) found that distressed couples also had significantly more listener not tracking codes on the MICS, a code that assesses listener withdrawal. There were no gender effects on this code.

3.8.3.3. Sequential Analyses

The results Schaap (1982) found with the sequential analyses were far too detailed to completely summarize here. Hence, I only mention a few results. Schaap (1982) found greater likelihood of cross-complaining sequences with one sequential analysis, but not with another. He found a greater likelihood of validation sequences, which he necessarily had to define somewhat differently than Gottman (1979), because of his use of the MICS. Validation sequences were defined as problem description followed by consenting, in which consenting included accepts responsibility, agrees, assents, approves, and complies. Validation sequences were more common for nondistressed couples, which replicated Gottman (1979). The role of the nondistressed wife in validation was particularly salient in Schaap's (1982) data.

He found a greater likelihood of reciprocated humor, especially for distressed couples. After joking by the husbands, validation sequences were likely. Humor increased the consequent probability of positive and decreased the consequent probability of negative affect. Contracting sequences were more likely for the nondistressed couples, which also replicated Gottman (1979). He did not find evidence of the counterproposal sequences in distressed couples.

The dimension of defensiveness also emerged in Schaap's (1982) data, defined as chains of dissenting (combines the MICS codes of command, deny responsibility, disagree, and noncomply). He summarized this as a "yes-but" sequence, but it appeared more like a "no-no" sequence.

3.8.3.4. Point Graphs

Schaap (1982) did not construct point graphs in the same way as Gottman (1979). Gottman identified types of marital interaction from the shape of the point graphs. Instead, Schaap constructed his own typology of six groups, ranging from extremely negative to extremely positive. The shape of his curves generally related to marital satisfaction and agreement-to-disagreement ratios. Schaap's results replicated the notion that more positive graphs are more likely to represent more positive sequences identified in Gottman such as contracting and validation (to a lesser degree), as opposed to cross-complaining and counterproposal sequences. Schaap also analyzed "yes-but" sequences and "yes-dear" and "no deal" sequences between these groups. He did not replicate Gottman's results between flat-beginning and flat-ending point graphs. This failure to replicate was a reflection of the fact that there were no flat-beginning or flat-ending couples in his sample, not that these patterns were not reflective of validation or negotiation deficits as Gottman (1979) found. Schaap (1982) found the nonverbal data more useful in these discriminations than the verbal data.

3.8.3.5. Summary

In reviewing this complex dissertation, I conclude that many, but not all, of the observational results reported in Gottman (1979) were replicated. It is fair to conclude that the essential findings were replicated.

3.8.4. Ting-Toomey (1982)

Designed in part as a replication attempt of Gottman's (1979) studies, in a carefully executed study of 34 married couples, Ting-Toomey (1982) designed a new observational coding system (the Intimate Negotiation Coding System, INCS) and conducted sequential analyses of two types: Markov model fitting to determine order and homogeneity, and lag-sequential analysis (see Gottman & Roy, 1990, for a discussion of these methods). Hers was a sophisticated, exemplary approach to sequential analysis.

She divided her couples into three groups: low, moderate, and high in marital satisfaction. She found that the interaction in the high marital satisfaction group could be characterized by "communication strings of coaxing, confirming and socio-emotional questioning in a unilateral direction, while acts of task-oriented question and description were reciprocal or bilateral" (p. 16). In the low marital satisfaction group, the interaction sequences could be described as defensive. One common sequence was the confront → defend → confront → defend → confront sequence "with the sequential trend running toward complain and defend when confront was the criterion behavior" (p. 17). Another common pattern in the low marital satisfaction group was the complain → defend → complain → defend pattern, which "runs through lag 10 (10 events away from the criterion) when complain was used as the criterion behavior; and, (3) consequently, when defend was used as the criterion code, the sequential loop of defend → complain → defend → complain also runs through the entire ten lags" (p. 17). In the moderate satisfaction group, she found three patterns: chains of questioning and agreement when agreement was employed as the criterion code, chains of confirm and agreement when confirm was the criterion code, and chains of coaxing when coaxing was employed as the criterion code.

3.8.5. Revenstorf et al. (1984)

Using the MICS in a lag-sequential analysis, these authors identified four patterns: distancing, which was an alteration of negative responses; problem escalation, which was an alternation of problem description and negative responses to it; acceptance, which was problem description and positive responses in alternation; and attraction, which were patterns of alternating positive responses. Distressed couples showed long chains of negative reciprocity before therapy. Distressed and nondistressed couples had been distinguished by these sequences (Revenstorf et al., 1980), and these authors found that marital therapy changed each of these patterns considerably.

3.8.6. Schaap (1984) and Weiss and Heyman (1990)

The reader is referred to Schaap's (1984) review of the literature for additional conclusions about the relationship between concurrent marital satisfaction and marital interaction. An excellent recent review by Weiss and Heyman (1990) summarized the marital interaction literature since the Schaap (1984) review. The reader is referred to that article for another recent update of the marital interaction literature.

3.8.7. Fitzpatrick (1989)

Fitzpatrick (1989) studied 51 couples. She employed the CISS content codes and performed lag-sequential analyses. She concluded: "These results offer strong support for the importance of the conflict resolution sequences originally proposed by Gottman (1979) and found by Schaap, Buunke, and Kerkstra (1987)" (p. 152).

3.9. THEORETICAL IMPLICATIONS OF GREATER NEGATIVE RECIPROCITY AMONG DISSATISFIED COUPLES

In this section, I underline that greater reciprocated negative affective interaction as an absorbing state for dissatisfied couples has profound implications for the discussion of interaction process. As I suggested, this means that negativity becomes an absorbing state for dissatisfied couples (i.e., it is a state that is difficult to exit once entered).

What are the potential implications of this fact? One needs to know two additional facts about marital interaction. Vincent, Friedman, Nugent, and Messerly (1979) studied the interaction of distressed and nondistressed couples in a problem-solving task (the IMC). The two groups could be discriminated from one another on five out of six MICS summary codes, positive problem solving, and verbal and nonverbal positive and negative codes. They then asked distressed and nondistressed couples to fake good or bad during the next 10 minutes. Both groups of couples were unable to fake their nonverbal behaviors. Hence, nonverbal behavior may be a better discriminator of distressed and nondistressed groups than verbal behavior alone.

Second, most couples expressed the most negative affect during the middle arguing phase of the conflict resolution and their major attempts at repair of the interaction usually are delivered in this phase as well. Attempts at interaction repair often are delivered with negative affect. For example, statements like "Stop interrupting me !" or "We're getting off the subject" may be accompanied by irritation, tension, sadness, or some other form of distress. Thus, repair attempts usually have two components: a negative affective nonverbal component and a metacommunicate content component attempting to repair the interaction.

The implication of greater negativity being an absorbing state for dissatisfied couples is that they may attend primarily to the negative affect component of repair attempts, whereas satisfied couples attend primarily to the repair component. Thus, I conclude that repair processes do not work very well in dissatisfied marriages. Instead, what will predominate in dissatisfied couples' attempts to use these social processes is the negative affect. Hence, in various sequential analyses of the stream of behavior, if one spouse attempts a repair mechanism with negative affect, the other spouse is more likely to respond to the negative affect component with reciprocated negative affect in a dissatisfied marriage than in a satisfied one. The usual social processes that are present during conflict that repair the interaction (such as metacommunication) do not work in unhappy marriages. These processes are the mechanisms used by satisfied couples for exiting a negative state (Gottman, 1979). They include metacommunication, feeling probes that explore feelings, information exchange, social comparison, humor, distraction, gossip, finding areas of common ground, and appeals to basic philosophy and expectations in the marriage.

What goes hand in glove with this phenomenon is a constriction of social processes. The constriction of available social processes is the fascinating structural dynamic that maintains the absorbing state. How does this work? For example, assume that a message has two parts, one positive and one negative (e.g., the message "Stop interrupting me," which is an attempt to repair the interaction, may have been said with some irritation). In a happy marriage, there is a greater probability that the listener will focus on the repair component of the message and respond by saying, "Sorry, what were you saying?" On the other hand, in an unhappy marriage, there is a greater probability that the listener will respond only to the irritation in the message and say something like, "I wouldn't have to interrupt, if I could get a word in edgewise." In this case, the attempted repair mechanism does not work. The response to the negativity continues for long chains of reciprocated negative affect in dissatisfied marriages. Negativity as an absorbing state implies that all these social processes have less of a chance of working, because what people attend to and respond to is the negativity.

Interestingly, a side effect of this analysis is that the interactions of dissatisfied couples show a higher degree of interaction structure, more predictability of one spouse's behaviors from those of the other, and less statistical independence than is found in the interactions of satisfied couples. The interaction of happily married couples is more random than that of unhappily married couples. This is precisely what Raush et al. (1974) predicted. One interesting finding that may be related to this phenomenon is that this greater structure may come to pervade positive as well as negative interaction. This latter result is not found consistently across laboratories, but this may not be so much a failure to replicate as the inconsistency across laboratories in conceptualizing, generating, and measuring positive affect and in the lack of studies that do sequential analyses of their data.

To summarize, I noted that the finding of greater global negativity or less positivity in unhappy couples compared with happy couples is not necessarily a robust result. However, the finding of greater negative reciprocity appears to be somewhat more robust. Furthermore, I suggested why it is not at all trivial, but can be understood how it can act as a short circuit of other important constructive social processes (such as repair mechanisms) by the absorbing state of negativity.

3.10. OVERALL SUMMARY

The major point I wish to make in this review of the marital interaction literature is that by examining *specific* codes and code *sequences*, the results of the early research on the relationship between marital inter- action and marital satisfaction do not seem to be trivial. I can identify a number of replicated, distinct patterns that discriminate dissatisfied from dissatisfied couples. Among dissatisfied couples, there is:

1. Greater negativity and less positivity during conflict: (a) enhanced levels of negative interaction and affect; (b) low levels of agreement compared to disagreement; (c) lower levels of humor and laughter, and less reciprocated laughter; (d) fewer assents, agreements, approval, and compliance; and (e) more disagreement, criticism, and put downs (verbal contempt).

2. Greater reciprocity of negativity and greater probability that negativity is an absorbing state: (a) a lack of validation (or positive acceptance) of expressed feelings about a problem; (b) greater likelihood of cross-complaining; (c) a deficiency in contracting sequences and negotiation; (d) enhanced listener withdrawal from interaction; (e) enhanced defensiveness, such as denying responsibility, yes-butting, and mindreading with negative affect, followed by disagreement or chains of defending oneself against complaints and confrontations; (f) reduced likelihood of editing sequences among both males and females (editing refers to chains of negativity interrupted by neutral statements; it can be indexed by a negative listener who is then surprisingly not negative when it is the listener's turn to speak); (g) reduced feeling probes and metacommunication sequences that work to repair the communication; (h) structural differences—a constriction of social processes that can repair interaction during conflict and that are related to the absorbing state of negative affect; (i) pervasiveness of the conflict across interactional tasks—Gottman (1979) and Birchler et al. (1975) reported that unhappily married couples' interactions are more negative, less neutral, and less positive even when they are not resolving a conflict task. Hence, their conflictual interactions are more pervasive across situations than the interactions of their happily married counterparts; and (j) increased dominance among husbands in distressed couples (Gottman, 1979, time-series analysis of point graphs).

This list shows that observational research on marriage has learned a fair amount about the answer to the Terman question.

3.10.1. What Is Missing from This List and What Is to Come

You have just read a list of general conclusions that I have deduced from the literature on the observational marital interactional correlates of marital satisfaction. I have tried to be precise in constructing this list because, as you see later in this book, I believe that vague constructs do not help build theory. Theory comes from good observation and good observation comes from both precision and intuition.

What is really missing from the previous list is theory. My goal in this book is to build a new process theory of marriages. What makes things happen in a marriage? What are the dynamics? What makes things get better or worse over time? In the chapters that follow I plan to slowly and inductively build this theory. Its final formulation will be in chapter 15. I am proceeding in this way because I first need to build the elements of the theory so that it will be understandable later. I hope that the reader will be able to bear with me until chapter 15 so that the preceding list will take on some vitality in describing how I think that things operate in marriages.

3.11. MY OBSERVATIONAL MEASURES

I have employed five different observational systems in my work. I use some systems in some studies and other systems in other studies. Like the proverbial blind man feeling different parts of the elephant, each coding system highlights some particular aspect of marital interaction. No system is ideal by itself. I do not describe the systems in detail here. Instead, I refer to the codes the results are discussed. However, a section in the appendix of this book describes each system. The appendix is an introduction to the actual business of observing couples for the interested reader.

3.11.1. Pervasiveness of Marital Conflict and Rebound from Conflict

It seems likely that as marital conflict becomes more severe and problems remain unsolved, negative affect will become increasingly more pervasive in all the couples' interactions, and that they will be less likely to rebound from a conflict discussion. Hence, two additional criteria employed in this book to discriminate groups of couples are the pervasiveness of the marital conflict across situations, and couples' abilities to rebound from a conflict discussion to a positive conversation. Nearly all the research on marital interaction has involved the observation of conflict resolution. There are only three exceptions. The first is a study by Birchler et al. (1975), which included a brief 4-minute beginning period of free conversation during which couples "were instructed to talk about anything 'while we're setting up the equipment' " (p. 352).

They found that negative behaviors discriminated distressed couples from nondistressed couples in both casual conversation and the conflict task, but that positive behaviors discriminated couples only on the conflict task. In a dissertation in Gottman's laboratory, Rubin (1976) designed a fun deck task in which couples were instructed to have a good time discussing a set of items that a set of couples said represent good times. As reported in Gottman (1979), the ratio of agreement to disagreement discriminated distressed couples from nondistressed couples on the fun deck task, as did the proportion of problem feeling statements and the amount of neutral affect (distressed couples had lower ratios of agreement to disagreement, more problem feeling statements, and less neutral affect than nondistressed couples). Even on the fun deck task, distressed couples talked about problems in their marriage. Schaap (1982) also employed a nonconflict task. Couples were asked to talk about the time they met one another. Once again, unhappily married couples could be discriminated from happily married couples on this task. Hence, it appears that the pervasiveness of the conflict across interactional situations has been found to be a potent discriminator of happily from unhappily married couples. I employ one variable, the pervasiveness of negative affect, as a risk factor.

In my research, couples typically start by discussing how their days went. They have been separated for at least 8 hours before they have this conversation. They then are interviewed about areas of disagreement in their marriage, and they discuss one or several of these areas. They then are interviewed about things they like to talk about, and they then have this conversation, which I hope is enjoyable. I call the first conversation the events of the day (or events, in brief) conversation, the second conversation the conflict conversation, and the third the positive conversation. Before each conversation, there is a 5-minute silent period. When I talk about the pervasiveness of conflict, I mean that on the events conversation dissatisfied couples will be less positive or more negative than satisfied couples. When I talk about rebound, I mean that on the positive conversation dissatisfied couples will be less positive or more negative than satisfied couples.

4

Longitudinal Change in Marital Happiness: Observing Physiology as Well as Marital Interaction

The field of social psychophysiology is introduced. This chapter reviews results in predicting and understanding longitudinal change in marriages, particularly with physiological measures.

So far, many of the results I have discussed about marriage point to the fundamental role that affect or emotion plays in understanding marriage and how it changes over time. In 1980, Levenson (University of California, Berkeley) and I began to study seriously the question of longitudinal change in marriages. We began a collaboration designed to collect data about as many aspects as we could of emotion during marital interaction. We designed procedures that made it possible to obtain videotapes of the interaction synchronized with indexes of physiological activity.

Couples also returned and viewed their videotapes again and rated how they recalled having felt in the interaction. During this recall session, we also obtained physiological data. We discovered that couples tended to "physiologically relive" their interaction as they watched the video; as they watched and rated their videotapes, their hearts beated faster, their blood flowed faster, and they sweated more and moved more at the same times that they did during the actual interaction (Gottman & Levenson, 1985).

We were not the first to think of obtaining both physiological and social interaction data. In fact, there is a small field known as social psychophysiology, which has a fairly interesting history.

4.1. HISTORY OF SOCIAL PSYCHOPHYSIOLOGY

Social psychophysiology was born in the study of psychotherapy, but it did not leave a lasting mark on that field, nor did it become established in its own right as a result of its use in psychotherapy research. Like the Phoenix, it has had to rise from its ashes several times. Now it is considered a respectable field, and there are several textbooks about it.

In one of these texts, Waid (1984) noted that research on social psychophysiology had its roots in the study of social and physiological processes in the 1950s. An initial flurry of excitement accompanied the observation by Dittes (1957b) that a patient gave less electrodermal responses when the therapist was more permissive about an embarrasing sexual statement than when the therapist was unpermissive. This was a fairly interesting result, although it may seem intuitively obvious. Still, the notion that physiology could be affected so strongly by psychological processes was very exciting.

However, the new field was dealt its first death blow in a review by Lacey (1967). Lacey suggested that, because of the sensitivity of autonomic measures to immediate social contact, these measures "would not be reliable indications of the patients progress" (Ward, 1984, p. 4). Lacey's review led to a decline in the interest of autonomic correlates of therapy. The Phoenix went up in flames.

However, in the late 1960s, behavior therapy returned to the use of physiological measures to evaluate the success of treatment. Unfortunately, physiological measures were not very effective in this role, as Lacey had suggested. Still, even if they could not tell if the therapy was successful, they might be good indicators of processes occurring during treatment, or what are known as process variables. Yet, despite these early uses of psychophysiology in an interpersonal context, social psychophysiology had to wait for another 25 years to be born properly.

Our inspiration came from a study published in 1963. Kaplan, Burch, Bloom, and Edelberg (1963) examined the electrodermal activity (EDA) of interacting four-member groups in which people were paired on a sociometric that measured whether they disliked, liked, or felt neutral toward one another. They found that behavior and physiology related most for the groups that disliked one another. It seemed that negative social affect mediated the effect. In 1964, Liederman and Shapiro edited an important volume on social psychophysiology, in which Kaplan, Burch, and Bloom (1964) reported that there was high physiological linkage (i.e., covariation) in EDA only for the groups that disliked one another.

As Cacioppo and Petty (1983) noted, the 1940s saw technical advances in electronics that set the stage for quantifying mechanical and electrical events with a person. Before then, scientists used major stimulus events to obtain a physiological reading on their galvanometers. They used stimuli like a gunshot going off behind a subject's head, electric shock, suddenly and unexpectedly putting the subject's feet in a bucket of ice water, or putting excrement suddenly under the subject's nose. With the advent of better equipment, far smaller changes in physiology could be reliably detected, and this made it possible to study more subtle psychological events. Cacioppo and Petty (1983) pointed out that "The experimental treatments to which subjects are now commonly exposed need not be nearly as traumatizing as was the case several decades ago, and the sample and sensitivity of the electrophysiological measures are greatly improved" (p. 7). In short, it is now possible to reliably detect much smaller effects, and, hence, to study more interesting, everyday events, like those that occur when a married couple is conversing.

By the 1960s, the first influential books on psychophysiology began appearing, and these methods became widely available to researchers. Since the 1960s, the sophistication, simplicity, and cost of equipment have improved. With the availability of small computers for real-time data acquisition, the design of small psychophysiology laboratories is now feasible.

The potentially unfortunate result of this historical change is likely to be a compounding of the errors of equating psychological with physiological domains of measurement. For example, electrodermal activity can be created by a variety of stimuli, including a click to the ear; intense stimuli; a startle stimuli; and emotionally laden stimuli of lower intensity. Heart rate may decrease with some attentional tasks and increase with others. As Cacioppo and Petty (1983) noted: "[T]he *pattern* of physiological responses, rather than the intensity of the output of any single physiological effection, is in many instances regarded as the most informative 'physiological response' for study" (p. 10).

It is important to avoid the logical error that physiological variables are more fundamental indexes of psychological constructs. I suggest that the peripheral physiological measures most psychophysiologists employ must be viewed as crude measures of physiological processes. It is important to interpret them with a keen awareness of physiology. Also, it is essential in interpreting a physiological variable to be keenly aware of context (Kahneman, Tursky, Shapiro, & Crider, 1969). The psychological interpretation is usually highly suspect.

4.2. SOCIAL PSYCHOPHYSIOLOGY OF CHANGE IN MARRIAGE: AN OVERVIEW

In the past 10 years, Levenson and I have embarked on a series of studies of marriage in which we are trying to understand how marriages change over time. These studies were motivated by our adding a related longitudinal question to the oldest question in the research literature on

marriage: What distinguishes a marriage that will become more satisfying over time from one that will become less satisfying over time? At
first glance, it might seem that the same set of features would provide
the answer to both the contemporary question as well as the longitudinal one, but on further consideration, the possibility of different
answers becomes quite strong. For example, behaviors that are functional for "keeping the peace" in the present could leave unresolved
critical areas of conflict that might undermine the relationship over time.

Given our interest, it is inadequate to examine only the contemporary
correlates of marital happiness or misery. Once we started doing
longitudinal research on marriage, we found, much to our surprise, that
the correlates of concurrent marital satisfaction are not identical with the
correlates of change in marital satisfaction over time.

With respect to marital interaction, several variables are important in
longitudinal prediction of change in marital satisfaction. These are
*complain/criticize, defensiveness, disgust and contempt, and listener withdrawal
from interaction.*

4.2.1. Studies of Affect and Physiology During
Marital Interaction

The patterns that related to marital satisfaction described in chapter 3
were the phenomena that we set out to explain in our first collaborative
study in 1980. In our early thinking, there was a certain emphasis on
negative affect. This emphasis had multiple sources. Positive affect and
positive affect reciprocity had not proved to be very useful in discriminating satisfied from dissatisfied marriages (e.g., Gottman, 1979). In
addition, greater cross-situational consistency in marital behavior had
been found for measures of negative affect and negative affect reciprocity than for measures of positive affect (Gottman, 1980a). Finally,
we expected that our autonomic nervous system (ANS) measures would
be primarily responsive to the negative emotions (e.g., anger and fear)
by virtue of the role that the sympathetic nervous system plays in
preparing the organism to deal with emergency situations (e.g., those
requiring fighting or fleeing).

4.2.2. The Initial Levenson–Gottman Marital Interaction Study

When we first embarked on this collaboration, we both were interested
in studying emotion. Ekman, Friesen, and Ellsworth's (1972) classic
book *Emotion in the Human Face* suggested social interaction as an
important context for studying emotion, but most investigators in the
field still were using single-subject paradigms. As described earlier, we

were interested particularly in marital dissatisfaction, especially in relationship to negative affect, negative affect reciprocity, and ANS activation. We also saw this collaboration as an opportunity to collect a unique multimeasure, multimethod database that could be explored in a number of different ways.

Our first study was conducted in 1980 (Levenson & Gottman, 1983). Thirty couples came to the laboratory at the end of the day after at least 8 hours of separation and had two conversations. The first was a relatively low-conflict discussion in which they discussed the events of their day, and the second was a high-conflict discussion in which they attempted to resolve an issue in their marriage that had been a major source of disagreement for both spouses (the problem inventory and play-by-play interview procedures described earlier were used to facilitate this inter-action). Each spouse returned to the laboratory on a separate occasion to view the videotape of these interactions and to provide a continuous self-rating of his or her own affect on a rating dial that utilized a "posi-tive–neutral–negative" scale. During both sessions, we measured four physiological variables: heart rate, pulse transit time to the finger, skin conductance, and general somatic activity. All physiological, self-report, and video data were synchronized to the same time base (for full details on these procedures, see Levenson & Gottman, 1983).

The interactions that occurred in this study were powerful, emo-tional, and generally unconstrained. Questions of generalizability can be raised about any laboratory procedure, but, much to our relief, the interactions seemed quite natural and real. Previous work that com-pared marital interaction in the laboratory with marital interaction at home had indicated that differences between satisfied couples and dissatisfied couples observed in the laboratory underestimate those that would be obtained from home recordings without an observer present (Gottman, 1979). The naturalness of the interactions, coupled with this tendency to underestimate differences, gave us a degree of confidence in the generalizability of the findings that emerged from our analyses.

The database we collected in this study allowed us to ask a number of questions. We began by exploring ways in which the interactions of satisfied couples and dissatisfied couples differed. Two kinds of differ-ences emerged. First, as in previous research, marital dissatisfaction was associated with higher levels of negative affect and negative affect reciprocity. Second, we explored the notion that the interactions of dissatisfied couples not only would be characterized by reciprocity of negative affect, but also by a kind of temporal predictability and reciprocity in physiology as well. *Physiological linkage* was the term we used to describe this hypothesized physiological marker of marital dissatisfaction.

Recall that the notion of physiological linkage had been implied by the results of the small study by Kaplan et al. (1964). They paired people on the basis of sociometric measures of mutual like, dislike, and neutrality and found that predictability from one person's galvanic skin response (GSR) to another's only existed for people who disliked one another. It seemed reasonable to expect that dyads that disliked each other would express greater amounts of negative affect, and that it was this negative affect that was activating the GSR. Hence, we predicted that unhappily married couples would show the most physiological linkage.

In the Kaplan et al. (1964) study, simple correlations were used to measure the extent of physiological relatedness between people. There are serious problems with this statistical approach, because physiological data can be autocorrelated highly (e.g., cyclical). This means that data can be forecast from their past. If data can be forecast from their past, it is difficult to make inferences about linkages between variables. For example, if annual U.S. military spending and annual Russian military spending each can be predicted from previous values, it is hard to estimate how military spending in the two countries affect each other. There are better statistical approaches to this problem (for discussions and computer programs, see Gottman, 1981; Gottman & Ringland, 1981; Williams & Gottman, 1981).

In our study, when we used a more appropriate time-series analysis to assess predictability from one spouse to the other (controlling for autocorrelation), we actually found that the conclusion of Kaplan et al. (1964) held. *In fact, we were amazed that we were able to account for the majority of the variation in marital satisfaction with our physiological linkage variables.*

We found evidence for the relationship between physiological linkage and marital satisfaction only for the high-conflict problem-solving discussion. We think the physiological linkage variable reflects the ANS concomitants of cycles of negative emotional activation and deactivation, which are particularly prevalent in problem-solving conversations of dissatisfied couples. As evidence has accumulated that different negative emotions have different patterns of ANS activation (e.g., Ekman, Levenson, & Friesen, 1983), it seems likely that a fuller understanding of physiological linkage will require the consideration of which specific negative affects are being exchanged between spouses and which specific ANS variables are becoming linked.

In physiological linkage, we have a physiological parallel for negative affect reciprocity that may provide a more complete understanding of how the behaviorally absorbing state of negative affect we have noted in dissatisfied couples becomes a somatic state as well as a behavioral state.

Perhaps negative affect reciprocity, or the absorbing state discussed in chapter 2, continues because of heightened autonomic arousal in both people.

4.2.3. Predicting How Marriages Change in Happiness

4.2.3.1. The Follow-Up Study

In 1983, we completed a longitudinal follow-up study of the 30 couples that had participated in the 1980 study. We successfully located 21 of these couples and had them complete questionnaires concerning their current levels of marital satisfaction. We then computed a simple change score that indicated the amount and direction of change in marital satisfaction that had occurred between 1980 and 1983. Using partial correlations (to control for initial levels of marital satisfaction), we determined which of the affective and physiological variables measured in 1980 were predictive of changes in marital satisfaction that had occurred during the ensuing 3 years. Two strong findings emerged (see Levenson & Gottman, 1985, for a complete report of these findings). First, negative affect reciprocity was a strong predictor of change in relationship satisfaction. Second, physiological arousal (in all measures) was highly predictive of declines in levels of marital satisfaction. The sizes of these correlations were quite encouraging. For example, the correlation between the husband's heart rate during the conflict discussion and decline in marital satisfaction was quite high (see Table 4.1).

When we obtained these high correlations, we were encouraged that physiology might be teling us something about processes related to change in marital satisfaction. We also worried that in our next study we would find that nature was quite a bit more complex than she had led us to believe at first.

TABLE 4.1
Physiological Predictors of Changing Marital Satisfaction

Content	Husband				Wife			
	IBI	PTT	SCL	ACT	IBI	PTT	SCL	ACT
Events of day								
Baseline	.77**	.71**	−.39	−.21	.02	−.27	−.50*	−.34
Interaction	.80**	.76**	−.56*	.10	.08	−.16	−.62*	−.26
Conflict Area								
Baseline	.92**	.37	−.49*	−.22	.01	.23	−.58*	−.53*
Interaction	.92**	.48	−.48*	.08	−.11	.40	−.76**	−.02

Note. IBI = heart rate divided by 60,000; PTT = pulse transmission time; SCL = skin conductance level; ACT = general somatic activity.
* $p < .05$. ** $p < .001$.
From Levenson and Gottman (1985. Reprinted with permission)

4.3. A NEW THEORETICAL CONCEPT: DIFFUSE PHYSIOLOGICAL AROUSAL

What was conceptually appealing about our first longitudinal results was their simplicity. The results predicting decline in marital satisfaction over time could be summarized in one sentence: "Controlling for the initial level of marital satisfaction, the more autonomically aroused couples were at Time 1, the more their marital satisfaction declined in 3 years."

Relevant to our findings was some new research by Ekman, Levenson, and Friesen (1983). They asked whether specific pure emotions, either relived intensely in memory or just mimicked by the appropriate facial muscle contractions, would have specific autonomic effects. By this they meant that anger might have one effect and fear another. In fact, this is exactly what they found. Anger raised the temperature of people's fingers, whereas fear lowered it. They called this the specific autonomic signature of emotion. By this they meant that each emotion leaves its signature or characteristic pattern in the autonomic nervous system (ANS).

How is this relevant to our findings? Based on the specificity of the autonomic responses to specific emotions discovered by Ekman, Levenson, and Friesen (1983), it is possible that diffuse autonomic arousal in conflictual marital interaction is created by blends or close temporal sequencing of negative emotions. For example, we may expect that the emotions of anger, fear, and sadness, blends of these emotions and their close temporal sequencing, are diffusely physiologically arousing, whereas the emotions of interest, amusement, humor, and affection are more likely to be calming.

Based on other research in psychology that relates nervous system activity and stress to thoughts and feelings, it is also likely that several specific kinds of social and cognitive processes accompany physiological arousal. These processes include a reduced ability to process new information, a reliance on overlearned behaviors and cognitions, and a tendency to invoke fight and flight behaviors (e.g., the escalation of aggression and threat, and withdrawal from interaction).

Two other processes also may be suggested. First, Ekman (1984) recently introduced the concept of flooding, by which he meant that through emotional conditioning a wide range of stimuli eventually become capable of eliciting blends of anger, fear, and sadness. I add that the term *flooding* also suggests that the emotional state becomes disregulating in that a person can attend to or do little else when flooded. In this manner, flooding may be highly disruptive of organized behavior. Second, I suggest that people in relationships that chronically generate negative affect blends that lead to flooding may become hypervigilant to potentially threatening and escalating interactions. They may become likely to misattribute threat potential to relatively neutral or positive acts. All of these processes have implications for the course of a conflictual marital interaction.

4.4. BEYOND STUDYING CHANGES IN MARITAL SATISFACTION

So far, Levenson and I have limited ourselves to measuring change in marital satisfaction over time. With our next study, we had many more couples, and we learned how to improve our longitudinal follow-up so we could start studying the process of marital dissolution. It was not clear from the research literature whether the deterioration of marital satisfaction and separation and divorce were the same processes. There was reason to doubt that they were the same processes, because we all know many unhappily married couples who stay together. In our approach to this question of predicting separation and divorce, we searched for types of marital interaction that could predict different longitudinal courses.

5

Marital Processes That Predict Dissolution

The question of the longitudinal health and stability of a marriage may seem, at first blush, to be the same question as what makes some marriages happy whereas others are unhappy. In this chapter, the longitudinal question is introduced, particularly related to issues of marital stability. Previous research on marital dissolution rarely has been based on prospective research studies. Previous prospective studies have not done very well in predicting dissolution, nor have they yielded a consistent theoretical formulation of the marital processes that may be related to stability or dissolution. First, a cascade model of marital dissolution is presented that links work on marital unhappiness to work on marital dissolution. Second, a balance theory of marriage yields a first cut at prediction of a trajectory toward dissolution versus stability. Process cascades also are explored that are related to the cascade toward marital dissolution.

5.1. PREVIOUS STUDIES PREDICTING DISSOLUTION

Despite the importance of marital dissolution, empirical research has not been very successful at predicting which married couples will separate or divorce and which married couples will stay together. The epidemiological attempts at understanding the changes in divorce in the 20th century have not tried to predict which couples in a cohort might divorce. Instead, demographic correlates of stability have been studied, and epidemiologists have attempted to discover variables that would show the same kinds of patterns over time as the divorce rate time series and that could reasonably account for variation in divorce rates over time (Cherlin, 1981).

Several comments are in order about this research. First, it is very important work. Specifying variations in marital patterns and marital stability as a function of ethnicity, race, parental divorce or stability, age at marriage, cohabitation, length of courtship, education, fertility, and other such variables is a necessary part of understanding marital stability or dissolution. It is important to know that African Americans are significantly more likely to divorce than White Americans. It is also important to know about historical patterns and variations across countries in the law, premarital courtships, marital arrangements, family structures, and stability and dissolution. Without this knowledge, one never will know how general are the lawful relationships that may be discovered. Cherlin (1981) suggested that the evidence that exists shows that liberalized attitudes toward divorce and the liberalization of divorce laws were effects, rather than causes, of increased divorce rates. He also noted that the concomitant increase in women's employment beginning in 1950 cannot be a cause of the increased divorce, but rather would serve to make it easier for women who were unhappy to leave their husbands.

However, one needs to be keenly aware that these variables do not suggest a mechanism that can explain stability or dissolution. One must be skeptical when reading suggested accounts of divorce rate time series that suggest mechanisms of marital dissolution without empirical test and without reference to the marital literature. For example, consider an analysis by Easterlin (1980). In his theorizing, decreased expectations about financial opportunities in the young men and women in the baby-boom generation led them to postpone marriage and led wives to work. This led to increased marital conflict, which led to increased divorces. However, there are several missing pieces in this analysis. Does increased financial stress on a couple lead to increased conflict about finances? The evidence suggests that this is not necessarily the case; there is no substantial relationship between income and marital satisfaction (Burgess, Locke, & Thomes, 1971b). Elder's (1984) analysis of the effects of the United States' Great Depression on marriages and families suggested that families that were unhappy before the Depression were the ones that fared the worst in terms of increasing marital distance and isolation. Also, even in the cases of increased marital misery, divorce was not necessarily the result. In no prospective study of divorce has family income, or the discrepancy between the husband and wife's income, been a predictor of dissolution. Hence, these accounts of divorce in terms of demographic trends over time are valuable in suggesting possible correlates of changes in divorce rates, but they tend to be very weak in suggesting a mechanism that would explain why some marriages are stable, whereas others follow a trajectory toward dissolution.

5.1.1. Accounting for Variation in Divorce Rates Across and Within Nations

Trent and South (1989) used 1983 data on 66 countries and attempted to account for variance in the crude divorce rate, which is the number of divorces per 1,000 population. These authors admit that the crude divorce rate is only a rough estimate of actual divorce rates, because it is influenced by such factors as the age and the marital composition of the population. Trent and South used the following indices to account for variation in the divorce rate: (a) an index of socioeconomic development (a factor made up of the log of gross national product per capita, the infant mortality rate, life expectancy at birth, and the percentage of the population that is urban), as well as the square of this index; (b) the female average age at marriage; (c) the sex ratio (number of males per 100 females at ages 15 to 49); (d) the female labor force participation (percentage of adult women defined as economically active) and the square of this variable; (e) the percentage Catholic; and (f) whether the country was predominately Muslim. They explored three equations, and the second of these accounted for 43.9% of the variance in divorce rates. Based on beta weights, the divorce rate increased with development, decreased with female age at marriage, decreased with sex ratio, and decreased with female labor force participation, decreased with percent Catholic, and increased with whether the country was Muslim.

They also found a linear and a curvilinear relationship between the divorce rate and the development index, and between the divorce rate and female labor force participation rate; this turned out to be a curvilinear interaction. When the economic development index is low, women's participation in the labor force has a buffering effect on the divorce rate (i.e., it lowers it), whereas when countries are more developed, the reverse is true, women's labor force participation increases the divorce rate. They offer no explanation for this curvilinear interaction effect. However, many hypotheses can be proposed for their results. For example, it is likely that when societies are at a low level of development, women's entry into the labor force reflects some liberalization of attitudes toward women, but the jobs women obtain are likely to be fairly routine, low status jobs. At higher levels of development, on the other hand, women may have access to jobs that are more interesting and professional; these jobs may provide both significantly more income and self-esteem. These more prestigious jobs may give women the freedom to leave a failing marriage that they do not have in countries at a lower level of development. Some support exists for this hypothesis (see Booth, Johnson, White, & Edwards, 1984).

The Trent and South study illustrates advantages and disadvantages of a sociological approach to the study of divorce. First, it is remarkable that so much of the variance is accounted for in the cross-national statistics by these variables. Second, it is clear that the regression models do not *explain* the phenomenon, nor do they come anywhere close to suggesting theory that might account for variation in divorce rates across countries. This is quite unfortunate.

A similar model had been developed by Brinton-Lee's (1980) cross-national analysis of 15 highly developed countries. Brinton-Lee also examined variation within one nation that has a relatively low divorce rate (this was, however, not always true—the divorce rate in Japan in the years 1884 to 1888 was 36.7%, see Burgess & Locke, 1945; Kumagai, 1983). Furthermore, Brinton-Lee examined variation within Japanese prefectures found consistency with cross-national models. She wrote:

> Japanese prefectures with high rates of female employment, especially in wage-earning positions as opposed to positions in family enterprises, tend to have higher divorce rates than prefectures in which women participate less in the market economy. (p.55)

Would these models indexing development and female labor partic-ipation also hold in a country that had a high divorce rate such as the United States? A study by Yang and Lester (1991) attempted to account for the statewide variation in the crude divorce rate and separation rate within the United States (using 1980 Census data). They used a Principal Components analysis with a varimax rotation of 36 variables designed to measure "social instability," obtaining seven nonorthogonal factors. Factor 3 correlated very highly with the separation rate ($r = 0.71$), whereas Factor 4 correlated very highly with the divorce rate ($r = -0.82$). Correlated with separation rate were the variables that loaded highly on Factor 3, which were: percent in poverty, latitude (negative loading), percent Black, homicide rate, southerness, percent Roman Catholic (negative loading), and infant mortality. Correlated with the divorce rate were the variables that loaded highly on Factor 4 (recall the negative correlation of this factor with the divorce rate), which were: suicide rate (negative loading), interstate migration (negative loading), church attendance (positive loading), alcohol consumption (negative loading), longitude (negative loading), the reciprocal of the sex ratio (positive loading), the percent born in state (positive loading), and the strictness of the gun control laws (positive loading). Individual variables also were highly correlated with the divorce rate; for example, the correlation with suicide rate was 0.78, the correlation with the rate of interstate migration was 0.74, the correlation with church attendance was -0.49, and the correlation with alcohol consumption was 0.40. This pattern of results portrays quite a different picture from the cross-national results of Trent and South (see also Glenn & Shelton, 1985).

5.1.2. Variations Across Samples

It is important to realize that a clear and replicable pattern of factors at a macrolevel associated with divorce may be difficult to obtain from any one study or group of studies. For example, an interesting retrospective study of divorce by Thornes and Collard (1979) obtained a random sample of people divorcing in England, in the West Midlands, and a sample of intact marriages from the same geographic region. On the basis of interviews and questionnaires, these investigators found that the couples who divorced differed from the intact marriages in some very dramatic ways. In particular, the divorcing couples had married quite young; in 44% the bride was under 20 years old, compared to a 28% figure for the intact marriages, that 32% of the brides from the divorcing group were pregnant at the time of marriage, compared to 19% of the intact marriages, and that of the divorcing women, 51% reported that their parents were opposed to the marriage at its outset, compared to 13% of the intact marriages. This sample reveals one dramatic sample of failed marriages: Those couples who married very young were likely to be pregnant, and married despite parental disapproval. Despite the fact that this study highlights one set of risk variables for marital instability, the high risk pattern they identified is probably not a very general pattern across countries, and perhaps not even across regions within England.

However, there may be some generality in the fact that an early age at marriage can be a risk factor for dissolution; for example, a similar finding was reported by Wong and Kuo (1983) for divorce among Muslims in Singapore (see also Broel-Plateris, 1961, for the United States). This factor of age at marriage and unplanned premarital pregnancy has been identified as a consistent high risk factor for marital dissolution. It can be found quite pervasively in the countries in Europe described in the book *Divorce in Europe*, edited by Chester and Kooy (1977). In fact, the factors that accompany marrying at a young age may underly another consistently observed relationship between lower socioeconomic status (SES) and divorce. The pattern was well described by Rubin (1976): One common way for a teenage girl to get out of a difficult conflict-ridden lower SES family is to marry. Teenage pregnancy may be more of a high risk factor for Whites in the United States, and not for African Americans, due to a different culture surrounding extended intergenerational families among Blacks.

5.1.3. Contributions From Historians

Much can be learned through insightful historical analyses of marriages and divorces. For example, consider Rawson's (1991) fascinating edited work on marriage, divorce, and family relations in pre-Christian ancient Rome. In the introduction to his book, Rawson wrote that historians had successfully refuted the idea that there was no concept of childhood as a distinct phase of life and no sensitivity to children's needs in Europe before the 17th century. Indeed it appears that families were very similar to our own in emphasizing emotional closeness and affectional ties between both parents and the children. Also, the nuclear family pattern was the norm in Ancient Rome rather than the extended family pattern (see Rawson's chapter on adult–child relationships).

Treggiari (1991) described a culture that is not very different in some respects from our own in the way it approached marriage and divorce. For example, marriage was not arranged, but based on the consent of both partners, and apparently for love. Women had a relatively high degree of power, financial independence, and legal rights. The consent of both partners was sufficient for divorce, although by the time of Cicero both husbands and wives could divorce one another unilaterally. Fidelity for both husband and wife was valued by the society, and yet the infidelity of a wife would cost her only one sixth of her dowry. Unlike our own culture, however, was the commonly accepted practice of infanticide, and the fact that children tended to remain with the husband after divorce. From reconstructions of marriage and divorce in Ancient Rome it appears that the affectional nature of the marriage had a lot to do with whether or not the marriage survived.

5.1.4. Contributions From Studies of Law and Public Policy

Much can also be learned about marriage and divorce from insightful studies of the law, its daily application, its variation across cultures, and public policy. For example, Rheinstein's (1972) penetrating analysis of whether a reform of existing divorce laws would affect the divorce rate noted that prior to a liberalization of the divorce laws, there were extremely high rates of family abandonment by males. After a thoughtful analysis of law, marital stability and divorce in many cultures, Rheinstein concluded that:

> For the strengthening of marriage stability, then, effective tools are available. Laws tending to make divorce difficult should not be considered one of them. Social policy and, above all, family counseling and family life education are effective means at our disposal. (p. 443)

A case study of the divorce law in different cultures can provide insight into the workings of marriages and their problems as cultures vary in their basic beliefs about marriages, families, and the correct roles for men and women. Nakamura (1983) reported detailed cases of divorce hearings among Muslims in Java. The courts are likely to act in ways that appear surprising given the stereotypes one has about cultural norms. For example, in what was apparently a male-dominated society, in actual cases women were given a great deal of consideration, and the court appeared to be operating on a principle of deciding wisely for the best welfare of all parties, without thought of punishment or sin. For example, one case concerned a man whose marriage had been arranged and was fairly loveless. When he discovered that his wife was having an affair with his best friend, he asked her if she loved the best friend and she said that she did. The husband petitioned the court to approve the divorce so that his wife and friend could marry one another and be happy. He wished to marry again and he also wished to keep his loving friendship with his friend. The court decided in his favor, and approved the subsequent union of the wife and best friend.

A similar analysis showing the differences between the formal and informal application of rules in marriages can be found in Cohen's (1971) anthropological analysis of Kanuri marriage in an African Islamic culture in which the women are supposedly completely subordinate to the men, and in which the divorce rate is quite high. In fact, despite lip service paid to wifely obedience, the women actually have a great deal of economic and social independence. Cohen described the tension that exists between the legitimacy of the husband's dominance and the actual fact of the wife's defiance and struggle for power.

It is important for scholars of divorce to know the correlates that have been explored to date. White's (1990) decade review article on the determinants of divorce noted that parental divorce, premarital cohabitation, age at marriage, premarital pregnancy, and marital fertility are all significantly positively correlated with divorce. However, most of these effects are relatively small, even if they are statistically significant with large samples. Also, as noted earlier, they do not suggest a mechanism for dissolution. In prospective studies, when they have been employed (as has parental divorce in the Kelly & Conley's, 1987, study) they have not been significant predictors of divorce.

Lamentably, studies attempting to specify interactional behaviors and processes that are antecedents of marital dissolution have been quite rare (for a review, see Newcomb & Bentler, 1981). The current lack of knowledge concerning which patterns of marital interaction lead to marital dissolution stems, in part, from the fact that, in most studies, divorce and separation have been viewed as independent rather than dependent variables. These studies have been concerned primarily with the effects of marital dissolution on other variables and on the adjustment of spouses and children to marital dissolution.

Of the many published studies with the terms *marital separation* or *divorce* in their titles, I know of only six prospective longitudinal studies that have attempted to predict future separation and divorce (Bentler & Newcomb, 1978; Block, Block, & Morrison, 1981; Constantine & Bahr, 1980; Fowers & Olson, 1986; Kelly & Conley, 1987; Sears, 1977).[1]

What did these studies find? Fowers and Olson (1986) were completely unable to predict divorce or separation with their instrument called Prepare, which assesses disagreements between prospective spouses in 11 different areas. Unfortunately, these authors also combined separated and divorced couples into one group. This was a mistake, because the correlates of separation may not be identical to the correlates of divorce, and it is important to keep them separate for the time being until more is known. The Prepare instrument could not discriminate between couples that were less happily married but stayed together and couples that separated or divorced. The authors reported only a discriminant analysis between the happily married and those who separated or divorced, thus confounding two factors—marital status and marital happiness. They claimed as validity evidence for Prepare its high correlations with marital satisfaction, so it is likely that

---

[1]I have not included a recent longitudinal study by Schaninger and Buss (1986) because this study only compared happily married and divorced couples, thus confounding marital satisfaction with marital stability.

The results of a new study by Kurdek (1993) were recently published as we were in the copy-editing process. Kurdek's is a longitudinal study of dissolution and stability with newlyweds, using questionnaires. The stable and unstable couples differed in the following ways. Among couples likely to dissolve their marriage, compared to stable couples:

1. the husband had a lower income,
2. the husband was a stepfather,
3. the wife had low income and low educational level,
4. the couple had a history of divorce,
5. the couple did not pool finances,
6. the couple knew each other only a few months,
7. the husband and wife held dysfunctional beliefs about relationships (examples: disagreement is destructive to relationships, mindreading is expected, sexual perfection is expected),
8. the wife was low in self-reported conscientiousness (examples: describes self as conscientious, self-reliant, reliable, self-sufficient),
9. the wife was low on satisfaction with perceived social support,
10. the husband had many external motives for being married, and
11. the couple had large discrepancies on autonomy and external motives for being married.

what they are measuring with Prepare is one aspect of marital satisfaction (probably consensus, because the instrument ostensibly assesses consensual agreement on 11 areas of marriage).

The prospective study by Sears (1977) has an interesting history. Terman and Oden (1947) reported that a self-report measure of emotional stability administered to their gifted subjects when they were 7–14 years old was related to marital happiness 18 years later (the relationship, although statistically significant, was only 0.25). In fact, in 1940, Terman actually developed a marriage aptitude test to give to his young geniuses. The concurrent correlation of Terman's marital aptitude score with marital satisfaction was 0.62, and the relationship was mainly due to what he called neuroticism items, not childhood family background. In fact, it turned out that the members of the couples that divorced between 1940 and 1946 had marital aptitude scores that were a standard deviation below those who stayed married. Sears later related these 1940 marital aptitude scores to marital outcome in 1972 (when the average age of the subjects was 62). The correlations were 0.28 for females and 0.12 for males. Although for females this correlation was statistically significant, the prediction was quite weak. Kelly and Conley (1987) were influenced strongly by the weak Sears result, and added the commendable innovation that the personality variables of their subjects were not assessed by self-report, but by other people in the subjects' friendship networks.

The next prospective study of divorce emerged from the landmark longitudinal study of child development by the Blocks. The Blocks used these data to search their data to see if they had any precursor predictors of parental divorce. In the Block et al. (1981) study, parental disagreement about childrearing practices from 57 families when the child was 3.5 years old discriminated between the intact and divorced groups 10 years later.

Constantine and Bahr (1980), in a 6-year longitudinal study, found that men who divorced had a greater internal orientation on a measure of locus of control than men who remained married. It is hard to know what to make of this result.

Bentler and Newcomb (1978) used the Bentler self-report personality test. They found that couples that remained married were more similar in age, interest in art, and attractiveness than couples that separated or divorced. Separated and divorced couples were combined into one category. Men who separated or divorced described themselves as more extroverted, more invulnerable, and more orderly than males who stayed married. Women who separated or divorced described themselves as less clothes conscious and less congenial than women who stayed married. Although these personality dimensions are interesting, they tell us little about the dynamics of a marriage that might be associated with a longitudinal course toward dissolution.

Kelly and Conley (1987) used acquaintances of the couple, who rated the partners' personalities. Theirs was a prospective 35-year longitudinal study of marital stability. They reported that the men who remained married were more conventional, less neurotic, and had greater impulse control than those who divorced. A similar pattern was found for women, although women who stayed married were judged as higher in emotional closeness and lower in tension in their families of origin. Unfortunately, Kelly and Conley (1987) reported no statistical tests in their published article. In the prepublication version, they reported that the married and divorced groups differed by about two thirds of a standard deviation on the discriminant function. It is frustrating not to have statistical tests for this important study, so this latter result can be translated into an equivalent point-biserial correlation coefficient of 0.25 (see Glass & Stanley, 1970, p. 163, Equation 9.5).[2] These results suggest that adjusted people have more stable marriages, or perhaps relationship quality at Time 1 in this study is tapping a dimension similar to that tapped by the adjustment measures.

The findings from these studies are not conclusive. In fact, they are somewhat hard to integrate. Perhaps they suggest that spouses in these cohorts who were most traditional, with spouses most similar and least neurotic, were most likely to stay married. Although effect sizes in these studies were not particularly large, that they did have some ability to predict dissolution is encouraging for additional efforts at longitudinal prediction using the same and other methods. From my perspective, an important methodological improvement would be the addition of direct observation of marital behavior, which could provide greater descriptive clarity in prospective longitudinal research and might account for greater amounts of variance in marital dissolution.

5.1.1. The Inadequacy of a Psychopathology Approach to the Prediction of Marital Dissolution

When Kelly began his longitudinal research on marriage in the 1950s, it probably seemed quite logical to use personality inventories that were presumed to measure individual psychopathology and expect these

---

[2]Because the N was 300 and 50 couples were divorced, the point-biserial correlation coefficient was estimated as:

$$(2/3)\text{sqrt}\{[(50)(250)]/[(300)(299)]\}.$$

scales to be predictors of divorce. However, 35 years later, the kind of results Kelly obtained pose some serious problems in interpretation. With the divorce rate near or above 50%, it seems strange to suggest that it is neurotic people who get divorced. Is the base rate of neurosis, whatever that construct may be, over 50% in the population?

It is far more likely that what was tapped by Kelly's measures was some kind of wellness, distress, or negativity dimension that acquaintances had to record as a personality dimension. This generally has turned out to be the case for most measures of individual psychopathology. Hence, what Kelly may have been tapping at Time 1 was a dimension similar to what is tapped by measures of marital satisfaction of measures of the quality of life. Even if this is true, and all Kelly was measuring was some aspect of well-being, the fact that there is some prediction over 35 years is very interesting, even if the prediction is not very high.

A second problem raised by personality research that purports to assess individual psychopathology is what is really learned about marriage and marital dissolution by such research. What is the advice that results from the prediction that neurotic people have unstable marriages? Is it, "Don't marry a 'neurotic' "? Or is it, "First cure your 'neurosis' and then get married"? It seems that research based on an individual psychopathology model, particularly one that is global and not specific, has little to say about the possible mechanisms that lead to marital dissolution. Even if the prediction were good, which it is not, the understanding of the prediction that results from this kind of research is small.

Prospective longitudinal research on marital dissolution needs to rely on a multimethod approach. It is important to know as precisely as possible exactly what one is measuring. The research also needs to be based on a broad theory that can generate hypotheses about the possible mechanisms that underly marital dissolution. If prospective longitudinal research accomplishes both the goal of prediction and the goal of generating hypotheses about the mechanisms of the effect, it may lead to real experiments about the mechanisms through which marriages change over time. Of course, without these experiments, one will never know how marriages work or fail to work.

5.2. THE PROBLEM OF LOW BASE RATES OF DIVORCE IN SHORT-TERM LONGITUDINAL STUDIES

Ironically, although many marriages ultimately end in divorce, attempts to predict marital dissolution over short 3- to 5-year periods often are plagued by low base rates of divorce. In part, this problem simply reflects the fact that it can take many years before an unsatisfying marriage formally dissolves, but it also may reflect sampling issues (e.g., couples that are willing to participate in these kinds of research projects may be those that are least likely to divorce). Examples of low base rates for divorce in short-term longitudinal studies are common. In Kelly and Conley's (1987) study of 278 couples that were married in 1935, the divorce rate was approximately 0.5% per year. There is evidence that the divorce rate is somewhat higher among more contemporary cohorts. For example, in the more recent Block et al. study, the divorce rate was 2.8% per year (16 of 57 couples in 10 years). My own rates are between 3% and 4% of the sample divorcing per year of the study. However, even with somewhat higher divorce rates, the problem of low base rates of divorce can function as a major deterrent for short-term longitudinal studies of marital dissolution.

5.3. A CASCADE MODEL OF MARITAL DISSOLUTION

What one needs to do is identify different trajectories toward divorce or stability. In the prediction of heart attacks, research also is plagued by this problem of very low base rates of the event in any reasonable longitudinal study. It would be ideal if there turned out to be a set of lead indicators of heart attacks, such as certain kinds of chest pain, treadmill tests, and so on that reliably spelled out different trajectories for persons. Then the job of prospective research would be to predict progress along the high-risk or low-risk pathway, instead of having to predict only the low base-rate event.

This is the approach Levenson and I have taken. To accomplish this goal, we hope to identify some variables with relatively high base rates of occurrence that are likely precursors of the relatively low base-rate variable of primary interest, namely, divorce. Conceptually, these precursor variables could be arranged in the form of a scale that suggests a cascade or stage model, in which couples that are destined ultimately to reach the final stage of divorce are likely to pass through the earlier stages on the way. Using such a model, a short-term longitudinal study of divorce could attempt to predict the hypothesized precursor variables, assuming that a larger proportion of couples that are found to be in these earlier stages ultimately will precede on to divorce, compared with couples that are not in these earlier stages.

We hypothesized a simple *cascade model*: decline in marital satisfaction, which leads to consideration of separation or divorce, which leads to separation, which leads to divorce. We consider this model highly likely to reflect the modal course of marital dissolution. The model does not imply that this is the course of dissolution for every couple.

We need long-term longitudinal data to test this model. So far, we have only two studies: one 4-year follow-up study and one 3-year longitudinal study. Nonetheless, a preliminary test of the model's viability is provided using those data that are currently available and by utilizing a statistical method called structural equations modeling.

Our remaining research strategy would then be conceptually quite simple. Once we accomplish the goal of identifying the cascade toward marital dissolution, we can ask if there are any other cascades that we can identify at our Time-1 assessment that would be predictors of the cascade toward dissolution.

5.4. METHODS OF THE STUDIES

I go into considerable detail about these studies, because they are the major database I discuss. In my laboratory, the two studies are called "DU083" and "DU086," named after the computer program that Levenson wrote, which acquires the physiological data and sycnchronizes it to the video time code.

5.4.1. Study 1: DUO83

This study is described in considerable detail elsewhere (Gottman & Levenson, 1992). Hence, I am quite brief here.

5.4.1.1. Subjects

Couples originally were recruited in 1983 in Bloomington, Indiana, using newspaper advertisements. Approximately 200 couples that responded to these advertisements took a demographic questionnaire and two measures of marital satisfaction, for which they were paid $5. From this sample, a smaller group of 85 couples was invited to participate in the laboratory assessments and to complete a number of additional questionnaires (including measures of health). The goal of this two-stage sampling was to ensure a distribution of marital satisfaction in which all parts of the distribution would be represented equally. Complete sets of usable physiological data were obtained from 79 of these 85 couples. These 79 couples could be described as follows: Husbands were about 32 years old ($SD = 9.5$ years); wives were about 29 years old ($SD = 6.8$ years); they were married an average of 5 years ($SD = 6.3$ years); the average marital satisfaction for husbands was (average of Locke–Wallace and Locke–Williamson scales) = 96.80 (SD = 22.16); and for wives the average marital satisfaction was 98.56 (SD = 20.70).

5.4.1.2. Procedure

5.4.1.2.1. Interaction Session

The procedures employed in this experiment were similar to those used in previous studies. Couples came to the laboratory after having not spoken for at least 8 hours. After recording devices for obtaining physiological measures were attached, couples engaged in three conversational interactions: (a) discussing the events of the day, (b) discussing a problem area of continuing disagreement in their marriage, and (c) discussing a mutually agreed on pleasant topic. Each conversation lasted for 15 minutes, preceded by a 5-minute silent period. During the silent periods and discussions, a broad sample of physiological measures was obtained and a video recording was made of the interaction. For purposes of the present study, only data from the problem area discussion were used.

Prior to initiating the problem area discussion, couples completed the Couple's Problem Inventory (Gottman et al., 1977), in which they rated the perceived severity of a set of marital issues. The experimenter, a graduate student in counseling psychology, then helped the couple select one of these issues to use as the topic for the problem area discussion. The Couple's Problem Inventory also provided an index of each spouse's ratings of the severity of problems in the relationship.

5.4.1.2.2. Recall Session

Several days later, spouses separately returned to the laboratory to view the video recording of their interaction. The same physiological measures were obtained and synchronized with those obtained in the interaction session. Spouses used a rating dial to provide a continuous self-report of affect. The dial traversed a 180-degree path, with the dial pointer moving over a 9-point scale anchored by the legends *extremely negative* and *extremely positive*, with *neutral* in the middle. Subjects were instructed to adjust the dial continuously so that it always represented how they were feeling when they were in the interaction.

5.4.1.2.3. 1987 Follow-Up

In 1987, four years after the initial assessment, the original subjects were recontacted and at least one spouse (70 husbands, 72 wives) from

73 of the original 79 couples (92.4%) agreed to participate in the follow-up. These 73 participants represented 69 couples in which both spouses participated, one couple in which only the husband participated, and three couples in which only the wife participated.

Spouses completed a set of questionnaires assessing marital satisfaction, health (using the Cornell Medical Index), and items relevant to other stages of the hypothesized cascade model (i.e., during the 4-year period had the spouses considered separation or divorce, had they actually separated or divorced, and the length of any separation). There is evidence to suggest that serious thoughts about divorce are predictors of dissolution (Booth, Johnson, & Edwards, 1983; Booth & White, 1980; Bugaighis, Schumm, Jurich, & Bollman, 1985).

5.4.1.2.4. Physiological Measures

Five physiological measures were obtained. These were: (a) heart rate; (b) skin conductance level; (c) general somatic activity—an electromechanical transducer attached to a platform under the subject's chair generated an electrical signal proportional to the amount of movement in any direction; (d) pulse transmission time to the finger. The interval was timed between the R-wave of the EKG and the upstroke of the finger pulse; and (e) finger pulse amplitude—the trough-to-peak amplitude of the finger pulse was measured.

This set of physiological measures was selected to sample broadly from major organ systems (cardiac, vascular, electrodermal, somatic muscle), to allow for continuous measurement, to be as unobtrusive as possible, and to include measures utilized in our previous studies (Levenson & Gottman, 1983).

5.4.1.2.5. Nonphysiological Data

Two remotely controlled, high-resolution video cameras that were concealed partially were used to obtain frontal views of each spouse's face and upper torso. These images were combined into a single split-screen image. The DEC computer enabled synchronization between video and physiological data by controlling the operation of a device that imposed the elapsed time on the video recording.

5.4.2. Study 2: DUO86

5.4.2.1. Subjects

The procedures of this study are described elsewhere (Buehlman, Gottman, & Katz, 1992), hence, again I am brief. I followed most of the procedures described in Gottman and Levenson (1992). This study was designed primarily to assess the effects of marital conflict resolution patterns on the socioemotional development of children from ages 5 to 8. Subjects consisted of 56 families that were recruited for participation by newspaper advertisement. Half of the families had a female and half had a male 5-year-old child. This age range was sampled due to previous theorizing that the ability to regulate emotion develops during this period (Maccoby, 1980). It was reasoned that emotion regulation ability is likely to be affected by marital interaction patterns, and that this variability would be reflected 3 years later when the children were in the early elementary school grades. Interested families were telephoned by a survey research company for an initial assessment of marital satisfaction. Assessment of marital satisfaction was based on a modified telephone version of the Locke–Wallace Marital Inventory (Locke & Wallace, 1959; developed by Krokoff, 1984). Unfortunately, the sample was biased in the direction of higher marital satisfaction, with a mean marital satisfaction score of 111.1 ($SD = 29.6$). However, the range of marital satisfaction was large.

5.4.2.2. Procedure

5.4.2.2.1. Interaction Session

Couples were seen in a laboratory session whose main function was to obtain a naturalistic sample of the couple's interaction style during only the high-conflict task of the Gottman and Levenson (1992) study. The high-conflict task was modified for this study so that it consisted of a 15-minute discussion of two problem areas in the marriage. Both behavioral and physiological data were monitored in both spouses and synchronized in time.

5.4.2.2.2. Recall Session

The recall session in the DUO86 study was conducted in the same way as it was in the DUO83 study.

5.4.2.3. Time 1 Assessments

5.4.2.3.1. Marital Satisfaction

Marital satisfaction was assessed using the telephone version of the Locke–Wallace Marital Satisfaction Inventory, and the paper-and-pencil forms of the Locke–Wallace Inventory and the Locke–Williamson Marital Satisfaction Inventory (Burgess, Locke, & Thomes, 1971a).

5.4.2.4. Time 2 Assessments

Families were recontacted 3 years later for follow-up assessments of marital outcomes. Ninety-three percent (52 out of 56) of the families in the initial sample agreed to participate in the Time 2 assessments.

5.4.2.4.1. Marital Satisfaction and Marital Dissolution

To assess marital satisfaction at follow-up, couples again completed the Locke–Wallace and Locke–Williamson Marital Satisfaction Inventories. Assessments of marital dissolution were conducted using telephone interviews. Interview questions were aimed at assessing whether couples had separated or divorced during the intervening 3-year period or had any serious considerations of separation or divorce. Each spouse was interviewed individually and was asked the following five questions: "In the last 3 years, have you seriously considered separation?"; "In the last 3 years, have you seriously considered divorce?"; "In the last 3 years, have you and your spouse separated?"; "If so, how many months have you been separated, or how long was your separation period?"; and "In the last 3 years, have you and your spouse divorced?"

5.5. CODING AND ANALYSIS OF THE DUO83 DATA

5.5.1. Observational Coding

The videotapes of the problem area interaction were coded using several observational coding systems. The Rapid Couples Interaction Scoring System provided the means for classifying couples into regulated and nonregulated types. The Marital Interaction Coding System and the Specific Affect Coding System were used as measures of concurrent validity.

5.5.1.1. Rapid Couples Interaction Scoring System (RCISS)

The Rapid Couples Interaction Scoring System (RCISS; Krokoff et al., 1989) employs a checklist of 13 behaviors that are scored for the speaker and 9 behaviors that are scored for the listener on each turn at speech. A turn at speech is defined as all utterances by one speaker until that speaker yields the floor to vocalizations by the other spouse (vocalizations that are merely backchannels such as "Mm-hmm" are not considered as demarcating a turn). RCISS behavioral codes can be scored in terms of an underlying positive–negative dimension. In the present study, only speaker codes were used to classify couples. These speaker codes consisted of five positive codes (neutral or positive problem description, task-oriented relationship information, assent, humor-laugh, other positive) and eight negative codes (complain, criticize, negative relationship issue problem talk, yes-but, defensive, put down, escalate negative affect, other negative).

It is important to point out that, because of the design of the RCISS as a checklist employed at every turn of speech, coders are not deciding between codes, but choosing all that apply to a turn at speech. Thus, theoretically (and empirically), positive and negative codes are logically independent of one another.

5.5.1.2. Using RCISS Point Graphs to Classify Couples as Regulated or Nonregulated

RCISS speaker codes were used to classify couples into two types: (a) regulated and (b) nonregulated. This classification scheme was based on a method proposed originally by Gottman (1979) for use with the Couples Interaction Scoring System, a predecessor of the RCISS. On each conversational turn, the total number of positive RCISS items minus the total number of negative items coded was computed for each spouse. Then the cumulative total of these points was plotted for each spouse. The slopes of these plots were determined using linear regression analysis. Regulated couples were defined as those for whom both husband and wife speaker slopes were significantly positive; nonregulated couples had at least one of the speaker slopes that was not significantly positive. Thus, regulated couples showed fairly consistently that they displayed more positive than negative RCISS codes. Classifying couples in the current sample in this manner produced two groups consisting of 42 regulated couples and 31 nonregulated couples.

An example of the speaker point graphs for one regulated and one nonregulated couple is presented in Fig. 5.1.

5.5.1.3. Testing the Validity of the Point Graphs

To test the validity of my classification of couples with the RCISS point graphs, I employed two additional observational coding systems: the Marital Interaction Coding System (MICS) and the Specific Affect Coding System (SPAFF). The MICS was designed in Oregon and the SPAFF was designed in my laboratory.

5.5.1.3.1. Marital Interaction Coding System (MICS)

The Marital Interaction Coding System (MICS; Weiss & Summers, 1983) contains codes that tap many of the same aspects of marital

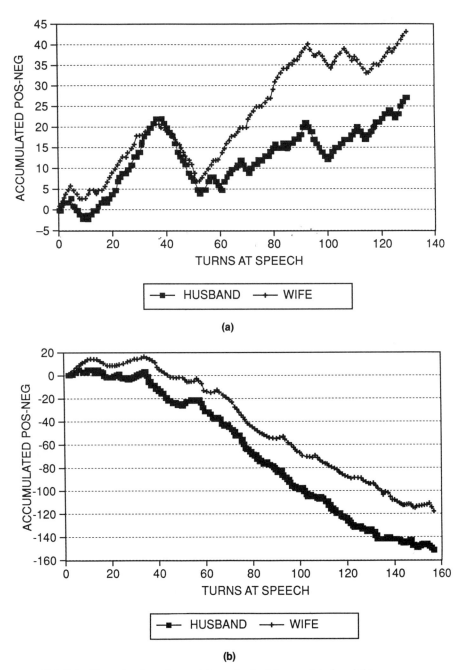

FIG. 5.1. Example of speaker point graphs for (a) a regulated and (b) a nonregulated couple. (From Gottman & Levenson, 1992; Reproduced with permission.)

interaction as does the RCISS. MICS coding was carried out in a separate laboratory, with an entirely different group of coders, under the supervision of Dr. Robert Weiss at the University of Oregon (see Weiss & Summers, 1983, for a discussion of the MICS codes and a review of literature that has employed the MICS). For my purposes, the MICS codes were collapsed into the four negative summary codes employed by Gottman and Krokoff (1989): (a) defensiveness—sum of excuse, deny responsibility, negative solution, and negative mindreading by the partner; (b) conflict engagement—sum of disagreement and criticism; (c) stubborness—sum of noncompliance, verbal contempt, command, and complaint; and (d) withdrawal from interaction—sum of negative listener behaviors no response, not tracking, turn off, and incoherent talk. Codes were assigned continuously by coders for 30-second blocks.

5.5.1.3.2. *Specific Affect Coding System (SPAFF)*

For greater precision in the description of the affective portion of the interactions beyond the positive–negative dimension, the Specific Affect Coding System (SPAFF, Gottman & Krokoff, 1989) was employed. The videotapes were coded independently by a third team of coders using the SPAFF, which dismantled affect into specific positive and negative affects. SPAFF is a cultural informant coding system in which coders consider a gestalt consisting of verbal content, voice tone, context, facial expression, gestures, and body movement. In the version of SPAFF used on these data, only the speaker's affect was coded: Coders classified each turn at speech as affectively neutral, as one of five negative affects (anger, disgust/contempt, sadness, fear, whining), or as one of four positive affects (affection/caring, humor, interest/curiosity, joy/enthusiasm).

5.5.2. Results[3]

5.5.2.1. Incidence of Separation and Divorce

During the 4-year period between 1983 and 1987, 36 of 73 couples (49.3%) reported considering dissolving their marriage. Eighteen of the 73 couples (24.7%) actually separated; their average length of separation was 8.1 months. Nine of the 73 couples actually divorced (12.3%). Thus,

---

[3]The $p = .05$ rejection level was adopted unless otherwise stated. All reported probabilities for statistical were two-tailed except for three z tests of proportions for dichotomous dissolution variables, which were hypothesized and were conducted one-tailed. For t tests, pooling was utilized unless the variances of the two samples were found to be significantly different. Those t tests in which pooling was not utilized can be identified in the text by having fewer than 71 degrees of freedom.

the low annual base rate of divorce and the short 4-year period resulted in a fairly small pool of divorced couples.

5.5.2.2. Support for the Hypothesized Cascade Model of Marital Dissolution

As indicated earlier, it would be a considerable help in the problem of predicting marital dissolution if events with higher base rates than actual divorce (i.e., marital dissatisfaction, considering dissolution, separation) were precursors of divorce. The concept of a cascade toward marital dissolution implies that events that are precursors to divorce exist. My data were consistent with this notion. Figure 5.2 summarizes these results. Couples that had divorced were more likely to have separated than those who had not. In addition, couples that had separated were more likely to have considered dissolution than those who had not. Finally, couples that had considered dissolution were more likely to be lower in marital quality in 1987 and 1983 than those who had not.

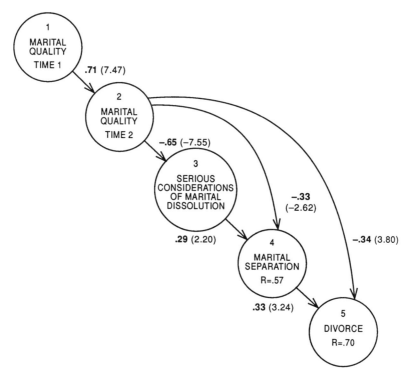

FIG. 5.2. Structural equation model of the cascade model of marital dissolution. χ^2 = 7.09, p = 0.13, with Bentler–Bonett goodness of fit statistic = 0.994. (Reprinted by permission from Gottman & Levenson, 1992.)

An alternative model was tested (see Fig. 5.3) that states there is actually no cascade (i.e., that we cannot predict the separation and divorce variables from the supposed precursor variables). This alternative model did not fit the data well.

5.5.2.3. Validity of the Regulated Versus Nonregulated Distinction

Regulated (N = 42) and nonregulated (N = 31) couples were compared in terms of dissolution, questionnaire, physiological, affect rating dial, MICS, and SPAFF variables.

5.5.2.3.1. Dissolution Variables

Nonregulated couples were at greater risk for marital dissolution than regulated couples on most measured variables. As Fig. 5.4 shows, 71% (22 of 31 couples) of nonregulated couples reported considering marital

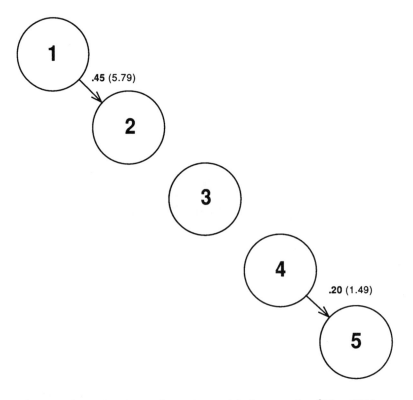

FIG. 5.3. Alternative structural equation model of no cascade. $\chi^2(4) = 22.59$, $p <$ .001. (Reprinted by permission from Gottman & Levenson, 1992.)

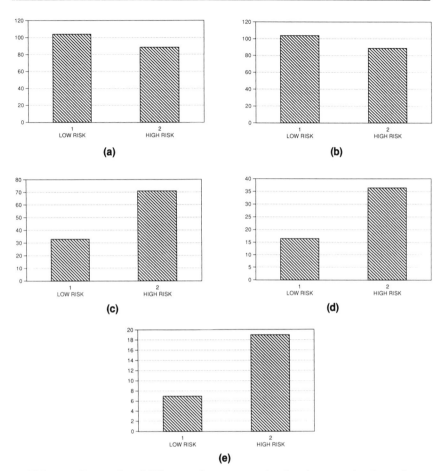

FIG. 5.4. Bar graphs of differences between regulated and nonregulated couples on the cascade variables (a) marital quality Time 1, (b) martial quality Time 2, (c) percent considered dissolution, (d) percent separated in 4 years, and (e) percent divorced in 4 years.

dissolution during the 4-year period between 1983 and 1987, which was significantly greater than the 33% (14 of 42) of regulated couples. Thirty-six percent (11 of 31) of nonregulated couples actually separated, which was significantly greater than the 16.7% (7 0f 42) of regulated couples. Nineteen percent (6 of 31) of nonregulated couples actually divorced, which approached being significantly greater than the 7.1% (3 of 42) of regulated couples.[4]

---

[4]A re-analysis of these data in Gottman (1993) using a split of couples by listener as well as speaker RCISS point graphs found that divorce was significantly more likely for nonregulated couples than for regulated couples.

Table 5.1 portrays the means for 1983 and 1987 marital satisfaction. Compared with regulated couples, nonregulated couples had lower levels of marital satisfaction at both times of measurement.

5.5.2.3.2. Other Questionnaires

Wives in nonregulated couples rated marital problems as more severe and reported more health problems than wives in regulated couples (see Table 5.1). Husbands in the two types of marriages did not differ on these variables.

5.5.2.3.3. Physiological Variables

Wives in nonregulated couples had faster heart rates (i.e., shorter cardiac interbeat intervals) and greater peripheral vasoconstriction (i.e., smaller finger pulse amplitudes) during the problem area interaction than did wives in regulated couples (see Table 5.1). Husbands in the two types of marriages did not differ physiologically.

TABLE 5.1

Comparison of Regulated and Nonregulated Couples on Dissolution, Other Questionnaires, Physiological, and Affect Rating Dial Variable

Variable	Regulated	Nonregulated	t
Dissolution			
1983 marital satisfaction	104.02	91.44	2.83**
1987 marital satisfaction	104.28	87.78	3.73**
Other Questionnaires			
Hus. severity of problems	16.62	20.61	−1.20
Hus. illness	15.76	21.00	−1.46
Wife severity of problems	13.33	21.51	−2.89**
Wife illness	18.68	28.55	−2.57*
Physiological			
Hus. cardiac interbeat interval	800.07	811.45	−.43
Hus. activity	.98	.97	.37
Hus. skin conductance	12.34	11.15	.73
Hus. pulse transmission time	243.26	244.03	−.16
Hus. pulse amplitude	7.74	7.87	−.16
Wife cardiac interbeat interval	789.48	731.10	2.08*
Wife activity	1.78	1.78	−.17
Wife skin conductance	11.39	8.97	1.50
Wife pulse transmission time	239.07	233.13	1.41
Wife pulse amplitude	9.38	6.58	2.11*
Recall Session Affect Rating Dial			
Hus. rating	3.51	2.95	2.86**
Wife. rating	3.33	2.95	1.86

$*p < .05.$ $**p < .015.$

5.5.2.3.4. Affect Rating Dial

Husbands in nonregulated couples rated the problem area interaction more negatively than did husbands in regulated couples (see Table 5.1). The difference between wives in the two types of marriages was in the same direction, but was not significant.

5.5.2.3.5. MICS Coding

Husbands in nonregulated marriages were coded as being more conflict engaging, more stubborn, and more likely to withdraw from interaction than were husbands in regulated marriages (see Table 5.2). Wives in nonregulated marriages were coded as being more stubborn

TABLE 5.2
Comparison of Regulated and Nonregulated Couples on Behavioral Coding Variables

Variable	Regulated	Nonregulated	t
Marital Interaction Coding System (MICS)			
Hus. defensiveness	1.58	2.16	−1.19
Hus. conflict engagement	2.43	5.72	−4.20**
Hus. stubbornness	.58	1.34	−2.74**
Hus. withdrawal from interaction	4.71	9.56	−4.36**
Wife defensiveness	1.80	3.24	−1.85
Wife conflict engagement	4.03	5.64	−1.67
Wife stubbornness	.77	2.04	−3.43**
Wife withdrawal from interaction	5.03	8.28	−2.87**
Specific Affect Coding System (SPAFF)			
Hus. neutral	21.21	20.07	.38
Hus. humor	4.19	3.16	1.21
Hus. affection/caring	1.56	1.09	1.05
Hus. interest/curiosity	5.85	4.73	.93
Hus. joy/enthusiasm	.57	.24	1.46
Hus. anger	4.73	8.88	−2.52*
Hus. disgust/contempt	2.49	2.42	.09
Hus. whining	.58	1.80	−2.64*
Hus. sadness	1.02	1.50	−.90
Hus. fear	7.72	5.48	1.04
Wife neutral	18.88	13.51	1.92
Wife humor	4.33	2.94	1.54
Wife affection/caring	1.21	.68	1.64
Wife interest/curiosity	6.83	3.43	3.00**
Wife joy/enthusiasm	.62	.16	2.98**
Wife anger	5.41	12.75	−3.75**
Wife disgust/contempt	1.85	4.48	−2.30*
Wife whining	1.36	3.39	−2.49*
Wife sadness	1.04	2.66	−1.35
Wife fear	8.56	6.63	1.00

$^*p < .01.$ $^{**}p < .015.$

and more likely to withdraw from interaction than were wives in regulated marriages.

5.5.2.3.6. SPAFF Coding

Husbands in nonregulated marriages were coded as showing more anger and whining than were husbands in regulated marriages (see Table 5.2). Wives in nonregulated marriages evidenced less interest/ curiosity, less joy/enthusiasm, greater anger, greater disgust/contempt, and greater whining than did wives in regulated marriages.[5]

5.5.2.3.7. Generality of Negativity Across Conversations: Pervasiveness and Rebound

Table 5.3 summarizes two types of analyses: nonsequential that measure and the analyses for the pervasiveness of marital conflict for the two types of couples (the events of the day discussion) and rebound (the positive conversation).

1. *Pervasiveness.* The two groups of couples could be distinguished in terms of pervasiveness. Regulated wives showed significantly more joy and interest during the events of the day conversation than did their nonregulated counterparts. The effect for interest was similar for husbands, but only marginally significant. It is not that conflict was more pervasive, but that conflict took its toll in diminishing positive affect and increasing disengagement in nonconflictual conversations. Hence, in the area of positive affect, nonregulated wives, even in nonconflict

---

[5]I note, in passing, the strange behavior of the SPAFF code for fear/tension/worry. This code is not acting reliably as a negative affect. Although regulated and nonregulated couples do not differ significantly on this code, regulated couples are higher than nonregulated couples on this code (husbands in regulated marriages = 7.72, husbands in nonregulated marriages = 5.48; wives in regulated marriages = 8.56, wives in nonregulated marriages = 6.63). One possible reason for this may be a subcode of the fear/tension/worry code, which is called "non-ah speech disturbances." These behaviors involve incomplete phrases, repetitions of words, fragments, or phrases, omissions, slips of the tongue, and other errors of speech that do not have to do with holding the floor as a speaker (which are called "ah speech disturbances"). Although in many contexts these non-ah disturbances are indicative of stress or tension, they also can occur during excitement or other intense positive affects, or when a person's thoughts come faster than he or she can express them. Although the observer's manual tries to be clear about distinguishing this code from excitement and joy, this may be a source of unreliability in the fear/tension/worry affect. With these data, fear/tension/worry cannot reliably be considered as either a positive or negative affect. Perhaps this problem can be cleared up in later versions of the SPAFF training materials.

TABLE 5.3

Generality of the Regulated/Nonregulated Distinction for the Other Conversations: Pervasiveness and Rebound

Variable	Regulated	Nonregulated	t	df	p
		Events of Day (Pervasiveness) SPAFF			
Husband					
HNEU	57.86	57.45	.06	66	ns
HHUM	9.17	10.33	−.50	57	ns
HAFF	1.94	2.12	−.24	52	ns
HINT	31.09	22.64	1.80	66	.076
HJOY	4.29	2.64	1.53	66	ns
HANG	1.11	2.73	−1.57	40	ns
HDIS	4.03	3.09	.76	54	ns
HWHI	.37	.61	−.67	48	ns
HSAD	.91	1.97	−1.11	45	ns
HFEA	6.57	6.67	−.05	59	ns
Wife					
WNEU	54.09	53.03	.16	61	ns
WHUM	10.26	11.48	−.51	66	ns
WAFF	2.43	2.85	−.49	66	ns
WINT	34.49	22.70	2.02	61	.048
WJOY	6.09	3.36	2.26	61	.028
WANG	2.46	2.94	−.43	66	ns
WDIS	2.57	3.03	−.59	66	ns
WWHI	1.51	1.64	−.19	60	ns
WSAD	.57	.67	−.28	66	ns
WFEA	6.11	9.42	−1.60	66	ns
		Positive Conversation (Rebound) SPAFF			
Husband					
HNEU	51.40	50.02	.08	66	ns
HHUM	10.00	10.18	−.08	66	ns
HAFF	2.83	1.73	1.44	48	ns
HINT	26.89	26.27	.13	66	ns
HJOY	10.57	9.33	.50	66	ns
HANG	1.94	2.88	−.57	66	ns
HDIS	2.71	3.39	−.48	66	ns
HWHI	.17	.82	−1.53	35	ns
HSAD	.80	1.42	−1.10	52	ns
HFEA	6.54	5.45	.57	66	ns
Wife					
WNEU	47.23	44.64	.38	66	ns
WHUM	10.66	11.52	−.37	66	ns
WAFF	2.89	3.27	−.40	66	ns
WINT	30.23	24.70	1.18	66	ns
WJOY	10.43	10.94	−.16	66	ns
WANG	2.69	3.76	−.63	66	ns
WDIS	1.94	2.88	−.92	66	ns
WWHI	.74	1.64	−1.61	66	ns
WSAD	1.20	1.00	.39	66	ns
WFEA	6.97	5.94	.51	62	ns

discussions showed less positivity and more disengagement (less interest) than regulated couples.

2. *Rebound.* The two groups of couples could not be distinguished in terms of rebound (i.e., they could not be distinguished on the positive conversation that followed the conflict discussion).

5.5.3.2.8. Start Up, Continuance, and Positive Reciprocity

Table 5.4 summarizes the results for the sequences in each conversation described as start up (from neutral to negative affect across spouses), continuance (from negative to negative affect across spouses), and positive reciprocity (positive affect to positive affect across spouses). In terms of the sequences identified, there were no significant differences on the positive conversation. There was one marginal difference on the conflict conversation, and there was more positive reciprocity for regulated couples from husband to wife. However, there were two significant differences on the positive conversation: There was more

TABLE 5.4

Sequences Identified to Measure Start Up, Negative Continuance (Negative Affect Reciprocity), and Positive Continuance

	Group				
Sequences	Regulated	Nonregulated	t	df	p
Positive Conversation					
Start up HO → WN	−.25	.00	−.82	57	ns
Start up WO → HN	.33	.00	1.06	57	ns
Continuance HN → WN	3.06	3.30	−.29	57	ns
Continuance WN → HN	2.44	2.86	−.55	57	ns
Pos. recip. HP → WP	2.95	3.02	−.13	57	ns
Pos. recip. WP → HP	2.53	2.86	−.65	57	ns
Conflict Conversation					
Start up HO → WM	1.23	1.62	−.97	66	ns
Start up WO → HN	.79	.58	.62	66	ns
Continuance HN → WN	5.38	5.93	−.54	66	ns
Continuance WN → HN	5.56	5.81	−.23	66	ns
Pos. recip. HP → WP	4.38	2.94	1.72	66	.090
Pos. recip. WP → HP	4.16	3.00	1.40	66	ns
Positive Conversation					
Start up HO → WN	.00	−.01	.05	56	ns
Start up WO → HN	.23	.21	−.69	56	ns
Continuance HN → WN	2.61	4.20	−2.04	65	.046
Continuance WN → HN	2.44	4.26	−2.23	65	.029
Pos. recip. HP → WP	4.14	3.93	.43	65	ns
Pos. recip. WP → HP	3.73	4.04	−.59	56	ns

negative continuance (negative affect reciprocity) and less positive affect reciprocity for nonregulated couples compared with regulated couples. Hence, even on the positive conversation, increased negative continuance and decreased positive affect reciprocity is evident for nonregulated couples. Because the positive conversation followed the conflict conversation, this is evidence of a reduction in the couple's ability to rebound from a conflictual discussion. Hence, there is evidence that the differences observed in the conflict–resolution discussion extend into interaction in other areas of the marriage and affect the quality of the emotional exchanges in general.

5.5.2.4. A Two-Group Marital Typology Based on Behavioral Observation

The utility of a new method for identifying two kinds of marriages was evaluated. It was demanded that the typology be able to distinguish marriages in a number of domains including health, physiology, behavior, affect, marital satisfaction, and the risk for marital dissolution. It was encouraging to find that these two marital types, regulated and nonregulated couples, were quite different at the time of their classification and followed quite different courses over the ensuing 4 years.

As indicated earlier, despite the existence of a large number of proposed classification schemes, there have been relatively few attempts to classify marriages based on direct observation of behavior. The classification system offered here, which is based on the coding of a 15-minute snapshot of the couples' behavior as they attempted to resolve a marital conflict, has a number of advantages. First, the RCISS coding, upon which it is based, is relatively economical compared with other coding systems. It takes about 6 hours to code 15 minutes of speaker behavior. Second, RCISS coding can be carried out with quite high reliability by coders after about 2 months of training. Third, the classification rules for defining the two marital subtypes are simple, requiring no inference. Fourth, as is seen later, other distinctive subtypes are likely to emerge from this system, especially if point graphs of listener codes also are considered. Fifth, the RCISS point graphs are somewhat unique in that they take account of both the balance between negative and positive affective behavior as well as changes in the balance that occur over time. Sixth, the RCISS codes sample emotions (e.g., humor, escalate negative affect), emotional behaviors (e.g., put down, complain), and task-related behaviors (e.g., problem description), thus encompassing a number of different (albeit related) characteristics of the interaction.

5.5.2.5. The Dysfunctional Qualities of Nonregulated Marriages

Nonregulated couples, those for whom the balance between positive and negative affective behavior fails to increasingly favor positive affective behaviors over time, have marriages that appear, in many ways, to be much more dysfunctional than those of regulated couples.

In the realm of quality of the marital relationship, nonregulated couples reported lower levels of marital satisfaction (both at the time they were classified and 4 years later), and nonregulated wives rated marital problems as being more severe. Over the 4-year period of this study, nonregulated couples were more likely to consider marital dissolution and more likely to actually separate. Self-report measures of marital satisfaction were among the most widely accepted barometers of marital quality; consideration of dissolution and actual separation were arguably among the clearest behavioral signs of marital distress. Thus, in terms of both kinds of criteria, the relationship quality of nonregulated couples was lower than that of regulated couples.

In the realm of interaction, MICS coders rated the behavior of nonregulated couples as characterized more by negatively tinged behaviors such as conflict engagement, stubbornness, and withdrawal from interaction. SPAFF coders rated nonregulated wives as less likely to express the positive emotions of interest/caring and joy/enthusiasm and more likely to express disgust/contempt. Both nonregulated husbands and wives were found to be more likely to express the negative emotions of anger and whining. These results from observational coding were consistent with husbands' rating dial data, which indicated that nonregulated husbands felt more negative during the interaction. This combination of MICS behaviors, the character of which made them unlikely to lead to constructive resolution of problems, coupled with SPAFF emotions, which indicated a lack of positive affect and a surplus of negative affect, are likely to make marital interaction an unpleasant and unproductive aspect of marital life for nonregulated couples. Unpleasant and unproductive interaction does not bode well for the ultimate stability of a marriage.

In the physiological realm, nonregulated wives showed evidence of greater sympathetic nervous system arousal in their cardiovascular responses during their problem-area interactions. Because both faster heart rates and greater vasoconstriction were observed in nonregulated wives, it is likely that they were evidencing heightened arousal in both the alpha-sympathetic and beta-sympathetic branches of the sympathetic nervous system. Although the association was not as strong in the present data, it is worth remembering that in earlier longitudinal work with a different sample of couples, physiological arousal during marital interaction was a strong predictor of future declines in marital satisfaction (Levenson & Gottman, 1985).

In another biological realm, nonregulated wives reported being in poorer health in 1987 than did regulated wives. The basis for this finding is unknown. However, a possible contributor to this finding could be the greater cardiovascular sympathetic nervous system arousal during the 1983 interactions on the part of nonregulated wives. Sustained high levels of sympathetic nervous system activity and/or sympathetic nervous system hyperreactivity often have been suggested as possible mediators of the relation between stress and disease (e.g., Henry & Stephens, 1977). Of course, the present data are only suggestive in this regard. Any causal link between marital dissatisfaction and poor health could go in either direction, especially given that comparable health data in 1983 were not obtained. Even if conclusive data were available linking these kinds of patterns of cardiovascular arousal to illness, one cannot know, based on brief 15-minute samples of physiological data, whether nonregulated couples are hyperaroused chronically. Nonetheless, regardless of etiology, poorer health on the part of nonregulated wives could be yet another factor reducing the quality of these marriages.

5.5.2.6. Gender Differences in Regulated and Nonregulated Couples

A number of interesting differences emerged in the pattern of findings for husbands and wives, an issue that was explored previously (Gottman & Levenson, 1988).

One such finding was that the relation between the nonregulated marital style and poor health was more apparent for wives than for husbands. Given that the present study revealed nonregulated couples to be lower in marital satisfaction, a finding from an earlier longitudinal study (using a different sample of subjects) is supportive of this gender difference. In that study, the correlation between marital dissatisfaction in 1980 and lower health scores in 1983 was found to be stronger for wives than for husbands (Levenson & Gottman, 1985).

Assuming that self-reports of illness are reasonable indicators of actual illness (McDowell & Newell, 1987), the results suggest that men might be better buffered from the negative health consequences of dysfunctional marriages than women. Along these lines, it has been speculated (Gottman & Levenson, 1988) that a partial explanation for the often-observed tendency of husbands to withdraw and stonewall during stressful marital interaction is that the male becomes hyperaroused physiologically when experiencing negative affect. The listener withdrawal seen in the laboratory when couples are constrained to remain seated probably is reflected by actual avoidance of interaction at home. Because this hyperarousal is aversive, men engage in behaviors that help reduce arousal, usually by avoiding interaction, with the attendant benefit of minimizing the associated adverse health consequences. Following this line of argument, women, who are far less likely to engage in these avoidant behaviors and far more likely to pursue their men so that issues can be resolved, would be exposed more directly to the adverse health consequences of distressed marital interaction.

A second area in which gender differences were observed was in the SPAFF coding of emotional behavior. Husbands and wives in the nonregulated and regulated groups differed in anger and whining, but only nonregulated wives showed more disgust/contempt. It is my impression (and that of marital therapists) that contempt and disgust are particularly dysfunctional behaviors in a marital conflict resolution, probably indicative of a higher level of rejection of the relationship at Time 1 by nonregulated wives. Whereas both nonregulated husbands and wives displayed more negative affect than their regulated counterparts, only nonregulated wives showed less positive affect. This finding suggests an interesting dynamic. Observations of hundreds of marital interactions over the years has led me to hypothesize that wives are much more likely than husbands to take responsibility for regulating the affective balance and keeping the couple on problem-solving task during the problem-area marital interaction. Wives do this by interjecting humor, caring, and concern at appropriate moments of high tension, thus dissipating negative affect and allowing the couple to return to the task of working toward a solution of the designated problem. Perhaps one reason that nonregulated couples are so dysfunctional and at such heightened risk for dissolution is that nonregulated wives no longer assume the responsibility for using positive affect in this regulatory manner. Thus, like a powerful heating system without a thermostat, the unregulated marital interaction is much more likely to self-destruct.

5.5.2.7. A Cascade Model of Marital Dissolution

Thirty-six percent (11 of 31) of nonregulated couples actually separated, which was significantly greater than the 16.7% (7 of 42) of regulated couples. Given that the 12.3% incidence of divorces over the 4-year period reported here produced a group of only nine divorced couples, it would be difficult to consider this to be a definitive study of divorce until a larger group of divorces has accumulated. Nonetheless, the number of nonregulated couples that divorced during this period (i.e., six) was twice as large as the number of regulated couples that divorced (i.e., three), despite the larger sample size for regulated couples. Furthermore, the difference in percentage of divorces between the two groups approached statistical significance. In terms of the variables hypothesized to be precursors of divorce, nonregulated couples had significantly lower marital satisfaction scores in 1983 and 1987, were more likely to consider dissolution, and were more likely to separate than regulated couples. These findings, by themselves, suggest that nonregulated couples are at heightened risk for marital dissolution. I attempted to explore this matter further by utilizing structural equations modeling.

The use of structural equations modeling to explore models of causality in correlational data is controversial, and I wish to align myself with the most conservative interpretation of these methods. When applied to the cascade model of marital dissolution portrayed in Fig. 5.2, these analyses supported the hypothesis that declining marital satisfaction led to considerations of dissolution, eventual separation, and divorce. Of course, except for the 1983 marital satisfaction, all data used to test this model were obtained in 1987. Thus, this notion of the temporal cascade must be considered only hypothetical.

One reason that the issue of a cascade model is important is because of the aforementioned problem of low base rates of separation and divorce in short-term longitudinal samples. Although some success was had in predicting these outcomes, my data suggest that, consistent with a cascade model, it is easier to predict variables such as declining marital satisfaction and considerations of dissolution than to predict separation and divorce.

In considering this cascade model, a likely first reaction is that it is not very profound. Is not it obvious that couples that divorce are likely to have separated previously, and, before that, to have considered dissolution, and, before that, to have been unhappily married? In reality, this kind of progression has never been demonstrated empirically, and, further, it may be only one of a number of possible progressions. For example, marital dissatisfaction may be an independent process from marital dissolution (Lederer & Jackson, 1968). Everyone knows unhappily married couples that continue to stay together for a variety of reasons (e.g., religiosity; see Bugaighis et al., 1985). Levenson, Carstensen, and I are currently studying a group of such unhappy couples, many of whom have been together for over 35 years. It is currently unknown whether the dissolution of marriages is part of the same process as the deterioration of marital satisfaction (as was suggested by Lewis & Spanier, 1982) or whether these are independent processes. Given the lack of knowledge from prospective research concerning this issue, it is of some interest that in the present study it was possible to scale the events leading to marital dissolution as a cascade. This supports the notion that there is some continuity between these variables.

What of the relation between the typology of marriage proposed and the hypothesized cascade model of marital dissolution? As indicated earlier, compared with regulated couples, nonregulated couples were more likely to have entered the early stages of the model and thus can be thought to be more likely to reach the final stage of marital dissolution. By using observational methods to study the interactions of nonregulated couples while their marriages are still intact, I hope to have identified a profile of behaviors that are early warning signs of future marital dissolution. This kind of profile, if accurate, should be useful for researchers and clinicians alike.

5.5.2.8. A Marital Process Cascade That is Related to the Outcome Cascade: The Four Horsemen of the Apocalypse

The model to be tested is that couples at Time 1 vary in terms of their location on a set of marital processes, and that these processes predict the probability that couples will move toward dissolution. There is no need for these processes to form a cascade, but it would be elegant if this were the case. Indeed, it seems plausible that there is a cascade of process variables that are related to the outcome cascade.

Marital outcomes do indeed form a cascade. Hence, one can describe a couple as on a cascade toward marital dissolution, or not. Furthermore, one is able to predict precursor variables more easily than the rarer variables of separation and divorce. I show that there is a set of marital interaction processes and physiological variables that are related strongly to this cascade toward marital dissolution.

The point graphs provided some information about the marital interaction, and the typology that resulted (regulated and nonregulated couples) was useful in predicting the variables of the cascade model. The use of the one RCISS process variable to predict may be parsimonious, and of some interest, but it is intellectually unsatisfying as a description of the ailing marriage. The process cascade I propose, which predicts marital dissolution, is the following: Complaining and criticizing leads to contempt, which leads to defensiveness, which leads to listener withdrawal from interaction (stonewalling). I refer to these four corrosive marital behaviors as "The Four Horsemen of the Apocalypse." My assumption is that they are integral in powering the cascade toward marital dissolution, that is, I propose a causal connection here, for which I have no evidence. However, Gottman and Krokoff (1989) found that defensiveness and stonewalling predicted deterioration in marital satisfaction in a 3-year longitudinal study. Contempt, defensiveness, and stonewalling can be assessed with the RCISS. Each scale, which consists of several behaviors, has high Cronbach alpha and has been validated using as criteria marital satisfaction, other observational coding systems, and conflict interaction at home (Krokoff, Gottman, & Haas, 1989).

To check the validity of the RCISS, data also were coded by Dr. Robert Weiss at the University of Oregon with the Marital Interaction Coding System (MICS). The MICS summary codes validated by Gottman and Krokoff (1989) were employed. In each system, it was possible to define four parallel codes: (a) complain/criticize, (b) defensive, (c) contemptuous, and (d) stonewalling. For the sake of simplicity, and for these analyses, data were summed over husband and wife. Figure 5.5 shows that these four variables for both the RCISS and the MICS form a Guttman-like scale. For the RCISS, $\chi^2(2) = 0.02$, $p = 1.00$, whereas for the MICS $\chi^2(2) = 0.82$, $p = .66$. These figures show that there is considerable consistency in this Guttman-like scaling of processes. These analyses show that such a Guttman-like scaling model is consistent with these data.

5.5.2.9. Correlations with Cascade Model

Table 5.5 summarizes the correlations of these four process variables with the variables of the cascade model. For both the RCISS and the MICS, these four processes predict the variables of the cascade model. Furthermore, as expected, they do better for the precursors of divorce and separation.

5.5.2.9.1. Summary

Using the four observational variables, I identify a hypothesized process cascade that I have called the Four Horsemen of the Apocalypse:

COMPLAIN/CRITICIZE → CONTEMPT → DEFENSIVENESS → STONEWALLING

Hopefully, this process adds to the ability to diagnose couples at high or low risk for the trajectory toward marital dissolution.

5.5.2.9.2. A Questionnaire Package That Covaries with Behavior and Predicts Dissolution

Most couples do not have access to a laboratory in which their videotapes can be coded by trained observers. Hence, it would be useful

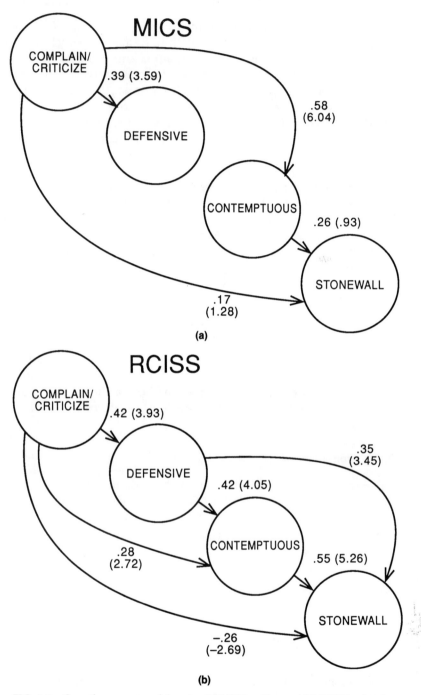

FIG. 5.5. Cascade process models using (a) MICS coding and (b) RCISS subscales.

TABLE 5.5
Correlation of the Four Process Variables with the Cascade Model Variables

Variable	Marital Quality Time 1	Marital Quality Time 2	Considered Dissolution	Separation	Divorce
MICS					
Complain/criticize	−.34**	−.32**	.23*	.18	.28**
Defensive	−.26*	−.18	.13	.13	.05
Contemptuous	−.27**	−.19	.11	−.01	.01
Stonewalling	−.37***	−.31**	.23*	.06	.09
RCISS					
Complain/criticize	−.24*	−.09	.11	.18	.16
Defensive	−.31**	−.39***	.25*	.14	.40***
Contemptuous	−.31**	−.35**	.14	.14	.26*
Stonewalling	−.34**	−.43***	.24*	.12	.19

*$p < .05$. **$p < .01$. ***$p < .001$.

to discover a self-report cascade that had some margin of predictability, even if it were less than the predictability from scoring a videotape. Then perhaps couples could decide for themselves if their marriage were at risk, and they could decide (if they so desired) to intervene to change the trajectory. I have discovered a set of five questionnaires that fits theoretically into a cascade called "The Distance and Isolation Cascade."

5.5.2.9.3. Distance and Isolation

At Time 1, I collected a set of five questionnaires from subjects. These questionnaires were designed to describe a process of increasing distance and isolation. The idea was that the underlying variable driving this increased distance and isolation was a concept called *flooding*. The five questionnaires were: (a) loneliness (sample item: "Sometimes I feel so lonely it hurts"), alphas = .79 and .82 for husband and wife, respectively (LONELY); (b) parallel lives (sample item: "My partner and I live pretty separate lives"), alphas = .95 and .95 for husband and wife, respectively; this scale assesses the extent to which husband and wife have arranged their lives so that they do not interact very much and do not do things together (PARALLEL); (c) severity of problems, computed from the Couple's Problem Inventory (Gottman et al., 1977), based on a subjective estimate of the severity of a set of issues in the marriage, alphas = .79 and .75 for husband and wife, respectively (PROB); (d) flooded by partner's negative affect is a scale that assesses the extent to which spouse A feels that spouse B's negative emotions arise unexpectedly and are overwhelming and disorganizing to spouse A, alphas = .82 and .73 for husband and wife, respectively (ESCAL); (e) works problems out alone, not with spouse is a scale that assesses the extent to which a person thinks it is better to avoid problems or work them out alone, rather than with the spouse, alphas = .88 and .76 for husband and wife, respectively (PHIL).

5.5.2.9.4. Summary

To review, the theoretical idea behind the design of these measures was that they would tap the increasing distance and isolation that might accompany marital dissolution, and that being flooded by one's partner's negative affect would drive this increased distance and isolation. The self-report data add conceptual clarity to the constructs about what describes the processes related to marital dissolution. Self-report measures also can be used cheaply by clinicians or clinical researchers. However, it is important to validate that these measures correlate with both behavior and marital outcome.

Thus, the theory is that what is driving the distance and isolation cascade is being flooded by one's partner's negative affect expressions, and that this leads to diffuse physiological arousal and increased avoidance of interaction.

5.5.2.9.5. Factor Structure

I performed a principal components analysis on the questionnaire data. The following two components were obtained (see Table 5.6). This analysis suggests that the five questionnaires are primarily one dimension, except for wife loneliness and wife parallel lives, which load on an orthogonal component. The parallel lives scale correlates with each person's own loneliness; for wives, the correlation is 0.61, $p < .001$, and for husbands, the correlation is 0.59, $p < .001$. This latter result implies that couples did not tend to view this state of parallel lives as a desirable state.

TABLE 5.6
Principal Components Analysis of the Distance and Isolation Cascade Variables

Variable	Component 1	Component 2
H PHIL	.59	.01
W PHIL	.49	.28
H ESCAL	.78	−.11
W ESCAL	.79	−.19
H PROB	.88	−.06
W PROB	.75	−.17
H LONELY	.89	.00
W LONELY	.26	.86
H PARALLEL	.59	−.19
W PARALLEL	.19	.83
Variance	44.00%	16.30%

5.5.2.9.6. Correlation with Behavior

Table 5.7 summarizes the correlations of the questionnaires with behavior. This table shows that the questionnaires correlate quite well with the behavioral measures.

5.5.2.9.7. Correlations of Questionnaires with Variables of the Cascade Model

Table 5.8 summarizes the correlations of the questionnaire variables with the variables of the cascade model. These data show that the questionnaires correlate with the variables of the cascade model in a manner that is consistent with expectations that these variables form a Guttman-like scale, in which precursor variables are easier to predict than rarely occurring criterion variables.

TABLE 5.7
Correlations of Questionnaires with Behavior

Variable	Complain/Criticize	Defensive	Contempt	Stonewalling
With MICS				
H PHIL	.19	.05	−.05	.19
W PHIL	.22	.11	.11	.17
H ESCAL	.35**	.26*	.43***	.32**
W ESCAL	.38***	.34**	.42***	.40***
H PROB	.26*	.14	.29**	.20
W PROB	.45***	.24*	.49***	.24*
H LONELY	.20	.17	.28*	.18
H PARALLEL	.24*	−.05	.11	.14
With RCISS				
H PHIL	.13	.09	−.03	.10
W PHIL	.22	.15	.19	.04
H ESCAL	.29**	.21	.38***	.35**
W ESCAL	.23*	.39***	.37***	.50***
H PROB	.04	.00	.12	.04
W PROB	.31**	.35**	.39***	.35**
H LONELY	.21	.11	.15	.21
H PARALLEL	.23*	.15	.22	.20
With Point Graph Variables	*Husband*		*Wife*	
H PHIL	−.15		−.07	
W PHIL	−.20		−.25*	
H ESCAL	−.39***		−.39***	
W ESCAL	−.40***		−.42***	
H PROB	−.14		−.12	
W PROB	−.36**		−.47***	
H LONELY	−.29**		−.27*	
H PARALLEL	−.31**		−.14	

Note. With point graph variables, husband = positive minus negative; wife = positive minus negative.
*$p < .05$. **$p < .01$. ***$p < .001$.

TABLE 5.8
Correlations of the Questionnaire Variables with the Cascade Model Variables

Variable	Marital Quality Time 1	Marital Quality Time 2	Considered Dissolution	Separation	Divorce
H PHIL	−.45***	−.33**	.17	.12	.15
W PHIL	−.39***	−.30**	.12	.13	.28*
H ESCAL	−.68***	−.46***	.39***	.10	.09
W ESCAL	−.72***	−.59***	.53***	.14	.21
H PROB	−.68***	−.40***	.33**	.05	.17
W PROB	−.62***	−.49***	.48***	.31**	.26*
H LONELY	−.78***	−.43***	.43***	.16	.16
H PARALLEL	−.16	−.24*	.07	.16	.31**

*p < .05. **p < .01. ***p < .001.

Table 5.9 shows that the Four Horsemen of the Apocalypse are correlated with emotional flooding by both spouses. There is also a suggestion that males become flooded by negative partner behaviors that are less intense than is the case for women. Complaining and criticizing were correlated with flooding for men but not for women.

5.5.2.10. The Questionnaires Also Form a Process Cascade

Recall that the theoretical idea that motivated the design of these questionnaires was that the perception of one's partner's emotions as overwhelming and unpredictable would be likely to drive the decay of the relationship and lead to avoidance. Using structural equations modeling, there is a model that is consistent with this theory that the experience of being flooded by one's partner's negative emotions may lead to withdrawal, the perceptions that the marital problems are severe, and loneliness in the marriage. To simplify the analysis, the ESCAL, PHIL, and PROB variables were added for husband and wife, and the parallel lives scale was dropped from the analysis. The model in

TABLE 5.9
Correlations of Feeling Flooded by Partner's Negative Affect as a Function of the Negativity of the RCISS Codes

Partner's Behavior	Husband Flooded (ESCAL)	Wife Flooded (ESCAL)	z
Complain/criticize	.25*	.15	1.81
Defensiveness	.24*	.36**	.68
Contempt	.29*	.41***	.68
Stonewalling	.45***	.35**	.74

*p < .05. **p < .01. ***p < .001.

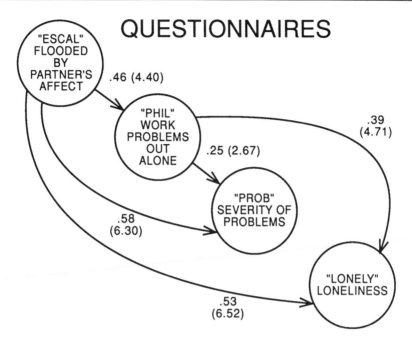

FIG. 5.6.   Cascade process model using questionnaire data.

Fig. 5.6 fit the data, with $\chi^2(1) = 1.69$, $p = .19$, Bentler-Bonnett Normed index = .998.

5.6. SUMMARY

It is possible to identify a set of interactive processes called the Four Horsemen of the Apocalypse, a set of processes that index distance and isolation with five questionnaires assessing: loneliness, parallel lives, severity of problems, flooded by partner's negative affect, and works problems out alone, not with spouse. These interactive behaviors and the questionnaires each form a process cascade, and covary with both behavior and the outcome cascade. The data are not inconsistent with the notion that what may be driving increased distance and isolation is the experience of being "flooded" by one's partner's negative emotions;[6] emotional flooding may lead to withdrawal, the perceptions that the marital problems are severe, and loneliness in the marriage.

---

[6]In support of the relationship between the husband's contempt/disgust behavior on the RCISS and her feeling flooded, in the area of facial expressions of negative affect, the wife's feeling flooded in significantly correlated with the number of the husband's contempt facial expressions ($r = .32$, $p < .05$).

6

In What Sense are Regulated Couples Regulated?

A question remains in suggesting that any system is regulated, namely, what is the error signal? This means that there must be some quantity that is being regulated, so that deviations from this set point results in the system restabilizing in some manner. The choice of this error signal is explored in this chapter.

In chapter 5, I reported the results of a study that Levenson and I conducted in which we classified married couples into two groups based on their interactive behavior during conflict resolution. Seventy-three married couples were studied in 1983 and 1987. The two groups were regulated (i.e., a group in which both spouses increased the cumulative difference of positive to negative behaviors over the course of a 15-minute discussion of a marital problem) and nonregulated (i.e., a group in which the couples did not). Thus, one variable was employed to divide couples into two groups, the slope of cumulative graphs of positive minus negative speaker codes on the Rapid Couples Interaction Scoring System (RCISS). Regulated couples had significantly positive slopes for both husband and wife, whereas nonregulated couples did not have both slopes significantly positive.

Compared with regulated couples, nonregulated couples were more dysfunctional in a number of domains: (a) marital problems rated more severe (wives), (b) there was poorer health at Time 2 (wives), (c) there was greater cardiovascular arousal (wives), (d) interactions were rated more negative (husbands), (e) there was more negative emotional expression (wives and husbands), (f) there was less positive emotional expression (wives), (g) there was more stubbornness and withdrawal from interaction (wives and husbands), and (h) there was greater defensiveness (husbands). Nonregulated couples were also at greater risk for marital dissolution, reported lower marital satisfaction both at Times 1 and 2, and reported higher incidence of serious considerations of dissolution and of actual separation. A cascade model of marital dissolution that considered marital dissatisfaction, consideration of separation, and actual separation as precursors of divorce received preliminary support in this report.

Surprisingly, this was the first prospective study of marital dissolution based on interactive behavior. The ability to predict dissolution and its precursors was an improvement over the previous four prospective longitudinal studies of marital dissolution (Bentler & Newcomb, 1978; Block et al., 1981; Constantine & Bahr, 1980; Kelly & Conley, 1987). The results also presented a reasonably coherent theoretical model of these precursors.

However, a problem with this model was that the variable used to divide couples into the two groups was a compound variable based on the difference between positive and negative speaker codes. It is unclear which variable—the total of positive codes, the total of negative codes, or some measure of their balance (as is represented by the difference variable employed)—is most effective at discriminating the two groups. The terms used to describe the groups, namely, *regulated* and *nonregulated*, suggest some balance between negative and positive codes. However, the question remains as to whether these terms actually are justified. This chapter attempts to answer this question.

This discussion is important, because the term *nonregulated* may be conceptually misleading. Recently, a relatively young man who weighed 500 pounds died. His weight was clearly dysfunctional for his health and longevity. However, his body defended that weight, and that weight became a set point around which other processes (e.g., hunger) were regulated. In a similar way, it may be the case that unstable marriages are, in fact, regulated, but their set point is dysfunctional for their longevity. If this is the case, then the term *nonregulated couples* is misleading terminology.

A second question I address in this chapter is whether all negative and positive codes of the RCISS are doing equivalent work in the discrimination. That is, are some negative codes more corrosive than others and some positive codes more buffering than others?

6.1. RCISS SUBSCALES

Recall that the videotapes of the problem area interaction were coded using the RCISS, which provided the means for classifying couples into regulated and nonregulated types.

6.1.1. Rapid Couples Interaction Scoring System (RCISS)

The Rapid Couples Interaction Scoring System (RCISS; Krokoff, Gottman, & Haas, 1989) employs a checklist of 13 behaviors that are scored for the speaker and 9 behaviors that are scored for the listener on each turn at speech. A turn at speech is defined as all utterances by one speaker until that speaker yields the floor to vocalizations by the other spouse (vocalizations that are merely backchannels such as "Mmmhmm" are not considered as demarcating a turn). RCISS behavioral codes can be scored in terms of an underlying positive–negative dimension. In the study reported in chapter 5, only speaker codes were used to classify couples. These speaker codes consisted of three positive speaker scales: (a) positive agenda building, which included the following behaviors—neutral or positive problem description and task-oriented relationship information; (b) response to partner's agenda building, which included the behavior called "assent";[1] and (c) positive affect, which included the behaviors humor-laugh. There were also three negative scales: (a) complain, criticize, (which also included negative relationship issue problem talk); (b) defensive, which included the behaviors yes-but and defensive; and (c) contempt, which included the behaviors put down, escalate negative affect, and other negative.

6.1.2. Positive and Negative Subscales of the RCISS

To answer the question posed in this chapter, the mean positive and negative speaker codes for husband and wife, their mean difference for husband and wife, and the ratio of negative to positive plus negative codes were computed. Ratios of positive to negative codes have been employed in the past in research on marital satisfaction using two variables, the ratio of agreement to agreement plus disagreement (Gottman, 1979), and the ratio of pleasing to displeasing events recorded in the Spouse Observation Checklist diary measure (Weiss, Hops, & Patterson, 1973). The ratio of agreement to agreement plus disagreement is a better choice than the ratio of agreement to disagreement, because it avoids the problem of dividing by zero for some cases, and the mean of the latter ratio can be computed from the mean of the former ratio.

---

[1]The code "assent" refers to short vocalizations (e.g., "Mmm-hmm," "Yeah") that usually communicate some form of mild agreement or acceptance of the speaker's point of view. However, a more impatient form of assent, in which the listener is only communicating that he or she wishes the speaker to express feelings or ideas but does not necessarily agree with what is being said, also is coded assent. Thus, assent is a fairly limited and low-level form of agreement and acceptance.

I used a statistical technique called Discriminant Function Analysis to answer these questions (Gottman & Levenson, 1992). In this technique, one tries to find a function that is a weighted sum of the variables that best discriminates the two groups (regulated and nonregulated). To answer the question of this report about which variables are doing the work of discriminating regulated from nonregulated couples, five stepwise discriminant function models were compared. The first model contained only negative codes, the second model contained only positive codes, the third model contained only the difference between positive and negative codes, the fourth model contained only the ratio codes, and the fifth model included all the variables.

To answer the question about whether specific subscales of the RCISS were more active in the positive and negative discriminations than others, two additional stepwise discriminant function analyses were conducted—one for the three positive subscales and one for the three negative subscales.

6.2. RESULTS

Table 6.1 is a summary of four of the five stepwise discriminant function models. The fifth model was not included in this table, because it selected only the variables of the fourth model and, thus, all the statistics were identical to the fourth model. As can be seen from these models, both positive and negative speaker codes are able to discriminate the two groups. Negative codes do slightly better than positive codes. The wife's positive codes is the only variable entered in the first model. Both spouses' negative codes contribute to the discrimination, with wives' negative codes entered first. Although the two models do equally well in overall classification, the negative codes do better at classifying the regulated couples (97.2% correct) than the positive codes (88.9% correct). The difference codes do better than either positive or negative codes, again with the wives' codes entered first; and the ratio codes do the best of all models, with a canonical R of .83 and percent correct classification of 95.5.

It is consistent with these comparisons to conclude that a better fit to the classification proposed is a balance model between positive and negative codes. Indeed, if one computes the mean ratio of positive to negative codes, for the husband it is much higher for regulated couples than for nonregulated couples, and the same is true for wives. This represents a dramatic difference in interaction balance. I say more about this idea of balance in a later chapter.

Table 6.2 is a summary of the discriminant function analyses of the

TABLE 6.1
Comparison of Four Stepwise Discriminant Function Models to Classify Couples as Regulated or Nonregulated

| | Means | | | | Step | | | | | |
Variable	Regulated	Nonregulated	t	df	Entered	F	df	R	χ^2	df
Positive Codes										
Wife	.92	.56	7.36***	65	1	54.11	(1,65)	.67	39.07	1
Husband	.91	.64	4.39***	65	Not entered	—	—	—	—	—
Percent correct	88.9	77.4								
Overall percent correct		83.6								
Negative Codes										
Wife	.28	1.09	8.31***	36	1	77.78	(1,65)	.75	52.31	2
Husband	.27	.81	6.65***	37	2	40.46	(2,64)			
Percent correct	97.2	71.0								
Overall percent correct		85.1								
Difference Codes										
Wife	.63	-.52	9.71***	39	1	104.91	(1,65)	.79	63.69	2
Husband	.63	-.17	6.66***	40	22	54.57	(2,64)			
Percent correct	100.0	87.1								
Overall percent correct		94.0								
Ratio Negative/(Negative + Positive)										
Wife	.23	.63	11.80***	65	1	139.13	(1,65)	.83	75.27	2
Husband	.23	.54	7.83***	46	2	71.73	(1,64)			
Percent correct	94.4	96.8								
Overall percent correct		95.5								

*p < .05. **p < .01. ***p < .001.

TABLE 6.2
Comparison of Two Discriminant Function Models for Specific Positive and Negative Subscales of the RCISS

Variable	Means		t	df	Step Entered	F	df	R	χ^2	df
	Regulated	Nonregulated								
Positive Codes										
Hus pos. agenda	.63	.45	2.71**	58	—					4
Hus. pos. response	.16	.12	1.18	63	—					
Hus. pos. affect	.12	.07	2.22*	62	4	18.70	(4,62)	.74	49.86	
Wife pos. agenda	.62	.42	3.89***	65	1	15.10	(1,65)			
Wife pos. response	.16	.07	3.46***	46	2	26.87	(2,64)			
Wife pos. affect	.14	.08	2.92*	62	3	23.96	(3,63)			
Percent correct	86.1	87.1								
Overall percent correct		86.6								
Negative Codes										
Hus. complain/criticize	.07	.29	3.76***	43	—					4
Hus. defensive	.18	.43	5.83***	42	2	43.61	(2,64)			
Hus. contempt	.09	.02	3.02***	32	3	30.64	(3,63)			
Wife complain/criticize	.08	.53	6.80***	38	1	51.54	(1,65)			
Wife defensive	.19	.43	5.86***	46	—					
Wife contempt	.02	.13	3.37**	31	4	23.57	(4,62)	.78	53.24	
Percent correct	100.0	74.2								
Overall percent correct		88.1								

*$p < .05$. **$p < .011$. ***$p < .001$

three positive and the three negative speaker subscales of the RCISS. The table reveals that it is the wife's positive codes that are the most important in the discrimination. Interestingly, they are not simply positive affect, which is not entered until Step 3. They are the wife's positive presentation of her views on an issue and her assent behavior when her husband presents his views on an issue. It may be that it is particularly wives in relationships that are on a course toward dissolution who have relinquished these particular behaviors.

The negative scales suggest that the discrimination particularly involves the wife's complaining and criticizing and the husband's defensiveness and contempt, which are most important in the discrimination.

6.3. CONTEMPT, DEFENSIVENESS, AND DIVORCE

The relationship between defensiveness and contempt with respect to marital dissolution can be explored by testing alternative path equations models in the direct prediction of divorce. Only three of the four correlations with divorce were significant[2] (husband defensiveness, husband contempt, wife defensiveness, and wife contempt). These three variables were then employed in the path modeling. Three path models were compared (see Fig. 6.1). In the first model, defensiveness and contempt were independent; in the second model, defensiveness affected divorce only indirectly, through contempt; in the third model contempt affected divorce only indirectly through defensiveness. The direction of the path from the husband's to wife's defensiveness was not important in the model, because the two variables correlated so highly.[3] Nor were different directions between these two variables discrernable or meaningful. Only the third model fit the data. Hence, a model that is most consistent with the data is that contempt works indirectly through defensiveness to predict marital dissolution. Hence, in the discrimination between regulated and nonregulated couples, not all negative codes

---

[2]For husband defensiveness, $r = 0.41$, $p < .001$; husband contempt, $r = 0.23$, $p < .10$; wife defensiveness, $r = 0.40$, $p < .001$; and wife contempt, $r = .32$, $p < .01$. These three variables were employed in the path modeling. Three path models were compared (see Fig. 6.1).

[3]The direction of the path from the husband's to the wife's defensiveness is not important in the model, because the two variables correlate so highly ($r = 0.84$). Nor would different directions between these two variables be discrernable or meaningful. Only the third model fits the data. The multiple R of this model in predicting divorce is 0.44. Path coefficients and z scores for each coefficient for this third model are presented in Fig. 6.1. Hence, a model that is most consistent with the data is that contempt works indirectly through defensiveness to predict marital dissolution.

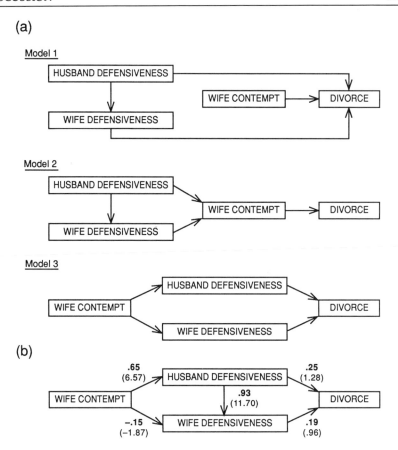

FIG. 6.1. Comparison of three path models in the prediction of divorce by defensiveness and contempt. (a) Model 1 proposes independent, direct effects for defensiveness and divorce. Model 2 proposes that defensiveness works indirectly through contempt. Model 3 proposes that contempt works indirectly through defensiveness. Only Model 3 fits the data. (b) Path coefficients and z scores (parentheses) for Model 3.

are equally corrosive in facilitating the cascade toward marital dissolution. Nor are all positive codes equally active as buffers against marital dissolution.

6.4. DISCUSSION

Based on these analyses, I am justified in suggesting that the RCISS point graphs are unique, because they take account of the balance between negative and positive behavior and affect. However, I left unanswered the question of whether a balance model, or one based on just positive or just negative speaker codes, would do as well in the classification. This chapter suggests that both positive and negative codes, but especially indexes of their balance, are most important in the discrimination. Hence, the two groups of couples appear to be named aptly.

The RCISS codes sample emotions (e.g., humor, escalate negative affect), emotional behaviors (e.g., put down, complain), and task-related behaviors (e.g., positive or neutral problem description) thus encompass a number of different (albeit related) characteristics of the interaction. Hence, it was possible to ask whether some positive codes and some negative codes were more active ingredients in the discrimination than others.

Here I encountered some interesting gender differences. In the area of positivity, the wife's positive codes, particularly in agenda building and the use of assents in responding to her husband's presentation of his views on an issue, were far more important in the discrimination than her general positive affect or the husband's positive codes.

On the other hand, Table 6.2 showed that the husband's defensiveness and contempt were quite important in the discrimination based on negative codes; they were stepped into the discriminant function following the wife's complain-criticize code.

It is my impression (and that of marital therapists) that defensiveness, contempt, and disgust are particularly dysfunctional behaviors in a marital conflict resolution, probably indicative of a higher level of rejection of the relationship at Time 1. In the area of negativity, both contempt, particularly the wife's, and the defensiveness of both partners were predictors of divorce. It appears that contempt and defensiveness do not operate independently and additively in predicting marital dissolution. Path equation models suggested that the wife's contempt has its effect on divorce through the defensiveness of both partners.

Taken together, these results suggest a dynamic of dissolution in which wives at Time 1 already have, to some degree, emotionally rejected the marriage. This emotional rejection is manifested in the following dynamic: Wives in marriages that are dissolving do not provide specific positive behaviors in presenting a problem and responding to their husband's views; instead, they complain and criticize in presenting a problem, and the contempt they feel combines with their own and their husband's defensiveness to amplify emotional distance and rejection.

In chapter 5, I noted that although both nonregulated husbands and wives displayed more negative affect than their regulated counterparts, only nonregulated wives showed less positive affect. This finding suggested an interesting dynamic. Our observations of hundreds of marital interactions over the years have led us to hypothesize that wives are much more likely than husbands to take responsibility for regulating the affective balance and keeping the couple problem solving on task during the marital interaction. Wives do this by interjecting humor, caring, and concern at appropriate moments of high tension, thus dissipating negative affect and allowing the couple to return to the task of working toward a solution of the designated problem. Perhaps one reason that nonregulated couples are so dysfunctional, and at such heightened risk for dissolution, is that nonregulated wives no longer assume the responsibility for using positive affect in this regulatory manner. This pattern, combined with the specific pattern of negativity involving complaining, criticizing, contempt, and defensiveness, may create a marriage that is like a powerful heating system without a thermostat, and the unregulated marital system is much more likely to self-destruct.

6.5. OUTLINE OF THINGS TO COME

Since chapter 5 I have been discussing one rough cut at a typology of couples, regulated and nonregulated. The two types differed in their risk for marital dissolution (i.e., progress on the cascade model). A balance theory of marriage yielded this first cut at prediction of a trajectory toward dissolution versus stability. Process cascades were also explored that were related to the cascade toward marital dissolution. In this chapter I explored the question that if the marital system is regulated, namely, what is the error signal? I suggested that there must be some quantity that is being regulated, so that deviations from this *set point* result in the system restabilizing in some manner. The choice of this error signal was explored in this chapter and I suggested that it was a balance between positive and negative interaction.

In the next three chapters I introduce three very different types of stable marriages, conflict-avoiding couples, volatile couples, and validating couples. Because conflict avoidance was such a strong and salient issue in the Raush et al. (1974) work, I begin by discussing this issue. Actually, each of the three stable styles of marriage address a different issue first raised by Raush et al. In chapter 10, I return to the general theoretical question of a balance theory of marriage. Chapter 11 shows that there are actually two types of nonregulated couples, and this chapter rounds out the theoretical discussion of balance in its presentation of predator-prey models for describing the ecology of behavior in a marriage. I later suggest that the set point is the ratio of positivity to negativity.

7

Is Conflict Avoidance Dysfunctional?

Raush et al. (1974) struggled with the issue of whether avoiding conflict was functional or dysfunctional. This chapter explores what might be meant by conflict avoidance and what about it would be functional or dysfunctional in a marriage.

In my research on marriage, I have studied primarily how couples resolve conflict. This assumes that, in all marriages, there will be areas of continuing disagreement and that the way these disagreements are handled by the couple is critical. This is a logical assumption. However, over the years, investigators have discovered that there is a group of couples that claim they really never disagree very much and are generally in harmony most of the time, or who say that they "agree to disagree." By this they usually mean that they avoid talking about areas that they know will result in a deadlocked disagreement. Is this "agree to disagree" style dysfunctional or not? The book by Raush et al. (1974) was the first to seriously consider these couples and to wrestle with questions about whether this type of marriage was somehow pathological or basically okay.

7.1. PREVIOUS SPECULATIONS ABOUT CONFLICT AVOIDANCE

Raush et al. (1974) apparently found quite a few couples in their sample who refused to take their experimental procedures seriously. These were cases in which one or the other spouse simply refused to conflict and tried to avoid the conflict or withdraw from it.

They were quite disturbed about these couples and were not sure

128

what to conclude about their marriages. I have no idea of the prevalence of this pattern in their data, nor do I have a clear idea of precisely what these couples were doing in their interactions. As best I can determine, these couples were not very psychologically minded about feelings or very introspective. They also tended to emphasize basic agreement and unanimity in the marriage.

Actually, a close reading suggests that their concept of conflict avoidance was quite vague. It included "distrust" that was "played out communicatively in symmetrical, competitive guilt-induction, against a background of passive resentment at the partner's intrusive manipulations" (Raush et al., 1974, p. 73). It also included repression and denial, in which neither partner "admits to awareness of any childhood problems; according to their reports neither set of parents ever fought or showed signs of marital strain" (p. 78). It included "entirely bland" descriptions of their interaction. About one couple, the Millers, Raush et al. (1974) wrote:

> Despite the interviewer's perplexity, probings, cajoling, enticements, and skepticism, there is never a break in the bland denial of difficulties. Their values and tastes are exactly the same, their marriage is entirely happy; when either one might be upset, the other simply leaves him or her alone. They "try not to worry each other with complaints"; they "never have hurt one another." Mrs. Miller places consistent emphasis on her easygoing nature, Mr. Miller on his responsible self-control. According to them they have no disagreements, they understand each other, their relationship has not changed at all in almost four years, and it is exactly as they expected it to be. *Neither partner is at all introspective about his or the other's feelings* [italics added]. Both are involved in many social activities, sometimes jointly but often separately. (p. 78)

They felt that their experimental procedures provided a misleading portrait of the Millers, because the improvised scenes bound them into conflict, "whereas in their daily lives the Millers offer one another ready escapes from the possibilities of confrontation" (p. 78).

This style of marriage is so important to Raush et al. (1974) that there is a long, two-chapter essay about this issue of conflict avoidance. Basically, they suggested that there are two kinds of avoidance of conflict: one in which one person (the husband in their example) avoids the conflict by skirting confrontation with the partner in a defensive manner, and one in which there is a joint contract to avoid disagreements.

The first pattern of avoidance can be done in a variety of ways. They listed the following: avoiding responsibility, agreeing quickly without disagreements being aired, committing covert acts that they interpret as being defensive, externalization, denial, and disqualification. In these instances, one person is the pursuer of the conflict and the other is the avoider (or the one who wishes to withdraw). There is an inherent asymmetry.

These mechanisms for asymmetries in conflict avoidance are contrasted with avoiding as a conjoint defensive contract in the case of the Millers. Raush et al. (1974) suggested that the Millers tended, in general, to deny difficulties. The Millers also had clear role definitions that supported this avoidance of conflict. Raush et al. (1974) suggested that this pattern of conflict avoidance may not be functional in the long run. They wrote:

> That the Millers might come to want something more of one another, as is hinted in the confines of the Improvisation scenes, is, of course, possible. In that case one might expect the marriage to become severely strained, since neither can cope with his own or the other's feelings. (pp. 78–79)

Their final word about conflict engagement versus avoidance is that either approach works, *"Given the context of continuing positive affection . . .* engagement does offer a greater prospect for growth, but it may, as suggested elsewhere . . ., place greater burdens on both of the individuals and the dyad" (p. 106).

7.2. GOTTMAN AND KROKOFF (1989)

In 1989, Gottman and Krokoff reported the results of two longitudinal studies on the relationship between marital interaction and marital satisfaction. This research was conducted before the cascade model was discovered, hence in its proper context this work speaks to correlates at the top of the cascade. As I speculate about the meaning of the results that have emerged from my laboratory, I suggest that the bottom line of these two studies was that, for most marriages, the best advice one can give husbands who want to preserve their marriages is "Embrace her anger," and the best advice one can give wives is to not be overly compliant, but to persist in getting her husband to face areas of continuing disagreement. I qualify this advice later.

The studies reported in Gottman and Krokoff (1989) were based on the observational coding of couples attempting to resolve a high-conflict issue. The two time points were 3 years apart for both studies. The major finding of these two longitudinal studies was that a different pattern of results predicted concurrent marital satisfaction than predicted change in marital satisfaction over 3 years. The specific results were that some marital interaction patterns, such as disagreement and anger exchanges, which usually have been considered harmful to a marriage, may not be harmful in the long run. There is a difference between temporary misery in the marriage and what is healthy for the marriage in the long run.

In one study that Gottman and Krokoff described, the interaction of couples at home, as well as in the laboratory, also was studied. They found that a set of marital interaction patterns related to happiness and positive interaction at home concurrently, but were predictive of deterioration in marital satisfaction longitudinally. In particular, an agreeable and compliant wife was dangerous for improvement in marital happiness. It seemed that it is necessary for disagreements to be aired in a marriage, and that is usually the role of the wife in this society.

For both spouses, three interaction patterns were identified as dysfunctional in terms of longitudinal deterioration: "defensiveness," which includes whining; "stubborness"; and "withdrawal from interaction." Withdrawal from interaction appeared to be a particularly male phenomenon, for the most part.

7.3. EMBRACE HER ANGER

Much to our surprise, Krokoff and I found that anger and disagreement was not the monster it was supposed to be. In fact, we were led to suggest that anger is a resource for the long-term improvement of the marriage, particularly the wife's anger. For this reason, I called this section "Embrace Her Anger." In Gottman and Krokoff's (1989) paper, we tried to understand variation in three variables: Time 1 marital satisfaction, change in marital satisfaction over time, and the amount of husband and wife negative affect in couples' interaction at home at Time 1.

7.3.1. Marital Satisfaction

It was found that concurrent marital satisfaction and change in marital satisfaction were well predicted by global codes of positivity and negativity (using the MICS). The data also replicated the well-known result that, in the resolution of marital conflict, there is a stronger relationship between concurrent marital satisfaction and negative interaction than for positive marital interaction. However, upon closer examination, the signs of the correlations between the husband's negative interaction and marital satisfaction and change in marital satisfaction were opposite. The husband's negative interaction predicted concurrent distress, but it predicted improvement in marital satisfaction over time. The same direction of results held for the wife's negative interaction, although they failed to reach significance.

To understand these results, the subscales of the MICS were analyzed. For the positive interaction scales, the interesting results were that, for the wife, positive verbal behavior strongly predicted concurrent marital satisfaction, but it predicted deterioration in marital satisfaction over time. Compliance by the wife also predicted deterioration in marital satisfaction over time. However, for the negative codes, conflict engagement predicted, for both partners, concurrent marital dissatisfaction, but also improvement in marital satisfaction over time. The wife's withdrawal was more predictive than the husband's of concurrent distress, whereas the husband's withdrawal was more predictive than the wife's of declines in marital satisfaction over time.

7.3.2. Home Interaction

In general, the MICS codes predicted primarily the husband's negative affect at home (coded with the voice codes of the CISS). The husband's negative interaction in the laboratory—defensiveness, conflict engagement, and stubborness—positively predicted his negative affect at home. His positive interaction—positive verbal behavior, positive nonverbal behavior, and compliance—all correlated negatively with his negative affect at home. In contrast, only the wife's defensiveness predicted his negative affect at home. The home interaction variables made another contribution: They demonstrated that these relationships are robust to variations in the method used to collect the data. I am confident that this phenomenon can be observed outside of laboratory conditions.

7.3.3. Summary

Gottman and Krokoff (1989) suggested that positive verbal behavior and compliance expressed by wives may be functional in the short run, but problematic in the long run. The opposite was true for both partners' conflict engagement, which predicted concurrent dissatisfaction with the marriage, but improvement over time. On the other hand, some codes appeared to give some evidence of being dysfunctional in both concurrent and longitudinal terms, namely, defensiveness, stubborness, and withdrawal from interaction. Thus, conflict engagement of a specific kind may be functional longitudinally, but conflict that is indicative of defensiveness, stubborness, and withdrawal may be dysfunctional longitudinally.

7.4. FURTHER SPECIFICATION OF THE MARITAL INTERACTION VARIABLES

Because the MICS did not separate content, or what is being said from affect or how it is being said, it was not possible to determine which of the aspects of the MICS interaction codes of the MICS were doing the work in predicting the criterion variables. Therefore, Gottman and Krokoff employed the CISS system to partial out affect and examine variation in content codes delivered with neutral affect. The SPAFF system code affect was employed in greater detail, independent of content.

7.4.1. CISS Results

Gottman and Krokoff employed the CISS to test only two hypotheses. First, whether the results obtained with the MICS Conflict Engagement subscale would be obtained with the CISS by examining the wife's disagreement with neutral affect. They decided to focus on disagreement, because it is most similar to the MICS conflict engagement code. If the same pattern of predictions were obtained for concurrent versus change in marital satisfaction independent of negative affect, it was argued, this would demonstrate that raising disagreements, per se, is constructive in a longitudinal sense. Second, the CISS also permits further elaboration of the husband's mindreading by examining only mindreading with neutral affect, which Gottman (1979) reported as a functional behavior ("feeling probe") in that it may function as a probe for clarification of the other's feelings. Mindreading with neutral affect should not show the same pattern as other MICS defensiveness codes (negative correlations with concurrent marital satisfaction and negative correlations with change in marital satisfaction). Instead, neutral mindreading should correlate positively with the criteria.

To assess these possibilities, the husband and wife's disagreement with neutral affect only and the husband and wife's mindreading with neutral affect only were correlated. Disagreement with neutral affect showed the same pattern of correlating negatively with concurrent marital satisfaction, but positively with change in marital satisfaction over time. Hence, the MICS results about conflict engagement held independent of negative affect.

What these analyses may mean is that the confrontation of disagreement by itself may be functional for marriage in a longitudinal sense. Hence, for marriages in general, conflict avoidance is dysfunctional for the long-term course of marital satisfaction over time.

7.5. SUMMARY AND DISCUSSION

The major finding of Gottman and Krokoff (1989) was that conflict engagement of a specific kind may be functional for a marriage longitudinally, but conflict that is indicative of defensiveness, stubbornness, and withdrawal (particularly on the part of husbands) may be dysfunctional longitudinally. Perhaps one cannot assume that the correlation of interaction patterns with concurrent relationship satisfaction is adequate for labeling these interaction patterns as *functional* or *dysfunctional*. This fact has implications for the design of therapeutic interventions with unhappily married couples. It is possible that couples that engage in conflict may pay a price in terms of concurrent dissatisfaction and negative affect at home; but the strife may pay off in the long run, provided that the conflict does not invoke stubbornness, defensiveness, or withdrawal from interaction.

These results were similar to those of a former student of mine, H. Markman. Markman is a pioneer in the longitudinal study of marriages. His doctoral thesis showed that he could predict, from a brief interaction of couples planning to marry, the relationship satisfaction of the couples 6 ½ years later. This was the first theoretically based study that predicted change in marital satisfaction.

Markman's (1984) more recent longitudinal results also support the conclusion that predictors of later marital satisfaction may change over time, some becoming more powerful when initially they were not. Talktable impact ratings are such an example. They were uncorrelated with Time 1 relationship satisfaction, but correlated highly with Time 2 and Time 3 relationship satisfaction. Markman (1984) wrote: "We see once again that predictors of premarital happiness are different from predictors of future marital happiness" (p. 262).

There were interesting spouse differences in the results of Gottman and Krokoff (1989). Wives who were positive and compliant fared better in terms of their husbands' concurrent negative affect at home and concurrent marital satisfaction, but the marital satisfaction of these couples deteriorates over time. On the other hand, the stubbornness and withdrawal of husbands may be most harmful to the longitudinal course of marital satisfaction. In terms of specific emotions, the marital satisfaction of wives improves over time if wives express anger and contempt during conflict discussions, but declines if wives express sadness or fear. For husbands, only whining predicted change in marital satisfaction over time, and it predicted the deterioration of both partners' marital satisfaction. Thus, one may not be able to say that the same negative affects are equally positive or negative, in a longitudinal sense, for husbands and wives. In terms of recommendations for marriages, the results suggested that wives should confront disagreement and not be overly compliant, fearful, and sad, but express anger and contempt. Husbands also should engage in conflict, but not be stubborn or withdrawn. Neither spouse should be defensive. How can one make sense of these spouse differences?

7.6. THE SPECIAL ROLE OF WOMEN IN MARRIAGES

Several studies have suggested that wives are more likely than husbands to confront disagreements in their marriage (e.g., Burke, Weier, & Harrison, 1976; Huston & Ashmore, 1986; Wills, Weiss, & Patterson, 1974). In my laboratory, I generally have noticed that, in most conflict discussions, either the wife begins by stating the issues or the husband begins and quickly defers to his wife for elaboration. However, there is another pattern in the marital research literature. In interview and questionnaire-based research, wives in unhappy marriages are described as conflict engaging, whereas husbands are described as withdrawn. For example, there is a consistent spouse difference in marital complaints: Unhappily married women complain about their husbands being too withdrawn, whereas unhappily married men complain about their wives being too conflict engaging (Locke, 1951; Terman et al., 1938). Komarovsky (1962) reported that blue-collar husbands are self-disclosing in happy marriages, but withdrawn in unhappy marriages. Rubin's (1976) interviews with married couples suggested that these unhappily married husbands may have withdrawn from intense negative affect. In research based on observational methods, these differences were mirrored. For example, when discussing disagreements, wives acted in ways designed to confront the issue and enforce their feelings about it, whereas husbands relied on more conciliatory and factual explanations (Margolin & Wampold, 1981; Raush et al., 1974). When Gottman and Krokoff's (1989) results were added to this picture, they suggested that the wife, as the manager of marital disagreements, has to manage a complex dialectic.

I suggested that this dialectic is as follows. If the wife introduces and elaborates disagreements in marriages, the data suggest that, for the sake of long-term improvement in marital satisfaction, she may need to do this by getting her husband to confront areas of disagreement and to openly vent disagreement and anger. This much will be functional for the longitudinal course of relationship satisfaction, but only if the interaction does not also result in the husband whining, being stubborn, withdrawing from interaction, or both partners being defensive. These interaction patterns of whining, stubborness, and withdrawal in a marriage are more deleterious if they are characteristic of husbands. On the other hand, the husband may need to view his wife's disagreement and confrontation as a resource in the marriage for improving marital satisfaction over time, even if such interactions are related to concurrent distress.

I investigate the hypothesis that withdrawal from intense negative affect is more likely among males than females in chapter 12.

7.7. A TYPOLOGY OF MARRIAGE

Having said all this about the possible dysfunctional nature of conflict avoidance for most marriages, I now dispute this conclusion in the subsequent typological analysis of types of marriages that are stable over time. I examine a group of marriages that apparently have a style of marital interaction that is designed contractually to avoid conflict. I study the anatomy of this conflict avoidance and see that it is quite different in some ways from the speculations of Raush et al. (1974). First of all, conflict avoiders do not think of themselves as avoiders. They think of engagement in conflict as characteristic of their interaction. But, by this "engagement," they mean fully expressing their feelings about an issue. Conflict avoiders in my research do in fact do this. However, and this is a crucial discovery, conflict avoiders never seem to engage in attempts to persuade one another. Also, based on their behavior, they seem to lack the ability to metacommunicate. This is probably what Raush et al. (1974) had in mind when they talked about an absence of psychological mindedness among conflict avoiders.

7.7.1. Overview of the Typology

In this book, I present five types of couples. Three of the types have marriages that, as far as I have studied them, are stable. By stable I mean that they are not on a path toward separation and divorce. I differentiate these three types with one key theoretical variable, although they differ on many other important variables as well. The key variable is the degree to which and the timing of their attempts to influence one another. Conflict-avoiding couples (I actually call them "conflict-mini-mizing" couples) are one type of stable couple. They are fairly flat emotionally and somewhat distant from one another. Another type is just the opposite. They have a great deal of intimacy and also a great deal of autonomy in their marriage. They seem to thrive on combat, and they try to influence one another about most everything. This type of couple is quite passionate and emotionally expressive. They fight a lot, but they also laugh a lot. They have a wide range of emotional expression. The third type of couple uses influence attempts sparingly, and only after they have heard, without much disagreement, one another's feelings about the issues under discussion. They are emotionally close, and a sense of "we-ness" seems to be critical to them, but their level of emotional expression is also fairly low and generally more neutral than the passionately volatile couples. My work on these three types of couples has parallel with the work of Mary Ann Fitzpatrick, who described three pure types of happily married couples that are remarkably similar to the three types I have discovered. Independent replication and corroboration is one of the rare joys of scientific work.

I also describe two types of unstable marriages. The nature of conflict in these two types of couples is very different than in the three stable types. Of particular importance are three patterns of interaction: contempt, defensiveness, and withdrawal. The conflict in these two types of unstable marriage is very different than conflict in the three stable types.

8

Conflict Avoidance and the Behavior of the Listener: Toward a Typology of Marriage

In this chapter, the idea of types of marriages is explored, as opposed to a dimensional view. A 2 × 2 typology is proposed, using RCISS speaker and listener slopes. The issue of conflict avoidance and conflict engagement is investigated empirically.

8.1. MARITAL TYPOLOGIES

It should come as no surprise that the history of research on marriage is replete with suggested systems for marital classification. For example, Cuber and Harroff (1965) described five marital types (i.e., conflict-habituated, devitalized, passive-congenial, vital, and total), whereas Bell (1975) described four types (i.e., patriarchal, matriarchal, companionship, and colleague). Other classification schemes have been proposed more recently (e.g., Fitzpatrick, 1989; Margolin, 1988; Olson, 1981).

Most of these classifications of marriages were not based on direct observations of how couples behaved, but rather represented more impressionistic global attempts to organize a vast array of self-report data concerning beliefs, lifestyles, and interaction patterns (Gottman, 1979).

Although several classification systems have been based on direct observation of behavior (e.g., Fitzpatrick, 1989; Hawkins, Weisberg, & Ray, 1977; Raush et al., 1974) none of these classifications had to do with predicting the longitudinal course of the marriage. As with any assessment procedure, criteria need to be established for evaluating the utility of any marital typology.

My goal was to develop a typology that had both concurrent and predictive validity. That is, the typology should concurrently distinguish couples that differ in the realms of behavior, emotion, physiology, and marital satisfaction. It also should be able to predict the future course of the marriage, especially whether the marriage will remain intact or dissolve.

8.2. THE SCIENTIFIC MEANING OF TYPES AS OPPOSED TO DIMENSIONS

It is important to point out that there is a very important scientific meaning to believing that there are types of marriages as opposed to dimensions of marriage. The distinction is very much like Niels Bohr's model of the atom compared with early views of the atom. In the Bohr model of the atom, the electron is far more likely to be at only certain locations from the nucleus of the atom. These positions are called shells. Furthermore, when an electron gains or loses energy, it moves out to a new shell further from the nucleus of the atom, or into a shell closer to the nucleus. Orbits in between shells are unstable. In the model of the atom before Bohr's, the electron could occupy any position with respect to the nucleus. Its position was continuous or what would be called dimensional in personality psychology. The Bohr model of the atom was discrete or quantized, and such views formed the basis of the branch of models in physics that has come to be known as Quantum Mechanics.

By trying to construct a typology of marriage, I suggest something very similar to what Bohr suggested about orbits of electrons around the nucleus. I suggest the following kind of theory: Marriages come in discrete adaptations, and there are no in-between adaptations that are stable over time. The adaptation I propose involves balancing negative and positive interactions in the marriage.

8.3. MARITAL DISSOLUTION AS A CRITERION VARIABLE

Perhaps the ultimate test of any proposed typology of marriage is its ability to designate couples that are at heightened risk for future marital dissolution. There are currently over 1 million divorces a year in the United States, with estimates that almost 67% of marriages ultimately will end in divorce (Martin & Bumpass, 1989). Marital dissolution is a serious social issue in terms of its negative consequences for the mental and physical health of spouses (Levinger & Moles, 1979) and their children (Emery, 1988).

I eventually suggest that there are five groups of couples. There are three kinds of stable, regulated couples and two types of nonregulated couples (whose marriages are dissolving). The three types of stable, regulated couples consist of two kinds of conflict engagers: volatile couples and validating couples and another group of stable marriages called conflict-avoiders group (in which both partners are defensive), and a hostile detached group that is both defensive and stonewalling.

8.4. THE BEHAVIOR OF THE LISTENER: THE IMPORTANCE OF STONEWALLING

The RCISS has two menus for the listener's behavior: a positive menu which describes a positive, engaged listener; and a negative menu, which describes a negative and disengaged listener. This part of the RCISS was designed to describe in greater detail than the MICS a set of listener withdrawal behaviors called *stonewalling*. In stonewalling, the listener presents a stone wall to the speaker. He or she does not provide the usual backchannels (Duncan & Fiske, 1977) that tell the speaker that the listener is tracking. There are no small vocalizations of the kind that get coded "assent" by the MICS, nor are there the usual head nods. In fact, the neck tends to be quite rigid, and there is little gaze at the speaker. If the listener does gaze at the speaker, the gaze is usually brief (i.e., a monitoring gaze). There is little facial movement, but when there is, it is a negative facial code that shows displeasure with the speaker. The content and affect of the speaker's talk must be considered in this coding. Not all negative facial codes imply negativity toward the speaker. For example, if the speaker is complaining about a colleague at work, a contempt facial code could reflect empathy with the speaker's plight.

Visual gaze in most human conversation has a rhythmic quality (Kendon, 1967; Kleinke, 1986). It is known that a speaker looks away as he or she begins to talk. The looking away is part of the signal for switching turns at speech. The length of time the speaker looks away is known to be a function of the perceived cognitive complexity of the conversation (Dabbs, personal communication, 1992). The listener usually provides all kinds of cues to the speaker that he or she is tracking the speech: head nods, brief vocalizations, facial movements, and small movements of the head at the neck. It is easy to manipulate gaze parameters experimentally. A status differential (e.g., a job interview situation) reveals an asymmetry in gaze; this asymmetry has been called the "social structure of attention" by Chance and Larsen (1976) in their studies of dominance in nonhuman primates.

Negative affect is another parameter that affects gaze probabilities. It is hard to look at someone who is upset or angry with you; it seems to be far more comfortable to look away. In stonewalling, the listener does not produce the usual cues for the speaker that the speech is being tracked. Emotionally, stonewalling often is perceived by the speaker as detachment, disapproval, smugness, hostility, negative judgment, disinterest, and coldness. In fact, this depends on the type of marriage one has. In some marriages, it is fine, but it usually is accompanied by very positive speaking behavior; that is, the stonewalling listener demonstrates that he or she is positive and engaged during the speaking turn. The inner experience of the stonewaller is largely unknown; it is something I explore when I discuss gender differences on withdrawal from marital conflict. Stonewalling turns out to be primarily a male thing to do in most marriages; about 85% of my stonewallers were male. This means that when women stonewall, it is a very significant act.

To study the behavior of the listener, I constructed listener point graphs analogous to the speaker point graphs described previously. In other words, at each turn at speech, I computed the total positive minus the total negative listener points for each spouse and cumulated this value across turns. I then plotted these graphs and computed the slopes of these curves. Table 8.1 shows the resulting classification as a 2 × 2 table.

8.5. CONFLICT ENGAGERS AND CONFLICT AVOIDERS

I present an analysis that begins to classify different types of regulated couples. Hence, in this chapter, I do not confound conflict avoidance with marital instability. What follows is an analysis of conflict avoidance or engagement within stable marriages. I talk here about two different styles or adaptations toward having a stable marriage.

Using the RCISS point graphs, I classified a group of couples that had positively sloped husband and wife speaker curves, but who had at least one flat or negatively sloped listener curve as conflict avoiders. Recall that a flat or negatively sloped listener curve is a good way to identify a

TABLE 8.1

	Listener Slopes		
Speaker Slopes	Both Positive	Other	Type
Both Positive	Engagers $N = 26$	Avoiders $N = 11$	Regulated
Other	Hostile $N = 16$	Hostile Detached $N = 19$	Nonregulated

stonewalling listener. Of these 11 couples, 9 were husband stonewallers and 3 were wife stonewallers (82% of the males and 27% of the females, $\chi^2 = 4.55$). I decided that this group was most likely to be a good candidate for conflict avoiders, because their discussion of the conflict was generally positive, but nonetheless they (mostly the men) somehow tended to avoid looking at their partners throughout the discussion. Because of this stonewalling in the face of generally positive and agreeable interaction, these couples could be described as positive but relatively disengaged, and hence they seemed to be a good candidate for the conflict-avoider group.

If this surmise were true, I would expect that this group would show considerably less conflict engagement than the two engager groups. I also would expect that the situation of asking them to resolve an area of continuing disagreement would pose some definite stress that should be evident in the physiological data. I also should find evidence of this stress in the difficulties my interviewers would have in setting up the conflict discussion in the play-by-play interview that precedes the conflict discussion.

Before labeling this group, I conducted some qualitative analyses similar to those of Raush et al. (1974) using our play-by-play interviews. On the basis of these observations, it may be better to call this a "conflict-minimizing" group rather than a "conflict-avoiding" group.

8.6. QUALITATIVE DATA

Following in the Raush et al. (1974) tradition, I examined the qualitative data obtained in this study in the play-by-play interview. This interview is designed to set up the conflict discussion. It begins with each partner separately filling out the problem inventory, in which they rate a set of 10 problems in severity and chronicity. They have spaces to add two other problem areas if they choose to do so.

8.6.1. Conflict Minimizing Versus Conflict Avoiding

Although I continue to speak of conflict avoiders, it is important to point out that the couples in this group are probably best thought of conflict minimizers. Why? They did not describe themselves as avoidant of conflict. For example, when interviewed, they referred to discussing topics of disagreement at great length at home, rather than avoiding the issue. Two couples referred to an asymmetry in avoiding discussions when there were negative feelings. In one couple (No. 160), the wife said: "I know when I'm mad at him, just leave me alone and then I'll sit there for a while and think about it, just let time solve the problem." However, the husband added: "I feel pretty distant. It's kind of hard to figure out what move to make to alleviate the problem because I don't know what the problem is a lot of the time." In another couple (No. 153), the wife said:

> Well Jim says he just likes to let things go and "go with the flow" and just let problems work themselves out and that problems usually work themselves out without a lot of deep discussion about it, and I say that I think it's better to talk about problems or things that are upsetting about me or about him or vica versa.

However, closer examination reveals that talking things out has a particular character. First, there was an emphasis on common ground rather than differences. Second, there was an acceptance of differences and disagreements as not very important, so they could be ignored. Third, the interactions tended not to be very psychologically minded or introspective. Hence, once each person had stated his or her case, they tended to see the discussion as close to an end. They considered accepting these differences as a complete discussion. Once they understood their differences, they felt that the common ground and values they share overwhelmed these differences and made them unimportant and easy to accept. Hence, there was very little give and take and little attempt to persuade one another. There was a pervasive view, which they communicated to the interviewer, that although they discussed things and talked things out, they did not fight, argue, or have continuing disagreements. They emphasized their similarities, tolerance of differences, and going separate ways on things.

In a sense, all of these conversations were like standoffs. They reached some understanding that they disagree, but they did not explore the precise emotional nature of the disparities, and they did not attempt to persuade their partner of the validity of each of their viewpoints. Often the proposed solutions to issues were quite nonspecific. For example, they may have agreed to ignore their differences, or they may have agreed to be more like the other person (e.g., if there is a difference of opinion on disciplining the children), or more often to let time take its course. They tended to view the passage of time without raising the issue as a potential solution.

Among the unhappily married couples in this group, the standoffs generated a great deal of negative facial affect (No. 166), which was not expressed verbally. Among the happily married couples in this group, the standoff ended by them deciding that this entire issue was not too important in the whole picture of the positiveness and affection in their marriage. Some general observations and examples follow.

1. *It was very difficult for the interviewer to set up the conflict discussion.* Recall that the interviewer must find an area on continuing disagreement in the marriage. The following is one example of the trouble the interviewer had:

> W: And the recreation area I don't see much. He likes to do what he likes to do and I like to do what I like to do and they're not the same things (she laughs, he smiles), so there's not much problem there.

The interviewer then went on to discuss the area of sex, which they had rated high on the problem inventory.

> Int: Do you feel it's resolved and you just haven't talked about it for a while?
>
> W: When we talked about it when it's a problem just in 1 or 2 weeks there'll be a minor, ahh, just a problem that comes up and then it'll come up and then everything's all right and then in a couple of months . . .
>
> H: It gets . . .
>
> W: Huh?
>
> H: It gets pushed out of the way for a while.
>
> W: Yeah, the thought, the topic never comes up for a while and then it'll come up. Nothing is ever resolved because there's no way of resolving it. It's just a conflict that we accept in a way. Sometimes we do hash back over it and figure out if there's something we can do, but so far it's just ended up the same, you know, that's, you know, well, just the way it's gonna have to be for now. We haven't come up with a solution.

2. *The interviewer may have been persuaded to accept an area of trivial disagreement.* After a while, the interviewer may settle on a topic that they have both rated as a "problem," even though it was clearly not a source of disagreement. An example was not having enough money. They both agreed this is a problem, that they do not have enough money. For example, one couple (No. 143) noted that all the problems they had checked were problems, but they agreed completely about them all:

> H: Like on money for instance we never get into any arguments about what we're gonna do, we don't get into any arguments as far as a problem for both of us. There's

always something she wants she can't get you know, and
that's the only problem there is.

W: It's not really a problem between us, it's a problem with the
money.

In one couple (No. 112), the wife suggested to the interviewer that
a serious problem she had was that her husband always decided
what restaurant they went out to and what they would eat at home
as well. He said he just got these definite ideas and cravings. He
expressed dissatisfaction that they were having chicken for dinner
tonight instead of pizza. He wanted pizza. The interviewer accepted this as a problem area. Their conversation was quite brief.

H: What made you decide on chicken tonight instead of
pizza?

W: Because it was too difficult to make the pizza at the time I
was comin' home.

H: That's true.

W: And I had to feed Ryan before I left. And if I made the
pizza before it'd be yucky for us to eat.

H: Oh, so you . . .

W: It's frozen anyway so you can't . . .

H: That's no big deal . . .

W: I don't, what are we gonna make pizza on? The chicken is
sitting there wasting. We're gonna eat chicken.

H: Well I know we're gonna eat chicken.

W: If anything you can go out and buy some pizza but you're
not gonna sit there and make a big mess.

H: (laughs and mouths silently) Well I want pizza.

W: We've got chicken made. Eat the chicken.

H: I guess.

That was the end of the discussion of the disagreement. They
managed to get the interviewer to allow them to discuss an
innocuous topic that was resolved easily.

3. *The couple agreed that their differences were not important and the
topic was dropped.* For example, one couple (No. 163) discussed a
sexual problem. He wanted intercourse more frequently than
she did. She told the interviewer that this problem had been
discussed recently, because she had an intimate conversation
with her sister-in-law, Jennifer, who said that she refused to
simply comply to her husband, Al, whenever Al wanted sex.

Both husband and wife in this couple deplored Jennifer's attitude. They decided to discuss the sexual problem between them. They began the discussion with the wife asking the husband if he felt better about their "situation." He proceeded to agree with her criticism of Jennifer's attitude. After they spent some time unified in their mutual criticism of Jennifer's attitude, he said that he did not think that they had resolved their own problem. She asked if he thought that things had changed a great deal since they married. He said no. She said she used to consider it a threat to their marriage, that it might break up their marriage. He said he never thought that. She said she agrees that it will not break up their marriage. She continued:

W: I consider it almost not a real problem anymore as that's part of us.
H: That's just accepted.
W: That's kind of the way we function now.
H: Sure. That's the way I view it now. I guess from that respect, maybe I did view it differently then.

They went on to suggest that it really was not a problem as such anymore, so it sort of has been solved, or accommodated to. They then considered that they had resolved the issue.

4. *They agreed to accept discomfort at the lack of a the solution rather than face the discord of argument.* For example, one couple (No. 153) discussed their sexual problem. The basic issue was that he wants to have intercourse more frequently than she does. They discussed the issue with the interviewer:

Int: How do you each feel? Are you comfortable? Is it frustrating?
H: No, it's more of an ideological dispute in some ways than frustrating emotionally or physically.
Int: How about for you?
W: I think I've sort of come to the point of feeling resigned about it or maybe a little wistful, I mean, that's one thing I'm pretty sure is just not gonna be any different for us. Sometimes I wish it would.
Int: So you're the one who wants the change, Jane?
H: Mmm-hmm.
W: I guess so. Sometimes I think we don't talk about things that are, I don't know quite what the, we don't talk about

some things that we probably should, or that would be better if we did.

They finally settled on discussing the sexual issue. He said he is extreme in not showing affection. She said she is less responsive in bed because it is the only time he does show affection. He thought that was a problem too. He said he is wrapped up in his work, not relaxed. She said she has responded over the years by becoming detached, and that sometimes she feels terrible about her detachment. They continued:

H: If sex didn't seem like something so out of, I don't mean, I shouldn't say, out of the ordinary, but it's sort of separated in a way from regular life and it's the place for intimacy and the other isn't.
W: I guess.
H: Well, you know neither of us comes from families that do very much, have very much physical contact among themselves and I always felt . . .
W: We kids always did with my mother.
H: You kids did?
W: Not with my father.
H: Well we never did.
W: And I have a lot of physical contact with Nick (their child).
H: So do I at this point.
W: I don't know. It doesn't bother me as much as it used to. I mean, people make a big deal about having sex, sexual compatibility and so on, but I think in the long run it's probably more important that we have our other compatibilities.
H: Yeah.
W: If our sex life was wonderful and we disagreed about everything else, we'd probably be considering divorce.

5. *Persuasion was minimized during the conflict discussion.* In sharp contrast to the conflict engagers, there was little attempt to persuade one another of the validity of a point of view. Anchoring the scale at the other end, the volatile engagers were doing this kind of persuasion even at the feeling expression stage of the discussion of a marital disagreement. The conflict avoiders rarely engaged in this kind of persuasion.
6. *They seemed to lack basic conflict–resolution skills that involve compromise or psychological mindedness.* Although conflict avoiders

expressed their views about issues, they did not engage in the give and take of an ordinary discussion. They did not really problem solve. For example, they did not imagine a compromise solution to their problem. What was more striking was that they did not comment about the process of trying to solve the problem and how it made them feel and think. Hence, they did not try to improve their ability to solve the problem. They acted as if they were stuck with the problem forever and must learn to live with it.

An interesting example of this kind of interaction occurred on one tape in which a conflict-avoiding couple discussed a house they were building. Most people agree that building a house is an unusually stressful experience. In this case, there was added stress because the operation was being funded by her father. Furthermore, her father was not the kind of dad who says, "Here's the money kids, do it any way you like." Instead, her father was at the site on a regular basis, telling the construction crew that he didn't think a light was needed over this kitchen counter, and so on. As one might imagine, a great deal of conflict was generated by this situation. Yet the couple's discussion never included one comment such as, "I feel caught between you and my dad, always in the middle." Or even, "This is very hard, but it will pass." Instead, the conversation focused on the tiny details of the construction, and a great deal of unverbalized pain was evident in their discussions about such things as the kitchen cabinet doors. Instead of being able to metacommunicate, or comment about their own communication patterns, the conversation stumbled along until they found something they could agree about. They stayed on this small point of the construction of their house until they felt a little better about one another. What was so striking about this conversation, in which the couple was clearly unhappy and under a great deal of strain, was that it appeared as if they lacked the basic tools for resolving conflict.

Couples in the conflict-avoider group appeared to act as if once they had discovered their differences in opinion, the discussion was nearly at an end. What was left was learning how to accept and live with these differences. To do this, they tended to emphasize the positive aspects of the marriage, the areas of fundamental agreement and shared values, and became philosophical about the relatively small importance of these revealed differences. This was in sharp contrast to conflict engagers, whose discussion reached a high point once they discovered their differences. For conflict engagers, once they discovered their differences, they began trying to persuade their partner. They each argued for their point of view, gave reasons, disagreed with one another's reasons, and generally tried to influence one another. If feelings got hurt along the way, or if the topic strayed or the discussion became chaotic, they employed repair tactics (either of feelings or of the content of the discussion). Finally, with a knowledge of common ground and differences, they began to negotiate and compromise. Essentially, the conversation began for conflict engagers where it ended for conflict avoiders.

8.7. QUANTITATIVE ANALYSES: AVOIDERS VERSUS ENGAGERS

The quantitative analyses proceeds in five steps. First, I examine problem-solving behavior using the RCISS codes and the MICS codes. Second, I examine affective behavior using both the SPAFF and the EMFACS. Third, I examine physiological data during the conflict discussion. Because both avoiders and engagers are regulated couples, I do not expect to see a difference between them in physiological activity. Recall that physiological activation predicted deterioration in marital satisfaction (Levenson & Gottman, 1983). However, because the amount of negative affect expressed between the two groups should differ markedly, I predict that the two groups differ significantly on the amount of physiological linkage. Fourth, I examine differences between avoiders and engagers in pervasiveness and rebound. Fifth, I examine two sequential variables of start up and continuance for all three conversations.

8.7.1. Problem-Solving Behavior

8.7.1.1. RCISS Subcodes

Recall that the classification of the regulated couples as avoiders or engagers was based entirely on the *listener* point graphs. However, if the characterization of the two groups as "conflict avoiders" and "conflict engagers" is correct, then one would expect that the two groups of couples would differ on subcodes of the speaker RCISS codes, as well as the listener point graph slopes. Table 8.2 is a summary of these analyses.

This was indeed the case. Engagers were significantly more likely than avoiders to complain and criticize (both husbands and wives). Engager wives were more likely than avoider wives to display verbal

TABLE 8.2
Problem-Solving Differences Between Engagers and Avoiders

Variable	Engagers	Avoiders	t	df	p
MICS					
Hus. defensive	1.70	2.07	-.52	13	ns
Hus. engages	3.43	1.22	2.78	33	.009
Hus. stubborn	.82	.80	.06	34	ns
Hus. withdrawn	4.46	5.21	-.56	12	ns
Wife defensive	1.60	1.80	-.32	34	ns
Wife engages	4.92	2.82	1.70	32	.099
Wife stubborn	1.12	.69	.96	29	ns
Wife withdrawn	5.11	5.36	-.24	34	ns
Number turns	112.04	84.55	2.89	32	.007
RCISS					
Hus. complain/criticize	.12	.01	3.08	27	.005
Hus. defensive	.17	.19	-.62	35	ns
Hus. verbal contempt	.02	.01	.45	35	ns
Hus. stonewall	.65	1.36	-4.99	35	.000
Hus. pos. agenda bldg.	.70	.49	2.57	35	.015
Hus. assent	.13	.20	-1.50	35	ns
Hus. pos. affect	.14	.08	1.69	35	ns
Hus. lis. pos.	2.07	1.06	5.23	30	.000
Wife complain/criticze	.12	.02	3.28	28	.003
Wife defensive	.19	.19	.06	35	ns
Wife verbal contempt	.02	.01	1.77	35	.086
Wife stonewall	.54	.93	-3.43	35	.002
Wife pos. agenda bldg.	.68	.52	2.11	35	.042
Wife assent	.13	.21	-1.47	35	ns
Wife pos. affect	.14	.13	.32	35	ns
Wife lis. pos.	2.29	1.49	3.84	34	.001

contempt (this was a marginal effect). The conflict engagement of engagers was not entirely negative, however. Engagers also were more likely than avoiders to display positive agenda building (this also was true for both husbands and wives).

The fact that these differences held for both negative and positive codes indicative of tackling the problem is strong evidence that the characterization of these two groups as engager and avoider is justified. It also fits my conjectures about the rewards and costs of the two styles (engagement vs. avoidance). A conflict-engaging style makes both positive problem-solving codes and negative (complain and criticize) more likely than a conflict-avoiding style.

Conflict engagers took more turns at speech than conflict avoiders. This is indicative of a more lively conversation among the conflict engagers than among the conflict avoiders. This means that engagers are less likely than avoiders to hold forth with long monologues.

8.7.1.2. MICS Data

The MICS conflict engagement summary code should discriminate among the two groups. This summary code is a good index of attempts to persuade one's partner (Gottman, 1993). Indeed, engagers showed significantly more MICS conflict engagement codes than avoiders (husbands and wives, although the effect was only marginally significant for wives).

8.7.2. Affective Behavior

8.7.2.1. SPAFF Data

Table 8.3 shows that, during the conflict discussion on the SPAFF, engagers displayed significantly more disgust and contempt (both husbands and wives) and more whining (wife only); there was a marginally significant difference for engager husbands to show more tension/fear than avoiders. In general, there is evidence from the SPAFF data that there is more negative affect generated in the conflict discussion of engagers than avoiders.

8.7.2.2. Facial Data

Table 8.4 shows that conflict-engaging husbands tended to display more facial expressions than conflict avoiders (marginal effect), although there were no significant differences between wives. Conflict engaging husbands displayed more contempt (marginal), fear, and Duchenne smiles than conflict-avoiding husbands. A Duchenne smile is a complete smile that involves the mouth corners being turned up by zygomaticus major, and there is eye involvement in the smile by involvement of orbicularis oculi. It contrasts with a smile that is more unfelt, which has no eye involvement (the kind of smile that is more likely to be posed for photographers). Conflict-engaging wives displayed more contempt facial expressions than conflict-avoiding wives. Hence, the two groups of couples were quite different in facial affect, with conflict engagers showing both more positive and more negative affect than conflict avoiders.

8.7.3. Physiological Data

Table 8.5 shows that, as predicted, conflict-engaging couples showed significantly more physiological linkage than conflict-avoiding couples. Recall that we previously had discovered that linkage was a variable mediated primarily by negative affect. Again, as expected, because all

TABLE 8.3
SPAFF Affect Differences Between Engagers and Avoiders

Variable	Engagers	Avoiders	t	df	p
Events					
Hus. neutral	55.48	63.80	−.83	33	ns
Hus. humor	10.28	6.40	1.38	33	ns
Hus. affection	1.88	2.10	−.26	33	ns
Hus. interest	35.44	20.20	2.20	33	.035
Hus. joy	5.00	2.40	1.54	33	ns
Hus. anger	1.20	.90	.38	33	ns
Hus. disgust/contempt	3.60	5.10	−.63	33	ns
Hus. whining	.28	.60	−.63	10	ns
Hus. sadness	.96	.80	.18	33	ns
Hus. fear	8.00	3.00	1.77	32	.086
Wife neutral	52.68	57.60	−.42	33	ns
Wife humor	11.52	7.10	1.78	33	.084
Wife affection	1.64	4.40	−1.85	11	.092
Wife interest	37.28	27.50	1.16	28	ns
Wife joy	7.60	2.30	2.64	33	.013
Wife anger	2.56	2.20	.21	33	ns
Wife dis/contempt	3.28	.80	2.90	33	.007
Wife whining	1.40	1.80	−.34	33	ns
Wife sadness	.72	.20	1.46	30	ns
Wife fear	6.68	4.70	.83	25	ns
Conflict					
Hus. neutral	33.28	42.82	−1.07	34	ns
Hus. humor	11.24	6.64	1.55	33	ns
Hus. affection	2.80	3.45	−.51	34	ns
Hus. interest	12.84	8.91	1.42	34	ns
Hus. joy	1.68	.82	1.04	33	ns
Hus. anger	15.12	7.27	1.51	34	ns
Hus. dis/contempt	8.00	2.45	2.19	33	.036
Hus. whining	1.48	.82	.81	34	ns
Hus. sadness	2.36	1.64	.88	34	ns
Hus. fear	24.28	11.55	1.93	34	.063
Wife neutral	29.36	40.18	−1.12	34	ns
Wife humor	11.60	7.73	1.24	31	ns
Wife affection	2.56	1.27	1.36	34	ns
Wife interest	14.64	10.55	1.26	34	ns
Wife joy	1.52	.82	1.00	34	ns
Wife anger	17.04	11.00	.91	34	ns
Wife dis/contempt	5.68	1.45	2.34	30	.026
Wife whining	5.08	1.45	2.20	32	.035
Wife sadness	2.56	1.55	1.27	33	ns
Wife fear	22.88	13.27	1.25	34	ns
Positive					
Hus. neutral	51.60	50.90	.06	33	ns
Hus. humor	11.72	5.70	2.21	31	.034

(continued)

152

TABLE 8.3 (continued)

Variable	Engagers	Avoiders	t	df	p
Hus. affection	3.28	1.70	1.43	33	ns
Hus. interest	30.36	18.20	2.06	33	.047
Hus. joy	12.60	5.50	2.62	30	.013
Hus. anger	1.84	2.20	−.15	33	ns
Hus. dis/contempt	2.84	2.40	.26	32	ns
Hus. whining	.16	.20	−.21	33	ns
Hus. sadness	1.08	.10	2.43	27	.022
Hus. fear	6.56	6.50	.02	33	ns
Wife neutral	46.84	48.20	−.13	33	ns
Wife humor	11.72	8.00	1.08	33	ns
Wife affection	3.28	1.90	1.19	33	ns
Wife interest	33.28	22.60	1.58	33	ns
Wife joy	12.72	4.70	2.79	31	.009
Wife anger	3.20	1.40	.82	32	ns
Wife dis/contempt	2.20	1.30	.88	31	ns
Wife whining	.96	.20	1.45	31	ns
Wife sadness	1.44	.60	1.11	33	ns
Wife fear	7.40	5.90	.42	33	ns

three groups were regulated couples, there were no other differences between the groups on any other physiological variable. Thus, the groups did not differ in levels of physiological arousal on the conflict discussion, despite the pervasive differences in affect between groups.

8.7.4. Pervasiveness of Negative Affect

How pervasive is the greater negative affect displayed by conflict-engaging couples? Recall that all three conversations were coded with the SPAFF, and that by pervasiveness I mean the affect on the events conversation, which occurs before the conflict discussion is set up by the interviewer.

Table 8.6 shows that on the events-of-the-day conversation, conflict-engaging husbands showed more interest and more tension/fear (marginal) than conflict-avoiding husbands; conflict-engaging wives showed more humor (marginal), less affection (marginal), more joy, and more disgust and contempt than conflict-avoiding wives.

Hence, except for the affection code, conflict-engaging couples were coded as more affectively expressive of both positive and negative affects than conflict-avoiding couples, even when discussing the events of their day. Thus, one sees that the differences between the two kinds of couples in the way they resolved conflict also were pervasive. The differences generalized to how they discussed the events of their day

TABLE 8.4
Facial Expression Data for Engagers and Avoiders

Variable	Engagers	Avoiders	t	df	p
Husband					
Anger	7.85	8.36	−.20	35	ns
Contempt	1.77	3.18	−1.79	35	.082
Disgust	1.65	1.00	.77	33	ns
Fear	4.12	1.82	2.08	34	.045
Sadness	1.92	1.82	.07	32	ns
Duchenne smile	20.92	9.36	2.95	33	.006
Other smiles	14.23	11.64	.68	31	ns
Total action units	153.73	106.00	1.82	34	.077
Wife					
Anger	12.77	13.27	−.16	35	ns
Contempt	2.50	1.00	2.06	34	.047
Disgust	2.03	2.73	−.56	35	ns
Fear	8.15	5.64	.76	35	ns
Sadness	2.35	2.27	.06	35	ns
Duchenne smile	19.15	18.36	.18	35	ns
Other smiles	18.08	14.09	.85	35	ns
Total action units	204.12	166.64	1.29	33	ns

TABLE 8.5
Physiological Activity and Linkage During Conflict for Engagers and Avoiders

Variable	Engagers	Avoiders	t	df	p
Physiological Linkage	.44	.30	2.40	35	.022
Physiological Activity					
Hus. heart period	784.27	815.00	−.76	35	ns
Hus. activity	.99	.95	1.27	35	ns
Hus. skin cond.	11.70	12.24	−.25	35	ns
Hus. pulse transit time	241.50	247.00	−.77	35	ns
Hus. finger amplitude	7.08	7.82	−1.37	35	ns
Wife heart period	782.31	735.55	1.23	35	ns
Wife activity	1.77	1.76	.04	35	ns
Wife skin conduct.	9.53	11.74	−1.50	35	ns
Wife pulse transit time	242.65	235.00	1.14	35	ns
Wife finger amplitude	9.00	9.82	−.38	35	ns

after having been separated for at least 8 hours. This result also was consistent with our conjecture about the rewards and costs of both types of marriage.

8.7.5. Rebound

Table 8.6 also presents results on rebound by examining differences in affect on the positive conversation, which followed the conflict conver-

TABLE 8.6
Sequences of Affect for Engagers and Avoiders: Start Up and Continuance[a]

Variable	Engagers	Avoiders	t	df	p
Events					
Startup H → W	−.20	−.35	.33	28	ns
Startup W→ H	.66	−.32	2.07	28	.048
Continuance H → W	3.36	2.45	.71	28	ns
Continuance W → H	2.19	2.94	−.67	28	ns
Conflict					
Startup H → W	1.36	.93	.77	33	ns
Startup W → H	.57	1.27	−1.58	33	ns
Continuance H → W	6.11	3.77	2.08	33	.046
Continuance W → H	6.42	3.69	2.26	33	.030
Positive					
Startup H → W	−.02	.04	−.19	32	ns
Startup W → H	−.04	.00	.14	32	ns
Continuance H → W	2.78	2.23	.51	32	ns
Continuance W → H	2.56	2.14	.34	32	ns
Events					
Positive reciprocity H → W	3.27	2.30	1.16	28	ns
Positive reciprocity W → H	2.78	2.01	.97	28	ns
Conflict					
Positive reciprocity H → W	4.93	3.17	1.31	33	ns
Positive reciprocity W → H	4.90	2.56	1.90	33	.066
Positive					
Positive reciprocity H → W	4.31	3.73	.71	32	ns
Positive reciprocity W → H	4.10	2.83	1.34	32	ns

[a]z scores are given, computed according to Allison and Liker (1982).

sation. On the positive conversation, conflict-engaging husbands showed more humor, interest, joy, and sadness than conflict-avoiding husbands; conflict-engaging wives showed more joy than conflict-avoiding wives. This is a reasonably clear picture. On the positive conversation, conflict- engaging couples were again more affectively expressive of both positive and negative affects than conflict-avoiding couples. Except for the greater expression of sadness by engaging husbands, engagers were more interested in one another's conversation, laughed more, and displayed more joy than avoiders. Thus, according to my definition, except for the husband's sadness, engagers showed more rebound than avoiders.

8.7.6. Sequential Variables

8.7.6.1. Conflict Task

Table 8.6 shows that, during the conflict task, conflict-engaging couples showed a greater likelihood of negative continuance. There also was some weak support for the existence of greater positive affect reciprocity (a marginal effect, and only for reciprocity from wife to husband, W → H).

8.7.6.2. Events of the Day

During the events-of-the-day task, conflict engagers differed from avoiders in a greater likelihood of negative start up (only by husbands) for conflict engagers compared with avoiders. This means that engager husbands were more likely to engage in sequences that brought them from neutral to negative affect.

8.7.6.3. Positive Conversation

On the positive conversation, the two groups did not differ on the sequential variables.

8.7.6.4. Summary of Sequential Variables

Thus, on two of the tasks, the sequential structure of the interaction demonstrated that conflict engagers were more likely to start up and continue in negative affect cycles, and some weak evidence that engagers were more likely to reciprocate positive affect.

8.8. SUMMARY AND SPECULATION ABOUT THE PHYSIOLOGY OF AVOIDERS

Conflict engagers expressed more emotion, both positive and negative, and not just during the conflict discussion. They expressed more emotion on their faces. They had a more lively exchange and took more turns at speech. Conflict engagers started negative affect exchanges more than avoiders, and they continued them more than avoiders, even during the events-of-the-day discussion.

Perhaps the greater physiological linkage of avoiders is a clue to understanding their avoidance of emotional expression (both positive and negative) and their reluctance to conflict. In a previous study (Levenson & Gottman, 1983), Levenson and I found that physiological linkage was related strongly to marital unhappiness. We also found that linkage was positively related to the amount of negative affect expressed. We speculated that linkage may be the physiological basis of negative affect becoming (at times) an absorbing state, which is typical of unhappy marriages. Perhaps avoiders are avoiding this negative affective absorbing state, which would be their lot because of their greater physiological linkage. In other words, their greater physiological linkage may put them at greater risk for negative affect expression becoming an absorbing state. In this case, the best strategy is to avoid expressing very much negative affect. If this is so, we have seen that the cost of down-regulating the expression of negative affect is that it also down-regulates the expression of positive affect.

9

There are Two Types of Conflict Engagers

In this chapter, I introduce a second type of conflict-engaging couple called a "volatile" couple. These couples are highly emotional. They appear, on the surface, to resemble the dysfunctional conflict-escalating style of marriage described by Raush et al. (1974). However, they balance a high level of negativity with a high level of positivity. Also, the amount and timing of persuasion attempts differentiate the three types of stable marriages. The striking similarity of these results to Fitzpartick's (1989) typology is reviewed.

Raush et al. (1974) speculated about the detrimental aspects of excessive conflict engagement, especially about relatively trivial disagreements escalating into quarrels. They suggested that in such marriages what was at stake was not the ostensible conflict itself, but conflict about some other issue (i.e., symbolic conflict). They then discussed the nature of this conflict and the nature of possible symbols. Their conclusion was that these kinds of marital interactions would surely be dysfunctional.

In this chapter, I introduce an adaptation to having a stable marriage that appears to fit the bill for the kind of dysfunctional conflict engaging couple that Raush et al. described. However, I suggest that this volatile style of conflict engagement is quite functional and stable longitudinally.

9.1. QUALITATIVE DATA

As in Gottman (1979), the point graphs are employed to classify couples on the basis of their interactions. In that book, one group of couples was identified whose point graphs generally had a positive slope. The RCISS point graphs make it possible to separately identify listener as well as speaker point graphs. Using the RCISS point graphs, it was possible to identify a group of 25 couples that had positively sloped cumulative positive minus negative listening and speaking curves. These curves are illustrated in Fig. 9.1.

The point graphs have a severe limitation. At any interact (a unit in which both partners have taken a turn), the total positive minus the total negative points for that interaction is added to the curve. Thus, a

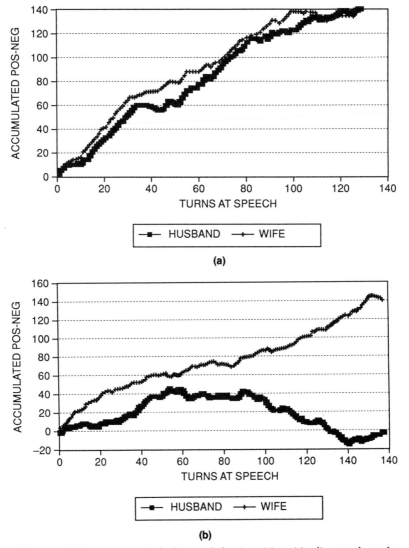

(a)

(b)

FIG. 9.1. RCISS point graphs for listener behaviors: (a) positive listener slopes for a regulated couple, (b) nonpositive listener slopes for a nonregulated couple.

husband who earns 3 positive points gets the same score as one who earns 11 positive and 8 negative points. However, the latter husband is far more affectively expressive, both positively and negatively, than the former. Thus, these are unlikely to be the same kinds of exchanges. Hence, for conflict engagers, it is necessary to further examine the point graphs in terms of this dimension of volatility. In fact, in watching the videotapes of the engager group, there appears to be two styles of conflict resolution within the group, which the RCISS curves were not discriminating.

One group consisted of couples that were generally good listeners, who validated their partner's expressions of emotion, and who were calm receivers of their partner's expression of feelings about a marital issue. The second group of couples was far more emotional. These couples often were angry, belligerent, and domineering. I begin by describing these groups anecdotally.

9.1.1. Sketch of Volatile Couples' Interaction

These couples have marriages that are intensely emotional. They are the hot kind of romantic marriage one often reads about between Holly-wood stars, like Elizabeth Taylor and Richard Burton. They have big fights and great times making up afterward. There is a lot of jealousy in these relationships, and also a lot of protectiveness and love. The husbands are extremely expressive and involved, and there is a high level of both positive and negative affect in these marriages.

One example involves a couple in which the topic of conflict is the husband's jealousy (No. 224). The husband says that he is very insecure and that he is afraid of his wife leaving him. She says that she does not understand why he is even jealous of her sister's visit. He agrees that he is and says, "You don't have to spend every waking moment with her. Why am I such a sleeze that you want to spend it away from me?" She says, no, that he is welcome to join them. He says that he is not comfortable with her family's teasing him and picking on him. She says that she hates his jealousy, but that she does also enjoy his jealousy in a way, that it is romantic, that he is sort of always courting her. He agrees that he courts her so she won't leave him. He is also quite provocative, controlling, and angry throughout this conversation, but he is also quite charming and funny. There is laughter, tension, and anger expressed.

Another example involves a couple (No. 258; 1987 tape) in which the husband is a lawyer. The wife complains that she feels very despairing about not seeing her parents more often, and that she would like her husband to be more involved. He says he doesn't care to be more involved with her parents. She tells him that she is quite upset about his being so contemptuous toward her parents. He says that he doesn't believe that. She says, incredulously, "Don't you care about me? I'm your wife. Aren't you interested in things that bother me?" He replies, "I don't see it as affecting you negatively." In this example, he invalidates her feelings, in effect telling her that he does not accept her statement that she is upset as evidence that she is upset. He tells her that he wants to see some more negativity to believe that she is really upset.

What appears to be characteristic of these couples is that the usual persuasion part of the discussion comes early—it pervades the entire discussion, even the agenda-building phase, when feelings usually are being expressed. As a result, there are many communications that say, in effect, your feelings are wrong. For example, a wife may express her concern about the family budget, saying that she thinks that they do not save enough. The volatile husband may respond by saying something like, "You are wrong. We do not have a problem with finances." Then the persuasion begins, but it sorrounds her expression of feelings.

9.1.2. Sketch of Validating Couples' Interaction

These couples have conversations that involve conflict, but there is a lot of ease and calm in the discussions. A typical conversation is characterized by the one spouse validating the other's description of a problem. Validation can be as minimal as vocal listener backchannels (coded assent by the MICS) such as "Mmm-hmm," "Yeah," and so on. When listening to this interaction, it does not necessarily seem that the validating husband is in agreement with his wife, but simply saying, "OK, go on, I'm interested and I'm listening to your feelings. I may have my own point of view on this issue, but I want to hear you out." That is sufficient to count as validation. At a more extreme level, the validating spouse provides support, perhaps empathy, for his partner's feelings, communicating that he or she understands expressed feelings and that it makes sense to him for her to feel that way, given his or her position and vantage point. The validator still may not feel the way the partner does, but he or she communicates, verbally or nonverbally, that he or she understands and accepts the expressed feelings as valid. This communication can be nonverbal, as in mirroring facial expressions of worry and distress, or it can be direct and verbal.

An example (No. 237) is a conversation in which the wife is advocating that the husband be practical in his choice of a career. There is a great deal of good-natured kidding and teasing as she tries to help him figure out what he should specialize in of all his interests. She says that she is quite concerned that he make a reasonable and practical choice. He is quite validating of her concern. He suggests that she become a corporate vice president while he pursues the life of a scholar: "I have it planned that way," he says. She laughs and says that she would like to start her own business someday and he quips, "Why don't you start with a conglommerate?" Still, the conversation does include some confrontation on both their parts about this problem. He conveys respect for her intuitions and practicality and she conveys affection for him.

In the conversations of validating couples, there is often the sense that, although there is disagreement, the spouses are both working together on a problem.

9.2. QUANTITATIVELY BREAKING THE ENGAGER GROUP INTO TWO GROUPS

Based on qualitative observations that the volatile groups are much more emotionally expressive than the validators, I employed the following criterion to break the engagers into two groups. I divided the couples at the median on the sum of husband and wife SPAFF neutral affect on the conflict discussion. How are these volatile engagers different from the more affectively neutral validators, and how are these types different from the avoiders? Thus, by splitting at the median on neutral SPAFF affect, I sought to divide the engager group into two groups: one that I called volatile and one that I called validating. This split is illustrated by Table 9.1.

9.3. QUANTITATIVE ANALYSES: DIFFERENCES AMONG REGULATED TYPES

The quantitative analyses of differences between the three types of regulated couples proceeds in five steps. The first is a test of whether one can discriminate the three groups on the basis of qualitative observation that they differ on the extent to which and the timing with which they attempt to influence one another.

TABLE 9.1
Listener Slopes

Speaker Slopes	Both Positive	Other	Type
Both Positive	Volatile (12) Validator (14)	Avoider N = 11	Regulated
Other	Hostile N = 16	Hostile Detached N = 19	Nonregulated

The second step determines whether there is evidence of differences in conflict engagement and indexes of affect and problem solving between the groups.

The third step tests a precise hypothesis about physiological differences between the groups. Because indexes of physiological arousal appear to predict the longitudinal deterioration of marriages (Levenson & Gottman, 1985), and because these three marriages are stable longitudinally, one would expect conflict engagers and conflict avoiders not to differ on indexes of physiological arousal. However, because physiological linkage reflects the amount of negative affect and conflict engagement, one would expect conflict engagers and conflict avoiders to differ on physiological linkage, with avoiders showing less linkage.

Fourth, one expects that both conflict engagement and conflict avoidance have their respective costs and benefits. One expects to measure these costs and benefits in analyses of pervasiveness and rebound. From my observations, I notice that the costs of conflict avoidance appear to be low levels of positive as well as negative interaction. Fitzpatrick (1989) also noted this in her typology. She found that conflict-avoiding couples (whom she called separates) were not as self-disclosing with one another. On the other hand, one expects conflict-engaging couples to demonstrate higher levels of negativity, both on the events conversation (pervasiveness) and the positive conversation (rebound).

The fifth step assesses the differences between types on the affect sequences of start up and continuance in the three conversations.

9.3.1. Step 1: Influence Attempts

It is possible to discriminate all three regulated groups of couples from one another by using only one variable, which indexes the amount and timing of attempts at persuasion. Recall that Gottman (1979) identified three phases to a conflict discussion. The first phase was the agenda-building phase: Among happily married couples, both people tended to present their views and feelings on a problem. Among happily married couples, there were validation sequences in this phase, whereas among unhappily married couples there were cross-complaining sequences in this phase. The second phase was the arguing phase, in which couples tended to argue for their own point of view. There were long sequences of disagreement in this phase, as well as repair mechanisms such as feeling probes and metacommunication, followed by agreement. Unhappily married couples differed from happily married couples by having more disagreement and less agreement in this phase, and repair mechanisms did not work because negative affect had become an absorbing state. The third phase was called the negotiation phase, and its goal appeared to be compromise. Happily married couples were characterized by negotiation sequences, whereas unhappily married couples were characterized by counterproposal sequences.

To index the amount of persuasion attempts in each phase, I computed, for each third of the interaction, the amount of conflict engagement, which is the sum of disagree and criticize codes on the MICS. If my qualitative observations are correct about the three groups of couples, I should see a graph like that in Fig. 9.2. In this figure, the volatile couples are highest in persuasion attempts; these begin right away in the agenda-building phase. What this means is that they are trying to persuade one another even at the stage of expressing feelings. For example:

W: I'm worried that we're not saving enough money. We seem to live hand to mouth.
H: I don't agree. We do not have a problem with finances. You're wrong.
W: No, you're wrong. I would feel more secure if we had some savings.
H: Don't be ridiculous.

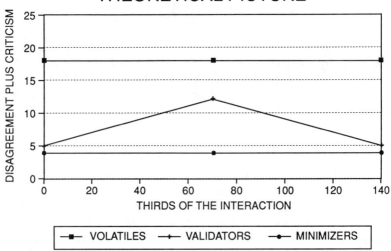

FIG. 9.2. Theoretical predictions of how volatile, validating, and conflict minimizing couples differ in influence by thirds of the interaction.

Volatile couples then are expected to continue their persuasion attempts unabated throughout all parts of the interaction. The shape of their curve should be a straight line on a higher elevation than the other two groups.

Validating couples are expected to listen to one another in the agenda-building stage and to validate feelings with agreement or assent; and their persuasion attempts should be high only in the middle third, or arguing phase, of the discussion. The sequence analagous to the one earlier might sound like this:

W: I'm worried that we're not saving enough money. We seem to live hand to mouth.
H: Uh Huh. So you'd like to save more. Well I think we do not have a problem with finances.
W: I see.
H: I think you're wrong about our finances.
W: Um-Hmm. I just would feel more secure if we had some savings.
H: I see.

Validating couples also are expected to compromise and negotiate in the final third of the interaction. Hence, the amount of influence attempts should fall for this group, and it should have a characteristic inverted-V shape.

Avoiders are expected to avoid influence attempts throughout the interaction, so their curves should be at a low level, and it should be flat throughout the interaction.

This explains the theoretical expectations of the amount of persuasion attempts of the three groups, as illustrated by Fig. 9.2. These expectations are based on qualitative observations of the groups.

Figure 9.3 is a summary of the results. This figure, by visual inspection, generally follows the predictions made in Fig. 9.2. Essentially, the same pattern of results holds for husbands and for wives. If one examines the proportion of conflict engagement in each phase of the discussion (Table 9.2), it shows that validators and volatile couples showed essentially no gender differences across the three phases of the discussion. However, avoiders did show a gender difference. Most of the persuasion attempts by avoiding wives were in the first third, whereas most of the persuasion attempts of avoiding husbands were in the last third.

An analysis[1] of the data in Fig. 9.3 revealed the following. Overall, the groups were statistically different, as were husbands different from wives. Consider the data separately by spouse for each third of the

---

[1]A loglinear analysis.

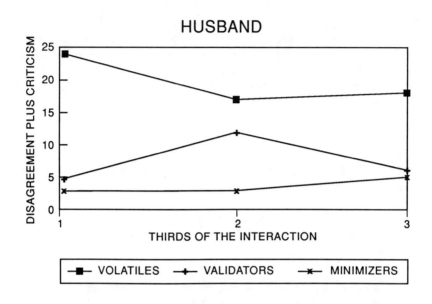

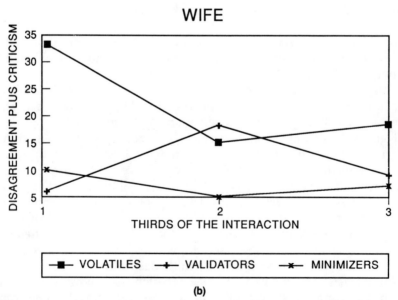

(b)

FIG. 9.3. Actual data of the index of influence attempts of how volatile, validating, and conflict-minimizing couples differ in influence by thirds of the interaction.

TABLE 9.2
Proportions of Conflict Engagement Across the Interaction for Each Group, for Each
Third of the Interaction

	Husbands			Wives		
Group	First	Second	Third	First	Second	Third
Validators	.22	.52	.26	.18	.55	.27
Volatiles	.41	.29	.31	.50	.23	.27
Avoiders	.27	.27	.45	.45	.23	.32

interaction. First, consider husbands. In the first third, the data for volatile husbands were significantly greater than those for validating husbands, volatile husbands were greater than avoiders, but avoiders and validators were not significantly different. In the second third, the data for volatile husbands were not significantly greater than those for validating husbands, volatile husbands were greater than avoiders, and validators significantly exceeded avoiders. In the third third, the data for volatile husbands were significantly greater than those for validating husbands, volatile husbands were greater than avoiders, but avoiders and validators were not significantly different.

Now consider wives. In the first third, the data for volatile wives were significantly greater than those for validating wives, volatile wives were greater than avoiders, but avoiders and validators were not significantly different. In the second third, the data for volatile wives were not significantly greater than those for validating wives, volatile wives were greater than avoiders, and validators significantly exceeded avoiders. In the third third, the data for volatile wives were significantly greater than those for validating wives, volatile wives were not significantly greater than avoiders, and avoiders and validators were not significantly different.[2]

---

[2]In this footnote, I include statistical tests. These are likelihood ratio chi-square tests for main effects, interactions, and specific contrasts (Gottman & Roy, 1990). A loglinear analysis of the data in Fig. 9.3 revealed the following. Overall, there was a statistically significant effect for groups [$\chi^2(2) = 65.44$, $p < .001$], a statistically significant effect for gender [$\chi^2(1) = 4.26$, $p < .05$], but no significant effect by thirds [$\chi^2(2) = 2.41$, ns]. The group by thirds interaction was statistically significant [$\chi^2(2) = 19.20$, $p < .001$].

Next, consider the data separately by spouse for each third of the interaction. I employed contrasts (Gottman & Roy, 1990). First consider husbands. In the first third, the data for volatile husbands were significantly greater than those for validating husbands ($z = 3.19$), volatile husbands were greater than avoiders ($z = 3.41$), but avoiders and validators were not significantly different ($z = 0.73$). In the second third, the data for volatile husbands wre not significantly greater than those for validating husbands ($z = .92$), volatile husbands were greater than avoiders ($z = 2.78$), and validators significantly

9.3.2. Step 2: Problem Solving and Affect

9.3.2.1. Problem Solving

Table 9.3 is a summary of the analysis of the MICS and RCISS data. The MICS did not discriminate the two groups of engagers. However, the RCISS discriminated the two groups. Volatile couples were more positive than validators in their presentation of their views on a problem, but they were less likely to assent to their partner's views, and they were less engaged listeners. They were also marginally more likely to stonewall than validators. Volatile wives also were more defensive than validator wives.

The RCISS codes showed volatile couples to be more positive in presentation of their views, but less responsive toward their partner's presentations of their views. They also were more positive in affect toward their partners than validators. Hence, volatile couples were more confronting (but positively) than validators, but they were less responsive to their partners than validators. Furthermore, volatile wives were more defensive than validator wives.

9.3.2.2. Affect

Table 9.4 is a summary of the SPAFF affect differences between volatiles and validators. On the conflict task, volatile husbands showed more tension/fear and marginally more joy than validating husbands. Volatile wives were more joyful as well as more angry and more tense/fearful than validating wives.

Table 9.5 is a summary of the facial expression data during the conflict discussion. The groups were not very different in dispaying affect facially. The only significant differences between the groups were a few

---

exceeded avoiders ($z = 2.15$). In the third third, the data for volatile husbands were significantly greater than those for validating husbands ($z = 2.29$), volatile husbands were greater than avoiders ($z = 2.51$), but avoiders and validators were not significantly different ($z = 0.29$).

Now consider wives. In the first third, the data for volatile wives were significantly greater than those for validating wives ($z = 3.82$), volatile wives were greater than avoiders ($z = 3.33$), but avoiders and validators were not significantly different ($z = 1.14$). In the second third, the data for volatile wives were not significantly greater than those for validating wives ($z = .50$), volatile wives were greater than avoiders ($z = 2.14$), and validators significantly exceeded avoiders ($z = 2.51$). In the third third, the data for volatile wives were significantly greater than those for validating wives ($z = 2.10$), volatile wives were not significantly greater than avoiders ($z = 1.70$), and avoiders and validators were not significantly different ($z = 0.48$). Wives were significantly greater than those for validating wives ($z = 2.10$), volatile wives were not significantly greater than avoiders ($z = 1.70$), and avoiders and validators were not significantly different ($z = 0.48$).

TABLE 9.3
Problem-Solving Differences Between Volatile and Validating Engagers

Variable	Volatile	Validators	t	df	p
MICS					
Hus. defensive	1.91	1.52	.74	23	ns
Hus. engages	3.87	3.02	.61	18	ns
Hus. stubborn	.95	.71	.53	19	ns
Hus. withdrawn	4.70	4.24	.64	23	ns
Wife defensive	2.14	1.11	1.42	17	ns
Wife engages	6.45	3.50	1.60	23	ns
Wife stubborn	1.56	.71	1.33	23	ns
Wife withdrawn	6.06	4.23	1.61	16	ns
Number turns	109.50	114.21	−.32	24	ns
RCISS					
Hus. complain/criticize	.07	.16	−1.52	17	ns
Hus. defensive	.20	.14	1.69	24	ns
Hus. verbal contempt	.03	.01	1.26	24	ns
Hus. stonewall	.78	.54	1.87	24	.073
Hus. pos. ag. bldg.	.84	.57	4.19	18	.001
Hus. assent	.06	.20	−3.40	20	.003
Hus. pos. affect	.19	.10	2.25	24	.034
Hus. listener pos.	1.69	2.39	−2.18	15	.046
Wife complain/criticize	.10	.15	−.76	21	ns
Wife defensive	.25	.14	2.77	24	.011
Wife verbal contempt	.03	.01	1.66	24	ns
Wife stonewall	.66	.43	1.93	24	.066
Wife pos. ag. bldg.	.81	.57	3.51	19	.002
Wife assent	.04	.21	−3.60	16	.002
Wife pos. affect	.18	.10	2.25	24	.034
Wife listener pos.	1.95	2.58	−2.13	15	.050
HSPK (Positive minus negative)	.79	.56	2.40	24	.024
WSPK "	.65	.58	.68	24	ns
HLIST "	.91	1.85	−2.38	15	.031
WLIST "	1.28	2.16	−2.41	15	.029

marginally significant differences. Volatile husbands and wives displayed more non-Duchenne smiles than validator husbands and wives. Volatile wives also moved their facial muscles more than validating wives. This was a marginally significant effect.

9.3.2.3. Pervasiveness of Negativity

Table 9.4 also summarizes the SPAFF affect results on the events-of-the-day conversation. The two groups were very different in terms of pervasiveness. Volatile husbands were more tense/fearful and more disgusted/contemptuous toward their wives. They displayed more interest in their wives' conversation about how their days went than

TABLE 9.4
Volatile Engagers Compared with Validators on SPAFF Affect

Variable	Volatile	Validators	t	df	p
Events					
Hus. neutral	35.67	73.77	−4.51	23	.000
Hus. humor	9.83	10.69	−.25	23	ns
Hus. affection	.75	2.92	−2.99	14	.010
Hus. interest	42.67	28.77	1.86	23	.076
Hus. joy	3.75	6.15	−1.31	23	ns
Hus. anger	2.08	.38	2.00	12	.069
Hus. dis/contempt	6.25	1.15	2.30	13	.039
Hus. whining	.42	.15	1.20	17	ns
Hus. sadness	.67	1.23	−.55	17	ns
Hus. tension/fear	14.67	1.85	3.31	12	.006
Wife neutral	30.08	73.54	−4.58	23	.000
Wife humor	12.00	11.08	.22	23	ns
Wife affection	1.17	2.08	−1.11	16	ns
Wife interest	49.67	25.85	1.98	16	.065
Wife joy	7.92	7.31	.26	23	ns
Wife anger	2.82	2.31	.28	23	ns
Wife dis/contempt	3.17	3.38	−.14	23	ns
Wife whining	1.08	1.69	−.56	16	ns
Wife sadness	1.25	.23	1.53	12	ns
Wife tension/fear	10.83	2.85	2.73	23	.012
Conflict					
Hus. neutral	12.08	52.85	−6.52	17	.000
Hus. humor	8.83	13.46	−1.00	18	ns
Hus. affection	2.42	3.15	−.55	23	ns
Hus. interest	11.17	14.38	−.66	23	ns
Hus. joy	2.92	.54	1.83	12	.092
Hus. anger	20.17	10.46	1.52	16	ns
Hus. dis/contempt	8.50	7.54	.21	23	ns
Hus. whining	1.42	1.54	−.12	23	ns
Hus. sadness	2.50	2.23	.27	23	ns
Hus. tension/fear	40.33	9.46	3.10	15	.007
Wife neutral	7.92	49.15	−5.88	13	.000
Wife humor	9.08	13.92	−1.03	23	ns
Wife affection	2.58	2.54	.04	23	ns
Wife interest	12.17	16.92	−.85	23	ns
Wife joy	2.58	.54	2.55	13	.025
Wife anger	26.58	8.23	2.42	16	.027
Wife dis/contempt	5.75	5.62	.04	23	ns
Wife whining	5.00	5.15	−.05	23	ns
Wife sadness	2.17	2.92	−.58	23	ns
Wife tension/fear	39.00	8.00	4.18	13	.001
Positive					
Hus. neutral	27.18	70.79	−3.81	23	.001
Hus. humor	14.55	9.50	1.11	15	ns

(continued)

170

TABLE 9.4 (continued)

Variable	Volatile	Validators	t	df	p
Hus. affection	3.27	3.29	−.01	23	ns
Hus. interest	33.55	27.86	.94	23	ns
Hus. joy	12.09	13.00	−.21	23	ns
Hus. anger	3.82	.29	1.16	23	ns
Hus. dis/contempt	5.27	.93	1.30	10	ns
Hus. whining	.18	.14	.20	23	ns
Hus. sadness	1.27	.93	.43	23	ns
Hus. tension/fear	12.09	2.21	2.55	13	.024
Wife neutral	23.36	65.29	−4.28	23	.000
Wife humor	13.91	10.00	.98	23	ns
Wife affection	3.36	3.21	.08	21	ns
Wife interest	34.64	32.21	.34	23	ns
Wife joy	13.45	12.14	.24	23	ns
Wife anger	7.18	.07	1.90	10	.087
Wife dis/contempt	3.82	.92	1.42	12	ns
Wife whining	.64	1.21	−.65	16	ns
Wife sadness	2.27	.79	1.71	12	ns
Wife tension/fear	14.00	2.21	3.39	12	.005

validating husbands (marginal effect). However, they were also less affectionate toward their wives than validating husbands. Volatile wives were more interested in how their husbands' day went than validating wives (marginal effect), and showed more tension/fear during the conversation than validating wives.

9.3.2.4. Rebound

Table 9.4 also presents the SPAFF affect analyses for the positive conversation. Volatile husbands were again less affectionate toward their wives than validating husbands, and more interested in their conversation (marginal effect). They also expressed more disgust/contempt and anger toward their wives (marginal effect), and more tension/fear than validating husbands. Volatile wives showed more interest in their husbands' conversation, and more tension/fear than their validating counterparts.

9.3.2.5. Physiological Data

Table 9.6 presents the physiological data. The two groups were not very different in their physiology during the marital conflict interaction. They did not differ in physiological linkage, and they differed only in husband finger pulse amplitude. Volatile husbands had less blood in

TABLE 9.5
Facial Expression Differences for Volatile and Validators

Variable	Volatile	Validators	t	df	p
Husband					
Anger	9.42	6.50	.98	24	ns
Contempt	1.92	1.64	.32	24	ns
Disgust	2.42	1.00	1.01	13	ns
Fear	3.08	5.00	−1.14	18	ns
Sadness	1.17	2.57	−.65	14	ns
Duchenne smile	26.50	16.14	1.48	24	ns
Other smiles	20.50	8.86	2.04	13	.062
Total action units	195.17	118.21	1.64	15	ns
Wife					
Anger	14.50	11.29	.84	24	ns
Contempt	2.42	2.57	−.13	24	ns
Disgust	3.00	1.21	1.25	13	ns
Fear	8.50	7.86	.17	24	ns
Sadness	3.08	1.71	.90	24	ns
Duchenne smile	19.75	18.64	.21	24	ns
Other smiles	23.33	13.57	2.04	24	.052
Total action units	247.42	167.00	1.87	24	.074

TABLE 9.6
Physiological Activity and Linkage During Conflict for Volatile and Validating Engagers

Variable	Volatile	Validators	t	df	p
Physiological Linkage	.42	.46	.58	24	ns
Physiological Activity					
Hus. heart period	784.42	781.57	−.14	21	ns
Hus. activity	1.00	.99	−.33	24	ns
Hus. skin conductance	10.78	12.49	.70	24	ns
Hus. pulse transit time	242.17	240.93	−.16	24	ns
Hus. finger amplitude	6.50	7.57	2.14	14	.050
Wife heart period	790.08	775.64	−.38	24	ns
Wife activity	1.80	1.73	−1.16	13	ns
Wife skin conductance	10.91	10.91	−1.62	24	ns
Wife pulse transit time	247.92	247.92	−1.43	24	ns
Wife finger amplitude	7.33	7.33	1.39	24	ns

their periphery than validating husbands, which usually suggests greater alpha-sympathetic physiological arousal.

9.3.2.6. Sequential Analyses

Table 9.7 shows that the two groups of couples also were quite different in continuance and positive reciprocity. Volatile couples were

TABLE 9.7
Sequences of Affect for Volatile and Validating Conflict Engagers

Variable	Volatile	Validators	t	df	p
Events					
Start up H → W	−.08	−.27	.34	18	ns
Start up W → H	.69	.64	.08	18	ns
Continuance H → W	5.32	2.05	2.48	18	.023
Continuance W → H	4.58	.60	5.04	18	.000
Pos. reciprocity H → W	4.64	2.36	2.48	18	.023
Pos. reciprocity W → H	3.41	2.37	1.02	18	ns
Conflict					
Start up H → W	1.35	1.37	−.04	22	ns
Start up W → H	.43	.69	−48	22	ns
Continuance H → W	8.99	3.69	3.03	14	.009
Continuance W → H	9.15	4.11	2.88	15	.012
Pos. reciprocity H → W	7.34	2.89	3.14	22	.005
Pos. reciprocity W → H	6.59	3.47	2.21	22	.038
Positive					
Start up H → W	−.12	.06	−.62	22	ns
Start up W → H	−.06	.12	−.46	22	ns
Continuance H → W	4.76	1.36	3.36	22	.003
Continuance W → H	4.74	1.01	2.99	22	.007
Pos. reciprocity H → W	5.19	3.69	1.55	22	ns
Pos. reciprocity W → H	5.34	3.22	2.01	22	.057

not more likely to initiate negative affect, but they were more likely to turn it into an absorbing state. Interestingly, they did this for both positive and negative affect. Furthermore, these patterns held across all three conversations. Hence, for volatile couples, both positive and negative affect had a greater likelihood of becoming absorbing states than was the case for validating couples. The affective behavior of validating couples, in addition to being more neutral (by definition), also were less latched sequentially.

9.4. SUMMARY

Volatile couples were more positive in presentation of their views, but they also were less responsive toward their partners' presentations of their views. They also were affectively more positive toward their partners than validators. Hence, volatile couples were more confronting (but positively) than validators, but they were less responsive to their partners than validators. Furthermore, volatile wives were more defensive than validator wives. On the conflict task, volatile husbands showed more tension/fear and more joy than validating husbands. Volatile wives were more joyful as well as more angry and tense/fearful than validating wives. However, volatile husbands and wives displayed more negative non-Duchenne smiles than validator husbands and wives. Volatile wives also moved their facial muscles more than validating wives. The two groups were very different in terms of pervasiveness. Whereas volatile husbands were more tense/fearful and disgusted/contemptuous toward their wives, they also displayed more interest in their wives' conversation about how their day went than validating husbands. However, they also were less affectionate toward their wives than validating husbands. Volatile wives were more interested in their husbands' conversation about how his day went than validating wives (marginal effect), but they showed more tension/fear during the conversation than validating wives. In terms of rebound, on the positive conversation volatile husbands were again less affectionate toward their wives than validating husbands, but more interested in their conversation. They also expressed more disgust/contempt toward their wives and more anger and tension/fear than validating husbands. Volatile wives showed more interest in their husbands' conversation, but more tension/fear than their validating counterparts.

The two groups of couples also were quite different in continuance and positive reciprocity. Volatile couples were not more likely to initiate negative affect, but they were more likely to turn it into an absorbing state. This was suggested as an extremely negative interaction pattern with respect to marital happiness (chapter 3). However, volatile couples also turned positive affect into an absorbing state. Furthermore, these patterns held across all three conversations. Hence, for volatile couples, both positive and negative affect had a greater likelihood of becoming absorbing states than was the case for validating couples. The affective behavior of validating couples, in addition to being more neutral (by definition), also were less latched sequentially. The two groups differed in husband finger pulse amplitude. Volatile husbands had less blood in their periphery than validating husbands, which suggested greater alpha-sympathetic physiological arousal.

9.5. FITZPATRICK'S (1989) TYPOLOGY

In a careful series of investigations, Fitzpatrick (1989) made a case for the existence and replicability of three pure types of couples. She called these three types "traditionals," "independents," and "separates." The three types initially were defined by using self-report measures of what the couples' values were. In fact, Fitzpatrick developed a questionnaire called the Relationship Dimensions Instrument (RDI), which she used to create her subgroups. In a typical study, Fitzpatrick recruited a group of couples, administered the RDI, and then formed subgroups. She then had the couples interact using some task, and then employed or designed an observational coding system that gets at some theoretical aspect of marriage she thinks should discriminate the three groups.

There is a remarkable convergence between Fitzpatrick's three pure types and the three types of regulated couples identified here. I need to make the equation: validating = traditional; volatile = independent; and avoider = separate.

9.5.1. Differences in the Values of the Three Types

Traditionals (validators) tend to avoid conflict, but will argue about the most important issues in their marriage. They tend to have very few conflicts, and usually "sweep discord under the rug." There is a fair amount of stereotyping by gender roles in their marriages. Each spouse has his or her own spheres of influence. Her's is usually the home and the children. He is usually the final decision maker. He tends to see himself as analytical, dominant, and assertive. She tends to see herself as nurturant, warm, and expressive. They both emphasize "we-ness" over individual goals and values. They tend to finish one another's sentences. They value communication, verbal openness, being in love, displaying affection, and sharing time, activities, and interests. There is a high degree of sharing of space. They tend to have a regular daily schedule.

Independents (volatiles) are quite different from traditionals (validators). They believe that individuality should be emphasized and strengthened by the marriage. They believe that in a marriage, each partner should be allowed privacy and independence. They thrive on conflict, and neither spouse is openly afraid to express disagreement. There is no gender role stereotyping. The marriage is egalitarian and each spouse sees him or herself as androgynous. He views himself as both analytical and expressive. They engage in conflict, bargaining, and negotiation. They disclose a lot of positive and negative feelings. They tend to interrupt one another with questions, rather than finishing one another's sentences and emphasizing "we-ness." In their home, they tend to have separate physical spaces and control accessibility to them. They have no regular daily schedule.

Separates (avoiders) are characterized by separateness and interpersonal distance. There is a low level of companionship and sharing. Their values resemble those of traditionals (validators), but they value separateness and maintain autonomy in the use of space. They tend to avoid all marital conflicts.

Fitzpatrick (1989) also discussed mixed types, but this work is not reviewed here. However, the three types that Fitzpatrick (1989) identified are all high in marital satisfaction. The average Spanier DAS scores are 158 for the traditionals (validators), 139 for the independents (volatiles), and 122 for the separates (avoiders). All these scores are well above the usual cutoff for the Spanier (115).

Fitzpatrick (1989) investigated various aspects of marital interaction for the three types. I briefly summarize her findings.

9.5.2. Power

Fitzpatrick (1989) had couples discuss two issues: one high in salience and one low in salience. In other words, one issue was emotionally "hot" and the other was not. She employed two observational coding systems (Ellis, Fisher, Drecksel, Hoch, & Werbel, 1976; Rogers & Farace, 1975). Power is one of the most elusive constructs in the marital interaction literature. Although most investigators think that power is an important construct, attempts to measure it have met with mixed success. To illustrate the difficulties, consider the codes' agreement and disagreement. In many observational coding systems (e.g., Roger & Farace, 1975), agreement is viewed as a positive interaction. However, in coding power, agreement may be viewed as submission rather than positive interaction. In the Ellis et al. (1976) system, agreement can be any of three control moves: Simple agreement is considered deference, agreement with extension is considered structuring, and conditional agreement is considered equivalence. Disagreement is viewed as a "one-up bid for dominance." All of these views of agreement and disagreement do not distinguish their affective and problem-solving functions from their potential value as indexes of power.

Fitzpatrick (1989) distinguished two kinds of power sequences: competitive symmetrical exchanges (CSE) and complimentary exchanges (CE). In the CSE, one spouse refuses to give in to the control moves of the other spouse, so that a one-up move is met with another one-up move. For example:

Paul: You know I want you to keep the house picked up during the day.
Margie: I want you to help sometimes!
or,
Spouse 1: You are a lousy lover!
Spouse 2: I'd be a better lover if you weren't so fat!

Complimentary exchanges (CE) involve accepting control moves of the other spouse. There are clearly strong affective elements of the exchanges in these examples, but they are ignored intentionally for the analysis of power, rather than coding both affect and power and exploring how they interact. This may be an unfortunate choice. Fitzpatrick (1989) assumed that they were independent aspects of marital interaction, but her own examples demonstrate that this need not be the case. The results were as expected. Independents (volatiles) had more CSEs than the other types. Regardless of the salience of the problem, separates (avoiders) used proportionally fewer CSEs than the other types. Hence, separates (avoiders) and independents (volatiles) anchored opposite ends of a scale in terms of CSEs. Traditionals (validators) were in between. They used CSEs, but mostly for the hot issues. In terms of CEs (accepting spouse's control moves), separates (avoiders) were higher than the other couple types, whereas traditionals (validators) used CEs mostly when the issues were hot. Independents (volatiles) did not vary their use of CEs as a function of the problem's salience.

In another study, Fitzpatrick (1984) examined sequences of power moves. Her conclusions based on this analysis were these: Traditionals (validators) resolved their disagreements quickly, they refused to relinquish control in a conflict, they exchanged commands (e.g., Husband: "You've got to let me have that encyclopedia!"; Wife: "You have got to get rid of that defensive tone!"), and they used agreement less and information seeking more than other couples. Independents (volatiles) used dominance more and information seeking less than other couple types. She wrote that independents (volatiles) showed:

> strong assertiveness and resulting conflict, yet through equivalence arises a sense of mutual regard and interdependence. The Independents (Volatiles) demonstrate that they are very expressive with one another . . . Even in a casual conversation Independents (Volatiles) challenge and justify. (p. 130)

Separates (avoiders) appeared to be adept at avoiding potentially explosive communication patterns. Fitzpatrick's (1984) summary of these analyses was:

> In all marriages, there is a change from issue attack to personal attack when a conflict occurs. All couples use personal nonsupport statements as linguistic attempts to assert dominance in conflict. *What differs among couples is how a spouse responds to that personal attack*, not the occurrence of the attack in the first place. These results parallel those of Gottman (1979), who finds that in happy marriages, one spouse de-escalates a conflict by not responding in kind to the negative communication acts of his or her partner. (p. 133)

9.5.3. Avoidance, Cooperation, and Confrontation

In one study, Fitzpatrick (1984) attempted to directly code communications as avoidance, cooperation, or competition. This global coding was quite unsuccessful at discriminating among the couple types. After more coding and analysis, she concluded that withdrawal was characteristic of separates (avoiders). She wrote: "Separates (Avoiders) psychologically withdraw from conflict by speaking to their spouses less often, for shorter periods, and with fewer interruptions than other couples. This inaction is an extreme form of avoidance" (p. 145). Sillars, Pike, Jones, and Redman (1983) found that independents (volatiles) used more negative voice tones (i.e., cold, angry, accusing) when discussing tense issues. The independent (volatile) relationship is committed to the open expression of negative feelings and conflicts. Burgaff and Sillars (1976) found no gender differences in confrontation or evasiveness.

Some of Burgaff and Sillars' (1986) data were contrary to Fitzpatrick's (1984) data. They found that it was the traditionals (validators) who used more avoidance, less confrontation, and more conciliation than expected by chance, whereas it was separates (avoiders) who used significantly more confrontations than expected by chance. The replication problem in this study may come from not controlling marital satisfaction. Support for this possibility comes from Fitzpatrick's (1984) description of separates (avoiders) as "subtly hostile," a style that "depends on confrontation and depresses analytical and conciliatory moves. . . . Separates (Avoiders) tend to initiate confrontational acts when there was no immediate antecedent act by the spouse. Separates (Avoiders) do not reciprocate confrontational acts" (p. 131). This is a kind of "sniping" style, which she called a "hit and run" style. This description is quite opposite to her initial characterization of these couples as conflict avoiding. Perhaps happily married separates (avoiders) avoid conflict effectively, but unhappily married separates (avoiders) use the hit and run style. It also may be that they are more complex than initially thought.

In the Burgaff and Sillars (1986) study, independents (volatiles) did not come out quite as predicted. They were less likely to be supportive, to make concessions, and to accept responsibility for the conflict. They were more likely to use analytical tactics. They did not initiate confrontation, but did if provoked. They reacted negatively to avoidance by the spouse.

In the Fitzpatrick and Kalbfleisch (1988) study, the Couples Interaction Scoring System (CISS) was employed with lag sequential analysis. Gottman (1979) identified cross-complaining sequences (e.g., Wife: "At the end of the day when you come home I want some relief from you because I've been with the kids all day!"; Husband: "When I come home I'm tired and just want to unwind."). These sequences were found only among separates (avoiders) and independents (volatiles). Gottman (1979) also coded metacommunication, which are statements about the nature of the communication itself, such as "You're interrupting me." Fitzpatrick and Kalbfleisch (1988) found that metacommunication was not used by separates (avoiders). Also, Gottman (1979) and Gottman and Krokoff (1989) identified a form of defensive pattern called negative mindreading. In this sequence, one partner attributes motives, feelings, or behavior to the other spouse (e.g., "You don't care about how we live!"; or "You never want to go to the shore for vacations.") and the other spouse disagrees with this attribution. This sequence was characteristic of independents (volatiles), with the wife disagreeing with her husband's mindreading statements.

9.5.4. Obtaining Compliance

Fitzpatrick's (1984) analysis of compliance broke the interaction down to detailed categories, using the Verbal Interaction Compliance-Gaining Scheme (VICS), which then were summarized as comply, refute, discount, agree, and other. She found that independents (volatiles) used significantly greater than chance levels of refute and discount and less than chance levels of comply and agree. Separates (avoiders) used significantly greater than chance levels of comply, refute, and discount; and less than chance levels of agree. Traditionals (validators) used significantly greater than chance levels of comply, and less than chance levels of refute and discount. Fitzpatrick (1984) wrote:

> Independents (Volatiles) demand compliance from their spouses in that they rely on "you" strategies and power plays when attempting to persuade their spouses. Independents (Volatiles) are likely to offer compromises and to *question their spouse about their needs and wants*. Independents (Volatiles) use fewer compliance-gaining techniques overall, yet do engage in *defending themselves* and refuting what the spouse says [italics added] (p. 172). Separates (Avoiders) are not without intensity in their interactions but have a guerrilla-like communication style that demands acquiescence from the spouse without verbally staying to fight the whole battle. (p. 173)

9.5.5. Self-Disclosure

Fitzpatrick (1984) also studied self-disclosure in marriage. Self-disclosures are very personal and intimate statements about one's self.

She used Gottman and Rubin's "fun deck" task to elicit self-disclosure. She analyzed the middle 4 of 10 minutes. The independents (volatiles) had the highest proportion of disclosure, acknowledgment, and confirmation. Separates (avoiders) had the least disclosure, advisement, and confirmation. Separates (avoiders) "engage in a higher proportion of questioning of the spouse and are not likely to express their feelings, state their opinions to the spouse, or to give the spouse advice" (p. 184).

Fitzpatrick (1984) also conducted a brilliant round-robin study in which spouses talked to strangers as well as to their partners. This design made it possible to see if self-disclosure was a function of the individual or the relationship. Her data provided overwhelming support that the relationship, and not the individual, was most important in predicting the amount of disclosure. She also correlated her RDI scale with the amount of disclosure. She reported that:

> Those who subscribe to the ideology of Traditionalism and have high degrees of companionship in the marriage (Traditionals (Validating)) are less likely to self-disclose to the spouse, whereas those with a less conventional ideology (Independents (Volatiles)) use more self-disclosure. *Avoiding conflict is related to suppressing self-disclosure in marriage.* (p. 196, italics added)

9.5.6. The Use of Language

Fitzpatrick (1984) studied couples' use of linguistic and pragmatic forms in speech and did a content analysis of their speech. She found that traditionals (validators) used more references to themselves as a couple ("we" references), whereas independents (volatiles) used more personal pronouns. Independents (volatiles) used significantly more references to themselves ("I" references) and embroidered their conversations with more complex verb forms.

These findings were echoed by the content analyses. Traditionals (validators) emphasized togetherness; expressed communal themes, expressive communication, and sharing; and referred to romantic themes such as being in love and mutual affection. Separates (avoiders) were conventional, but deemphasized togetherness; they presented marriage as a product of separate identities or roles. They talked about their individual and distinctive activities, hobbies, personalities, traits, habits, and skills.

It seems quite remarkable that my data and Fitzpatrick's (1984) data appear to converge in many ways to identify three types of stable marriages. In the following chapter, I put these typology results together and suggest a theory of stable and unstable marriage.

10

A Balance Theory of Marriage

In this chapter, I suggest and find evidence for the contention that what is regulated in marriages that are stable is some ratio of positive to negative problem solving or positive to negative purely affective behaviors. Furthermore, it appears that there are only three distinct possible adaptations to regulating this ratio: one by using a lot of negative and positive affect, another by using a moderate amount of positive and negative affect, and the other by using a small amount of positive and negative affect. The ratio of positivity to negativity is a constant of about 5.0 in the three types of stable marriages, and less than 1.0 in the unstable marriages. This is true across conversations and coding systems. I argue that these three stable adaptations are distinct types rather than dimensions, because there are so many concomitants of each style or type. I speculate about the benefits and risks of each adaptation.

It is possible that the three types of regulated couples described previously represent the range of adaptations that exist to balance or regulate positive and negative behaviors in a marriage. If this were the case, then other adaptations would prove to be unstable longitudinally.

I examine the nature of the three stable adaptations to balancing negativity and positivity. In the volatile case, the adaptation includes a lot of negativity. This tends to be balanced by a lot of laughter, positive presentation of issues, and passionate romance. This is the adaptation with a lot of nonneutral affect.

There are two other adaptations that involve much less negative and positive affect and much more neutral interaction. One adaptation, represented by the validators, involves carefully picking and choosing when to disagree and confront conflict, and then conveying some measure of support when one's partner expresses negative feelings about an issue. There is a great deal of warmth and "we-ness" in this type of marriage, but little heat in the form of either quarrels or passion.

The other adaptation with high levels of neutral affect is the avoider adaptation. It appears to involve a minimization of the importance of disagreement. It results in a good deal of calm interaction, but pays the price with emotional distance in the marriage.

10.1. A THEORY OF BALANCE

One may think of these three adaptations as balancing some quantity of positivity against negativity. In the case of the volatile marriage, this is managed by a lot of negativity offset by a lot of positivity. In the case of the validating couple, this is managed by a moderate amount of negativity balanced by a moderate amount of positivity. In the case of the avoiding couple, this is managed by a small amount of negativity balanced by a small amount of positivity. I hypothesize that all three types of regulated marriages might have a constant ratio of negative to positive interaction.

If this were true, *stable marriages would be like ecologies, in which there is a balance* between life forms, and predator and prey populations are in stable opposition. The balance in regulated marriages is between behaviors rather than species. In the case of marriage, negative interaction is considered the predator and positive interaction is the prey. It is known from research on marriage that negative interaction can be both a mighty predator, and (Gottman & Krokoff, 1989) that negative interaction also can be functional in a longitudinal sense if it is of a particular nature. Negative interaction has two faces: one potentially constructive and one potentially destructive. Which face it shows may depend on its balance with positive interaction.

10.2. QUANTITATIVE TEST

Using only RCISS codes, if one adds up all positive husband and wife speaker codes and all husband and wife negative speaker codes, and takes the ratio, one finds that the ratio of positive to negative codes is about 5 for couples whose marriages are regulated or stable. This ratio is less than 1.0 for nonregulated, or unstable, marriages.[1]

---

[1] The statistical comparison between regulated and nonregulated couples resulted in an $F(1,70) = 29.20$, $p < .001$.

10.3. A UNIVERSAL CONSTANT?

On the basis of these results, I suggest that there is a rough universal constant that is stable across each of the three types of regulated couples. This constant, the ratio of positive to negative RCISS speaker codes during conflict resolution, is about 5, and it is not significantly different across the three types of marriage.[2] This constant also can be obtained if one computes the ratio for husbands and wives separately. For husbands across all three groups, the ratio was 5.10, and the three groups did not differ significantly.[3] For wives, the ratio was 5.06, and, once again, the three groups did not differ significantly.[4] These ratios also discriminated regulated from nonregulated marriages. For husbands, the mean positive to negative RCISS ratio for nonregulated marriages was 1.06.[5] For wives, the mean positive to negative RCISS ratio for nonregulated marriages was 0.67.[6]

On the basis of these analyses, I suggest that each adaptation to having a regulated marriage, or each regulated couple type, represents a similar kind of stable adaptation. The volatile couples reach the ratio of 5 by mixing a lot of positive affect with a lot of negative affect. The validators mix a moderate amount of positive affect with a moderate amount of negative affect. The avoiders mix a small amount of positive affect with a small amount of negative affect. Each do so in a way that achieves roughly the same balance between positive and negative.

One also can speculate that each type of marriage has its risks, benefits, and costs. I speculate about these risks, costs, and benefits based on what I know about each type of marriage.

10.3.1. Notarius, Benson, Sloane, Vanzetti, and Hornyak (1989)

In this study, the conflict interaction (low- and high-conflict interactions were combined) of nine distressed couples and nine nondistressed couples was coded with the affect portion of the Couples Interaction Scoring System (CISS; Gottman, 1979; Notarius & Markman, 1981). Couples interacted using the talk table paradigm (Gottman et al., 1976). A positive-to-negative ratio was reported for wives' coded behavior: The ratio was 0.67 for distressed wives and 5.32 for nondistressed wives. These ratios are quite close to those reported above for discriminating stable from unstable couples.

---

[2]$F(2,34) = 0.93$, ns.
[3]$F(2,34) = 0.15$, ns.
[4]$F(2,34) = 2.31$, ns.
[5]Comparing regulated and nonregulated husbands, $F(1,70) = 19.51$, $p < .001$.
[6]Comparing regulated and nonregulated wives, $F(1,70) = 24.69$, $p < .001$.

10.4. RAUSH'S QUESTION ABOUT QUARRELING
REVISITED

Recall that Raush's question was "What makes conflict dysfunctional?" When I first reviewed the discussion of this issue, I mentioned that we have all known couples whose interactions consist of a lot of bickering about very trivial matters. I reviewed the idea that most investigators have been convinced that such issues that escalate out of control have to be about something else, other than the seemingly trivial issue being discussed. Raush et al. (1974) thought that trivial discussions that became heated actually were arguments about symbols of something else, that the conflicts were symbolic conflicts. Symbolic conflicts were thought to be dysfunctional.

However, the volatile couple's marriage appears to be based on persuasion attempts that begin at the feeling expression stage of the discussion: It is a heated, affectively expressive interaction. It seems to fit the bill for what Raush et al. (1974) thought of as a relationship that would be beset with symbolic conflict. Indeed, volatile couples demonstrate fairly high levels of negative continuance, but they also demonstrate high levels of positive continuance. From everything that has been seen, it is not a dysfunctional marriage in terms of the cascade model.

Thus, that the volatile marriage is regulated flies in the face of prior notions that this kind of interaction is dysfunctional. Hence, neither conflict avoidance or high levels of negative conflict are, by themselves, dysfunctional in terms of the marriage.

Therefore, I have to modify the thinking of Raush et al. (1974) somewhat in the light of my data. What is consistent with my results, and those of Fitzpatrick (1989), is that *what is dysfunctional is the response to one's partner with criticism, disgust, contempt, defensiveness, and stonewalling.*

If one recalls the other half of the speculations by Raush et al. (1974) about what makes discussions of disagreements dysfunctional, one sees that the notion of defensiveness is there. Recall that by drawing on the work of Deutsch (1969), Raush et al. (1974) expanded on this notion of symbolic conflict. They suggested that threat leads to increased reliance on threat, coercion, and deception, which are, in turn, reciprocated. They wrote that threat leads to defensiveness and excessive tension, which leads to the closed mind. I now can underscore their speculations with some data.

10.5. REVISITING THE SCIENTIFIC MEANING OF TYPES AS
OPPOSED TO DIMENSIONS

I pointed out earlier that there is an important scientific meaning to believing that there are types of marriages as opposed to dimensions of marriage. I borrowed from the history of physics to make this point, reviewing Niels Bohr's model of the atom compared with early views of the atom. In the Bohr model of the atom, the electron is far more likely to be at only certain locations from the nucleus of the atom. These positions are called shells. Furthermore, when an electron gains or loses energy, it moves out to a new shell farther from the nucleus of the atom, or in to a shell closer to the nucleus. Orbits in between shells are unstable. In the model of the atom before Bohr's, the electron could occupy any position with respect to the nucleus. Its position was continuous or what would be called dimensional in personality psychology. The Bohr model of the atom was discrete or quantized, and such views formed the basis of the branch of models in physics that has come to be known as Quantum Mechanics.

In trying to construct a typology of marriage, I suggest something similar to what Bohr suggested about orbits of electrons around the nucleus. I suggest the following theory: *Marriages come in three discrete adaptations, and there are no in-between adaptations that are stable over time.* One now sees that the adaptation I propose is an adaptation to balancing negative and positive interactions in a marriage. I state this idea by discussing another analogy, that of an ecological system in balance. In this case, the elements that are in balance are behaviors and not species. I suggest that types of marital interaction coded as negative with the RCISS and the SPAFF are like predators of those types of interaction coded as positive. The choices of what are to be considered positive and what are to be considered negative are not trivial. For example, Gottman and Krokoff's (1989) longitudinal studies revealed that disagreement, especially by wives, may be unpleasant in the short run, but positive in the long run. I am interested in the idea that positivity has to do with avoiding the cascade toward marital dissolution. It means that the marriage continues over time and that both partners find it satisfying.

There is a further analogy to the Bohr atom that may be useful to discuss. The various adaptations to the balance between negative and positive interaction in marriage is related to some construct that could be called energy. The amount of energy exchanged in the marital interaction is highest in the volatile marriage, intermediate in the validating marriage, and lowest in the avoider marriage. The best way to measure this energy was attempts at persuasion during conflict resolution. Volatile couples engaged in the most persuasion attempts, validators were intermediate, and avoiders were at the lowest level.

What does energy mean when it comes to behavior? One can employ a definition that comes from a branch of statistics called time-series analysis. In time-series analysis, there is an equation of energy and variance. In a simple case, this is very easy to understand. If one considers a pendulum oscillating at a particular frequency with amplitude A, the amplitude of oscillation depends on how hard the pendulum is shoved initially. How hard the pendulum is shoved is the energy imparted to it for its swing. The amplitude of its oscillation is the amount of a circle that it takes up from its maximum amount of swing on one side to its maximum amount of swing on the other side. The variance of its motion is proportional to the square of this amplitude, and therefore is the energy of the pendulum's swing. Hence, variance and energy can be equated in this simple case. It turns out that this simple case is generalizable for most situations. Over time, most data can be well represented by sums of oscillations, with weights for each oscillations determined by the data. This kind of analysis is called Fourier analysis, a method that is named for the great French mathematician, Jean Baptiste Fourier, whose theorem in 1822 led to this branch of mathematics. There have been extensions of the mathematics in the 20th century that have led to the field of modern spectral analysis.

Hence, there is a mathematical basis for equating energy with variance in behavior. Therefore, there is a sense in which a theory of marital types is very much like Bohr's model of the atom. It suggests that three specific adaptations are much more likely to occur than any others, and that others, like the positions of the electron intermediate to the shells, are unstable, or what I have called nonregulated.

10.6. TWO CAVEATS

The first caveat I discuss is that the concept of regulated versus nonregulated couples is misleading. Both groups of couples are likely to represent regulated systems, but these systems have different set points. Recently in the news, there was the story of a very famous obese man who weighed 500 pounds when he died. Dick Gregory had worked with him at one time and helped him to lose an enormous amount of weight. I am certain that his body defended his weight, and many of the normal mechanisms to maintain weight were functional in essentially the same way in his body as in another body. However, despite that his weight was regulated, his set point was dysfunctional. In a similar way, the interactive behavior of couples whose marriages are on a trajectory toward dissolution have a set point that regulates their interactive behavior. However, the set point is dysfunctional in terms of the life of their marriage and probably also dysfunctional in terms of their physical health. This caveat is designed to distinguish between regulated and chaotic processes. I have no evidence presently that chaotic processes characterize marriages that are on a trajectory toward dissolution.

The second caveat concerns the seemingly trait-like nature of the marital typology. I cannot suggest, at this point, that the three adaptations toward having a stable, regulated marriage are like unchangeable traits. Indeed, my use of the term *adaptations* to regulated marriage was intended to be reminiscent of a Darwinian notion of the adaptation of species and their balance to a particular ecological niche. In this case, I discuss populations of behaviors rather than species. It is certainly sensible to suggest that couples can change their adaptations. I eventually plan to report on my longitudinal data of marital interaction to determine how stable marital interaction patterns are over time. I expect to find some evidence of both change and stability. Most therapists currently seem to hold the model of the validating marriage as the one toward which they try to move couples. This may be an excellent model, but, at this point, I cannot recommend it as the only model.

10.6.1. Why Do People Choose Some Types of Marriages Over Others?

It is an interesting mystery to consider why some individuals are drawn to some kinds of relationships and not others. There may be an emotional comfort level that individuals have with emotional expression. I expect that, to some extent, I will discover that people tend to seek levels of affect or affective intensity consistent with their own physiological reactivity (Matthews et al., 1986), and that these variables will have a large genetic component. However, at present, this is merely speculation.

10.6.2. Cultural Variation

Also, I am sure that I will find cultural variation in the distribution of marital types. Rabin (personal communication, 1992), who is an Israeli marital therapist and researcher, recently told me that most Israeli couples she treated had "volatile" marriages. How well will my results replicate in different cultures? I expect that some things will hold. For example, I predict that, regardless of how a culture communicates contempt (the British may do this in a manner different from Italians or Indians), contempt will be corrosive in a marriage and it will be corrosive of marital bonds regardless of how the culture approaches mate selection (e.g., arranged marriages).

10.7. EXTENSIONS INTO THE REALM OF PURE AFFECT: FURTHER QUANTITATIVE TESTS

The results I have described have been interesting and encouraging, but they have been specific to one observational coding system—the RCISS.

The RCISS is a combination of both problem solving and affect. There are two questions one may ask. First, would the results I have obtained hold if I examined only affect with the SPAFF? Second, an advantage of the SPAFF is that I can examine all three interactions. Would the results I have obtained hold for interactions other than conflict resolution? Is there evidence for some other constant in these contexts? Or would roughly the same constant be obtained?

To answer the first question, I computed the ratio of positive to negative SPAFF affects for the conflict interaction.[7] As I predicted, there were no significant differences between types of couples within the regulated group.[8] However, again according to prediction, the ratio discriminated regulated from nonregulated couples on the conflict interaction.[9] Furthermore, the mean for regulated husbands was 4.16, and for nonregulated husbands was 0.91; the mean for regulated wives was 5.26, and for nonregulated wives was 0.46. Hence, on the conflict interaction, what I jokingly call "Gottman's constant" (see chapter 13) holds as characteristic of regulated couples when only pure affect is considered, as measured by the SPAFF.

To answer the second question, I computed the same ratio for the events-of-the-day interaction and for the positive interaction. On the events conversation, the husband ratio did not discriminate among regulated types. The same was true for the wife ratio.[10] However, again as predicted, the ratios discriminated regulated from nonregulated couples. For husbands, the regulated mean was 4.16 and the nonregulated mean was 0.91.[11] For wives the regulated mean was 5.26 and the nonregulated mean was 0.46.[12] Again, the constant of nearly 5 was obtained as the ratio of positive to negative affects for regulated couples

---

[7]In these computations, I did not include the affect of fear/tension/worry. Hence, the ratio is (humor + affection + interest + joy) divided by (anger + disgust/contempt + whining + sadness). The reason for excluding the fear code is that I have noticed that the fear/tension/worry code of the SPAFF acts inconsistently as a negative affect. The code is based largely on non-ah speech disturbances, such as sentence fragment repetitions, omissions, and slips of the tongue. These disturbances also occur during fast-paced interaction, and do not seem to be reliable as indicators of negative affect. The fear/tension/worry code did not discriminate regulated from nonregulated couples, and it is not correlated reliably with marital unhappiness. It may be that greater precision is necessary with this code. For example, it may be mixing excitement with fear inadvertently.

[8]For husbands, $F(2,32) = 0.39$, ns; and for wives $F(2,32) = 0.40$, ns.

[9]For husbands, $F(1,64) = 7.93$, $p < .01$; for wives, $F(1,64) = 6.16$, $p < .05$.

[10]For husbands, $F(2,21) = 0.37$, ns; the same was true for the wife ratio, $F(2,27) = 0.22$, ns.

[11]$F(1,64) = 7.93$, $p < .01$.

[12]$F(1,67) = 6.16$, $p < .05$.

on the events-of-the-day conversation, and a ratio less that 1 for non-regulated couples.

In the positive conversation, once again the ratio did not discriminate among regulated subtypes. For husbands, the ratio was not significantly different across the groups,[13] as was the case for wives.[14] Once again, the ratio discriminated between regulated and nonregulated subtypes, for both husbands and wives.[15] The mean for regulated husbands was 4.16, whereas for nonregulated husbands the mean was 0.91. The mean for regulated wives was 5.26, whereas the mean for nonregulated wives was 0.46.

10.8. SUMMARY

In this chapter, I suggested and found evidence for the contention that what is regulated in marriages that are stable is the ratio of positive to negative problem solving or positive to negative purely affective behaviors. Furthermore, it appears that there are only three distinct possible adaptations to regulating this ratio: one by using a lot of negative and positive affect, another by using a moderate amount of positive and negative affect, and the other by using a small amount of positive and negative affect. I argued that these three adaptations are distinct types rather than dimensions, because there are so many concomitants of each style or type. Fitzpatrick (1989) explored many of these. I speculate later about the costs, benefits, and risks of each adaptation.

I also saw that Gottman's constant of about 5 also is obtained for regulated couples using both RCISS and SPAFF data, and that it also is obtained for the other two interactions sampled here. Hence, my results are not limited to conflict resolution, nor are they limited to the very specific codes of the RCISS.

The most important aspect of my theory is that something very precise is regulated in regulated marriages. I found one such quantity, which is not significantly different across regulated types, but very different from nonregulated marriages. I need to be cautious in concluding that the variable I discovered is the regulated variable. It may very well be.[16] Nonetheless, the fact that one exists suggests that

---

[13]$F(2,22) = 0.68$, ns.

[14]$F(2,24) = 0.58$, ns.

[15]For husbands, $F(1,64) = 7.93$, $p < .01$, whereas for wives, $F(1,67) = 6.16$, $p < .05$.

[16]These results are reasonably robust for another way of computing a balance between positive and negative speaker RCISS codes. If I use the difference between positive and negative RCISS speaker codes, I can discriminate regulated from nonregulated couples [for the husband $F(1.70) = 58.95$, $p < .001$; for the wife, $F(1,70) = 112.26$, $p < .001$].

regulated marriage is like an ecology, in which behaviors between people, rather than species, are in balance.

I need to be cautious about believing in the universality of this particular constant. There is no theoretical reason that a constant of 5 should emerge. However, it could emerge as an eigenvalue for an equation yet to be discovered. Still, I am confident that if I were to observe couples in other contexts, and with other methods, I might obtain results that are somewhat different (see chapter 13). For example, some early marriage research was conducted using a method that has been criticized for its reliability (Elwood & Jacobson, 1982, 1988; Jacobson & Moore, 1981): a diary record-keeping system called the Spouse Observation Checklist. In attempting to discriminate happily from unhappily married couples, positive to negative ratios of about 18 were obtained for happily married couples, whereas ratios of about 5 were obtained for unhappily married couples (Jacobson, Follete, & McDonald, 1982). Couples are not very reliable recorders, especially in areas related to communication (Jacobson & Moore, 1981). Still, although these diary data are of questionable usefulness, even if these data are indexes of people's perceptions of the events that occur in the marriage, it appears that the mix of positive to negative codes needs to be perceived as quite rich in favor of the positive to make a marriage feel right. This may be true independent of the kind of adaptation that stable couples select.

10.9. SPECULATIONS ABOUT THE RISKS OF EACH TYPE OF MARRIAGE: AN OVERVIEW

Each adaptation to having a stable marriage has its own set of rewards and costs. In pursuing this notion, I tried to use the data available about each type of marriage to speculate about what these rewards and costs might be. This qualitative essay about the risks of each adaptation to having a stable marriage is intended for purely hypothesis-generating purposes.

It seems clear that the volatile marriage has the potential for a great deal of turmoil and upset at times. Usually these are repaired with a

---

However, although the three types of marriages are not significantly different for wives [$F(2,34) = 0.27$, ns], they are different for husbands [$F(2,34) = 3.57$, $p < .05$]. In the case of the husband, volatile husbands are more positive than negative compared with the other two groups (volatile mean = 0.79, validator mean = 0.56, avoider mean = 0.56). At the time of this writing, the ratio is still the best candidate for the regulated variable.

great deal of positive passion, but some hurts could arise that are difficult to heal in this manner, if at all. For example, they could be viewed as basic betrayals. In this case, the volatile marriage has the potential for great reciprocity of negativity, defensiveness, and even violence. I have seen some violent couples cast in this mold. They are distortions of the volatile marriage.

The validating marriage seems to have the opposite kind of risk (i.e., that the marriage will become a passionless arrangement). This is dramatized in a film called *The Arrangement*, in which the couple has grown far apart emotionally. Although sharing and friendship are emphasized in the validating marriage, there is a danger that the marriage will stop being romantic and satisfying. This is the challenge for the validating marriage. It may be particularly vulnerable at major life transitions, such as the transition to parenthood.

The avoiding marriage has the same risks that the validating marriage has in terms of the loss of passion (assuming it was ever there in the first place). Loneliness is a great danger for this marriage. There is another danger. Couples in avoiding marriages, unlike validating couples, lack the social skills necessary to resolve conflicts that are unavoidable. In these cases, they are, like fish thrown on the beach, in danger of dying. They cannot metacommunicate or discuss their problems and solve them. When the problem cannot be minimized, they are in a great deal of pain. This marriage is in danger, in these circumstances, of becoming hostile and detached, and also in some danger of becoming violent. Some of the violent marriages I have seen are also in the avoider mode. In fact, after a violent episode, they may entirely deny the event and avoid any conflict for a time, until the pain builds up once again.

Avoiders tend to suppress problems and minimize their importance, but they do so at some cost. There is evidence that the suppression of emotions leads to physiological arousal. Hence, it is possible that avoiders may have somatic problems that result from living with unresolved and unresolvable problems that have no channel of expression.

10.9.1. Detailed Qualitative Analysis of Risks

10.9.1.1. Speculations About the Risks of Conflict Avoidance

In the following three excerpts from the conflict–resolution discussions of conflict avoiders, I illustrate some of my speculations about the risks of this adaptation to having a stable marriage.

10.9.1.1.1. Risk 1: They Live with the Pain of Unsolved Solvable Problems

It is interesting that 30% of the couples in this study in the avoider group had sexual problems, with the problem being that the husband wanted sex more often than his wife. This was a remarkable coincidence, and it would be interesting if this unusually high frequency of this problem held up in subsequent studies for avoiders. This may be a particular risk for a marriage in which relatively little negative emotion is expressed. One of the functions of dealing with negativity may be that it manages to regulate intimacy so it does not decay.

The following couple discusses a sexual problem. Again, he wants to have sex more often than she does. For couple No. 163 in the DUO83 study, this discussion begins with the wife first bringing up a conversation she had with their sister-in-law about her attitude. They then unite in gossip against the attitude of the sister-in-law, and this unity helps them to feel good about their own marriage.

W: . . . just because (her husband) Dave is a man and she is a woman, she's not gonna drop everything she wants to do just to satisfy . . .
H: Just to please him. Yeah.
W: . . . his needs. . . . You were saying that if I had that attitude . . .
H: Yeah, that, oh, I don't know, that, that'd disturb me with that kind of attitude, uh, she would really be thinking about it like that, like it's disturbing her and . . .
W: Well, that's, you know, in in contrast to that, do you think that we have, I don't know, do you feel better about ours? Or about, I guess, our conclusions or agreements or, you know, maybe stop and think back, uh, three years ago, right after we first got married.
H: Yeah.

They agree that their marriage has improved greatly, and that especially The Problem, a sexual problem, has gotten somewhat better, particularly in comparison with their sister-in-law's marriage.

W: And think about how you felt about it then and maybe how you feel about it now, you know, have we come to some kind of agreement or something?
H: Oh, I think better than they had.

They also agree that they are more secure with one another now, but the husband adds:

H: . . . the actual problem, we haven't dealt with it, anymore, any differently since then, I don't believe, I don't know if we really changed.

But the wife says that she is certain that they are both feeling different about the problem, because they are so much more secure with one another. She and he then agree that the problem probably has diminished in importance. They spend the rest of their conversation minimizing the relative importance of the problem, both agreeing that it would never break up the marriage. However, the husband adds that the problem is something he simply tolerates.

W: Tolerate?
H: Ahh, yeah, that's the word. I'd say more of a tolerate, I tolerate the situation and I don't rebel against it, against it and say, you know, beg and plead, you know whatever.

They discuss whether this deprivation would ever lead the husband to be unfaithful, and he affirms that it would not.

H: . . . (it's) something I . . . I guess I put out of my mind but . . . oh, I . . . maybe that's one of the things I fantasize over, I suppose, you know, just . . . goin' along with . . .

10.9.1.1.2. Risk 2: Negative Emotions Are Frightening

In the following discussion of couple No. 161 from DUO83, one can see how conflict avoiders view the expression of negative emotions.

W: But I mean I guess that we just have to expect every once in a while somebody's gonna have an outburst. Probably it'll be me, too. As a reaction to what we're going through.
H: Hmm.
W: And just be ready for it, I guess. We'll have to tolerate it, I suppose . . .
H: But, yeah, it depends on the severity of your, I know, if, if you can tell sometimes it's building up to that.
W: Well . . .
H: For example, when,
W: When I was talking last night?
H: Or even the other day when we came home from the trip and I thought everything was OK and you were kind of frustrated with

the fact that we went to a ball game and . . . you actually . . . uh . . . that experience was pleasant that night. That was . . .

W: Well, I'm . . . sometimes I'm angry at myself. . . . Well I knew last night when I was saying those things and being kind of I knew halfway I was saying some irrational things and even as I said them I was aware of what I was saying and I was almost ready to laugh about it . . .

H: . . . I was kind of overwhelmed by the whole thing because I went down with that approach of, you know, we were talking about not having enough frequency of sex and I was trying to be nice and then your attitude just went the other way and started off on all this other stuff. And this negativism. . . . I was trying to be nice and extending myself and you came back the other way and I said what the hell is going on with her? Or second, What is she so bitchy about? . . .

W: . . . It was almost funny, though, 'cause I, I could almost laugh when you called me "Bitch!" as you went down the stairs . . .

They talk about how they keep avoiding issues and then "things build up" and they "lash out at each other," with the wife being the one "who finally blows," by which they mean expressing anger.

10.9.1.1.3. Risk 3: Not Having the Skills to Work Out Unavoidable Conflict

In life, there are unfortunately times when conflict may be unavoidable. Conflict avoiders try to minimize these times, and, failing that, they minimize the importance of the conflict when it is unavoidable. The following example is from the conversation of couple No. 166 in DUO83.

They are building a house that her father is financing. Building one's own house is recognized as a stressful experience, even under the best of circumstances. When one's in-law is financing the operation, the complications can be enormous, even if the father-in-law is not intrusive. In this case, however, the father-in-law is extremely involved with all the details of the construction and has strong opinions about what his daughter's house should look like. They talk about when the workmen are coming.

H: So that I doubt if they're home, so we don't know when they're coming . . .

W: That's what I mean. I thought they said Tuesday or Wednesday.

H: Well, I wasn't around for any of that conversation.

W: You were the one who told me.

H: How can I tell you when I'm not even around when any of the conversation is made? Your father's doing the deal, not me.
W: No, he didn't talk with Ed. You talked with Ed.
H: I didn't even know they couldn't get anybody to finish. I've never even met this finisher.

Notice that in this clip of interaction, there is implicit conflict involving her father, but neither of them say anything like, "This is stressful having your father so closely involved" or "I feel caught between you and my Dad."

W: . . . you can't have bare wires. They won't close on it with bare wires.
H: Well, cause I figured, like the bathroom lights, the makeup lights, maybe Wicks or somebody less expensive can . . .
W: Well, then you gotta figure out how.
H: Your father picked some out at Wicks for the bathroom I think already, so . . .
W: No, he knows what I wanted . . . 'cause I told him I didn't like any of the lights they had.

It is clear from this discussion that the husband feels cut out of the decision-making process.

W: . . . and then we're gonna have Mom's mirror in the center of it. So we don't have to buy a mirror.
H: Mom's mirror? What mirror?
W: She's got an antique mirror.
H: Well, why should we take her mirror?
W: 'Cause she doesn't have a place to put it, so she said I could have it.
H: Um.
W: It's just a mirror.

As they continue, she describes her plans for the house's lighting. Again, he voices his objections, which clearly have to do with being left out of the decision making.

W: . . . 'cause the outside lights, we can go with a cheaper light, or something, but, um . . .
H: What about sixty-three thousand dollars and I allotted five hundred for lights. And everything else is fixed prices that we can't change.

However, instead of addressing this concern directly, the wife deals with it indirectly by continuing to discuss specifics.

W: Umm-hmm. What are we gonna do, 'cause you see track lighting's only on sale 'till the end of this month, also, right?

This approach of not dealing with her husband's feelings does not work. Instead, it leads to negative affect getting expressed within the context of a discussion that continues on and on about the details of the lighting. This is the hit-and-run sniping that Fitzpatrick (1989) described.

H: I think it's probably over with. Probably lost that.
W: You said until July 31st.
H: It was in the paper. It's in the paper there's two days that they had a special on.
W: That's not what you told me.
H: If you can't read the paper, you don't have enough interest, that's okay.
W: I haven't had time to sit down and read the paper. I have other things to do, like you.

Unable to deal with this escalating negative affect, they continue to discuss the details of the lighting sale.

W: But you read it to me and you said July 31st, the end of the July.
H: It's two days, I think, the 29th and 21st, or some days like that.
W: Well we haven't come to that yet.
H: I think. I don't remember what the two days were but there were two Saturdays.
W: . . . 'cause today is only the 24th.
H: There's two Saturdays it was gonna be.
W: Well if it was the 29th, that's this coming Saturday.
H: But I'm not sure it was the 29th. I know it was two days.
W: Was it in today's paper?
H: No. I ain't seen today's paper, so it's, you know . . . I had to get the insulation done.

After this frustrating exchange, he changes the topic. However, notice again how the father's authority slips in as an issue for him.

W: Well maybe there was . . . Hmm?
H: Your father said we had to get the insulation done, so I, we went and did insulation yesterday.

W: When was the sale in the paper?

H: I think it was in during the week this past week, I think I saw it, when I come home and read all the papers, or looked through 'em. Think it was in there, telling what days.

W: Now I read some of this week's papers and I didn't see it.

The conversation then continues on about what kind of deal she can get on lighting, again ignoring the feelings that surround the father's directing the pace at which the house will be built, and even selecting lighting for intimate parts of the house.

How do they deal with the negative affect generated by this style of discussing details and ignoring feelings? What they do is try to end up on a good note by discussing other aspects of the construction that do not seem to involve her father. It is not a very successful attempt. At the end of the conversation, they both seem very tired.

10.9.1.1.4. Risk 4: Violence—The Rushe Hypothesis

Regina Rushe, a graduate student in my laboratory, formulated the hypothesis that one type of violent couple could be described as conflict avoiding in between episodes of violence. Her hypothesis is that, lacking the skills to deal with negative events, negative feelings build up and are suppressed, only to be vented eventually in an explosive manner. Horrified about the ensuing violence, the couple then becomes highly avoidant of conflict, letting suppressed negative feelings build up until the tension is so great that another violent or nonviolent fight occurs. Depending on when in this cycle the couple is observed, Rushe suggested that they will appear different, sometimes seeming quite avoidant of conflict, and sometimes quite tense and hostile.

10.9.1.2. Speculations About the Risks of the Volatile Style

10.9.1.2.1. Risk 1: There Are No Private Negative Feelings: No Hurt Is Spared

There is a relentless commitment in this marriage toward ferreting out the real honest truth about feelings, at whatever cost. This can be very exciting and brave, and it can lead to a great deal of intimate bonding, but it also can be terrifying. It is a style that permits very little to remain hidden and unexplored, even some scary or ugly truths about the relationship.

The following couple (No. 297) discusses their sexual problem, and the husband will not accept his wife's attempts to attribute the problem to situational factors. He insists that the problem lies more in enduring traits that are related to fundamental differences between them.

W: You have to think of all those extenuating circumstances we've had too, I think.

H: Yeah, but this time in my life, I've come to the realization that life is one long set of extenuating circumstances.

She makes a second attempt to attribute their problem to the circumstances of their children coming into their bed for comfort. He will have none of this. Instead, he sees her feelings as the central problem and one that needs to be changed.

H: I think we have a basic . . .

W: No.

H: A kind of basic, I don't know, difference in philosophy or something about it, that we almost approach it backwards, like you see it as a natural outgrowth or expression of the way that you feel about the other person and you have to demonstrate that feeling, before you can have the expression.

W: Mmm-hmm.

H: And I see it more like in terms of what that guy was saying last night on the otherwise vapid show we were watching, that, uh, . . .

W: Don't touch my chair (laughs).

H: (laughs) that uh . . .

W: They don't want you to.

H: I know, I know, that it's designed to be a pleasurable experience and that it's designed to and can, and can change the way you feel about yourself.

W: I know, and sometimes I feel that way, I mean sometimes I think I could probably, you know, I don't know.

H: Go ahead, complete the thought. That was going to be interesting, I think.

The husband senses that his wife is concealing something that is potentially interesting and powerful. He feels excited and compelled to explore what has up to now remained unsaid.

W: (Laugh. Sigh)

H: They're going to erase all of this later.

W: Sometimes I think I could have sex with a perfect stranger, not every stranger, and enjoy, and just have no strings attached to it that would be enjoyable, but sometimes there's so much other things between us.

H: It might not actually be enjoyable, but it, certainly the idea of it somehow is . . .

W: . . . but because other times there's so many other things between us, that that gets in the way.

H: Mmm-hmm

W: I guess, somehow . . .

H: Mmm-hmm

W: You know . . .

H: Mmm-hmm Mmm-hmm, yeah.

W: . . . that sometimes I think it would be enjoyable just to go and yeah just to go and have sex with somebody I don't know

H: Well . . .

W: . . . and just enjoy it on a physical, you know, just physically, and not have any of the other worries that go along with.

H: That's, that's what I thought our disagreement was, that I, that I could think of it uh in terms of gratification.

W: But I can't think of it that way with *you*.

H: Uh-huh.

W: Because there's a whole lot of other things that get in the way, if I'm a little peeved with you about something, sometimes if we're making love, I just get, rrrrr, you know if there's some vestige of of . . .

H: I'm surprised that you've ever made love to me when you feel that way.

The wife now feels that she has gone too far, that she must discuss the fact that she frequently fantasizes about having sex with a total stranger, and that she feels weary in their relationship because of all the conflict.

W: . . . argument. . . . And that's why the other will appeal to me. I don't want to deal with other problems that are interfering with my sexual feelings and and . . .

H: You don't want to work on problems, you just want to get it on.

W: (laugh) and that's why the other way may be, I don't know, but . . .

H: Mmm-hmm . . .

W: I don't know, sometimes I'm feeling frustrated with the other things in life, or it's occurring to me how long we've been together, sometimes that seems sometimes I think Gees, twenty two is really young to have committed oneself, almost, you know, I don't know, I'm going through a mid-life crisis, I guess.

H: Yeah, I know, sometimes during the day when I daydream and watch all the women by on campus though, not in quite those, uh, terms of imagining a sequence of acts . . . just admiring the fit of those jeans, uh. Now lately you've been getting these feelings, I remember there were periods where I felt that way, and we'd get into a fight or something and one or the other of us says something to the effect of, well that did it, if you're going to be that way about it, then we'll have to separate or something like that. And I'll actually entertain the possibility of you know, the same sort of way, but invariably I don't like the feeling, the idea of, if I imagine that, you know.

W: Yeah, well, yeah, there's some aspects just to . . .
H: There are . . .
W: Like I think, Oh freedom sounds good, but there are other aspects that are just too unsettling.
H: But then yeah I figured.

Although they have restated their commitment to one another, there is a lot that is tentative in it. Thus, the volatile style can run the risk of an emotional brinkmanship, as part of a relentless commitment to completely exploring their differences.

10.9.1.2.2. Risk 2: Deterioration to Endless Quarreling and Bickering

This is perhaps the most obvious risk of a confrontative relationship, in which it is fair game to persuade one another about everything, including feelings. The quarreling and bickering can become much worse if it begins to include defensiveness and contempt. That is always a danger when attempts at persuasion meet stubborn active or passive resistance. This kind of relationship is often parodied in comedy, as with the famous couple, "The Bickersons," or the comic strip "The Lockhorns."

The following couple's (No. 267) conflict discussion is so uniform that it is possible to start anywhere in the transcript and take a nearly identical excerpt. I illustrate this by sampling from various portions of the interaction. I begin at the beginning.

H: OK, you start.
W: No, I did before.

Even in these first two lines, there is evidence that they will disagree about anything.

H: OK, what's your view on the money, as if we didn't know.

This sarcastic question is an example of mild contempt.

W: You got butter on your hands and you know it.

The contempt is reciprocated with an insult.

H: Don't (laugh). That's it?
W: Yeah. Well you know that.
H: (large sigh) I'm what?
W: Well, you, Herman, you know you got butter in your hands, you can't have a nickel if you . . .
H: Well don't keep saying that, it's stupid.
W: . . . you'd spend it.
H: I had a nickel one time and I didn't spend it.
W: Oh sure.
H: On what?
W: Fish.
H: How many did I buy? Two since I've been here that's it.

They are off and running in this pattern of him being defensive and sarcastic and her being attacking, belligerent, and contemptuous. To her, his tropical fish are a waste of money. They also disgust her. She contends her purchases are for the whole family, not selfish purchases like his. He disagrees with her about how altruistic her purchases are.

W: When I buy something it's because we all use it or it's for somebody.
H: The *Inquirer*?
W: Yes, because you read the *Inquirer*.
H: Only because it's there.
W: Oh, excuse me.

She is offended at his suggestion that she also buys selfishly. Actually, as the discussion unfolds, it becomes clear that they have a great deal of financial autonomy from one another.

W: . . . you have to give me some money.
H: I don't have any money.
W: In the checkbook. You have to give me some money. I know you don't have that much at least I need $10 'cause I have to buy some, uh . . .
H: Well take it out of the checkbook, cause my blood money I'm using.

W: Well, I'm not asking for your blood money. I'm asking for the checkbook.

He is referring to the fact that he literally makes some money selling his blood. He is defensive about his use of this money.

H: Well . . . it's not enough to pay, pay any really, any of the bills.
W: Well, but it helps. When my mother sends some money I put it in for the house. I could keep it all for myself.

Mention of her mother's money opens up a new Pandora's box.

H: I think you oughta, I think you oughta sell your share of the house (chuckles).
W: No.
H: It's your mother's house.
W: I will not.
H: I bet you we could pay off all our bills.
W: That is out of the question.

She later explains that the house is her mother's only security and she will not sell it or take out her share of it. The husband then relents.

H: Ahh, nobody's saying you that, but I'm just saying it's too bad that that didn't happen.
W: . . . It's not going to solve any problem because whatever money you get you spend and then you don't have a thing. . . .

After more discussion of her reasons for being adamant about the house, she then accuses him of not buying anything for their child.

W: But I get, I get mad when you go out and buy a stupid fish and . . .
H: But I what?
W: And you don't get Tracy something.
H: I haven't done any of that for a long time so now you're talking about . . .
W: Poor Tracy.
H: . . . things to the behind. You buy enough for both of us.
W: (laugh) . . . well because I have to buy for you too.

There is a brief break in the antagonism, but it returns quickly to the same pattern.

H: So you admit you spend some too?
W: Yeah, but I buy it for Tracy, most of the stuff.
H: OK, so we're even.
W: Most of the stuff I buy for *her*.
H: There's always a good reason for you to spend money but when I spend it (laugh) it's not a good reason.
W: If you buy something for her I don't say anything.
H: But so (laugh) so you shouldn't say anything if I buy something for me either . . .
W: Well the things you don't buy things for you itself like clothes or stuff, you just buy like cigars, stinkin' cigars and stuff like that.

10.9.1.2.3. Risk 3: Violence

In a research project with Neil Jacobson, I saw examples of physically violent couples whose pattern of interaction appears to be a distortion of the volatile couple. In one example of this interaction, the wife begins by stating her opinion that they do not save anything and she is worried about their finances. The husband responds that she is completely wrong, that they do not have a problem with their finances, and that he has been investing for both of them by his purchases of old coins. He presents a view of himself that appears somewhat ego-maniacal, as a great entrepreneur and investor. Actually, he holds two minimally paying jobs and has very little education. In contrast, she is quite educated and has a professional level job.

He continues persuading her that her feelings of anxiety about their finances are wrong in an interesting fashion. His pattern of behavior led Rushe to develop an exciting new observational scheme for coding power. To develop this scheme, Rushe reviewed diverse literature on power and persuasion, including such diverse areas as brainwashing techniques and styles of salesmanship.

One of these styles of salesmanship is called *lowballing* and one is called *highballing*. In lowballing, the salesperson gets the potential customer to start agreeing and saying yes, usually to platitudes with which anyone would agree. "If I could show you how you could make a profit, and still buy this encyclopedia, you'd want to do it right?" Then the persuasion begins by showing the customer how he is essentially making a profit with his purchase. In the same way, the husband in this couple begins by saying, "Wouldn't you agree, honey, that marriage is a partnership?" She says "Yes." "Well, Ok," he says, "and haven't I invested far more than you have in the coins?" And so the persuasion goes. By the way, in highballing, the salesperson may begin with something like, "Would you pay $10,000 for this encyclopedia?" No, says the customer. "Would you pay $5,000?" Absolutely not. "Well, then, say that you were going to buy one and money was no object, what would you expect to pay? Go on, take a guess." As the conversation proceeds, the customer is amazed that the cost is as little as $3 a day. This is the idea in highballing.

In this interaction, the husband also employs a particular kind of domineering style. He lectures his wife. He has a patronizing voice tone, as if he is being very patient with someone who is not very smart. He leans forward, never breaking off eye contact, and he lowers his head and raises his eyes so that he appears strong and menacing to most viewers. There is a charismatic quality to this kind of interaction.

On the other hand, his wife, speaks softly, disagrees with him quietly under her breath, and tries hard not to rile him. She qualifies everything she says by adding such phrases as, "I know you've been trying hard to invest in things. . . ." She is clearly upset if one studies her facial expressions. There are brief indications of anger and contempt (see appendix for more details of how to code these emotions on the face), but these emotions are not expressed verbally.

In Rushe's new observational coding scheme, she described various kinds of persuasion in marital interaction, including those that undermine a person's sense of what is real and what is not real. These insidious persuasion techniques at times resemble brainwashing techniques, in which the goal is to make over the self of the prisoner. An example of this pattern involves the use of what I usually code as validation. In one example of lowballing, validation is used after criticisms to short circuit the partner's retaliation and instead elicit agreement. It is a tactic to control the other person by squelching their response to the criticisms. When the partner responds to the criticisms, the lowballer complains that the partner was agreeing all along and that he (or she) now feels betrayed. All of this argument can become a very tangled knot, so that the person being lowballed can become very confused and overpowered.

In some dramatic recent trials, such as the child abuse Steinberg/Nussbaum case in New York City, there was a strong case made that the charismatic personality of Mr. Steinberg had in fact brainwashed the child's mother and led to her becoming passive about the abuse by Mr. Steinberg, which eventually led to the child's death. The phenomenon is similar to transformations that have been reported when people are kidnapped and held hostage, in which they come to identify with the aggressor. In literature on concentration camps, this phenomenon was called "identification with the aggressor" by psychoanalysts.

Dutton (1988) speculated that in violent marriages there is a kind of intense negative and intense positive affect he referred to as "traumatic bonding." He reviewed animal research that suggested that mixing intense rewards and punishments in training dogs results in greater loyalty and attachment of the dog to its master than purely positive or negative techniques.

I do not suggest that the volatile marriage is violent, but that one form of violent marriage may resemble the volatile style gone wrong, and, as such, perhaps violence is one potential risk of the volatile marriage.

10.9.1.2.4. Risk 4: Teasing and Its Pitfalls

Teasing is a common part of most marital interaction. However, in the volatile couple my observation is that teasing is much more common than in the three other stable types. There is a risk inherent in this teasing, namely, that it may escalate.

In many couples, teasing itself may lead to diffuse physiological arousal. However, in volatile couples this is generally not the case unless the teasing touches upon a raw nerve or if one partner feels cornered. The following two examples of discussions that involve teasing are annotated with some data on heart rates.

Male resting heart rate is usually about 72 beats per minute (BPM). My data suggest that when it goes up about 10%, to about 80 BPM, there is evidence for the start of *diffuse physiological arousal* that makes it hard to process information, leads to increased defensiveness or hostility, and begins the flooding process. So look for my notes at any heart rate increase beyong 80 BPM. The next marker for heart rate increases occurs at near 100 BPM. This tends to be the point at which the sympathetic nervous system cuts in ("fight or flight" response) and adrenaline is secreted in relatively large doses (Rowell, 1986).

In the first example (DUO87, No. 134), the couple tease each other often. They enjoy this style of interaction. Here we see the aftermath of this teasing. She has teased him about his not being able to parallel park, and he then retaliated with a tease about her not being a very good lover. She is hurt and he is trying to convince her that he didn't mean it.

H: I'm sorry about this morning.
W: Well, I think we should talk about this morning. (chuckling) I mean, we have 15 minutes we have to fill up.
H: Okay.
W: Ever since the other night, you've been making fun of what I said.
H: I just think it's, uh— it was funny. You know? Nothing real personal. It was just funny.
W: What was funny about it?

H: The sequence in your— in which you said it.

W: Well, if— I mean . . . we tease each other a little bit about sex all the time, anyway. And make remarks that the other have said. But you've been like really teasing me about it. Not like in loving little jabs, but like "Muh-muh-muh, muh- muh-muh."

H: Well, sometimes I don't realize what I'm . . .

W: Watch your hand.

H: . . . I don't realize that I'm teasing, because I love to tease so much. And, uh, I get an issue that's, uh, sticky with you, you know, and I tease you about it alot. And, uh . . . it's just my own mean satisfaction I guess.

W: Uh, what do you get from it?

H: Ahhh. I don't know. Just laughter. Humor.

W: To see somebody else squirm?

H: (exhaling) No. Yeah, I suppose.

W: You en— you, you enjoy that?

H: Sometimes.

W: Well—

H: But it's a fully mean of me to do that, and I'm sorry. And I don't think I'll do that no more. Anymore.

W: Well . . . and then this morning . . . you made a nasty remark about—

H: That was just because I wanted— you made me awful about 'cause I couldn't parallel park.

W: (chuckles)

H: And that—

W: (chuckles) I can't help it. You can't parallel park.

H: And I have to get back at you somehow. And that's just another step meaner than what you did.

W: But there must be some truth to what you said.

H: No, no. There's not any truth to it at all.

W: But there is truth to the fact that you can't parallel park. You said that yourself.

H: (burps) That's right. ((Excuse me.))

W: ((And I was trying)) to— I was just trying to . . . (((laughs)))

H: (((chuckles)))

W: I was just trying to point out that if there's something you can't do, that if you take a little time to practice, or let someone instruct, you could do it better.

H: Can you parallel park the truck?

W: Yes. Dave, I do. In downtown Indianapolis. Almost every day.

H: (exhales) Oh, I can never do that.

W: But you can. See, if you say "I can't do it," then that means "I won't try." And my point of telling you about that, was that you— if you say "I won't try," then you can't.

H: Right. **HIS HEART RATE: 80 BPM; this is already aroused**

W: But if you make an effort, then you can.

H: Right.

W: But that's not the point. The point is, you then made a very negative comment about my sexual abilities.

H: (laughs) But I didn't mean it. That's what you gotta understand. **HIS HEART RATE: 96.3 BPM. His heart rate has gone up 16 beats a minute in 0.35 seconds! This is extreme arousal, and it is around the level when adrenaline starts getting secreted at high levels.**

W: But how do I know that?

H: But I'm telling you, and we're supposed to be honest with each other, and I am.

W: (sigh) But you know— I mean, sex is probably one of the issues that we have recurring problems about.

H: It's, it's one of the least. Let's put it that way, 'cause we have other recurring problems such as money and so forth, and in-laws.

A little while later, in this discussion his heart rate exceeds 100 beats a minute:

W: Yeah. I mean, obviously it's real sensitive. Or your teasing wouldn't upset me. 'Cause it doesn't up-upset me about anything else that you say. And Lord knows, you say some pretty crude things.

H: Well . . . I think some of it is probably because of our size.

W: That's probably part of it.

H: Which is neither here nor there, but it probably affects us, you know.

W: And you think that makes it harder for us to talk about?

H: Uh-huh. It, it probably doesn't hurt— you know, help it any. I mean . . .

W: What else?

H: And the fact that our upbringing was different. And we have different . . . you know, points of view on it. I know I do. **HIS HEART RATE EXCEEDS 100 BPM**

W: How so?

H: Well, I was told, always taught that it was a— never, uh, to be discussed or anything ((like that.))

W: ((Hmmm.))

H: And, uh, it was, uh . . . and it was never discussed, with me.
W: You think my family's more open about that?
H: Uh-huh.
W: Yeah. They really are. I mean, I think they have a pretty healthy attitude about it. Not that they sit around and talk about sex, when I was growing up. But they do so more now that we're adults.
H: Umm. Uh-huh?
W: The way they, you know, make jokes and tease and stuff.
H: And I think perhaps that's probably what it basically, you know . . . ((the bottom line.))
W: ((You know, I hadn't thought)) about that.
      HIS HEART RATE NOW HAS GONE DOWN TO 82.4 BPM, still high, but *a bit* **more relaxed.**

The second example (DUO87 No. 224) is a volatile couple in which the husband does a great deal of teasing and does not validate his wife's feelings at all. She says that she would like to save some of their money and not live so much from hand to mouth. This transcript shows that for a volatile couple the confrontation and the total lack of validation need not at all lead to physiological arousal or flooding.

W: . . . to pay the bills, and still have enough extra when it comes somebody's birthday, that we can just go out and buy something. It's always, (inhales) we don't have the cash so we have to charge it. And then the bills come, and then it's just worse than ever.
H: Katherine, I took . . .
W: (swallows)
H: . . . a hundred and fifty dollars out of the savings, so that you could pay your nieces and nephew. And that languished, for days and days and day. It ((could have been in the bank . . .)) **HIS HEART RATE: 63.3 BPM. HER HEART RATE: 71.3 BPM. NEITHER ONE IS PHYSIOLOGICALLY AROUSED**
W: ((((inhales))))
H: . . . earning interest. ((But I got it . . .))
W: ((I, uh−))
H: . . . so that you could send it to them, and you didn't do anything.
W: I am sometimes careless about letting things slide. But it's ((usually when I'm being feelin . . .))
H: ((((sniff) (clears throat) (faint) Excuse me.)))
W: . . . pressured by other things, in my life.
H: But you feel pressured all the time about ((something or other.))

He continues to invalidate her feelings and to tease her. She is thinking about how she can save more money. But his joke about getting rid of the baby does get a rise in heart rate from her.

W: . . . how to stretch thing— well, that's, ((I've explained all of that. That's for two weeks. (sniff) And for how many people?))

H: ((And that— that isn't— that doesn't count if you— that doesn't count the thirty-some dollars that I spent on)) baby stuff.

W: That's— yes, but, uhh, how many people does, does that feed? You, and me, and Crystal, and Eve, and Erin . . . lots of times. And the baby. That's . . . a lot of people. ((For— and most of it, for two weeks. Not all of it.))

H: ((Well, we always think we can't afford the baby. We should get rid of the baby.)) **HIS HEART RATE: 69.2 BPM; HER HEART RATE: 89.2 BPM, SLIGHTLY AROUSED.**

W: (inhales) (chuckling) Well, we can't get rid of the baby.

H: ((No.))

10.9.1.3. Speculations About the Risks of the Validating Style

I suspect that there are two risks associated with this type of marriage. The first is a loss of romance, and the second is a loss of self. The two probably are related to the strong sense of "we-ness" that this type of marriage attempts to create (see Fitzpatrick, 1989).

In the following conversation, the couple (No.229) discusses the fact that the wife does not like her husband's friends.

H: But see, the thing that sometimes I think about, sometimes I feel guilty that I've, you know, gone out with my friends.

W: Well, I, that's your own thing, because I don't think that you shouldn't go out with your own friends. And I don't hold that against you and you know I don't.

H: I know you don't hold that against me but . . .

W: I don't care.

H: I'm just telling you sometimes the way I feel.

W: I know. I know you feel guilty about it and I, I really don't care, I, you know, in fact, I think it's kind of good you have people that you like to be with that aren't necessarily friends of mine. I think it's OK.

Yet she is critical of his friends, says she feels uncomfortable with them, and disapproves of some of their habits. He says that he thinks her feelings are hurt if he chooses to be with his friends for an evening, which excludes his being with her.

H: I have these real mixed feelings about how to deal with that when I go out, you know, with my own friends, I think I'm afraid I'm gonna hurt your feelings.
W: I know you are. I know and I, I really mean it that I don't, I, I even get that way with you sometimes. I think I'm gonna hurt you feelings and, and you tell me, you know, that it's not hurting your feelings. Maybe we . . .
H: It doesn't, 'cause I like to know that we are, you know, we can maintain independence.
W: I do too.

In another couple (No. 144), the issue appears to be his insecurity with her support of his development as an artist.

H: . I'm painting for myself, and hopefully the people will pay for it
W: But doing bank portraits isn't painting for yourself.
H: . . . Until I can paint what I want for money, then I have to do bank portraits on the side. You see?

She is quite supportive of his explorations in theater, writing, and painting. Yet she expresses concern about how he will do all this and still be with the family, particularly the children. He senses this.

H: But, you know, there's no way I could ever be an actor and be a family man too. There is, but not to the potential of acting that I want. So I pretty well have to put it out of my head. But it's still there. It still bothers me every time I see West Heaven, it bothers me and I can't explain it.
W: I believe you. I know.

Despite this understanding, there is conflict about these separate identities.

H: But I see years down the road getting into acting or theater, writing plays. I do.
W: I know.
H: What do you think about that? You hate it. I know you. You hate it.
W: It's not that I hate it. I don't hate it. It's just that I hate to see your art going to waste.

Still she adds an air of practicality to his deliberations that frightens him.

H: . . . You'd like to see me doing lily portraits and landscapes and.
W: Yeah. Not all the time. But for the State Fair, yeah.
H: See, you don't believe in what I believe in.

Eventually she brings up the issue. She says she believes he will get into acting someday.

W: That eventually you'll get into it someday.
H: And you think I'll be a big fool.
W: No, I just don't think we'll . . .
H: Live off of it.
W: No, I just don't . . .
H: See there, again, I think that comes back into believing of I believe I could do it . . .
W: Yeah, but what about us?
H: . . . Well, you're gonna be there. I'm not gonna abandon you.
W: Well, you're gonna have an acting career and an art career and a wife and kids all at the same time. And a writing career.

This is the issue. How can they be a family and have the kind of "we-ness" that validators seek, and how can he simultaneously explore and realize his full potential as an individual?

10.9.1.4. Risks of All Types

If my theory is correct that each type of marriage represents an equilibrium, a kind of adaptation to balancing positivity and negativity in marriage, then any disequilibrium places the marriage at risk for entering the cascade toward dissolution. Each marriage has inherent safeguards against this possibility. The validators' safeguard is that they are excellent at resolving important conflicts. They may experience negative affect, but it does not become an absorbing state. They have all sorts of repair mechanisms for solving problems. The volatile couple has an extremely strong attachment, one that Dutton (1988) called traumatic bonding. Traumatic bonding results from extremes of both negativity and positivity. Dutton (1988) reviewed both animal and human research that suggests that relationships based on such extremes have much stronger attachments than other combinations (e.g., only positivity). I also noticed that volatile couples are bonded very strongly to one another. The avoiders tend to have extremely strong social supports and a traditional value system that keep the marriage together.

11

There are Two Types of Nonregulated Couples

If I am right that the volatile couple is not a candidate for the dysfunctional interaction patterns that Raush et al. (1974) had in mind, what, in terms of the longitudinal stability criterion, is a dysfunctional interaction pattern? In this chapter, I suggest that the key dimension involves extremely high levels of defensiveness, and that there are two styles of highly defensive couples: engaged and detached.

Recall that I discovered that the typology of regulated versus nonregulated couples made it possible to distinguish marriages in a number of domains, including health, physiology, behavior, affect, marital satisfaction, and the risk for marital dissolution. I was encouraged to find that these two marital types, regulated and nonregulated couples, were quite different at the time of their classification and followed quite different courses over the ensuing 4 years.

Nonregulated couples, those for whom the balance between positive and negative affective behavior failed to increasingly favor positive affective behaviors over time, had marriages that appeared to be much more dysfunctional than those of regulated couples.

In the realm of quality of the marital relationship, nonregulated couples reported lower levels of marital satisfaction (both at the time they were classified and 4 years later), and nonregulated wives rated marital problems as being more severe. Over the 4-year study period, nonregulated couples were more likely to consider marital dissolution and more likely to actually separate. Self-report measures of marital satisfaction were among the most widely accepted barometers of marital quality; consideration of dissolution and actual separation were arguably among the clearest behavioral signs of marital distress. Thus, in terms of both kinds of criteria, the relationship quality of nonregulated couples was lower than that of regulated couples.

212

In the realm of interaction, MICS coders rated the behavior of nonregulated couples as being characterized by negatively tinged behaviors such as conflict engagement, stubbornness, and withdrawal from interaction. SPAFF coders rated nonregulated wives as less likely to express the positive emotions of interest/caring and joy/enthusiasm and more likely to express disgust/contempt. Both nonregulated husbands and wives were more likely to express the negative emotions of anger and whining. These results from observational coding were consistent with husbands' rating dial data, which indicated that nonregulated husbands felt more negative during the interaction. This combination of MICS behaviors, the character of which would make them unlikely to lead to constructive resolution of problems, coupled with SPAFF emotions, which indicate a lack of positive affect and a surplus of negative affect, are likely to make marital interaction an unpleasant and unproductive aspect of marital life for nonregulated couples. Unpleasant and unproductive interaction does not bode well for the ultimate stability of a marriage.

In the physiological realm, nonregulated wives showed evidence of greater sympathetic nervous system arousal in their cardiovascular responses during their problem-area interactions. Because both faster heart rates and greater vasoconstriction were observed in nonregulated wives, it is likely that they were evidencing heightened arousal in both the alpha-sympathetic and beta-sympathetic branches of the sympathetic nervous system. Although the association was not as strong in the present data, it is worth noting that in my earlier longitudinal work with a different sample of couples, physiological arousal during marital interaction was a strong predictor of future declines in marital satisfaction (Levenson & Gottman, 1985).

In another biological realm, nonregulated wives reported being in poorer health in 1987 than did regulated wives. The basis for this finding is unknown. However, a possible contributor to this finding could be the greater cardiovascular sympathetic nervous system arousal during the 1983 interactions on the part of nonregulated wives. Sustained high levels of sympathetic nervous system activity and/or sympathetic nervous system hyperreactivity often have been suggested as possible mediators of the relation between stress and disease (e.g., Henry & Stephens, 1977).

11.1. THE TWO TYPES OF NONREGULATED COUPLES DEFINED

I next split the nonregulated couples into two groups using the RCISS listener point graph slopes. This split was done in the same way as for regulated couples when I formed engaging and avoiding couple types. When I do this for nonregulated couples, I also obtain two groups, which I call hostile and hostile/detached.

11.2. QUALITATIVE DATA

11.2.1. Hostile Couples

The conversations of hostile couples are characterized by a great deal of direct engagement in conflict and an attentive listener, and by a great deal of defensiveness, usually on the part of both people. One sequence that indexes defensiveness is the mindreading → disagreement sequence. In this sequence, one person attributes a motive, feeling, or behavior to the other person. At times, this statement is accompanied by a "you always" or "you never" phrase, and usually it has a negative voice tone or facial expression that gives the mindreading a blaming or judgmental quality. For example, one person may say, "You never clean up the house. You just don't care how we live!" This is followed by disagreement and elaboration, such as, "I do so clean up a lot. Just the other day I straightened the house before your mother came over!"

An example of a hostile couple follows. There is a great deal of whining and defensiveness in this couple's conversation. They are quite engaged with one another. He is on the attack and she is on the defensive. Throughout the discussion, he never hears her point about how much effort it takes her to take care of their child.

W: Now I know you said something about—you know you go—but it's always been this way, but I remember, okay, listen, before I had Aaron, I remember every single Friday I would clean the house, ya know. I had a day set a week when I would move all the furniture, I'd sweep, I'd polish the table, I'd take out the books from the bookshelf, sweep behind there, then you'd come home from work and say, Oh honey, the house looks so nice, smells like polish and the floors were shiny.

H: All right, but wait a minute, you didn't let me finish.

W: Okay.

H: Uhm, you know, the problem is, not that, well first, that hasn't been gotten for years, ya know.

W: Honey.

H: That was like the first year of our marriage, that was like two years since it was . . .

W: Ever since Aaron was born because when I was pregnant, I remember movin' furniture and stuff, and your Mom told me that, you know, I better stop, you know.

H: Okay.

W: . . . movin' so much furniture or I was gonna cause . . .

H: Yeah, occasionally, occasionally. But that was, that's just like I said, ya know, the dust and stuff like that, but anyway, uh, the problem now is not that, the problem now is that how much effort does it take to move a wet dishrag out of the sink, ya know, and how much effort does it take to pick up . . .

W: Mmm-hmm.

H: . . . can ya know, if it doesn't go in the trash, ya know.

W: I do.

H: No you don't.

W: Honey . . .

H: I see them lying around the kitchen all the time.

W: Just because the trash can runs over, and the thing is . . .

H: No, it's not because it just runs over.

W: Honey, I always put trash in the trash can. The thing is the trash can gets split a lot. But then I pick it up maybe something will roll up I don't see.

H: Well, I guess . . .

W: (Groan) Oh.

Throughout the discussion, he avoids her point that she has much less time to keep the house neat now that she is taking care of their child and in school.

W: I pushed all those books . . .

H: Well that's what I'm saying, you're not using them either. You might as well take the most recent ones and put them away, because—that ya know—

W: The thing is though, the thing is . . .

H: . . . rather than going through the stuff that is already put away.

W: Honey, listen. The thing is for summer session I missed that test so I want to keep that book to study, and then I made two then I had to take two incompletes because I got sick and missed . . .

H: (Inaudible)

W: . . . my finals so I've got notebooks for three classes so that whenever I've got an hour I just like to have the book out, have this book out, you know, refer to it, because I am trying to keep studying. So I like having all those books handy so I can, ya know, Aaron's asleep, I have a half-an-hour, so I can grab one of those books, or grab one of the notebooks and start reviewing.

H: Well, then, I think you need to get rid of the other stuff . . .
W: Mmm-Hmm

The argument proceeds in the same manner, with him offering no support or understanding, and her whining and on the defensive. He tells her she should find the time to clean up, and she finally expresses her feelings.

W: Yeah, honey, listen to me. I know when do I have time? I mean, it irritates me that you know that you act like, well you should do this, you should do that, you know, you should do this, this that, and then everybody else is like, I don't know how you do it, you make such good grades, you take care of your family, you know, you work, you know, and then it's like you Roxanne why don't you do this, why don't you do that. And then everybody else is like giving me the opposite I don't see how you do it, you know we go to family reunions or something and talkin to your aunts, need to take those guys and in there and they say well I couldn't go to school and take care of a kid.
H: Well . . .
W: And I say you should see my house, it's just a mess you know, that's what gets the scars and they say well how can you expect to clean a house when you're doing all this?
H: Well, it's, you know . . .
W: And everybody's like well does Randy help you with housework and stuff? And I'm like well . . .

He protests that he does help and she confronts him.

H: And I do the laundry and I wash the dishes and I . . .
W: Honey, you never, you've washed the dishes twice since we've been married.
H: Oh, c'mon.
W: You have you never go in there and wash dishes. One time you started, too, and then you didn't finish it.

11.2.2. Hostile/Detached Couples

The hostile/detached couple fits Fitzpatrick's (1989) characterization of "sniping" and "hit-and-run" "guerrilla warfare." These people seem quite detached and emotionally uninvolved with one another, but they get into brief episodes of reciprocated attack and defensiveness.

For example, in the following dialogue, the conversation begins innocently, with the wife suggesting that she thinks that they communicate better these days. The husband expresses disgust and contempt facially and tells his wife that he hates her complaining about the hot weather. He tells her he does not want to hear her talk about anything unless it is pleasant. The affect rapidly escalates, and she hears this as a major rejection. There is a great deal of stonewalling on the husband's part during this interaction.

W: Don't you think we get along a little better?
H: Yeah
W: What do you think . . .
H: But I get but I get tired of hearing how hot it is.
W: Well, those are the things people talk about. I'm sorry.
H: They talk once, twice a day at the most. Third time, person like me will scream. Fourth time, it is hot for everybody, not just for you.
W: Well, I'm sorry.
H: Not just the weather, I, uh, talking isn't necessary. I'll listen to something, uh, I'll, I'll listen is pleasant. Otherwise, fighting, fighting is communication, too. Verbal fighting.
W: You lost me there, brother.
H: What?
W: I said you lost me there.
H: If there isn't anything I, I don't enjoy, I don't want to talk about it.
W: You're not particularly enjoying yourself, you just don't wanna talk.
H: Right.
W: That's . . .
H: If it's not pleasant, anything pleasant, I don't wanna talk about. If the subject isn't pleasant.
W: Yeah, you're the only family I've got and damn it, if I have to keep all my problems to myself, I might as well live by myself.

The interaction continues in this manner.

W: . . . aren't those cigarettes something else? I don't particularly like them, do you?
H: (disgusted) Then why do you buy them?

And a second later:

H: . . . when are you going to take care of that damn cauliflower? It's molding again.
W: Really?

H: Yeah, really.
W: It was molding when I bought it. That's why it was so cheap. Cut off parts that I could use.
H: Are you going to use it or not?
W: Look, as long as I'm working, uh, 12, you know, 10 and 11 hours a day, why don't you make . . . cut up some of those vegetables? Wouldn't kill you. You've got 2 hours to kill before you pick me up from work. It really wouldn't and it'd save me time. I could reach in the ice box and grab something in the af . . . uh . . . when I go to work in the morning. It's a really good idea.
H: Instead of reading your five and penny novels, you can spend five minutes a day and do that yourself.

This example illustrates some of the interaction patterns characteristic of the hostile/detached marriage.

11.3. QUANTITATIVE ANALYSES

11.3.1. Problem Solving

Table 11.1 summarizes the problem-solving differences between the two groups of nonregulated couples. In addition to being described as more withdrawn by MICS coders, husbands in hostile/detached marriages, compared with husbands in hostile marriages, were more defensive (marginal effect), more verbally contemptuous, and less positive in presenting their views about the problem. Husbands in the two groups also differed in the slope of their speaker point graphs. The slope was more positive for husbands in hostile marriages than for husbands in hostile/detached marriages. This result is notable, because the groups were divided on the basis of listener point graphs, and yet husbands differed on speaker point graph slopes as well. Wives also were more verbally contemptuous in the hostile/detached compared with the hostile group.

11.3.2. Affect

As Table 11.2 shows, husbands in hostile marriages were more interested in their wives, showed more affection (marginal), and showed less disgust/contempt than husbands in hostile/detached marriages. Wives in hostile marriages showed more interest, whined more, but expressed less disgust/contempt than wives in hostile/detached marriages. Table

TABLE 11.1
Problem-Solving Differences Between Hostile and Hostile/Detached Couples

Variable	Hostile	Hostile/Detached	t	df	p
MICS					
Hus. defensive	2.40	2.19	.25	32	ns
Hus. engages	5.00	6.65	−1.32	32	ns
Hus. stubborn	1.06	2.27	−1.64	22	ns
Hus. withdrawn	7.95	10.87	−1.65	32	ns
Wife defensive	2.54	3.90	−1.10	32	ns
Wife engages	5.28	6.22	−.58	32	ns
Wife stubborn	1.91	2.21	−.47	32	ns
Wife withdrawn	5.86	10.05	−2.36	29	.025
Number of turns	97.06	89.16	.61	33	ns
RCISS					
Hus. complain/criticize	.31	.34	−.31	33	ns
Hus. Defensive	.36	.50	−1.93	33	.063
Hus. verb. contempt	.04	.15	−3.06	22	.006
Hus. stonewall	.82	1.82	−5.51	33	.000
Hus. pos. ag. bldg.	.58	.33	2.95	33	.006
Hus. assent	.12	.12	−.15	33	ns
Hus. pos. affect	.07	.06	.67	33	ns
Hus. pos. listening	2.12	1.18	4.05	20	.001
Wife complain/criticize	.62	.49	1.12	33	ns
Wife defensive	.40	.45	−.65	33	ns
Wife verbal contempt	.06	.21	−2.46	23	.022
Wife stonewall	.69	1.43	−4.72	31	.000
Wife pos. ag. bldg.	.46	.37	1.21	33	ns
Wife assent	.07	.07	−.17	33	ns
Wife pos. affect	.09	.05	1.52	33	ns
Wife pos. listening	2.14	1.49	2.44	22	.023

11.3 shows that husbands in hostile marriages moved their facial muscles more and smiled more (other smiles; marginal) than husbands in hostile/detached marriages. Wives in hostile marriages smiled more and showed less sadness (marginal) than wives in hostile/detached marriages.

11.3.3. Pervasiveness and Rebound

The two groups of husbands could be discriminated in the events-of-the-day conversation. Husbands in hostile marriages showed more interest than husbands in hostile/detached marriages. Wives also could be differentiated. Wives in hostile marriages showed more humor and more interest than wives in hostile/detached marriages. In the positive conversation, which assesses rebound from conflict, there was mixed

TABLE 11.2
Affect Differences on the SPAFF Between Hostile and Hostile/Detached Couples

Variable	Hostile	Hostile/Detached	t	df	p
Events					
Hus. neutral	54.60	59.83	−.58	31	ns
Hus. humor	13.93	7.33	1.65	18	ns
Hus. affection	1.13	2.94	−1.48	28	ns
Hus. interest	30.73	15.89	2.26	20	.035
Hus. joy	2.33	2.89	−.40	29	ns
Hus. anger	2.27	3.11	−.43	31	ns
Hus. disgust/contempt	2.87	3.28	−.33	31	ns
Hus. whining	.73	.50	.34	16	ns
Hus. sadness	1.27	2.56	−.79	22	ns
Hus. tension/fear	8.20	5.39	1.21	31	ns
Wife neutral	52.07	53.83	−.23	31	ns
Wife humor	16.33	7.44	2.43	17	.026
Wife affection	3.60	2.22	.98	20	ns
Wife interest	32.00	14.94	2.62	20	.016
Wife joy	3.07	3.61	−.38	31	ns
Wife anger	2.27	3.50	−.76	26	ns
Wife disgust/contempt	3.40	2.72	.62	20	ns
Wife whining	1.40	1.80	−.34	33	ns
Wife sadness	.72	.20	1.46	30	ns
Wife tension/fear	6.68	4.70	.70	33	ns
Conflict					
Hus. neutral	38.63	32.76	.67	31	ns
Hus. humor	7.56	5.39	.70	31	ns
Hus. affection	.63	2.41	−1.86	18	.080
Hus. interest	10.69	4.41	2.98	25	.006
Hus. joy	.81	.18	.91	16	ns
Hus. anger	17.75	30.82	−1.39	22	ns
Hus. disgust/contempt	3.19	8.94	−2.80	22	.011
Hus. whining	3.31	2.59	.50	22	ns
Hus. sadness	2.38	1.88	.42	31	ns
Hus. tension/fear	13.56	8.53	.92	31	ns
Wife neutral	28.50	21.88	.88	31	ns
Wife humor	8.19	3.71	1.48	31	ns
Wife affection	.88	1.12	−.41	31	ns
Wife interest	10.19	3.24	2.74	20	.013
Wife joy	.25	.24	.07	25	ns
Wife anger	23.25	35.35	−1.44	31	ns
Wife disgust/contempt	4.69	9.29	−2.46	31	.020
Wife whining	5.08	1.45	2.20	32	.035
Wife sadness	2.56	1.55	1.27	33	ns
Wife tension/fear	22.88	13.27	1.53	31	ns
Positive					
Hus. neutral	43.53	56.89	−1.42	28	ns
Hus. humor	11.20	9.33	.55	31	ns

(continued)

220

TABLE 11.2 *(continued)*

Variable	Hostile	Hostile/Detached	t	df	p
Hus. affection	1.80	1.67	.20	31	ns
Hus. interest	32.07	21.44	1.48	31	ns
Hus. joy	10.13	8.67	.39	31	ns
Hus. anger	1.20	4.28	-1.34	18	ns
Hus. disgust/contempt	2.00	4.56	-1.57	21	ns
Hus. whining	.40	1.17	-.98	24	ns
Hus. sadness	.47	2.22	-2.01	19	.059
Hus. tension/fear	8.20	3.17	2.42	31	.022
Wife neutral	42.53	46.39	-.39	31	ns
Wife humor	14.00	9.44	1.28	20	ns
Wife affection	3.27	3.28	-.01	31	ns
Wife interest	27.20	22.61	.64	31	ns
Wife joy	10.40	11.39	-.21	26	ns
Wife anger	2.20	5.06	-1.43	29	ns
Wife disgust/contempt	.87	4.56	-2.64	31	.013
Wife whining	.96	.20	1.45	31	ns
Wife sadness	1.44	.60	1.11	33	ns
Wife tension/fear	7.40	5.90	.42	33	ns

TABLE 11.3
Facial Affect Differences Between Hostile and Hostile/Detached Couples

Variable	Hostile	Hostile/Detached	t	df	p
Hus. anger	10.63	7.32	1.13	33	ns
Hus. contempt	2.69	1.95	.95	33	ns
Hus. disgust	1.00	2.05	-1.34	25	ns
Hus. fear	5.19	3.68	.94	33	ns
Hus. sadness	.81	.79	.07	33	ns
Hus. Duchenne smiles	16.44	9.95	1.38	23	ns
Hus. other smiles	18.13	9.68	1.90	20	.073
Total action units	170.44	107.63	2.05	38	.049
Wife anger	12.88	11.84	.33	33	ns
Hus. contempt	2.88	2.16	.72	33	ns
Hus. disgust	3.06	3.21	-.10	33	ns
Hus. fear	5.88	4.89	.62	33	ns
Hus. sadness	1.19	2.84	-1.72	26	.097
Hus. Duchenne smiles	12.88	11.58	.43	33	ns
Hus. other smiles	20.81	9.32	2.46	18	.024
Total action units	182.06	154.16	.89	33	ns

evidence of less rebound for hostile/detached compared with hostile couples. Although hostile/detached couples showed more sadness (marginal), they also showed less tension/fear than hostile couples. However, wives in hostile/detached marriages showed more disgust/ contempt than wives in hostile marriages on the positive conversation.

TABLE 11.4
Physiological Differences Between Hostile and Hostile/Detached Couples

Variable	Hostile	Hostile/Detached	t	df	p
Physiological Linkage	.39	.39	−.03	33	ns
Physiological Activity					
Hus. heart period	814.63	792.00	.55	33	ns
Hus. activity	1.00	.95	1.66	33	ns
Hus. skin conductance	9.78	13.10	−1.45	28	ns
Hus. pulse transit time	243.94	241.84	.28	33	ns
Hus. finger pulse amplitude	8.13	7.79	.23	19	ns
Wife heart period	749.88	710.21	1.15	24	ns
Wife activity	1.77	1.77	−.15	33	ns
Wife skin conductance	7.19	12.29	−2.20	25	.032
Wife pulse transit time	236.56	230.16	1.16	33	ns
Wife finger pulse amplitude	5.06	7.50	−1.51	27	ns

11.3.4. Physiology

Table 11.4 shows that the two groups of couples differed on one physiological variable: Wives in hostile/detached marriages had higher skin conductance than wives in hostile marriages.

11.3.5. Sequences

The only sequential difference between the two groups was that there was more positive affect reciprocity on the positive conversation for hostile compared with hostile/detached couples (see Table 11.5).[1]

11.3.6. Ratios of Positive to Negative

The ratio of positive to negative RCISS codes was not significantly different for the two groups of husbands or wives.[2] For the SPAFF coding system, the two groups could be distinguished only on the conflict task, and only wives' ratios could be distinguished. During conflict, the wives in the hostile group had a higher ratio of positive to

---

[1]Both groups of couples show high average z scores (greater than 1.96) for continuance on all three conversations. These continuance z scores are highest for the conflict discussion.

[2]For the hostile group, the ratio was 1.23 for husbands and 0.76 for wives. For the hostile/detached groups, the ratio was 0.91 for husbands and 0.60 for wives. The F ratios were $F(1,33) = 1.31$, ns for husbands; and $F(1,33) = 0.69$, ns for wives.

TABLE 11.5
Sequential Analyses Comparing Hostile/Detached and Hostile Couples

Variable	Hostile	Hostile/Detached	t	df	p
Events					
Start up H → W	.19	−.13	.68	27	ns
Start up W → H	−.02	.01	−.06	27	ns
Continuance H → W	2.90	3.58	−.59	27	ns
Continuance W → H	2.39	3.19	−.71	27	ns
Positive reciprocity H → W	3.05	3.00	.07	27	ns
Positive reciprocity W → H	3.07	2.70	.53	27	ns
Conflict					
Start up H → W	1.60	1.63	−.06	31	ns
Start up W → H	.51	.65	−.27	31	ns
Continuance H → W	6.22	5.67	.37	31	ns
Continuance W → H	6.08	5.55	.34	31	ns
Positive reciprocity H → W	3.34	2.57	.70	31	ns
Positive reciprocity W → H	3.09	2.91	.15	31	ns
Positive					
Start up H → W	.36	−.32	1.50	31	ns
Start up W → H	.14	.27	−.31	31	ns
Continuance H → W	3.80	4.53	−.59	31	ns
Continuance W → H	4.31	4.21	.08	31	ns
Positive reciprocity H → W	4.50	3.45	1.58	31	ns
Positive reciprocity W → H	4.75	3.44	2.52	31	.017

negative affects than wives in the hostile/detached group (0.73 compared with 0.20).[3]

11.3.7. Summary

In general, it appears that there is some evidence of greater negativity, particularly contempt and disgust as well as greater detachment, of both husbands and wives in the hostile/detached compared with the hostile group.

11.4. SUMMARY OF ALL FIVE TYPES OF COUPLES

I have described five types of marriages. Three types were regulated and two types were nonregulated. I found that nonregulated couples were

---

[3]The F ratios for the conflict conversation were $F(1,31) = 10.03$, $p < .003$ for wives; and $F(1,29) = 0.95$, ns for husbands. For the events-of-the-day conversation, $F(1,23) = 0.20$, ns for wives; and $F(1,23) = 3.46$, $p = .076$ for husbands. For the positive conversation, $F(1,22) = 2.69$, ns for wives; and $F(1,22) = 3.81$, $p = .064$ for husband.

more likely to be on a course toward marital dissolution than were regulated couples. I suggested that the variables being regulated were a balance between positive and negative codes, both in problem solving (with the RCISS) and in affect (with the SPAFF). The regulation held even when the couple was not discussing an area of continuing disagreement, but also for the events-of-the-day and the positive conversations.

I also suggested that the idea of types rather than dimensions made sense. In this view, there are three stable adaptations to obtaining a ratio of 5 between positive and negative codes. One adaptation is the volatile couple, which has a lot of both types of codes. Another adaptation is the validating couple, which has a moderate amount of both types of codes. A third stable adaptation is the avoider couple, which has a small amount of both codes. I discussed each adaptation in terms of its benefits and risks. Next, I described the two types of unstable adaptations I observed—the hostile and hostile/detached couples.

The results of these discussions can be summarized with contour graphs that display all five groups on one graph and show the degree of separation I achieved with my measures. Before doing that, it is necessary to summarize briefly how population ecologists plot their data.

Figure 11.1 is an illustration of a standard predator–prey diagram; it shows that "a stable limit cycle" actually is composed of regions of changing predator and prey populations. Region "A" is one in which both populations are low and the population of the predator decreases due to lack of food, whereas the population of the prey increases due to the lack of predation. The figure explains how one obtains a closed loop, or "limit cycle," in this manner. Figure 11.2 shows a predator–prey model illustrating two stable limit cycles, one drawn inside the other. Figure 11.3 illustrates two predator–prey limit cycles, one favoring the predator and one favoring the prey.

I now apply these plots to my own data. In my data, the species population is replaced by a behavior frequency. In this case, negativity is the predator and positivity is the prey. Figure 11.4 illustrates the predator–prey contour plots of positive and negative RCISS points for husband. Each point represents the husband's data for one particular couple. The figure illustrates the five groups of couples; contours have been drawn to encircle each group. Figure 11.5 illustrates the predator-prey contour plots of positive and negative RCISS points for the wife. Again, the figure illustrates the five groups of couples. The figure demonstrates that, even with two measures, I can discriminate the five groups reasonably well.

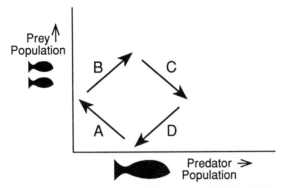

Region A: Both populations are low, and the population of big fish decreases due to the lack of food (small fish) while the population of small fish increases due to the lack of predation. This is shown by vector A.

Region B: In this region there are lots of small fish but relatively few predators, and hence both populations can increase. This is shown by the direction of the vector B.

Region C: In this region both populations are large. The big fish are multiplying, which results in a dramatic reduction of the number of smaller fish. This is illustrated by the direction of vector C.

Region D: In this region there are few little fish but many big fish. Both populations must decline. This fact is illustrated by vector D.

FIG. 11.1. Predator–prey diagram showing a stable limit cycle actually is composed of regions of changing predator and prey populations.

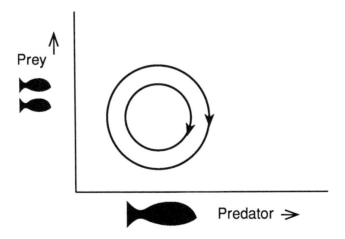

FIG. 11.2. Predator–prey model illustrating two stable limit cycles.

225

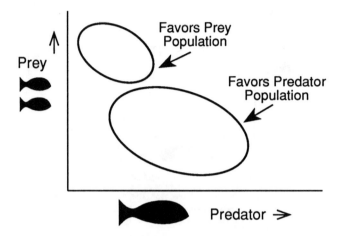

FIG. 11.3. Predator–prey limit cycles: one favoring the predator and one favoring the prey.

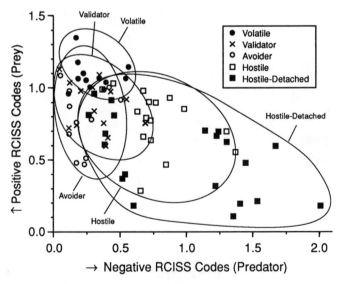

FIG. 11.4. Predator–prey contour plots of positive and negative RCISS points for husband. Figure illustrates the five groups of couples.

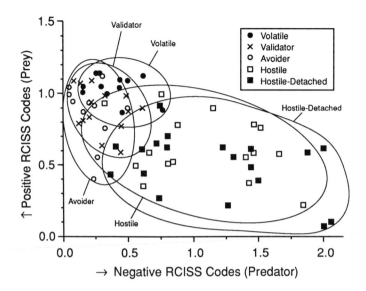

FIG. 11.5. Predator–prey contour plots of positive and negative RCISS points for wife. Figure illustrates the five groups of couples.

11.5. MATHEMATICAL MODELING OF THE RCISS GRAPHS IN THE FIVE TYPES OF MARRIAGE

In a collaboration with Murray, Cook, White, Tyson, and Rushe, we developed a mathematical model for the RCISS point graphs. The goal was to represent the data with an equation that contained only a small number of parameters that would be descriptive of how the five types of marriages function. The method for developing the representation of the data was quite different from the methods of mathematical statistics. In Murray's (1985) approach, the equations generated a small number of assumptions about the processes that underlie the phenomenon of interest. That is the goal of the mathematical process. The process is more deductive than inductive; data also come into this process to obtain some reasonable estimates for the parameters of the equations, and then to determine if these parameters seem reasonable. The form of the equations is determined by reasoning about the processes that are operative in creating the phenomenon to be simulated. The basic outline of this approach is spelled out in Murray's (1985) book entitled *Mathematical Biology*.

This project is summarized briefly here. The equations developed by this team worked on the unaccumulated RCISS point graphs. The equations were:

$$H_{t+1} = I_{W \to H} + K_H*H_t + L_H'$$

$$W_{t+1} = I_{H \to W} + K_W*W_{t+1} + L_W$$

The models represented by the equations are quite general and very simple. The first equation states that the unaccumulated RCISS point-graph behavior of the husband at Time $t+1$, H_{t+1}, is the sum of three parts: (a) the influence of the wife on the husband, $I_{W \to H}$; (b) the emotional inertia of the husband when he is not being influenced (i.e., when the influence of his wife is zero), K_H*H_t; the constant K_H is the husband's emotional inertia; emotional inertia is the tendency of a person to continue in a positive or negative state when uninfluenced by one's partner; and (c) the steady state or natural set point of negativity or positivity of the husband, L_H, when he is not being influenced. The second equation is similar to the first, except that the model assumes, arbitrarily, that the wife speaks first.

Think about these equations for a moment. Once one starts thinking in terms of the parameters of the equations, one automatically gets an organization for theorizing. Here are some examples. The equations suggest looking at the times that the husband is not being influenced by his wife and ask what his set point and his inertia are. That is, what is his propensity for positive and negative action, and how likely is he to continue in this state once he gets started? Does this inertial parameter vary as a function of gender and whether the marriage will last or not? What about his steady state set point? Is his set point when he is uninfluenced less positive than when he is being influenced by his wife? Perhaps this is an operational definition of a successful marriage.

Once one starts thinking in terms of the parameters of the equations, one expects that wives generally would have higher inertia than husbands, which means that, when uninfluenced, they would be more likely to continue in an emotional state for more turns at speech than the husbands, whose emotional behavior would be more fleeting. That seems consistent with the literature (see chapters 3 and 12 of this book).

The influence function is defined as a graph of the RCISS point graph values at Time t versus the change in the partner's value from t to $t+1$. For example, to compute the husband's influence on the wife, at Time t = 15 the husband's value was -3 and his wife's value was 2 at that time and 1 at Time t = 16. The influence the husband had would be $1-2 = -1$ at that point; to compute his influence at his RCISS value of -3, average his influence at all points for which he was at -3.

The beauty of the mathematical modeling is that it makes it possible to examine interesting model parameters in relief so that one can generate hypotheses about principles that may underly the data. To see how this works, examine Table 11.6. Table 11.6 summarizes the model parameter estimates that were obtained from the DUO83 data from the five groups of couples, using these equations. Several hypotheses emerge from this table. The parameter estimates are treated as if they are population parameters, and statistical tests are not performed.

I begin by examining the behavior of the husbands. First, I examine the regulated marriages. Volatile and validator husbands have more emotional inertia than conflict-avoiding husbands. Volatile and validator husbands also have a more positive natural set point than conflict-avoiding husbands. One also may notice that husbands have more emotional inertia in volatile and validating marriages than wives. The natural set point of volatile husbands is more positive than the natural set point of either validating or conflict-avoiding husbands. The emotional inertia of husbands in nonregulated marriages is not different from the emotional inertia of husbands in regulated marriages, but the set points are less positive or more negative than that of husbands in nonregulated marriages. Husbands in hostile/detached marriages have a more negative emotional set point than husbands in hostile marriages.

I now examine the behavior of the wives. First, I examine the regulated marriages. Unlike husbands, volatile, validator, and conflict-avoiding wives did not differ in emotional inertia. As noted, husbands had more emotional inertia in volatile and validating marriages than did wives. The natural set point of volatile wives was also more positive than the natural set point of either validating or conflict-avoiding wives. The emotional inertia of wives in the three regulated marriages was not different. However, in nonregulated marriages, wives had more emo-

TABLE 11.6

Parameter Estimates in the Murray et al. (1993) Group's Mathematical Modeling of the RCISS Unaccumulated Point Graphs

Group	Husbands		Wives	
	Emotional Inertia	Natural Set Point	Emotional Inertia	Natural Set Point
Regulated couples				
Volatile	.33	.68	.20	.68
Validator	.37	.38	.14	.52
Avoider	.18	.26	.25	.46
Nonregulated couples				
Hostile	.32	.10	.51	−.64
Hostile/detached	.40	−.42	.46	−.24

tional inertia than they did in regulated marriages. Also, the set points of wives in nonregulated marriages was negative, and more negative than the set points of wives in regulated marriages. Wives in hostile marriages had a more negative set point than wives in hostile/detached marriages.

The behavior of the wives was quite different from that of the husbands. Wives in regulated marriages had a set point that was equal to or more positive than husbands in regulated marriages. However, wives in hostile marriages had a set point that was more negative than their husbands, whereas the reverse was true in hostile/detached marriages. The notion that wives have a more positive set point than husbands in regulated than in nonregulated marriages suggests that wives as well as husbands in these marriages may play a central role of regulating positivity. However, in the hostile marriage it appears to be the wives who have reversed this role, and whose set point is now negative. They also have a very high emotional inertia. Thus, in hostile marriages wives, and not so much husbands, have shifted to a negative balance, and their high inertia suggests long runs of this negativity characterize their interaction with their husbands. In hostile/detached marriages, on the other hand, both husbands and wives have a negative set point and high inertia. This may be further indication that the hostile/detached marriage represents a deterioration beyond the hostile marriage.

To compute the influence functions we assumed that when the RCISS value is zero (equally positive and negative) there is no influence. This assumption made it possible to compute *influenced* and *uninfluenced* set points. The addition of this parameter now makes it possible for one to determine if a marriage is more positive when influenced by the partner. Figure 11.6 shows the results that for validators and avoiders the influenced set point is more positive than the uninfluenced set point. However, for the volatile and combined hostile and hostile/detached groups this is not the case; their interaction is driving them toward greater negativity than they would exhibit when they are not influenced.

I computed the slope of the influence function separately for negative and positive value of the partner's behavior. The x axis represented the range of positivity or negativity in each group. Only data close to the natural set point for each group could be trusted to avoid infrequent numbers of instances of RCISS values within a group. This means that more reliable information is obtained for regulated couples in the positive ranges and for nonregulated couples in the negative ranges of the x axis. My results then were used to induce hypotheses about what kind of processes might be generating the data.

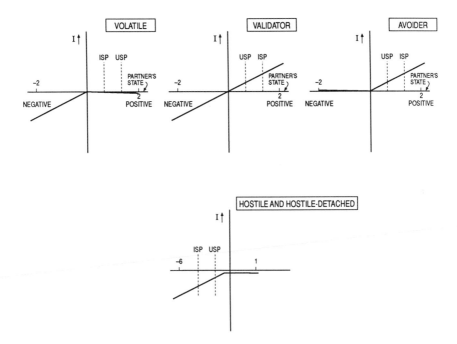

FIG. 11.6.   Theoretical influence functions for each of the types of marriage and their influenced and uninfluenced emotional set points. Note that the three regulated marriages have a narrower range of negativity and a broader range of positivity than nonregulated marriages. Note that the regulated set points are positive, whereas the nonregulated set points are negative. The volatile couple has a more positive uninfluenced set point; this is also true for nonregulated couples. ISP = influenced set point; USP = uninfluenced set point.

From examining the data, I proposed that validating couples were able to influence their spouses with both positive or negative behavior; positive behavior had a positive sloping influence, whereas negative behavior also had a positive sloping influence. This means that the negative x-axis values had a negative influence, whereas the positive x-axis values had a positive influence. For validators, across the whole range of RCISS point values, the slope of the influence function was a constant, upwardly sloping straight line.

However, avoiders and volatile couples were opposite in the shape of their influence functions. Avoiders influenced one another only with positivity (the slope was flat in the negative RCISS point ranges), whereas volatile couples influenced one another only with negativity (the slope was flat in the positive RCISS point ranges). The influence of hostile and hostile/detached couples was similar to the influence function for volatile couples.

It seems that the data was generated by the following process: In validating regulated marriages, there is a uniform slope of the influence function across both positive and negative values. Overall, negative behavior has a negative influence, whereas positive behavior has a positive influence in regulated marriages. Hence, a full range of emotional balance is possible in the interaction. However, in nonregulated marriages, it is likely that the curve flattens out in the positive ranges near the natural set point, which is negative. This means that in nonregulated marriages, people generally are able to influence one another only with negativity; they have almost no influence on one another with positivity relative to their negative set point. If this is correct, this can suggest an explanation for the more negative natural set point in nonregulated marriages. Could the greater negativity and reduced positivity of nonregulated marriages be a result of the lack of influence of positivity? The ability to have an effect on one's partner must be one of the necessary ingredients of having a relationship that is interdependent (for a theoretical analysis of this point, see Kelley et al., 1983). It is natural to assume that the ability to influence one's mate is an intrinsically reinforcing aspect of social interaction. If negativity is the only way that nonregulated couples can influence one another, it seems obvious that they naturally would drift toward a more negative set point.

This analysis appears complicated by the fact that the shape of the volatile couple's influence functions looks like that of nonregulated couples. Their influence also lies in the negative ranges and in a negative direction. Hence, they should look like nonregulated couples, except that they maintain a high level of uninfluenced positivity. That is, they have a highly positive set point instead of a negative one. Hence, theirs is a high-risk strategy: If they became less positive, their interaction might drift toward that of the nonregulated couples. This makes sense. Their style of confrontation, when not coupled with high levels of positivity, could reasonably lead to defensiveness. Then they would resemble the hostile or hostile/detached couple.

The influence function of avoiding couples is the reverse of that of volatile couples. They have influence only in the positive ranges around their positive set point; the curve flattens out in the negative ranges. As paradoxical as it may seem at first, I suggest that theirs is also a high-risk strategy: They are flirting with the danger of avoiding negativity. The problem, as seen, is that, like predators who cull the prey species, negativity can improve the marriage. Without it, problems remain unresolved. They simply become reprioritized as unimportant as the basic beliefs of the couple are reinforced and reaffirmed. The problem is minimized by a low level of emotionality; positivity is never very positive and negativity is never very negative. Hence, the avoiders' strategy for adapting to having a stable marriage is quite the mirror image of the volatile strategy.

This discussion of the theoretical shapes of the influence functions for the five groups is summarized in Fig. 11.6. The top three graphs in the figure represent the influence functions for the three regulated marriages. The validators have an influence function that creates an influence toward negativity in a spouse if the partner's behavior is negative, and an influence toward positivity if the partner's behavior is positive. Volatile and validator influence functions are, respectively, one half of the validators', with volatiles having the left half and the validators having the right half. For validators and avoiders, the uninfluenced set point is less positive than the influenced set point, but this is reversed for volatile couples. The very positive uninfluenced set point is the way that volatile couples balance the negative influence function. The nonregulated couples' (hostile or hostile/detached) influence function looks remarkably like that of the volatile couples', with a few differences. First, the range of positivity is narrowed, whereas the range of negativity is broadened in the nonregulated compared with the volatile couple. Second, both the uninfluenced and influenced set points are negative, although, like the volatile couple, the influenced set point is more negative than the influenced set point. This summarizes my hypotheses about the set points and influence functions.

11.5.1. A Word About the Point of All This Mathematics

The beauty of the type of mathematical modeling we have employed here is that it has provided a *theory* of what may be driving the RCISS point graphs that gives them their predictive power. Writing down the mathematical equations has required us to state our best guesses at such a theory. In doing this we decided that several parameters were necessary to describe the RCISS data. These parameters were the *emotional inertia* of each spouse, the *influenced and uninfluenced set points* in the marriage, and the influence function over the range of positivity/ negativity exhibited. Actually, although I have not portrayed this here, these parameters and functions can be computed separately for each spouse. The very existence of these parameters now gives us a quantitative language for discussing the types of marriages we have discovered.

When we take a look at what the data tell us about these functions and parameters, we can see some things more clearly. For example, we see that all the other influence functions are distortions of the validator's influence function. This was a complete surprise. The avoider seems to have only the capability of positive influence. The volatile couple seems to have only the capability of negative influence. Furthermore, volatile and nonregulated marriages have similarly shaped influence functions; they differ only by the much more positive set points of the volatile couple. This reveals in quantitative terms what a high-risk strategy the volatile couple's style represents. Take away the high balance of positive over negative RCISS codes and the interaction of the volatile couple is likely to resemble, in some ways, the interaction of nonregulated couples.

In one figure, the mathematics makes it possible for us to portray the different types of marriages dynamically. The initial writing down of the equations forced us to build a theory for the different types of couples' RCISS data. We then examined the data and estimated parameters and influence functions. Now we can return to the initial equations and write down the influence functions in functional algebraic, theoretical (and not empirical) form. Thus, the process of creating these mathematical (and not statistical) models has given us a mini-theory about the RCISS data. Now we can state some hypotheses about the dynamic nature of the positive/negative regulation that may be taking place in each of our types of couples.

The mathematics represented by this process might aptly be called *qualitative mathematical modeling*. It is well described in Murray's (1985) book. Only part of the process was described here. The remainder of the process has some exciting possibilities. Once the equations are written down with the influence functions in functional form, it is possible to attempt to solve the equations and to describe their steady states and attractors. In a number of examples in Murray's book what emerges from these solutions are descriptions of the system that go beyond the data collected. The solutions could conceivably reveal possibilities in the system's behavior under conditions different than those that generated the original data and equations in the first place. These new solutions may then suggest new experiments for understanding the system of interest. In some cases, these solutions have suggested ways of controlling the system; for example, in one problem modeling the bud-worm infestation of trees, a solution suggested a means of regulation of a bud-worm epidemic that had hitherto been unimagined by forest maintenance policies. In the case of couples, these solutions could have impact on the therapeutic interventions that are generated by the mini-theory. This represents an approach to modeling that has yet to be explored in the social sciences.

In a discussion of what must be a related phenomenon, Jacobson and Margolin (1979) called attention to reinforcement erosion. They referred to a tendency in some marriages to interact in ways that may have been rewarding once, but are no longer rewarding. Reinforcement erosion may be the result of the inability of positivity to influence one's mate in nonregulated marriages. The inability to have an influence with positivity may produce negativity. For example, if repeated attempts at humor are a failure in a marriage, this could produce hostility and lead to the gradual erosion of reinforcement.

Thus, in terms of the model, the idea emerges from the data that the natural influenced emotional set point in a marriage follows from the nature of the influence function. The natural influenced emotional set point was precisely what was involved in the predator–prey plots examined earlier in this chapter, which suggested the parameter of regulation in marriages. The uninfluenced set point can counterbalance this process, as seen in the case of the volatile marriage.

Although this is a compelling analysis, it still leaves many unanswered questions. Why does positivity have such little influence in nonregulated marriages? Did these marriages begin this way? If not, why did the power of positivity wear off in these marriages? Could it be that the four horsemen of criticism, contempt, defensiveness, and withdrawal, and the resultant emotional flooding, were corrosive of precisely this branch of the influence function? Is this an operational definition of the erosion of love in some marriages?

11.6. MISMATCH THEORY: THE POSSIBILITY THAT UNSTABLE MARRIAGES ARE THE RESULT OF FAILED ATTEMPTS AT CREATING A PURE TYPE

In this section, I propose that all the data in this chapter can be organized by the hypothesis that hostile and hostile/detached couples are simply failures to create a stable adaptation to marriage that is either volatile, validating, or avoiding. In other words, the results of this chapter are an artifact of the prior inability of couples to accommodate one another and have one of the three types of marriage. For example, a person who wishes a volatile marriage may have married one who wishes a validating or avoiding marriage. There are three possible types of mismatches: volatile/validating, volatile/avoiding, and validating/avoiding.

Unfortunately, it is easier to propose this hypothesis than it is to test it. The problem in testing this hypothesis is that I have employed the marital interaction as a means for classifying couples. As a result, the marriage is described as volatile, validating, or avoiding, rather than each person's style or preferences. An independent method for classifying each person's conflict-resolution style is needed to test this hypothesis.

To begin to test this hypothesis, I computed the difference between husbands and wives on the RCISS positive negative and the difference between positive and negative speaker codes. If the hypothesis were true, one would expect the results of an analysis of variance between the groups to show greater discrepancies between husbands and wives for the hostile and hostile/detached group than for the three stable groups. This was indeed the case. Pooling the stable groups into one group and the unstable groups into one group, for the positive speaker code, $F(1, 70) = 4.12$, $p < .05$ (stable = $-.01$, unstable = $.08$); for the negative speaker code, $F(1, 70) = 10.42$, $p < .01$ (stable = $-.02$, unstable = $-.26$); for the difference between positive and negative speaker codes, $F(1, 70) = 8.57$, $p < .01$ (stable = $.01$, unstable = $.34$).[4]

Thus, it may be that the unstable groups are examples of discrepancies in interactional style between husbands and wives that are reflective of their differences in preferred type of marital adaptation.

There also is the possibility that the two types of nonregulated couples are actually one type of marriage at two different stages of relationship dissolution. This makes some intuitive sense, because the hostile couples are still engaged with one another and their interactions still show active engagement. The hostile/detached couples may represent a later stage of dissolution, in which couples are still quite defensive with one another, but have increased their distance and isolation from one another. There are no data at present to support this speculation.

---

[4]For the positive speaker code, $F(4,67)=3.32$, $p<.05$ (volatile = $.05$, validating = $-.01$, avoiding = $-.08$, hostile = $.16$, hostile/detached = $.01$); for the negative speaker code, $F(4,67)=4.05$, $p<.01$ (volatile = $-.09$, validating = $.01$, avoiding = $.01$, hostile = $-.38$, hostile/detached = $-.16$); for the difference between positive and negative speaker codes, $F(4,67)=4.00$, $p<.01$ (volatile = $.14$, validating = $-.02$, avoiding = $-.08$, hostile = $.53$, hostile/detached = $.17$).

12

Male Withdrawal From
Marital Conflict

Gottman and Levenson (1988) theorized that many commonly noted gender differences in relationships can be derived from a hypothesis about gender differences in autonomic nervous system (ANS) reactivity. The weak form of this hypothesis is that males recover more slowly from ANS arousal than females. Their review of the literature on gender differences in physiological responses to stress provided some support for this hypothesis. If this gender difference is true, and if chronic ANS activation is considered to be harmful, unpleasant, and undesirable, then men might be more inclined than women to avoid situations that would be associated with repeated high levels of ANS activation, and to withdraw from negative affect in marital conflict. Taking this argument a step further, if intense negative affect is seen as activating high levels of ANS activation (especially in men), then men may try to manage the level of negative affect to which they are exposed. They may try to create a rational, as opposed to an emotional, climate in relationships (Kelley et al., 1978), which can be a major source of repeated high level negative emotions and of concomitant high levels of ANS activation; they may become more conciliatory and less conflict engaging than females; and they may try to terminate negative affect encounters by withdrawing, that is, by stonewalling. Gottman and Levenson (1988) presented instances from the marriage research literature that show that each of these behavioral characteristics has been ascribed to men. In direct contrast, women in this literature have been described as being less conciliatory, more conflict engaging, and less likely to withdraw from negative affect.

12.1. INTRODUCTION

Throughout this book, I have noted differences between husbands and wives wherever they occurred in my data and in the data of other investigators. In general, these differences are quite pervasive and

237

profound in their implications. In previous research, I also found evidence (Gottman & Krokoff, 1989) that it is important for the longitudinal satisfaction of couples that wives confront disagreements and not be overly compliant. In some investigations, this special role that wives play in getting the couple to confront their disagreements may be observed as the greater negativity of wives compared with husbands. The elucidation of these gender roles and the possible reasons that they exist is the subject of this chapter. As is seen, there is a powerful difference between husbands and wives in the way they respond to intense emotion in the handling of continuing disagreements in a marriage.

12.2. EVIDENCE FOR GENDER DIFFERENCES IN MARITAL INTERACTION

In a recent paper, Gottman and Levenson (1988) reviewed evidence for a consistent gender difference in the way married men and women handle marital conflict in unhappy marriages: Men tend to withdraw from conflict, whereas women tend to engage.

12.2.1. Gender Differences in Marital Grievances

Even in the earliest studies on marriage, it is possible to find evidence for gender differences in the subjects about which husbands and wives complain. Terman et al. (1938) noted that the grievances of husbands concerned their wives' complaining, criticizing, and escalating emotion ("criticizes me," "wife nervous or emotional," "quick tempered," "wife's feelings too easily hurt," "wife nags me"), whereas wives' grievances concerned their husbands' emotional withdrawal ("does not talk things over," "does not show affection") or aggressiveness ("husband is argumentative," "quick tempered"). Locke (1951) found that divorced men complained of constant bickering more than did divorced women, even when gender differences were controlled by comparing them to happily married husbands and wives. Locke also suggested that in unhappy marriages, it is men and not women who withdraw in terms of discussing issues in the marriage. Locke wrote: "women tend to place a higher value on talking things over than do men. . . Moreover, divorced women reported much more frequently than divorced men that they and their spouses almost 'never' talked things over together" (p. 251).

Is it the case that men are generally more reserved or withdrawn socially than women, and this gender difference in marriage is simply a reflection of this fact? This question can be asked in another way. Are men generally more withdrawn than women in marriage, or does this gender difference only emerge in unhappy marriages?

12.2.2. In Unhappy Marriages Men Withdraw Emotionally, Whereas in Happy Marriages They Do Not

Komarovsky's (1962) study of 58 blue-collar couples concluded that the blue collar husband is generally not emotionally expressive, not self-disclosing, and does not talk things out with his wife. This is the author's summary of her findings as stated in her 1976 book *Dilemmas of Masculinity*. However, she did not analyze her data statistically, and her conclusion is wrong. A re-analysis of her tables reveals a strong statistical relationship between marital happiness and self-disclosure for both men, χ^2 (1) $= 14.09$, and women, χ^2 (1) $= 16.25$. These results show that, in her sample, blue-collar husbands do self-disclose when they are happily married. Further analysis reveals that, in happy marriages, there are no statistically significant differences between husbands and wives in the amount of self-disclosure.

This remarkable conclusion flies in the face of what generally is believed about men and self-disclosure. Komarovsky (1962) also investigated what she called areas of emotional reserve. These are areas or concerns that are not shared with the spouse. Wives hold back most in personal areas (i.e., worries about health, dissatisfactions with self, hurts, dreams and aspirations for herself and the family, transgressions, and reminiscences). In contrast, husbands hold back only in areas concerned with work and money (i.e., satisfactions, dissatisfactions, worries about bills, and economic concerns). Komarovsky's (1962) interviews revealed that men do not think it is "manly" to complain about work, to bring the job home, or to worry the family. Hence, men's self-disclosure in happy marriages is far more intimate than that of their wives, and, in fact, appears to be more *personal*, judging by Komarovsky's (1962) own use of the term. Furthermore, whereas wives disclose to a fairly wide support network that includes their husbands, their close female friends, and their relatives, husbands, in essence, only disclose to their wives. In unhappy marriages, they tend, on the whole, to disclose to no one.

Thus, Komarovsky's (1962) own data suggest that blue-collar men have a smaller, but more intense social world than their wives, and that their self-disclosure is: (a) limited to their wives when they are happily married and (b) nonexistent if they are unhappily married. This is not a picture of an inexpressive male, and depicts males whose degree of disclosure is highly dependent on the emotional climate of the marriage.

Males are very self-disclosing in happy marriages; in unhappy marriages, they disclose to no one. On the other hand, females are self-disclosing in the most personal areas primarily outside the marriage, regardless of their marital satisfaction.

What happens in unhappy marriages? Komarovsky (1962) noted that unhappily married men conceal their feelings; she referred to "a striking tendency on the husbands' part to 'clam up' in the face of conflict" (p. 143). She wrote:

> . . . confronted with a marriage conflict, a greater proportion of the husbands than the wives withdraw, either physically or psychologically, by such means as walking out of the house ("I say what I have to say and then I go zoom out of the house") or by silence ("I don't pay any attention until she cools off"). (p. 193)

This same pattern of husbands' withdrawal in the face of intense negative affect was described by Rubin (1976). For example, in a typical quote, a husband in her study said: "When she comes after me like that, yapping like that, she might as well be hitting me with a bat" (p. 115). This is precisely the concept of flooding, which I view as central to marital dissolution. Can it be that there is some gender difference related to flooding? This possibility is explored in chapter 15.

From this discussion, the hypothesis emerges that it is intense negative affect (or negative affect that is perceived as intense) that may be responsible for the emotional withdrawal of men in unhappy marriages. Although Komarovsky's (1962) data about the history of the marriages in her study are retrospective accounts, many of the quotes from her couples suggest that husbands were not always withdrawn in their marriages. For example, one wife said: "I used to talk to him a lot when we were first married, but now I can't talk to him at all. He kinda draws away from me" (p. 138).

In terms of self-disclosure in happy marriages, men are very different than in unhappy marriages, whereas women appear to be fairly consistent regardless of marital satisfaction. Males have a much smaller network for self-disclosure than females, and their partners are in the center of the network, but only if they are happily married. Females have a wider network of self-disclosure than males, and in some senses their partners are not in the center of this network, regardless of their marital satisfaction. This discussion is quite consistent with the study of support networks in which gender differences are not based on comparisons within the marriage as the unit of analysis (House, 1981).

12.2.3. Gender Differences in Marital Conflict

I have discussed complaints and self-reports about marriage. How pervasive is the gender difference in marital behavior, not the perception of this behavior as reflected in grievances? Raush et al. (1974) found that the instrumental/affective hypothesis about gender differences produced by Parsons and Bales (1955) did not hold true. Men were not more instrumental and task-oriented than women, nor were women more affective or expressive than men in marital conflict resolution. This may be a reflection of a general result that gender differences cannot be generalized to spousal differences in marriages. In high-conflict (relationship-oriented) improvisations, the significant gender differences that Raush et al. reported were that women were more coercive (one of their coding categories) and personally attacking than men (this was true regardless of the antecedent behavior), and that men were more resolving and reconciling than women. Wives also were more prone to use coercion as a response to reconciling behavior. Raush et al. (1974) wrote that: "Wives tend more than husbands to follow reconciling behavior on the part of their husband with efforts to attain their own aims" (p. 142). They also reported that wives generally used more pressure on husbands in response to any act, wives used twice as many coercive acts on husbands; and husbands used about three times as many resolving and reconciling acts in response to rejection as wives. Raush et al. wrote: "Wives appear to behave in ways designed to enforce their own point of view. . . . Thus, generally husbands behaved in more pacifying ways than wives even in the closeness–distance scenes. Wives showed a fairly consistent tendency toward greater use of emotional pressure" (pp. 144–145).

These closeness–distance scenes induced a high level of conflict for most couples, and the observed gender differences became even more pronounced during pregnancy. When the conflict is even higher than in the improvised scenes of Raush et al. (1974) the gender differences are even greater. Schaap's (1982) study of Danish couples employed what must have been the most highly conflictual interaction situation in the literature. He asked couples to sequentially resolve their marital problems one after another, and they were asked to resolve as many as they could within 25 minutes. Indeed, the behavioral coding suggests that this situation induced a remarkable degree of conflict in unhappily married couples. What were the results in this situation on gender differences? Using the same coding scheme for classifying affect that Gottman (1979) used, Schaap (1982) found that, among distressed couples, it was the wife who "compared to her husband delivers the most negative and longest [negative affect] sequences" (p. 91). Schaap (1982) wrote: ". . . generally wives deliver more codes with negative affect, and the husbands more codes with positive affect" (p. 72).

To summarize, it appears that wives could be described behaviorally as conflict engaging and husbands as conflict reducing (and, in the face

of high conflict, as withdrawing), and that these differences are increased during pregnancy (Raush et al., 1974) and high conflict.

The greater use of reconciling and resolving acts on the part of
husbands compared with wives in the Raush et al. (1974) study raises
the question of whether husbands tend to assume an unemotional
attitude toward the resolution of differences, and tend to be more active
in the de-escalation of conflict. The answer is no. Gottman (1979)
defined *editing* as a reduced sequential probability that a negative
listener would turn into a negative speaker once speaking turns
switched. This is a specific form of conflict de-escalation. He reported
that wives in satisfied marriages play this editing role in de-escalating
tensions, but only in discussions that induce the highest conflict,
whereas husbands in satisfied marriages play this role, but only in
low-conflict discussions. Essentially, no one plays this de-escalation role
in dissatisfied marriages. The conclusion is that men cannot edit very
well in high-conflict situations regardless of how happily married they
are. This suggests the hypothesis that, in resolving marital conflict of
low-intensity negative affect, men may be positive, reconciling, and
resolving to avoid the escalation of negative affect, because in high-
conflict interaction even happily married men cannot successfully edit
their own negative affect, whereas their wives can. Thus, the research
evidence suggests that, regardless of the level of marital satisfaction,
men do not seem to function as well as women (i.e., in de-escalating
conflict) in the context of high negative affect.

There are two additional sources of evidence that men and women
differ in terms of their capacity to function in the face of negative affect.
One source comes from a study by Ginsberg and Gottman (1986) on the
conversations of male and female college roommates. For women, there
were several affect–behavior sequences that began with the expression
of negative affect that were correlated positively with greater relationship satisfaction (e.g., negative affect followed by asking a question,
negative affect followed by acknowledgment). For men, this was not
true at all; all affect–behavior sequences that started with the expression
of negative affect were correlated with lower relationship satisfaction.
Speculating on the meaning of these results, the authors concluded that
both men and women tend to avoid negative affect in their interactions
with close roommates; but once negative affect is expressed, women can
follow it with a number of behaviors that function to preserve relationship satisfaction, whereas men cannot. Levenson and I currently are
studying the closest love relationships of gay males and lesbians to test
the generality of these gender differences. We expect that the interaction
of gay males is very male—low in conflict and high in reconciling
behavior—whereas the interaction of lesbian couples will be very

female—high in both positive and negative emotional expression and very confronting.

A second piece of evidence is a study by Gottman and Porterfield (1981), in which spouses were asked to deliver ambiguous, pre-written verbal messages (e.g., "I'm cold, aren't you?") in a way that conveyed a specific meaning (e.g., "I would like to snuggle" vs. "Please turn up the heat"). Receivers had a list of the possible meanings of the ambiguous message and had to guess the meaning being sent. Wives' abilities to accurately decode their husbands' messages were equally good in satisfied and dissatisfied marriages. Husbands' abilities were much worse in dissatisfied marriages. Further, the decoding deficit of husbands in dissatisfied marriages was specific to messages sent by their wives. When the sender was someone else's wife, these dissatisfied husbands showed no impairment in decoding ability. Noller (1980) reported identical results with Australian couples. Males were fine at decoding the nonverbal behavior of other men's wives and at decoding the nonverbal behavior of their own wives if they were happily married. These results support an interpretation that the deficits in decoding ability found in men in dissatisfied marriages are the results of marital dissatisfaction, rather than inherent deficits in decoding ability. The gender differences in decoding nonverbal behavior in these studies suggests that husbands withdraw emotionally in dissatisfied marriages, and thus became less attentive to their wives' nonverbal cues, whereas wives do not withdraw emotionally.

To summarize, the results of these observational and interview studies that examined spouse differences in the domain of negative affect lead to three hypotheses: First, in the face of strong negative affect, men tend to withdraw from interaction, whereas women tend to engage. Second, women can function within the context of strong negative affect much more competently than can men. Third, men are more reconciling in conflictual interactions to manage the level of conflict and to keep it from escalating.

12.3. EVIDENCE FOR GENDER DIFFERENCES IN PHYSIOLOGICAL RESPONSES

Gottman and Levenson (1988) argued that there are distinct gender differences in the way men and women respond to negative affect in close relationships. They proposed that these differences probably are socialized as a function of biological differences that may be related to the superior health and resilience of premenopausal women.

There is undoubtedly far more conflict and far more intense negative affect in unhappy marriages than in happy marriages. Phillips (1975) found that the sheer amount of conflict per month reported by spouses in satisfied versus dissatisfied marriages was dramatically different. Based on his data, satisfied couples reported spending about 16 hours per year in conflict, whereas dissatisfied couples reported spending about 180 hours per year in conflict. Heated conflicts were described as more frequent (1.3 per month vs. 3 per month) and lasting longer (5.11 hours vs. 0.52 hours) for dissatisfied versus satisfied couples.

There are numerous lines of evidence that indicate that negative affect of this type produces widespread physiological activation. Within the autonomic nervous system (ANS), Cannon's (1927) classic "flight or fight" sympathetic nervous system activation pattern is well known, consisting of such changes as increases in cardiac rate and cardiac contractility; sweating; deepened breathing; and direction of blood flow toward large skeletal muscles and away from the periphery, and shutting off arterial blood flow to the renal and mesentery arteries. Associated with these changes is the release of catecholamines from the adrenal medulla (e.g., epinephrine and norepinephrine). In addition to this activation of the ANS, it also is well established that negative emotions are associated with activation of the pituitary-adrenocortical axis, resulting in the release of adrenocortical hormones such as cortisol (e.g., Mason, 1975a). Henry and Stephens' (1977) model suggested that the specific affects associated with anger and hostility may be related to this sympathetic-adrenal medullary axis (release of catechoamines), whereas the specific affects related to sadness and depression may be related to the pituitary-adrenal cortical axis (release of cortisol).

Previously I reviewed the longitudinal data reported by Levenson and Gottman (1985), in which the physiological activation of husbands was able to predict changes in marital satisfaction over 3 years. The results also were there for wives, but somewhat attenuated. These results showed that the more physiologically aroused couples were at Time 1, the more their relationship satisfaction dropped over 3 years; the converse (expressed in terms of the increase of marital satisfaction over time and low arousal) was also true. Negative affect also can produce physiological interrelatedness between members of an inter-acting dyad. Levenson and Gottman (1983) reported the results of a study that obtained a broad range of psychophysiological measures during conversational interactions between husbands and wives. They found that high-conflict interaction (a) increased the level of self-reported negative affect, and (b) increased the amount of physiological linkage, which is the ability to predict one person's physiological responses from the other's, controlling for autocorrelation. As noted earlier in this book, Kaplan et al. (1964) found a similar linkage in skin conductance during interactions between persons who disliked each other.

There is yet another way in which negative affect in marital interaction could produce physiological activation: when the negative affect is inhibited (e.g., stonewalling) or masked (e.g., unfelt, false smiles). Stonewalling involves controlling and suppressing verbal and emotional expressive behavior and suppressing the usual listener backchannels, such as head nods and eye contact.

However, I suspect that the effect is more complex than mere inhibition. Stonewalling probably leads to even more enhanced autonomic arousal if the suppression is accompanied by cognitions that rehearse the upset (e.g., that the partner is not being fair). It may be that this enhanced autonomic response form of stonewalling occurs more often for men than for women. It could account for the sometimes noted negative association between overt expression of emotion and physiological responding, which has been labeled the *hydraulic model* (Buck, 1980).

This view of spouse differences in autonomic responding also is supported by the results of a small study by Notarius and Johnson (1982). They compared the skin conductance responses of spouses in periods in which their partners were complaining and in which they were neutral listeners. Husbands had higher skin conductance levels than did wives during these periods. It could be that what Notarius and Johnson (1982) coded neutral were actually moments of this type of stonewalling for the men. Notarius considered this to be a reasonable interpretation of his results (Notarius, personal communication, 1985). In addition to being inhibited, negative affect also can be masked by other expressions, such as with a smile. Shennum and Bugental (1982) proposed that females are more likely to learn to mask negative affect with smiles or other expressions, whereas males are more likely to learn to inhibit the display of negative affect by having no facial expression. The autonomic effects of masking are unknown.

There is some indirect support for the contention that some attempts to control negative affect are productive of enhanced physiological arousal. Subjects who do not manifest the expected facial expressive responses when under stress have been shown to be more aroused physiologically than facially expressive subjects (e.g., Notarius & Levenson, 1979). In addition, there is evidence that repression and denial are associated with heightened ANS responses to stress (e.g., Weinberger, Schwartz, & Davidson, 1979; also see recent work by Gross & Levenson, 1990).

If specific affects have a distinct "autonomic signature" (Ekman et al., 1983), then general, diffuse autonomic arousal could result from blended negative affects, or affects in close temporal sequence. It is also not known if blends are a necessary concomitant of more intense affects. For example, grief may not be intense sadness, but sadness blended with other affects such as anger and fear, and a similar situation may exist for affects like rage. I believe that the physiological arousal produced by the kind of negative affects in an unhappy marriage can be quite long lasting, especially when the arousal is sufficient to cause the release of large amounts of stress-related hormones, such as norepinephrine, epinephrine, and corticosteroids. The effects of these hormones may continue long after the initial stimulus has subsided, because the removal of these hormones from the system requires some time. Under these conditions of extended arousal, spouses may experience prolonged feelings of upset, derived in part from the conflict itself and in part from subjective sensations resulting from the physiological arousal (Pennebaker, 1983). In much the same way as high levels of anxiety are associated with decrements in performance (i.e., the "inverted-U" Yerkes-Dodson, 1908, relationship), negative affect during marital interaction and the concomitant physiological arousal may interfere with higher order cognitive functions such as problem solving, planning, and creative thinking. Such a reduction in flexibility of cognitive functioning may result in a reliance on automatic and overlearned cognitive routines, and thus a tendency to resort to well-rehearsed, but highly maladaptive, behaviors that adversely affect the couples' ability to resolve conflicts. This view could be part of the mechanism that accounts for the Levenson and Gottman (1985) effects in which autonomic arousal predicts decline in marital satisfaction over time.

To summarize, strong negative affects during marital interaction can produce widespread physiological activation that is long lasting. This activation probably is related to subjective feelings of upset and reduced abilities to engage in new behaviors and creative problem solving, all of which bode ill for marital conflict resolution.

12.3.1. Gender Differences in ANS, Endocrine, and Emotion-Related Behavioral Reactivity

Gottman and Levenson (1988) reviewed a large number of studies in which the physiological responses of men and women were compared. There is not a great deal of relevant research, because historically most experiments have utilized subjects of only one gender. Still, among studies using both male and female subjects, the most common finding is that men are more reactive physiologically to a given stressful stimulus than are women. This relative heightened physiological reactivity of men and relative physiological "imperturbability" of women may provide a biological basis for understanding the consistent differences between husbands and wives found in the marital research: (a) wives function more effectively in a climate of negative affect, (b) husbands are more likely to withdraw emotionally in conflictual distressed marriages, (c) wives are more likely to escalate conflict, and (d) husbands are more likely to attempt to reduce conflict by conciliation.

Gottman and Levenson (1988) also reviewed the evidence for greater ANS, endocrine system, and emotion-related behavioral reactivity in men. In all of these studies, it was not possible to separate nature from nurture, and they did not claim that they were able to make this separation.

12.3.1.1. Autonomic Nervous System

From age 15 on, casual systolic blood pressure is higher in men than in women (Eichorn, 1970). In terms of reactivity, Liberson and Liberson (1975) found that men's systolic blood pressure responses to shock were more than those of women. A similar pattern of results holds for skin conductance. In a study of the habituation of the electrodermal orienting response, Korn and Meyer (1968) reported that males habituated more slowly than females over the first set of tones. Their results supported a previous experiment by Kimmel and Kimmel (1965), who used visual instead of auditory stimuli. Fisher and Kotses (1974), in a study of subjects' basal skin conductance levels and their responses to bursts of white noise, found significantly higher basal skin conductance levels in males than in females. Eisdorfer, Doerr, and Follette (1977) studied males' and females' skin conductance levels during the Valsalva maneuver (i.e., exhalation against 40 mm of Hg for 12 seconds). Males had higher skin conductance levels than females. van Doornen (1985) studied the physiological reactions of males and females on a routine day and on the day of an examination. On examination day, males showed a larger adrenaline reaction than females, but the gender did not differ on serum cholesterol level, systolic blood pressure, and heartrate. Finally, there is evidence that heart rate levels during a waiting period that followed an episode of provocation were less likely to decrease in males than in females (Sapolsky, Stocking, & Zillmann, 1977).

Blood pressure and persuasion. There is further evidence of gender differences in physiological response to stress and to intense marital conflict from a research tradition that stems from the study of Type A personality and cardiovascular risk. In a series of studies, Smith and his colleagues have studied the relationship between blood pressure responses and interpersonal influence (Brown & Smith, 1992; Sanders, Smith, & Alexander, 1991; Smith & Allred, 1989; Smith, Allred, Morrison, & Carlson, 1989; Smith & Brown, 1991). Brown and Smith (1992) studied 45 married couples and found that husbands attempting to persuade their wives showed the greatest increase in systolic blood pressure before and during the discussion. In males, physiological effects were accompanied by increased anger and a hostile and coldly assertive interpersonal style. Although wives showed behavior patterns that were similar to some degree to the husbands, they displayed neither elevated systolic blood pressure or anger. Also, Fankish (1992) found that both the size of the systolic blood pressure responses of husbands during marital conflict and their recovery times exceeded those of their wives.

12.3.1.2. Endocrine

A similar pattern of results exists for stress-related hormones released from the adrenal medulla (norepinephrine, adrenaline) and the adrenal cortex (corticosteroids). Frankenhaeuser (1975) found a gender difference among both adults and 12-year-old children in their adrenaline response to challenge. Tasks such as mental tests and examinations led to greater elevation of adrenaline in males than in females. Frankenhaeuser (1975) wrote: "in this case, as among adult males and females, there was a slight difference between the sexes, in favor of the female group. Hence, a sex-linked difference in motivation does not appear to be a likely explanation of the endocrine sex difference" (p. 229). As part of a longitudinal study, Rauste-von Wright, von Wright, von Wright, and Frankenhaeuser (1981) studied the stress and coping patterns of 18-year-old males and females. Obtaining measures of urinary catecholamine secretion under the stress of a 6-hour matriculation examination, they found that men excreted more adrenaline than did women. Men and women did not differ in their adrenaline secretion in response to a control condition. These results are consistent with findings reported elsewhere by Frankenhaeuser (1976, 1978, 1982). However, Gunnar's (1987) review of developmental psychoneuroendocrinology suggested that more recent studies provide evidence of a link between cognitive-motivational factors and endocrine differences between the genders. Nonetheless, Gunnar (1987) pointed out that, ". . . even when girls and women show an increase in adrenaline secretion, only the boys and men showed a rise in excretion of cortisol" (p. 85; see also Collins & Frankenhaeuser, 1978; Frankenhaeuser et al., 1978; Gunnar, 1989; Lundberg, de Chateu, Winberg, & Frankenhaeuser, 1981). Second, even when the women clearly had chosen to compete in male-dominated spheres, the rise in their adrenaline excretion was significantly smaller than that observed in males (Collins & Frankenhaeuser, 1978).

Most of this research was done with early adolescents. However, it was found that 3-year-old boys secrete more adrenaline than girls during the regular day-care activities (Lundberg, 1983).

In an investigation of a powerful life stressor, Friedman, Mason, and Hamburg (1963) studied corticosteroid excretion rates in parents of children admitted to a hospital with a diagnosis of a malignant disease. Fathers' corticosteroid excretion rates were significantly higher than those of the mothers (7.1. mg per 24 hours vs. 5.0 mg per 24 hours). It is possible that the higher excretion rates of fathers were due to their not having as great a role in assisting their child as mothers. However, this failure of active coping hypothesis also has been offered to explain the lower excretions of adrenaline of adolescent girls in examinations. Finally, Valtysson, Vinik, Glaser, Zohglin, and Floyd (1983) examined the plasma human pancreatic polypeptide (HPP) response to beta-adrenergic stimulation (which mimics sympathetic nervous system activation). The rise in HPP concentration produced in males was six times that produced in females.

12.3.1.3. Emotion-Related Behavior

In the area of behavioral differences in excitability and emotionality, there is evidence that males across a wide range of excitable species tend to be more emotional under stressful conditions than females. Becker (1971) studied isolation and crowding effects in newborn male and female rats, finding that males were more sensitive than females to the effects of deviations from normal postweaning social stimulation. Masuri, Schutz, and Boerngen (1980) found similar gender differences in behavior in the open field situation in young rats. Although there were no significant differences at 30 and 45 days of age, by 60 days, male rats had higher defecation scores and more ambulation than females.

Sackett (1974) reviewed research on gender differences in the effects of partial and total social isolation in Rhesus monkeys. Males under both deprived rearing conditions exhibited more self-aggression (in normal Rhesus monkeys, there are no gender differences in aggression; Sackett, 1974), reduced activity, less exploration (in normal Rhesus monkeys, males explore more than females), and more fear than females. Sackett (1974) noted that, in general, isolated females were less affected than their male counterparts, and referred to females as "the buffered sex" (p. 116). In particular, he proposed that the

deprivation-rearing effects are due to a developmental failure of inhibitory response mechanisms . . . [and that differences between genders result from] a deficiency in inhibiting those responses that are inappropriate and maladaptive in post-rearing situations. . . . The isolate cannot or will not inhibit these incompatible, competeing behaviors that developed during infancy. (pp. 120–121)

He suggested that "females may develop the physiological basis for response inhibition prenatally and therefore are not as adversely affected and persistently affected by abnormal rearing environments as are males" (p. 121).

Not all the studies they reviewed found gender differences (e.g., Frodi, Lamb, Leavitt, & Donovan, 1978; van Olst & ten Kortenaar, 1978). However, in sum, there was enough evidence to entertain seriously the hypothesis that *under extreme stress males become more physiologically and behaviorally aroused and are slower to return to prestressor levels than are women.* Clearly, the definitive work on this hypothesis has yet to be done. Nonetheless, the hypothesis organizes a considerable amount of the literature on gender differences that I have discussed. There are at least four components of the response with respect to physiological reactivity to stresses (such as strong negative affect in marital interaction) on which men and women may differ: (a) higher basal levels, (b) faster rise time after the onset of stress, (c) greater peak response, and (d) slower recovery. It is not known precisely what the pattern of differences is that discriminates men from women, but not all components of the response are needed for the hypothesis to be useful. They suggested that the most robust component will turn out to be slower recovery after arousal.

12.3.2. Implications of Gender Differences in Physiological and Behavioral Reactivity for Interactive Style and Health

Gender differences in reactivity, amplified by gender differences in socialization, provide some basis for understanding gender differences in marital interactive style and even may shed some light on observed gender differences in health.

12.3.2.1. Interactive Style

To reiterate a portion of our hypothesis, the reconciling and resolving interactive style of husbands in distressed marriages may represent an attempt to manage the level of negative affect in marital interaction and to keep it from escalating. The hypothesis that men are more physiologically reactive to stress than women provides a theoretical rationale for this effect. If negative affect is more physiologically punishing for males than for females, then men will be more inclined to engage in behaviors designed to minimize negative affect and to keep it from escalating. If this is true, it can help explain a number of observed gender differences in interactional style. Take the characterization of men as "rational" and women as "emotional" as an example.

There is good evidence for the existence of these rational versus emotional gender differences in the context of close heterosexual relationships. For example, Rubin (1976) wrote about blue-collar couples: "Thus, they talk *at* each other, *past* each other, or *through* each other— rarely *with* or *to* each other. He blames her: 'She's too emotional.' She blames him: 'He's always so rational' " (p. 116). Support also comes from a questionnaire study reported by Kelley et al. (1978). They concluded:

> The female is expected and reported to cry and sulk and to criticize the male for lack of consideration of her feelings and for insensitivity to his effect on her. The male is expected and reported to show anger, to reject the female's tears, to call for a logical and less emotional approach to the problem, and to give reasons for delaying the discussion. . . . The results are interpreted in terms of the interaction between a conflict-avoidant person (the male) and his partner (the female), who is frustrated by the avoidance and asks that the problem and the feelings associated with it be confronted. (p. 473)

It may be that males use whatever means possible (which are usually withdrawal, avoidance, and rationality) to manage the level of negative affect so it does not escalate.

12.3.2.2. Health

There is evidence linking negative affect to health. Bereavement following loss of a loved one has been associated with diminished immune system response, increased somatic illness, and increased risk for mortality (Van Dyke & Kaufman, 1983). Anger, hostility, and suppressed rage have been shown to be related to hypertension and coronary heart disease (Appel, Holroyd, & Gorkin, 1983). Also, the Type A coronary prone personality profile, which is thought to relate to heightened risk for coronary heart disease, is associated with a lifestyle characterized by negative affects such as hostility, contempt, and anger (Dembroski, MacDougall, Eliot, & Buell, 1983). There are clear health implications of these hypothesized gender differences in physiological reactivity, because they cut across the major ANS and endocrine systems that have been implicated in the functioning of the body's immune system (Jemmott & Locke, 1984). A review of Russian and European work on the precise biological mechanisms relating autonomic and endocrine functioning with immunocompetence (e.g., the relation of sympathoadrenal activity and antibody formation by B lymphocytes) is now available in translation from Russian in Korneva, Klimenko, and Shkhinek (1985).

The greater physiological imperturbability of women has clear implications for understanding the consistent finding that premenopausal women are overwhelming superior to men in their resistance to most infectious diseases and environmental stresses (Hoyenga & Hoyenga, 1979). These differences are worldwide, they hold across age, and they appear generalizable to psychological as well as to nonpsychological stressors (e.g., see Hetherington et al., 1982, on the effects of divorce on young children). Females appear to be put together better psychobiologically to deal with life's stresses than men. Women appear to be tougher, more resilient, and better able to recover more rapidly from upset than males. This latter effect appears to hold among the more excitable primates as well (Soumi, personal communication, 1980). This is not to say that women are invulnerable, but rather that they are somewhat less vulnerable than men. However, these gender differences in health need to be examined within the context of marriage; it is here that I run into a problem concluding that women's health is superior to that of men.

12.3.3. Is There a Contradiction Here?

However, things do not seem to be this simple and clear cut (e.g., see Verbrugge, 1985, 1989). There is other evidence suggesting the it is women, and not men, who are the potential victims in marriage. Indeed, Bernard's (1982) hypothesis was that marriage provides more of a buffering effect for men than it does for women. In terms of protection from mortality, the Berkman and Syme (1979) study supported Bernard's (1982) hypothesis (but see Ferraro & Wan, 1986). Marriage conferred a buffering effect for men against mortality, but it was friendship that supplied this buffering effect for women.

Also, in my DUO83 data (reported in chapter 5), it was seen that women, and not men, seem to be at greatest health risk 4 years later when the marriage was classified at Time 1 as on a trajectory toward dissolution.

Work on immune functioning and marital stress to date supports the idea that women are at greater risk than men. Kiecolt-Glaser et al. (1987) employed in vitro assessments of immunocompetence of 38 married women and 38 separated/divorced women. Immunocompetence was correlated with the marital satisfaction of the married women and the amount of attachment to the ex-partner for the separated or divorced women. Among the married women, lower marital satisfaction was associated with immunosuppression. Also, women who were separated a year or less had poorer immune function than married women, and among the separated/divorced group, shorter periods of separation and greater attachment to the ex-partner were associated with poorer immune function.

The equivalent work now has been done with men (Kiecolt-Glaser et al., 1987), and the data suggest that men undergoing marital dissolution are less at risk than women in terms of measures of immune functioning. In the Kiecolt-Glaser et al. (1987) study, recently separated or divorced women were compared with married women. The separated/divorced women had significantly higher EBV VCA titers, significantly lower percentages of natural killer (NK) cells, and lower percentages of T-lymphocytes than married women. There were also differences in the blastogenesis data between the two groups for PHA and the higher doses of ConA. Furthermore, although the two groups differed on self-report psychological variables, they did not differ markedly on other variables assessing sleeplessness, nutrition, or weight loss. Relationships undergoing separation that differed in the emotional conflict surrounding the separation also could be discriminated using the in-vitro immune measures. Separated or divorced women who were still high in attachment to their husbands had lower lymphocyte proliferation to ConA and PHA than similar women who were less attached. Attachment was assessed by self-reports of preoccupation and disbelief about the separation or divorce. Kiecolt-Glaser et al. (1988) attempted to extend their findings to males. I briefly summarize these results by noting that there were significant, but markedly smaller, effects or marital quality on immunocompetence in males. Using a hierarchical multiple regression, after education and years married were partialled out, there was a significant relationship as predicted between marital quality and EBV VCA antibody titers and the helper/suppressor ratio. Nonetheless, this set of results is considerably weaker than the equivalent results for the study of women. Furthermore, when the greater stress of relationship dissolution was employed, predicted results only were obtained as a function of whether men claimed to have initiated or not initiated the dissolution. Initiators had significantly lower antibody titers to EBV VCA than noninitiators, suggesting poorer cellular immune system control over virus latency for noninitiators.

These gender differences are interesting, particularly because they are consistent with other data that suggest that marriage provides greater health and mortality benefits to men than to women (Bernard, 1982). Whereas married males report less illness than unmarried men, married females report more illness than unmarried females (Cleary, 1987; Gove,

1978). A similar pattern holds for mortality; in this case, mortality shows a large main effect for marital status for males. Recently, however, Schmoldt, Pope, and Hibbard (1989), in reviewing evidence for these effects, concluded that it is not marital status that is related to health, but marital quality. Thus, studies that found the gender effect may have oversampled unhappy marriages inadvertently. If the Schmoldt et al. (1989) criticism was correct, it suggested that, consistent with the Kiecolt-Glaser results for women and for men, women are at greater health risk in unhappy marriages than men. Other research (Floyd & Markman, 1983) suggested that women are the barometers of unhappy marriages. Berkman and Breslow (1983) collected data on marital quality. The marital quality effect on mortality for men was most pronounced in the 50–59 age group, whereas for women the benefit was nonexistant throughout the life span. The buffering effect for women was friends and relatives. Of course, mortality is quite an extreme dependent measure.

12.3.4. Gender and Physiological Indexes of Stress in General: An Update

Polferone and Manuck (1987) wrote an excellent review of gender differences in cardiovascular and endocrine responses to stress. The cardiovascular measures were most commonly heart rate and blood pressure elevations above a baseline, whereas the endocrine measures were generally urinary or plasma measures of catecholamines (epinephrine and norepinephrine) and cortisol. Epinephrine has been more responsive to psychological stresses, whereas norepinephrine has been more responsive to physical stresses such as exercise (Dimsadale & Moss, 1980a).

The evidence they reviewed suggested that females have a smaller elevation in urinary and plasma concentration of epinephrine than males; the heart rate reactions of men usually are not different from those of women; but when differences are observed, the heart rate reactions of men usually are smaller than those of women; women have smaller blood pressure responses than men, particularly systolic blood pressure. In the study of Type A and Type B personality patterns, the Type A cardiovascular response pattern tends to be more consistently observed for male than for female subjects. However, there is some evidence that among women interpersonal as opposed to achievement-like challenges are more effective at detecting the Type-A/Type-B distinction using physiological indices of reactivity. Dimsadale and Moss (1980a) also concluded that the evidence does not strongly or consistently support the hypothesis that these gender differences are a function of female reproductive hormones.

In an ambitious dissertation, Emde (1991) studied the heart rate and blood pressure responses of maritally satisfied and maritally dissatisfied couples during marital conflict resolution. There were two tasks given in the same sequence: The first was conflict resolution with Markman's (1979) communication box, and the second was a conflict discussion without the communication box. The communication box involves spouses rating the intent and impact of their messages and taking turns at speech; it is a modification of the talk-table procedure (Gottman et al., 1976). The communication box procedure has been found to produce lower levels of negativity (Lindahl & Markman, 1990). Emde found that systolic pressure was higher for unhappily compared with happily married males during the communication box conflict discussion (see Fig. 12.1a). Unhappily married males also had higher diastolic blood pressures, particularly during the interview that preceded the conflict discussions. The heart rate data revealed no gender differences, but dissatisfied spouses differed from satisfied spouses across baseline as well as interaction conditions. This pervasive difference across conditions is quite consistent with my results. The baseline differences for males seem to be somewhat greater than those for females (the two groups of males differed by about 10 beats per minute, whereas the females differed by about 5 beats per minute), with dissatisfied subjects having higher heart rates than satisfied subjects (see Fig. 12.1b). Hence, the unhappily married males showed a more diffuse physiological response to marital conflict than the unhappily married females.

12.3.5. What Is One to Conclude?

There is evidence to suggest that females are the victims of ailing marriages, and that males are also the victims of ailing marriages. In some studies, with some physiological measures, the data support one conclusion, whereas in other studies with other physiological measures, the data support the opposite conclusion. However, it is encouraging that in no studies was it found that people in ailing marriages are *physiologically* less stressed than people in more satisfied and stable marriages.

However, in terms of these arguments of which gender is at most risk in terms of physiological arousal and illness, the data remain equivocal at this point. The definitive research has yet to be done on this issue. Part of the problem is probably methodological. In these studies, there tends to be little analysis of physiological response within the interaction, linked to specific behaviors within the interaction; instead, aver-

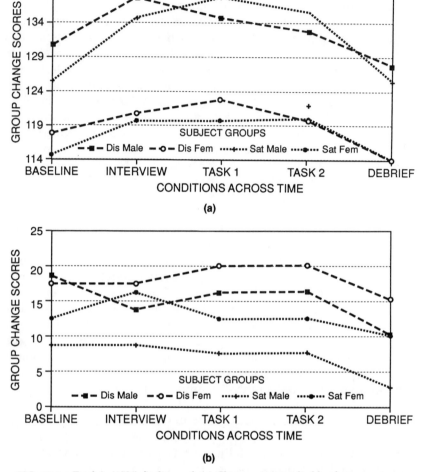

FIG. 12.1. Emde's (1991) findings of: (a) Changes in systolic blood pressure as a function of gender and marital satisfaction; (b) changes in heart rate as a function of gender and marital satisfaction. (Reproduced with permission.)

ages of both behavior and physiology across time have been studied. I am as guilty of this potential methodological error as anyone else. The reason for this methodological problem is that it is quite a complex programming and statistical task to go inside an interaction to study the synchronization of behavior and physiology. However, this is clearly the next step in this research.

With respect to health, in the sections that follow, I attempt to reconcile these disparities by developing a model that shows that the withdrawal of males from marital conflict is an effective health buffer unless it results in loneliness. The model suggests that male illness is mediated by loneliness. Because the cascade toward marital dissolution often implies loneliness (as part of the distance and isolation cascade), it is reasonable to expect that both husbands and wives are victims of a dissolving marriage, although their pathways to illness are different. Because loneliness is only a probable concomitant of marital dissolution for men, it is reasonable to expect inconsistencies across studies in terms of which spouse appears to be the identified victim of ailing marriages.

The model I propose is that diffuse physiological arousal and illness results from an ailing marriage for both men and women, but that it is mediated by different mechanisms for women than it is for men. I suggest that for women in an ailing marriage, illness results from their enhanced engagement and increased sense of responsibility—an enhanced desire to engage and reconcile the problems in the marriage, when coupled with a hostile and/or stonewalling husband who withdraws from the intense negative affect of this increased confrontation. In such a marriage, women experience physiological arousal and subsequent illness. Their physiological arousal can be predicted from their husband's stonewalling behavior. For men, illness in an ailing marriage is mediated by their being flooded by their wives' negative affect, their own stonewalling and withdrawal from the marriage, and their own subsequent loneliness as they progress down the distance and isolation cascade. I suggest that if men do not become lonely as part of this withdrawal from their ailing marriages, they will be buffered from physical illness. I suggest that this is not true for women.

Perhaps the role that loneliness plays for men, but not for women, in mediating illness exists because, for many men, withdrawal from their ailing marriages often spells complete social isolation, given their tendency to have extremely lean social support systems. For women, withdrawal from their ailing marriages implies calling on a rich social support system of friends and kin that are known to provide buffers against illness and mortality (Berkman & Syme, 1979). I have preliminary evidence from my study of distressed and nondistressed families with children that when a man withdraws from a distressed marriage, he withdraws from both his wife and children, whereas a woman withdraws from her husband but not from her children (in fact, she may become more involved with her children than previously). For many men, then, this withdrawal from an ailing marriage can involve an enormous emotional loss. Interestingly, the husband's participation in housework and child care are an index of his engagement with the marriage, and his lack of fear of his wife's expressions of negative affect toward him.

Before building this model of male illness as a function of marriage, I first examine the evidence for these gender differences in complain/ criticize and stonewalling in my own data, and the possible concomitants of these differences.

12.4. DUO83 DATA: MALE WITHDRAWAL FROM MARITAL CONFLICT

What is the evidence from my data for male withdrawal from marital conflict? In the DUO83 study, I found that there were spousal differences for the RCISS stonewalling listener code, $t(72) = 4.78$, $p < .001$, with husbands stonewalling significantly more than wives (husbands = 1.09, wives = 0.86). Also, there were differences in the complain/ criticize scale, $t(72) = -3.51$, $p < .001$, with wives complaining and criticizing more than husbands (husbands = .20, wives = .31).

Hence, there is evidence from this behavioral coding that anecdotally observed gender differences in marital complaints were paralleled by observations of marital interaction in the present study; husbands stonewalled more than wives, whereas wives complained and criticized more than husbands.

There were no spousal differences in the other negative RCISS codes of defensiveness, $t(72) = -.23$, ns, or contempt, $t(72) = -1.50$, ns.

12.4.1. Physiological Correlates of Husband's Stonewalling and Wife's Complaining and Criticizing

I next assessed whether there were physiological correlates of the two behaviors for which gender differences were found (i.e., husband's stonewalling and the wife's complaining and criticizing). Table 12.1 shows that, during marital conflict, the husband's general somatic activity was related negatively to his stonewalling and his skin conductance was related positively to his stonewalling. Thus, for the husband, stonewalling was associated with lower somatic activity (as would be expected) and greater electrodermal arousal. For the wife, the husband's stonewalling was correlated negatively with her cardiac interbeat interval and correlated positively with her skin conductance. Thus, the husband's stonewalling was associated with greater cardiovascular and electrodermal arousal on the part of his wife. Table 12.1 also shows that the wife's complaining and criticizing was not associated with any of the husband's physiological variables. However, the wife's complaining and criticizing was correlated negatively with her cardiac interbeat interval, as was her finger pulse amplitude. Thus, the wife showed greater cardiovascular arousal (increased heart rate and greater peripheral vaso-

TABLE 12.1
Relationships Between Physiological Variables, Husbands' Stonewalling, and Wives'
Complaining and Criticizing

Variable	Husband Stonewall	Wife Complain/Criticize
Husband		
Interbeat interval	.14	−.07
Skin conductance	.31**	.03
General somatic activity	−.26*	−.10
Finger pulse amplitude	−.02	.02
Pulse transit time	.01	−.12
Wife		
Interbeat interval	−.34**	−.26*
Skin conductance	.30*	.04
General somatic activity	.16	−.03
Finger pulse amplitude	−.05	−.31**
Pulse transmission time	−.09	−.19

*$p < .05$. **$p < .01$. ***$p < .001$.

constriction) when she complained and criticized. This kind of peripheral vasoconstriction, associated with withdrawal of the blood from the periphery, is consistent with the general "alarm" response, probably indicative of greater alpha-sympathetic activation.

Interestingly, the physiological impact of "spouse-atypical" behavior was much less profound. Thus, when the wife stonewalled, it was associated with greater skin conductance on her part,[1] but was associated with no signs of greater arousal on her husband's part. In fact, the only significant relation between the wife's stonewalling and her husband's physiology was an association with lower levels of his somatic activity.[2] Similarly, when the husband complained or criticized, it was unrelated to all indexes of his or his wife's physiology.

12.4.2. Relations Between Male Withdrawal and Negativity of Interaction

I next addressed the question of whether male withdrawal was related to the intensity of negative marital interaction (see Table 12.2). For these analyses, male withdrawal was assessed using the RCISS stonewalling code, whereas negativity of the interaction was assessed using the other negative RCISS behavioral codes of defensiveness, contempt, and complain/criticize.

The husband's stonewalling was related significantly to his defensive-

---

[1] $r = 0.30$, $p < .05$.
[2] $r = -0.27$, $p < .05$.

TABLE 12.2

Relationships Between Measures of Negativity of Marital Interaction and Husbands'
Stonewalling

Variable	Husband Stonewall
Husband	
Complain/criticize	.08
Defensiveness	.55***
Contempt	.57***
Wife	
Complain/criticize	.24*
Defensiveness	.50***
Contempt	.51***
Stonewall	.78***

*$p < .05$. **$p < .01$. ***$p < .001$.

ness and his expressions of contempt. The husband's stonewalling also
was related significantly to his wife's complaining and criticizing,
defensiveness, contempt, and stonewalling. Thus, it appears that the
husband's stonewalling is related to the intensity of behavioral codes
related to the negativity of the interaction, and also to the listener
withdrawal of the wife.

12.4.3. Gender Differences in Stonewalling and in Complaining and Criticizing

Thus, these results provide empirical support for the anecdotal reports
of gender differences between husbands and wives that have appeared
in the marital literature over the past 50 years (Gottman & Levenson,
1988). I found evidence that, during conflictual marital interaction,
husbands stonewalled more than wives and wives complained and
criticized more than husbands. Observed gender differences in the
present study were limited to these two behaviors; husbands and wives
did not differ in the other negative behaviors of contempt and defensiveness.

I consider these spousal differences as having the potential to
produce a vicious cycle in those marriages that are characterized by high
levels of conflict: The more wives complain and criticize, the more
husbands withdraw and stonewall; the more husbands withdraw and
stonewall, the more wives complain and criticize. How to break out of
this cycle of criticism and withdrawal is likely to be a central problem
that must be solved if conflict-engaging marriages are to avoid dissolution.

The relationships I found between the husband's stonewalling and increases in the wife's heart rate and skin conductance were consistent with the notion that the husband's withdrawal is stressful (i.e., more physiologically arousing) for the wife. This result fits with reports in the literature regarding wives' complaints that they find husbands' withdrawal highly aversive (Komarovsky, 1962; Rubin, 1976).

The husband's stonewalling was related to the intensity of the wife's negative RCISS codes and to his own defensiveness and contempt, as well as his wife's stonewalling. This suggests that stonewalling occurs within a negative interactive context, in which both partners become withdrawn listeners and complaining, criticizing, defensive, and contemptuous speakers. This interaction can be described as a hot-withdrawn or hostile/detached pattern.

It is probable that the greater likelihood of male stonewalling is independent of whether the conflictual issue was raised by the husband or the wife. Recent work by Christensen (1988) and Christensen and Heavey (1990) examined observers' ratings of withdrawal when a childrearing issue under discussion was raised by the husband or the wife. In both instances, husbands were significantly more likely to be rated as withdrawing from the interaction than were wives.

There was evidence in my data that the husband's stonewalling also is associated with his physiological arousal (i.e., increased levels of skin conductance). I have hypothesized in an earlier paper (Gottman & Levenson, 1985) that a major reason males engage in stonewalling behavior is to reduce high levels of physiological arousal. Compared with females, males have a constitutionally heightened vulnerability to sustained levels of physiological hyperarousal and males experience such states as being highly aversive.

These results are consistent with those of Notarius and Johnson (1982), who compared the physiological responses of husbands and wives during moments when wives' speech was coded as negative but husbands were coded neutral, versus moments when husbands' speech was coded as negative but wives were coded neutral. Husbands had higher skin potential responses during the husband neutral moments than wives did during their respective neutral moments. The inexpressivity of males may represent a different process than the inexpressivity of females. Perhaps males are rehearsing distress-maintaining cognitions during these moments, whereas wives are soothing themselves. This interpretation would be consistent with the research of Zillmann (1979). Sapolsky et al. (1977) experimentally provoked anger in males and females, who then were given an opportunity to retaliate either immediately after provocation or after a 6-minute wait. Waiting did not reduce arousal in males, but it did in females. Zillmann (1979) wrote that: "This difference in the effect of waiting on recovery suggests that males may be more prone than females to ruminate about mistreatments they have suffered and/or about their inability to retaliate against their annoyer" (p. 321). Evidence shows that brooding and rehearsal of grievances impedes recovery from annoyance-produced excitation. Also, Zillmann (1979) noted that "Communications involving contents that relate to the individual's acute emotional state potentially reiterate arousal-maintaining cognitions" [italics removed from in original] (p. 321). Also, during the wait period, the autonomic arousal (usually blood pressure and heart rate) of males remained high, but reduced in a retaliation condition; in general, the reverse was true for females: They were able to calm down during the wait period, but became aroused when they were forced to retaliate. Males may be worse at self-soothing than females, and more socialized to maintain distress for the purpose of later counterattack.

Gaelick, Bodenhausen, and Wyer (1985) used a technique in which men and women reported on how they perceived salient moments in a problem discussion. They discovered an interesting gender difference, consistent with my discussion. They wrote:

> Men tend to distort their partner's message in a negative direction. Consequently, they interpret a failure to convey positive affect as an indication of hostility. In contrast, women show a bias to interpret their partner's communications positively, perceiving their partner's lack of hostility to be an indication of positive feelings. (p. 1255)

These results could be related to gender differences in self-soothing during a problem discussion.

Zillmann's (1979) transfer of excitation phenomenon also suggests that people think that they have calmed down long before they actually have, and during that period when they seem unaware of their autonomic arousal almost any affect can be transferred to them. This suggests two possibilities: (a) calming down completely may have an added advantage in discussing a marital conflict of avoiding unwanted transfer of emotions that are not helpful; and (b) it may be possible, during the period when transfer of excitation is most probable, to transfer helpful positive affects such as humor. These possibilities await further exploration.

Although male stonewalling might represent a "shutting down" to control high levels of physiological arousal, some evidence suggests that such strategies may be ineffective. For example, in correlational studies, subjects who characteristically did not behaviorally express emotion during stressful situations were found to have larger physiological responses than those who did express emotion (e.g., Buck, 1979;

Notarius & Levenson, 1979). Similarly, using an experimental approach, subjects who were instructed to suppress behavioral signs of emotion also showed signs of heightened physiological reactivity when exposed to an emotional stimulus (e.g., Gross & Levenson, 1990; Lanzetta, Cartwright-Smith, & Kleck, 1976). In addition, there is evidence that a coping style of repression and denial may be associated with heightened physiological responses to stress (e.g., Weinberger et al., 1979).

Of course, the actual situation is likely to be considerably more complex than such a simple hydraulic model suggests. The physiological effects of stonewalling may depend on specific cognitions, the specific affects involved, as well as the inhibition of expression. I have interviewed couples about the moments in their own interaction that they rated as most negative. In those negative moments in which husbands stonewalled, spouses tended to rehearse cognitions of righteous indignation (reporting feeling blends of hurt and anger) and innocent victimhood (a kind of internal whining), which usually were accompanied by increases in their physiological arousal. On the other hand, in those negative moments in which wives stonewalled, they tended to rehearse cognitions of self-soothing, which usually were accompanied by reductions in physiological arousal. These informal observations suggest that subjects should be interviewed regarding their cognitions during all stonewalling moments that are coded during a marital interaction, perhaps using a video recall method (Gottman & Levenson, 1985). I hope to obtain these kinds of data in future experiments to further my understanding of stonewalling behavior and its physiological consequences.

12.5. LONELINESS, HOUSEWORK, HEALTH, AND PHYSIOLOGICAL AROUSAL

12.5.1. Loneliness

Loneliness is a potential correlate of withdrawal from marital conflict. Loneliness generally has not been studied in the context of a close relationship such as marriage, but I speculated (Gottman, 1990) that the experience of loneliness in a marriage might be a long-term consequence of male withdrawal. Recently, attention has been drawn by a number of writers to loneliness and its correlates (Peplau & Perlman, 1982). Loneliness has been distinguished from depression and described as a distinct set of psychological states (Weiss, 1973). Lonely people have been found to display distinct patterns of social behavior with a stranger of the opposite gender; they differed from nonlonely subjects in asking fewer questions, changing the topic more frequently, responding more slowly to their partner's statements, and making fewer personal attention statements (Jones, 1982). Hence, loneliness appears to have correlates other than the self-reports that define it.

Loneliness also may have negative consequences over time for physical health. The relationship between loneliness and poor physical health is by no means well established (Peplau & Perlman 1982). For example, a review by Weiss (1975) cited an unpublished study by Maisel that found the correlation between loneliness and health to be − .13. However, Kiecolt-Glaser et al. (1988) reported direct evidence of immunosuppression from in vitro assays of peripheral blood among lonelier medical students; lonelier students had significantly lower levels of natural killer cell activity and higher Epstein-Barr virus capsid antigen titers than less lonely students. In the DUO83/87, the assessment of health was included, using self-report measures that have been found to be reliable and valid (McDowell & Newell, 1987).

12.5.2. Husband's Participation in Housework

Based on Oakley's (1975) work on the sociology of housework, I adopted the husband's participation in housework as an index of how egalitarian the marital relationship is in terms of gender role specialization. Past research has suggested that husbands are inaccurate reporters of their own housework; they tend to overestimate it. For this reason, only the wives filled out a questionnaire rating their husbands' participation in housework. In previous research, it has been suggested that traditional gender role arrangements actually may reduce conflict and be functional for the marriage. I thought that the opposite also could hold, namely, that husbands who do housework could be more involved in their marriages and, correspondingly, less lonely. Hence, the husband's doing housework was adopted as an index of the husband's involvement in the marriage.

12.5.3. Other Questionnaires

I refer to five questionnaires: (a) loneliness (sample item: Sometimes I feel so lonely it hurts, alphas = .98 and .98, for husband and wife, respectively; (b) husband does housework, a questionnaire filled out by the wife on the extent to which the husband does household chores (alpha = .96); (c) chronicity of problems computed from the Couple's Problem Inventory (Gottman et al., 1977), based on a subjective estimate of how long a set of issues in the marriage have been problems (alphas

= .92 and .80, for the husband and wife, respectively); (d) escalation, which assesses the extent to which the partner's negative emotions are perceived as aversive, irrational, unexpected, and overwhelming (alphas = .95 and .96, for husband and wife, respectively); and (e) avoid conflict, which assesses the extent to which the subject believes that negative feelings and problems are best worked out alone rather that by talking things over (alphas = .82 and .78, for husband and wife, respectively).

A construct called Husband Conflict Avoider was created using the chronicity of problems, escalation, and avoid conflict questionnaires by converting each to z-scores and adding them.

12.5.4. Observational Coding

To test the hypotheses described in the anecdotal accounts about gender differences in marital interaction, I assess three constructs. These are: (a) criticism; (b) withdrawal from marital interaction; and (c) a construct called "hot marital interaction." The anecdotal evidence predicts that wives should complain and criticize more than husbands, whereas husbands should withdraw more than wives. First, I used the Marital Interaction Coding System (MICS) to measure one variable, which I call stubbornness (Gottman & Krokoff, 1989). The summary code stubbornness is a sum of the MICS codes noncompliance, verbal contempt, command, and complaint. The videotapes were coded by Dr. Robert Weiss' laboratory at the University of Oregon (see Weiss & Summers, 1983, for a discussion of the MICS codes and a review of literature that has employed the MICS). Double codes, which are used with the newest version of the MICS, were treated merely as additional single codes for this research. A sample of every videotape was coded independently by a second observer. The mean weighted Cohen's kappa of this observational coding system employing all the subcodes of the MICS was .60. Every z-score for each tape that compared kappa to its standard error was significantly greater than chance. A second observational coding system, the Rapid Couples Interaction Scoring System (RCISS), was designed in my laboratory to code three negative scales: (a) complain or criticize, (b) verbal contempt or escalate negative affect, and (c) stonewalling listener. This scale included the following listener withdrawal behaviors: no vocal or nonvocal backchannels (Duncan & Fiske, 1977) that usually convey to the speaker that the listener is tracking; no facial movement; no gaze or monitoring (brief glances) gaze pattern toward the speaker and a rigid neck. A second observer independently scored a random sample (10%) of each videotape. The average interobserver correlation for these scales was 0.75. On the basis of previous research (Gottman & Krokoff, 1989), a construct called Hot Marital Interaction was created by converting to z-scores and summing several variables derived from observational coding of the videotapes. These variables were husband stubborn, wife stubborn, husband put down or escalate negative affect, wife put down or escalate negative affect, and wife complain and criticize. Because these scores are summed across the interaction session, a correlation across observers was computed; this correlation was 0.82.

12.5.5. Results

12.5.5.1. Structural Models

Table 12.3 is a correlation matrix of the variables that were employed in building a structural equations model of these interrelations. Figure 12.2 is a diagram of a structural equations model of these data. If the model fits the data, a nonsignificant chi-square is obtained and the Bentler–Bonnett index is close to unity. The model fit the data well, with $\chi^2(32) = 39.79$. The Bentler–Bonnett index was 0.978. In Fig. 12.2, the z test for each path coefficient is given in parentheses. For significance at the $p < .05$ alpha level, the z-score must exceed 1.96.

One must be cautious about making causal inferences from these kinds of correlational data, and in the discussion that follows I recognize this caveat. Arrows in the model represent hypotheses about causal relationship that are consistent with the data. These data are well represented by a model that suggests that both stonewalling and physiological arousal (in skin conductance) follow from hot marital interaction. Furthermore, stonewalling in the model leads to the cardio-vascular arousal of wives and to higher scores on the husband avoider construct. The husband avoider construct is related to the husband's loneliness, which significantly predicts his illness 4 years later[3]. Further-more, the husband's participation in housework as assessed initially predicts less illness 4 years later. The housework construct also is related to lower heart rate for the husband during the initial problem area interaction.

The housework variable was designed to index the husband's greater engagement and involvement in the marriage: To test the possible indirect effect of this variable, an additional structural model was tested in which the arrow from the housework variable to the husband's illness was replaced by an arrow to the husband's conflict avoider construct.

---

[3]$r = 0.30, p < .05$

TABLE 12.3
Correlation Matrix of Variables in Structural Equations Model

Variables	V1	V2	V3	V4	V5	V6	V7	V8	V9	V10
V1: Hot marital interaction										
V2: Hus. skin conductance level	.36***									
V3: Hus. stonewalling	.52***	.20								
V4: Hus. conflict avoider	.27*	.11	.35**							
V5: Wife cardiac interbeat interval	-.17	-.06	-.39***	-.16						
V6: Hus. loneliness	.25*	.03	.25*	.71***	-.17					
V7: Hus. health at Time 2	.06	.11	.00	.06	-.05	.35**				
V8: Hus. does housework	-.04	.10	-.19	-.39***	.09	-.40***	-.23*			
V9: Hus. cardiac interbeat interval	-.13	-.13	.08	-.17	.13	-.12	-.13	.31**		
V10: Wife skin conductance level	.42***	.57***	.15	.09	-.06	.02	-.08	.21	.03	

*p < 0.05. **p < 0.01. ***p < 0.001.

267

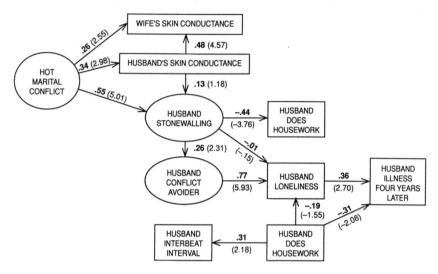

FIG. 12.2. Structural equations model of the variables relating to husband stonewalling.

This analysis is summarized in Fig. 12.3. This model also fit the data well, $\chi^2(32) = 33.28$, Bentler–Bonnett index = 0.982. As predicted, the path coefficient from the housework variable to the husband avoider construct was negative and statistically significant.

12.5.5.2. Summary

I have direct evidence that intense marital conflict is related to husband's withdrawal during conflict interaction, and that this withdrawal is associated with physiological arousal for both spouses. In the everyday environment, when they can escape, this male stonewalling pattern probably is associated with real escape and avoidance of interaction with the wife. In an ailing marriage, women are the ones who take responsibility for the state of the marriage, and not men. Several studies have suggested that wives are more likely than husbands to confront disagreements in their marriage (e.g., Burke et al., 1976; Huston & Ashmore, 1986; Wills et al., 1974). I also have noticed in most marital conflict discussions either the wife begins by stating the issues or the husband begins and quickly defers to his wife for elaboration.

12.5.5.3 Other Potential Benefits of Men Doing More of the Household Chores

Rabin et al. (in press) reviewed research that inequities in housework and child care have profound implications for the marital satisfaction of

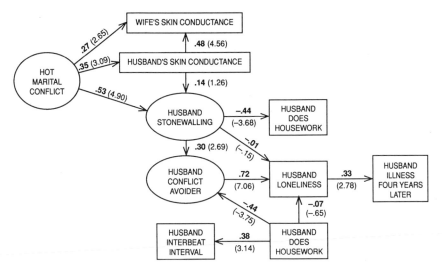

FIG. 12.3. Structural equations model with the husband housework effect on Time 2 husband's health as an indirect effect mediated through the conflict avoider construct.

wives. Such inequities cannot help but eventually (probably with some time lag) affect the quality of the marriage for husbands. However, the evidence suggests that there is an intransigence among many men that is difficult for most marriages to cope with. Rabin et al. (in press) noted that inequality in decision making and lack of shared parenting have been related to wives' depression (Mirowsky, 1985), and that inequity in relationship with the spouse was associated with depression for employed women, particularly for those who experienced role overload, but not for men (Vanfossen, 1981). The amount of housework and child care that men do is related to how wives evaluate them and their marriage (Barnett & Baruch, 1987; Staines & Libby, 1986). There are no similar correlations for men.

Rabin et al. (in press) noted that husbands resist sharing household and parenting chores and rate their marriage as happier when they perceive their wives as demanding less change (Harrell, 1986). Even women having a career is not typically met with increased involvement by husbands in household chores and child care. Men are quite aware that their working wives expect them to do more at home (Pleck, 1985), but the evidence is that they do not help more when their wives work (Crosby, 1991). For example, men with employed wives spent an average of 4 minutes more per day on household tasks than other men (Berk, 1985). Furthermore, a "liberated rhetoric" espoused by males may be unrelated to their actual behavior. In a study of 50 "liberated" men who claimed that their wives' careers were as important to them as their own, Gilbert (1985) found that not one man had discussed with his wife how household tasks were to be handled or divided. However, when men and women feel that the allocation of household chores is equitable (whether it is actually equal), both men and women benefit (Rabin & Schwartz, in press). There may be an intriguing link between men's doing household chores and child care and their involvement in the emotional life of the family. Rabin and Schwartz (in press) found, in interviews with self-acclaimed equalitarian marriages, that the emotional availability of both partners was central to the couple's feelings that the marriage was equitable; she found that this was particularly true for husbands not fleeing from their wives when their wives expressed negative affect (Rabin, personal communication, 1992).

12.6. INTERACTION OF STONEWALLING AND COMPLAIN/CRITICIZE AND MARITAL DISSOLUTION

I analyzed my data to see if the gender differences in stonewalling and complaining as a function of whether the couple was regulated or nonregulated. Regulated and nonregulated couples were quite different on both behaviors, for both husbands and wives. Nonregulated couples stonewalled and criticized/complained more than regulated couples. Also, across both groups of couples, wives complained and criticized more than husbands, and husbands stonewalled more than wives. Husbands always stonewalled more than wives, but this gender difference was not exacerbated among nonregulated couples. However, wives complained and criticized more than husbands, and this gender difference was exacerbated among nonregulated couples.[4] Hence, the

---

[4]I conducted a multivariate repeated measures analysis of variance of stonewalling and complaining and criticizing. In this analysis, there were four repeated measures: the wife's complaining and criticizing and stonewalling and the husband's complaining and criticizing and stonewalling. There was also a between-subjects factor of regulated versus nonregulated couples. The results were: (a) there was a significant multivariate effect for the between-subjects group factor, with Hotellings' $F(2,69) = 40.12$, $p < .001$; the multivariate spouse effect was also statistically significant, with Hotelling's $F(2,69) = 20.17$, $p < .001$; the multivariate spouse by group interaction was also statistically significant, with Hotelling's $F(2,69) = 6.86$, $p < .01$. The univariate F ratios revealed that, among nonregulated couples, there was more complaining and criticizing and more stonewalling than among nonregulated couples, and this was true for both husbands and wives [for husband stonewalling, $F(1,70) = 4.55$, $p < .001$; for wife stonewalling, $F(1,70) = 3.48$, $p < .001$; for husband complain/criticize, $F(1,70) = 19.59$, $p < .001$; for wife complain/criticize, $F(1,70) = 59.04$, $p < .001$]. Husbands always stonewalled more than wives, but this gender differences was not exacerbated among nonregulated couples. However, wives complained and criticized more than husbands, and this gender difference was exacerbated among nonregulated couples.

typical wife gender difference was exacerbated in marriages that were on a trajectory toward marital dissolution.

12.7. GENDER DIFFERENCES IN ADRENALINE SECRETION AND RECOVERY FROM ADRENALINE SECRETION DURING MARITAL CONFLICT

In an unpublished paper,[5] Gottman, Kiecolt-Glaser, Rushe, Glaser, and Malarkey (1992) discussed the results of a recent study with 90 newlywed couples. In this study, the couples were studied during a standard conflict task. After adaptation to the Clinical Research Center at the hospital at the Ohio State University Medical Center, blood samples were drawn periodically from an indwelling catheter. For frequent, unobtrusive sampling during the interaction tasks, a long polyethylene tube was attached to the heparin well, so nurses could draw blood samples at set intervals out of subjects' sight. The baseline blood draw occurred about 90 minutes after the heparin well was inserted, after subjects had been sitting quietly in chairs in front of the curtain for 10 minutes. At the end of the play-by-play interview, and immediately before the half-hour conflict interview, the second sample was drawn; the third and fourth samples were drawn 15 minutes after conflict began, and again at the end of the 30-minute conflict task. The blood was assayed for concentrations of the adrenal hormone adrenaline (in the United States, adrenaline typically is called epinephrine, abbreviated EPI).

Based on the Gottman and Levenson (1988) hypothesis, Gottman et al. (1992) expected to find gender differences both in the secretion of EPI and in the recovery from the secretion of EPI. Specifically, they expected that males would secrete more EPI than females during marital conflict, that males would recover more slowly than females, and that less intense negative affective events would lead to secretion of EPI in males than in females.

They found that husbands secreted more EPI than wives at each time point of measurement, including baseline (see Fig. 12.4). Also, there was a significant positive relationship between recovery and the time course of EPI secretion. The recovery of husbands and wives was

---

[5]The following is a reference to the unpublished report discussed in this chapter: Gottman, Kiecolt-Glaser, Rushe, Glaser, and Malarkey (1992): specific affects and recovery from plasma epinephrine secretion during marital conflict in newlywed couples. University of Washington, 1992. Copies will be sent upon request to the first author.

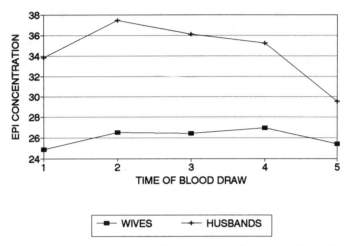

Fig. 12.4. Ohio State Study—epinephrine secretion by gender (from Gottman, Kiecolt-Glaser, Rushe, Glaser, & Malarkey, unpublished).

uncorrelated. Videotapes of the first 15 minutes of the interaction were coded with the SPAFF for the expression of specific emotions. The average kappa was equal to 0.64 for wives and 0.62 for husbands for the entire SPAFF coding system. Couples were first grouped into whether husbands recovered at least to baseline levels. Then the time course of EPI secretion was compared for husbands and wives. Couples were then grouped into whether wives recovered at least to baseline levels. Then the time course of EPI secretion was compared for husbands and wives.

They asked the question of which affects were associated with recovery from EPI secretion for each gender. Specific affects were related to recovery from EPI secretion, and these affects differed as a function of gender. There were gender differences in specific affects. Women exceeded men in the expression of disgust, whining, sadness, and belligerence. Women also exceeded men in listening with anger, disgust, and sadness. There was a linear spouse-by-time effect for stonewalling. There was a steeper increasing linear trend in stone-walling for men compared with women. Men eventually exceeded women in stonewalling [first third, $t(89) = 1.63$, ns; second third, $t(89) = 1.58$, ns; third third, $t(89) = 2.05$, $p < .05$].

For the wife's recovery from EPI secretion, there were significant group main effects for contempt, belligerence, and listening with belligerence. Couples that were contemptuous or belligerent, or that listened with facial displays of belligerence, had wives who did not recover from EPI secretion.

For the husband's recovery from EPI secretion, there were significant group main effects for anger and for listening with anger. Couples that expressed anger or listened with facial displays of anger had husbands who did not recover from EPI secretion.

Gottman and Levenson (1988) proposed that males would have slower recovery to negative affect in marital interaction than women, and that physiological activation of males would result from less intense negative affect than for females. The first part of the hypothesis was not supported, but the second part of the hypothesis was supported.

In this study, hostility was discriminated along a dimension of intensity, from direct expressions of anger, to belligerence and domineering, to contempt. Recovery from EPI secretion for wives could not be predicted from husbands' recovery. Hence, one might expect that different psychological processes might govern the time course of recovery from EPI secretion as a function of gender. This was indeed the case. The recovery of wives from EPI secretion was related to more intense expressions of hostility, to expressions of contempt and belligerence, and to belligerent listening by both partners (this was a group effect, not a group by spouse interaction). On the other hand, the recovery of husbands from EPI secretion was related to less intense expressions of hostility, to direct expressions of anger, and to listening with anger by both partners (again, this was a group effect, not a group by spouse interaction).

The pattern of the specific affects associated with husbands' versus wives' recovery from EPI secretion is interesting. The distinction between anger, on the one hand, and belligerence and contempt, on the other hand, may be quite important. In the coding system used in the present study, anger is coded when it is a direct expression of anger, either verbally, paralinguistically, vocally, or facially. This expression of anger is unencumbered by either domineering (effective at squelching the partner's response) or belligerence (effective at escalating and provoking a hostile retort). Thus, belligerence is a far more insidious and escalated form of anger expression. It is this escalated form of anger expression that affects wives' recovery from EPI. Also, consider the case of contempt, which often is an insult, derogation, mockery, or what has been termed a *character assassination* (e.g., "You are worthless as a lover").

I have noted elsewhere in this book that contempt is associated particularly with the risk of marital dissolution over time. Thus, it appears that the recovery of wives from EPI is associated with more escalated forms of anger and hostility than the recovery of husbands, and, furthermore, that these escalated forms of hostility that affect wives probably are related to the future time course of the marriage.

12.8. THE MALE FIGHT RESPONSE INSTEAD OF OR IN ADDITIONAL TO THE MALE FLIGHT RESPONSE

This chapter has highlighted male withdrawal from marital conflict as if it were the only typical male response to an ailing marriage or intense negative affect. Domestic violence is such a common problem today that this portrayal is an obvious oversimplification (Dutton, 1988). With Jacobson, Rushe, Holtzworth-Munroe, and Fehrenbach, I recently have begun studying the marital interaction of three groups of couples, a group in which the husband is physically assaultive toward his wife, a maritally distressed but nonviolent group, and a group of couples that is neither distressed nor violent. It is clear at this preliminary stage of research that the male tendency to aggress verbally or physically in a marriage also must be studied systematically. We are finding that, compared with maritally distressed males, violent males begin a marital interaction higher in contempt, domineering, and belligerence, and they stay that way throughout the interaction. Interestingly, violent men and men in distressed nonviolent marriages did not differ in anger, but only in the more aggressive and provocative negative affects. The emphasis on anger management for violent men may need to become more specifically focused on provocativeness, belligerence, and contempt instead of on the direct expression of anger.

One of the major puzzles in the clinical lore of domestic violence is why these marriages seem so stable longitudinally; not that they last, but that they seem to last longer than anyone thinks they should. Dutton (1988) suggested the concept of traumatic bonding as an explanation for the apparent longevity of these relationships. However, at present, there is very little prospective longitudinal research on these highly violent marriages. For very different reasons, we also need to know what factors are associated with the stability or dissolution of these marriages.

12.9. DEVELOPMENTAL ROOTS OF GENDER DIFFERENCES IN THE SOCIALIZATION OF EMOTION

In this section I explore the potential developmental root causes for the difficulty men and women have in emotional communication in close relationships. Can we identify differences in the natures of males and females or in the ways that boys and girls are socialized that may be related to difficulties that the sexes have in getting along? I propose a set of hypotheses that seem to converge to suggest that these roots exist. I also analyze the results of a longitudinal study of marriage and see if there are any recommendations for each gender that can be deduced from the correlates of marital stability and marital happiness.

12.9.1. The Sex-Segregation Effect in Childhood

Interestingly enough, in most cultures courtship follows a long period of segregation between the sexes whose causes are poorly understood. The explanation of this sex segregation has the potential for generating hypotheses about the troubles that many men and women will eventually have in their marriages.

Maccoby (1990) reviewed evidence that showed that, as far as we know, the sex-segregation effect is cross-culturally universal. She noted that the same-sex playmate preference is a widespread effect, and that its roots can be observed as early as the preschool period and that it grows stronger over time. The sexes do not begin life avoiding one another. In fact, Gottman (1986) reported an unpublished study by Rickelman (done in my laboratory) from a door-to-door survey in several types of socioeconomic neighborhoods in a midwestern city while about 36% of mutual friendship choices in preschool (ages 3 to 4) were cross-sex, this rate dropped to 23% for 5- to 6-year-olds and was nonexistent for 7- to 8-year-olds; the effect held. Hence, the evidence is that the sex-segregation effect is weaker in young children, but grows toward middle childhood, reaching it zenith by age 7.

Surprisingly, the evidence for a same-sex preference of some sort has roots that considerably precede the preschool period. Lewis and Brooks (1975) reported that 12-month-old infants prefer to look more at a slide of a same-sex child than a cross-sex child. Aitken (1977) obtained similar effects even when the children in the slides were dressed to look like their opposite gender (boy models were dressed in frilly dresses and shown holding a doll and girl models were dressed in dark-colored dungarees and shown banging a drum). Bower (1989) reported the effects of movement when the models were babies. There was a clear same-sex preference for the full color films of these models. Bower then did a clever experiment. Lights were attached to the joints of the children, so that in the film of the models' movements nothing was visible but 12 lights; this was less information than that provided by an animated stick figure; in a still frame the lights were not even recognizable as a human. Bower (1989) wrote:

> Nevertheless, when the films were set in motion, babies had little trouble in identifying the gender of the babies who had modeled the display; twelve-month-old boy babies looked more at the pattern generated by the baby boy, girl babies more at the pattern generated by the baby girl. (pp. 34–36)

Furthermore, the light pattern produced better discrimination of boy and girl baby viewers than the full color film. This study demonstrates a remarkable ability of babies to detect same-sex movement patterns, and it also demonstrates a preference for these movement patterns. These effects are not understood, but they suggest a biological basis for the same-sex preference effect.

Why are the sexes segregated for so long and then suddenly expected to be able to form and maintain an intimate life-long liaison? Let us take a look at possible explanations of this cross-sex segregation and discuss the implications of these causes for the stability and satisfaction of marriages. Do these explanations suggest any hypotheses about how the worlds of boys and girls are different in childhood that may lead to later difficulties between men and women? Are there any correlates of marital satisfaction within areas that are generally considered central to the maintenance of the marriage?

12.9.2. Possible Explanations of the Sex-Segregation Effect

Maccoby (1990) ruled out parental influences as causal in creating the sex-segregation effect. She then reconsidered a number of the conclusions that she and Jacklin had reached in their book on sex differences (Maccoby & Jacklin, 1974). The reconsideration was a rethinking of gender differences within the context of relationships. Maccoby and Jacklin had, by and large, decided in that 1974 book that, in general, there was little evidence for gender differences that were consistently greater than variation within each gender. However, Maccoby now suggested that within the context of social relationships there were some important and consistent phenomena that distinguish young men from young women.

Actually, there are two phenomena that need to be explained. The first is a same-sex preference, and the second is an increasing sex-segregation effect. I discuss only the second phenomenon here. Maccoby reviewed evidence for two factors that she suggested may account for the early segregation of the genders. The first factor is the preference of boys for rough-and-tumble play and for play that involves competition and dominance. The second factor is that girls find it difficult to influence boys. For example, Serbin, Spraflein, Elman, and Doyle (1984) reported that the developmental increase in influence attempts by girls involves increases in polite suggestions, whereas for boys it involves increases in direct demands. The influence styles of girls was effective with other girls and adapted for teachers and other adults. Maccoby noted that these factors would account for why girls would avoid boys but not for why boys would avoid girls.

In a study conducted by Jacklin and Maccoby (1978) with 33-month-old children, females paired with males interacted less than they did when paired with other females and they were more likely to passively observe while the boys monopolized the toys. Passivity in the girls was not a trait but a characteristic of cross-sex interaction. Maccoby suggested that the idea was that girls would not wish to associate with persons they have no influence with, so therefore it is reasonable that girls would avoid boys.

Maccoby also suggested that child and adult male social interaction can be described as *constricting*, whereas female interaction can be described as *enabling* (constructs she credited to Hauser et al., 1987). Maccoby (1990) wrote:

> A restrictive style is one that tends to derail the interaction—to inhibit the partner or cause the partner to withdraw, thus shortening the interaction or bringing it to an end. Examples are threatening a partner, directly contradicting or interrupting, topping the partner's story, boasting, or engaging in other forms of self-display. Enabling or facilitative styles are those, such as acknowledging another's comment or expressing agreement, that support whatever the partner is doing and tend to keep the interaction going. *I want to suggest that it is because women and girls use more enabling styles that they are able to form more intimate and more integrated relationships.* (p. 517, italics added)

How true is this very negative view of males? There is indeed some truth to her contention. For example, there is no question that males, even at a very young age, are more aggressive than females (e.g., see Hoyenga & Hoyenga 1979). However, there is also evidence that this aggressiveness is part of a cluster of behaviors that have to do with males having less ability than females to recover from strong negative emotions; for example, an early study by Goodenough (1931) showed that boys exceeded girls in the frequency of temper tantrums and anger outbursts and that this sex difference persisted through age 7. (For a detailed review of the question of sex differences in aggression and emotionality see Patterson, 1982.) Hence, we can conclude from the research literature that males have more trouble regulating their own negative emotions than females.

However, this view of young males must be qualified by data that show that young males make and maintain different kinds of peer social relationships than young girls. There is evidence that elementary school boys are more likely to choose activities that involve unrestrained movement or pretend assault (e.g., cops and robbers) more often than girls (see Sutton-Smith, 1979). Girls tend to choose activities that involve restrained movement (dolls, dressing up, house, school, hopscotch). Thorne (1986) also noted that during recess boys prefer run and chase games that require larger spaces and more children, whereas girls tend to play in smaller groups closer to the school building. Lever (1976) reported that there were sex differences in children's play. She concluded that boys more often play outdoors, in larger groups, and that their games last longer than girls' games. Gilligan (1982), reviewing this work, wrote:

> Boys games appeared to last longer not only because they required a higher level of skill and were thus less likely to become boring, but also because, when disputes arose in the course of a game, boys were able to resolve the disputes more effectively than girls: "During the course of this study, boys were seen quarreling all the time, but not once was a game terminated because of a quarrel and no game was interrupted for more than seven minutes. In the gravest of debates, the final word was always, to 'repeat the play,' generally followed by a chorus of 'cheater's proof'" (p.482). In fact, it seemed as if the boys enjoyed the legal debates as much as they do the game itself, and even marginal players of lesser size or skill participated equally in these recurrent squabbles. In contrast, the eruption of disputes among girls tended to end the game. (p.9)

Now recall the relative deficit that boys appear to have in regulating their negative emotions. In the context of this deficit, I suggest that the goal of the games that boys play in large groups is figuratively to keep the ball in play, that is, to keep the game moving. For boys *the game* is the object of the play, as is a fascination with negotiating the rules of the game as it is played. I have noticed on school playgrounds that an emotional event (e.g., one boy's crying) that threatens to disrupt a large group of boys' game is dealt with quickly by the boys in a perfunctory fashion. Emotion may be displayed but it cannot be allowed to be disruptive. The game must continue. So, in a sense, boys are working at containing their emotions by using the outside structure of the rules of the game, in which emotions are subordinated to another, more important goal, namely, the game.

In contrast, I suggest that for girls emotions are the substance of the interaction and the relationship is the context for bringing up, exploring, expressing, and understanding emotions. When conflict occurs that the girls cannot handle they discontinue the play because the object in a game like hopscotch is not hopscotch but the relationship the girls have when playing hopscotch. Hopscotch is an excuse for talking, feeling, and interacting. The relationship is the thing, not the game, and emotions are the substance of the relationship. Thorne's (1986) anthropological observations of different gender group play on playgrounds supports such a view.

These are complex differences between boys and girls because they involve both differences in the size of the group and the nature of the play. Gilligan took this evidence and suggested that boys do not learn how to relate in smaller, more intimate groups such as the best friend dyad, which is more likely to foster role-taking and empathy rather than competition. However, this is not true. Although boys play in larger groups than girls on playgrounds, a great deal of the play of both boys and girls occurs in groups of two, with best friends, and usually at home. However, even in the dyadic context there are some striking sex differences that can reliably be observed.

12.9.3. Further Exploration of the Causes for the Childhood Sex-Segregation Effect

Gottman (1986) reported the results of research comparing the dyadic conversations of boy–boy, girl–girl, and cross-sex best friendships among preschool children. In that report I noted that young boys played in ways that were very different from the play of young girls, and these differences concerned emotion. The boys tended to introduce danger and fear into their play and then to use mastery or humor to deal with their fears. In contrast, the girls tended to avoid introducing danger into their fantasy play, and when fear arose they would discuss the feelings and comfort one another in a parental manner. In cross-sex friendships, this difference was quite dramatic. In one tape of a pair of cross-sex best friends, the girl wanted to play with a doll, pretending that the two children were a married couple with a new baby whom they were taking around to show to their friends. After a period of this domestic play, the boy suddenly observed that the baby was dead and had to be rushed to the hospital with a very fast ambulance that he pretended to drive, and then at the hospital he turned into the surgeon who operated on the baby and brought the baby back to life. The girl protested that he was driving the pretend ambulance too fast and that she was afraid. He said not to worry, that it was OK and they would soon be at the hospital. This type of interaction difference was typical of the conversations of these young best friends.

Furthermore, it was not the case that the conversations of the boys could be described as "constricting," whereas those of the girls could be described as "enabling." For example, here are some excerpts from the conversation of two boys who were best friends, Billy and Jonathan (4 and 3 years old, respectively). They started out playing with water and then ended up talking about what they used to believe about soap when they were babies all then discussing all the things that can kill. Discussions of dangerous things is a common theme in conversations surrounding all young children's best-friend play.

[p. 161]
B: We'll go wash our hands, OK? Let's pretend we go wash our hands, Jonathan.
J: OK.
B: 'Cause I like it that way.
J: Why do you?
B: I just, well, because, I thought of soapy when I was a baby; then I started to like it.
J: You know what I thought when I was a baby?
B: What?
J: That it was poison.
B: Yes, and it was.

This last suggestion about soap being poison is rapidly taken up by Billy because the word "poison" for children has a delightfully dangerous and forbidden quality and they know it is tinged with great danger.

J: I did not want to have any [soap] when I was a baby.
B: Yeah, like kryptonite hurts Superman? And that's poison.
J: Yeah.

This leads to a discussion of all the things that can kill. Boys are quite eager to engage in an extensive discussion of these things, whereas girls are much less likely to extend such discussions in their play. Billy and Jonathan also become quite excited and worked up emotionally as they talk about these dangerous things.

B: And rattlesnakes are poison.
J: Ark!
B: Yes, they are.
J: No, they rattle their tail before they bite people.
B: Yeah, that makes them sick.
J: Or a person shot the snake. The snake would hurt.
B: Yeah, 'cause I hate snakes.
J: Yech!

In the fever pitch of this excitement they pick what they consider the ultimate fearful object, the shark. They then employ a strategy of dealing with the evoked pretend fear that is characteristic of boys—they either pretend to be the terrifying objects, or they devour it, or they kill it and conquer it.

B: And I hate sharks. But I love to eat sardines.
J: I love to eat SHARK.

B: Yeah, but they're so big!

J: But we can cut their tail.

They continue exploring the great power of the shark, realizing that they have imagined a terrible opponent, one that will require special efforts to subdue.

B: Yeah, what happens if we cut them to two?

J: It would bite us, it would swim, and we would have to run. Run very fast, run to our homes.

B: Yeah, but ummm . . .

J: By the trees. Mr. Shark bited the door down and we would have to run away into the forest.

B: Yeah, but . . . but if he bited all the trees down . . .

J: And then we would have to shoot him. Yeah, and the shark is poison.

B: But pink is. Red is, yellow is.

B: Yeah, but people are too. What happened if the shark ate us?

J: We would have to bite him, on his tongue.

B: Yeah, what happened if we bite him so far that we made his tongue metal?

J: Yeah.

B: Then he couldn't have breaked out of metal.

J: He can eat metal open. Sharks are so strong they can even bite metal.

B: Yes.

J: How about concrete? Concrete could make it.

Here is the ultimate means of resolving the fear. The creature is capable of nearly infinite metamorphosis—capable of moving from sea to land, capable of biting down trees in a forest so that no one can hide, capable of turning into metal or biting through metal obstacles. But concrete finally will subdue it, they decide.

When young girls introduce the discussion of dangerous things into their play with best friends they cope with the fears generated in entirely different ways than boys. They encourage the direct expression of these fears and then take a parental, comforting role, empathizing with the fear, and then soothing it away with words of comfort, love, loyalty, and affection. Again, the boys have dealt with the emotion indirectly and by subduing and conquering it (humor is another favorite indirect young male strategy). The emotion is dealt with externally and its direct expression is not encouraged; in Billy and Jonathan's conversation, instead of the fear of the shark being discussed, Mr. Shark's qualities and how to defeat him are discussed. Hence, these differences in dealing with emotion in the dyadic context appear to be consistent with the differences in group play previously discussed.

12.9.3.1. Summary

What do the selected findings I have reviewed suggest about gender differences related to sex segregation? First, the dyadic conversation of boys is clearly not describable by a "constricting" code, as Maccoby suggested. Boys' interaction is facilitative, but it is facilitative of a high energy and adventurous kind of exploration. It is also an exploration that avoids emotions. Boys are learning to employ external exploration to deal with their relative inability to calm themselves in the context of negative emotions. They are learning to suppress emotion and make it unimportant, to consider it disruptive to productive play, adventure, mastery, and exploration. Billy and Jonathan do not express their fear of the shark directly. Instead, they figure out how to kill the shark.

I am suggesting that the style of young boys' interaction downplays the direct expression and exploration of emotion, although this is not true for young girls. There is evidence from the work of Buck (1975, 1977) that boys between 4 and 6 years old are learning to inhibit the *facial* expression of emotion, although this is not true for girls. Buck used a procedure in which mothers (looking at a closed-circuit video of their child's face) had to guess which slides their children were viewing. Mothers of 4-year-old boys and mothers of 4-year-old girls did equally well on this task; mothers of 6-year-old girls also did well, but mothers of 6-year-old boys did significantly worse than the other three groups. We have direct data that corroborates this result; from both directed and spontaneously elicited facial expressions of 5-year-old girls and boys, girls produced more and more varied facial expressions under both conditions than boys (Shortt et al., in press; Wilson, Katz, & Gottman, 1993).

Why would boys be socialized to inhibit the expression of emotion and to deal with emotion indirectly through structures that encourage mastery? The hypothesis I am suggesting then is that because young boys are far worse than young girls at regulating their own negative affects, and because young boys' greater aggression is part of a greater interest in danger and adventure than girls, boys become socialized to suppress their own emotionality in the service of an external goal, which usually involves exciting play, combat, and competitiveness. Maccoby has suggested reasons for why girls would avoid boys. I suggest that because the play of girls does not afford the opportunities boys need for suppression of emotional expression, for high levels of excitement in pretend adventure, and for a mastery approach to fear, and because girls prefer the direct expression of emotion, boys also avoid girls. If this is true, young girls find young boys quite annoying, and young girls are just not much fun for young boys.

What are the implications of these hypotheses for later cross-sex interaction? The same-sex preference does not suddenly end with the emergence of adolescence; it continues well into young adulthood. If my hypothesis is correct, this avoidance over a period of about 14 years (from age 7 to 21) will have serious consequences when love relationships bloom and become serious in young adulthood.

12.9.4. In Public Settings Women Defer but in Marriages They Confront

Throughout life, boys are encouraged to explore wider physical spaces (Thorne, 1986) to have looser ties with the family than is the case for girls, who are kept close to the family and encouraged to make close social ties with kin (e.g., see Elder, 1984). As a result, it may be the case that initial differences in social behavior in childhood are amplified by socialization.

There is evidence that the social behavior of women in stranger groups is tentative, polite, and subordinate (Aries, 1976). Adult women clearly differ from men in social influence, dominance, and power in stranger group interaction. They are also more emotionally expressive than men and far more competent with close socioemotional relationships than men.

Interestingly enough, in close personal relationships, these gender differences have a surprising effect. Women have been socialized to be experts in close personal relationships. Hence, it should come as no surprise that women's *public* tentativeness and deference, the acceptance of a subordinate role and politeness in women in stranger groups does not hold in marriages. In the research literature on marital interaction that has used observational methods, women's marital interaction, in fact, has been consistently described as more confronting, demanding, coercive, and highly emotional (both positive and negative emotions) than the interaction of their husbands (e.g., Gottman, 1979; Raush et al., 1974; Schaap, 1982). The evidence also suggests that women in marriages have considerable influence (Gottman, 1979; Raush et al., 1974; Revenstorf et al., 1980; Schaap, 1982; Schaap, Buunk, & Kerkstra, 1988). Men, on the other hand, have been described as conflict-avoiding, withdrawing, placating, logical, and avoidant of emotions (Kelley et al., 1978; Raush et al., 1974).

13

Replication and Extension

This chapter explores the replication of the results with another sample, as well as extensions of the results using a new on-line SPAFF system. Effects of the SPAFF marital processes that correlate with the RCISS speaker slopes are explored using the longitudinal effects of marital interaction on children as dependent variables.

Until now, I have discussed the results of Study 1, the DUO83 study. Study 2, the DUO86 study, was designed, in part, to test the replicability of my results. The study also was designed to extend and consolidate previous results. One of its major goals was also the study of the effects of marital conflict on young children.

In this chapter, I discuss the results of this second study. Additional studies are currently underway with two other Seattle cohorts: a replication of DUO86 with 63 couples and a study with 140 newlyweds.

The DUO86 study was only a partial replication of the DUO83 study. Its main purpose was to study the effects of marital conflict on children's emotional and social development. The DUO86 study sampled only the conflict discussion, and it did not employ the same set of questionnaires as the DUO83 study. Like the DUO83 study, DUO86 also included the Oral History Interview, but it focused for the first time in my laboratory on coding the couple's behavior during this interview.

13.1. RAPID CODING OF AFFECT IN THE MARITAL INTERACTION

One of the most serious problems in doing this kind of research is the great deal of time the observations take. Toward the end of streamlining this portion of the research, I began experimenting with more rapid methods of coding.

The videotapes of the DUO86 study were coded with the RCISS and SPAFF systems. The RCISS coding was done in a fashion identical to that used with the DUO83 study. However, the SPAFF coding used a new modification of this coding system, called on-line SPAFF. This system was designed and built by Alan Ross, research engineer of the Instrument Development Laboratory at the Child Development and Mental Retardation Center of the University of Washington. Two observers were employed simultaneously for on-line SPAFF; one coded the wife and one coded the husband. For reliability checking, they both coded the same person for a time. In on-line SPAFF, observers used an affect wheel for the coding. They literally turned a small wheel, which lit up the appropriate code on a panel under the video monitor. This sent a signal to an A to D converter in a laboratory computer, the signal was sampled at 128 Hz, and a computer program then averaged the data into the most prominent SPAFF code for each second. The codes were perfectly synchronized to the computer-readable video time code on the videotape, so synchronization of behavior and physiology was accomplished with this system.

In the affect wheel version of the SPAFF, many changes were made to incorporate the knowledge that had been gained from DUO83's coding. All SPAFF codes had a low and high intensity (these were combined for my analyses of the oral history codes). Contempt and disgust were separated. This made it possible for me to test whether it was disgust or contempt that was most salient in the discrimination of couples into regulated and nonregulated groups using the RCISS. Positive and negative surprise categories were added later.

Also, patterns of behavior that appeared to be useful in the DUO83 study with other observational systems (RCISS, MICS) were added, to be coded directly by the SPAFF. These patterns were domineering, belligerence, defensiveness, stonewalling, and validation. In another version of the on-line SPAFF I currently am using in my laboratory in the study of spouse abuse, I am trying to make many distinctions in the listener's affect. Undoubtedly there will be other versions of the SPAFF in years to come, particularly as a function of new populations of couples I study.

I now have another version of on-line SPAFF. This version uses computer-assisted video coding stations and software designed by James Long. Both versions of the SPAFF considerably speed the coding. In fact, it now takes approximately twice real time to code a videotape with SPAFF (i.e., the tape is viewed first, then coded, so the total observer time is one-half hour, not including reliability checking); the previous time for SPAFF coding was approximately 20 hours for 15 minutes of videotape; hence, time is saved by a factor of 40. Even with training time with the new affect wheels (observers already were trained SPAFF coders), it took two observers about 1 month to code all 56 tapes from the DUO86 study; it would have taken approximately 2.5 years with the old version of the SPAFF. Reliability was acceptable for this version of the SPAFF system.

13.1.1. New SPAFF Codes

The Appendix summarizes the notes to coders about the new SPAFF codes when using on-line SPAFF. Briefly, new code definitions actually were devised for every SPAFF code, because on-line SPAFF has two intensities (low and high). The new codes were designed to capture the important information of all the other productive codes used in previous longitudinal studies, including the RCISS, MICS, and CISS. Also, there are added codes: (a) separation of contempt from disgust; (b) adding validation to the positive codes; (c) belligerence, which is on an anger axis, but has a provocative quality; (d) domineering, which is opposite to belligerence in that it attempts to control and squelch anger expression in the partner rather than provoke it; (e) defensiveness, which includes examples of this from the MICS, RCISS, the CISS; and (f) stonewalling.

13.2. REPLICATION OF THE CASCADE MODEL

Figure 13.1 is a representation of the results of the structural equations modeling of the variables of the cascade model. This model fit the data well, with $\chi^2(3) = 4.63$, $p = .20$, and Bentler–Bonnett norm = .998. The figure shows that the variables of the cascade model again form a Guttman-like scale. The 2-year follow-up data in this study differed from the 4-year follow-up data in the DUO83 study; they showed a tighter linkage between separation and divorce and a stronger correlation between marital separation and considerations of dissolution. Marital satisfaction, even at Time 2, was a weaker predictor of separation and divorce than was the case for the DUO83 study. Nonetheless, the cascade model replicated its general structure. Marriages that dissolve generally go through an orderly progression represented by the cascade model.

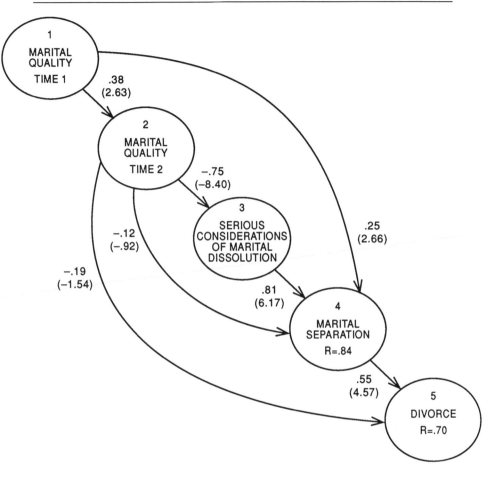

FIG. 13.1. Cascade model for Study 2 (DUO86).

13.3. DO MARITAL PROCESS VARIABLES PREDICT
THE CASCADE?

Table 13.1 summarizes the correlations between the RCISS variables, including the speaker point graph slopes, the SPAFF codes, and the variables of the cascade model. In general, the results are consistent with those of the DUO83 study (Study 1).

13.3.1. RCISS Results

For the RCISS, Time 1 marital satisfaction was related negatively to complain/criticize for the husband, defensiveness for both husband

TABLE 13.1

Correlations of RCISS and SPAFF Variables with Variables of the Cascade Model, Study 2

Variables	Marital Quality Time 1	Marital Quality Time 2	Serious Considerations of Dissolution	Separation	Months Separated	Divorce
RCISS						
Hus. complain/criticize	−.28*	−.22	.24	.05	.00	−.14
Hus. defensiveness	−.39**	−.35**	.26	.12	.05	−.12
Hus. contempt	−.25	−.37**	.39**	.29*	.18	.01
Hus. stonewall	−.09	−.06	.11	−.02	.19	−.07
Wife complain/criticize	−.26	−.11	.22	.01	−.04	−.16
Wife defensive	−.32*	−.25	.15	.03	.05	−.13
Wife contempt	−.37**	−.27*	.46***	.33**	.30*	.02
Wife stonewall	−.10	−.17	.20	.06	.18	−.11
Hus. speaker slope	.40**	.32*	−.32*	−.14	−.09	.10
Wife speaker slope	.31*	.21	−.29*	−.10	−.08	.10
SPAFF						
Hus. disgust	−.07	−.01	−.10	−.07	−.04	−.05
Hus. contempt	−.32*	−.22	−.29*	−.07	−.03	−.03
Hus. belligerence	−.27*	−.41**	.41**	.28*	.41**	.15
Hus. domineering	−.13	−.35**	.26	.12	.00	−.10
Hus. anger	.09	.13	−.08	−.07	−.04	−.08
Hus. tension	−.09	.37**	.10	.09	.27*	.21
Hus. defensiveness	−.19	−.09	−.02	−.02	−.10	−.04
Hus. whining	−.09	.01	−.12	−.12	−.01	−.06
Hus. sadness	−.18	.12	.21	.20	.39**	.31*
Hus. stonewalling	−.03	.01	−.04	−.09	−.08	−.07
Hus. interest	.11	.18	−.05	−.05	−.10	−.08
Hus. validation	.15	.23	−.18	−.07	−.08	−.06
Hus. affection	.28*	.16	−.18	−.02	−.11	−.10
Hus. humor	.44**	.13	−.11	.00	.08	.02
Hus. joy	.17	.12	−.10	−.07	−.04	−.05
Wife disgust	−.14	.11	−.14	−.10	−.03	−.06
Wife contempt	−.31*	−.27*	.34**	.11	.32*	.15
Wife belligerence	−.28*	−.19	.20	−.02	.16	.03
Wife domineering	−.24	−.05	.30*	.27*	.11	.00
Wife anger	−.31*	−.17	.16	.13	.24	.07
Wife tension	−.25	−.13	.00	.03	.05	−.09
Wife defensiveness	−.39**	−.07	−.06	−.03	−.03	−.03
Wife whining	−.11	.00	.17	−.07	−.03	−.06
Wife sadness	−.19	−.22	.20	.08	.23	.02
Wife stonewalling	−.23	−.18	.18	−.01	.06	.01
Wife interest	.11	−.01	.05	.27*	−.02	.23
Wife validation	.05	.21	−.17	−.04	−.06	.03
Wife affection	.17	.18	−.17	−.06	−.09	−.06
Wife humor	.51***	.22	−.22	−.04	.07	−.03
Wife joy	.24	.30*	−.17	−.15	−.08	−.11

*p < .05. **p < .01. ***p < .001.

288

and wife, and contempt for the wife; and positively related to the speaker point graph slopes. Time 2 marital satisfaction was related significantly negatively to husband complain/criticize, contempt, wife contempt; and positively related to the husband's speaker point graph slope. Serious considerations of marital dissolution were correlated with Time 1 husband contempt and wife contempt, and negatively related to the speaker point graph slopes. Marital separation was predicted by both husband and wife contempt; months separated were predicted by the wife's contempt. Divorce was not predicted significantly by any RCISS variable.

13.3.2. SPAFF Results

Time 1 marital quality was related negatively and significantly to the husband's contempt and belligerence; the wife's contempt, belligerence, anger, and defensiveness; and positively related to the husband's affection and both the husband's and wife's humor. Time 2 marital quality was predicted negatively related at Time 1 to the husband's belligerence and domineering, and the wife's contempt; and positively related to the husband's tension and the wife's joy. Serious considerations of marital dissolution were predicted by Time 1 husband contempt and belligerence, and wife contempt and domineering. Marital separation was predicted by the husband's belligerence at Time 1, the wife's domineering, and (curiously) the wife's expressed interest. Months separated were predicted by Time 1 husband belligerence, husband tension, husband sadness, and wife contempt. Divorce was predicted only from Time 1 husband sadness, and this result probably is not general; it appears to be due to one outlier couple that divorced, and in which the husband was coded at Time 1 as extremely sad.

13.3.2.1. Replication of the Process Cascades

Once again, structural equations modeling was employed to test whether the four MICS and the equivalent four RCISS process variables formed a cascade. For the MICS variables, the same model held, with $\chi^2(2) = 3.21, p = .20$, Bentler–Bonnett Normed Index = .993. Figure 13.2 summarizes this analysis. Although the path coefficients are somewhat larger than in the DUO83 study, the same model fit. For the RCISS data, a simpler model fit the data. Recall that only a nearly saturated model fit for the DUO83 data, with zero chi-square. For the DUO86 data (portrayed in Fig. 13.2), it was possible to drop the link between complain/criticize and stonewalling; this simpler model fit, with $\chi^2(1) = 2.70, p = .10$, Bentler–Bonnett Normed Index = .992. Hence, the replication data

Study 2 (DUO86)

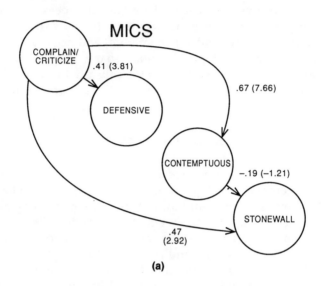

(a)

Study 2 (DUO86)

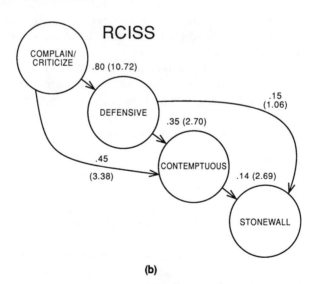

(b)

FIG. 13.2. Structural equations models for the (a) MICS and (b) RCISS data, Study 2, showing replication of the Guttman-like scale of the interaction process variables.

are consistent with the notion that the process variables for both the MICS and RCISS form a Guttman-like scale, that is, a process cascade.

13.3.3. Physiology

Table 13.2 presents the correlations of the mean levels of physiological activity during the marital interaction with the RCISS speaker point graph slopes. Consistent with Study 1, there were no significant correlations with husband physiology and either the husband's or the wife's slope. However, for the wife's physiology, a positive husband slope was significantly related to longer interbeat intervals (slower heart rates), and lower skin conductance levels; there was a marginal effect for activity: Positive slopes were associated with less wife somatic motor activity during the interaction. In general, these results suggest that less positive speaker slopes are associated with more wife physiological arousal. There was no effect for husbands. This pattern replicates the pattern of the physiological data in Study 1.

13.4. TYPOLOGY RESULTS

Applying the same criteria as in the DUO83 study (Study 1) yielded 26 validators, 12 volatile couples, 2 conflict minimizers, 12 hostile couples, and 4 hostile/detached couples. Because of the low cell sizes for some of the categories, comparisons only were conducted between validators, volatile, and hostile marriages. These one-way analyses of variance

TABLE 13.2
Correlation of Physiological Variables with RCISS Speaker Point Graph Slopes, Study 2

Variable	Husband Speaker Slope	Wife Speaker Slope
Husband		
Cardiac interbeat interval	.03	.00
Activity	.08	.16
Skin conductance level	− .20	.00
Pulse transmission time	− .11	.03
Finger pulse amplitude	− .23[a]	− .06
Wife		
Cardiac interbeat interval	.27*	.19
Activity	− .23[a]	− .22[a]
Skin conductance level	− .30*	− .09
Pulse transmission time	.03	− .13
Finger pulse amplitude	.14	.14

[a]$p < .10$. *$p < .05$.

results are shown in Table 13.3. As can be seen from this table, these three groups differ, as expected, from the previous discussion of these types of couples in Study 1. On the SPAFF, for husband and wife contempt, husband and wife belligerence, husband domineering, husband defensiveness, wife anger, and wife defensiveness, the hostile group far exceeds the other two groups. One also can see that the volatile couples, as expected, are both more positive and more negative than the validators (see husband validation and defensiveness, wife belligerence, wife defensiveness, and wife validation). Similar patterns hold for the RCISS subscales; hostile couples complain and criticize more than validators and volatiles, they are more defensive, and they express more contempt.

In a test of the universal constant, for the RCISS, a constant near 5.0 held for the validators and volatile couples, whereas the equivalent ratio was 1.73 for husbands in hostile marriages and 2.38 for wives in hostile marriages. Hence, the constant near 5.0 held for this study for the stable groups. Note that the RCISS was used without modification in DUO86 (Study 2). However, the SPAFF was modified in going to the on-line version. Many negative affect patterns were added. For example, domineering, belligerence, and defensiveness were added, and contempt and disgust were coded separately. With this new SPAFF, the ratio was about 2.4 for husbands in regulated marriages and 0.16 for nonregulated; for wives in regulated marriages, the ratio was 0.63, whereas for wives in nonregulated marriages, the ratio was 0.11. The nature of the relationship for both ratios remained the same. In fact, it may be that a universal constant may be found in the ratio of the two positive to negative ratios (regulated vs. nonregulated marriages). However, it is clear from these numbers that the actual value of the positive-to-negative ratio is a function of how finely one breaks down negativity and positivity.

13.5. GENDER DIFFERENCES

Table 13.4 summarizes the gender differences obtained with the complain/criticize and stonewalling. Once again, the differences obtained in Study 1 were replicated. Wives complained and criticized significantly more than husbands, and husbands stonewalled significantly more than wives. Because the new SPAFF coding system has a code for stonewalling, a test of its validity would be if gender differences were obtained using this code with the affect wheel version of SPAFF. Indeed, using the on-line SPAFF, males stonewalled an average of 15.48 seconds, whereas females stonewalled an average of 1.07 seconds (out of 15 minutes), $t (55) = 2.29$, $p < .05$.

TABLE 13.3

One-Way Analyses of Variance for Typology with RCISS and SPAFF Variables, Study 2

	Means			
Variable	Volatiles	Validators	Hostiles	F(2, 47)
		SPAFF		
Husband				
Disgust	.08	.00	.00	1.62
Contempt	2.08	2.73	16.67	7.52***
Belligerence	7.58	3.23	25.75	20.32***
Domineering	.58	.19	39.00	6.12**
Anger	2.42	.85	10.92	2.01
Tension	22.67	12.65	5.00	1.01
Defensiveness	144.25	31.92	126.92	12.15***
Whining	.50	.08	.08	4.90
Sadness	42.92	2.77	.83	3.13[a]
Stonewalling	.00	15.50	15.67	.78
Interest	1.00	1.35	.17	3.00[a]
Validation	47.00	12.77	7.17	3.76*
Affection	5.17	5.15	.58	1.27
Humor	21.75	24.77	9.25	3.43*
Joy	.00	.04	.00	.45
Wife				
Disgust	.83	.31	.00	1.21
Contempt	3.75	2.35	11.25	4.87*
Belligerence	11.58	6.73	62.17	7.33**
Domineering	10.92	4.96	41.67	1.43
Anger	9.00	1.54	3.42	4.90*
Tension	38.25	8.50	38.67	2.30
Defensiveness	129.83	50.15	129.33	9.17***
Whining	2.17	1.31	9.58	2.09
Sadness	17.75	9.42	5.83	1.06
Stonewalling	.75	1.58	.08	.41
Interest	1.33	1.73	1.67	.08
Validation	22.42	9.50	5.17	5.86**
Affection	6.67	4.23	.17	1.57
Humor	24.08	22.27	10.83	2.24
Joy	.17	.42	.33	.20
		RCISS		
Husband				
Complain/criticize	.04	.02	.32	47.74***
Defensiveness	.33	.15	.51	29.16***
Contempt	.01	.00	.05	14.00***
Stonewalling	.67	.74	.99	2.21
Wife				
Complain/criticize	.10	.03	.38	35.92***
Defensiveness	.25	.16	.44	29.46***
Contempt	.01	.00	.06	6.53**
Stonewalling	.49	.58	.76	1.78

Note. Means are seconds for which code was dominant.

[a]$p < .10$. *$p < .05$. **$p < .01$. ***$p < .001$.

293

TABLE 13.4
Gender Differences on RCISS Subscales, Study 2

Variable	Means			
	Husband	Wife	t(55)	p
Complain/criticize	.12	.17	−2.76	.008
Defensiveness	.31	.28	1.78	.081
Contempt	.02	.03	−1.49	ns
Stonewalling	.88	.71	3.18	.002

13.6. FURTHER PRECISION ABOUT THE AFFECTIVE NATURE OF THE RCISS POINT GRAPHS: CORRELATIONS BETWEEN NEW SPAFF SYSTEM AND RCISS SPEAKER SLOPES

Table 13.5 summarizes the correlations obtained between the RCISS speaker slopes and the new on-line SPAFF codes. This table is interesting, because it enables a test of greater specificity in correlating the new SPAFF codes with the RCISS codes. This permits greater precision in inferences about which behaviors may be implicated in the RCISS's prediction of dissolution. As can be seen from the table, contempt (not disgust) is related strongly to RCISS speaker slope. Both intensities of contempt, for both spouses, are related significantly to the point graph slopes. The husband's low-intensity anger was related only to his wife's RCISS speaker slopes, but the wife's anger of both intensities was related to both slopes. Once again, fear was an uninteresting code in the SPAFF. Belligerence turned out to be a very important code in accounting for variation in RCISS speaker slopes, particularly the husband's belligerence. To a lesser degree, a similar statement could be made for the husband's domineering. Defensiveness (low intensity) was related to the husband's RCISS slope; the wife's low-intensity defensiveness was related to both slopes, whereas her high-intensity defensiveness was related to her slope only. Whining lost some of its usefulness with the added code of defensiveness. Interestingly, the wife's sadness and the husband's and wife's neutral affect were related to the RCISS slopes, but this was not true for the husband's sadness.

Of the positive affects, validation, affection, and humor were related to the RCISS speaker slopes, although the relationship was weaker than it was for the negative affects and neutral affect. Thus, the new on-line SPAFF added some clarity to the old SPAFF, and it reduced the coding time by an enormous amount.

TABLE 13.5
Correlations of Online Affect Wheel SPAFF and RCISS Speaker Slopes, Which Were
Predictive of Marital Dissolution

Husband Code		Husband Slope	Wife Slope	Wife Code		Husband Slope	Wife Slope
Disgust	1	–	–	Disgust	1	.21	.16
	2	.05	.04		2	.05	.04
Contempt	1	−.53***	−.46***	Contempt	1	−.47***	−.65***
	2	−.42***	−.47***		2	−.55***	−.66***
Belligerence	1	−.69***	−.62***	Belligerence	1	−.37**	−.35**
	2	−.60***	−.60***		2	−.33*	−.22
Domineering	1	−.33*	−.11	Domineering	1	−.14	−.14
	2	−.36**	−.13		2	−.17	.15
Anger	1	−.18	−.37**	Anger	1	−.31*	−.44***
	2	−.20	−.13		2	−.40**	−.51***
Fear	1	.18	.17	Fear	1	−.09	.10
	2	−.05	−.06		2	.01	.09
Defensiveness	1	−.33*	−.13	Defensiveness	1	−.41**	−.39**
	2	−.16	−.08		2	−.22	−.34**
Whining	1	−.04	−.22[a]	Whining	1	−.26[a]	−.30*
	2	−.04	.10		2	.15	.17
Sadness	1	.10	.12	Sadness	1	−.30*	−.37**
	2	.14	.13		2	−.23[a]	−.40**
Stonewalling	1	−.07	−.23[a]	Stonewalling	1	−.04	−.02
	2	−.07	−.27*		2	.08	−.12
Neutral		.37**	.23[a]	Neutral		.57***	.57***
interest	1	.24[a]	.20	interest	1	.09	.07
	2	–	–		2	−.18	−.08
Validation	1	.19	.22[a]	Validation	1	.31*	.29*
	2	.23[a]	.29*		2	.15	.02
Affection	1	.28*	.26[a]	Affection	1	.30*	.24[a]
	2	.16	.13		2	.12	.10
Humor	1	.37**	.33*	Humor	1	.29*	.22[a]
	2	.21	.21		2	.15	.18
Joy	1	−.03	−.02	Joy	1	.09	.06
	2	–	–		2	–	–

Note. 1 = low intensity, 2 = high intensity.
[a]$p < .10$. *$p < .05$. **$p < .01$. ***$p < .001$.

13.7. LONGITUDINAL EFFECTS OF MARITAL PROCESSES ON CHILDREN

The parents' marital interaction was video-taped when the children were preschoolers, averaging 5 years of age. Three years later, the teachers completed the Child Adaptive Behavior Inventory (CABI; Cowan & Cowan, 1990). The CABI was employed as a measure of child outcomes for several reasons. First, the CABI, based on a normal sample, contains subscales that are less pathological in nature than measures such as the Achenbach scale (Achenbach & Edelbrock, 1981,

1984), and may be sensitive to more subtle behavior problems than the Achenbach scales. Second, the CABI controls for teacher rating bias by having teachers complete the scale on all same-gender children in the classroom and deriving z-scores for the target child. The CABI has good internal consistency (average alpha = .81; range = .66–.90) and predictive validity (Cowan & Cowan, 1987). Candidates for child problems are usually either externalizing problems involving aggression or internalizing problems involving depression, anxiety, and somatic complaints. At this follow-up time, children also were administered the Peabody Individual Achievement Test.

Table 13.6 summarizes the correlations between those on-line SPAFF codes that correlated with the RCISS speaker slope variables (obtained when the children were 5 years old) and the z-scores of the teacher ratings on the antisocial factor, depression, and academic achievement, and the Peabody scales when the children were 8 years old. There were no significant child gender effects in this study (Katz & Gottman, 1993). In one case, the child's antisocial ratings by the teacher at age 8 were predicted significantly by the husband's belligerence and anger toward his wife and his wife's contempt, belligerence, anger, and lack of validation toward her husband when the child was 5 years old. The child's depression ratings by the teacher at age 8 were predicted significantly by the husband's anger toward his wife and his wife's belligerence toward her husband when the child was 5 years old. The child's academic ratings by the teacher at age 8 were predicted significantly by the wife's belligerence toward her husband when the child was 5 years old. The child's math achievement was not predicted by the marital interaction. The child's reading recognition scores were predicted only by the husband's validation of his wife when the child was 5 years old. The child's reading comprehension scores at age 8 were predicted significantly by the husband's belligerence toward his wife and his wife's contempt and defensiveness toward her husband when the child was 5 years old.

The prediction involves multimethod correlations, and the correlations suggest that there is a substantial relationship between the marital interaction of the parents when the children are preschoolers and how children do in school 3 years later. The mechanisms for these correlations remain to be explored, but it is reasonable to suggest that there is direct modeling of aggression by the children. There is evidence that this is the case by examining correlations between the marital interaction and the child's interaction with a best friend at home. There also is evidence that parent–child interaction mediates some of these effects (Katz, Kramer, & Gottman, 1992). There also is evidence that the children of unhappily married parents were acutely more autonomically aroused

TABLE 13.6

Correlations Between Parents' Marital Interaction When Child Was 5 Years Old and Teacher Ratings on the Adaptive Behavior Inventory and Peabody Achievement Test Scores When Child Was 8 Years Old

Marital Behavior at Age 5		Child Outcome at Age 8					
		Antisocial	Depression	Academic	Math	Reading Recognition	Reading Comprehension
Husband							
Contempt	1	.15	.13	−.25	.06	.02	−.01
	2	.14	−.07	−.16	.01	−.08	−.27
Belligerence	1	.11	.26	−.22	−.16	−.09	−.22
	2	.45**	.28	−.33*	−.22	−.24	−.31*
Domineering	1	−.07	.11	−.11	.08	−.05	.04
	2	−.10	.20	−.15	.04	−.10	−.03
Anger	1	.26	.30*	−.17	.19	.02	.03
	2	.31	.26	−.27	.12	.00	.14
Defensiveness	1	.14	.10	−.10	.16	.03	.07
	2	.14	.23	−.12	−.02	−.11	−.12
Validation	1	−.03	.16	−.11	.24	.27*	.30*
	2	.05	.01	−.28	.00	.08	.10
Affection	1	.19	−.19	−.23	−.18	−.21	−.19
	2	−.06	−.12	−.06	.03	.01	−.02
Humor	1	.12	−.08	−.11	−.23	−.10	−.07
	2	−.03	−.13	−.09	−.04	.10	.04
Wife							
Contempt	1	.47***	.20	−.25	−.20	−.24	−.47***
	2	.25	.04	−.13	−.03	−.19	−.36**
Belligerence	1	.35*	.28	−.35*	−.18	−.13	−.25
	2	.38**	.40**	−.35**	−.04	−.07	.06
Domineering	1	−.03	−.06	.12	.08	.02	.08
	2	−.06	.23	.03	.15	.09	.12
Anger	1	.33*	.28	−.16	−.14	−.22	−.26
	2	.38**	.26	−.20	.04	−.09	−.16
Defensiveness	1	.08	.00	.01	.26	−.18	−.13
	2	.07	−.13	.08	.08	−.21	−.31*
Validation	1	−.36*	−.13	.24	.01	−.04	.06
	2	−.05	.19	−.04	.11	.10	.05
Affection	1	−.21	−.14	.15	.06	.00	.07
	2	−.13	−.13	.16	.11	.01	.01
Humor	1	−.03	−.13	.03	−.25	−.01	−.01
	2	−.09	−.13	−.04	−.01	.06	.04

Note. 1 = low intensity, 2 = high intensity.
*p < .05. **p < .01. ***p < .001.

during parent–child interaction when they were 5 years old. They were aroused chronically as well. Children of unhappily married parents had higher levels of urinary catecholamines when they were 5 years old (Gottman & Katz, 1989). Furthermore, when they posed facial expressions of emotion at age 5, children of unhappily married parents had greater heart rate reactivity than children of more happily married parents (Shortt et al., in press).

13.8. SUMMARY

The results of Study 2 were quite consistent with those of Study 1. The general form of the cascade model held, and the same sets of variables predicted the dissolution cascade. The typology, to the extent that it could be studied, seemed consistent with the results of the first study. The pattern of physiological results also paralleled those of Study 1, and the same gender differences in behavior were obtained again. Furthermore, there was evidence that the marital processes that correlated with the RCISS speaker slopes were predictive of a wide range of deleterious outcomes in children once they entered school.

13.9. APPENDIX

13.9.1. New SPAFF Codes: Notes to Coders Using On-Line SPAFF

13.9.1.1. Validation

The observer needs to distinguish couples that express real feelings and have them validated by their partner, from those couples that do not give any validation. It is important to consider the context of the topic of conversation. RIPFT refers to Relationship Information, Problems, Feeling Talk. *Validation* occurs in the context of RIPFT. Validation can be coded when the couple is talking about one of the partner's feelings, or about a topic pertaining to the marriage. Even if the topic begins to stray away from a subject related to the marriage, if validating behavior occurs, it can be coded. For example, if one member of the couple starts talking about problems she or he is having with a co-worker, and the listener validates the speaker's feelings, it is coded as validation.

A good cue that validation has taken place comes from the reaction of the partner to the statements by the other member of the couple. If the individual seems to open up, or expand more in response to something said by the person who is a candidate for a validation code, then validation probably has taken place. *Expansiveness* is defined in this context as someone opening up to someone else. When the partner is validated, he or she is much more relaxed and is able to talk longer as a result of the validation. It is like a door opening, through which the speaker can walk. It becomes much easier for him or her to talk about feelings or concerns. Therefore, one should look at how the other person reacts to the validation. Even minimal validation can have a dramatic effect on another person. However, it is important to watch out for a defensive or begrudging tone to backchannels. These would not be coded validation.

13.9.1.1.1. Low Intensity

Backchanneling by the listener refers to head nods, "Umm-hmms," or other physical and vocal assenting behaviors that indicate that the person is listening in an affirmative fashion. Backchannels are coded validation only when there is eye contact. This can occur in statements that are neutral by the speaker or that are critical of the listener. For example:

H: "I'm upset when you don't call me when you are going to be late."
W: "Umm-hmm."
W: "It makes me upset when you don't call me when you are going to be late."
H: "I know." (neutral affect in tone)

There is a sense here that there is an acceptance of the partner's point of view or feelings. There is support for the partner's affect; there is acknowledgment of the partner's point of view or feelings as being valid.

13.9.1.1.2. High Intensity

A stronger expression of validation would be a direct expression of understanding of the partner's feelings. For example:

W: "I'm upset about the childrens' grades."
H: "Yes, I know that upsets you."
W: "It makes me upset when you don't call me when you are going to be late."
H: "I really made you angry didn't I?"

Any agreement with a direct complaint, or an apology to the complaint, is considered high-intensity validation. It is very difficult for a person to validate a complaint made against him or herself.

Respect that is expressed directly is another strong expression of validation. The validator agrees with his or her spouse's suggestions for solving a problem or for a course of action. Acceptance of the partner's attempts to repair communication negotiates or summarizes the partner's point of view. An apology is also a strong form of validation.

If there is a lot of warmth in the voice, the response should be coded affection. If the response includes feelings that the partner is feeling in resonance with his or her spouse (e.g., being happy when the partner is happy, or being sad when the partner is sad) then it is empathy and belongs under affection.

13.9.1.2. Belligerence

Belligerence has a provocative quality. Instead of repudiating, withdrawing, or stifling, belligerence provokes a response. It may look as if one partner is trying to start a fight, challenge his or her spouse, or get a rise out of the other partner. Belligerence in marital interaction usually is seen as a dare, a taunting question, or unreciprocated (sometimes mean) humor. Often the jaw is thrust forward and mouth open as if the speaker is daring the other person to hit him or her on the jaw. Watch for finger pointing. Sometimes people use cruder language when being belligerent than in other parts of the conversation (as if challenging the rules of language). A telltale belligerent tone is the rising inflection of the challenging question. There is a "poke" in this question. The question is set up so the partner's position is challenged (e.g., the partner is not supposed to have an answer, there is no answer, or the question is meant to put the partner into an untenable situation). The ultimate belligerence is the challenge to the rules of the marriage. An example is a couple talking about the husband's drinking, and the husband says "What are you going to do if I go out and drink anyway?"

13.9.1.2.1. Low Intensity

Low-intensity belligerence includes unreciprocated, inappropriate laughter; unreciprocated joking, probably regarding something that is serious or sensitive for the partner, especially the kind with a tag on question such as "aren't you?" or "do you?"; challenges such as "so?" or "so what?"; taunting questions that express disbelief "so you get home by five?" (taunting, not sarcastic); insistently coming up with unanswerable questions with the intention of provoking partner (e.g., "Well, what are you going to do about . . .?" or "Where are you going to find the money for that?!"); and taunts such as "See?!" "See, I told you!"

13.9.1.2.2. High Intensity

High-intensity belligerence is the dare that challenges the tacit or agreed upon limits or rules of the relationship. This interpersonal terrorism ups the ante and the stakes are the relationship (e.g., "What would you do if I *did* drink?"; "Just how would you stop me?"; "Maybe I should have a girlfriend?!").

13.9.1.3. Domineering

The goal of domineering behavior is to dominate by stifling the partner. The domineering person insists on winning, and there may be a desperate quality to his or her insistence. Winning a conversation may consist of merely not allowing the other person physical space to speak (with incessant speech and interruptions, talking over partner), or it may be a concerted, elaborate effort to shut the partner up by glowering, lecturing, patronizing, persuading, invalidating, threatening, or some combination of these maneuvers. The domineering person insists on maintaining the floor and does not yield it easily. There is a repetitious quality to domineering. This person may refuse stubbornly to give any ground while summarizing the self repeatedly (not partner or couple). Behaviors accompanying and enhancing domineering may be glowering, forehead tilted toward listener (the "rattlesnake pose"), and a deliberately slowed, adamant manner of speech. Look at the gaze in particular. A domineering gaze is usually steady and intense with a fixed quality, as if the eyes alone will convince of the speaker's authority.

Very important in this code is invalidation of the partner's feelings. This is a communication that the person's feelings are wrong. For example, the spouse may say that he or she thinks that there is a problem with them not saving enough money. The response may be something like, "We do not have a problem with money." There is no acknowledgment that the spouse's feelings could be correct.

Don't get invalidation confused with not validating the partner's feelings. Validating is simply a communication that it could make sense to feel the way the spouse says he or she feels. It's easy to not validate. For example, common forms of not validating are yes-butting, cross-complaining, and mindreading with negative affect. These are coded defensiveness. Invalidation is an active undermining and denial of the partner's feelings. A rule of thumb for distinguishing high and low intensity is to look at whether the speaker insists the listener agree with him or her. Look for lots of "you" statements.

13.9.1.3.1. Low Intensity

As a general guideline, low intensity is the speech-making, floor-maintaining, lecturing qualities of domineering. Look for simultaneous speech or interruptions not due to excitement, but intended to cut off the other person. The partner insists on maintaining the floor and does not yield it easily. Look for stubbornness and no accommodation to the partner's point of view. The speaker insists on being right. He or she may attempt to maintain authority by patronizing, quoting authorities, contradicting, or invalidating the partner's point of view (but mostly by validating speaker's own contradictory view). Look for platitudes, cliches, patronization, repetition of the speaker's point of view, and quotes from authorities or the ambiguous "everyone" (as in "everyone knows").

13.9.1.3.2. High Intensity

Again, think direction and intensity. High intensity is exaggerated: more demanding, a more intense gaze, an absolute refusal to give credence to partner's point of view, or an invalidation of partner him or herself. Domineering frequently is escalated by "enrolling" the listener. Instead of merely insisting on his or her own point of view, the speaker insists on the partner agreeing with his or her point of view. Notice the "you" messages (e.g., "You know better than that"; "You know that's not true!"; "You can't say I don't want what's best"; or "You yourself can see . . . you're a very intelligent person"). The speaker may insist on the listener's agreement by setting up questions in such a way that the listener is forced to, or unknowingly agrees to, invalidate his or her previous position. This is called lowballing and usually is begun with a platitude or simple innocuous statement that the partner agrees to: "You believe marriage is a partnership, don't you?" That agreement is used to prove the speaker's point. For example, the domineering individual might say, "Then you can see why I have to. . . ."

Another way the listener is pulled in is when the speaker makes direct demands about his or her behavior or speech: "I don't want to hear you say that again!" or "You will not work outside the home!" Threats and ultimatums are also high-intensity domineering.

13.9.1.4. Defensive

In many ways, this is the verbal counterpart to whining. There is an innocent victim kind of stance, a communication of blamelessness, as if to say, "Leave me alone. What are you picking on me for? I didn't do anything wrong. It's not my fault." Some cues are: a raise in voice pitch (up to and including whining), a false smile (no 6s), or a shifting side to side as if the person is trying to avoid being hit. Often a cue for defensive behavior in women is when they play with their neck as if they had a necklace. Folding one's arms across the chest is a clue of defensive behavior. Defensiveness takes precedence over whining as a code.

13.9.1.4.1. Yes-Buts

A yes-but is a statement that starts off sounding like an agreement, but ends up being a disagreement. A simple disagreement does not qualify for this description. The speaker views this behavior as agreeing, but with some elaboration. In this case, the speaker is surprised when the listener takes it for disagreement. For example, one person tells the other, "I think it would help if you got home earlier." The other person replies *"Yes, but* if I do I won't get all my work done." Once again there is a claimed innocence to this response that qualifies it as defensive.

13.9.1.4.2. Cross-Complaining

This involves meeting a complaint with a countercomplaint. Be careful. This happens without any assent, head nodding, or vocalization such as "Yeah" or "Mmm-hmm" to count as cross-complaining. There is a direct meeting of a complaint with a cross-complaint. For example:

H: "You never help with the dishes."
W: "Well neither do you."
W: "I stay at home alone with the kids and then you come home and want to be alone."
H: "Well I'm tired from working all day and want a little time to unwind from all the tension."

13.9.1.4.3. Rubber Man or Rubber Woman

This refers to communications that express the message of "Whatever you say bounces off of me and gets you." The individual defends him or herself from attack, but also blames the partner. The message tries to suggest that the guilt or blame is the other person's.

13.9.1.4.4. Countercriticism or Counterattack

There is a juvenile quality to this kind of response. The speaker acts pouty and victimized. When distinguishing levels of intensity for defensiveness, look primarily for how it functions to shift blame in the couple. Where does the blame go? If the speaker's purpose is to shift blame from him or herself, but is in no way blaming the partner, code low intensity. When the blame is being shifted from self to partner, code high intensity.

Occasionally defensiveness is so exaggerated or intense that it is coded high intensity even though the partner is not being blamed. This is particularly true with a high-pitched whine of speech.

13.9.1.4.5. Low Intensity

The following are examples of low-intensity defensiveness:

1. Denies responsibility or blame. "It's not my fault" and "I didn't do it" kinds of statements qualify for this denial of responsibility. The individual denies a connection between his or her behavior and a problem ("It's not my fault"). The particular behavior already should have been defined in the discussion. For example:

   H: "The house is always dirty."
   W: "It's not my problem, I can't do everything."

   W: "You didn't pick up my clothes at the cleaners."
   H: "Well, I never said I would."

   W: "What you said last night hurt my feelings."
   H: "I didn't say anything wrong."

2. Makes excuses. Gives an excuse for why something was or was not done and this excuses his or her behavior in the situation. The excuse need not be implausible, but any implausible explanation, spurious reason, or weak rationale also is coded as making excuses. There may be a "poor me" attitude to the excuses.
3. Disagreement within a defensive loop that does not blame the partner. A defensive loop is a cycle of accusation and defense that may or may not be initiated by negative mindreading.

13.9.1.4.6. High Intensity

High-intensity defensiveness is when whatever is wrong is the partner's fault. This may be established through cross-complaining, yes-butting (when the "but" is about the partner), rubber man/woman (when the return complaint is about partner), or negative mindreading. Negative mindreading may not seem like defensiveness initially, because it initiates a defensive loop instead of necessarily being a response to an accusation. To cue into mindreading, look for global statements such as "you always" or "you never."

Negative mindreading and its denial are both coded defensive. A mindreading statement is any attribution that the partner makes about the other's feelings, behaviors, motives, or assumptions about the other. If done with neutral affect or positive affect, this functions as a sensitive "feeling probe." For example, "You always get tense when my mother talks about how to raise children"; if it is delivered with neutral or positive affect, it functions as if it were a question (i.e., "How do you feel when my mother talks about how to raise children?"). Usually this is responded to with agreement and elaboration. For example, "Yeah, she does make me nervous because I think she is going to start criticizing the way we are raising Jamie."

Note that it is only coded defensive if the mindreading statement is delivered with negative affect. These mindreading statements often include the phrases "you always" or "you never." For example, "You never take out the garbage and I always end up having to do it myself." If the mindreading is delivered with negative affect, it appears as an accusation or attack to the partner. The response tends to be disagreement and elaboration. For example, "I don't always feel that way. It is just that your mother is so sanctimonious."

13.9.1.5. Whine

This is a code that refers only to the voice tone quality of whining. It accompanies behavior that cannot be coded defensive, usually in the form of a complaint. Use the intensity code to code the extent or intensity of the whining quality in the voice.

13.9.1.6. Stonewall

Look for this behavior only as a response to something aversive the partner is saying or has said. Stonewalling is a listener behavior and a refusal to respond to the partner. This usually is in response to one of two things: (a) the partner is complaining, blaming, criticizing, raising an issue, or otherwise upset or expressing negative affect; or (b) the partner is dreaming impracticably (usually being what the listener considers financially irresponsible or some other violation of role responsibility).

13.9.1.6.1. Low Intensity

There is a lack of feedback in addition to away behavior (away behavior refers to focusing on something other than speaker, such as something in room), or an automanipulation such as playing with hair or hands. Other low-intensity examples of stonewalling include: placing hands over face, looking down or leaning down, or keeping face or neck rigid when partner is expressing negative affect. There may be monitoring gaze, although when monitoring gaze is added it usually is coded high intensity (because there are usually other stonewalling behaviors accompanying monitoring gaze). Low-intensity stonewalling with monitoring gaze occurs when the person is looking at the partner and the monitoring gaze is the main clue that stonewalling is taking place. The stonewalling listener is conveying to the speaker, "I'd rather not be here right now."

13.9.1.6.2. High Intensity

High-intensity stonewalling is when all the main stonewalling behaviors are taking place: no vocal backchannels, no nonverbal backchannels, little eye contact (gaze is away) or monitoring gaze, and rigid face and neck (no facial movement, no facial mirroring). In addition, the body is turned away and there is (rarely) muttering under the breath to self.

14

Physiology During Marital Interaction

This chapter explores the hypothesis that physiological arousal is related to the cascade toward marital dissolution. The results of these studies are encouraging, but not entirely consistent. The husband's arousal, particularly his heart rate, was a predictor of variables in the cascade toward dissolution in the DU080 and DU086 studies, but the wife's and not the husband's heart rate was a predictor of variables in the cascade toward dissolution in the DU083 study. It is not clear at this time why these inconsistencies exist. However, a conservative conclusion from the data of three studies would be that physiological arousal in general is associated with marital dissolution variables.

The question of the role of the couple's physiological responses has considerable practical as well as theoretical import.

14.1. WHAT PHYSIOLOGICAL AROUSAL MAY IMPLY FOR THOUGHT, EMOTION, AND MARITAL INTERACTION

In this section, I briefly review autonomic nervous system physiology as a background for discussing one physiological construct of interest in building theory of how marriages change over time. This construct is called diffuse physiological arousal (DPA; Gottman, 1990).

14.1.1. Overview of Autonomic Measures

Our physiological measures were selected as a compromise of two considerations: (a) we wanted to sample from a reasonably wide range of physiological responses, and (b) we wanted to minimally encumber the subjects. We measured heart rate as the interval between R-waves of the electrocardiogram (EKG), pulse transit time to the middle finger of the nondominant hand as the time between the R-spike and the maximal amplitude of blood volume in the finger as measured by the finger photoplethysmograph (the photoplethysmograph passes a cool red light through the finger), skin conductance using a constant voltage method from the middle phalanges of the first and third finger of the nondominant hand, and gross motor movement using a highly sensitive jiggleometer in the base of the subject's chair that measures movement in all three planes. These measures were amplified with an 8-channel Lafayette polygraph, synchronized to the video time code, and averaged over 10-second intervals with a DEC LSI 11/23 laboratory microcomputer.

14.1.1.1. Anatomy

These peripheral physiological measures were selected to provide various information about the autonomic nervous system (ANS), which has at least two anatomically and functionally distinct subsystems: the parasympathetic branch (PNS) and the sympathetic branch (SNS). Both subsystems are characterized by a two-neuron linkage from the brain or spinal cord. The first preganglionic neuron is joined to a second neuron that innervates the target organ. In the SNS, the neural fibers leave the spinal cord from the chest and saddle regions (thoracolumbar); in the PNS, the fibers leave the spinal cord from the brain stem and tail regions (craniosacral). However, the nature of the two-neuron linkage is reversed completely in the SNS compared with the PNS. In the SNS, the two-neuron chain is a short connection that is preganaglioic and a long connection that is postganglionic, whereas in the PNS, the anatomy is reversed—long fibers from the spinal cord to the vicinity of the target organ, and then short fibers into the target organ. In the SNS, the short preganglionic fibers go from the spinal cord to a chain (called the sympathetic ganglia) that runs alongside the spinal cord. One implication of these different anatomical features is that there is great potential for the mixing of sympathetic ganglia and the possibility of more "cross talk," which implies that the SNS is capable of diffuse action. On the other hand, for the PNS, the anatomy appears to be designed for little mixing and thus fairly specific action.

Although there are no main SNS nerves, due to the amount of SNS mixing, there are two main nerves of the PNS and the organs it serves. The first is the vagus nerve (Xth cranial nerve), which serves the heart, bronchioles of the lung, stomach, small intestine, liver, pancreas, and large intestine. The second is the pelvic nerve (sacral nerves 2, 3, and 4), which serves the colon, kidney, bladder, sex organs, and exterior genitalia. PNS fibers also are found in the following cranial nerves: oculomotor (III), facial (VII), and glossopharyngeal (IX).

14.1.1.2. Chemistry

The stimulation chemistry of the two branches of the ANS also are different. Preganglionic fibers in both systems stimulate postganglionic targets using acetylcholine (ACh) released at the synapse. However, in the SNS, the primary neurotransmitter from postganglioic fibers to target organs is norepinephrine (NE), whereas in the PNS, it is acetylcholine. Two exceptions are: (a) the SNS innervation of the adrenal medulla, which is stimulated by SNS preganglionic fibers and hence ACh; and (b) the sweat glands, which are stimulated by SNS postganglioic fibers, but the neurotransmitter is ACh. Hence, sweat gland activity, which in the emotionally responsive eccrine glands, still is innervated by the SNS and has a different stimulation chemistry than is SNS innervation of the heart.

14.1.1.3. Function

The two branches of the ANS usually act in reciprocal and contrasting fashion throughout the body. However, there are a few well-established gross functional differences that can be described, albeit with some qualifications:

1. The SNS is a fight/flight system that acts in an energy-expending or catabolic fashion, whereas the PNS acts in an energy conserving, or anabolic, fashion. For example, whereas the SNS is responsible for converting the carbohydrate glycogen stored in the liver to glucose for energy, the PNS is responsible for the conversion of glucose to glycogen.
2. The SNS generally acts diffusely, whereas the action of the PNS usually is specific.
3. The SNS has a slow onset (i.e., 2 seconds), whereas the PNS has a more rapid onset (i.e., 0.5 seconds).
4. The action of the SNS is longer lasting than the action of the PNS, because NE is not degraded as readily by body tissue, whereas ACh is. The time for recovery of some effects of the SNS (e.g., on left ventricle contractility; see Berne & Levy, 1981) can be long—2-3 minutes.
5. In the cardiovascular system the main effect of the PNS is on heart rate, whereas the main effect of the SNS is on myocardial contractility (actually both branches affect both aspects of car-

diac function; see Levy, 1983a, 1983b; Levy, Martin, & Stuesse, 1981).

These general contrasts have to be qualified in some ways. First, the effects of the two branches of the ANS usually are reciprocal. For example, it is tricky to tell whether a heart rate increase resulted from less PNS activity or more SNS activity. This problem holds throughout, although there is evidence that the vagus can affect the SNS effect on myocardial contractility in a synergistic and reciprocal manner. Second, the SNS is quite capable of specific functioning. For example, in the human sexual response, there is a temporal orchestration of PNS and SNS responding. The excitement phases that regulate the engorgement and lubrication of sexual tissue usually are controlled by the PNS; SNS activation during these phases of the sexual response results in sexual dysfunction. However, orgasm and ejaculation are regulated by the SNS. It is as if the SNS were the cymbalist who came in at the conductor's signal only at the crescendo and in very specific fashion. Another example concerns the functioning of the PNS and SNS during pure emotions (Ekman et al., 1983). Nonetheless, these general and gross contrasts are useful.

14.1.2. Diffuse Physiological Arousal (DPA)

In their original finding about longitudinal change in marital satisfaction, Levenson and Gottman (1985) reported that a fairly diverse set of physiological measures of autonomic arousal led to declines in marital satisfaction over a 3-year period. These findings were the inspiration for the concept of diffuse physiological arousal (DPA). For purposes such as marital therapy, it is important to have a viewpoint about the nervous system. I propose that DPA is a useful organizing variable. To describe this variable, consider an ordinal pattern of autonomic nervous system (ANS) activation, arranged from high to low:

1. *Emotion specific patterning.* I already have noted that both branches of the ANS are potentially able to function with great specificity. The form of action most important to building a theory of marriage is the specificity that results from specific patterns of emotional responding of the kind described by Ekman et al. (1983).
2. *Multiple negative emotions in close temporal sequence, constrained emotions, negative emotion blends.* Here activation in terms of physiology is likely to be more diffuse, so that the specific

profiles Ekman et al. (1983) found are likely to produce a more general elevation of autonomic activity.

3. *Sympathetic nervous system (SNS) Global Discharge.* This kind of general activation of the SNS is the kind that Cannon (1927) described as part of the fight or flight syndrome.

4. *SNS and PNS discharge.* There is some evidence that the parasympathetic nervous system (PNS) is activated as a negative feedback mechanism to regulate SNS's effects on discharge (e.g., vagal action can reduce SNS effects on myocardial contractility).

5. *Stress-related hormones and adrenal involvement.* When the adrenal medulla is activated by the SNS, there is a general increase of systemic levels of stress-related hormones epinephrine and norepinephrine. There also is evidence that the pituitary-adrenocortical axis is important as a second axis in relation to the body's response to stress (Selye, 1975).

It is reasonable to suggest that DPA is a highly unpleasant and aversive subjective bodily state. The evidence for this contention is weak, but some support comes from Pennebaker (1982) on the psychology of physical symptoms.

There is some evidence beyond my own results to suggest that the DPA construct is useful. For example, Henry and Stephens (1977) suggested that the two adrenal endocrine processes associated with stress are connected to specific emotional states. They reviewed a great deal of human and animal research that supported the notion that the sympathetic-adrenomedullary system (which results in the increased secretion of the catecholamines) is related to anger, hostility, and active coping, whereas the pituitary-adrenocortical system (which results in the increased secretion of cortisol) is related to sadness, depression, and helplessness. Taggart and Carruthers (1971) found that plaque formation in arteries was predicted by both catecholamine secretion (which increases the amount of free fatty acids in the blood) and cortisol secretion. Thus, there may be a fairly interesting emotion-based theory of myocardial infarction due to atherosclerosis, namely that it is related to chronic life situations that generate blends or temporal sequences of both states (anger, hostility, active coping and sadness, depression, and helplessness). Unfortunately, distressed marriages provide a rich resource for this kind of configuration.

What does all of this physiology have to do with marital interaction? The following hypotheses show why a biologically based theory of marital functioning contributes knowledge that cannot be obtained from a study of social behavior alone. I suggest that the state of DPA has powerful implications for cognitive and social behavior. These implications are:

1. DPA reduces the ability to process information. This distinction is one that is akin to the Lacey (1967; see Coles, Jennings, & Stern, 1984) and Sokolov (1963) stimulus intake/rejection hypothesis in psychophysiology. This hypothesis in psychophysiology has linked the intake of stimuli to cardiac deceleration and the rejection of stimuli to cardiac acceleration (Obrist, 1981).
2. DPA makes overlearned behaviors and cognitions more likely than newly acquired behaviors and cognitions. If this hypothesis were true, it would explain why it is difficult for marital therapy clients to have access to new learnings during times of heated controversy that resulted in DPA.
3. DPA increases the likelihood of the same behaviors that are engaged during fight or flight, that is, withdrawal and aggression. This would make sense as having been the result of past emotional conditioning; it states that, in effect, emotions that result in DPA become linked to the primitive fight or flight diffuse SNS response.
4. Gender differences exist in recovery time from DPA: Males take longer than females. There are clear-cut implications of this hypothesis, which are spelled out in Gottman and Levenson (1988). These are that males are more likely than females to manage the level of negative affect in marital interaction and to take steps to keep it from escalating. In particular, males are more likely than females to inhibit the expression of emotion, to appeal to rationality, and to compromise (Raush et al., 1974).

14.2. DIFFUSE PHYSIOLOGICAL AROUSAL AND THE HISTORY OF THE AROUSAL CONSTRUCT

Because I am resurrecting an old construct that has been sharply criticized when I talk about DPA, I review the history as well as current views of the construct of physiological arousal within psychophysiology. This review shows that DPA is entirely consistent with current notions of the possibility that the sympathetic branch of the autonomic nervous system is capable of specific responding. This is true because no one denies that it is still capable of diffuse action, nor that, as arousal increases, more and more systems in the body are called into play that prepare the organism for emergency action. Furthermore, I show that, from a historical perspective, the existence of this type of arousal state was never criticized or denied by the classic critiques of arousal theory.

14.2.1. History of the Arousal Construct: Review of Duffy (1957)

Arousal as a concept comes from notion of energy mobilization, which is based on notion of the intensity of behavior, independent of its direction. Duffy (1957) was perhaps the most articulate proponent of an arousal view, which also was proposed by D. Lindsley in 1934 (see Lindsley, 1952). Lindsley linked arousal to EEG asynchrony and the inverted U-shaped performance-anxiety curve of Yerkes and Dodson (1908). Duffy's (1957) idea was a broader one than Lindsley's, (1957) but it retained all of his ideas. Duffy (1957) expressed her idea of arousal conservatively as follows:

> Among the physiological measures which may be employed are skin conductance, muscle tension, the electroencephalogram (EEG), pulse rate, respiration, and others. These measures show intercorrelations, although the correlation coefficients are not always high since there is patterning in the excitation of the individual, the nature of which appears to depend on the specific stimulus situation and upon organic factors within the individual. Nevertheless, there is evidence also of "generality" of the excitation. Hence a concept of arousal, or energy mobilization, appears to justified. (p. 266)

She included measures of autonomic and somatic functioning, saying: "It is clear that it is the *organism*, and not a single system, or a single aspect of response, which shows arousal or activation" (p. 266). Roots of this use of arousal by Duffy's (1957) may be found in Cannon's (1915) concept of energy mobilization during emotion. However, Duffy (1957) expanded the concept to describe the intensity aspect of all behavior. The "degree of excitation" was another phrase that was used.

Duffy (1957) pointed out that there is a confusion between the degree of internal arousal and the vigor and extent of overt responses. She suggested that these two are probably negatively related. Here are shades of what is later discussed as the hydraulic model of emotion. Duffy (1957) cited evidence of the nature of the situation and its significance for arousal. For example, men undergoing flight training show more muscle tension during solo stage of training than others. People's galvanic skin response (GSR) is higher if questions about social problems are in disagreement with the group than in harmony. She then discussed the notion of optimal level of arousal, suggesting that emotion results from too high a degree of arousal, and anxiety disorders can be conceived of as overarousal or hyperresponsiveness. This notion of an optimal level of arousal resurfaces again and again in what has come to be known as the Yerkes–Dodson law. A part of Duffy's (1957) idea was that high levels of activation increase disorganization.

14.2.2. Lacey's (1967) Critique of Arousal

Duffy's (1957) arousal concept equated arousal across physiological channels, particularly behavioral, cortical, and autonomic. In 1967, Lacey published a book chapter that proved to be a definitive attack on the arousal concept. I review Lacey's (1967) argument in some detail.

First, Lacey (1967) argued that it is possible to create dissociation across physiological channels (either surgically or pharmacologically). For example, in cats, atropine produces (Bradley, 1958) high-amplitude, slow EEG waves similar to those seen in sleep, but the cat is neither drowsy nor behaviorally unresponsive. If amphetamine is added to the atropine, the wave pattern stays the same, but the cat is alert or excited. It is also possible to produce an alerted cortex in a behaviorally drowsy dog with the drug physostigmine (it inhibits acetylcholinesterase [AChE], which breaks down acetylcholine [ACh]). Cortical desynchronization (a usual index of activation) can be produced by stimulating the midbrain reticular formation in the complete absence of behavioral arousal. Hence, it is possible, experimentally, to separately induce behavioral, autonomic, or cortical arousal in animals.

Second, under normal conditions, one generally obtains low correlations across different physiological measures. The sizes of these correlations vary. For example, Elliott (1964) found correlations across channels in adults of about .35 to .36, and in children the correlations were almost zero (he employed HR, respiration rate, palmar conductance, muscle potentials, and EEG in three bands: 2–4 H_z, 8–12 H_z, 17–28 H_z.)[1]

Actually, Lacey (1967) argued that there is evidence for both association across physiological channels and disassociation. He wrote: "The evidence seems clear, however, that somatic and behavioral arousal consists of dissociable components, mediated by separate neural mechanisms, but that "commonly" these appear simultaneously" (p. 20). However, he admitted that extreme laboratory conditions such as electric shock, intellectually demanding tests, situations that induce the affects of flight or fight, or anxiety-producing stimuli create high

---

[1]Lazarus, Speisman, and Mordkoff (1963) argued for averaging to obtain more precise means for increased reliability (as in using many items on a test). Even with these suggestions, one obtains only about 0.5 correlations.

correlations between measurement domains. He also suggested that one would not obtain such strong association across channels for pleasant affects. Thus, even in Lacey's (1967) original critique of arousal, he noted that, under typically strong negative conditions produced in most psychophysiology laboratories, all bodily systems designed to cope with emergency would fire together rather than be dissociated. Dissociation occurs under mild, neutral, or positive conditions.

Third, he then discussed his results of what he called individual response stereotypy. In this notion, some people respond characteristically to stress with heart rate (HR) increase and some with a skin conductance (SC) increase. The idea is that within subjects these individualistic responses are stable.

Fourth, Lacey (1967) noted that evidence exists for specificity of responses across channels, that is, of patterning. For example, specific situations produce specific autonomic response profiles (e.g., Ax's, 1964, study of anger and fear). He suggested that the act of noting and detecting stimuli results in a HR decrease, whereas SC increases and activity decreases. Graham also noticed specific profiles of autonomic activity for hypnotic responses to different affective states (Graham, Stern, & Winokur, 1960).

Fifth, he remarked that BP and HR do not always increase together. In fact, there exists a response called the baroreceptor reflex. If blood pressure increases sharply, then there are stretch receptors in the aortic arch and the carotid sinus that join the vagus and glossopharyngeal nerves, which terminate in the lower brain stem and act to inhibit cortical activity and lower HR.

Sixth, he discussed his data on directional fractionation. Directional fractionation relates to behavior in specific ways. Reaction time (RT) is faster with greater HR deceleration. Correlations are not high ($-.2$ to $-.4$), but the prediction is not made by arousal theory if behavioral activation equals attention. Actually attention is related to inhibited motor activity during orienting. In this research, he noted that attentive observation to the external environment produces cardiac deceleration, cardiac stabilization, BP decreases, or diminution of BP increases.

Why did Lacey's (1967) points contradict Duffy's (1957) version of arousal theory? The answer may be found in Duffy's (1957) inclusion of attention. One often observes increases in respiration and SC, but decreases in BP and HR during orienting and attention (although Lacey noted that the HR response was part of a polyphasic curve).[2]

More recently, Lacey (1967) related the orienting reflex to the contin

---

[2]Note that directional fractionation effect must be PNS, because one gets immediate cardiac slowing.

gent negative variation found in the EEG (denoted the CNV). Lacey's (1967) directional fractionation effect was related to the CNV, which is presumed to reflect the readings of the organism to respond and the organism's evaluation of reinforcement contingencies. There is a direct relationship between cardiac deceleration and the magnitude of the CNV.

Lacey (1967) also reported that if the stimulus that leads to orienting occurs early in a cardiac cycle, more cardiac slowing results. This occurrence can be tied to the P300 wave of the EEG evoked potential. The P300 is presumed to be related to aspects of event significance.

14.2.3. Diffuse Physiological Arousal and Stimulus Response Stereotypy (or Specificity)

The notion here is that there is a specific pattern of physiological responses unique to a particular stimulus situation. There are two versions of this idea. One version is individual response stereotypy, in which an individual's profile of responses across physiological measures is consistent across similar situations, but that this pattern differs from individual to individual. A well-known paper by Lacey (1967) presented profiles of idiosyncratic response patterns over five occasions of measurement (resting, anticipation of a cold pressor test, the actual cold pressor test, a mental arithmetic, and a word fluency task). He presented drawings for six variables ranked as systolic blood pressure, diastolic blood pressure, plamar conductance, heart rate, HR variability, and pulse pressure. Reasonably high concordance was found for most people. Lacey (1967) wrote:

> Thus, in five studies of autonomic activation by physiological and psychological stressors, and in the study of spontaneous resting autonomic activity, we have uniformly found the two basic phenomena of fractionated or patterned autonomic response, and tendency to reproducible profile of reaction. In the data presented in an earlier section concerning heart rate and palmar conductance responses, we found that patterning of response can even extend to complete failure of response in one physiological variable, while another simultaneously recorded variable indicates "arousal." The results seem to have considerable generalizability, for various subject populations have been used—maturing children of both sexes, male college freshmen, and adult women—in experiments in which details of experimental design, recording techniques, and mathematical modes of evaluation of magnitude of response have all differed. For the kinds of stressors we have employed, and for the physiological measures used, we believe that the evidence is conclusive that individual differences

in the organization of response hierarchies exist, and that these differences are reproducible over long periods of time and from one stressor to other different stressors. (pp. 190–191)

This suggests that some people in stressful situations are HR responders, whereas others are SC or BP responders. This has led to the introduction of the baloon stress test, in which a baloon is suddenly burst to see which channel is the one of maximum activation for each subject (Levis & Smith, 1987).

An analogous and more general concept of individual response stereotypy is that of specificity of response that generalizes across subjects, but not across situations. One active area of research, with a long history, is related to emotion. In the emotion literature this has been referred to as the arousal versus specificity question.

Cannon (1927) suggested that, in strong negative emotions like fear, anger, and pain, there was accompanying general massive and diffuse SNS discharge that also involved the SNS and the adrenal medulla (which secretes the catecholamines epinephrine and norepinephrine). The SNS lends itself to this diffuse arousal interpretation, with its anatomical potential for interneuronal cross talk. This is the famous fight or flight reaction attributed to Cannon (1927). It is the organism's adaptive preparation for emergency and the mobilization of the body's fuels. It also theoretically involves peripheral vasoconstriction, increased blood supply to the muscles, increased attention, higher HR and BP, and higher SC. The increase in palmar and plantar sweating has been the subject of much adaptive evolutionary speculation (e.g., it is adaptive to sweat for increased ability to grip a weapon, or it is adaptive to sweat so that one will be too slippery to be grabbed).

Cannon's (1927) view was elaborated by Selye in the 1940s, who focused more on long-lasting stimuli and chronic stressors and implicated what has come to be called the pituitary-adrenocorical axis. I discuss the pituitary and the adrenals in detail in the section on behavioral endocrinology. The adrenal cortex secretes steroids such as cortisol.

In emotion research, this idea of diffuse, general arousal was picked up by Schachter and Singer (1962). They used the notion to propose that this kind of physiological arousal was the underlying substance for all emotions, hence implying that the discrete emotions, such as joy and anger, differed only by the cognitive labels persons applied to explain themselves and their perception of their own bodily cues of arousal. This view was elaborated as a cognitive theory of emotion by Mandler (1975) and was applied recently by Berscheid (1983).

14.2.4. Recent Thinking About Arousal

The general physiological arousal notion has been challenged recently by Ekman, Levenson, and Friesen (1983), who found evidence for an autonomic signature for some emotions (see also Levenson, Ekman, & Friesen, 1990; Levenson, Carstensen, Friesen, & Ekman, 1991; Levenson, Ekman, Heider, & Friesen, 1992). This research challenges the classic experiment in emotion by Schacter and Singer (1962). Ekman et al. (1983) found that HR decreases in facial expressions of disgust, but increases in anger, fear, joy, and sadness. Anger and fear are differentiated by the fact that hands get hot in anger and cold in fear facial expressions.

How can these specificity results be integrated conceptually with Lacey's (1967) individual response stereotypy notion? The integration would be very important. Levenson had an idea that potentially could perform this integration. Levenson (personal communication, 1989) speculated that people may have a characteristic emotional reaction to laboratory stressors, which could determine their physiological profile. This would then make individual response stereotypy a subphenomenon of the autonomic signature hypothesis.

The arousal-specificity question is considerably broader in psychophysiology than the area of emotion. The question of arousal versus specificity is related to two factors.

The first factor is the set of physiological variables sampled, and the second factor is the range of situations sampled. First, I discuss the situation. Lacey (1967) recognized the importance of this factor. He wrote:

> It bears repeating, I think, that *the widely held opinion that autonomic, electroencephalographic, and skeletal-motor activation occur simultaneously and in equal measure may be traceable partially to the fact that the experimental conditions commonly used by psychophysiologists and neurophysiologists are all too limited. Enormously popular manipulations are used in the vast majority of studies of arousal: aversive physical simuli, intellectually demanding tasks, convenient perceptual-motor tasks, affects of "fight or flight," and "anxiety-producing" stimuli. We do not as often use nonaversive stimuli, "pleasant affects," tasks without the appeal to the need for academic achievement, or tasks which emphasize set to perform rather than the performance itself. It may be that as we braoden our scope of observation we will be able to begin to meet the need voiced by Wikler to specify the precise conditions under which the phenomena of arousal are concomitant and those under which they are dissociated. Perhaps also we can begin to understand the "why" both of dissociation and association. (p.21; italics added)

It is clear from the literature that, if the situations are varied and if their range is extreme, physiological variables move together in a predictable fashion. However, once the range of situations decreases, physiological responses become uncorrelated. This is quite reasonable. One would want various components of the nervous system to be able to function independently under most everyday conditions. However, under conditions of energy mobilization for emergency, they should work together toward a common purpose.

The second factor is which variables were included. Perhaps the most controversial is the EEG. Cortical desynchronization, or alpha-blocking, certainly is characteristic of a wide range of behavioral states, varying from drowsy to active. However, if this range is restricted, cortical patterns do not necessarily accompany *behavioral arousal*, a term that needs more precise definition. In other words, the original subtler functions of the reticular activating system probably were overstated in terms of their sympathetic downward connections.

The mobilization for energy expenditure characteristic of the fight-or-flight response may not involve increased attention. In fact, organisms are less efficient at processing new information in a defensive posture. This becomes evident once the differences between orienting and defense are investigated.

Several researchers recently have employed paradigms that speak to the notions of a general arousal concept. Cantor, Zillmann, and Bryant (1975) suggested a transfer of excitation model. They used an exercise bicycle in which subjects increased their heart rate. They then were presented with a second stimulus designed to elicit emotion. The second stimulus occurred before the subject's heart rate has returned to baseline, but after the subject thought that the heart rate had returned to baseline. This was referred to as residual excitation. Cantor et al. (1975) found that the second stimulus affected the decay of excitation. They argued that, during this period, it was possible to obtain transfer of excitation between nearly any two emotions.

Anderson sudied SNS nerve activity in humans by direct recording of blood to muscles increasing and blood to skin decreasing. The direct neural recording of an SNS nerve was done on the forearm and the calf (the radial and the pereneal nerve of the leg). It was necessary to occlude the outflow of blood briefly. Anderson (see Johnson & Anderson, 1990) found that mental arithmetic caused increased blood to arm, but not to the leg. Increased SNS activity was obtained to the leg, but not to the arm. Vasoconstriction was due to NE, so it was primarily evidence of specific SNS patterning. Hence, Anderson provided direct evidence of specificity in SNS action.

14.2.5. A Hierarchy of Arousal

It is possible to organize the recruitment of physiological systems as a function of increasing arousal if one reviews the evidence for such a notion in a variety of stimulus situations. Probably the lowest level of activation of physiological systems is related to orienting.

14.2.5.1. The Orienting Response

The orienting response was first described by Pavlov. It is the general response of orienting to a mild novel stimulus. The response is quite complex. It involves general behavioral stilling, cessation of breathing, and a small but reliable cardiac deceleration (heart rate decrease) of a few beats per minute. This decrease is transient, but can be sustained for longer periods if it is relevant to keep attending. Graham and Clifton (1966) suggested that HR decrease is a component of orienting.

The orienting response habituates rapidly, which means that the response decreases rapidly over repeated presentations of the same stimulus. Pavlov probably did not come into his lab very often, because he said that when he did the dogs oriented to his presence, so they obviously had not habituated to his entry. Pavlov called the orienting the "what is it?" response.

In 1963, Sokolov wrote a classic paper on the orienting and defense reflex (I discuss the defense response in a moment). The orienting reflex has two functions: (a) the adequate processing of new stimuli, and (b) the preparation for fast action. The response has been investigated in detail, and it has a number of other physiological components. For example, it has a concomitant skin conductance increase, constriction of cutaneous tissue at the periphery, and cephalic dilation. Reaction times are lower, there is increase in muscle tension and tonus, pupil dilation, and a P300 evoked potential response.

14.2.5.1.1. Sensory Intake and Rejection

John and Beatrice Lacey initially proposed a hypothesis related to the heart rate decrease in orienting in terms of responses to positive and negative stimuli. Their idea was formulated in terms of environmental intake of positive stimuli or environmental rejection of negative stimuli. Lacey (1967) later moved away from the positive–negative stimulus dimension in favor of a view that environmental intake involves a quieting of thinking versus effortful cognitive elaboration.

In other words, if the subject's attention to the stimulus involves orienting, but no effortful information processing, one obtains an HR decrease. However, if it evokes thinking, one obtains an HR increase.

Autopsy slides (not a positive stimulus) evoke an HR decrease, beautiful scenes evoke an HR decrease, and even positive tasks that require thinking evoke an HR increase (Lacey, Kagan, Lacey, & Moss, 1963). The result initially was noticed with respect to reaction time, in which a number of investigators found that HR decreases in the fixed foreperiod of simple reaction time (RT) experiments, and that greater magnitudes of HR decreases were associated with shorter RTs (Andreassi, 1989).

14.2.5.1.2. Cardiac–Somatic Coupling

An alternative exploration was offered by Obrist (1981). Obrist suggested that the HR deceleration reflects the requirements of the muscles. He agreed that there is a cardiac–somatic integration center, and that the HR deceleration reflects the behavioral quieting of orienting and attending. However, the situations used by Lacey (1967) are ones in which subjects do not move very much. Hence, the question arises, How much movement is necessary to obtain cardiac–somatic coupling? Exercise is capable of eliciting this coupling, but what about the kinds of tasks the Laceys were studying?

Cacioppo (personal communication, 1987) pointed to a problem with the Obrist (1981) work. Obrist (1981) tried EMG measurements at many different sites and had luck with a chin placement, which was used as an index of general somatic activity because the chin placement showed the greatest relationship to HR.

However, Cacioppo noted that there is an alternative hypothesis. Silent language processing is accompanied by a perioral EMG response (e.g., silent text processing). Cacioppo noted that if one quiets oneself cognitively, one sees the greatest decrease in chin placement and a greater relationship between chin EMG and HR decrease the faster the reaction time.

Obrist (1981) was aware of the problem of arguing that eye blinks and chin (and neck) EMGs are responsible for cardiac adjustments. In fact, Obrist, Webb, and Sutterer (1969) wrote:

These results are relevant to several issues which require some elaboration. The first concerns how the concomitance between heart rate and somatic-motor activity is to be understood. As suggested previously (Obrist & Webb, 1967; Obrist, 1968), a rather strong argument can be made that cardiac and somatic activity are truly interrelated events representing different aspects of the same response process. The problems such a position raises are several. Perhaps the most important of these concerns whether the relationship is one in which the cardiac event is dependent on the occurrence of the somatic event, in that it is afferent feedback from the musculature that modifies the cardiac response. The alternative to this is that both responses have a common central origin, in that both are initiated by the same processes. There has been considerable recent interest in this problem as indicated by the curarization studies. As a whole, these studies indicate that in the classical conditioning as well as operant conditioning situation, cardiac changes can be demonstrated when no striate response can occur and when respiration is controlled (Black, 1965, 1967; Miller, 1967). This could be interpreted to mean that to a significant extent, cardiac changes can be related to somatic activity at a central level and not to the peripheral occurrence of somatic events (see Black, 1967). There are two lines of evidence from the present study which support this. First, *it is hard to conceive that cardiac deceleration could be significantly influenced by feedback from such non-extensive motor acts as eye movements and blinks.* Second, the decrease in EMG and eye movements which accompanied the larger cardiac deceleration when respiration was suspended clearly suggests the possibility of common central mediating mechanisms. This does not deny that feedback from respiratory maneuvers or other types of somatic acts can influence the cardiac response; there is evidence that it can (Obrist & Webb, 1967). But it would appear no longer feasible to view the heart rate deceleration as strictly dependent on respiratory maneuvers, other somatic activities, or for that matter other peripheral events such as blood pressure induced reflex mechanisms (Obrist et al., 1965). Overall, it is likely that theirs is a complex interaction between cardiac and somatic processes which cannot be treated as an either–or type of relationship. It would seem that until such time as the respective roles of peripheral and central influences on the heart can be more definitively ascertained, it is theoretically most parsimonious and useful to treat these cardiac-somatic effects as interrelated concomitant events. As such, cardiac effects might serve as the most useful aspect of this interrelationship because we may have in cardiac muscle a faily accurate depiction of what the complete striate musculature is doing. (pp. 718–719)

However, in later writings (e.g., Obrist, 1976), these distinctions become obscure, and HR deceleration in the Lacey (1967) situations is related to somatic quieting. In fact, Cacioppo (personal communication, 1987) noted that it is possible to ask subjects to move or tense various other muscles in these situations and show little HR change.

14.2.5.2. Defensive Responses (DR) and the Startle

If the intensity of the stimulus keeps increasing, eventually one obtains an entirely different response than orienting. In some ways, this response is opposite to the orienting response. This response is called the defense response. For example, if you keep increasing the dB of a tone at 50 to 80 dBs you will get an OR, but at 110 dBs you will get a DR. The components of a DR are: (a) increased SC (1–3 sec); (b) increased HR

(2–4 sec), the notion being that it is to facilitate action; (c) postural changes away from the stimulus (the opposite of orienting); (d) pupil dilation; (e) skin vasoconstriction; and (f) cephalic vasoconstriction. Unlike the orienting response, the defense response habituates slowly.

The startle response is similar to the DR, but somewhat different. To get a startle, the stimulus must have a sharp rise time. The responses commonly (but not always) obtained are: (a) blink; (b) moves forward; (c) shoulders hunch; (d) flexor (arms and legs move away from gravity) versus an extensor response; (e) gasp; (f) increase in SC and HR; and (g) pupil dilation. On the basis of very stereotyped responding across subjects, Ekman, Friesen, and Simons (1985) suggested that the startle be considered a reflex instead of an emotion. Emotional responses, they suggested, have far less steroetypy in the temporal form of the response. All component behaviors of the startle tend to habituate quickly except for the blink.

The stimuli used to create diffuse physiological arousal need not be traumatic. For example, stressors such as mental arithmetic (e.g., count backward out loud to a metronome from some start number such as 1873 by 17s) are used in the stress literature to create reliable increases in both heart rate and blood pressure. Obrist (1981) found that reliable increases in both heart rate and stroke volume could be obtained by situations in which the subject had a perceived sense of control (regardless of whether there was actual control).

14.2.5.3. Making Inferences About Underlying Neural Activity Using What Is Known About the Heart and Its Response to Exercise

Often we wish to get the maximum amount of information from peripheral physiological methods. A lot can be inferred with the proper selection of physiological measures and knowledge of physiology. I review a few of these inferences here.

Under normal conditions, the heart's rate is under control of the parasympathetic nervous system through the action of the vagus nerve. Generally, resting heart rates are about 70 beats per minute (BPM) for men and somewhat higher for women (closer to 80 BPM). The frequent tonic action of the vagus slows the heart by causing the secretion of acetylcholine; this tonic action of the vagus nerve is referred to as vagal tone. If the vagus were cut, the heart would speed up within a heartbeat to what is called its intrinsic rhythm—the rhythm of the atrial pacemakers, approximately 105 BPM. The vagus thus acts on the heart's rate very quickly, and it speeds the heart by inhibiting its activity. Vagal tone can be estimated from the subject's heart rate and respiration using the amount of covariation in the heart rate spectrum that is due to respiration (Porges, 1972, 1983, 1984, 1985; Porges et al., 1980). Time-series analysis is employed in this computation; to obtain reasonably stable estimates, about 30 seconds of data are necessary. Porges (1972, 1983, 1984, 1985) also reported correlations in the 0.90s by using only the heart rate data (interbeat intervals) and the standard ranges of respiration for subjects (which varies with age and gender).

Rowell (1986) studied the response of the cardiovascular system to exercise. During the start of exercise, the initial increase in the heart's rate is the result of vagal inhibition. However, this action is not capable of taking the heart's rate beyond the heart's intrinsic rhythm, so that increases in heart rate beyond about 105 BPM are not due to vagal inhibition. Rowell (1986) pointed out that, during continued exercise at around 100 BPM (in males; Robinson, Epstein, Beiser, & Braunwald, 1966), two additional effects speed the heart. One is the action of sympathetic nerves (which are asymmetrically richer on the left side of the heart), and the other is the secretion of catecholamines by the adrenal gland (and norepinephrine by sympathetic nerves). This is illustrated in Fig. 14.1.

It is well known that the sympathetic nerves that innervate the heart are also primarily responsible for increases in myocardial contractility and concomitant decreases in systolic time intervals. The heart increases its output in two ways: by increasing its rate and/or by increasing stroke volume. The sympathetic nerves that innervate the heart act through beta receptors.

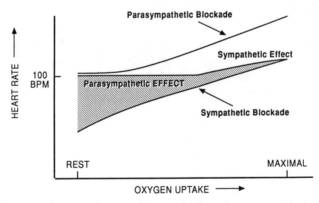

FIG. 14.1. Relative contribution of sympathetic and parasympathetic nervous system to the rise in heart rate during exercise. The hatched region shows that the relative magnitude of vagal withdrawal (parasympathetic effect) predominates at low levels of exercise; the initial cardioacceleration is due almost entirely to this mechanism. At higher levels of exercise the sympathetic effect predominates (shown by open region). From Rowell (1986, p. 221. Used with permission).

Sympathetic nerves also innervate the vasculature, through the action of alpha receptors. The alpha branch of the sympathetic nervous system exerts a tonic influence that keeps arteries and arterioles tonically contracted. Inhibition of alpha SNS influence opens arteries and arterioles. Blood pressure is a function of a heart that has a large stroke volume (usually this implies high beta SNS activation) and high alpha SNS activation (constricted arteries result from increased alpha activity). Hence, if one measures blood velocities, the blood's velocity to the periphery (e.g., to the fingers) is proportional to beta and proportional to minus alpha. However, if one measures blood flow to the head (e.g., pulse transit time to the ear), it is a different story. Because that vasculature to the head is more likely to remain open, pulse transit time to the ear is more a function of beta sympathetic activation.

Hence, the peripheral physiological responses that are collected, even of just the cardiovascular system, can be employed to support the construct of diffuse physiological arousal.

14.3. WHAT IS THE ROLE OF PHYSIOLOGY IN PREDICTING THE MARITAL DISSOLUTION CASCADE?

Levenson and Gottman (1985) found that a general pattern of physiological arousal at Time 1 predicted declines in relationship satisfaction over a 3-year period, controlling for initial levels of marital satisfaction. These correlations were summarized in Table 4.1. As can be seen from this table, we found that cardiovascular measures for the husband that indicated higher arousal (faster heart rate and faster pulse transit times), both in baseline and during the events-of-the-day conversation, predicted declining marital satisfaction, controlling initial levels. This also was the case for the husband's skin conductance and for the wife's skin conductance, and baseline activity level before the conflict task. In each case, higher activation predicted declines in satisfaction, whereas lower levels predicted increases. The changes in marital satisfaction over 3 years represented by these data were clinically significant; a number of couples increased or decreased by as much as 2 standard deviations over the 3 years. How general are these initially encouraging results about the role of physiological arousal in predicting the cascade toward marital dissolution?

At the moment, one can examine the database of couples' physiological responses in three studies. The first study (DU080, with 30 couples) was conducted with Levenson in 1980; and there were 4-year and 8-year follow-ups of the couples in 1983 and 1987 (Levenson & Gottman, 1983, 1985). In the first study, a smaller set of physiological variables was averaged over 10-second intervals. The data were SPAFF coded with an early version of the SPAFF. Very little was known about longitudinal follow-up then, and at Times 2 and 3 we were able to recontact only 63% and 60% of the couples, respectively. None of the recontacted couples had divorced or separated by Time 2, and only one couple had divorced by Time 3. I already have described the other two studies (DU083 and DUO86).

Because it was not possible to analyze the divorce and separation data for the DU080 study, analyses were conducted between the Time 1 physiology during the events-of-the-day discussion and the conflict discussion, with serious considerations of dissolution by husbands and wives (sum of serious considerations of separation and serious considerations of divorce) at Times 2 and 3.

At Time 2, there were significant correlations with the wife's serious considerations of dissolution and the mean of the husband's cardiac interbeat interval for the baseline before the events-of-the-day discussion ($r = -.53$, $p < .01$), the mean of the husband's cardiac interbeat interval during events of the day discussion ($r = -.51$, $p < .05$), the husband's mean pulse transit time during the events-of-the-day discussion ($r = -.45$, $p < .05$), the wife's mean skin conductance level during the events of the day discussion ($r = .45$, $p < .05$), the husband's mean cardiac interbeat interval for the baseline before the conflict discussion ($r = -.59$, $p < .01$), the wife's gross motor movement for the baseline before the conflict discussion ($r = .62$, $p < .01$), and the husband's cardiac interbeat interval during the conflict discussion ($r = -.53$, $p < .01$). Serious considerations of dissolution by the wife at Time 2 were predicted by greater autonomic activation at Time 1. None of the correlations with serious considerations of dissolution by the husband was significant.

A set of t tests conducted on the husbands' heart rates for couples whose wives had or had not thought of dissolution revealed that the husbands' heart rates were, respectively, 73.16 BPM and 95.92 BPM in the baseline before the events discussion [t (18) = 2.62, $p < .05$], 75.32 BPM and 95.16 BPM during the events discussion [t (18) = 2.52, $p < .05$], 70.21 BPM and 93.31 BPM in the baseline before the conflict discussion [t (18) = 3.09, $p < .01$], and 72.94 BPM and 87.66 BPM during the conflict discussion [t (18) = 2.67, $p < .05$]. These are very large effects in the literature on autonomic physiology, where laboratory effects tend to average less than 5 BPM. By Time 3, a similar pattern of results held, but there was not adequate power to achieve significance, except for the wife's activity during the events and the conflict discussion.

In the DUO83 study, a sufficient number of separations and divorces present a more complete table. For the wife's serious considerations of dissolution, the only results were that the following correlations were significant: the husband's finger pulse amplitude during the conflict discussion ($r = -.23$, $p < .05$) and the wife's interbeat interval during the conflict discussion ($r = -.23$, $p < .05$). There were no significant results for the husband's considerations of dissolution (except for the husband's finger pulse amplitude; $r = -.21$, $p = .058$), nor for predicting actual separation (except for the wife's interbeat interval; $r = -.20$, $p = .080$) or divorce. A t test was conducted for the wife's interbeat interval for wives who seriously had or had not considered dissolution. During the conflict discussion, the mean heart rates of wives, who in the next 4 years were to seriously consider dissolution, was 82.44; whereas for other wives the mean heart rates were 76.08 [t (77) $= 2.31$, $p < .05$].

In the DUO86 study, I included an eyes-closed baseline before the interview that set up the conflict discussion. I thought that arousal differences on this baseline would be a more reliable reflection of chronic activation than the eyes-open baseline obtained after the interview and before the conflict discussion. In the DUO86 study, I found a significant result for the husband's heartrate in correlation with actual divorce. This also was true in the eyes-closed baseline that preceded the interview about the marital conflict, when, presumably couples would be less likely to be autonomically aroused. No other physiological variable was correlated significantly with divorce. However, the husband's baseline eyes-closed heartrate was also a significant predictor of separation ($r = -.28$, $p < .05$). The wife's baseline activity level was a significant predictor of the husband's later considerations of dissolution ($r = .41$, $p < .01$); this was also the case for her activity level during the interaction ($r = .44$, $p < .01$), and with her considerations of dissolution for the eyes-closed baseline ($r = .29$, $p < .05$).

A set of t tests conducted on the husband's interbeat interval showed that these correlations were associated with large Time 1 differences in heartrate between couples that eventually divorced in DUO86 and couples that stayed together. For the eyes-closed baseline, $t(51) = 2.62$, $p < .05$, see Fig. 14.2; or the eyes-open baseline, $t(51) = 2.69$, $p < .01$, divorced mean $= 84.49$ BPM and stable mean $= 73.43$ BPM; for the conflict interaction, $t(51) = 2.57$, $p < .05$, divorced mean $= 85.50$ BPM and stable mean $= 75.20$ BPM. As in the DUO80 study, these are large effects, and they were obtained for the husband's heart rate.

14.4. SUMMARY

The results of these studies are encouraging, but not entirely consistent. The husband's arousal, particularly his heart rate, was a predictor of

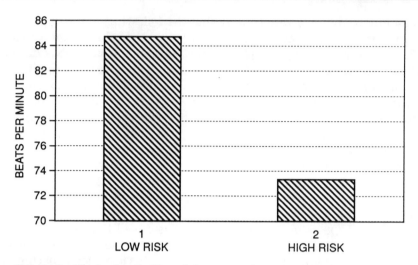

FIG. 14.2. The husband's Time 1 heart rate during an eyes-closed baseline between couples who eventually divorced (in DUO86) and couples who stayed together.

variables in the cascade toward dissolution in the DUO80 and DUO86 studies, but the wife's and not the husband's heart rate was a predictor of variables in the cascade toward dissolution in the DUO83 study. The wife's activity level was fairly consistently a predictor of declines in relationship satisfaction and considerations of dissolution. It was not clear why these inconsistencies existed.

A conservative conclusion from the data of these three studies is that physiological arousal is, in general, associated with marital dissolution variables. Although, these results are a long way from proving the validity of the DPA theory presented in this chapter, they are encouraging, and they suggest the potential value of further research on the construct and its potential theoretical usefulness. Bernard's (1982) idea that it is women who are the victims in marriage and men who are buffered physiologically is not supported consistently by these results. A conservative conclusion is that marriages are systems; when they are ailing, both men and women suffer, although they suffer in distinct ways (see chapter 16).

This chapter, and chapter 12 on gender differences, have provided a foundation for an integrated formulation of the role of physiological activation in understanding why some marriages are on a trajectory toward dissolution, whereas others are on a stable trajectory. In the following chapter, I expand the discussion to include the important concept of physiological reactivity and its significant relationship to the

Oral History variables, which were highly predictive of marital dissolution in the DUO86 replication study. Hence, a final suggestion of the potential role of physiological variables in predicting the cascade toward marital dissolution and possible mechanisms for this cascade are discussed in the following chapter.

15

Toward a Comprehensive Theory of Marital Stability

In this chapter, a theoretical formulation is proposed that is designed to link the outcome cascade (cascade toward dissolution), the process cascade (the Four Horsemen of the Apocalypse), the distance and isolation cascade, and concepts of physiological arousal and reactivity. The basis of this formulation is the definition of conjugate spaces, P-space that assesses behavioral flow of cumulated negativity minus positivity, and Q-space that assesses the perception of well-being or distress (operationalized as the rating dial in the video recall procedure). The additional goal of this formulation is to surmise how a person might go from thinking negatively about an interaction to more globally and stable negative attributions about the partner and the relationship. Flooding is suggested as the variable that provides the intervening link. Data are presented that suggest that these linkages exist. New data are presented from 156 couples using a self-report of affect procedure developed by Rushe during interviews with couples about their most negatively and positively rated moments. These data support the idea of linkages between self-report of affect, negative attributions about the spouse, and flooding. The structure of Q-space is examined for positive and negative moments. The results of an Oral History Interview are presented to show that global perceptions of the spouse and the history of the relationship are highly predictive of divorce in then DUO86 study, correlated with interaction during marital conflict and indexes of physiological reactivity. Data also are reviewed about the negative consequences of negative affect and the buffering effects of positive affect (particularly interest, humor, and validation) on adrenaline secretion during marital conflict. Results are integrated into a model that posits a core triad of balance with bidirecional relationships between P-space, Q-space, and physiological responses.

15.1. OUTLINE OF THE THEORETICAL FORMULATION

In this chapter, I propose a theoretical formulation about marital stability and dissolution that is an attempt to integrate behavior, cognition, and physiology in marital interaction.

I am not interested in the long-standing debates about what has "primacy," affect, or cognition (see Izard, Kagan, & Zajonc, 1984; Zajonc, 1980). In fact, it is quite clear to me that the two are intricately connected. From a measurement standpoint, cognition can be assessed from behavior, as Buehlman et al. (1992) demonstrated, by coding behavior during an interview. There are also independent methods for assessing couples' perceptions, as Levenson and Gottman (1985) showed using the rating dial during video recall. Instead of debates such as the primacy of cognition and affect, I suggest a mechanism through which the outcome and process cascades may be linked.

The first step in this theorizing is to suggest a mechanism for how the distance and isolation cascades are related to behavior. Recall that the cascade model suggested that there are separate trajectories for couples whose marriages are dissolving (nonregulated couples) and couples whose marriages are stable (regulated couples). Couples generally go through a process of dissolution that involves being unhappily married for a time, seriously considering separation and divorce, and then actually separating and divorcing.

I suggested that there is a process that is related to this outcome cascade that can be based on a balance theory of marriage. Dissolution is related to positive-to-negative ratios of less than one (there is more negative than positive), whereas stability is associated with ratios that are around 5.0. I also suggested that all negatives are not equally negative, and that there are Four Horsemen of the Apocalypse, namely criticism, defensiveness, contempt, and stonewalling.

I also suggested that marital stability is not uniform, but, in fact, there are three separate types of stable marriages, all of which have a positive-to-negative ratio of about 5.0.

Before I discuss the theoretical formulation, I discuss the task of the integration of cognition and emotion in the context of the study of marriage. Fortunately, Fincham et al. (1990) provided a guide for theoretical development of the study of cognition in marriage. They suggested that it is important to understand how cognition is used in marriage. They wrote:

> [W]e argue that a central function of cognition in marriage is to understand past and present relationship events and to predict and guide future relationship behaviors . . . a cognitive account of marriage must include cognition that occurs between marital interactions and cannot be limited to cognition that occurs during interaction. . . . Cognitions that occur between interactions necessarily involve constructions of previously experienced events (memory) and these constructions are most likely to reflect the deliberate attempts at recall that dominate the study of memory in psychology. . . . A second factor that influences recall is affect . . . nega-

tive material is more easily retrieved by distressed than nondistressed spouses and is therefore more likely to influence cognitive processing. . . .

Thus far we have emphasized deliberate recall and processing of marital events that occur between interactions. However, it is important to acknowledge that recall of marital events often is not effortful. . . . However, marital cognition research has not focused on the immediate perception of behavior but on cognitions available via controlled processing. (pp. 135–139)

Fincham et al. (1990) went on to discuss Weiss' (1980) concept of sentiment override, in which a spouse's responses toward the partner's behavior are determined not by the behavior, but by the spouse's general sentiment toward the partner. They then suggested a broad research agenda for studying the relationship between automatic and effortful information processing. They wrote: "What may distinguish distressed and nondistressed spouses is not how they consciously process partner behavior but what aspects of partner behavior gain attention and are made available for controlled processing" (p. 140). They suggested that "there are numerous methods for 'getting inside the head' " (p. 141), such as "clustering and sequencing of recalled material . . . , which can reveal much about the structure of representations" (p. 141).

In this chapter, I hope to outline a theoretical formulation that is guided by the insights of Fincham et al. (1990).

15.1.1. Elements of the Theory

I construct this theory within a theoretical framework of systems recently devised by the Swiss theoretical physicist, Roland Fivaz (in press, 1991). Some of my theoretical formulation is speculative. I propose the theory, because I believe it is parsimonious and it integrates all of my results into a relatively simple framework.

Fivaz's (1991) thinking was based on a generalization of thermodynamics, and the physical basis for his ideas are not my concern here. My ideas were inspired by his writings and my conversations with him, but I take responsibility for any misinterpretations. I do not go into much detail about Fivaz's ideas in this chapter. However, Fivaz's thinking included a simple set of conjugate variables that is required to describe the behavior of a wide class of systems. I do not define the term *conjugate* in general, but in Newton's mechanics, position and momentum are conjugate variables.

Fivaz's general notation for these conjugate sets of variables are P and Q, and I speak in this theory of "P-space" and "Q-space." He called the

Q variables the "order variables" and the P variables the "flow variables." This probably is very abstract, except for those readers who are familiar with some physics. Therefore, I bring it down to the realm of marriage and make it all concrete.

In the theory I wish to formulate, the P variables are simply the cumulative (or integrated) sum over time of positive minus negative behaviors. This ought to be very familiar to readers of this book, because examples of these are the speaker RCISS point graphs. In general, one can think of each partner in a marriage having a built-in meter that measures the totality of accumulated negativity in this interaction. As in the case of the point graphs, negativity is reduced or balanced by the positivity expressed or received. To summarize, the P variables measure the total flow and accumulation of overall negativity over time, as the interaction proceeds.

I suggest that there is a threshold slope of these cumulated variables; if the threshold is exceeded, this affects the perception of the interaction. These perception variables are the Q variables. In my theorizing, they are operationalized using the rating dial and my video recall procedure, as well as techniques like thought listing.

I discuss the general character of the Q variables further. In physics, the P variables reflect kinetic energy (or flow) and the Q variables reflect potential energy (or order). The Q variables, the equivalent of potential energy, in my theory, must represent some form of displacement from an equilibrium state of perceived well-being.

In this formulation, the Q variables are dichotomous, but that need not be the case. I think of them as either the perception of well-being and safety in the relationship (feeling loved and respected, in which case one can think of $Q = +1$) or the opposite perception. I think, on the basis of pilot work using a video recall interview, that this perception of "non-well-being" can be made up of moments of feeling hurt and under attack, that is, perceived threat ($Q = -1$) or moments of hurt and anger. Later I discuss empirically where this notion comes from. In one kind of moment fear is central, and in the other anger and contempt are central; both kinds of moments are blended with sadness and disappointment.

The Q-space represents the subtext in a person's perception as the interaction unfolds. Generally, this is a quiescent subtext, as long as $Q = +1$; the perception of neutrality and well-being is a subtext that is not very prominent in awareness. When $Q = -1$, perceptions flip and a new cognitive–emotional process is engaged.

In my theoretical framework, the Q-space value of -1 is the entry point for the flooding variable, which I propose is the driving force of the distance and isolation cascade. So, the first theoretical link I make is between the behavior process cascade and the distance and isolation cascade. I do not suggest that every perception that "all is not OK" leads to flooding, but rather that the negativity needs to exceed some threshold before $Q = -1$, and that the occupation time in this $Q = -1$ state determines flooding.

Figure 15.1 shows a graph of a P variable and a Q variable. The link between them is the axiom that when the P variable passes a threshold slope, the Q variable flips. The flip represents a catastrophic change in perception. A parameter in P-space (the slope of the cumulated graph) undergoes smooth changes, but, at some critical value, the Q variable undergoes a major discontinuity. Thus, the relationship between P-space and Q-space is simply a threshold model. When the slope of the cumulated P variable passes a particular threshold, the Q variable jumps from $+1$ to -1. This represents a departure from the perception of well-being in the interaction.

15.1.2. Perceptual Shifts as Catastrophic Changes in Cognition

Figure 15.2 presents two well-known perceptual illusions: one in which a vase can look like two faces, and another in which a young woman can look like an old woman. In these examples, the perceptual flip is symmetrical. It can go back and forth between seeing the illusion one

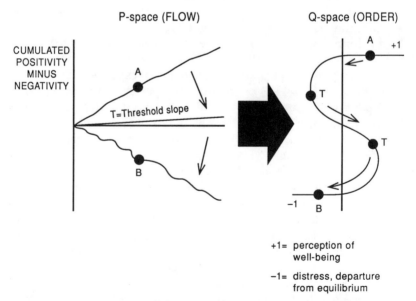

P-space (FLOW)   Q-space (ORDER)

CUMULATED POSITIVITY MINUS NEGATIVITY

A

T=Threshold slope

B

A   +1

T

T

-1 B

+1= perception of well-being

−1= distress, departure from equilibrium

FIG. 15.1. The relationship between P-space and Q-space is a threshold relationship that illustrates a cusp catastrophe (two choices for Q); for example, when the threshold in P-space exceeds a critical value, Q makes a sudden jump.

FIG. 15.2. Two common reversible perceptual illusions that also flip suddenly: left—two faces or a vase, right—old lady or young woman.

way or the other. It is possible to create other illusions that are less symmetrical; once they are seen one way, it is very difficult to see them any other way. In the same way, perceptions about an interactional moment, the partner, or the entire relationship may be symmetrical to varying degrees. For example, a violent act or knowledge of a secret extramarital affair are more likely than other acts to permanently transform the perception of one's partner. Catastrophe theory (Arnold, 1986; Saunders, 1990) is the study of "abrupt changes arising as a sudden response of a system to a smooth change in external conditions" (Arnold, 1986, p. 2). In my formulation, some parameter in P-space (the slope of the cumulated curve) changes smoothly, but then, at some threshold slope, there is an abrupt flip in the perception of well-being (much like the flips depicted in Fig. 15.2). This is the initial catastrophic change.

15.1.3. Examples from Interaction in Which Q-Space Represents the Subtext

15.1.3.1. The Idea of a Subtext

Before going further with this formulation, I show how this might work in an actual interaction. In the following transcript of a conversation from the film *Annie Hall*, one can think of a hidden subtext of thoughts in Q-space that are unrevealed to the viewer. The scene subtext is in parentheses. The man (Alvie) and the woman (Annie) have just met during a doubles tennis match, and they are in her apartment on the rooftop balcony having a drink.

Alvie: So, did you do those photographs in there, or what?
Annie: Yeah, I sort of dabble around.
         (I dabble? Listen to me—what a jerk)
Alvie: They're wonderful. They have a quality.
         (You are a great looking girl)
Annie: I would like to take a serious photography course.
         (He probably thinks I'm a yo-yo)
Alvie: Photography is interesting because it's a new art form and a set
         of aesthetic criteria that's not emerged yet.
         (I wonder what she looks like naked)
Annie: Aesthetic criteria? You mean whether it's a good photo or not?
         (I'm not smart enough for him. Hang in there)
Alvie: The medium enters in as a condition of the art form itself. (I
         don't know what I'm saying—she senses I'm shallow)
Annie: Well, to me it's all instinctive, you know. I just try to feel it. I try
         to get a sense of it and not think about it so much.
         (God, I hope he doesn't turn out to be a shmuck like the others)
Alvie: Still, you need a set of aesthetic guidelines to put it in social
         perspective, I think.
         (Christ, I sound like an FM radio. Relax.)

In this well-known example, the subtext roughly represents events in the Q-space, whereas the text represents events in the P-space.

15.1.3.2. Subtext as Flips in Q-Space

To illustrate a more precise usage of these two spaces of variables, consider another transcript, taken from a couple discussing the issue of jealousy. This time, instead of a subtext in parentheses, I put the wife's suggested value of Q, with commentary.

Husband (H):   Well the issue is your jealousy.
Wife (W):   Which has gotten a lot better lately. (Q = +1, nonverb-
               ally she reflects a sense of well-being)
H: Yes it has. Since I made a commitment to my family it
               has gotten better. Now if you saw me during the day
               driving in my car with a woman you wouldn't get
               jealous probably.

W:	Why? Is there a woman in your car? (Q = +1, she sounds a bit alarmed, but not very much)
H:	No.
W.	Good. (Q = +1, She is relieved)
H:	Actually, Laura Neville and I are going to ride together to a workshop.
W:	A workshop? What about? (Q = +1, She is neutrally asking for information)
H:	Commercial real estate. It's business.
W:	Oh. No I wouldn't be jealous of that because I know it's purely professional. (Q = +1, She is quite calm)
H:	You know it does bother me though, just for a hypothetical, that say I wanted to see Jeannie again, just say for lunch, you know.
W:	No, that's Jeannie is a different story. You were lovers. (Q = +1, There is a bit of alarm in her voice, but it is slight. Still, she may be drifting to an in-between zone, where there is a higher probability of a shift to Q = −1)
H:	But that was way before I met you. And you know that I have made a commitment to our family. It is just not an issue. It's like seeing an old chum.
W:	It doesn't matter. That's a very different kind of relationship. She simply has no place in our lives. It's not like a chum. She's a woman. (Q = +1. She accepts this as a hypothetical discussion and is relaxed talking about it, giving her views)
H:	See that's where I think you're wrong. She's a person that I once liked a lot, and it's a shame to lose touch with her. As a friend. As an acquaintance.
W:	Why should she come into our lives, into our home? Why should my children know her? (Q = −1, There is suddenly clear alarm in her voice and on her face)
H:	She's very interesting, you know. You both went to the same college. You'd have a lot in common.
W:	Wait a minute! Do you want to see her? Is that what you are saying? (Q = −1, She looks and sound fearful)
H:	Yes I would. Why not? I'd like to find out how she's doing, talk to her again. Yes.
W:	Then I think we have a serious problem. We need counseling. (Q = −1. She has clearly left the region of well-being, and may be becoming flooded)
H:	Well, maybe we do.

Gradually, through these perceptual flips in Q-space, her sense of well-being is displaced by the threat she feels his desire to see an old flame has on their relationship. Once the negativity has passed a threshold value, Q flips from $+1$ to -1. This is, in rough outline, the way that P-spaces and Q-spaces can work.

The link I make is between behavior and this perception of being flooded by one's partner's behavior. I review some evidence that there is, in fact, a correlational link.

15.2. EMPIRICAL EXPLORATIONS: CORRELATES OF FLOODING (Q-SPACE) IN RELATION TO BEHAVIOR FLOW (P-SPACE)

In chapter 5, I reviewed evidence for the fact that there is a cascade of variables that measure distance and isolation in the marriage. I showed that behavior was, in general, related to this cascade, and that this cascade also covaried with the trajectories leading toward marital stability or marital dissolution. In this section, I reexamine these relationships in light of the gender difference reviewed in chapter 12. Is there any evidence that behavior is related to flooding?

15.2.1. Behaviors Are Correlated with Flooding

The first question I ask is whether the RCISS point graphs are related to flooding. The multiple correlation of the slope of the husband's and wife's RCISS speaker graphs was 0.41 [$F(2,67) = 6.84$, $p < .01$] for the husband feeling flooded, and 0.44 [$F(2,67) = 7.93$, $p < .001$] for the wife feeling flooded. Both point graphs contributed equally to this multiple correlation; for the husband's feelings of being flooded, the correlations with his wife's and his own slopes were $-.39$ ($p < .001$) and $-.39$ ($p < .001$), respectively; for the wife's feelings of being flooded, the correlations with her husband's and her own slopes were $-.42$ ($p < .001$) and $-.40$ ($p < .001$), respectively. Table 15.1 reports the results of multiple regressions with MICS and SPAFF codes as the independent variables. The eight MICS codes had a multiple correlation of 0.52 [$F(8,66) = 3.09$, $p < .01$] with the husband feeling flooded, and a multiple correlation of 0.61 [$F(8,65) = 4.75$, $p < .001$] for the wife feeling flooded. The strongest univariate correlations were the wife's stubbornness for the husband and the husband's withdrawal for the wife. The SPAFF codes were analyzed separately into positive and negative affects. Both positive and negative affects were related significantly to

TABLE 15.1
MICS and SPAFF Codes and Husbands' and Wives' Feeling Flooded

Variable	Husband Flooded	Wife Flooded
	R	R
MICS		
Wife withdrawn	.23	.19
Wife defensive	.26*	.32**
Hus. stubborn	.32**	.39***
Hus. withdrawn	.30**	.47***
Hus. defensive	.17	.24*
Wife engages	.36**	.30**
Wife stubborn	.42***	.30**
Hus. engages	.27*	.37***
SPAFF positive affect: buffering		
Wife joy	−.26*	−.01
Wife humor	−.36**	−.41***
Hus. neutral	−.20	−.32**
Wife affection	.04	−.15
Wife interest	−.15	−.12
Hus. affection	−.25*	−.24*
Hus. interest	−.11	−.06
Hus. joy	−.22	−.08
Wife neutral	−.25*	−.29*
Hus. humor	−.37***	−.41***
Wife fear	−.08	.05
Hus. anger	.41***	.47***
Hus. sad	.12	.10
Wife sad	.20	.05
Wife disgust/contempt	.07	.15
Hus. disgust/contempt	.28*	.03
Wife whining	.29*	.34**
Hus. whining	.23	.18
Hus. fear	.02	.04
Wife anger	.39***	.49***

Note. R = Correlation
*p < .05. **p < .01. ***p < .001.

the feelings of being flooded, and thus there was evidence that positive affect may act as a buffer against flooding for both husbands and wives. More specifically, as a buffer for the husband's feelings of being flooded, the multiple R was 0.57 [$F(10,65) = 3.17$, $p < .01$], and for the wife's feelings of being flooded, the multiple R was 0.55 [$F(10,65) = 2.90$, $p < .01$]. For both the husband and wife, the strongest buffers were the husband and wife's humor. For the relationship between negative affect and the husband's feelings of being flooded, the multiple R was 0.56 [$F(10,65) = 2.98$, $p < .01$], and for the wife's feelings of being flooded, the multiple R was 0.57 [$F(10,65) = 3.09$, $p < .01$]. For both the husband and wife, the strongest univariate relationship to feeling flooded was the husband and wife's anger, with her whining a close second.

To summarize, there is an orderly relationship between behavior and flooding, with positivity acting as a buffer.

15.2.2. Gender Differences in Feeling Flooded by Partner's Negative Affect

Gottman and Levenson (1988) suggested that men are physiologically more reactive to negative affect than women, that their recovery times are longer than women's, and that they react to negative affective stimuli of lower intensity than women. To explore these kinds of potential differences in the subjective feeling of being flooded by one's partner's negative affect, I correlated the ESCAL ratings of husbands and wives with their partners' actual behavior during conflict resolution. The prediction was that different RCISS scales would predict the ESCAL ratings for husbands more than for wives. The complain/criticize scale should be correlated with husbands feeling flooded by their wives' negative affect, whereas behaviors of higher negativity (defensiveness, contempt, and stonewalling) should be related to wives feeling flooded by their husbands.

Table 15.2 is a summary of these correlations. As can be seen, for husbands all four negative wife behaviors were correlated significantly with husbands feeling flooded. However, the husbands' complain/criticize was uncorrelated with wives feeling flooded, whereas hus-

TABLE 15.2
Husbands and Wives Feeling Flooded and Their Partners' and Their Own Behavior
Using the RCISS Coding System

RCISS CODE	Husband Feels Flooded (HESCAL)	Wife Feels Flooded (WESCAL)
Husband		
Conplain/criticize	.26*	.15
Defensiveness	.16	.36**
Contempt	.45***	.41***
Stonewall	.32**	.45***
Wife		
Complain/criticize	.25*	.25*
Defensiveness	.25*	.39***
Contempt	.29*	.30*
Stonewall	.35**	.50***

*$p < .05$. **$p < .01$. ***$p < .001$.

bands' defensiveness, contempt, and stonewalling were correlated significantly with their wives feeling flooded (comparing correlations between feeling flooded and the complain/criticize code of the partner, $z = 1.81$). For both husbands and wives, stonewalling had the strongest correlations with flooding. It is logical that feeling flooded is related to withdrawal from interaction; it is also likely that the relationship is bidirectional.

Table 15.3 presents separate correlations for husbands and wives for the variables of the distance and isolation cascade. The correlation matrices are quite similar for husbands and wives, except for the striking differences in correlations with respect to loneliness. For husbands, all the other variables were strongly correlated with their loneliness. For wives, only parallel lives were correlated with their loneliness. For example, feelings of loneliness were correlated with feeling flooded by the partners' negative affect 0.71 ($p < .001$) for husbands and $-.01$ (ns) for wives ($z = 5.54$). If the distance and isolation cascade is an accurate reflection of the stages a person goes through in withdrawing from the marriage, and loneliness is the final stage, these differences in correlations suggest that husbands withdraw sooner in the process, perhaps when they feel flooded, whereas wives withdraw much later in the process, when their lives are actually working in parallel.

15.3. SPECULATIONS ABOUT THE PRINCIPLES OF P-SPACE AND Q-SPACE

I return from these empirical explorations to the formulation of P-space and Q-space theory. What principles may operate?

TABLE 15.3
Correlations Between the Variables of the Distance and Isolation Cascade Separately for Husbands and Wives

Variable	1	2	3	4	5
Flooding					
Problems severe	.61***				
	(.56***)				
Work problems out	.33**	.30**			
alone	(.34**)	(.34**)			
Parallel lives	.17	.04**	.20		
	(−.01)	(−.03)	(.14)		
Loneliness	.71***	.63***	.54***	.59***	
	(−.01)	(−.01)	(.20)	(.61***)	

Note. Wives' correlations in parentheses.
*$p < .05$. **$p < .01$. ***$p < .001$.

15.3.1. Dimensionality of Q-Space is 1.0 When Interaction is Positively Perceived

Most of the perceptions that people have as they interact in a marriage are effortless processing of information and emotion. I suspect that this automatic information processing in marital interaction is generally quite simple (see Fincham et al., 1990).

The Q-space usually is not very differentiated, but tends to be unidimensional and usually $Q = +1$ (the perception is one of well-being). Hence, the factor structure of Q-space when $Q = +1$ suggests unidimensionality. The dimension of the Q-space is probably a positive-negative dimension (perhaps well-being vs. perceived threat [danger] or anger/hurt).

Is it possible that Q-space becomes more differentiated under some conditions, and the information processing mode becomes more effortful and less automatic? I suggested that when the accumulated negativity in P-space passed a threshold (catastrophe machine), information processing shifted to $Q = -1$. It also might be that when the length of occupation time in $Q = -1$ exceeds a critical threshold, information processing becomes more complex and Q-space becomes more dimensionalized. As the length of occupation time in $Q = -1$ passes a critical threshold, perhaps negative cognitions (attributions) become more global and stable. This shift, in turn, probably affects behavior flow; behaviors are more likely to shift from complaint to criticism, and from neutral and positive mindreading to negative mindreading. "You always" and "you never" statements become more likely.

In some pilot work, Carrere, Bush, and McCoy (1992) interviewed newlywed couples in Seattle about specific moments in their marital interaction and had them fill out a questionnaire about what they were thinking and feeling. The moments were either moments of physiological arousal, or selected from behavioral coding of the interaction as moments of stonewalling, defensiveness, or hostility. In all moments, there seemed to be the same two dimensions of internal perception of the negative moment: (a) anger blended with hurt, or (b) perceived attack. Thus, perhaps there are times when Q-space becomes differentiated. I suggest it becomes differentiated only during negative states. This may be a function of the intensity of the negativity, the occupation time in the $Q = -1$ state, or the surprise value of the negative event.

15.3.2. Symmetric–Iterative Property

As I already have suggested, the Q-space can become a P-space. That is, order variables can become flow variables, and a new set of Q variables can be defined. How is this done? One way is to suggest that the new

P- variables be defined as simply the cumulated occupation time in the previous state $Q = -1$. By virtue of this transformation, the entire Q-space becoming a new P process can then repeat. Why is this transformation necessary? It is the mechanism by which momentary perceptions of the interaction become more stable and global perceptions of the partner's traits and of the relationship's characteristics in general. It is the basis for the development of overlearned and lasting cognitions and behaviors in the marriage that have far more globality and stability than brief perceptual flips.

15.3.3. Role of DPA and Physiological Reactivity

I also suggest that physiological reactivity plays a role in the emotional conditioning of wider cues to the perception of danger, perceived threat, and attack. With concomitant diffuse physiological arousal and physiological reactivity, the distance and isolation cascade is well underway. This process works through the mechanism by which flooding is related to hypervigilance. The result is that there is selective inattention to disconfirming evidence of positivity in the marriage. A similar process of selective inattention to disconfirming evidence has been suggested as a basis for marital therapy by Segraves (1990). Berley and Jacobson (1984) proposed a fascinating cognitive–behavioral approach to marital therapy that utilized knowledge from the marital attributional literature.

Physiological responses associated with positive affect also can buffer people from ill effects. Figure 15.3 illustrates a segment from the rating dial and interbeat interval of a husband during the events-of-the-day discussion in the DUO83 study. The rating dial is multiplied by 100 so that it is easier to plot both variables in one graph. There is a dramatic increase in this husband's ratings after minute 7, second 25. There also is a dramatic increase in his interbeat interval (i.e., a decrease in his heartrate). These shifts in rating and interbeat interval were statistically significant with an interrupted time-series analysis using a first-order autoregressive model [for the rating variable, $t(9) = 8.08$, $p < .01$; for the interbeat interval variable, $t(9) = 3.55$, $p < .05$]. This is an example of a significant flip in the husband's Q-space, in this case related to his physiology.

15.3.4. Talk Table, Communication Box, and Video Recall Rating Dial as Operational Procedures for Studying Q-Space

15.3.4.1. The First Two Talk-Table Studies

Gottman et al. (1976) reported the results of two studies with a talk table, a double-sloping table that constrained the interaction of couples, so that only one partner could talk at a time, and required each person

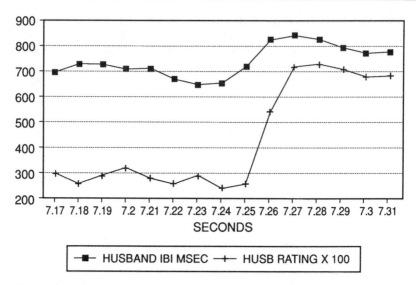

FIG. 15.3. Relationship between heart rate and rating dial data within an interaction suggests that there is order within interactions over time, which I have ignored to date.

to rate the positivity/negativity of the intent of messages sent and the impact of messages received. Several behavior-exchange models were tested with this paradigm, the critical test being the discrimination between distressed and nondistressed couples. The overall results of these two studies was support for a model in which nondistressed couples rated their partners' messages as having a more positive impact than distressed couples, and less discrepancy between intent and impact. Gottman et al. (1976) also reported that a positive reciprocity model was not supported by the data, and, instead proposed a bank account model. In the bank account model, the idea is that over a macro rather than a micro time period, the amount of positive acts generally exceeds the amount of negative acts in nondistressed couples' marriages, but there is not an immediate "tit-for-tat" exchange. Gottman's (1979) re-analysis of these data showed that although positive reciprocity did not distinguish between groups, negative reciprocity did distinguish between groups, with negative reciprocity more common in nondistressed couples than distressed couples. There were no intent differences between groups.

15.3.4.2. Rating Dial During Video Recall

I referred to the fact that Levenson and I developed a procedure in which couples view the videotape of their interaction and provide a continuous rating of the positivity or negativity of their recall of their own affect during the interaction. The rating dial is synchronized to the original video time code during the interaction. I believe that the rating dial paradigm provides a general approach to the study of Q-space. It is a generalization of the talk table that was developed to operationalize behavior exchange models in the study of naturalistic marital interaction (Gottman et al., 1976).

15.3.4.3. The Markman Studies with the Talk Table and the Communication Box

Subsequent studies with the talk table have replicated the talk-table impact results (Ferraro & Markman, 1981, with deaf couples; Floyd & Markman, 1983; Markman & Baccus, 1982, with Black couples). Markman also undertook a series of prediction studies with premarital couples (couples planning to marry). In one study, there was a significant prediction of Time 1 talk-table impact ratings and Time 3 (2.5 years later) relationship satisfaction ($r = 0.67$, $p < .01$), and Time 1 talk-table impact ratings and Time 4 (5.5 years later) relationship satisfaction ($r = 0.59$, $p < .05$). Problem intensity and relationship satisfaction ratings at Time 1 had no predictive power. Talk-table impact ratings with a small sample of couples also were found to be reasonably stable over time [$r(T1,T2) = 0.39$, ns; $r(T1,T3) = 0.78$, $p < .05$; $r(T2,T3) = 0.82$, $p < .05$].

The talk-table intent ratings were computed using the relative frequency of each button press (from supernegative to superpositive). Time-3 relationship satisfaction was predicted by the relative frequency of male negative intent ratings ($r = -0.73$, $p < .001$) and female negative intent ratings ($r = -0.62$, $p < .01$). This turned out to be the best Time 1 predictor of relationship satisfaction at Time 3.

Also, Markman and his colleagues improved on the Gottman et al. (1976) method of testing the intent–impact discrepancy model by using point-for-point discrepancies instead of averages across the interaction. There was no predictive power for the intent–impact discrepancy model for earlier times, but 5.5 years after the initial talk-table data were collected, the correlation was -0.66, $p < .01$ (three couples that provided Time 4 data, but who missed Time 2 were rightly included in this prediction). The less the discrepancy between intent and impact at Time 1, the greater their relationship satisfaction 5.5 years later.

Markman and Floyd (1980) and Markman and Poltrock (1982) replaced the talk table with a handheld communication box that provided the same data, but more conveniently. They found (Markman, personal communication, 1989) that communication box ratings were predictive of later relationship stability upon 6-year follow-up; initial relationship satisfaction was correlated weakly with stability for males ($r = -.14$, $p < .05$) and uncorrelated for females ($r = -.04$, ns).

15.3.4.4. The Notarius, Benson, Sloane, Vanzetti, and Hornyak (1989) Study with the Talk Table and the CISS Affect Codes

In an important methodological advance, Notarius et al. (1989) explored the relationship between the behavior of person A in a marital interaction, the perception of that behavior by person B, and the subsequent behavior of person B. They used the talk table for the perception ratings, and something akin to the CISS affect codes for the behavior. They used log-linear analysis to test models that might discriminate between the nine distressed and nine nondistressed couples in this study, pooling data across couples and across low- and high-conflict tasks. Distressed and nondistressed husbands did not differ in their talk-table scores, nor was their behavior coded differently by the observers. However, this was not the case for wives.

They evaluated three models that have been proposed in the literature as discriminating distressed couples from nondistressed couples: (a) a positive sentiment override model (Weiss, 1980), in which nondistressed couples discount negativity and emphasize positivity in their partners (rose-colored glasses); (b) a negative sentiment override model (Weiss, 1980), in which distressed couples discount positivity and emphasize negativity in their partners; and (c) editing model (Gottman et al., 1976), in which distressed wives (compared with nondistressed wives) fail to edit their negative cognitions in response to their partners' negative act, and thus act negatively when it is their turn to speak. Notarius et al. (1989) found evidence to support all three models. They wrote:

> Even when a negative antecedent was received negatively, nondistressed wives were about nine time as likely as distressed wives to offer a positive as opposed to a negative response in reply; nondistressed wives, compared to distressed wives, displayed a greater likelihood of editing out a negative response to a negative message that was received as negative. (p. 56)

Distressed wives also evaluated husbands' negative acts as negative 64% of the time, compared with nondistressed wives who evaluated their husbands' negative acts as negative 36% of the time. This was evidence for a positive sentiment override in nondistressed couples. They also suggested that distressed wives were the most accurate coders of their husbands' negative acts (agreed with observers more). There also was evidence for a negative sentiment override in distressed couples: If the husbands' behavior was coded neutral, distressed wives evaluated this message as negative 37% of the time, compared with nondistressed wives who evaluated this message as negative 14% of the time. Once these messages were coded negative, the subsequent act of distressed wives also was far more likely to be coded negative (72%), compared with distressed wives (38%). These methods are extremely provocative and innovative, because they permit the test of specific models of the behavior–cognition interface during reasonably naturalistic interaction.

15.3.4.5. Validity of the Levenson-Gottman (1983) Rating Dial Self-Report of Affect Procedures

Levenson and Gottman (1983) extended the talk-table procedures using a rating dial that couples employed to rate their interaction as they later viewed their videotape. The goal was to develop a procedure for obtaining the subject's self-report of affect with a procedure that did not constrain the interaction the way the talk table did.

To assess the validity of this self-report of affect procedure, Gottman and Levenson (1985) devised five tests. The first three were: (a) the measure should discriminate between high-conflict and low-conflict interactions, (b) the measure should discriminate between satisfied and dissatisfied couples, and (c) spouses' ratings of the same interaction should show evidence of statistical coherence. The fourth test required agreement between the self-reports of affect and the ratings of objective coders (Specific Affect Coding System, SPAFF, was used to code all of the videotapes in terms of specific affects; and these ratings were then collapsed into positive and negative affect codes). The fifth and final test was designed to assess the power of the video recall procedure. If subjects experienced the same sequence of emotions when viewing the videotapes as they had experienced during the actual interaction, an indication of similar patterns of ANS activity in the video recall session as had occurred in the interaction session would be seen.

The self-report of affect procedure passed all five of these tests (see Gottman & Levenson, 1985, for a full report of these results). I think one reason it passed the first four tests was because it passed the fifth test, which was termed *physiological reliving*. I assessed this by computing the coherence between the interaction session and the video recall session for each of the 30 couples for each of the four physiological measures (e.g., interaction session heart rate vs. recall session heart rate). I found that the spouses relived the original physiological experience as they watched and rated the videotapes. Not only were these two sets of responses strongly correlated, but the time series were usually in-phase. When a spouse watched the tape of the interaction, sweating, changes in cardiovascular functioning, and changes in movement all occurred at the same times as they had occurred when he or she was in the actual interaction.

15.3.4.6. Subsequent Work by Griffin with the Rating Dial Used to Operationalize Negative Affect as an Absorbing State

Griffin (1993) used the rating dial to define the negative absorbing state as staying in a negatively rated affective state. He used survival analysis to examine the hazard rate of transitions out of this negative absorbing state, and then constructed models for what the correlates were for this transition. As already reviewed (chapter 3), this choice of a central variable of Griffin's was quite insightful; Griffin asked a vital question in the study of marriage. In effect, he asked the question, "What keeps couples in this destructive negative absorbing state, and what is related to their transitions out of it?"

Griffin found that gender had a significant effect on the critical hazard rate. Wives had fewer, but longer episodes of negative affect than husbands. This gender difference was not significant in the positive task, although the trend was there, but it was significant in the conflict task. If the duration of wives' negative episodes was consistent, they tended to have longer stays in the negative state. As expected, the hazard rate for exiting negative affect was 72% larger in the positive than in the conflict task. Also, for each additional year of the wife's education, the probability of staying in a negative state was increased by 18%. Happily married wives were quicker to exit the negative state. For husbands, as for wives, the hazard rate was lower during the conflict than the positive task (in the positive task, it was 57% of the conflict task). The effect of education on the husband's hazard rate was opposite to its effect on the wife; each year of education shortened durations of negative affect; each year of education reduced the probability of staying in a negative state by about 15%. Also, for the husband, the effect of education was greater the longer the negative affective state had lasted.

Griffin's work was groundbreaking in its application of an exciting statistical method to the study of Q-space. It also contributed to the conclusion that these kinds of Q-space data have general validity and great potential in understanding the couple's affective perception of the interaction.

15.4. ATTRIBUTIONS IN MARRIAGE

There is a phenomenon in marriage that has to do with how spouses in happy and unhappy marriages think about positive and negative actions of their partners.

In a happy marriage, if the someone does something negative, the partner tends to think that the negativity is fleeting and situational. For example, the thought might be something like, "Oh, well, he's in a bad mood. He's been under a lot of stress lately and needs more sleep." The negativity is viewed as unstable, and the cause is viewed as situational; it is some external and fleeting situation that caused the negativity. On the other hand, in an unhappy marriage, the same behavior is likely to be interpreted as stable and internal to the partner. The accompanying thought might be something like, "He is inconsiderate and selfish. That's the way he is. That's why he did that."

On the other hand, in a happy marriage, if someone does something positive, the behavior is likely to be interpreted as stable and internal to the partner. The accompanying thought might be something like, "He is a considerate and loving person. That's the way he is. That's why he did that." On the other hand, in an unhappy marriage, the same positive behavior is likely to be seen as fleeting and situational. The accompanying thought might be something like, "Oh, well, he's nice because he's been successful this week at work. It won't last and it doesn't mean much." The positivity is viewed as unstable, and the cause is viewed as situational; it is some external and fleeting situation that caused the positivity.

Holtzworth-Munroe and Jacobson (1985) used indirect probes to investigate when couples might naturally search for causes of events and what they conclude when they do search for causes. They found that distressed couples engaged in more attributional activity than nondistressed couples, and that attributional thoughts primarily surrounded negative impact events. Nondistressed couples engaged in relationship enhancing attributions, whereas distressed couples engaged in distress maintaining attributions. Distress maintaining attributions maximized the impact of negativity and minimized the impact of positivity of the partner's behavior. Moreover, there was an important gender difference. Distressed husbands generated more attributions than nondistressed husbands, but the two groups of wives did not differ. The researchers suggested that normally males may not engage in much attributional activity, but that they outstrip women once relationship conflicts develop.

Relationship enhancing attributions were responses to positive partner behavior in both groups of couples. Relationship enhancing attributions minimized the impact of negative and maximized the impact of positive behaviors of the partner. In an experimental study by Jacobson, McDonald, Follette, and Berley (1985), distressed and nondistressed couples were assigned randomly to instructions to act positive or act negative. They found that distressed coupes were likely to attribute their partners' negative behavior to internal factors, whereas nondistressed couples were likely to attribute their partners' positive behavior to internal factors. Thus, once established, these attributions make change less likely to occur. Behaviors that should disconfirm the attributional sets tend to get ignored, whereas behaviors that confirm the attributional set receive attention.

Attributional processes may tap the way couples think in general about the marital interaction as it unfolds in time. For example, Berley and Jacobson (1984) noted that Watzlawick, Beavin, and Jackson (1967) talked about attributional processes when they discussed the punctuation fallacy. The punctuation fallacy is that each spouse views him or herself as the victim of the partner's behavior, which is seen as the causal stimulus. Attributions and general thought patterns about negative behaviors may, thus, be theoretically useful in providing a link between the immediate patterns of activity seen in behavioral interaction and physiological response and more long-lasting and global patterns that span longer time periods. It might be that these more stable aspects of the marriage are better at predicting long-term outcomes, such as divorce, than can be obtained from behavioral observation. In this chapter, it is seen that that is indeed the case.

The content dimensions of negative attributions that have been studied include locus (partner, self, relationship, or outside events), stability (e.g., due to partner's trait, a state that is situationally determined), globality (how many areas of the marriage are affected), intentionality (negative intent−selfish vs. unselfish motivation), controllability, volition, and responsibility (e.g., blameworthiness).

Fincham, Bradbury, and Scott (1990) reviewed experimental evidence for this phenomenon; they concluded that, by and large, these patterns had been well established by research. For attributions about negative events, 100% of the studies reviewed supported differences between happily and unhappily married couples on the two dimensions of globality and selfish versus unselfish motivation.

In my view, these attributional phenomena make the self-report measurement of any aspects of the quality of the marriage strongly related. They also are what become problematic in attaching any specificity to the measurement of marital satisfaction or marital quality (see Fincham & Bradbury, 1987).

15.4.1. Further Empirical Explorations in Q-Space

In this section, I test some speculations about the structure of Q-space and report some of the results of a larger study with three groups of couples: violent, distressed nonviolent, and happily married. This study was conducted with Jacobson, Holtzworth-Munroe, Fehrenbach, and Rushe (1993). For the past 3 years, we have studied the marital relationships of couples engaging in domestic violence (DV). From January 1990 through July 1991 (Time 1), we collected data on 57 DV couples (an additional) 28 that were maritally distressed but not physically violent (DNV), and (an additional) 20 (couples) that were happily married as well as nonviolent (NDNV). We also collected data from pilot couples and low-level violent couples, many of who went through all the procedures in the Gottman laboratory, but did not go through all the final procedures in the Jacobson laboratory. The total N was 156 couples. The data included videotapes of couples discussing areas of conflict, psychophysiological recordings of them during these conversations, detailed structured interviews, and numerous questionnaires. In January 1992, we began the longitudinal (Time 2) component of this research: an extensive 2-year follow-up.

In this study, we used the Levenson–Gottman video recall procedure and rating dial. After rating the conflict task, couples were interviewed about their most negative and positive moments, as well as a randomly selected neutral moment. In addition to having couples complete the Fincham and Bradbury attribution questionnaire for these moments (and for the interaction as a whole), couples filled out a Likert-type self-report designed by Rushe about their subjective experience of specific affects, including the negative affects of anger, disgust, contempt, sadness, whining, and worry; the positive affects of affection, humor, interest, and joy; and the neutral affects during each moment. Couples also rated their partners' moments, but these ratings are not discussed here. Couples also filled out the flooding questionnaire in this study. Of particular interest are three questions: (a) What is the structure of the subjective perception of highly negative and highly positive moments? (b) Is there any relation between these perceptions and flooding? and (c) Is there any relation between these perceptions and attributions?

15.4.1.1. The Structure of Q-Space Explored Empirically: Factor Structure of Perceived Affect During Positive and Negative Moments

Table 15.4 summarizes the results of the principal component analyses of husbands' and wives' ratings of these affects for positive and

TABLE 15.4

Principal Components Analysis of Husbands' and Wives' Ratings of Perceived Emotion During Their Most Negatively Rated and Most Positively Rated Moments

	Loadings	
Perceived Affect	Factor 1	Factor 2
Most Negative Moment	47.0%	20.0%
Hus. sadness	.61 (.12)	.67 (.89)
Hus. whining	.61 (.51)	−.02 (.33)
Hus. worry	.66 (.20)	.60 (.87)
Hus. anger	.72 (.75)	−.27 (.18)
Hus. contempt	.80 (.85)	−.35 (.17)
Hus. disgust	.71 (.84)	−.45 (.04)
	47.5%	23.3%
Wife sadness	.64 (.18)	.52 (.80)
Wife whining	.62 (.24)	.39 (.69)
Wife worry	.54 (.01)	.68 (.87)
Wife anger	.77 (.82)	−.35 (.20)
Wife contempt	.78 (.88)	−.43 (.15)
Wife disgust	.76 (.88)	−.46 (.11)
Most Positive Moment	54.0%	(Eigenvalue <1)
Hus. affection	.86	
Hus. humor	.62	
Hus. interest	.55	
Hus. joy	.86	
	56.5%	(Eigenvalue <1)
Wife affection	.86	
Wife humor	.73	
Wife interest	.49	
Wife joy	.86	

Note. Varimax rotation loadings in parentheses.

negative moments. The structure of perceived positive affect can be considered essentially one dimensional for both men and women; the first principal component has over 50% of the variance, and the second principal component has eigenvalue less than 1.0. No rotated solution is possible (or necessary). However, negative affect, seems to have two orthogonal components: For husbands, one component contains anger, contempt, disgust, and whining, and the other contains essentially only worry and sadness; for wives one component contains anger, contempt, disgust, whining, and sadness, and the other contains essentially only worry and sadness. Thus, Q-space is more differentiated for highly negative moments than it is for highly positive moments. Based on earlier pilot work done with newlyweds, I suggest that these two dimensions be named hurt/anger-hostility and hurt/perceived attack. This can be represented by amending the figure on the structure of

Q-space as shown in Fig. 15.4. This figure represents the perceptual flips in Q-space as two cusp bifurcations, or stable catastrophic changes.

Table 15.5 summarizes analyses on the general validity of the SPAFF self-ratings of positive and negative moments. Clearly, as expected, negative moments were rated less positively and more negatively by both husbands and wives than positive moments. Two other non-SPAFF dimensions were included in the ratings: control (how much subjects were controlling their emotions) and jealousy. Neither control nor jealousy discriminated positive from negative moments for husbands [$t(131) = 1.35$, ns; and $t(131) = 1.30$, ns], but for wives control did discriminate positive from negative moments [with more self-ratings of control for negative moments $M = 2.87$ than for positive moments $M = 2.57$, $t(134) = 2.93$, $p < .01$] and jealousy was marginally significant [with more self-ratings of jealousy for negative moments $M = 1.27$ than for positive moments $M = 1.13$, $t(134) = 1.87$, $p = .063$].

15.4.1.2. Relationship of Q-Space Perceived Affects to Flooding

The goal of this section is to make links between momentary perceptual flips in Q-space and more global and stable cognitions about the partner and the marriage. The link I wish to make at this point is between Q-space and flooding.

Table 15.6 is a summary of the correlations between the Rushe self-ratings of specific negative affects during the most negative moments and the flooding variables. The husband's ratings of his wife's emotions as flooding were significantly related to his experience of

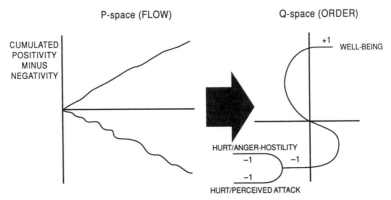

FIG. 15.4. Revision of Fig. 15.1 showing that the relationship between P-space and Q-space is a threshold relationship that illustrates a butterfly catastrophe (three choices for Q).

TABLE 15.5

Validity of the Self-Report of Affect: Comparison of the Most Positive with the Most Negative

| | Rating | | | |
Variable	Negative Moment	Positive Moment	t	df
Husband				
Affection	2.38	3.19	−7.68***	132
Interest	3.32	3.91	−5.55***	132
Joy	1.50	2.56	−9.04***	132
Humor	1.78	2.56	−6.23***	132
Anger	2.80	1.81	8.17***	132
Contempt	2.10	1.62	4.77***	132
Disgust	2.11	1.56	5.55**	132
Sadness	2.35	1.69	5.92***	132
Whining	1.35	1.23	2.21*	132
Worry	2.05	1.66	3.93***	132
Wife				
Affection	2.15	3.12	−9.77***	136
Interest	3.46	3.86	−4.46***	135
Joy	1.23	2.42	−10.08***	136
Humor	1.44	2.65	−10.28***	136
Anger	3.21	2.01	10.79***	136
Contempt	2.78	1.61	6.86***	136
Disgust	2.37	1.66	7.08***	136
Sadness	2.85	1.95	7.44***	136
Whining	1.54	1.26	3.64***	136
Worry	2.45	1.88	4.45***	136

*$p < .05$. **$p < .01$. ***$p < .001$.

anger, contempt, disgust, whining, and worry during his most negative moment; they also were related to his wife's ratings of her own anger, contempt, disgust, and whining during her most negative moment. The wife's ratings of her husband's emotions as flooding were related to her experience of anger, contempt, disgust, and whining (not worry or sadness) during her most negative moment; they also were related to her husband's ratings of his anger, contempt, disgust, whining, and worry (not worry or sadness) during his most negative moment.

Hence, there is support for the conjecture that the Q-space subjective perception of emotion during negative moments is related to feelings of being flooded by one's partner's negative emotions. This is the evidence needed for the necessary theoretical link I wish to make between Q-space during the marital conflict interaction and flooding (a rating that transcends a specific interaction and represents a more global perceived characteristic of the marriage).

TABLE 15.6
Self-Ratings of Affect During the Most Negative Moment and Feelings of Being Flooded
by Partner's Negative Affect

Perceived Affect	Husband Feels Flooded	Wife Feels Flooded
Husband		
Anger	.28**	.51***
Contempt	.31***	.51***
Disgust	.26**	.57***
Sadness	.18[a]	.09
Whining	.19*	.33*
Worry	.19*	.25[a]
Wife		
Anger	.40***	.41**
Contempt	.32***	.44***
Disgust	.39***	.31*
Sadness	.12	.21
Whining	.22*	.39**
Worry	.11	.19

[a]$p < .10$. *$p < .05$. **$p < .01$. ***$p < .001$.

15.4.1.3. Relationship of Q-Space Perceived Affects and Flooding to Attributions

In this study, we also interviewed subjects about the attributions they made for their partners' perceived specific negative behaviors during these negative, positive, and neutral moments. We asked each subject to suggest a specific behavior of his or her partner in each moment that the subject felt explained his or her perceptions of this moment. We then used the Fincham and Bradbury questionnaire, which asks subjects for ratings on the following dimensions: (a) locus in partner: Was cause due to something about the partner (e.g., partner's mood)? (b) locus in self: Was cause due to something about you (e.g., your mood)? (c) stability of cause for partner's behavior: Was cause unlikely to change? (d) globality: Did cause extend to other areas in the marriage? (e) intentionality: Was partner's behavior intentional or unintentional? (f) selfish: Was partner's behavior selfish rather than unselfish? and (g) blame: Was partner responsible for her or his behavior?

Table 15.7 shows that feelings of being flooded were related significantly to the husband's attributions of selfishness of his wife during his most negative moment in the marital conflict discussion. They also were related to his attributing responsibility for his wife's negative behavior in himself. They were not related to any other type of attribution (e.g., stability, globality). The wife's feelings of being flooded were unrelated to any of her attributions (except marginally to her rating her husband as

TABLE 15.7
Attributions During the Most Negative Moment and Feelings of Being Flooded by Partner's Negative Affect

Attribution	Husband Feels Flooded	Wife Feels Flooded
Husband		
Attribution of locus in partner	.10	.15
Attribution of locus in self	.03	.28*
Stability	.11	.17
Globality	.12	.27[a]
Intentionality	.10	.04
Selfishness	.32***	.52***
Blameworthiness	.01	− .01
Wife		
Attribution of locus in partner	− .05	− .19
Attribution of locus in self	− .05	− .07
Stability	− .03	− .14
Globality	.06	.17
Intentionality	.16[a]	− .17
Selfishness	.44***	.24[a]
Blameworthiness	.10	− .23

[a]$p < .10$. *$p < .05$. **$p < .01$. ***$p < .001$.

selfish). However, when I correlated all the attributions made with the attribution of partner's selfishness, the husband's ratings of her behavior as selfish correlated significantly with his ratings of her behavior as global ($r = .17$, $p < .05$), intentional ($r = .38$, $p < .001$), and blameworthy ($r = .25$, $p < .01$); and the wife's ratings of her husband's selfishness correlated significantly with her ratings of his behavior as global ($r = .17$, $p < .05$), intentional ($r = .32$, $p < .001$), and blameworthy ($r = .26$, $p < .001$). Principal component factor analyses of specific attributional scale items suggested that, for both men and women, locus in partner, stability, globality, selfishness, and blame were considered factors in these data.

The perception of specific negative affects also was related to ratings of one's partner's behavior as selfish. The husband rated his wife's behavior as selfish if he reported feeling anger ($r = .39$, $p < .001$), contempt ($r = .38$, $p < .001$), disgust ($r = .35$, $p < .001$), sadness ($r = .24$, $p < .01$), whining ($r = .23$, $p < .01$), and worry ($r = .20$, $p < .05$). The wife rated her husband's behavior as selfish if she reported feeling anger ($r = .48$, $p < .001$), contempt ($r = .56$, $p < .001$), and disgust ($r = .41$, $p < .001$).

There also were significant correlations between perceived specific affects and the other specific attributions (see Table 15.8). Particularly striking were the husband's attributions of globality and his experience

TABLE 15.8
Correlations Between Perceived Specific Affects and Specific Attributions

Subject's Attributions	Subject's Own Affect					
	Anger	Contempt	Disgust	Sadness	Whining	Worry
Husband						
Locus in partner	.08	.11	.04	−.01	−.09	.00
Locus in self	−.12	.11	.04	−.08	.15	.04
Stability	−.05	.05	−.02	.07	.06	.04
Globality	.14	.11	.13	.19*	.08	.22**
Intentionality	.13	.20*	.10	.01	.06	.01
Selfishness	.39***	.38***	.35***	.24**	.23**	.20*
Blameworthiness	.18*	.24**	.05	.03	−.05	−.01
Wife						
Locus in partner	.07	.04	−.10	.09	.07	.14
Locus in self	−.03	−.17	−.12	−.06	−.01	−.04
Stability	.11	.20*	.12	.05	.16ᵃ	.04
Globality	.30***	.30***	.20*	.33***	.22*	.33***
Intentionality	.11	.04	.04	−.04	−.01	.06
Selfishness	.48***	.56***	.41***	.08	.04	.01
Blameworthiness	.07	−.01	.03	.20*	.15ᵃ	.16ᵃ

$^a p < .10.$ $^* p < .05.$ $^{**} p < .01.$ $^{***} p < .001.$

of sadness and worry, and the wife's attributions of globality and her feelings of any and all of the negative emotions. Her attributions of stability were related to her feelings of contempt. Her attributions of globality were related to all her negative affects, as were his attributions of selfishness. Her attributions of selfishness were related only to her anger, disgust, and contempt.

The pattern of results in these data suggests that Q-space has a fairly simple structure. Furthermore, people's perceptions of their own negative affects during their most negative moments are related to their feelings of being flooded by their partners' negative affect and to the attributions they make about their partners' behavior.

15.5. LONG-TERM COGNITIONS ABOUT THE MARRIAGE

It would be interesting to explore the transformation of these negative perceptions and attributions to even more lasting views of the partner and the marriage. For this exploration, I turn to the interview I developed for exploring how a couple views its entire past history together. What I would like to speculate about is how these stable and global attributions about negativity arise in a marriage, and the process through which perceptions become generalized from this situation and this interaction to the partner's personality and to the marriage in general. Clearly, there is evidence that specific marital interactions can affect the way a person sees his or her partner's negative emotional expression. This set of cognitions may affect a process of emotional withdrawal from the marriage.

I propose that as couples continue to feel flooded and increase the emotional distance between them, this is reflected in their cognitions about the entire marriage and its history, and not just particular kinds of interactions. The process of reacting to a partner's negative emotional expressions in one instance and then entering the distance and isolation cascade is a process of increasing globality in how one thinks of the marriage. It has long been recognized that, in unhappy marriages, negative attributions about one's partner have a characteristic of being global rather than specific. These global cognitions (and no doubt their reflection in behavior) appear to be hard to change. Furthermore, it may be that there is an additional stage in the progression toward global negative attributions about the marriage, and that these cognitions about long-term aspects of the marriage are far more predictive of the marital outcome cascade than either behavior or the distance and isolation cascade have been.

Another way to say this is in terms of Fivaz's (1991) formulation: that the person's occupation time in a -1 value in Q-space (e.g., perceived threat that may come from feeling unfairly attacked) turns a Q variable into a P variable. Then, a threshold model again operates on another Q variable, different from the first only in its stability and globality of negative perception. Gradually the shift in perception (and action) moves from "You are now making me feel this way" to become something like "This is the kind of relationship—and you are the kind of person—that makes me continually feel this way," to "This relationship is globally negative."

Theoretically, the transformation of a Q variable becoming a P variable can be continued, with greater units of organization (from perceiving this moment in a negative way to eventually perceiving the partner, the relationship, and its history in a negative way) being the theoretical result.

15.5.1. How Thoughts Become Cast in Stone: The Oral History Interview

Vaughan (1990) collected postdivorce accounts of individuals' stories of their breakups. She wrote about the people who initiated the divorce: "Not only do initiators redefine their partners in negative terms, but they also reconstruct the history of the relationship, reordering their reminiscences into a negative chronology of events. The good times are forgotten or explained away" (p.29). This reconstruction may happen before couples are aware that they wish to terminate the relationship. Their accounts of the history of their relationship turn out to be highly related to their actual functioning within the relationship, and suggest the hypothesis that *how a couple views its history will predict its future.*

I initially thought it would be useful for clinical work to have an interview that could tap processes that were predictive of marital dissolution. Such an interview would make these processes readily observable to the clinician. I developed such an interview. In the DUO86 study, I used an interview I developed with Krokoff called the Oral History Interview.

The Oral History Interview (see Fig.15.5) was modeled after the interview methods of sociologist/reporter Studs Terkel. It is a semistructured interview in which the interviewer asks a set of open-ended questions. The interviewer asks about the history of the couple's relationship; how the two people met, how they courted and married, what their bad times were, how they got over these bad times, what their good times were, and what the good times are presently. The interviewer also asks about the couple's philosophy of marriage: The spouses are asked to select a good and bad marriage they know and to talk about the differences. They also describe their parents' marriages and how they compare to their own. I have used the interview as the first thing couples do in my projects, to build rapport with the couple. Most couples love doing the Oral History Interview. I also have used it as the last thing couples do in our project, as a way for couples to leave my laboratory in a good mood.

Recently, Buehlman et al. (1992) developed a behavioral coding system based on couples' responses in this interview. Her coding system assessed several dimensions of marriage. In particular, she recently selected six variables that she thought would be interesting theoretically and predictive of marital dissolution. She noticed that husbands' behavior during this interview showed a striking degree of variation across couples. Hence, she decided that husbands' data would provide the best predictors of the longitudinal fate of the marriage. She coded three positive variables: (a) husband "we-ness," the amount of "we-ness" expressed by the husband in the recollections and philosophies; part of this construct is the use of "we sentences" rather than "I sentences," so this construct taps how unified the husband feels with his wife; (b) husband expansiveness, how expansive the husband was during the interview, as opposed to constricted; an expansive husband elaborated with detailed recollections and philosophy about the mar-

This interview is based on the work of Studs Terkel. Terkel was interested in creating radio programs, so he invented an interviewing style that is very different from a clinical interview. He avoided the usual vocal backchannels ("um hmm", etc.) that clinical interviewers and therapists employ, because these are annoying on a radio show. At the end of the subjects' responses Terkl would gesture and respond with great energy and emotion, and then ask another question and be quiet. He could then splice himself out of the tapes and have a long segment of just the subject talking.

This is a semi-structured interview, which means that you will memorize the questions. However, the subjects may answer Question 10 as they are answering Question 2, and that is OK in a semi-structured interview. The important thing is to get answers to all the questions, but the order is not important. You will go with the natural course of conversation, and try to get the subjects to be as expansive and involved as possible.

A bad interviewer merely gets answers to the questions, but a good interviewer makes sure to get into the subjective world of the people being interviewed. For example, suppose that a couple describe a period in their relationship when he went to college but she stayed in high school one more year to finish. She says that she visited him a few times during this year. A good interviewer wonders about the inner experience of this period. Was the situation one in which he was embarrassed by her visits, viewing her as a kid or a yokel, and she felt the rejection? If so, how did they cope with these feelings? Or, was this a situation in which he felt great showing her the world of college and she was proud and excited? We want to know about these inner experiences.

We-ness. You will find some couples who emphasize we-ness in these interviews, while some couples do not. Sometimes one person will be talking about the "we" while the other is emphasizing separateness and difference.

Glorifying the struggle. Some couples will express the philosophy that marriage is hard, that it is a struggle, but that it is worth it.

Gender differences. See if you can identify differences between spouses that relate to gender differences in emotional expression, responsiveness, and role.

Conflict-Avoiding versus Conflict-Engaging Couples. Some couples minimize the emotional side of their marital interaction, either positive or negative affect. They tend to avoid disagreements. They tend to speak about the events of the day in terms of errands rather than feelings. Self-disclosure is minimized. Their roles tend to be fairly stereotyped and prescribed by cultural norms.

Part I: History of the Relationship (about 45 minutes)

Question 1. Why don't we start from the very beginning....Tell me how the two of you met and got together.

Do you remember the time you met for the first time? Tell me about it.

Was there anything about (spouse's name) that made him/her stand out?

What were your first impressions of each other?

(continued)

FIG. 15.5.

riage; (c) husband fondness for his wife, was a simple affective dimension of the degree of affection and pride the husband expressed toward his wife (an opposite example is a husband who cannot think of anything that first attracted him to his wife). She also coded three negative variables: (a) chaos, a rating given to the couple about the extent to which it seemed to feel out of control of their lives, buffeted by events outside their control (e.g., they got married because she was suddenly pregnant, and this kind of thing seems to characterize their lives); and (b and c) husband and wife disappointment in their marriage, which was judged as having expectations of their marriage that are not met. The overall agreement across coders on these dimensions was acceptable, at about 80%. A principal components analysis was con-

Question 2. When you think back to the time you were dating, before you got married, what do you remember? What stands out?

How long did you know each other before you got married? What do you remember of this period? What were some of the highlights? Some of the tensions? What types of things did you do together?

Question 3. Tell me about how you decided to get married.

Of all the people in the world, what led you to decide that this was the person you wanted to marry? Was it an easy decision? Was it a difficult decision? (Were they ever in love?)

Question 4. Do you remember your wedding? Tell me about you wedding. Did you have a honeymoon? What do you remember about it?

Question 5. When you think back to the first year you were married, what do you remember? Were there any adjustments to being married?

What about the transition to being parents? Tell me about this period of you marriage. What was it like for the two of you?

Question 6. Looking back over the years, what moments stand out as the really good times in your marriage? What were the really happy times? (What is a good time like for this couple?)

Question 7. Many of the couples we've talked to say that their relationships go through periods of ups and downs. Would you say that this is true of your marriage?

Question 8. Looking back over the years, what moments stand out as the really hard times in your marriage? Why do you think you stayed together? How did you get through these difficult times?

Question 9. How would you say your marriage is different from when you first got married?
Part II. The Philosophy of Marriage

Question 10. We're interested in your ideas about what makes a marriage work. Why do you think some marriages work while others don't? Think of a couple you know that has a particularly good marriage and one that you know who has a particularly bad marriage. [Let them decide together which two couples these are] What is different about these two marriages? How would you compare your own marriage to each of these couples?

Question 11. Tell me about you parents' marriages. [Ask of each spouse]. What was (is) their marriage like? Would you say it's very similar or different from your own marriage?

FIG. 15.5 The Krokoff–Gottman Oral History Interview.

ducted on the variables of the Oral History coding system. These are given in Table 15.9. This table suggests that a great deal of the Oral History codes fall on one dimension.

15.5.2. Validity of the Oral History Coding

Buehlman et al. (1992) correlated the Oral History variables with both SPAFF and RCISS coding of the videotapes. The correlations with the RCISS are presented in Table 15.10. The first important part of the table is the correlation of the RCISS variables with the speaker slopes. Recall that the RCISS speaker slopes were used for the first classification of the couples as regulated or nonregulated. As can be seen from the table, husband and wife negativity, husband and wife "we-ness," and chaos on the Oral History Interview significantly correlated with RCISS husband and wife speaker slopes. As expected, there were no strong correlations

TABLE 15.9
Results of Principal Components Analysis of Oral History Variables

Oral History Variable	Loading on First Principal Component
Husband fondness	.85
Wife fondness	.59
Husband negativity	−.75
Wife negativity	−.52
Husband expansiveness	.73
Wife expansiveness	.40
Husband we-ness	.87
Wife we-ness	.82
Gender stereotypy	−.24
Volatility	.45
Chaos	−.78
Glorification	.75
Husband disappointment	−.77
Wife disappointment	−.74

with listener slope. There also were significant correlations of the Oral History codes with subscales of the RCISS, particularly with complain/ criticize, contempt, and defensiveness, for both husband and wife.

The correlations with the SPAFF codes are presented in Table 15.11. There are significant correlations of the Oral History codes with the SPAFF codes, particularly with husband contempt, belligerence, whining, and stonewalling; and wife belligerence, contempt, anger, defensiveness, whining, sadness, and stonewalling.

15.5.3. Prediction of Divorce

Table 15.12 is a summary of the correlations of the Oral History coding variables with the variables of the cascade model of marital dissolution. As can be seen from the table, the Oral History variables correlated significantly with the later phases of the cascade model.

Buehlman et al. (1992) also computed a discriminant function analysis to predict divorce upon the 2-year follow-up. The results are summarized in Table 15.13. This strong prediction of divorce (about 94% accuracy) was surprising. The accuracy of the Oral History coding variables in predicting divorce was 100%. Clearly, these results have to be replicated; I am in the process of doing so with three other cohorts who also have participated in an Oral History Interview. Preliminary analyses at the time of this writing suggest that the predictive power of the Oral History coding system variables in predicting separation and divorce is replicating. Table 15.14 summarizes the correlations of the Oral History variables with marital satisfaction.

TABLE 15.10

Correlations of the Oral History Codes with Problem-Solving Behavior (RCISS) During Marital Interaction

RCISS Variables	HFONDNESS	HNEGATIV	HEXPANS	HWE-NESS	WWE-NESS	CHAOS	GLORY	HDISAPPOIN	WDISAPPOIN
Husband									
Complain/criticize	-.11	.34**	.04	-.24	-.23	.38**	-.19	.12	.26
Defensiveness	-.20	.33**	.05	-.23	-.28*	.34**	-.23	.06	.23
Contempt	-.06	.24	.00	-.15	-.09	.32*	-.17	.13	.04
Stonewalling	-.15	.17	-.21	-.18	-.04	.18	-.18	.03	.02
Positive agenda	.17	-.40**	-.15	.42**	.31*	-.46***	.23	-.36**	-.43**
Assent	.04	.04	-.29*	-.15	.05	-.02	-.02	.09	.04
Humor	.17	-.19	.12	.21	.28*	-.31*	.00	-.11	-.19
Positive listening	.12	-.17	.21	.23	.05	-.24	.12	-.19	-.12
Speaker slope	.23	-.39**	.03	.31*	.32*	-.48***	.17	-.17	-.35**
Wife									
Complain/criticize	-.11	.36**	-.13	-.36**	-.32*	.52***	-.22	.08	.26
Defensiveness	-.14	.38**	-.11	-.37**	-.36**	-.38**	-.22	.07	.19
Contempt	-.16	.19	-.10	-.21	-.23	.42**	-.22	.13	.18
Stonewalling	-.16	.12	-.05	-.18	-.12	.17	-.13	-.03	-.03
Positive agenda	.16	-.19	-.01	.25	.19	-.42**	.21	-.19	-.29*
Assent	.09	-.30*	.25	.33**	.29*	-.27	.11	-.17	-.23
Humor	.20	-.19	.29*	.34**	.33**	-.26	-.01	-.18	-.19
Positive listening	.16	-.20	.30*	.35**	.22	-.29*	.06	-.12	-.07
Speaker slope	.20	-.40**	.18	.45***	.39**	-.53***	.25	-.18	.32*

Note. HFONDNESS = husband fondness, HNEGATIV = husband negativity, HEXPANS = husband expansiveness, HWE-NESS = husband we-ness, WWE-NESS = wife we-ness, CHAOS = couple describes life as chaotic, GLORY = glorifying the struggle, HDISAPPOIN = husband disappointment in the marriage, and WDISAPPOIN = wife disappointment in the marriage.

*p < .05. **p < .01 ***p < .001.

TABLE 15.11

Correlations of the Oral History Codes with Specific Affects (SPAFF)

SPAFF Variables	HFONDNESS	HNEGATIV	HEXPANS	HWE-NESS	WWE-NESS	CHAOS	GLORY	HDISAPPOIN	WDISAPPOIN
Husband									
Contempt	-.15	.30*	-.06	-.31*	-.32*	.34**	-.38**	.08	.17
Belligerence	-.34**	.40***	-.16	-.34**	-.30*	.46***	-.36**	.35**	.33*
Domineering	.03	.01	.20	.12	.09	.10	.13	.15	.06
Anger	-.11	.12	-.23	-.20	-.08	.27	-.13	-.06	-.02
Sadness	-.16	.07	-.10	-.13	-.03	.10	-.05	.21	-.02
Validation	.21	-.09	.03	.18	.20	-.26	.13	-.18	-.17
Affection	.12	-.03	.17	.28	.21	-.22	.13	-.22	-.24
Humor	.25	-.14	.21	.26	.22	-.23	.16	-.14	-.21
Wife									
Contempt	-.23	.51***	-.27	-.54***	-.50***	.57***	-.37**	.29*	.32*
Belligerence	-.02	.35**	-.07	-.31*	-.30*	.32*	-.25*	.06	.12
Domineering	.09	-.09	.08	.06	.03	.00	.06	-.06	-.01
Anger	-.27	.22	-.07	-.26	-.31*	.49***	-.17	.30*	.28*
Sadness	-.11	.16	-.08	-.18	-.12	.34**	.02	.17	.13
Validation	.08	-.11	.17	.10	.10	-.19	.11	-.01	.13
Affection	.25	.03	-.02	.23	.20	-.18	.14	-.09	.00
Humor	.24	-.10	.23	.24	.22	-.24	.09	-.19	-.22

Note. HFONDNESS = husband fondness, HNEGATIV = husband negativity, HEXPANS = husband expansiveness, HWE-NESS = husband "we-ness," WWE-NESS = "wife we-ness," CHAOS = couple describes life as chaotic, GLORY = glorifying the struggle, HDISAPPOIN = husband disappointment in the marriage, and WDISAPPOIN = wife disappointment in the marriage.

*p < .05. **p < .01. ***p < .001.

TABLE 15.12

Pearson and Point Biserial Correlations of Oral History Variables with the External
Validity Criteria, Months Separate

Oral History Variable	Months Separated	Divorce
Husband fondness	−.52***	−.51***
Husband negativity	.42**	.28*
Husband expansiveness	−.45***	−.46***
Husband "we-ness"	−.40**	−.42**
Wife "we-ness"	−.27	−.33*
Chaotic couples	.34*	.35**
Glorifying couples	−.32*	−.36**
Husband disappointment	.49***	.68***
Wife disappointment	.13	.42**

*$p < .05$. **$p < .01$. ***$p < .001$.

TABLE 15.13

Discriminant Function Analysis Predicting Divorce from the Oral History

Actual Group Membership	No. of cases	Predicted Group Membership	
		Married	Divorced
Married	40	37	3
		(92.5%)	(7.5%)
Divorced	7	0	7
		(0%)	(100%)

Note. Percent of cases correctly classified = 93.62%.

15.5.4. Summary

The way a couple thinks about its past and its philosophy of marriage as revealed in this brief interview is predictive of their future. Up to now in my predictions, I only could approach the prediction of the cascade toward divorce. The Oral History Interview data make it possible to predict accurately even my most fragile criterion variable.

If this prediction were isolated, I would have to think of it as only encouraging, but mysterious. What is particularly exciting about the Oral History Interview results is that they fit in so well with the process variables that predicted the cascade in both studies. The processes of marital dissolution probably have been identified with some precision in these two nonexperimental studies. Not only can I predict divorce and the process of marital dissolution with high accuracy, but I also may understand what drives the process.

TABLE 15.14

Correlations of Oral History Coding with Locke–Wallace Marital Satisfaction Scale

Marital Satisfaction	HFONDNESS	HNEGATIV	HEXPANS	HWE-NESS	WWE-NESS	CHAOS	GLORY	HDISAPPOIN	WDISAPPOIN
Husband									
Time 1	.55***	-.53***	.22	.43**	.55***	-.53***	.24	-.51***	-.53***
Time 2	.40**	-.34**	.20	.41**	.37**	-.42**	.39**	-.46***	-.23
Wife									
Time 1	.38**	-.25	.05	.34*	.45**	-.44**	.19	-.50***	-.42**
Time 2	.30*	-.19	.17	.30*	.23	-.30*	.33**	-.44***	-.18

Note. HFONDNESS = husband fondness, HNEGATIV = husband negativity, HEXPANS = husband expansiveness, HWE-NESS = husband "we-ness", WWE-NESS = wife "we-ness", CHAOS = couple describes life as chaotic, GLORY = glorifying the struggle, HDISAPPOIN = husband disappointment in the marriage, and WDISAPPOIN = wife disappointment in the marriage.

*p < .05. **p < .01. ***p < .001.

15.6. REFORMULATION OF P-SPACE AND Q-SPACE IN RELATION TO MORE LASTING PERCEPTIONS AND COGNITIONS ABOUT THE MARRIAGE

Figure 15.6 is a summary of the relationship between P-space, Q-space to flooding, and to perceptions of the marriage that are increasingly global and stable. I propose that these more stable and global cognitions about the marriage lead to the distance and isolation cascade and to the recasting of the history of the marriage in negative terms. All of these processes then make up the story of the trajectory of the couple toward divorce.

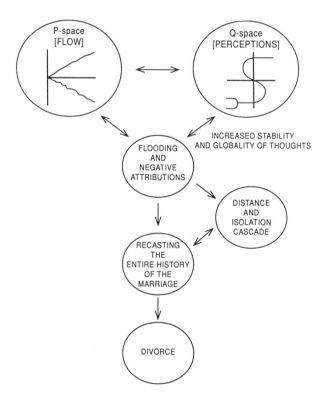

FIG. 15.6. Toward the full theory: A formulation for the relationship between P-space and Q-space, and the increased stability and globality of thoughts about the marriage, the relationship to flooding, the distance and isolation cascade, and the Oral History results, which predict divorce.

15.7. THE ROLE OF PHYSIOLOGY

Physiological responses can play a key role both as a negative accelerating or a positive buffering driving force in the cascade toward marital dissolution. In chapter 14, I proposed a theoretical formulation and reviewed evidence that diffuse physiological arousal (DPA) would affect the ability of the couple to process information and have access to newly acquired behaviors and cognition during a marital conflict. In chapter 12, I reviewed the Gottman–Levenson hypothesis of gender differences in recovery from diffuse physiological arousal.

In this section, I extend this thinking to include the role of physiological reactivity; I also review evidence that positive affect can act as a buffer against physiological arousal.

15.7.1. Physiological Reactivity and the General Role of Physiology in the Cascades Toward Dissolution

Physiological reactivity is a construct that has proved useful in the literature of Type A personality and cardiovascular disease (Matthews et al., 1986). In my research, it is a measure of increases in autonomic arousal over and above the baseline preconversation period. Table 15.15 summarizes the correlations of mean physiological reactivity, subtracting the 2-minute preconversation baselines, with the Oral History variables. The Oral History variables are related in an orderly fashion to the physiological reactivity variables. For example, "we-ness" is related to slower blood flow response in husbands (pulse transit times), and slower heart rate and activity response in wives. The husband and wife's disappointment in the marriage is related to faster wife heart rates in the interaction.

In my experience, it is remarkable that physiological reactivity would predict processes related to marital dissolution. This is the case, because baseline values of physiological activity predict the deterioration of marital satisfaction over time (Levenson & Gottman, 1985). It is, in fact, difficult to obtain a low-activity physiological baseline with married couples. Even an eyes-closed baseline shows quite a bit of physiological arousal; the very presence of the partner before marital interaction creates physiological responses during a supposed baseline that are related to what the marital interaction will be like several minutes or an hour later. Hence, these effects are over and above a level that is not a low-activity physiological baseline.

I suggest that physiological reactivity as well as chronic activation levels (reflected by DPA during marital interaction and during baselines with the spouse present) play a central role in driving the system from

TABLE 15.15
Correlations of Oral History Coding with Physiological Reactivity Variables

Physiological Variables	HFONDNESS	HNEGATIV	HEXPANS	HWE-NESS	WWE-NESS	CHAOS	GLORY	HDISAPPOIN	WDISAPPOIN
Husband									
Cardiac interbeat interval	-.10	.04	.18	-.06	.02	.02	-.11	.24	.21
Activity	-.10	.27	.01	-.16	-.07	.03	-.14	.11	-.03
Skin conductance	-.08	-.20	-.11	.14	.18	.07	.07	.13	.07
Pulse transit	.26	-.30*	.36**	.28*	.11	-.29*	.19	-.19	-.20
Pulse amplitude	-.09	.11	-.09	-.09	-.01	.10	-.01	.06	.00
Wife									
Cardiac interbeat interval	.23	-.46***	.23	.34***	.29*	-.20	.10	-.29*	-.50***
Activity	-.22	.32*	-.17	-.23	.34**	.17	-.26	.08	.10
Skin conductance	-.26	.20	-.35***	-.09	-.13	.06	-.22	.01	.05
Pulse transit	.00	.01	.20	.00	.06	.07	-.12	-.01	-.10
Pulse amplitude	.04	-.06	-.03	-.15	-.15	-.14	-.02	-.04	-.04

Note. HFONDNESS = husband fondness, HNEGATIV = husband negativity, HEXPANS = husband expansiveness, HWE-NESS = husband "we-ness", WWE-NESS = wife "we-ness", CHAOS = couple describes life as chaotic, GLORY = glorifying the struggle, HDISAPPOIN = husband disappointment in the marriage, and WDISAPPOIN = wife disappointment in the marriage.
*$p < .05$. **$p < .001$. ***$p < .001$.

369

momentary perceptions of non-well-being (either hurt/perceived threat or hurt/anger-contempt) to more stable and global negative thoughts about the spouse and the marriage. Figure 15.7 is a summary of the potential role of physiology in the theoretical formulation proposed in this chapter.

In the figure, I placed physiological responses in a bidirectional triad linking P-space and Q-space. I believe that the available research evidence on the linkages between behavior, cognition, and physiology

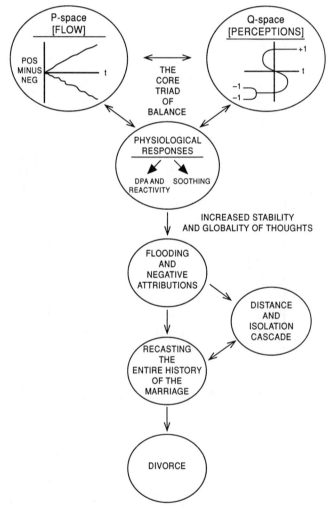

FIG. 15.7. The full theory: The core triad of balance suggests a unique role for physiology (and soothing) in mediating between P-space and Q-space and in predicting divorce.

support this bidirectional view (e.g., Cacioppo & Petty, 1983; Cacioppo & Tassinary, 1990; Gale & Edwards, 1983a, 1983b, 1983c; Grings & Dawson, 1978; Mandler, 1975; Reite & Field, 1985; Stellar & Stellar, 1985; Thayer, 1989; Vincent, 1990; Wagner, 1988; Waid, 1984). Until now, the physiological responses have been negative (DPA and physiological reactivity). However, I soon review evidence that suggests that positive affects can have a *soothing* effect on physiological activation. In the figure, I also have suggested that the linkages are bidirectional.

15.7.2. The Separate Physiologies of Positive and Negative Affect: Balance Within Physiology

In chapter 12, I cited some of the results of an unpublished paper based on the results of a recent study with 90 newlywed couples. This study was conducted in collaboration with Kiecolt-Glaser, Glaser, and Malarkey. Recall that the couples in this study were studied during a standard conflict task. After adaptation to the Clinical Research Center at the hospital at the Ohio State University Medical Center, blood samples were drawn periodically from an in-dwelling catheter. For frequent, unobtrusive sampling during the interaction tasks, a long polyethylene tube was attached to the heparin well, so nurses could draw blood samples at set intervals, out of subjects' sight. The baseline blood draw occurred about 90 minutes after the heparin well had been inserted, and after subjects had been sitting quietly in chairs in front of the curtain for 10 minutes. At the end of the play-by-play interview, and immediately before the half-hour conflict interview, the second sample was drawn; the third and fourth samples were drawn 15 minutes after conflict began, and again at the end of the 30-minute conflict task. The blood was assayed for concentrations of the adrenal hormone adrenaline (in the United States, adrenaline typically is called epinephrine, EPI).

In a second unpublished paper (Gottman et al., unpublished), the effects of positive versus negative affect were compared. Most reviews of the behavioral endocrinology of emotions equate emotion with emotional stress, rarely mentioning the positive emotions (e.g., Popp & Baum, 1989). In fact, the prevailing viewpoint currently is that the endocrine physiology of positive and negative emotions is probably the same. The view is that both positive emotions (such as humor and affection) and negative emotions (such as anger and contempt) have the same elevating effect on stress-related hormones such as epinephrine (Baum, Lundberg, Grunberg, Singer, & Gatchel, 1985; Thompson, 1988).

Historically, the idea stemmed from early notions of physiological arousal as a unidimensional construct. Although this notion has under gone major changes in psychophysiology since Lacey's (1956) paper, the unidimensional view has remained unchallenged in behavioral endocrinology since the work of Levi (1965), who employed emotion-eliciting films and measured urinary catecholamines; and the work of Patkai (1971), who employed a surgery film as a negative emotion-eliciting stimulus and a bingo game as a positive emotion-eliciting stimulus. Both Levi (1965) and Patkai (1971) reported that urinary catecholamines rose in both positive and negative emotion-eliciting situations.

Contributing to this monolithic view of the endocrine physiology of emotion was Schachter and Singer's (1962) classic experiment. Their view was that their injections of epinephrine created a general physiological arousal that could be channeled, in ambiguous informational circumstances, to either anger or amusement. There were later challenges to their conclusions about the effects of epinephrine (Plutchik & Ax, 1962). Despite these challenges and the specificity of their experimental conditions (with subjects uniformed or misinformed about the epinephrine injection), their work suggested to some theorists that the underlying physiology of humor and anger was the same (e.g., Mandler, 1975).

There are several reasons to challenge this monolithic conception of the endocrine response to emotion, and there are several reasons why such a challenge is now appropriate. First, theorizing has suggested that there may be specific negative psychological states associated with particular profiles of stress-related endocrine response. For example, Henry and Stephens (1977) proposed that: (a) the pituitary-adrenocortical axis (which involves the hormones ACTH and cortisol) is related to sadness, depression, and passivity; and (b) the sympathetic-adrenomedullary axis (which involves the catecholamines, primarily epinephrine, EPI) is related to anger, hostility, and active coping. Although Henry and Stephens' (1977) view is controversial, it has received some support in both human and animal literatures (Henry, 1986; Henry & Meehan, 1981). Other more specific hypotheses have been proposed in the stress literature. Some researchers have suggested studying the ratio of epinephrine to norepinephrine (NEP) for discriminating between active and passive coping (Henry, 1986), or between anger and fear (Woodman, Hinton, & O'Neill, 1978). However, proposals of the ratio of EPI to NEP as indexes of anxiety (primarily EPI) or anger (primarily NEP) have received only weak support. For example, Mason (1975a, 1975b) observed that EPI and NEP both increased during uncertainty, whereas NEP increased without EPI increasing in anger or fear (Baum et al., 1985). Also, Frankenhaeuser (1974) suggested (e.g., Lundberg, 1980) that effort plus distress would result in both an EPI and CRT increase, whereas effort without distress would result in an EPI increase and a CRT decrease.

Second, in the literature on the behavioral endocrinology of stress, a differentiated view has been reflected in recent endocrine research that has linked epinephrine with anxiety. For example, Dimsdale and Moss (1980a, 1980b) reported that epinephrine levels increased twofold during public speaking and norepinephrine levels increased significantly (but not as much), whereas norepinephrine levels increased threefold during physical exercise.

Third, there is increasing evidence to support a more differentiated view of peripheral physiological response in relation to emotion expression (e.g., Ekman et al., 1983). This differentiated view of physiological responses in relation to specific emotions also may be true for central nervous system processes. For example, asymmetries in frontal lobe EEG may be related to specific types of emotions, with more negative affects and withdrawal related to right frontal activation and more positive affects and approach related to left frontal activation (except for anger, which may be primarily left frontal; Davidson, 1984a, 1984b).

Fourth, there are methodological reasons to suspect the early work. Levi (1972) measured the urinary catecholamines EPI and NEP of 20 female office clerks to a set of films (shown at night) designed to evoke different emotions. The films were: "Day 1: neutral film, bland natural sceneries; Day 2: the war film *Paths of Glory*; Day 3 the comedy *Charley's Aunt*; Day 4: the hair-raiser *The Mask of Satan*" (Levi, 1972, p. 59). The urine samples were collected before the film, after the film, and later (all urinary voids were separated by 100 minutes). Subjects rated their emotions on 6-point scales, assessing the degree to which they felt expectant, engaged and carried away, frightened, uneasy, agitated, aggressive and angry, amused, and happy and cheerful; and whether they had laughed, felt bored, and felt tired. Subjects reported feeling frightened only during *The Mask of Satan*, aggressive only during *Paths of Glory*, amused and laughing only during *Charley's Aunt*, and bored and fatigued during the natural scenery films. EPI and NEP decreased significantly during the natural scenery films, but increased for all other films. Levi concluded that "In general, it was found that both types of emotional reactions, 'pleasant' as well as 'unpleasant' were accompanied by significant and similar changes in sympathoadrenomedullary activity as reflected in the urinary excretion of adrenaline and noradrenaline, and in renal function as indicated by changes in urine volume, specific gravity and creatinine excretion" (pp. 67–70). However, the conclusions about positive and negative emotions are flawed, because the EPI and NEP data are presented in units of ng/min which does not control for the significant increase Levi (1972) found in urinary output during all the emotion-eliciting films. Patkai (1971) also used a rate measure rather than a concentration measure, but did not provide comparable data on urinary output.

Couples were grouped by positive and negative SPAFF codes by splitting couples at the median. These analyses searched for a significant group effect or an interaction of the other factors with the grouping variable. Only the linear components of the group time interaction and group time gender interaction were studied.

Because the correlations between the amounts of husband and wife positive and negative emotions in this study were 0.50 ($p < .001$) and 0.75 ($p < .001$), respectively, positive and negative affects were added across husband and wife within each couple. Using a median split on total couple negative affect, a set of $2 \times 2 \times 5$ (group-by-gender-by-time) repeated-measures multivariate analyses of variance were conducted, with orthonormal polynomial contrasts for linear trend. The hypotheses concerned only general increases or decreases over time, so that the linear component was the only component discussed. The only hormone for which there was a significant group main effect or interaction effect for negativity was for EPI. There were no significant group effects as a function of negative affect, but EPI showed a significant group-by-time interaction, with significant linear trend-by-group interaction. These means are plotted in Fig. 15.8. The baseline (Time 1) difference between groups was not significant. Despite adaptation after the catheter was inserted, due to the novelty of the setting, the baseline levels of these hormones were somewhat elevated over actual resting levels. In marriages that were affectively highly negative, EPI increased over time during the interaction, and then returned to a level above the baseline level 30 minutes after the interaction. In less negative marriages, EPI had

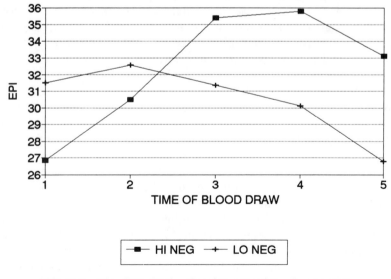

FIG. 15.8. Ohio State Study—Couple's epinephrine by negativity

a downward slope over time and returned to a level below baseline. The difference in linear trend for these two groups was significant [average $F(4,61) = 3.94, p < .01$]. The difference between the level EPI at the end of the conflict interaction level minus the level 30 minutes after the interaction (rebound) also was statistically significant [$F(1,67) = 5.48, p < .05$, negative group's rebound = 0.82; less negative group's rebound = 2.53].

The results for positive affect were similar to those for negative affect, except that couples that were highly positive showed a decrease in EPI over time rather than an increase. For these analyses, the amount of negative affect at each time point was employed as the covariate set. There were no significant group effects as a function of positive affect, but EPI showed a significant group time interaction. In highly positive marriages, EPI showed a downward trend, whereas in less positive marriages, EPI showed a positive trend. There were no significant differences in either baseline levels [$F(1,66) = 0.04$, ns] or rebound [$F(1,66) = 0.98$, ns].

The analysis of covariance on positive affect is problematic and must be treated cautiously, because positivity and negativity were correlated so highly ($-0.62, p < .001$). Gottman et al. performed an alternative analysis in which they tried to block subjects into a 2 × 2 design on positive and negative affect, using median splits on positivity and negativity. This resulted in 49 subjects who were low in negativity and high in positivity (the positive group) and 21 subjects who were low on positivity and high on negativity (the negative group). It also resulted in 19 subjects who were high on both positivity and negativity (the volatile group) and only 9 subjects who were low on both (the unemotional group). Because of the strong negative correlation between positivity and negativity, there was inadequate power for 2 × 2 analyses. However, in a two-group MANOVA comparing negative and volatile groups, the negative and volatile groups differed on EPI; there was a significant group-by-gender interaction [$F(1,30) = 4.49, p < .05$], with negative husbands greater on EPI secretion than volatile husbands (volatile husband mean = 29.12 and negative husband mean = 36.98), with no significant difference for wives (volatile wife mean = 29.32 and negative wife mean = 27.55). The MANOVA comparing the positive and the unemotional group had particularly low power, but the direction was the same, with the group-by-gender effect marginal [$F(1,31) = 2.91, p = .098$]; unemotional husbands were greater on EPI secretion than positive husbands (unemotional husband mean = 43.38 and positive husband mean = 32.53), with no evidence of even a marginally significant difference for wives (unemotional wife mean = 23.56 and positive wife mean = 25.29). In sum, they found that positivity made a difference in mean EPI secretion even within the context of negativity (and probably also in the context of no negativity), particularly for husbands.

The important contribution of this analysis is evidence that the effects of negativity and positivity are not the same. Also, they are not entirely redundant and due to the negative correlation between positivity and negativity. Although these results require replication, it seems that positivity can act as a buffer, particularly for males, even in the presence of high levels of negativity.

The unpublished paper also explored the separate effects of specific positive and negative affects. These results have to be considered highly exploratory, because these affects were not statistically independent. Also, there were many analyses here, and the results should be considered primarily exploratory, in the nature of hypothesis generation, rather than confirmatory. Instead of employing the nominal 0.05 alpha, they utilized an experiment-wise protection rate for alpha.

The specific negative emotions that were components of negativity were: (a) anger blends, (b) pure anger, (c) belligerence, (d) domineering, (e) contempt, (f) disgust, (g) sadness blends, (h) pure sadness, (i) whining, (j) fear, (k) defensiveness, and (l) stonewalling. The specific positive emotions and behaviors selected for study were: (a) humor, (b) affection, (c) joy, and (d) validation. Disgust and joy hardly occurred in these data. They tested only the hypotheses that there were significant group main effects or linear interactions of the group effect with time (GXT), gender (GXS), or a linear three-way interaction of group by gender by time (GXSXT).

15.7.2.1. Specific Negative Affects

Epinephrine secretion was related to several specific negative affects. For belligerence, there was a significant linear group-by-time effect for EPI $[F(1,64) = 7.18, p < .01]$. Couples high in belligerence showed no decline in EPI over time, whereas couples low in belligerence showed a decreasing slope over time. Initial differences in baseline were not significant $[F(1,60) = 2.00, ns]$. For contempt, there was a significant group-by-linear-time interaction for EPI. Couples lower in contempt showed a significantly steeper decline in EPI than couples high in contempt; again, the initial differences at baseline were not significant $[F(1,60) = 3.04, ns]$.

15.7.2.2. Specific Positive Affects

Epinephrine secretion also was related to specific positive affects. For interest, for EPI there was a significant group-by-time interaction $[F(1,64) = 6.04, p < .05]$. Couples low in interest had a positive slope in EPI, whereas couples high in interest had a negative slope in EPI. For humor, there was a significant group effect; couples low in humor secreted more EPI than couples high in humor [low humor mean = 34.66, high humor mean = 27.24; $F(1,64) = 6.41$, $p < .05$]. The group-by-time interaction was not significant. For validation, there was a significant group by time linear interaction for EPI [$F(1,64) = 10.19$ $p < .01$]. Couples high in validation declined in EPI secretion over time, whereas couples low in validation increased in EPI secretion over time.

15.7.2.3. Summary

Thus, it seems that the general conclusions made by Levi (1972) and Patkai (1971) about the similarity of the physiology of positive and negative affect must be challenged on the basis of these data, as well as methodological criticisms that they did not control for urinary output. The negative SPAFF codes of belligerence and contempt had significant effects on increasing EPI secretion. More important for our thinking about the implications of positive affect on marriage, we can be somewhat encouraged by these data: positive affects, particularly interest, humor, and validation.

15.8. THE CORE TRIAD OF BALANCE

If I return to Fig. 15.7, one can see that each element of *the core triad of balance* of P-space, Q-space, and physiological responses has both positive and negative aspects. The P-space component of the triad has positivity (and the central idea of behavioral balance). The Q-space component has the perception of well-being as a balancing force for perceptions of hurt/perceived-threat or hurt/anger-contempt. Physiological responses, linked to positive affects, have the potential to buffer arousal through physiological soothing. Each component can affect the other in a bidirectional fashion, and each component has the potential for balance.

15.9. INFLUENCE FUNCTIONS, PHYSIOLOGY, AND POSITIVE AFFECT

In chapter 11, I discussed a startling result that emerged from the graphs of the influence function based on the mathematical modeling by the Murray group of the RCISS point graphs. In regulated marriages, there was a uniform slope of the influence function across both positive and negative values: Negative behavior had a negative effect, whereas positive behavior had a positive effect in these marriages. However, in nonregulated marriages, the curve flattened out in the positive ranges near the natural set point. In nonregulated marriages, people were able to influence one another only with negativity; they had almost no influence on one another with positivity. These results could serve as an explanation for the more negative natural set point in nonregulated marriages. It is natural to assume that the ability to influence one's mate is an intrinsically reinforcing aspect of social interaction, and that if negativity is the only way that nonregulated couples can influence one another it would seem obvious that they naturally would drift toward a more negative set point.

It may be that in nonregulated marriages there is a biological basis to the ineffectiveness of positivity. In these marriages, positivity may not have the effect of reducing epinephrine secretion over time, as the conflict discussion proceeds.

15.10. THE NEED FOR A FAMILY LIFE-CYCLE MODEL OF STABILITY AND DISSOLUTION: MARITAL DISSOLUTION AMONG NEWLYWEDS

Dissolution can occur at any stage in the family life cycle. However, the processes that contribute to dissolution may not be the same at various stages in the marriage.

An unpublished paper by Gottman et al. examined the ability of SPAFF codes to predict the five divorces or separations that occurred among the newlywed sample in the first 2 years of the research project. The results were as follows. The canonical correlation for the discriminant function was 0.37, $p < .05$. The predicted and actual numbers of couples that separated or divorced or remained stable is given in Table 15.16 [$\chi^2(4)$ in the discrimination $= 12.51$, $p = .014$].

Table 15.17 summarizes the means for each group for the variables in

TABLE 15.16
Newlywed Study Classification Results

		No. of Cases	Predicted Group Membership	
Actual Group			1	2
Group	1 Div/sep	5	4 (80%)	1 (20%)
Group	2 Stable	85	13 (15.3%)	72 (84.7%)

Note. The diagonal represents correct prediction; Row 1 is the prediction of divorce or separation and Row 2 is the prediction of stability. Percent of "grouped" cases correctly classified = 84.44%.

the discriminant function analysis. Couples that stayed together were less likely to whine and more likely to validate their partners' feelings at the Time 1 assessment. To test whether these behaviors were more salient for husband or wife, t tests were conducted. For validation, there was a significant difference between groups for the husband's validation [nonpooled t ratio used to control for heteroskedasticity, $t(7) = -3.46$, $p = .010$], but this difference was not significant for wives [pooled t ratio used, $t(88) = -.38$, ns]. For whining, there was a significant difference between groups for the wife's whining [pooled t ratio used, $t(88) = 3.13$, $p = .002$], but this difference was not significant for husbands [nonpooled t ratio used to control for heteroskedasticity, $t(4) = .68$, ns].

Validation is the opposite of contempt, and whining is a central part of defensiveness. Hence, although the specific SPAFF codes here are different from the specific codes that predicted marital dissolution, they are actually part of the same constructs. Nonetheless, perhaps there is a stage model of dissolution that needs to be developed. What is critical in the early stages of marriages may not be the same as what is critical in later stages.

The effects of validation or invalidation may become more powerful predictors of marital dissolution over time. Notarius and Markman (1989) presented data at a national conference of the American Association of Marital and Family Therapy from a 6-year follow-up of approximately 100 young marriages. They used Time 1 interaction data to predict divorce or separation. They reported that a Couples Interaction Scoring System (CISS) code they called emotional invalidation (EI) significantly predicted divorce or separation. They also noted a sleeper effect in this prediction. For men, EI predicted divorce or separation with the following correlations for follow-up times 1–1½ years, 3 years, 4 years, 5 years, and 6 years, respectively: $-.01$, $.21$ ($p < .05$); $.19$ ($p < .05$); $.26$ ($p < .05$); and $.36$ ($p < .05$). For women, EI at Time 1 predicted divorce or separation as follows: $-.02$, $.17$, $.18$ ($p < .05$); $.39$ ($p < .01$); and $.55$ ($p < .001$).

15.11. SUMMARY AND A PARTIAL RESEARCH AGENDA

At the start of this book, I suggested that it is essential to know how to look at a marital interaction, and that this feat is not obvious to

TABLE 15.17
Group Means for Each Variable in the Discriminant Function

Group	WVAL	WWHI	HVAL	HWHI
1 Div/sep	1.49	1.40	.57	.43
2 Stable	1.81	.38	1.62	.20

Note. VAL = validation, WHI = whining.

researchers at the outset. It is essential to know what is negative and positive, and many very bright researchers and interesting theoretical formulations have turned out to be wrong. It also is essential to know how to look at behavior sequences, because the most stable differentiation of happy from unhappy marriage has to do with negative absorbing states, in which couples do not have access to natural repair mechanisms in their repertoire. I also suggested that diffuse physiological arousal and physiological linkage between partners may play roles in maintaining this negative absorbing state.

The three types of stable couples are proof that it is not obvious what should be considered negative and positive. Speculations by Raush et al. (1974) were prophetic. But it turns out that conflict avoidance is not dysfunctional, nor are the passionate, escalating quarrels typical of volatile couples. Rather, there are costs and benefits of each stable adaptation. Why people prefer one adaptation over another remains a mystery.

Unstable marriages are likely to be those that, over time, cannot work out one of the three stable adaptations. In their attempts to accomplish this feat, they fall into a pattern that does not maintain the balance of positivity to negativity at a high level. Not only that, but they tend to formulate their complaints as criticisms and contempt, they tend to respond defensively, and eventually they withdraw from one another.

At the core of this formulation is a balance theory, an ecology of marital behaviors in which a ration of positivity to negativity that is highly tilted toward positivity needs to be maintained. This ratio is suggested as the quantity that needs to be regulated at a high level of approximately 5.0.

If this balance is violated, I suggest that (in Q-space, $Q = -1$) the perception of well-being is replaced by one of distress, which is some combination of hurt anger and/or hurt and perceived attack.

I suggest further that the length of occupation time in the $Q = -1$ state determines the state of being flooded by one's partner's negative affect, diffuse physiological arousal, negative subjective affective states, and negative attributions of the partner. Flooding begins the distance and isolation cascade, which entails perceiving one's marital problems as severe, as better worked out alone rather than with the spouse, arranging one's lives so that they are more in parallel than they used to be, and loneliness within the marriage.

I suspect that eventually even one's perception of the entire relationship is affected. In the Oral History Interview, people (particularly husbands) expressed disappointment with the marriage, little fondness for the partner, and presented themselves as separate entities that did not see the past the same way or share a common philosophy of marriage. They also tended to see their lives as chaotic, out of control, and all the marital conflict as pointless and empty.

This grim formulation is balanced by the reverse results that couples whose marriages are stable use positive affect and persuasion in ways that buffer them from the physiological stresses of DPA, and from the perception of their partner's negative emotions as horrible, disgusting, terrifying, overwhelming, disorganizing, and impossible to predict. Tolstoy was wrong. Happy families are the ones who are varied. Unhappy families are unhappy in the same ways.

Of course, these data are only correlational. Nonetheless, the research agenda that is necessary at this time should begin by replicating and extending these results. I followed four cohorts of couples at different stages in the family life course. Marital interaction needs to be studied longitudinally so that sources of stability and change can be identified, and natural change processes can be identified. Replication and extension is essential to finding out if these speculations, models, and theories are repeated over time and samples.

In the next few years, I plan to develop the methodologies, statistics, and computer programs necessary for going inside an interaction and studying it as it unfolds over time. This seems like the essential way to study the relationship between P-space, Q-space, and physiology. I have waited 13 years to do these kind of analyses. I need to build process models of this unfolding over time.

I am extending this work in four other ways. I am studying long-term first marriages of couples in their 40s and 60s with Levenson and Carstensen. We also are studying gay male and lesbian relationships to examine the Gottman–Levenson hypotheses about gender differences in affect and physiology. With Jacobson we are studying violent relationships. With Katz we are studying the effects of marriages on children's social, emotional, and academic development, and searching for mechanisms of linkage in young, developing families.

What is missing is experimentation, particularly systematic research on interventions designed for divorce prevention. In the next chapter, I speculate about what this type of intervention should look like.

16

Eight-Year Longitudinal
Follow-up Study

This chapter reports the results of an 8-year follow-up of the couples originally studied in 1983. The levels of divorce and separation were quite a bit higher by 1991 than they had been in 1987. Results showed that Time 1 and Time 2 data were significantly correlated with separation and divorce, in ways consistent with the theory presented in chapter 15. Also, the Weiss Marital Status Interview was administered to couples who were still married in 1991. Results showed that the MSI formed a rough Guttman scale, and that the Time 1 and Time 2 data were correlated significantly with the MSI total scores and factors. The Oral History variables that predicted divorce over 8 years in this study were generally related to the same kinds of Time 1 variables as had been reported with the DUO86 study.

16.1. EIGHT-YEAR FOLLOW-UP STUDY

In 1991 an effort was made to recontact the couples in the DUO83 study. They had last been contacted in 1987 (Time 2). They were initially contacted by telephone, and later with a mailing of a questionnaire packet. This recontact took considerable detective work in many cases. The reader will recall that in 1987, 73 of the original 79 couples were recontacted (92.4%); in 1991, 69 couples completed questionnaire data (87.3% of the original sample); 72 had been recontacted by telephone in 1991.

Couples completed a questionnaire packet that consisted of:

1. our standard assessment of marital satisfaction (Locke–Wallace and Locke–Williamson);
2. the Carrere job environment scale (typical item: "My job requires that I almost never make a mistake");

3. the Cowan and Cowan Who Does What? scales (housework and parenting) (in a typical item the respondent is asked to specify on a 9-point scale who does more of a specific task, husband or wife, such as cleaning up after meals);
4. the Carrere Who Does What? in the maintenance of marital intimacy (e.g., initiating sex);
5. the Weiss Marital Status Inventory (Crane & Mead, 1980; Weiss & Cerreto, 1980), which is a Guttman-like scale assessing progress toward separation or divorce; items range from "I have occasionally thought of divorce or wished we were separated, usually after an argument or other incident," to "I have filed for divorce, or we are divorced";
6. the Holmes-Rahe (1967) Life Events Scale; and
7. several standard Illness and Health Questionnaire modified by S. Carrere (personal communication, 1993).

16.2. CODING OF THE ORAL HISTORY DATA

At the same time that we were conducting the 1991 follow-up, the Buehlman coding team, blind to the hypotheses, also coded the Oral History Interviews, which were (as is usual) administered at Time 1 in the DUO83 study. Again interobserver reliabilities were reasonable ranging from 0.70 to 0.86.

16.3. RESULTS

16.3.1. Marital Status

Based on the questionnaire data, by the Time 3 assessment, that is, by 1991, after 8 years, 20 couples had divorced. Of the original 79 couples, this was a divorce rate of 25.3%. Also, by 1991, 18 couples had separated (22.8%), and 29 couples had *either* separated or divorced (36.7%). These figures represent an unexpectedly high level of marital dissolution within an 8-year period and an increase in the rate of dissolution in this sample. The divorce rate, for example, had been 8.9% in the last 4-year period, or 2.22% per year, whereas the current rate was an additional 13 divorces of the still-married $(72 - 7 = 65)$ couples we were able to recontact by telephone, which represents a 20% divorce rate in the years from 1987 to 1991, or 5% per year.

16.3.2. Time 1 and Time 2 Prediction of Separations and Divorces by Time 3

How well did the Time 1 and Time 2 data predict dissolutions by 1987? Table 16.1 summarizes these point-biserial correlations.

16.3.2.1. Predictions of Divorce

16.3.2.1.1. Self-Report Measures

The severity of the marital problems at Time 1 as perceived by the wife significantly predicted divorce. Serious considerations of dissolution by either spouse at Time 2 significantly predicted divorce. This was true even when only new divorces were considered (correlations were husband considers separation 0.35, $p < .01$, husband considers divorce 0.32, $p < .01$, wife considers separation 0.43, $p < .001$, wife considers divorce 0.47, $p < .001$). This shows that these assessments of serious considerations of dissolution assessed at Time 2 did in fact predict actual new dissolutions at Time 3. Marital satisfaction at Time 1 did not predict divorce but marital satisfaction at Time 2 of both husband and wife did significantly predict divorce. These results are consistent with those of Booth and White (1980). Thinking about dissolution is a predictor of actual dissolution 4 years later.

16.3.2.1.2. Physiological Variables

Of the physiological variables, only baseline and interaction wife interbeat interval predicted divorce; at Time 1 a higher heart rate at baseline was observed for the wife who would eventually divorce; t tests revealed that the wives in couples who divorced had a baseline mean heart rate of 84.75 BPM compared to 76.79 BPM for couples who did not separate, which is an 8.2% increase over the nondivorced baseline heart rate [$t(77) = 2.16$, $p < .05$, t test done, as usual, on IBI data]. A higher heart rate was also observed for the wife who would eventually divorce in the conflict interaction; t tests revealed that the wives in couples who divorced had a mean interaction heart rate of 85.28 BPM compared to 77.47 BPM for couples who did not divorce, which is a 10.1% increase over the nondivorced interaction heart rate [$t(77) = 2.16$, $p < .05$, t test done, as usual, on IBI data].

16.3.2.1.3 Behavior

On the RCISS both the husband's speaker slope (marginal) and the wife's speaker's slope significantly predicted divorce; the husband's stonewalling also significantly predicted divorce. On the SPAFF, husbands who divorced showed less humor, whereas wives showed more contempt/disgust and more sadness. On the Oral History Interview there was significantly more husband disappointment and wife disappointment expressed on the part of couples who eventually divorced.

16.3.2.2. Predictions of Separation

16.3.2.2.1. Self-Report Variables

The husband's report of being flooded by his wife's negative emotional expressions predicted separations. The wife's description of their lives as parallel also predicted separations. The wife's descriptions of their marital problems as severe predicted separations. Serious considerations of dissolution at Time 2 by either spouse predicted separations; in fact, however, when only new separations and divorces since 1987 were considered, only the wife's considerations of dissolution in 1987 predicted actual separation (husband considers separation 0.18, ns, husband considers divorce 0.18, ns, wife considers separation 0.31, $p < .05$, wife considers divorce 0.29, $p < .05$). Time 2 but not Time 1 marital satisfaction predicted separations. Husbands rating dial means were higher for couples who did not separate compared to couples who did.

16.3.2.2.2. Physiological Data

Again, the wife's interbeat interval at baseline and marginally during the interaction predicted separation. A higher heart rate of the wife predicted dissolution; at baseline, t tests revealed that the wives in couples who separated since 1987 had a baseline mean heart rate of 84.02 BPM compared to 76.51 BPM for couples who did not separate, which is a 9.8% increase over the non separated baseline heart rate [$t(77) = 2.24, p < .05$, t test done, as usual, on IBI data]; a higher heart rate of the wife who would eventually be separated was observed in the conflict interaction; t tests revealed that the wives in couples who separated since 1987 had a mean interaction heart rate of 83.86 BPM compared to 77.39 BPM for couples who did not separate, which is an 8.4% increase over the nonseparated interaction heart rate [$t(77) = 1.96$, $p = .053$, t test done, as usual, on IBI data; the nonpooled t (38) was 2.11, $p < .05$].

16.3.2.2.3. Behavior

For couples who separated, at Time 1 wives were more defensive (on the MICS). On the RCISS, wives' speaker slopes were more positive for couples who did not separate; wives also criticized less and were less contemptuous. On the SPAFF, at Time 1 husbands who separated were sadder and wives were more contemptuous/disgusted and sadder than wives who did not separate. On the Oral History Interview, at Time 1 couples who separated had less expansive husbands who also expressed more disappointment in the marriage (see Table 16.1).

16.3.3. Couples Who Stayed Together

The Weiss Marital Status Inventory (MSI) was used to assess the extent to which couples who stayed together actually endorsed the items relating to dissolution, and to assess the extent to which variation on these items could be predicted from the Time 1 and Time 2 data.

Table 16.2 summarizes the extent to which separate items on the MSI were actually endorsed by couples who were still together at the 8-year follow-up. Table 16.2 shows that the MSI is roughly a Guttman-like scale. It also shows that even among those who were still together at the 8-year assessment, very specific thoughts of separation and discussions about it with friends or spouses were quite common.

The MSI data were factor analyzed for the entire sample separately for husbands and wives, and three clearly interpretable factors emerged. The factor analysis was a principal components analysis with varimax rotation, so that each factor accounts for decreasing amounts of the MSI variance. These factors are portrayed in Table 16.3. The factor analyses differed for husbands and wives because Items 10, 12, and 13 had no variance for wives. Also, Factor 1 for husbands is a factor of variables that specify actions taken toward dissolution, Factor 2 involves items of serious considerations of dissolution, and Factor 3 involves items toward an independent life. For wives, Factor 1 (most variance) was the serious considerations of dissolution factor, Factor 2 was the independent life factor, and Factor 3 was the factor of variables that specify actions taken toward dissolution. To summarize, three factors emerged for both husbands and wives, roughly organized by (a) serious thoughts about dissolution, (b) making plans to be independent, and (c) specific actions toward dissolution.

How well did the Time 1 and Time 2 data predict total MSI scores and these three MSI factors for the couples who were still together at the 8-year follow-up assessment? The data were analyzed in two ways.

TABLE 16.1
The Ability of the Time 1 and Time 2 Data to Predict Marital Dissolution

Correlations	Separation	Divorce
Self-Report Variables		
Husb Lonel	.03	.12
Wife Lonel	−.14	.02
Husb Flood	.26*	.10
Wife Flood	.11	.17
Husb PrAlo	.03	.02
Wife PrAlo	−.03	.12
Wife Paral	.35**	.11
Husb Paral	.05	.05
Husb Probs	.12	.04
Wife Probs	.27*	.26*
Husb CnDiv	.31**	.43***
Husb CnSep	.35**	.41***
Wife CnDiv	.44***	.43***
Wife CnSep	.50***	.45***
Husb Mar-1	−.20[a]	−.15
Wife Mar-1	−.17	−.22[a]
Husb Mar-2	−.35**	−.33**
Wife Mar-2	.39***	−.45***
Husb Ratng	−.26*	−.02
Wife Ratng	−.17	−.02
Physiological Variables		
Baseline		
Husband		
Heart Period	.05	.14
Activity	.12	.08
Skin Cond	−.02	−.04
Pulse Trans	−.04	.03
Finger Ampl	−.06	−.04
Wife		
Heart Period	−.25*	−.24*
Activity	.22[a]	.11
Skin Cond	−.10	−.09
Pulse Trans	−.12	−.20[a]
Finger Ampl	−.10	−.11
Interaction		
Husband		
Heart Period	.03	.13
Activity	.01	.05
Skin Cond	.00	−.02
Pulse Trans	−.02	.11
Finger Ampl	−.10	−.13

(continued)

TABLE 16.1 (continued)

Correlations	Separation	Divorce
Interaction		
Wife		
Heart Period	−.22[a]	−.24*
Activity	.06	.07
Skin Cond	−.11	−.09
Pulse Trans	−.11	−.18
Finger Ampl	−.08	−.10
Behavior		
MICS		
Husband		
Defensive	.03	.00
Confl Eng	.12	.09
Stubborn	.00	−.06
Withdrawn	.15	.14
Wife		
Defensive	.27*	.04
Confl Eng	.24*	.11
Stubborn	.13	−.13
Withdrawn	.12	−.02
RCISS		
HSPK	−.18	−.22[a]
HLIST	−.13	−.21[a]
WSPK	−.28*	−.25*
WLIST	−.08	−.12
Husband		
Compl/Crit	.14	.10
Defensive	.06	.20[a]
Contempt	.15	.01
Stonewall	.22[a]	.31**
Wife		
Compl/Crit	.27[a]	.19
Defensive	.11	.19
Contempt	.26*	.15
Stonewall	.13	.14

(continued)

TABLE 16.1 (continued)

Correlations	Separation	Divorce
SPAFF		
Husband		
Neutral	−.01	.12
Humor	−.13	−.22*
Affctn	−.05	.05
Interest	.13	.08
Joy	−.06	−.16
Anger	−.06	−.09
Cont/Dis	−.14	−.16
Whine	.15	.16
Sad	.23*	.17
Fear	−.04	−.10
Wife		
Neutral	−.02	.01
Humor	−.14	−.20
Affctn	−.08	−.10
Interest	−.06	−.11
Joy	−.05	−.15
Anger	.05	.05
Cont/Dis	.29**	.23*
Whine	.09	.03
Sad	.28*	.36***
Fear	−.16	−.12
Oral History variables		
Husb Fond	−.17	−.03
Wife Fond	−.07	−.20
Husb Neg	.07	−.12
Wife Neg	.13	−.01
Husb We	−.15	−.16
Wife We	−.14	−.08
Husb Expa	−.26*	−.23[a]
Wife Expa	−.08	−.13
Husb Disa	.25*	.31**
Wife Disa	.20[a]	.26*
H ORALTOT	−.22[a]	−.16
W ORALTOT	−.17	−.17
CHAOGLORY	−.09	−.23

[a]$p < .10.$ *$p < .05.$ **$p < .01.$ ***$p < .001.$

TABLE 16.2

Frequency With Which Specific Items on the MSI Were Endorsed by Couples Who
Were Still Together in the 8-Year Follow-Up

Item	Husband	Wife
1. Occasionally thought of divorce after argument or other incident (Item 8)	25.5	5.9
2. I have considered divorce or separation a few times, other than during or after an argument, although only in vague terms (Item 14)	13.7	21.6
3. Thoughts of divorce occur to me frequently as often as once a week or more (Item 3)	5.9	5.9
4. I have thought specifically about divorce or separation. I have thought about who would get the kids, how things would be divided, pros and cons, etc. (Item 5)	11.8	15.7
5. I have discussed the question of my divorce or separation with someone other than my spouse (trusted friend, psychologist, minister, etc.) (Item 7)	2.0	11.8
6. I have made specific plans to discuss separation or divorce with my spouse. I have considered what I would say, etc. (Item 1)	3.9	5.9
7. I have discussed the issue of divorce seriously or at length with my spouse (Item 9)	5.9	0.0
8. I have suggested to my spouse that I wished to be separated, divorced, or be rid of him/her (Item 4)	7.8	7.8
9. I have made inquiries of nonprofessionals as to how long it takes to get a divorce, grounds for divorce, costs involved, etc. (Item 11)	0.0	2.0
10. I have set up an independent bank account in my name in order to protect my interests (Item 2)	0.0	2.0
11. I have consulted with a lawyer or other legal aid about the matter (Item 13)	missing	missing
12. My spouse and I have separated. This is a (check one) trial separation or a legal separation (Item 6)	NA	NA
13. I have contacted a lawyer to make prelimininary plans for a divorce (Item 12)	missing	missing
14. I have filed for divorce or we are divorced (Item 10)	NA	NA

First, an overall MSI score was computed for husbands and wives. Second, factor scores were computed for these three factors for husbands and wives, and these factor scores were then correlated with the Time 1 and Time 2 data. The MSI factor scores were negatively keyed, so that, for example, a positive correlation of a predictor variable with serious considerations of dissolution indicated that increases in the predictor *lowered* the likelihood of considerations of dissolution. On the other hand the factor scores were positively keyed. The results are summarized in Tables 16.4 and 16.5.

TABLE 16.3
Factor Analysis of the Weiss Marital Status Inventory (Entire Sample)

Item #	Factor 1	Factor 2	Factor 3
		Husband	
1	.72	.24	.37
2	.21	.12	.69
3	.21	.75	.07
4	.14	.81	−.01
5	.06	.63	.61
6	.93	.06	.14
7	.15	.05	.91
8	−.04	.74	.22
9	.14	.41	.72
10	.89	−.11	−.12
11	.41	.19	.32
12	.93	.06	.14
13	.93	.06	.14
14	−.12	.75	.30
		Wife	
1	.37	.19	.54
2	.08	−.11	−.02
3	.45	.44	.05
4	.31	.29	.67
5	.84	.23	.24
6	.12	−.14	.89
7	.73	.24	.32
8	.80	.22	.13
9	.32	.71	−.13
11	−.04	.90	.16
14	.82	−.17	.11

16.3.3.1. Predicting Total MSI Scores

16.3.3.1.1 The Husband's MSI Scores

The husband's MSI scores were predicted by the following variables (see Table 16.4).

Self-report variables. The husband's loneliness, his feeling flooded and his wife's feeling flooded, his and his wife's rating of their marital problems as severe, his and his wife's serious considerations of separation at Time 2, both spouses' marital satisfaction at Time 1 and Time 2 his MSI scores predicted his MSI score.

Physiological variables. No physiological variables predicted the husband's MSI scores.

TABLE 16.4
Ability of Time 1 and Time 2 Variables to Predict the Marital Status Inventory (MSI)
Total Score of Couples Who Stayed Together

Correlations	HMSI	WMSI
Self-Report Variables		
Husb Lonel	.48**	.47**
Wife Lonel	.09	.10
Husb Flood	.50***	.47***
Wife Flood	.40*	.48**
Husb PrAlo	.15	.27[a]
Wife PrAlo	.18	.30[a]
Wife Paral	.14	.02
Husb Paral	− .14	− .13
Husb Probs	.42*	.51**
Wife Probs	.44**	.67***
Husb CnDiv	.27	.33*
Husb CnSep	.35*	.32*
Wife CnDiv	.15	.39**
Wife CnSep	.30[a]	.48***
Husb Mar-1	.40*	− .43**
Wife Mar-1	− .31[a]	− .60***
Husb Mar-2	− .68***	− .67***
Wife Mar-2	− .51***	− .60***
Husb Ratng	.12	− .12
Wife Ratng	.08	− .11
Physiology		
Baseline		
Husband		
Heart Period	.11	− .17
Activity	.06	.11
Skin Cond	.24	.33*
Pulse Trans	.30[a]	.06
Finger Ampl	− .12	− .18
Wife		
Heart Period	− .13	− .09
Activity	.08	− .04
Skin Cond	− .13	− .29[a]
Pulse Trans	− .09	− .02
Finger Ampl	.14	− .04

(continued)

TABLE 16.4 *(continued)*

Correlations	HMSI	WMSI
Interaction		
Husband		
Heart Period	.13	−.14
Activity	.02	.04
Skin Cond	.23	.31*
Pulse Trans	.26	.06
Finger Ampl	−.09	−.17
Wife		
Heart Period	−.08	−.07
Activity	−.10	−.14
Skin Cond	−.17	−.31*
Pulse Trans	−.05	.03
Finger Ampl	.09	−.05
Behavior		
MICS		
Husband		
Defensive	.13	.07
Confl Eng	.40*	.37*
Stubborn	.53***	.40**
Withdrawn	.14	−.01
Wife		
Defensive	.02	−.11
Confl Eng	.23	.21
Stubborn	.34*	.21
Withdrawn	−.02	−.09
RCISS		
HSPK	.07	.06
HLIST	.15	.16
WSPK	.17	.06
WLIST	.22	.15
Husband		
Compl/Crit	.01	−.08
Defensive	−.11	.00
Contempt	.05	.00
Stonewall	−.03	−.16

(continued)

TABLE 16.4 *(continued)*

Correlations	HMSI	WMSI
Wife		
Compl/Crit	−.12	−.09
Defensive	−.09	.07
Contempt	−.29[a]	−.22
Stonewall	−.11	−.15
SPAFF		
Husband		
Neutral	−.09	−.10
Humor	−.23	−.21
Affctn	−.10	−.18
Interest	−.02	.05
Joy	.11	.11
Anger	.01	.08
Cont/Dis	.37*	.14
Whine	.05	.07
Sad	−.07	−.01
Fear	.14	.14
Wife		
Neutral	−.14	−.17
Humor	−.30	−.22
Affctn	−.13	−.19
Interest	−.16	−.08
Joy	−.10	.00
Anger	.17	.14
Cont/Dis	.12	−.01
Whine	.45**	.28[a]
Sad	−.04	.13
Fear	.02	.09
Oral History variables		
Husb Fond	−.28	−.23
Wife Fond	−.39*	−.21
Husb Neg	.20	.11
Wife Neg	.47**	.32*
Husb We	−.33*	−.23
Wife We	−.32[a]	−.28[a]
Husb Expa	−.38*	−.36*
Wife Expa	−.48**	−.39*
Husb Disa	.31[a]	.42**
Wife Disa	.28	.41**
H ORALTOT	−.34*	−.31[a]
W ORALTOT	−.46**	−.38*
CHAOGLORY	−.32[a]	−.38*

[a]$p < .10$. *$p < .05$. ** $p < .01$. ***$p < .001$.

Correlations	HSERCON	WSERCON	HINDEP	WINDEP	HSEPDIV	WSEPDIV
Self-Report						
Husb Lonel	−.56***	−.45**	−.27	−.42**	−.13	−.41**
Wife Lonel	−.12	−.15	−.11	.05	.17	−.08
Husb Flood	−.57***	−.46**	−.29[a]	−.45**	−.11	−.42**
Wife Flood	−.46**	−.46**	−.20	−.48***	.07	−.38*
Husb PrAlo	−.23	−.28[a]	.01	−.18	.09	−.19
Wife PrAlo	−.20	−.28[a]	−.13	−.28[a]	−.10	−.27[a]
Wife Paral	−.17	−.01	−.03	−.11	.04	.07
Husb Paral	.13	.14	.14	.08	.06	.12
Husb Probs	−.49**	−.47**	−.24	−.52***	−.12	−.46**
Wife Probs	−.47**	−.61***	−.28[a]	−.66***	−.32[a]	−.59***
Husb CnDiv	−.33*	−.26[a]	−.08	−.32*	−.02	−.19
Husb CnSep	−.42**	−.28[a]	−.13	−.46**	−.03	−.23
Wife CnDiv	−.21	−.37*	.03	−.39*	.12	−.18
Wife CnSep	−.37*	−.47**	−.09	−.58***	.08	−.33*
Husb Mar-1	.50***	.46**	.18	.31*	−.03	.34*
Wife Mar-1	.36*	.65***	.18	.36	−.01	.49***
Husb Mar-2	.76***	.64***	.38*	.75***	.07	.66***
Wife Mar-2	.58***	.59***	.29[a]	.55***	.00	.48***
Husb Ratng	−.02	.19	−.28[a]	−.03	−.34*	.10
Wife Ratng	−.04	.13	−.22	.08	−.04	.04
Physiology						
Baseline						
Husband						
Heart Period	−.06	.16	−.22	.13	−.09	.11
Activity	−.10	−.09	.01	−.09	.07	−.07
Skin Cond	−.22	−.30[a]	−.23	−.33*	−.22	−.39*
Pulse Trans	−.20	−.03	−.44**	−.16	−.50***	−.10
Finger Ampl	.13	.20	.06	.12	.06	.15
Wife						
Heart Period	.19	.04	.00	.14	.01	.08
Activity	−.13	−.01	.01	.10	.23	.04
Skin Cond	.16	.29[a]	.06	.20	−.01	.28[a]
Pulse Trans	.12	−.02	−.02	.12	.04	−.02
Finger Ampl	−.09	.00	−.22	.06	−.15	.07
Interaction						
Husband						
Heart Period	−.08	.13	−.23	.09	−.10	.10
Activity	−.05	−.04	.05	−.03	.05	−.03
Skin Cond	−.21	−.27[a]	−.21	−.31*	−.21	−.36*
Pulse Trans	−.17	−.02	−.39*	−.16	−.43**	−.11
Finger Ampl	.13	.19	.00	.09	−.03	.14

(continued)

TABLE 16.5 (continued)

Correlations	HSERCON	WSERCON	HINDEP	WINDEP	HSEPDIV	WSEPDIV
Wife						
Heart Period	.13	.03	− .04	.11	− .02	.05
Activity	.07	.11	.13	.17	.22	.12
Skin Cond	.19	.31*	.11	.22	.03	.30[a]
Pulse Trans	.10	− .07	− .08	.07	− .07	− .05
Finger Ampl	− .06	.01	− .13	.08	− .07	.06
Behavior						
MICS						
Husband						
Defensive	− .11	− .06	− .14	− .06	− .13	− .07
Confl Eng	− .38*	− .24	− .31[a]	− .57***	− .45**	− .39**
Stubborn	− .54***	− .29[a]	− .39*	− .51***	− .41*	− .38*
Withdrawn	− .18	.00	− .11	.05	.13	− .03
Wife						
Defensive	.01	.16	− .06	− .04	− .15	.14
Confl Eng	− .21	− .11	− .19	− .41**	− .32[a]	− .22
Stubborn	− .36*	− .14	− .24	− .37*	− .24	− .24
Withdrawn	− .01	.10	.01	.10	.18	.09
RCISS						
HSPK	− .04	− .05	− .13	− .06	− .06	− .03
HLIST	− .14	− .11	− .11	− .26	− .15	− .18
WSPK	− .14	− .08	− .21	− .10	− .14	− .07
WLIST	− .24	− .08	− .10	− .28	− .16	− .16
Husband						
Compl/Crit	− .04	.12	.06	.00	− .05	.03
Defensive	.07	− .03	.21	.03	.16	.04
Contempt	− .10	− .01	.07	.02	.06	− .11
Stonewall	.01	.15	.03	.19	.11	.12
Wife						
Compl/Crit	.11	.14	.14	.10	.02	.11
Defensive	.02	− .09	.23	− .01	.19	.00
Contempt	.28	.23	.30[a]	.15	.16	.16
Stonewall	.12	.12	.02	.20	.12	.11

(continued)

TABLE 16.5 *(continued)*

Correlations	HSERCON	WSERCON	HINDEP	WINDEP	HSEPDIV	WSEPDIV
SPAFF (Proportions)						
Husband						
Neutral	.10	.12	.04	.10	.07	.07
Humor	.25	.21	.14	.25	.16	.16
Affctn	.13	.17	.00	.13	− .02	.15
Interest	.03	− .11	− .04	.03	.10	− .05
Joy	− .11	− .07	− .10	− .15	− .13	− .09
Anger	− .04	− .06	.09	− .15	.01	− .08
Cont/Dis	− .43**	− .07	− .15	− .34*	− .18	− .09
Whine	− .05	− .02	− .03	− .12	− .09	− .13
Sad	.13	− .03	− .02	.07	− .10	.06
Fear	− .13	− .19	− .11	− .05	− .10	− .12
Wife						
Neutral	.16	.17	.04	.16	.08	.13
Humor	.29[a]	.21	.25	.27[a]	.27[a]	.20
Affctn	.14	.18	.06	.16	.06	.23
Interes	.17	.03	.14	.10	.08	.16
Joy	.10	− .04	.08	.05	.08	.01
Anger	− .18	− .10	− .10	− .21	− .21	− .17
Cont/Di	− .14	.03	− .07	.01	− .08	− .05
Whine	− .49**	− .20	− .32*	− .41**	− .16	− .27[a]
Sad	.02	− .15	.02	− .08	.11	− .06
Fear	− .02	− .11	.01	− .01	− .01	− .03
Oral History variables						
Husb Fond	.37*	.23	.12	.19	− .05	.17
Wife Fond	.45**	.19	.27	.22	.10	.14
Husb Neg	− .29[a]	− .10	− .02	− .14	.11	− .03
Wife Neg	− .53***	− .32[a]	− .32[a]	− .29[a]	− .09	− .28[a]
Husb We	.42*	.23	.17	.18	− .03	.16
Wife We	.42*	.28[a]	.13	.21	− .04	.22
Husb Expan	.43*	.35*	.27	.31[a]	.13	.35*
Wife Expan	.56***	.34*	.30[a]	.41*	.19	.32*
Husb Disap	− .37*	− .46**	− .18	− .26	− .01	− .31[a]
Wife Disap	− .34*	− .43**	− .17	− .26	− .02	− .33*
H ORALTOT	.43**	.32[a]	.17	.25	− .02	.23
W ORALTOT	.55***	.38*	.27	.32[a]	.07	.30[a]
CHAOGLORY	.40*	.35*	.19	.33*	.05	.30[a]

[a]$p < .10.$ *$p < .05.$ **$p < .01.$ ***$p < .001.$

Behavior. As scored by the MICS, the husband's Time 1 conflict engagement and stubbornness and his wife's stubbornness predicted his MSI score. No RCISS code predicted the husband's MSI score. On the SPAFF, the husband's contempt/disgust, the wife's whining, and low amounts of wife humor predicted the husband's MSI score. On the Oral History Interview, the husband's MSI score was predicted by low expressions of fondness by the wife, high negativity by the wife, low levels of husband "we-ness," low levels of husband and wife expansiveness, high perception of chaos, and low overall global husband and wife positivity on the Oral History Interview, and (marginally) by the glorification/low chaos score.

16.3.3.1.2. The Wife's MSI Scores

The wife's MSI scores were predicted by the following variables (see Table 16.5):

Self-report variables. The husband's loneliness, his feeling flooded and his wife's feeling flooded, his and his wife's rating of their marital problems as severe, his and his wife's serious considerations of separation and divorce at Time 2, both spouses' marital satisfaction at Time 1 and Time 2 her MSI scores predicted her MSI score.

Physiological variables. The husband's baseline skin conductance and his skin conductance during conflict predicted his wife's MSI score; more physiologically aroused husbands had wives who had higher (less positive) MSI scores. In contrast, the wife's *low* skin conductance during conflict predicted her higher MSI scores.

Behavior. As scored by the MICS, the husband's conflict engagement and stubbornness predicted her MSI score. No RCISS code predicted the wife's MSI score. No SPAFF code predicted the wife's MSI score. On the Oral History Interview, the wife's MSI score was predicted by high negativity by the wife, low levels of husband and wife expansiveness, high perception of chaos, high levels of disappointment by both spouses, and by low overall global wife positivity on the Oral History Interview, and by the glorification/low chaos score.

16.3.3.2. Predicting the Three MSI Factors

16.3.3.2.1. Serious Considerations of Separation and Divorce by the Husband

Self-report variables. The husband's loneliness, the husband's and the wife's feelings of being flooded, the husband's and the wife's rating of their marital problems as severe, Time 2 serious considerations of separation and divorce by the husband, and serious considerations of separation by the wife, Time 1 and Time 2 marital satisfaction predicted the husband's serious considerations of dissolution factor on the MSI.

Physiological variables. No physiological variable predicted the husband's serious considerations of dissolution factor on the MSI.

Behavior. On the MICS, the husband's conflict engagement, stubbornness, and the wife's stubbornness predicted the husband's serious considerations of dissolution on the MSI. No RCISS variable predicted the husband's serious considerations of dissolution on the MSI. On the SPAFF, the husband's expressions of contempt/disgust, low levels of his wife's humor, and his wife's whining predicted the husband's serious considerations of dissolution on the MSI. On the Oral History Interview low levels of the husband's and wife's fondness, the wife's negativity, low levels of the husband's and wife's "we-ness," low levels of husband and wife expansiveness, high levels of chaos, high levels of disappointment by the husband and wife, and low global overall scores by wife and husband, as well as low glorification/chaos scores predicted the husband's serious considerations of dissolution on the MSI.

16.3.3.2.2. Serious Considerations of Separation and Divorce by the Wife

Self-report variables. The husband's loneliness, the husband's and the wife's feelings of being flooded, the husband's and wife's rating of their marital problems as severe, Time 2 serious considerations of separation and divorce by the husband (marginal), and serious considerations of separation by the wife, Time 1 and Time 2 marital satisfaction predicted the wife's serious considerations of dissolution on the MSI.

Physiological variables. No physiological variable predicted the wife's serious considerations of dissolution on the MSI.

Behavior. On the Oral History Interview the wife's negativity, low levels of husband's and wife's expansiveness, high levels of chaos, high levels of disappointment by the husband and wife, and low global overall scores by the wife, as well as low glorification/chaos scores predicted the wife's serious considerations of dissolution on the MSI.

16.3.3.2.3. The Husband's Actions to Become More Independent

Self-report variables. The only self-report variable that predicted the husband's actions to become more independent was Time 2 marital satisfaction.

Physiological variables. In both the baseline and during the interaction, husbands whose blood flowed *slower* were more likely to take actions to become more independent 8 years later.

Behavior. The husband's stubbornness and her whining were the only behavioral variables that predicted the husband's actions action to become more independent 8 years later.

16.3.3.2.4. The Wife's Action to Become More Independent

Self-report variables. Many more variables predicted the wife's compared to the husband's actions to become more independent was Time 2. These variables were: The husband's loneliness, the husband's feeling flooded, the wife's feeling flooded, the husband and wife report that their marital problems were severe, serious considerations of dissolution by both spouses, and Time 1 and Time 2 marital satisfaction.

Physiological variables. The husband's high baseline and within-session conflict discussion skin conductance predicted that wives were more likely to take actions to become more independent 8 years later.

Behavior. The wife's actions to become more independent 8 years later were predicted by: the husband's conflict engagement, his stubbornness, her conflict engagement and stubbornness, his expressions of contempt/disgust, her whining, and on the Oral History Interview by lower levels of expansiveness by the wife, and chaos.

16.3.3.2.5. The Husband's Actions Toward Dissolution

Self-report variables. Only lower ratings on the rating dial during the video recall interview predicted the husband's actions toward dissolution.

Physiological variables. In both the baseline and during the interaction, husbands whose blood flowed *slower* were more likely to take actions to dissolve their marriages 8 years later.

Behavior. The husband's conflict engagement, stubbornness were the only behavioral variables that predicted the husband's actions to dissolve the marriage 8 years later.

16.3.3.2.6. The Wife's Action Toward Dissolution

Self-report variables. Many more variables predicted the wife's actions toward dissolution than was the case for the husband. These variables were: The husband's loneliness, the husband's feeling flooded, the wife's feeling flooded, the husband and wife report that their marital problems were severe, serious considerations of separation by the wife, and Time 1 and Time 2 marital satisfaction.

Physiological variables. The husband's high baseline and within-session conflict discussion skin conductance predicted that wives were more likely to take actions to dissolve the marriage 8 years later; high arousal predicted these actions.

Behavior. The wife's actions to dissolve the marriage 8 years later were predicted by: the husband's conflict engagement, his stubbornness, her conflict engagement and stubbornness, and on the Oral History Interview by lower levels of expansiveness by the wife and the husband, disappointment by both wife and husband, and chaos.

16.3.3.3. Correlations of Time 1 Variables With Variables of the Oral History Interview That Predict Dissolution

In Buehlman, Gottman, and Katz (1992) the oral history variables organized the Time 1 variables as well as predicting divorce. Was this also true in this study? Table 16.6 summarizes the correlations of the Time 1 variables with the two Oral History variables that predicted divorce over an 8-year period, namely, husband and wife disappointment in the marriage. The variables that correlated significantly with these two Oral History variables were as follows.

Self-report variables. The husband's loneliness correlated with both husband and wife disappointment, as did the husband and wife's feelings of being flooded, the husband's and the wife's thoughts that it is not worthwhile to try to resolve problems with one's partner, the husband and the wife's perceived severity of marital problems, and Time 1 marital satisfaction.

Physiological variables. Correlated with both the husband and the wife's disappointment were the wife's baseline and within-conflict heart rate; a higher heart rate was related to greater disappointment.

Behavior. The husband's withdrawal (as coded by the MICS), the husband positive speaker slope, the husband's listener slope, the wife's speaker slope and the wife's listener slope were all correlated with the husband and wife disappointment in the marriage. The husband's contempt (RCISS) was related to his disappointment with the marriage (and this was marginally for the wife's disappointment). The wife's criticism (RCISS) and her stonewalling (RCISS) were related to the husband's disappointment with the marriage. On the SPAFF, disappointed husbands and wives tended to have husbands who were less affectionate and less humorous than less disappointed partners.

TABLE 16.6
Correlations of Time 1 Variables With the Oral History Variables That Predicted
Dissolution

Correlations	HDISAP	WDISAP
Husb Lonel	.56***	.62***
Wife Lonel	.14	.20
Husb Flood	.51***	.48***
Wife Flood	.55***	.58***
Husb PrAlo	.36**	.34**
Wife PrAlo	.26*	.24*
Wife Paral	.05	.11
Husb Paral	.10	.00
Husb Probs	.51***	.54***
Wife Probs	.48***	.53***
Husb CnDiv	.28*	.32*
Husb CnSep	.28*	.30*
Wife CnDiv	.34**	.24[a]
Wife CnSep	.35**	.30*
Husb Mar-1	− .62***	− .55***
Wife Mar-1	− .68***	− .66***
Husb Mar-2	− .51***	− .41***
Wife Mar-2	− .56***	− .53***
Husb Ratng	− .21[a]	− .16
Wife Ratng	− .09	− .05

Physiology

Baseline

Husband

Heart Period	− .21	− .22[a]
Activity	.12	− .12
Skin Cond	− .06	.01
Pulse Trans	− .16	− .09
Finger Ampl	− .01	− .05

Wife

Heart Period	− .31**	− .31**
Activity	.07	− .05
Skin Cond	− .09	− .03
Pulse Trans	− .13	.01
Finger Ampl	− .01	− .03

Interaction

Husband

Heart Period	− .19	− .21[a]
Activity	− .02	− .11
Skin Cond	− .06	.01
Pulse Trans	− .12	− .05
Finger Ampl	− .10	− .15

(continued)

TABLE 16.6 (continued)

Correlations	HDISAP	WDISAP
Wife		
Heart Period	− .32**	− .32**
Activity	− .12	− .13
Skin Cond	− .12	− .06
Pulse Trans	− .17	− .06
Finger Ampl	.07	.05
Physiological Reac-tivity		
HDELIB	.12	.08
HDELAC	− .11	− .03
HDELSC	− .06	.00
HDELFA	− .17	− .20
HDELPT	.14	.14
WDELIB	.03	.03
WDELAC	− .19	− .12
WDELSC	− .14	− .13
WDELFA	.19	.19
WDELPT	− .04	− .14
Behavior		
MICS		
Husband		
Defensive	.04	.04
Confl Eng	.10	.10
Stubborn	.06	.11
Withdrawn	.40***	.26*
Wife		
Defensive	.04	.02
Confl Eng	− .04	.06
Stubborn	.13	.12
Withdrawn	.19	.13
RCISS		
HSPK	− .33**	− .31*
HLIST	− .34**	− .29*
WSPK	− .29*	− .27*
WLIST	− .28*	− .27*
Husband		
Compl/Crit	.12	.13
Defensive	.16	.18
Contempt	.27*	.23[a]
Stonewall	.27*	.21[a]

(continued)

TABLE 16.6 *(continued)*

Correlations	HDISAP	WDISAP
Wife		
Compl/Crit	.13	.15
Defensive	.25*	.20
Contempt	.06	.09
Stonewall	.26*	.25*
SPAFF		
Husband		
Neutral	.05	.06
Humor	−.25*	−.23[a]
Affctn	−.28[a]	−.29*
Interest	−.14	−.04
Joy	−.18	−.20[a]
Anger	.17	.21[a]
Cont/Dis	.08	.07
Whine	.23[a]	.12
Sad	.15	.04
Fear	−.12	−.13
Wife		
Neutral	.04	.09
Humor	−.24[a]	−.22[a]
Affctn	−.18	−.15
Interest	−.06	−.02
Joy	−.21[a]	−.16
Anger	.19	.22[a]
Cont/Dis	.00	−.05
Whine	.17	.00
Sad	.08	.01
Fear	−.12	−.22

Note. Lone = Loneliness, Floo = Flooded, PrAl = Thinks it better to work out problems alone, Para = Parallel Lives, Prob = Perceived severity of marital problems, CnDi = Considered divorce in 1987, CnSe = Considered separation in 1987, Mar-1 = Time 1 marital satisfaction, Mar-2 = Time 2 marital satisfaction, Ratn = Mean interaction rating dial, Heart Per = interbeat interval, Activity = Somatic activity level, Skin Cond = Skin Conductance level, Pulse Tra = Pulse transit time, Finger Am = Finger pulse amplitude, Confl Eng = Conflict Engaging, SPK = mean positive minus negative RCISS speaker score, LIST = mean positive minus negative RCISS listener score, Compl/Cri = RCISS criticize/complain, Affctn = Affection, Cont/Dis = Contempt/Disgust, Fond = Fondness, Neg = Negativity, We = We-ness, Expa = Expansiveness, Disa = Disapointment, ORALTOT = Total positive minus negative Oral History score, CHAOGLORY = Glorifying the struggle minus chaos.

[a]$p < .10$. *$p < .05$. **$p < .01$. ***$p < .001$.

16.4. DISCUSSION

The 8-year follow-up data help allay any nagging problems one may have had that variables in the process and distance and isolation cascades were predicting a rare phenomenon, and that relationships may not have been reliable. By 1991, the divorce rate in the DUO83 study had reached 20% of the sample that could be recontacted (91.1% of the original sample); 36.7% of the original sample had either separated or divorced. These rates are quite high, consistent with (and exceeding, using yearly rates) the startlingly high Martin and Bumpass (1989) estimate of 67% dissolution rate within the lifetime of a marriage.

16.4.1. Predicting Dissolution

The relationships obtained suggest that Time 1 data are able to predict both separation and divorce. In general, as is to be expected, Time 2 marital satisfaction variables are better predictors than Time 1 marital satisfaction; Time 2 considerations of dissolution are also predictors of later dissolution.

Time 1 self-report variables were able to predict separation and divorce, and these predictions were consistent with the distance and isolation cascade. The only potent physiological variable that emerged as a predictor of dissolution was the wife's heart rate. Higher heart rates at Time 1 were predictors of dissolution. The percent difference between stable and unstable marriages is only about 10%. Also, the range of heart rates is well within the range of vagal inhibition because it is still considerably lower than the intrinsic rhythm of the heart (about 100 to 105 BPM). This effect for only wives is paralleled by an analogous effect for only husbands in the DUO86 study, and an effect that examined only changes in marital satisfaction primarily for husbands in the DUO80 study. Subsequent research will have to study these effects and this lack of consistency. It should be noted that our analyses collapse physiological responses and behavior over time, and this may be part of the problem in our inconsistency. Still, all the results suggest that physiological arousal during conflict resolution is a sign of an ailing marriage, and that this elevation in heart rate can be observed at baseline. This reflects either a chronic activation, or a chronic activation just in the presence of the spouse. We have reason to believe that it is very difficult to obtain a low level of functioning baseline when the partner is present.

Behavior that predicted divorce were generally also consistent with the previously suggested process cascade. Sadness at Time 1 was a surprise as a predictor of dissolution, but the rest of the variables that predicted were quite consistent with the predictions obtained previously. The Oral History variables again demonstrated an ability to predict dissolution. Furthermore, the Oral History variables in this study generally demonstrated the same kind of relationships with the Time 1 self-report and behavioral variables as they did in the DUO86 study.

16.4.2. The Marital Status of Intact Marriages

16.4.2.1. The Divorce Potential of Those Still Married

The Weiss Marital Status Inventory added a new dimension to our ability to forecast what processes toward dissolution may be operating at a subtler level in marriages that were still intact on 8-year follow-up. A surprisingly large proportion of these intact marriages seem to be on the road to dissolution. Our 1987–1991 data on the ability of the serious considerations of dissolutions variables to predict actual dissolution would suggest that these figures are alarming, and that continued follow-up of this sample is warranted; that is, we have not yet reached a ceiling.

16.4.2.2. Predictors of Total MSI Scores

It is important that the Time 1 data were able to predict the Weiss MSI data for these stable marriages, and that the direction of prediction was straightforward. The people who were lonelier at Time 1, who were more flooded, who perceived their marital problems as severe, and who were seriously considering dissolution in 1987 were also the same people who scored high in divorce potential on the MSI in 1991. The self-report data also suggest that Time 1 marital satisfaction may become a stronger predictor of dissolution over time, as the sample narrows due to attrition due to dissolution. One would usually expect that the opposite would be true. As the really unhappy couples leave the sample of the still-married, marital satisfaction should narrow its range and lessen in predictive power. Hence, these findings about the ability of Time 1 marital satisfaction, and other Time 1 variables to predict MSI scores of intact couples is quite encouraging for our belief in the orderliness of the processes related to stability and dissolution.

Husbands who at Time 1 were more physiologically aroused as indexed by higher skin conductance level had wives who scored higher on the MSI 8 years later. This was true for baseline as well as interaction skin conductance, so it suggests a chronic arousal effect rather than a reactivity effect. The negative correlation with the wife's interaction skin conductance level and her MSI 8 years later suggests that a dysfunctional pattern may be a physiological under-arousal of the wife at Time 1 coupled with her husband's over-arousal, but this notion is speculative at best.

Higher MSI scores were predicted by MICS codes of greater conflict engagement and stubbornness of the husband and greater stubbornness of the wife, greater contempt/disgust by the husband (SPAFF), and greater whining by the wife (SPAFF).

The Oral History variables predicted the husband's MSI score. Husbands who later scored high on the MSI were characterized 8 years earlier by low expressions of fondness toward them by their wives, high negativity by their wives, low levels of husband "we-ness," low levels of husband and wife expansiveness, high perception of chaos, and by low overall global husband and wife positivity on the Oral History Interview, and (marginally) by the glorification/low chaos score. The wife's MSI score 8 years later was predicted at Time 1 by her high negativity, low levels of husband and wife expansiveness, high perception of chaos, high levels of disappointment by both spouses, and by low overall global wife positivity on the Oral History Interview, and by the glorification/low chaos score.

These patterns are all clear and understandable.

16.4.2.3. Predictors of MSI Factor Scores

It is remarkable how well the self-report measures at Time 1 do in predicting all the MSI factors, even those that spell actual steps toward dissolution of these still intact marriages.

The husband's pulse transit time data suggest that the husband's *slower* blood velocity and lower skin conductance is associated with a better outcome (even on the steps toward dissolution factor) on the MSI 8 years later. This pattern of results is consistent with the global MSI results previously reported for the husband's Time 1 skin conductance level. We see that the opposite result of the wife's increased skin conductance level being associated with positive outcome on the MSI held only for the serious considerations factor; this clarifies the earlier results with the global MSI scores; these two patterns refer to different factors. In terms of hard prediction of actual actions toward dissolution, one would have to opt for the interpretation that the lower arousal of the husband is a protective factor.

Again on the MICS conflict engagement and stubbornness, particularly by the husband predicted not only serious considerations of dissolution, but actions toward that end, which was also somewhat the case for the SPAFF husband contempt/disgust and wife whining codes.

On the other hand, our results with the Oral History variables showed that these variables were better at predicting the considerations of dissolution factor than they were at predicting the actions toward independence and the actions toward dissolution factors. These Time 1 variables are most effective at predicting earlier parts of the Weiss–Guttman scale of a cascade of these intact marriages toward divorce.

17

Recommendations for a Stable Marriage

This chapter speculates about the implications of the research presented here for a marital therapy that has as its goal the prevention of marital dissolution. If such a therapy were to be devised, what would be its agenda, that is, its tasks and objectives? What would be its principles and its methods? This chapter summarizes current research on marital therapy and suggests a new marital therapy called minimal marital therapy.

In this age we have witnessed the triumph of chaos theory. We are discovering that we will never be able to predict tomorrow's weather any better than we can now, even if we have all the information in the world about weather patterns. Given this state of affairs about physical nature, how can we expect people's social relationships to be more orderly and predictable over time? Certainly the bias among the sciences is that the social sciences are particularly "soft" and will never be able to obtain the kind of understanding, prediction, and control that is the hallmark of true science.

Yet, surprisingly, the opposite appears to be the case. We are finding that if we observe behavior properly, people's closest relationships are predictable, even over a period of years. Furthermore, we can do all this prediction from just 45 minutes of videotape, a brief interview, and a few questionnaires. Despite the riot of people's personal lives, when we study them scientifically, the social world appears to be quite lawful, predictable, and understandable.

17.1. IMPLICATIONS OF THE TYPOLOGY

Of course, as it turned out, things are not so obvious, nor are they what they at first seem. Most of the reasonable hypotheses of our best

409

researchers in this area have turned out to be wrong. For example, we now have good evidence that conflict avoidance is not dysfunctional. Nor are hot blooded, passionate, and highly argumentative, conflictual volatile relationships dysfunctional.

Hence, the validating marriage, which is the current standard model for all marital therapies, is not the only stable adaptation to marriage. Marital therapists may have to broaden their visions about what works in marriage. There appears to be more than one adaptation to having a stable marriage.

Indeed, in this book there was evidence that there are but three stable adaptations. All three have positive to negative ratios of close to 5, whereas unstable marriages have ratios less than 1, that is, there is more negativity than positivity. The three marriages differed greatly in how emotionally expressive they were, with the volatile couple the most expressive, the validating couple the next most expressive, and the conflict-avoiding couple the least expressive. Also, the three stable adaptations could be discriminated with only one variable graphed over time. This variable was the timing and the extent to which they tried to influence their partner's opinions.

I speculated that all three stable adaptations had their risks and benefits, and at the present time we have no basis for favoring one over another. In subsequent research we can and will assess the effects on children of these three types of marriage. Fitzpatrick's work in conjunction with mine suggests that the three types of stable marriages are very different on almost any dimension that has been studied, including philosophy, intimacy, the way they use space at home, or the way they use language. Why people are drawn to one kind of relationship or another remains a mystery, but I have speculated that the optimal level of expressed emotion, desired intimacy, and conflict may be basic to this choice. This optimal level may be an individual differences variable determined in part by temperament and in part by the family of origin.

Unstable marriages are also quite lawful and orderly in both their progression toward dissolution and in the social processes that are predictive of this dissolution. The positive to negative ratio of less than 1 describes a lot about these marriages. They survive in a very lean behavioral ecology in which the deadly predator, negative affect and negative problem solving, is favored. Their negativity is also pervasive, it is an absorbing state, and they do not rebound easily. The fact that negativity is an absorbing state has profound implications about the viability of other social processes, such as being able to repair the interaction.

Not all seemingly negative behaviors in a marriage are actually negative in the sense of the longitudinal health of the marriage. I summarized this point with the phrase "embrace the anger." Also, not all negative behaviors and affects were equally corrosive. Particularly implicated were criticism, contempt, defensiveness, and stonewalling. I also suggested that unstable marriages are unstable because they were unable to work out one of the three stable adaptations to marriage; that is, "mixed types" are unstable longitudinally.

I believe it could also be the case that the hostile and hostile/detached types are actually different stages in the dissolution process. I think that detachment follows hot, hostile engagement. It seems then that Tolstoy was wrong. He said (in *Anna Karenina*) that happy marriages are all alike but that each unhappy marriage is unhappy in its own way. In fact, all unhappy marriages appear to be quite alike, whereas there are three ways of having a stable adaptation to marriage. In the future it would be interesting to determine what cultural differences exist with respect to the three types. Rabin (personal communication, 1992), who is an Israeli marital therapist and marriage researcher, noted that volatile couples are more common in Israel than validating or conflict-avoiding couples. The amount of emotion expression preferred by a culture may contribute to the preferences of people for one kind of adaptation or another, as may the culturally prescribed methods of mate selection. It would be important to determine whether the mechanisms I have proposed are cross-culturally universal. I suspect that the basic theory is universal. For example, although cultures may differ in how they verbally communicate contempt, I suspect that contempt will always have an extremely corrosive effect on marital stability and happiness.

17.2. SPECULATIONS ABOUT PRESCRIPTIONS FOR A STABLE MARRIAGE

What does all this say about the prescription for a healthy and happy marriage? I must be cautious because my data are entirely correlational. However, because it is unlikely that we will ever be able to (or want to) randomly assign people to marriage partners in a controlled experiment, we will have to rely on correlational data and cautious inferences for a long while. Intervention research is, unfortunately, not always very informative about the relationship between process and outcome, because couples in experimental groups do not generally change in the ways we hope they will by naming the experimental treatments. So, in point of fact, many intervention studies are still correlational studies. Despite these ugly truths, intervention research is still our best current test of the correlational models in this book.

Until such tests are done, it is interesting to speculate about what these results suggest about how one may wish to ensure having a stable marriage.

All the analyses presented lead me to formulate the following five hypotheses about unstable marriages:

1. Marital outcomes form a cascade. Hence, we can describe a couple as on a cascade toward marital dissolution, or not.

2. There are a set of marital interaction processes, perceptions, and physiological variables that form the *core triad of balance*. These processes are related to the cascade toward marital dissolution. I theorized that this works as follows: when a critical threshold in a regulated variable in marital interaction (slope of the cumulative sum of positive and negative interaction) is reached, there is a flip in Q-space that leads to the interaction being perceived in one of two ways: (a) hurt, disappointment, and perceived attack, the "innocent victim" perception in which a person is in a stance of warding off perceived attack or (b) hurt, disappointment, and "righteous indignation," in which a person is in the mode of rehearsing retaliation. The Four Horsemen of the Apocalypse are more likely than other marital behaviors to be related to these flips in Q-space (that is, not all negativity is equal).

3. Occupation times in these negative perceptual states are related in a bidirectional manner to increases in diffuse physiological arousal and reactivity, and increased physiological linkage.

This increased diffuse physiological arousal makes it unlikely that the couple will be able to process information very well, will have access to new learning, and more likely that they will rely on previously over-learned tactics for escaping from aversive bodily states.

4. Occupation times in these negative perceptual states are also related to increases in *flooding*. Occupation times in a flooded state, and repeated flooding is, in turn, related to the increasing likelihood that negative attributions about the interaction become more stable, more global, more insulting to the partner.

5. Flooding is related to the *distance and isolation cascade*. As marital interaction becomes increasingly aversive, we will see increases in the belief that one's marital problems are severe, that it makes little sense to try to work them out with one's partner, an increased arrangement of their lives as parallel, and, for some people, increasing loneliness. Loneliness for men is a possible link between marital strife and physical illness. The distance and isolation cascade leads, eventually, to a recasting of the entire history of the marriage in negative terms. From the Oral History Interview we can see potentially powerful precursors of marital dissolution in such simple affective variables as the amount of disappointment both spouses feel about their marriage.

Let us consider the implications of each of these hypotheses in turn.

17.2.1. The Primacy of Negativity: A Balance Theory of Marriage

The one variable that was employed to create the low- and high-risk groups was a variable that presumably tapped the balance between negative and positive codes of the RCISS. It was unclear from this initial analysis which variable was doing the work of discrimination. It could have been negativity, it could been positivity, or it could been some balance between the two. It turned out that the variable that did the best job of discrimination was a balance between positive and negative codes; of course, this does not "prove" that the balance theory is correct, but this result is not inconsistent with balance theory. In fact, the best discrimination was obtained by a ratio of positive to negative codes. The ratio was about 5 for stable marriages, and it was less than 1 for unstable marriages. Of course, we saw in the replication study that one needs to be cautious about believing in the universality of such constants, but the results are nonetheless provocative.

17.2.1.1. Steps Toward an Ecology of Behavior

Hence, these data suggest a balance theory between positive and negative may be one thing that contributes to marital stability. As we have seen, one way to understand this relationship is to view behaviors as if they were species in a kind of *ecology of interaction*. In population ecology, the survival of various species is modeled by three possible equations: (a) predator–prey; (b) competition-for-similar-food sources; and (c) symbiosis. In the predator–prey equation, predator and prey need to strike a balance or various instabilities will result. For example, if the predator population grows too much, the prey population diminishes until predators start to die due to lack of food. In the competition-for-similar-food equation, again there are only certain accommodations that produce stability. The same is true for symbiosis. The two species that are symbiotic also need to be regulated in any given ecology to ultimately survive.

The balance theory of marriage suggests that behavior in a marriage may be viewed as an ecology, with each kind of behavior as a species. Any pair of behaviors may have predator–prey, competitive, or symbiotic relationships. In our initial attempts at applying a balance theory, the predator is negativity, and the prey is positivity. Relationships that are themselves unstable have a balance that favors the predator of negativity. Relationships that are stable have a balance that hugely favors the prey of positive affect.

How far this analogy goes is anyone's guess at this point. For example, one may ask the fascinating question: Is negativity necessary in a marriage? Surprisingly, the Gottman and Krokoff (1989) results suggest that it may very well be necessary. Much more needs to be learned about conflict engagement and the functions it serves, for example in the maintenance of intimacy. Conflict may have many prosocial functions in families. In some cases, conflict may represent genuine disagreement over issues and the exploration of this disagreement may be stimulating and enriching for both people. The resolution of such a conflict may take many years instead of the 15 minutes we use for studying conflict resolution. Or the resolution may never occur. It could be the case that the struggle and the discussion itself is very enriching. Such was the case in the famous discussions that Albert Einstein and Neils Bohr had about quantum mechanics; the discussion lasted years and has become one of the most interesting parts of the history of modern physics for the science watcher to read about.

Conflict may also emerge periodically in a relationship as a mechanism for coping with stresses that build up and have no relationship to the marriage. Nonetheless, the marriage may be the arena where stress is vented, where irritation is expressed, and perhaps even understood.

I find that the most appealing speculation about the functions of negativity is that it creates a dynamic rather than a static equilibrium around the marriage's set point. This dynamic equilibrium has the capacity for change, adaptation, and renewal. It may be the very mechanism through which love changes and stays alive in long-term marriages. Levenson, Carstenson, and I are currently studying long-term marriages of couples in their 40s and in their 60s so that we can better understand how they function and change with age.

17.2.2. The Four Horsemen of the Apocalypse: Complain/ Criticize, Contempt, Defensiveness, Stonewalling

Not all forms of negativity are equivalent. Some negative acts may be far more corrosive than others. This is true, in particular, for the four processes that I called the Four Horsemen of the Apocalypse. Of course, we cannot yet say whether these four variables act together in some kind of sequence. However, the evidence of the Guttman-like scaling of these variables for both the MICS and the RCISS suggests that there may be some kind of chain. In fact, in one analysis to predict divorce, when I compared three structural equation models, only the model in which contempt acted indirectly through defensiveness to predict divorce fit the data. So it appears logical and consistent with the data to hypothesize that there is a chained effect of some sort, with complain/criticize → contempt → defensiveness → stonewalling. The four horsemen probably are related to physiological arousal, which has implications for the quality of the marital interaction possible.

What is inherent in this cascade, and what is its organization? The expression of anger and disagreement have a characteristic that is quite distinct from criticism and contempt. In the former a husband might say: "I'm upset that you didn't balance the joint checkbook. The bank called today about two bounced checks, and I was very embarrassed." In the latter, the husband may, in effect, be saying two things. First there is the implication that this problem reflects stable and global negative attributes of the partner; in effect, the husband says: "You are the kind of person that would do this to me." There is only a slight escalation from complaint to criticism, but it is a critical escalation. It may, in fact, arise naturally from repeated and frustrated attempts to change things. At first the complaints are specific; eventually, they become global, more blaming, and more judgmental. This analysis fits well as a behavioral counterpart to attribution theories of marriage.

Second, there is the derision or insult, with the implied superiority of contempt. Nothing could be designed in marital interaction that so perfectly would fit into the jigsaw puzzle in which *defensiveness* is the next piece of the puzzle. We know that defensiveness is symmetrical; seemingly one person's defensiveness leads to another's. As criticism, contempt, and defensiveness continue, withdrawal seems like the logical result.

To continue this analysis of the Four Horsemen, let us discuss the last horseman, stonewalling. We know quite a lot about stonewalling. First, we know that it is peculiarly a male thing to do. In our 1983 sample, 85% of our stonewallers were male. This result also held in the replication study. Second, we know that it is associated with high levels of negativity in the interaction. Third, we know that it is related to physiological arousal of both husbands and wives. How does this work sequentially? We do not know at this point, but we know enough to speculate.

It is likely that the stonewalling we see in our laboratories translates at home to actual avoidance of interaction by the male. This is likely to be related to the couple's inability to regulate physiological arousal in a discussion of problems. Hence, it is reasonable to expect that, in an ailing marriage, the male's inability to soothe himself, and the inability of the couple to soothe one another are important components of this pattern. A discussion of soothing brings us toward the physiological aspects of the research. This suggests that marital therapy cannot be symmetric with respect to gender!

17.2.3. Physiological Linkage and Physiological Arousal (Both Acute and Chronic)

Even though the data suggest that physiological arousal is the shakiest part of the theory, I believe that over time we will find that this is not the case. There are great limitations in the way I have analyzed my data to date, averaging physiological responses over time. I expect that there will be quite a bit more power in the physiological data once we go within an interaction. At any event, the inclusion of physiological variables adds something that will be useful theoretically.

Hence, let us take a little time to review some physiology. The reason I think this is important is that I will recommend as a new marital therapy agenda some kind of *couples' biofeedback*. What exactly do I mean when I am talking about physiological linkage and physiological arousal? Physiological linkage simply means that person A's physiological responses are predictable from person B's, and the prediction is even better than would be obtained by prediction from person A's past physiology. In other words, there is probably a causal effect of person B's physiology on person A. How is this possible? Well, it is clearly mediated by behavior. Physiological linkage is the physiological counterpart of cycles of negativity in behavior, or what has been called "negative affect reciprocity" (Gottman, 1979).

17.2.3.1. Negative Affect Reciprocity and the Core Triad of Balance

Negative affect reciprocity is very important because negativity becomes what has been technically named an "absorbing state." As I discussed in chapter 3, an absorbing state is one that is difficult to exit once it is entered. The existence of an absorbing state of negativity can have profound implications. The reason is that what an absorbing state implies is that the usual social processes that are present during conflict, some of which elaborate the conflict and processes that repair the interaction (such as metacommunication), do not work in ailing marriages. These processes include feeling probes that explore feelings, information exchange, social comparison, humor, distraction, gossip, finding areas of common ground, and appeals to basic philosophy and expectations in the marriage. Instead, what predominates in dissatisfied couples' use of these social processes is the negative affect.

Why is negative affect reciprocity so destructive? What goes hand in glove is *a constriction of other social processes* and the greater reciprocity of negative affect in dissatisfied couples than in satisfied couples. This means that sequential analyses of the stream of behavior reveal that if one spouse expresses negative affect, the other spouse is more likely to respond with negative affect in a dissatisfied marriage than in a satisfied one. However, the constriction of available social processes is the fascinating structural dynamic that leads to the absorbing state. What happens is that a message has two parts, one positive and one negative. For example, the message "Stop interrupting me!" is an attempt to repair the interaction, but it may have been said with some irritation. In a happy marriage, there is a greater probability that the listener will focus on the repair component of the message and respond by saying, "Sorry, what were you saying?" On the other hand, in an unhappy marriage, there is a greater probability that the listener will respond to the irritation in the message and say something like, "I wouldn't have to interrupt, if I could get a word in edgewise." In this case the attempted repair mechanism doesn't work. Negativity being an absorbing state means that all these social processes have less of a chance of working because what people attend to and respond to is the negativity.

The flip side of this coin is that many couples have a repertoire of repair tactics that can improve their marriages, but they do not have access to these repair mechanisms because negative affect has become an absorbing state. The prescription is to *drive a wedge* into the sequential bond of negativity, and thereby free up the repair mechanisms that the couple has in the repertoire.

How can one drive this wedge? I propose that this may be accomplished by a *minimal marital therapy*. Before I outline this minimal marital therapy, I briefly review marital therapy at this juncture. I limit myself to marital therapies that have been scientifically studied.

17.2.7. Marital Therapy: A Selected Recent History

In the 1960s and 1970s a number of books and papers began appearing that sought to revolutionize marital therapy. In hindsight it is clear that these books and papers were inspired by three distinct scholarly traditions: general systems theory, which had emerged in the mid-1950s (Bateson et al., 1956; Lederer & Jackson, 1968); behavior therapy, which began focusing on families during the 1960s (Patterson, 1982; Weiss et al., 1973); and behavior exchange theory (Thibaut & Kelley, 1959). The general systems theory approach emphasized interpersonal communication, and suggested that systems of interaction within relationships

should be the unit of analysis. At that time, behavior therapy emphasized negative reinforcement (coercion) and positive reinforcement,
social learning, and pinpointing changes that needed to be made in
behavior. Behavior exchange theory proposed a reward/cost, or "payoff" matrix that described the actual rewards and costs of behaviors
exchanged between people. Gottman et al. (1976) later interpreted these
rewards and costs to be perceived rewards and costs, and constructed a
talk table for marital interaction, which permitted couples to rate the
intent and impact of behaviors sent and received.

Implicit in these therapy approaches to ailing marriages is a theory of
what has gone wrong in these marriages, and what marriages need for
things to go right. I refer to each of these implicit theories as a *task
analysis of marriage*. This term refers to the tasks that need to be
competently accomplished (and the component skills that are part of
this competence) to make a marriage run successfully. We review a
number of influential therapy approaches and summarize their task
analyses of marriage. We then review outcome research on marital
therapy and suggest that most therapies have steadily increased the
complexity of their task analysis as they have encountered limitations in
therapy outcome results.

Behavioral approaches to marital therapy began being invented and
applied in the early 1970s (e.g., Azrin, Naster, & Jones, 1973; Weiss et
al., 1973). Whether behavioral approaches will eventually prove right or
wrong remains to be seen. However, a major contribution of the
behavioral approach to marital therapy was its empirical epistemology.
Before the early 1970s, the epistemology of marital therapy was the same
as it is for all nonempirically based intervention methods, an epistemology based on clinical folklore, mutual support, accreditation stan-
dards, reputation, clinical case presentations, and other ad hominums.
This is not meant to be pejorative; often many good ideas emerge from
this tradition, but there is, unfortunately, no way of sifting the wheat
from the chaff without hard, objective criteria and the replicability
criterion that scientific method brings with it.

The earliest paper in the behavioral tradition was one on contingency
contracting in couples (Azrin et al., 1973). Here the assumption was that
there was a deficit in ailing marriages, and that deficit was an inability to
work out mutually satisfying reciprocal agreements, or implicit "contracts." The therapy and the outcome criterion were one and the same
thing. The therapist helped the couple work out a contract, and then the
therapy was successfully concluded.

17.2.7.1. Lederer and Jackson

Where did this assumption come from? Clearly, it had little to do with
behavioral principles, nor did it have anything to do with empirical

research. Instead, it followed very quickly on the heels of a popular book by Lederer and Jackson (1968) called *Mirages of Marriage*. In that book Lederer and Jackson talked about the quid pro quo (literally "something for something") behavior exchange view (Thibaut & Kelley, 1959) as the fundamental problem that needed to be rectified in ailing marriages. The method of therapy recommended was something akin to reciprocal contingency contracting. The other assumption of this early work on contingency contracting was that the therapist's role was that of a teacher, or perhaps a coach in assisting the couple to acquire the appropriate social skills to be able to form a contract.

17.2.7.1.1. The Roles of Love and Trust: Lederer and Jackson

Lederer and Jackson's book, *Mirages of Marriage*, was an important historical landmark in marital therapy. It began by listing seven "false assumptions" about marriage. First, their false assumptions involved a debunking of the role of love in marriage, particularly romantic love. Their first false assumption was "That people marry because they love each other" (p. 41). Instead, they suggested that "during courtship individuals lose most of their judgment" (p. 42), that they often marry because society expects it, that there are other forces that impel people to marry, all of which have nothing to do with romantic love (parental pressure, romantic fantasies, social hysteria, loneliness, fear for their economic future, and other neurotic reasons). Their second false assumption was that most married people love each other; instead, they cynically suggested that married people " . . . usually are not aware they are murdering their marriage and mangling their partners under the guise of love." Their third false assumption was that "Love is necessary for a satisfactory marriage." What they meant was that romantic love, or continually being "in love," which they described as "essentially selfish," is neither necessary nor good in a marriage.

This apparently cynical view of the role of romantic love was counteracted by their discussion of trust in marriage. They wrote, "Those couples who enjoy trust, who give trust to each other, probably are among the most fortunate people alive" (p. 109). By trust they meant a reciprocal giving, coupled with honest and clear communication. They wrote:

> The practice of honesty and clear communication in marriage is likely to result in an extra dividend, for it encourages spouses to be generous, comforting, and consoling. . . . Tolerance and generosity in relation to others' mistakes become easier when one learns that others can be generous in return. . . . We are able to give to people we trust because we

have received from them and know that we will again; thus trust and generosity are both causes and results of a genuine give-and-take, or in our terms, quid pro quo. (p. 109)

The reader may also find it interesting to read the chapters on "how to drive your spouse crazy." In these chapters they describe destructive interaction patterns they have observed in therapy and ways to counteract these patterns.

Lederer and Jackson noted that, to have a successful marriage, one must choose well, and they suggested choosing someone with whom one has a lot in common. Presumably, the idea is that therapy cannot be very effective when a couple is mismatched. Once one has chosen reasonably well, they suggest that handling disagreements within a climate of respect and tolerance are the only other necessary ingredients of a successful marriage. In a short chapter titled "The Major Elements of a Satisfactory Marriage," they list three necessary ingredients. First is respect; they wrote "each spouse finds some important quality or ability to respect in the other . . ." (p. 198). Second, partners should be tolerant of each other. Third, "the key ingredient in a successful marriage is the effort of the spouses to make the most of its assets and minimize its liabilities" (p. 198). In their view, this process is accomplished by "learning to communicate in order to negotiate quid pro quo's" (p. 199).

Lederer and Jackson also discussed differences in affiliative versus independent preferences, and the need to find a match for the level of desired intimacy in the relationship. They avoided discussing possible gender differences in these preferences, and, in fact, their fourth false assumption was that "there are inherent behavioral and attitudinal differences between female and male, and that these differences cause most marital troubles" (p. 60). They denied that these "vast" gender differences exist, they claimed that the differences that do exist are small and arbitrary, vary greatly with culture, and, hence, are modifiable by the appropriate choice of sex roles.

To summarize, Lederer and Jackson emphasized the skill of being able to negotiate quid pro quos within a climate of respect and tolerance. They also suggest that the basis of trust is the expectation that, if you give to your partner, you will also receive.

17.2.7.2. Azrin, Naster, and Jones (1973)

Perhaps there is a Zeitgeist for new ideas, but the behavior therapy techniques of reciprocal contracting seem remarkably like Lederer and Jackson's recommendations. Thus, the Lederer and Jackson quid pro quo notion was either independently discovered or adopted whole heartedly as a therapy technique by Azrin et al. (1973). What was interesting about the Azrin et al. paper was the implicit, perhaps logically circular, suggestion that the reciprocal contract was both the treatment method and the outcome measure of the treatment. In their view all treatments in which the techniques was applied were, by definition, successful. Thus, we can see that Lederer and Jackson's task analysis of the necessary ingredients for a successful marriage had been accepted by behavioral therapy without an empirical test.

17.2.7.3. Weiss, Hops, and Patterson (1973)

This remarkably creative paper, which appeared in a set of conference proceedings published in 1973 (Weiss et al., 1973), presented a more complex set of outcomes than did Azrin et al. as tests of the effectiveness of the marital therapy, change in marital satisfaction (self-reported by the Locke–Wallace, 1959), and interaction behavior as measured by the new Marital Interaction Coding System (MICS). The "technology" they proposed for altering marriages was somewhat more complicated than negotiating a reciprocal exchange agreement. Social skills began being introduced into the behavioral picture.

They were also quite explicit about their task analysis. They wrote:

> Oversimplifying, three main areas are of concern in a behavioral approach to marital dyads: (a) the partners exchange affectional behaviors, (b) they problem solve over a wide range of specifics including the division of resources, and (c) they engage in behavior-change attempts toward one another. At any given time, one or more of these dimensions may be salient so that a total rehabilitation program would necessarily provide training in skills germane to all dimensions. (p. 310)

Thus, this paper expanded the Lederer and Jackson task analysis. First, the negotiation skills beyond the quid pro quo were required to include problem solving, in general. Second, explicit mention was made that the partners must exchange affectional behaviors. Third, spouses must be skillful at changing one another's behavior in a direction desired by each. Toward the latter end, the Spouse Observation Checklist (SOC; and later the Areas of Change questionnaire) was designed as both an assessment device and part of the therapy procedure.

17.2.7.4. Jacobson and Margolin (1979)

Perhaps the most sophisticated and complex task analysis of marriage proposed to date was Jacobson and Margolin's "behavioral-exchange model of relationship discord." Unlike their predecessors, Jacobson and

Margolin's model is based on their thorough and thoughtful review of the research literature. They list the ingredients they suggest for a task analysis of marriage.

First, they discussed the requirement of a rich climate of positive reinforcement; this included being able to handle "reinforcement erosion," in which, inevitably, the attractiveness of reinforcers diminishes over time in a marriage.

Second, they noted that reciprocal positive exchange is no more characteristic of distressed than nondistressed couples. They reviewed the Gottman et al. (1976) "bank account model," in which couples invest in a relationship:

> . . . which over time balance each other and thereby maintain the current rate of rewarding exchange. This aspect of reciprocity says nothing about any given interchange between a couple, nor does it preclude nonreciprocal exchanges at any given point in time. . . . Gottman's "bank account" model also explains this discrepancy between distressed and nondistressed couples. When the ratio of rewards to punishments in a relationship is low, as is the case with distressed couples, one is more apt to "balance the checkbook" regularly, to keep scorey. . . . It does appear that, in general, distressed couples are relatively dependent on immediate, as opposed to delayed, rewards and punishments (Jacobson, 1978e). Since happily married couples are accustomed to receiving a consistent, high rate of rewards from one another, nonreinforced behavior or nonequitable exchanges can be tolerated in the short run, since their shared reinforcement history offers promise of long-term equality and continued rewards. Perhaps this freedom from control by a partner's immediate consequences is an operational definition of "trust" (Jacobson, 1978e). (p. 16)

Here, once again, we have the notion of trust in a task analysis of marriage, but it seems to be quite the opposite definition that Lederer and Jackson proposed. The situation Jacobson and Margolin proposed to be the basis of trust is the *absence of contingency* or quid pro quo rather than its presence.

They noted that reciprocal *negative exchanges* are characteristic of distressed relationships, reciprocation far in excess of the higher base rates of negativity in distressed couples. However, this correct summary of the research literature does not seem to have led to any element of their task analysis.

Third, they reviewed contributions from social exchange theory, and suggested a modification. They wrote:

> It would be vastly oversimplified to suggest that each behavior in the repertoire of marital patterns is maintained by specific reinforcing stimuli

from the spouse on a point-for-point basis. Rather, it seems more realistic to posit a summation process such that classes of positive relationship behavior are maintained by a number of partner-initiated behaviors which are experientially summated by the receiver and integrated into an overall experience of the partner's behavior [pp. 18–19, italics added]. . . . The important point is that couples act in their marital environment to summarize and integrate the information provided by the partner, and that this cognitive processing affects the participant's subsequent responding, as well as his [or her] current evaluation of the quality of the marriage. (p. 20)

Fourth, they noted, as did Lederer and Jackson, that conflict is inevitable in a relationship, and, hence, the ability to manage that conflict is critical. They also noted (consistent with Weiss et al.) that the ability to change one's partner in a positive manner is also critical. They singled out coercive processes of influence as dysfunctional.

Fifth, they noted that all couples develop normative structures or "rules," which must be modified as necessary. They pointed out that some couples appear to have "lacunae" in their normative structure, and perhaps an inability to modify rules as new situational demands arise that challenge the old rules.

Sixth, they noted, under a category they called "skill deficits," a long list of skills:

Spouses need to be able to express their feelings, both positive and negative. They need to provide support and understanding to one another (Weiss, 1978). In the sexual realm, they need skills to maintain a viable sex life, particularly after the initial novelty has ended. Various instrumental skills are also necessary, including childrearing, household and financial management, and the like. (p. 26)

Later, they included the management of environmental stress as part of these skills.

Consistent with Lederer and Jackson, they discussed differences in affiliative versus independent preferences, and the need to find a match for the level of desired intimacy in the relationship.

17.2.7.5. Emotionally Focused Marital Therapy: Greenberg and Johnson (1988)

Greenberg and Johnson described a new approach to marital therapy called emotionally focused therapy (EFT). They noted that other approaches to marital therapy give a secondary role to emotion, emphasizing instead rational aspects of behavior such as the techniques the couples would use to negotiate agreements. They argued that what was needed in couples therapy was a direct approach to the emotions that were basic to the conflicts the distressed couple was experiencing.

They described two basic dysfunctional patterns of marital interaction (and their "variants"): the pursuer–distancer pattern (variants include mutual attack and mutual withdrawal) and the dominance–submission pattern (variants include mutual helplessness and mutual competitiveness).

Toward the end of their book they described a complex process of observational coding and couples reviewing their own tapes for the construction of a task analysis of successful conflict resolution. This is a summary description of what couples who successfully complete EFT do during conflict resolution. They described four stages:

> In the initial stage of the task, the partners are in conflict. The pursuer is engaged in blaming behavior and the withdrawer is either avoiding, protesting, or appeasing. The second component begins when either one of the partners openly discloses his or her feelings or needs, and the other partner responds with understanding, comforting, or helping behavior. One of the unexpected patterns that emerged, quite different from the hypothesized performance, was the third component, in which the pursuer temporarily reverted to blaming behavior, while the withdrawer did not revert to protesting or defending behavior but continued to affirm or understand the other partner. In each resolution event, the pursuers appeared to "test" their partners to see if their new, more understanding, behavior was genuine. If their partners held to their positive behavior, the couple proceeded to the next stage of resolution. In the fourth component, both partners trustingly disclosed feelings or needs while responding with empathic and affirming, protecting, or comforting behaviors. These four patterns were labeled escalation, deescalation, testing, and mutual openness. (p. 218)

The turning point about admitting vulnerability is considered to be quite important by these authors. To accomplish this pattern of competent conflict resolution, the designers of EFT use a variety of techniques, and they claim that some of the techniques are inspired by Gestalt therapy, and some by client-centered therapy. The therapy combines interpersonal and intrapsychic perspectives. They encourage the exploration and expression of feelings and empathic responses. They wrote:

> Major changes in interactional sequences can be brought about by reframing a negative interactional cycle in terms of the unexpressed aspect of the person's feeling and restructuring the interaction based on the need or motivation amplified by the emotional experience. A "pursue-distance"

interaction can therefore be reframed in terms of the pursuer's underlying caring or fear of isolation and the distancer's fear or unexpressed resentment. (p. 45)

They view emotions as basic to concepts of the marriage and self:

> Affect is very important in changing attitudes because affectively laden internal information appears to be closely linked to people's self-schemata and tends to override other cues and dominate the formation of meaning. (p. 46)

They believe that state-dependent learning suggests that it is essential to recreate the important emotions in therapy:

> Certain core cognitions, cognitive-affective sequences, and complex meanings learned originally in particular affective states are much more accessible when that state is revived. Accessing these "hot cognitions" (Greenberg & Safran, 1984, 1987) can be particularly important in clarifying couples' interactions because key construals that induce certain behaviors in the interaction are often not readily available when the problem is being discussed coolly, after the fact, in therapy. Helping couples re-create the situation and relive the emotions in therapy often makes the cognitions governing these behaviors more available for inspection, clarification, and modification. (p. 47)

Greenberg and Johnson described EFT as having nine steps:

1. delineate the conflict issues;
2. identify the negative interaction cycle;
3. access unacknowledged feelings underlying interactional positions;
4. redefine the problems in terms of underlying feelings;
5. promote identification with disowned needs and aspects of self;
6. promote acceptance by each partner of the other's experience;
7. facilitate the expression of needs and wants to restructure the interaction;
8. establish the emergence of new solutions; and
9. consolidate new positions.

17.2.8. Evaluation of Couples Therapy Programs to Date: Brief Review

As marital therapy based on a behavioral approach progressed, components were added to the original quid pro quo. As I have noted, implicit in this approach was the construction of a task analysis of successfully functioning marriages.

There have been a number of important reviews of the marital therapy literature to date (e.g., Baucom & Hoffman, 1986; Hahlweg & Markman, 1983; Jacobson & Addis, 1993). I summarize their major conclusions here. Baucom and Hoffman noted that the skills usually taught by behavioral marital therapy (BMT) are: (a) communication and problem solving, and (b) behavior change using contracts (e.g., based on the quid pro quo). They distinguished these communication skills as problem solving in nature, as opposed to communication skill programs oriented toward the expression of emotions and listening skills. Baucom and Hoffman concluded that: (a) couples receiving BMT (compared to a waiting list control group) improve significantly in negative communication, and self-reports of problems (Jacobson's program was the only one to report improvements in positive communication); (b) BMT is superior to nonspecific and attention control groups; (c) there are not major differences in the effectiveness of two components of BMT, nor in their order of administration. However, there is some evidence, reported by Jacobson et al. (1985, 1987), that the communication/problem-solving (CO) training was superior to the behavior exchange (contracting) (BE) condition. Upon 2-year follow-up, couples in the CO condition were most likely to be happily married and least likely to be separated or divorced. They also noted that, although statistically significant changes were obtained by BMT compared to a waiting list (and other) control groups, "60–65% of the couples either remained somewhat distressed or failed to change during treatment" (p. 605).

In a more recent review, Jacobson and Addis (1993) reached similar conclusions to those of Baucom and Hoffman (1986). They estimated that about 50% of couples cannot be considered successes. They are considerably more pessimistic than Baucom and Hoffman about the long-term effectiveness of BMT. They wrote:

> Little is known about these long-term effects, because very few studies followed their couples beyond a few months after treatment termination. The BMT literature *has* produced evidence regarding the course of relationship functioning following termination. One two-year follow-up found that about 30% of those couples who recovered during the course of therapy had relapsed (Jacobson, Schmaling, & Holtzworth-Munroe, 1987). In another study, a four-year follow-up revealed a 38% divorce rate, based on the entire sample of couples who received treatment (Snyder et al., 1991). (p. 7, ms.)

"Horse race studies" are those that compare "schools" of marital therapy. Jacobson and Addis concluded that very little has been learned from horse race studies, and that there is an effect (also noted by Baucom and Hoffman) that the relative outcome is strongly a function of the school to which the authors adhere. There are also problems in the purity of the treatments, particularly the least favored treatment. Jacobson and Addis noted that therapy manuals at times will take out of the least favored treatment those ingredients that proponents of that school think are the active ingredients of that form of therapy. They also pointed out that the first study with a new method obtains the largest results, and that there is a gradual decline of effectiveness upon replication.

Let us consider the two interesting findings of all this research. First, treatment gains are not generally maintained over time. Second, it doesn't seem to matter very much what one does in treatment; in general, the effect sizes are roughly the same, regardless of the exact nature of the intervention. This latter fact is remarkable in "dismantling" studies that are done within a school of thought (they have been done only in BMT). Rather than having identified an "active ingredient" of BMT, they suggest that any of the parts equals the whole. If this remarkable conclusion were true, it would suggest that a minimal marital therapy program may have equal success to a larger program. I now speculate about conditions under which a minimal marital therapy program might be more effective than the total program.

17.2.8.1. Divorce Prevention

We need to remember that not all couples should remain married, and that helping a couple to decide to divorce is a perfectly valid function of marital therapy. Interestingly, in our follow-ups we ask couples if they have had marital therapy and we find that the correlation between therapy and divorce is consistently about 0.50 across studies. This is probably true because for many couples therapy is a way to break up. There is nothing wrong with this if it is true. Therapists may be able to help a couple understand what went wrong with the marriage and assess whether it is possible to change the marriage and if they want to change it. Therapists may be able to help a couple deal with their anger, fear, and hurt, and they may be able to help with the many problems that will arise if there are children and co-parenting remains as an issue that binds the partners to one another even after divorce. The therapist may be able to help people through the usually difficult and stressful transition of divorce and help them in rebuilding their lives. These and many other possibilities exist for ways in which therapy can be helpful to people in the divorce process.

However, what if the couple and the therapist all decide to try to change the marriage and make it work as a stable adaptation? What do we know? Unfortunately, our results are quite premature with regard to our knowledge of how well our intervention programs function in preventing marital dissolution. Definitive research still needs to be conducted. However, the results to date are really quite encouraging. Gottman (1979, p. 271) reported the results of a small-N study in which the 2-year divorce rate in the control group was 50%, but it was 0% in the experimental group. Subjects in the experimental group received training by paraprofessional staff (they were not trained as therapists) who used only *A Couple's Guide to Communication* (Gottman et al., 1976).

Jacobson, Schmaling, and Holtzworth-Munroe (1987) reported the 2-year follow-up results of behavioral marital therapy. There were three treatment groups, behavior exchange (BE), communication problem solving (CPT), and the complete treatment (CO). After 2 years, the percentages of couples who separated or divorced were 55% in the BE treatment, 36% in the CPT treatment, and 9% in the complete treatment. Despite the small Ns, the CO couples were reported as significantly less likely to have separated or divorced than either BE or CPT couples ($p < .05$). They wrote: "Thus, there was much to indicate that treatment gains in the CO condition were holding up relatively well. In contrast, there was little indication of enduring changes in the two component treatment conditions" (p. 192). Hence, this is some evidence that a detailed and complete treatment of the kind spelled out in Jacobson's program or in the *Couple's Guide* may be helpful, in the short run, in preventing marital dissolution.

Markman et al. (1988) presented the 1 1/2-year and 3-year results of his Premarital Relationship Enhancement Program (PREP). Each of five sessions lasted approximately 3 hours. They wrote: "Each session was devoted to one or two major content areas, and homework assignments were completed between sessions that required couples to practice skills, read chapters, and complete exercises in *A Couple's Guide to Communication* (Gottman, Notarius, Gonso, & Markman, 1976)" (p. 212).

For purposes of analysis of the effects of the intervention on relationship stability, they combined those who were married or planning marriage into the stable group and those who were broken up before marriage or divorced or separated into the unstable group. Their results on relationship stability were as follows:

At Follow-up 1, results showed that no couple from the intervention group had dissolved their relationship, whereas 4 couples from the control group (19%) had done so. At Follow-up 2, 1 couple from the intervention group (5%) and 5 couples from the control group (24%) had dissolved their relationships. Chi-square tests indicated that the dissolution rate of intervention couples was lower than that of control couples at both Follow-up 1, chi-square (1, $N = 42$) = 10.4, $p < .001$, and Follow-up 2, chi-square (1, $N = 42$) = 6.8, $p < .01$. (p. 213)

We must be cautious about these results because they have considered couples who dissolved their relationships before marriage equivalent to couples who separated or divorced after marriage.

However, there is some evidence of continuity. Filsinger and Thoma (1988) conducted a 5-year longitudinal study of relationship stability and adjustment in 21 premarital couples. Marital instability was predicted from Time 1 interaction patterns of negative reciprocity. Eight couples out of 21 dissolved their relationships in the 5-year period (38.1%). Most couples who broke up did so at 1½ years. Filsinger and Thoma used the Bakeman lag sequential z-score analysis procedure to examine sequential dependencies. At 1½ years, the unstable couples were characterized by higher Time 1 negative reciprocity [$F(1,27) = 5.17$, $p < .05$] and higher Time 1 positive reciprocity [$F(1,27) = 5.78$, $p < .05$]. At 2½ and 5 years, the two groups differed only on Time 1 positive reciprocity [$F (1,24) = 4.63$, $p < .05$, and $F(1,19) = 4.58$, $p < .05$, respectively]. The finding that the unstable relationships were higher on Time 1 *positive* reciprocity is consistent with results reported by Gottman (1979). Gottman had suggested that both higher positive and negative reciprocity will characterize distressed relationships and that there is simply greater linkage and rigidity of interaction patterns in less happy relationships. Hence, this is some evidence of continuity. However, in an exploratory analysis, Filsinger and Thoma also found evidence that a higher Time 1 rate of the female's interruptions was predictive of instability as well as a higher rate of change toward instability. These results on interruptions have not been obtained in the marriage literature. Hence, it is unclear whether one can consider premarital dissolutions in the same category as marital dissolutions.

There were problems with the Markman experimental design because couples were able to refuse treatment. This resulted in a nonrandom subject selection effect in the experimental group; also it resulted in relatively low power to detect treatment effects. We must be cautious about these results because they have considered couples who dissolved their relationships before marriage equivalent to couples who separated or divorced after marriage. However, there is some evidence of continuity. A more recent paper (Markman, Renick, Floyd, Stanley, & Clements, 1993) reported the results of a 4- and a 5-year follow-up. In these analyses, separations and divorces that occurred only after marriage were examined. At the 5-year follow-up, two experimental couples (8.3%) had separated or divorced, whereas five control couples (16.1%)

had separated or divorced; these differences were not statistically significant, but there is very low power to detect differences of this magnitude with such small sample sizes. The results are in the right direction—couples in the control group separated or divorced at nearly twice the rate of the couples in the experimental group.

Nonetheless, the Markman results are encouraging. Taken together with the results of the *Couple's Guide* reported in Gottman (1979) and the Jacobson, Schmaling, and Holtzworth-Munroe (1987) study, the results suggest that it may indeed be possible to prevent marital dissolution by changing marital interaction patterns.

McCrady, Stout, Noel, Abrams, and Nelson (1991) treated 45 alcoholics and their spouses in one of three conditions, one of which was alcohol-focused spouse involvement plus behavioral marital therapy (reciprocity enhancement plus problem-solving skills training). The percent separations in this group were 11.1%, compared to 36.45% and 28.6% in the other two groups (which had no marital therapy); the authors also noted that the separations in the combined group were "quite short" (p. 1420).

Part of the problem in stating both the couple's divorce and the couple's stability as two possible successful outcomes of marital therapy is that it *defines* marital therapy as always successful. What is needed is an evaluation of the effectiveness of therapy as a function of the goals of the treatment. If divorce is the desired outcome, how effective was the therapy at reducing the problems that are usually entailed by this transition, compared to a control group for whom this was also the goal, but who did not receive the treatment? If a stable and satisfying marriage is the desired outcome, how effective was the therapy at changing the marriage and keeping the couple together compared to a control group for whom this was also the goal, but who did not receive the treatment? There is a clear need for primary and secondary intervention research in this area.

17.2.9. An Alternative Marital Therapy: "Minimal Marital Therapy"

I explore one reason why the outcome results I reviewed for the marital therapies may have been obtained, and suggest an alternative model of marital therapy. I offer this alternative with humility because I have no empirical data to support the suggestions. However, I hope to back up the speculations. The problem of divorce is so important that speculation about the most effective approach to the problem is to be encouraged.

One way to interpret the outcome results of marital therapy studies is that treatment effect sizes are relatively constant across schools of therapy, and that within schools, it makes very little difference which components are employed. Because it is well known that marital therapy is aversive (particularly for men), unlike some forms of individual therapy, creating a minimal therapy may have some advantages, and at no cost of effectiveness.

Thus, I suggest that a minimal marital therapy be created. Second, I suggest that the major reason for the lack of maintenance of effects over time may be that people do not have access to the learnings of therapy once they become physiologically aroused. Hence, I propose a soothing component to the therapy, and, second, that the minimal skills be overlearned. The basic suggestion I make here is based on the diffuse psychological arousal (DPA; acute and chronic) and physiological reactivity concepts.

17.2.9.1. Rationale for the Soothing Component for Minimal Marital Therapy

I noted earlier that Greenberg and Johnson (1988) stated that: (a) emotions are basic to people's core concepts of the marriage and the self; and (b) state-dependent learning suggests that it is essential to recreate the important emotions in therapy, " . . . because key construals that induce certain behaviors in the interaction are often not readily available when the problem is being discussed coolly, after the fact, in therapy" (p. 47). Gottman (1990) suggested similar ideas and then also related them to a concept he called diffuse physiological arousal.

17.2.9.1.1. Diffuse Physiological Arousal (DPA)

DPA simply means that more than one physiological system is activated to a significant degree above baseline levels (e.g., heart rate and blood velocity). It is well known in physiology that, as a negative stimulus becomes more intense and more aversive, more and more physiological systems become activated (e.g., see Rowell, 1986). Thus, at first heart rate will increase due to vagal restraint, and then the sympathetic will become activated to bring the heart rate to higher levels. Blood flow to the gut and kidneys will drop dramatically. Then the adrenal will begin secreting epinephrine and heart rate and myocardial contractility will increase. Then the kidneys will begin secreting renin, the renin-angiotensin system will become engaged, and blood pressure will rise. In most instances of normal functioning these systems function independently, and are fairly uncorrelated. However, the body is capable of the defense response and other responses to emergency (such as the alarm response) in which different systems operate in concert.

Gottman (1990) suggested that diffuse physiological arousal may accompany many heated marital conflict discussions. He suggested that this physiological state could be created by multiple negative emotions in close temporal sequence, by constrained emotions, and by negative emotion blends. He also suggested that DPA is a highly unpleasant and aversive subjective bodily state.

17.2.9.1.2. Implications of DPA for Social Interaction

Gottman (1990) also suggested that: (a) DPA reduces the ability to process information; (b) DPA makes overlearned behaviors and cognitions more likely than newly acquired behaviors and cognitions. If this hypothesis were true, it would explain why it was difficult for marital therapy clients to have access to new learnings during times of heated controversy that resulted in DPA; (c) DPA increases the likelihood of the same behaviors that are engaged during fight or flight, that is, withdrawal and aggression. This would make sense as having been the result of past emotional conditioning; it states that, in effect, emotions that result in DPA become linked to the primitive fight or flight response; (d) Sex differences may exist in recovery time from DPA: Males take longer than females. There are clear cut implications of this hypothesis, which are spelled out in Gottman and Levenson (1988). These are that males will be more likely than females to manage the level of negative affect in marital interaction and to take steps to keep it from escalating. In particular, males are more likely than females to inhibit the expression of emotion, to appeal to rationality and compromise (see Raush, Barry, Hertel, & Swain, 1974), and more likely than females to withdraw or aggress.

17.2.9.1.3. Automatic Versus Effortful Processing

17.2.9.1.3.1. Emotionality, anxiety, arousal, and performance. Probably the most famous hypothesis in psychology is the Yerkes–Dodson law (1908), the well-known inverted-U shaped function between arousal and performance. There have been many methodological critiques of this law, including the difficulty of defining arousal in a unidimensional way, and the difficulty of disproving the hypothesis. Kahneman (1973) showed that, in general, physiological arousal increases with task difficulty. There is no evidence of a decline in task performance that follows this increased arousal. A review of the literature by Eysenck (1982) concluded that there is more evidence favoring the law when the increased arousal has been produced by aversive stimulation than by incentives (p. 48).

Kahneman et al. (1969) suggested that the greater the processing demands, the larger are the physiological effects. A series of digits presented to the subject had to be transformed by adding 0, 1, or 3, after a 2-second pause. Three physiological measures (pupil diameter, heart rate, and skin conductance) all showed increases during the input and processing of the information, followed by a decrease. Pupil diameter grew steadily as task load (the number of serially presented digits) and task complexity (add 0, 1, or 3) increased. (See also Kahneman, 1973, for a review.)

17.2.9.1.3.2. Effortful processing, perceived control, and hypervigilance. Flooding will lead to the hypervigilance (and its concomitant distortions of reality and nondisconfirmable hypothesis of negativity). Hypervigilance is a state of wariness that comes from perceived control. Obrist (1981) has shown that even the *illusion* of control over aversive stimuli is adequate to create increases in heart rate and contractility. Actual control is sufficient but not necessary. Contractility of the heart is primarily under sympathetic nervous system influence. Thus, actual control or the illusion of control over aversive stimulation is probably adequate to produce diffuse physiological arousal. We continue to encounter this notion that the avoidance of aversive stimuli is responsible for disruption of attentional processes as well as being related to the sympathetic nervous system acceleration.

What do these results suggest about the efficacy of a minimal marital therapy program? They suggest that during marital conflict, vigilance and complex information processing should be kept to a minimum. Obrist's results also suggest that the sense of control that is usually part of vigilance will be adequate to create DPA, and, thus, perhaps somewhat paradoxically, subjects should enter a conflict discussion with a low sense of control. We say that this is paradoxical because therapy is usually thought of as providing people with a sense of control that comes with increased competence. The distinction between increased competence and lowered control and vigilance can be clarified somewhat by discussing effortful versus automatic information processing.

17.2.9.1.3.3. Information processing.   Posner (Posner & Snyder, 1975a, 1975b) suggested that there are two kinds of information processing: automatic processes and those requiring conscious attention. Automatic processes involve parallel processing, whereas conscious processes involve serial processing. Research then began on the processing of information without awareness. In such priming experiments (see

Eysenck's, 1982, citation of Marcel) it was discovered that a priming effect could take place without awareness even at a high level of semantic meaning. Conscious performance was impaired somewhat when unexpected events occurred, but nowhere near as completely disrupted as when unexpected expectations were applied to automatic processes.

Schneider and Shiffrin (1977) suggested a similar distinction between automatic and controlled processes. They used a different paradigm in which a small set of items are memorized and the subject has to find matches and mismatches in a set of serially presented items. Controlled processes are a linear function of the number of items in the memory set and involve serial comparisons, with each one occurring at the rate of 40ms. Automatic processes were not hindered by capacity limitations on short-term memory and do not require attention. They found that controlled processes are slower but far more adaptable than automatic processes.

Triesman and Gelade (1980) modified this theory by suggesting that objects that are perceived and attended to have features. If the subject is asked to attend to a conjunction of two features (A and B), then the processing is controlled, or serial. When there is no conjunction, the processing is parallel and automatic. They found that even extensive practice with detection of a combination of features did not result in automatic processing.

What do these results suggest for the possible efficacy of a minimal marital therapy? They suggest the need for overlearning so that the skills taught in therapy will become automatic, and less easily disrupted by diffuse physiological arousal. Combined with practical consider-ations of treatment, the possible need for overlearning also suggests the importance of teaching the couple only a minimal set of skills. We need to recall that the average number of sessions in BMT is only about 14.

How can we rely on only a small set of skills? It could still be the case that the task analysis for marriage is quite elaborate and complex, but that the best way into the task analysis is to teach *entry level skills*, and then hope that a self-guided and self-correcting system takes over after that. If my analysis of the absorbing state and its lack of access to repair mechanisms is correct, these entry level skills, if overlearned, may be adequate for many couples to put them back on a stable marital trajectory.

For other couples this may not be the case. The therapist will need to assess the level of skill that the couple has when they are at their best. Subsequent therapy could then be concerned with follow-ups and guiding the couples through the remainder of the task analysis. The hope in trusting a minimal set of a skills is in the couple driving a wedge into the reciprocity represented by the absorbing state of negative affect so that they have access to the range of repair messages that they normally employ, but that do not work at the moment because the negative affect component is responded to rather than the repair component.

17.2.9.2. The Nature of Minimal Marital Therapy

17.2.9.2.1. The Typology of Stable Marriage

The therapist needs to be aware of the fact that there may be more than one way to manage the task of talking about an area of disagreement than the validator's style. The three styles are particularly different in the way they attempt to influence one another and in what they regard as the close and the opening of the discussion. Conflict avoidance is not necessarily dysfunctional (for a conflict-avoiding couple), nor is direct conflict engagement necessarily dysfunctional (for a volatile couple). However, if you are doing marital therapy with conflict-avoiding or volatile couples, it is likely that some of their buffers may not be working effectively. For example, the balance of positivity and negativity in a stable volatile couple requires there to be a great deal of positive affect, and this may have eroded by the time a couple reaches therapy. The avoidance of conflict may be impossible for an avoiding couple by the time they reach marital therapy, so that they face an unavoidable conflict without the necessary skills to resolve it.

What the therapist needs to be aware of in considering the typology, is that the types differ most in their methods of persuasion. "Persuasion" in this book has been used in a limited way. It means a direct, overt attempt to convince one's partner that he or she is wrong and/or you are right. It need not be logical. Although in general, persuasion occurs in the second third of the interaction, we have discovered three distinct styles of persuasion that are equally viable from the standpoint of marital stability (Gottman, 1993). The three styles are called *validating*, *volatile*, and *avoiding*. The validating style listens for the first 5 minutes of the interaction, and then begins attempts at persuasion. The volatile style begins persuasion attempts right away (usually with a lot of interspersed positive affect, like laughter). The avoiding style never engages in persuasion. The therapist needs to be sensitive to these differences in persuasive style.

At this point, the research evidence is equivocal about the selection of entry level skills. The concept may even be wrong, and it may be arbitrary where one begins. However, we will assume that entry level skills exist and we will take a stab at suggesting what these skills are. If one assumes that the Four Horsemen of the Apocalypse represent a real cascade, the two places to intervene are in the presentation of complaints and in the response to complaints. What needs to change is the way complaints naturally become criticisms and contempt, and the characteristic defensiveness that follows. For the purposes of managing these two aspects of the four horsemen, I suggest that the entry level skills are: soothing, nondefensive listening, and validating. Details of these last two skills are readily available in the therapy literature; for example, see *A Couple's Guide To Communication* (Gottman, Notarius, Gonso, & Markman, 1976).

17.2.9.2.2. Selecting Entry Level Skills

These skills are not new, and are a part of almost all current marital therapy programs I have reviewed. What is different here is the suggestion that the therapy be limited to these skills, that the therapy involve overlearning and physiological soothing, so that the couple will have access to these skills when upset and aroused, so that flooding can be averted.

What about suggesting problem-solving training? The status of direct training in problem solving is unknown. I would guess that, in selecting which skills be considered "entry level skills," problem solving should be actively discouraged by the therapist because it will lead to effortful information processing and vigilance. Also, particularly regarding males, a commonly heard complaint from wives is that men rush in too soon to try to solve the problem without first having heard their wives' feelings and truly understanding her point of view. This is not to suggest that it isn't important to eventually solve the problem, but that it is the least important part of the therapy, a part that can be left to each couple. Conflict avoiders, for example, will have an entirely different idea of what a solution is than validators or volatile couples.

I would suggest, on the basis of our research experience, each marital interaction should be preceded by a 5-minute silence period in which couples can gather their thoughts, and it should be no longer than 15 minutes.

Let us begin by considering the *skill of soothing* (this can be self-soothing, or the couple can soothe one another; eventually, it should not be the therapist who does this). The couple needs to monitor their heart rates and stop the interaction when their heart rates increase more than 10 beats per minute over baseline, or if their heart rates exceed 82 for men 87 for women (these are guesses). The best methods for soothing physiological arousal are probably: (a) withdrawing from the interaction, that is taking a scheduled break (at least 20 minutes without negative arousal-sustaining cognitions, and a scheduled time to return, with a commitment to continue the discussion); and, (b) relaxation either separately, or, even better, with one another. There is some evidence that communications training of couples will reduce blood pressure reactivity (Ewart et al., 1984). We also have some unpublished evidence (Gottman, Kiecolt-Glaser, Rushe, Glaser, & Malarkey, 1992) that some positive affects are related to reductions in epinephrine secretion over time; these affects are mutual humor and validation.

17.2.9.2.3. Soothing and How to Know if One is in a State of DPA

Although research to date on the Yerkes–Dodson law would suggest that there are vast individual differences in the stimuli that create physiological arousal, there may be a simple, clear-cut, and inexpensive way to assess whether a client is in DPA. Rowell (1986), in his study of physical exercise, found that increases in heart rate above the intrinsic rhythm of about 100 BPM seem to be an important cutoff for men. This cutoff marks the point at which sympathetic nervous system activation and the secretion of stress-related hormones become involved in regulating the heart increasing rate; this is one cutoff for heart rate that suggests the point at which physiological arousal may become DPA. Since the base heart rate is about 70 BPM for males and 80 BPM for females, this suggests a critical cutoff of approximately 30 BPM increase will result in DPA. Our own research with violent and distressed nonviolent marriages (conducted with N. Jacobson, and as yet unpublished) suggests that, during marital conflict, heart rate increases far less than this cutoff, and more in the order of 12 BPM may create significant alterations in affective behavior. If these initial results are true, they suggest that having therapists should teach the couple a soothing ritual during marital conflict. The soothing ritual for withdrawal should be instituted when heart rate gets above +10 BPM over baseline (this might mean, perhaps, 80 for men, 85 for women). Heart rate can easily be monitored by having people take their first and second fingers of their right hand and count the pulses at the right side of the neck (near the carotid artery) for 15 seconds, and then multiplying by 4 to get their heart rate. A baseline heart rate should be taken before the conversation begins during a short period when the subjects' eyes are closed and they are more or less relaxed. We suggest the frequent use of "Stop Action" interventions, which can be called by the couple at any time (see Gottman et al., 1976).

17.2.9.2.4. Distress-Maintaining Cognitions

I have noted (in chapter 15) that distress-maintaining cognitions are of two types, the "innocent victim" and the "righteous indignation" set of thoughts. Both of these are likely to be involved in maintaining physiological arousal. I also noted (in chapter 12) that evidence suggests that men are more likely to maintain these thoughts than women. Self-soothing may therefore involve dealing with these kinds of thoughts and substituting thoughts that are calming. Examples of such thoughts that we have obtained from interviews with people who do calm themselves physiologically are:

1. "I love him; he is upset right now and I don't like this interaction, but I still love him."
2. "I'm not happy with things at the moment, but there's a lot I like about this marriage."
3. "I don't have to take this personally."
4. "Just relax and sit back."
5. "This is just not about me."
6. "There are still a lot of things I admire about him. I'll try to think of a time when things were much better between us. There was that vacation we took to Hawaii."

It will probably be necessary for the therapist to help each client with dealing with distress-maintaining cognitions and substituting calming thoughts.

17.2.9.2.5. Nondefensive Listening

Defensiveness involves self-protection and warding off a perceived attack. It includes whining, denying responsibility for a problem, rebutting mindreading attributions made by one's spouse (e.g., Spouse: "You always do or feel X," defensive rebuttal "I do not always do or feel X"), or cross-complaining. Listening to one's partner's complaints needs to exclude a defensive response and substitute an affectively neutral (or better yet an empathic) response. The requirement that a person validate his or her spouse's feelings and point of view decreases the possibility of a defensive response, so that nondefensive listening and validation are part of the same constructive response.

17.2.9.2.6. Validation

Validation is actually a scale of responses. At the low point of the scale we have simply providing listener backchannels that show that the listener is tracking (i.e., not stonewalling). These responses usually involve looking at the speaker, facial movement, occasional head nods, a nonrigid neck, relaxed breathing, and brief vocalizations (preferably assents such as "Yeah," "OK," "Mmm-hmm," and the like). These communicate to the speaker that the listener thinks what the speaker is saying could be valid and makes sense, that the listener could see things from the speaker's perspective. Validation at this lowest level on the scale does not necessarily imply that the listener agrees with the speaker. At highest end of the scale we have the kind of empathic understanding that Greenberg and Johnson (1988) described so ably.

17.2.9.2.7. Other Considerations

I suggest that all marital therapies need to be "gender sensitive," and take into consideration that during strong negative affect, men tend to withdraw and women tend to engage (Gottman & Levenson, 1988, 1993). Hence, the minimal set of skills may be different for men than for women. This has implications for how a therapist works with a couple. However, the minimal set of skills may need to be within the couple's interacting system, and hence, would be somewhat symmetrical for both spouses.

17.2.9.2.8. The Character of the Therapy

The therapy I suggest will probably be very dull for the therapist. The idea is to take this very small set of skills and have the couple apply the set over and over again, in many situations, until the skills become second nature and effortless. The therapy needs to be structured so that the skills are overlearned. The analogy to learning how to drive a car is apt. At first beginning drivers have to think about each part of the skill, but eventually the actions become automatic and effortless.

The hope of minimal marital therapy is that eventually the couple's manner of presenting complaints, responding nondefensively to them, validation, and physiological soothing will also become automatic, and that this fact will drive a wedge into the negative affect reciprocity that characterizes distressed marriages. Then they will have access to their repertoire of repair mechanisms for managing the interaction.

17.2.9.3. Research Agenda

There may be an added advantage to a research program that is based on a minimal marital therapy, that is, one can systematically investigate the nature of the failures one will have with this approach to determine what is missing (or wrong) in the minimal therapy. By systematically studying the kinds of couples who are helped or not helped, and the limitations in outcome, the therapy program can be modified over time. This may be an alternative to a research program that begins with multicomponent intervention program that has to first prove itself effective and then to be experimentally dismantled to be understood.

18

Epilogue

Usually voyages begin with great optimism and hope. It is as if a majestic sailing ship sets off on a bright blue day and all spirits run high. The ship hums with excited business, gear is stowed aboard, provisions are laid in, lines are secured, lists are checked and rechecked, and, finally, the anchor is weighed, the sails are raised and fill with wind, the prow begins cutting the crystal waters, and she moves out gracefully. So most marriages begin with a great celebration and with great expectations.

But on these voyages, no sailor expects the storm, and none is trained to deal with gales. There were no prior man-overboard drills. We are prepared only for the bright sunrises accompanied by the horn section of the orchestra singing our joyful gladness. We are prepared for the violins to accompany our romantic sunsets, and perhaps for the cellos to accompany our tender pathos.

So marriages begin as great journeys filled with faith or at least hope. Yet inevitably the gales come. We find that our ship does not perform perfectly. We are disappointed. Ingenuity is required, improvisation, and even work. Then come the storms, and the boat begins to leak. We wail as we repair it and continue all the while at breakneck speed on the journey. We become exhausted, and at times the orchestra is replaced by a lone oboe. Sometimes the sea seems vast, the gray clouds merge with the gray sea, and the waves are menacing, as if marriage were a powerful, relentless adversary. The waters may enter the boat faster than we can bail.

Yet people regroup. The sky eventually clears, the sun rises again, sails are repaired, and a small voice inside begins tentatively to sing again. The trials make the story more interesting and it becomes a tale of a real journey. So the couples in my research tell their tales of it all: the first glance, the first sight he had of her in a yellow dress in a green room, the first knowledge she had of his brave determination, the first flush of love, the blooming of admiration and respect. There are many journeys and as many ways to have an adventurous voyage as there are definitions of pleasure.

Yet, like the early explorers, researchers can now make some maps, and create some primitive charts that show that the way is not completely unknown. I can point to some of the beauties along the way and warn of the Scylla and Charibdis of this journey. Hopefully I have accomplished this much. Much of the detail in my maps is probably wrong. Many of the serpents may not be there, or maybe there are more of them than I thought. But the broad outlines of our continents will be there.

The potential is there in marriage for great joy and healing, as well as the potential for anguish. At the end of this research, I need to celebrate the triumph of the individual spirit, in an honest quest for a home, for peaceful resuscitation, for love, respect, adventure, and joy. If research can help in this quest, it surely will have assisted people in creating better homes in which to raise children. Perhaps fewer of these children will begin life with the wounds that come from seeing their parents struggling to find love in a harsh world.

Appendix: The Observational Coding Systems

I decided that I needed to employ four different observational coding systems to more fully understand marriage. In this appendix, I describe these observational systems.

A1. THE FACE AND EMOTION

A1.1. Coding Emotion in the Human Face

The face must hold a central place in any analysis of emotion. Indeed, as Ekman (1984) pointed out, the face is central to people's identities. It is the origin of speech, vision, taste, hearing, and smell. People do not carry around pictures of their own and loved ones' other body parts, such as feet and hands, nor do they put pictures of these body parts of loved ones on the walls of their homes. They tend to identify the face directly with the personality. Yet, until recently, this vital aspect of people's bodies has been virtually ignored by social scientists.

It is clear from chapter 3 that the most consistent discriminators between happily and unhappily married couples are negative affect and negative affect reciprocity. However, the coding systems that marital researchers have employed have been primitive. They are not based on what is currently known about coding emotion in human behavior. Perhaps the greatest failing has been in not attending to cues of emotion in the human face.

One of the most important advances in the study of human emotion was made in the 1970s by the systematic study of the human face. Two major research laboratories were involved in this advance: the laboratory of Paul Ekman and Wallace Friesen and the laboratory of Carroll

Izard. These researchers were influenced in large measure by the psychologist Sylvan Tomkins. Their work also has been influenced strongly by Darwin's (1972) book on the expression of emotions in humans and animals.

Considered by many researchers (e.g., Bruner & Tagiuri, 1954) prior to this seminal work to be a researcher's nightmare, the face was seen as an unreliable source of information about emotion. However, following Izard (1971) and Ekman et al. (1972), many of these ideas changed. In recent years, investigators have begun to learn how to observe facial movement. In many cases, they have had to begin by realizing that they are not born knowing how to read faces.

A1.2. How to Read Faces

Many researchers mistakenly think that they have no need to learn how to read faces—that they are socialized with this knowledge. Some people think that what they do not know is not worth knowing, and that, theoretically, only naive judges should be employed as raters of emotion. They have argued that reading faces with a microanalytic system will somehow bias naturalistic studies of emotion, and that naive raters should be employed instead. The decision about these issues depends on what one is studying. If one is interested in how naive raters perceive a social stimulus, clearly that is the measurement of choice. However, if one is concerned about knowing precisely what is being measured, an anatomically based observational system is needed.

Based on the author's experience, it appears clear that most people do not know how to read faces very well. Furthermore, training helps improve people's ability to read faces. However, learning a facial coding system is a major investment of time and energy. If one is interested in studying emotion, it seems clear that it is a necessity.

I am familiar with Ekman and Friesen's (1978) Facial Action Coding System (FACS), which is an anatomically based system for describing visual changes in groups of the facial muscles. There are other observational coding systems for describing facial action. Most prominent is an observational system devised by Izard called MAX (see Izard, 1982). For a review of different observational coding systems of facial expression, see Scherer and Ekman (1982).

In the FACS, the coding proceeds with a series of action units (AUs) that describe the muscle groups that probably are contracting to produce a particular action. The coding manual divides the face into two regions: the upper and lower face. Each group of muscles that produces a visible change in the face is referred to as an action unit (AU). Following this notation is a series of numbers that represents contractions of specific action units. For example, AU4 refers to the action unit called "brow lowerer," which brings the inner corners of the brow down and together, creating a vertical furrow between the brows. Table A.1 summarizes the action units of the FACS by facial regions. As can be seen, the mouth region is by far the most complex, and probably contains enormous information.

The next step after description of what action units have been observed in the faces over time is to reduce the data to a set of probable emotion predictions. This is a complicated business, because many facial actions are not emotional. For example, many accompany conversation and provide emphasis and punctuation. A good beginning guide are those expressions that have been found to have cross-cultural universality in recognition and production. These expressions are summarized in pictures in a book entitled *Unmasking the Face* (Ekman & Friesen, 1978) and discussed in Ekman et al. (1972).

The facial dictionary is the name that Ekman and Friesen (1978) gave to the basis they employ for making the emotion predictions. The dictionary continues to grow as researchers gain experience with the face in various contexts.

A1.3. EMFACS: A More Rapid Coding System

One drawback to the FACS as a research tool is that it is very time consuming. A recent observational coding system that operates in three times real time was devised by Ekman and Friesen (1978), called Emotion FACS (EMFACS). This system employs a more restricted set of AUs and provides emotion predictions based on combinations of AUs observed. An unpublished manual is available. To get some flavor for this manual, I review Ekman's (1984) discussion of the brow area of the human face.

A1.4. About Brows

Ekman (1984) distinguished between two types of facial signals: emotional expressions and conversational actions. He used an anatomically based catalog to describe facial action, centered on describing the muscles involved in creating any particular visible facial expression. To better illustrate this point, he focused on a rather salient part of facial expression: the eyebrow movement.

There are seven distinctly different eyebrow actions, each of which is the result of a different muscle or a combination of muscles. All seven eyebrow actions could be considered a social signal; five also are

TABLE A.1
Action Units of the FACS

Region of the Face	AU	Effect of the AU
Upper Face		
	4	Brow lowerer
	1	Inner brow raiser
	2	Outer brow raiser
	5	Upper lid raiser
	7	Lid tightener
	6	Cheek raiser and lid compressor
	41	Lid drooper
	42	Eye Slitter
	43	Eyes closer
	44	Squinter
	45	Blinker
	46	Winker
Combinations	4+5, 5+7, 1+4, 1+2, 1+2+4, 1+2+5, 6+43, 7+43	
Lower face		
Up/down actions		
	9	Nose wrinkler
	10	Upper lip raiser
	17	Chin raiser
	15	Lip corner depressor
	25	Lip parter
	26	Jaw dropper
	27	Mouth stretcher
Combinations	16+25	Lower lip depressor
	9+16+25, 9+17, 10+16+25, 10+15, 10+17, 15+17, 10+15+17	
Horizontal actions		
	20	Lip stretcher
	14	Dimpler
Combinations	20+26, 20+27, 14+17, 10+14, 10+20+25	
Oblique actions		
	11	Nasolabial furrow deepener
	12	Lip corner puller
	13	Sharp lip puller
Combinations	10+12+25, 12+16+25, 10+12+16+25, 12+15, 12+15+17, 6+12+15, 6+12+15+17, 12+26, 12+27, 12+17.	
Orbital actions		
	18	Lip pucker
	22+25	Lip funneler
	23	Lip tightener
	24	Lip presser
	28	Lip sucker

(continued)

TABLE A.1 (continued)

Region of the Face	AU	Effect of the AU
Combinations	10+23+25, 12+23, 12+24, 14+23 17+23, 17+24, 6+12+17+23, 12+17+23, 10+17+23, 18+23, 15+23, 23+26, 22+23+25, 20+23+25.	
Miscellaneous actions		
	8+25	Lips toward each other
	19	Tongue shower
	21	Neck tightener
	29	Jaw thruster
	30	Jaw sideways
	31	Jaw clencher
	32	Biter
	33	Blower
	34	Puffer
	35	Sucker
	36	Bulger
	37	Lip wiper
	38	Nostril dilator
	39	Nostril compressor
Head and eye positions		
	51, 52	Head turn right or left
	53	Head up
	54	Head down
	55, 56	Head tile, right or left
	57, 58	Head forward or back
	61, 62	Eyes turn left or right
	63, 64	Eyes up or down
	65	Walleye
	66	Cross-eye

involved in displaying emotional expression, and two of the eyebrow actions play an important part in many conversational signals.

To describe facial action, Ekman and Friesen (1978) spent 2 years studying anatomy, learning to move their own facial muscles in accordance with anatomical descriptions, and acquiring the ability to contract specific muscles. They also reviewed more than 5,000 different combinations of specific muscular actions. They then taught other people how to recognize facial actions, determining which actions could be distinguished reliably. The results of these findings were incorporated into a manual and other accompanying self-teaching materials (Ekman & Friesen, 1978) on how to score facial behavior. The following description of eyebrow movements is taken from this manual.

Ekman (1984) described the muscle units used in eyebrow movements as action units. Figure A.1 shows a baseline example of no action.

Non-verbal and verbal rituals in interaction

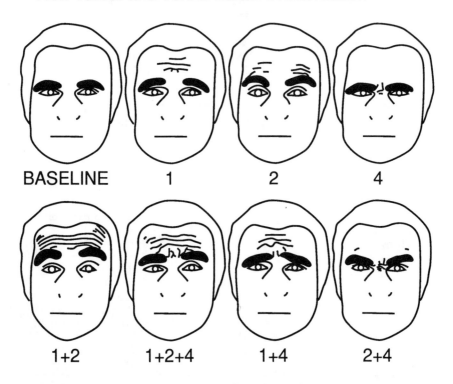

BASELINE   1   2   4

1+2   1+2+4   1+4   2+4

Action Units for the brow/forehead

FIG. A.1. *Action Unit 1* (denoted AU1) shows the change that occurs when just the medial portion of the frontalis muscle contracts. The inner corner of the eyebrow is raised, which may result in the appearance of short wrinkles in the center of the forehead. *Action Unit 2* (AU2) describes the appearance change when just the lateral portion of the frontalis muscle contracts. The outer corners of the eyebrows are raised. The skin in the lateral portion of the forehead is pulled up, which may cause short wrinkles to appear in the lateral portion of the forehead. *Action Unit 4* (AU4) describes the appearance changes when the corrugator, depressor gabella, and/or depressor supercilli contract. The eyebrows are pulled down and drawn together. The skin between the brows is bunched, often causing a vertical wrinkle between the brows. These three action units are the building blocks for the four combinations shown (from Ekman, 1984).

In describing emotional expression, there is cross-cultural evidence to support the theory that specific patterns of facial actions universally signify particular emotions. These studies include the work of anthropologists, ethologists, pediatricians, psychologists, and sociologists.

A1.5. Some Complexities of Context and Culture

However, some still argue that there are no universals in facial expression of emotion. They offer a linguistic analogy. In language, particular sounds are not associated with particular meanings. Because this is the case, there also may not be any consistent association between nonverbal signals and meaning in different cultures. Ekman (1984) explained that although a linguistic analogy is misleading concerning facial expression of emotion, it is useful in describing the function of facial conversation signals. He attempted to clarify this while offering a theoretical framework that incorporates the theory of those who argue for a linguistic analogy as well as those who argue from an evolutionary viewpoint.

Disagreement stems from many sources, such as the failure of universalists to explain what they mean by emotion terms such as *anger, fear, surprise, happiness,* and so on. Ekman (1984) considered that these emotive terms also imply an antecedent and classification system that includes the following:

1. elicitors—what stimulates the event to take place.
2. co-occurring response—refers to the skeletal muscular action, autonomic nervous system action, vocalizations, and so on, that occur.
3. subsequent interpersonal behavior—how a person copes with the source of emotional arousal.

Having discussed, to some degree, what he meant by emotion, Ekman (1984) then asked me to regard the seven eyebrow movements and consider their role in a few emotions for which there is clear-cut universal evidence of definition. In sadness, AU1 or 1 + 4 occur. In surprise, AU 1 + 2 is accompanied by raising the upper eyelid and dropping the jaw. In fear, the combination 1 + 2 + 4 is accompanied by raising the upper eyelid, tightening the lower eyelid, and horizontally stretching the lips (AU20). The 1 + 2 + 4 AU makes the brows appear horizontal. In anger, AU4, without brow raising, is accompanied by the same actions around the eyes as is described for fear, but the lips are pressed together, or tightened and squared.

The preceding has described and classified the role of eyebrow action in emotional expression. In comparison with emotional expression, there is little known about conversational signals. In focusing on eyebrow action, Ekman (1984) described the most frequent facial actions used as conversational signals.

Speaker conversational signals include what Ekman (1984) called the baton, underliner, punctuation, question mark, and word search. The baton usually coincides with voice stress (or with a word that is spoken more loudly). The usual accompanying facial expression for the baton is 1 + 2 and 4. The underliner is also for emphasis, but usually stretches out over more than a single word. Action units most common with the underliner are 1 + 2 and 4.

Punctuation is the term used when there is a pause, much like a comma, after each event in the series. Both 1 + 2 and 4 appear to be used as punctuation. The *question mark* refers to brow raising to indicate a question. Both 1 + 2 and 4 are used. In the word search, the speaker is holding the floor with "ah" while he or she searches for a particular word or turn of phrase. Facial expressions associated with this may include 1 + 2 (with eyes toward the ceiling in concentration) or 4.

In addition to the speaker's conversational signals, there are listener responses that are associated with facial expressions, and in particular with specific eyebrow movements. Agreement responses are associated with 1 + 2 with a smile or a head nod. Eyebrows can indicate a call for more information: AU4 or 1 + 2 can indicate perplexity, or that the individual does not understand and needs more explanation.

Although the previous signals involved spoken conversation, the following refer to emblems or conversational signals without speech: The eyebrow flash is a repeated brow raise (1 + 2) and it can be used as a greeting signal; disbelief is shown by 1 + 2 and pulling the corner of the lips down, relaxing the upper eyelid, pushing up the lower lip, raising the upper lip, and/or rocking the head from side to side; mock astonishment involves 1 + 2 with raised upper eyelid and a dropped open jaw; affirmation–negation is shown in two separate ways: Affirmation generally is associated with eyebrow raise (1 + 2) in most cultures, whereas negation often is associated with the drawing together of the brows (AU4).

Action Unit 1 + 2 and AU4 are the two eyebrow actions that appear most frequently. Because they are the easiest to perform, they might be the most prevalent social signals.

Thus, Ekman (1984) distinguished between emotional and conversational facial signals, although both occur in conversation. He chose to separate them on the basis of their differences. Emotional expressions are precursers of speech and conversational signals. Emotional expression is not always voluntary, whereas conversational facial signals usually are voluntary. Conversational facial signals only occur in the presence of others, although emotional expressions occur when a person thinks he or she is unobserved. Although there is much evidence for the universality of emotional facial signals, for conversational facial signals there may be no universals, although this is not known.

For both emotional and conversational signals, why do some actions rather than others become particular signals? Some investigators believe certain actions have been incorporated into the repertoire through natural selection, and that facial actions associated with emotional expressions originally served a biological function for our early ancestors (Darwin, 1872; Eibl-Eiblesfeldt, 1989). Through ritualization, a particular behavior is modified through genetic evolution to become an efficient signal. I illustrate this kind of comparative evolutionary speculation by examining what has been written about the adaptive value of certain facial expressions.

A1.5.1. The Adaptive Value of 1 + 2

Darwin (1872) offered the explanation that 1 + 2 helps raise the upper eyelid quickly, and that this movement increases the superior portion of the visual field.

A1.5.2. The Adaptive Value of 4

This action decreases the visual field, shutting out extraneous influences and aiding concentration.

A1.5.3. The Adaptive Value of 1 + 4

Darwin (1872) explained that when inhibiting crying, the only way to counteract the involuntary action of the depressor glabellae, which lowers the inner portion of the brows, is by the upward movement of AU1. But the corrugator muscle, which draws the brows together, cannot be completely prevented from movement by AU1, resulting in the combined action of brows being drawn together and raised at the inner ends.

A1.5.4. The Adaptive Value of 1 + 2 + 4

This merges two actions observed in other primates during threat behavior: 1 + 2 and 4. If one thinks of this action as anticipatory of fight or flight, it makes sense that the initial action of 1 + 2 increases the superior visual field in preparation for attack, whereas 4 narrows the visual field in concentration and makes the eyeball less vulnerable to blows.

I focused only on the brow region of the face. This summary only has touched the surface of what an investigator needs to know in coding emotion from facial expressions. For example, the most potential for different movements exists around the mouth region. To master observation of the face, the interested reader needs to engage in considerable study. To map the terrain that needs to covered, I end this chapter by briefly reviewing the muscles of the face.

A1.6. The Facial Muscles

The superficial muscles of the face can be grouped in relation to the orbital opening, the nasal aperature, and the mouth.

A1.6.1. The Eye and Brow

There are two parts to the muscle around the eye; the orbital portion is called *orbicualris oculi pars orbitalis* and the portion that raises the eyelids is called the *orbicularis oculi pars palpebralis*. The nerve supply of orbicularis oculi comes from temporal zygomatic branches of the facial nerve.

The *currogator* is a narrow band of muscle originating in the medial part of the superciliary arch. It draws the eyebrows medially, producing vertical wrinkles in the forehead.

There are two muscles of the frontalis, the medial and lateral frontalis.

A1.6.2. The Nose

Procerus is a muscle of the nose where fibers mix with the frontalis. It inserts in the lower forehead between the two eyebrows. It draws down the medial angle of the eyebrows and produces traverse wrinkles across the root of the nose. It is innervated by one of the superior buccal branches of the facial nerve. Lower on the nose are three muscles concerned with dilating the nasal aperature: (a) *Pars transversa* of the nasalis muscle arises from the upper part of the canine eminence of the maxilla and passes upward medially; (b) *Pars alaris* of the nasalia muscle arises from the maxilla above the lateral incisor tooth and inserts into the lateral portion of the lower margin of the ala of the nose (glabella); and (c) its more medial fibers are called *depressor septi*. The nasal muscles are supplied by the buccal branches of the facial nerve.

A1.6.3. The Mouth

Fibers of insertion enter at or near angles of the mouth. Three muscles are the principal elevators of the upper lip. These three muscles enter the upper lip from above. One muscle is *levator labii superioris alaeque nasi*, which lies in the sulcus between the nose and cheek (nasolabial furrow). It descends to indent partly into the ala of the nose and partly into the skin of the lateral half of the upper lip. *Levator labii superioris* lies away from the nose on either side of *alaque nasi*, inserting itself into the lateral half of the upper lip. *Zygomaticus minor* lies just away from the nose on either side of *labii superioris*.

Levator anguli oris is a thick muscle that elevates the angle of the mouth and draws it medially.

Zygomaticus major arises from the zygomatic bone descending obliquely where its fibers blend with *orbicularis oris*. This muscle turns the angle of the mouth upward and outward, as in smiling and laughing. *Risorius* is a muscle that runs transversely, arising from the fascia over the parotid gland, and widening the mouth. This muscle is often absent. *Buccinator* forms the principal substance of the cheek. It compresses the cheek, draws the corner of the mouth laterally, and forces the lips against the teeth. *Depressor anguli oris* lies below the mouth, is triangular in shape, and depresses the lip corners. *Depressor labii inferioris* is small and quadrilateral (i.e., it draws the lower lip down and lateralward). *Orbicularis oris* is an oral sphincter composed of interlacing fibers of other muscles, a deep stratum of fibers from the buccinator, and intrinsic bundles from the substance of the lips. The complex of muscle provides for sphincter action, flattening the lips, and protrusion.

This section was a brief introduction to the modern study of emotion. It introduced only one channel of information—the visible changes in facial movement. Although important in social interaction, the face is only one part of what needs to be studied when investigating emotion. For these and other reasons, I continue my discussion of emotion by introducing the detailed discussion of the SPAFF.

A2. THE SPECIFIC AFFECT CODING SYSTEM

A2.1. Coding Emotional Behavior During Marital Interaction

Previously I mentioned that the early attempts at observational description were quite crude, particularly in the extremely central area of describing emotion. This is understandable when one considers that only in the past 6 years have researchers had the basic tools for such essential tasks as measuring the anatomical basis of emotion facial expressions (Ekman & Friesen, 1978). In this section, I present a methodological discussion on how to code emotion. I hope to convince the reader that emotional behavior during marital interaction needs to be coded in two different ways for two different purposes.

A2.2. Coding Specific Affects

There are two approaches to coding emotions, which I call physical features and cultural informants. The physical features approach tries to detect specific cues that are cross-culturally universal, or at least reliably related to emotion in a given culture. The physical features identified are almost always nonverbal, and they are subdivided further into separate channels such as face, voice, gestures, paralinguistic features, and autonomic nervous system (ANS). Often an attempt is made to isolate the channels further; for example, the content of the verbal channel may be removed by the use of low-pass filtering or random splicing so that the coding of the acoustic properties of the voice can be done independently of the speech content. In contrast, the cultural informants approach is based on emotion judgments made by people judged to be competent readers of emotion in a particular culture. Usually these emotion judgments are based on an integrated gestalt of channels. I briefly discuss each approach.

A2.2.1. Specific Features

In the past decade, a great deal of progress has been made in identifying specific nonverbal behaviors that are good predictors of emotion. Headway is being made in the assessment of specific features in the voice for affective information. Unpleasant stimulation leads to constriction of the pharynx and the vocal pillars. Changes in vocal shape can be measured reliably from the glottal spectrum. For example, a chest register voice is deep, resonant, and relaxed, whereas a head register is tense, perhaps indicative of emotion or emotional control. The fundamental frequency and its shifts to higher levels gives reliable affective information (Scherer & Ekman, 1982). Speech disturbances also are indicators of emotion (Harper, Wiens, & Matarazzo, 1978).

Until 6 years ago, reliable, objective measurement of the face was not possible. Two major methods now exist: electromyography (EMG) and facial coding systems such as Ekman and Friesen's (1978) Facial Action Coding System (FACS). As reviewed, FACS is an anatomically based system for measuring visible facial movements; EMG can measure nonvisible changes in facial muscles, but it is more obtrusive and less precise in pinpointing which facial muscles have contracted. Nonetheless, both methods have been validated (Davidson, 1984). Empirical support for the emotional meaning of various facial configurations continues to accumulate. For example, Ekman and Freisen (1982) described the unfelt smile, which consists of contraction of the zygomatic major muscle (pulls the lip corners up) with no involvement of orbicularis oculi (muscle around the eye).

A2.2.2. Cultural Informants

Despite the importance of discoveries of the past decade based on the specific physical features approach, there are three problems with it as a method of coding affect. First, it attempts to extract emotional information only from the nonverbal channels. This view has arisen to emphasize evolutionary continuity in emotion expression, undoubtedly inspired by the important work of Darwin (1872). However, this practice obviously would be mistaken if used with marital interaction. Plays would not exist if words did not contain a great potential for communicating emotional information. As an illustration of this point, consider the following transcript of a marital interaction:

H: You'll never guess who I saw today. Frank Dugan!
W: So, big deal, you saw Frank Dugan.
H: Don't you remember I had that argument with him last week?
W: I forgot.
H: Yeah.
W: So I'm sorry I forgot, all right?
H: So it was a big deal to see him.
W: So what do you want me to do, jump up and down?
H: Well, how was your day, honey?
W: Oh brother, here we go again.
H: You don't have to look at me that way.
W: So what do you want me to do, put a paper bag over my head?

Considered by itself, the verbal content of this interaction has a number of indications that the couple was experiencing the emotion of anger. A great deal of emotional information would be lost if these indicators were ignored.

A second problem with the physical features approach is what might be called the additive channel assumption (Gottman, 1982), which assumes that specific features add emotional information to a substrate of emotion neutral language. Without such an assumption, techniques such as high-frequency voice filtering would not make sense. However, it is easy to show that physical features interact with language to convey emotional meaning; for example, consider the paralinguistic cue of stress; if the word *soon* is stressed in "I'd like this as soon as possible," it conveys impatience; if the word *possible* is stressed, it conveys the opposite. When speech is filtered electronically, reliability in emotion coding probably is obtained at the expense of coding most speech units as being emotionally neutral.

A third problem with this approach is that a great deal of emotional information is communicated in culturally specific ways. For example, Feld's (1982) research on the Kaluli noted that they use vestiges of specific tropical bird sounds to convey emotional meaning. A Kaluli will say, "my mother-in-law is coming to live with us" and use one bird-like sound to convey pleasure and another for sadness. Only a competent Kaluli informant would be able to detect this information. Because it is not cross-culturally universal does not imply that it is not useful emotional information.

Despite that it is possible to identify specific cross-culturally universal features that communicate anger, this certainly does not mean that there is only a single way to be angry. I believe that emotion in the stream of natural social interaction is conveyed by a nonadditive gestalt of information, which is detectable by competent cultural informants. In practice, it is wise to employ cultural informants who also have been trained to recognize the important physical features (e.g., can read the face using FACS), but who view them as only examples of how emotion may be expressed.

I believe that there are considerable scientific benefits to be obtained by maintaining a continual dialectic between the specific features approach and the cultural informants approach for coding emotion. I employ both methods in my work. I have developed a cultural informants method of coding specific affects and instances of emotional control (SPAFF) during marital interaction.

A2.3. The Dialectic Between the Global and the Molecular Approach to Observational Measurement

The basic problem with global coding systems is that one can never be sure what is being measured. Good examples of this problem are the literature on Type A/B ratings in psychiatric interview in the study of coronary heart disease, and ratings of a child's attachment classification in the Ainsworth strange situation.

Consider the attachment situation. There is a detailed codebook for making the judgment of which attachment classification a child is in.

However, raters of attachment in the strange situation may not be using the codes in the codebook, but actually may be rating something else, such as wellness or their own discomfort. Unless reliability is established for the component codes in the codebook, one never will be sure what is being measured in the attachment classification rating. One needs to know exactly what one is measuring. The goal is not to be narrow, but to be precise. Otherwise, one is in danger of confirming one's cherished beliefs without an adequate test.

One potential solution, one that I have selected in my work, is to engage in a dialectic between molecular and global coding. In creating a construct for analysis, one can then attempt to put together molecular and global codes. If they converge as a construct and function well with respect to criterion variables of interest, then one can have increased confidence that the description obtained is adequate.

A2.4. The Specific Affect Coding System (SPAFF)

In this section, I introduce the 10 specific affect codes. To train observers, there is a detailed manual, a set of voice training tapes, a training videotape, and a test tape. I provide a limited summary here. Although I list the specific subcodes of each affect, it is important to note that the subcodes are collapsed so that there are only 10 specific affects (includes neutral).

It is often possible to code these specific affects from the words and the voice, although the videotape adds a great deal of information that makes the judgment easier.

A brief description of each follows. In this summary, I begin by discussing cues in the words and the voice that are employed to illustrate each affect. The manual then goes on to suggest specific facial cues for each affect. All observers are now trained on the FACS and EMFACS7 before learning the SPAFF.

A2.4.1. Selecting Cultural Informants

Observers are selected if they appear to my laboratory staff to be good decoders of emotion. It is not possible for me to specify precisely what characteristics I use in choosing these cultural informants. I have found that a background in acting and an active interest in music are helpful. It also helps if candidates for the observer position can talk about emotion in test tapes I show them, and if they are oriented toward emotional experience in their own lives. If observers are not intimidated by imitating sounds they hear on tapes, such as whining, this also helps. Many of my coders are shy, and many are extroverted. I have not found any personality characteristic that is more indicative of a good observer. However, it is important that SPAFF coders be flexible and able to quickly arrive at an intuitive judgment based on their training and first impressions. It is helpful if they are not judgmental or moralistic about marriages. They are not there to code their own affective responses to each spouse, but to attempt to get inside the skin of each person. People who cannot avoid taking sides and identifying one partner as the victim and the other as the perpetrator will not make reliable SPAFF coders.

A2.5. The SPAFF Codes, Version 1.0

A2.5.1. Neutral

Most interaction contains portions of what could be called neutral speech. A lot of these conversations include information exchange that is not very emotional in tone. It is recognized as being nonemotional in content and voice tone. There is generally not a marked stress on individual syllables; the voice tone has a very even quality to it, as though the speaker is within a comfortable pitch range (as opposed to either extreme).

> *Type I:* Question and response.
> > H: Are we going out to eat?
> > W: No, I told them we'd meet them back at the house.
> *Type II:* Statement(s), information exchange (matter of fact).
> > H: I took the dog for a walk this morning.
> > W: Yeah, I guess that was after I left.
> *Type III:* Any other behavioral act can have accompanying neutral.

A2.5.2. Humor

This is a relaxed, good-natured expression of intimacy. It includes several subcategories that may overlap. These expressions of humor are neither sarcastic nor mocking, but always contain an underlying tone of affection. Humor cannot be coded when one person is laughing and the other is not enjoying the attempt at humor at all. Even if the observer thinks the humor is funny, but the spouse does not at all, the humor code is not used. SPAFF uses the humor code in a very special, limited way.

> *Type I:* Joking/good-natured teasing.
> > W: That stupid husband of mine . . .
> > H: Don't call your husband stupid. It's not nice.

Type II: Nonsensical speech/exaggeration/imitation.

H: I always thought Catholic schools were separated by sex . . .

H & W: Well, you're a *garden* of misinformation!

Type III: Laughing/giggling/chuckling/private joke. The humor in this interaction may be private and consequently elusive to the outside observer.

Type IV: Spontaneous wit, silliness, fun, recognizing absurdity.

Type V: Empathetic.

Type VI: We against others.

This is a case of both spouses laughing at something or someone else. They are united in appreciating the pomposity or foolishness of someone or something else.

Type VII: Private humor.

This is a reference to humor that is entirely private and not understood by outsiders.

Type VIII: Other.

A2.5.3. Affection/Caring

This is a direct expression of affection. The voice is sometimes rather slow, with a drop in amplitude, yet even then there remains a definite intensity of affect. There are three general categories under this code.

Type I: Direct statements. "I love you, you know I do."

Type II: Concerned question or statement. "What's the matter?" "You seem upset."

Type III: Compliment or general supportiveness. "You're really good at that."

Type IV: Other affection/caring.

A2.5.4. Interest/Curiosity

There must be a positive energy in relation to what the other person has said or done—a definite involvement on the part of the listener. The voice can be relaxed and calm here and still have this positive energy. However, the observer also scans for increased amplitude, tempo, rhythm, less pause time between people's utterances, pitch changes, and people interrupting or finishing each other's sentences. The couple has to show that they are actively interested and curious. These are not passive states, but active. The person must easily be communicating an active interest and curiosity in the other person.

A2.5.5. Joy (Anticipation/Surprise/Excitement-Enjoyment/Joy)

All the elements of this category are characterized by rapid fluctuations in pitch, volume, emphasis, stress, and rate of speech. There is exaggerated emphasis on certain words, often accompanied by a breathlessness. Positive energy level distinguishes between it and interest/curiosity.

Type I: Anticipation (childlike; future-oriented).
   (a) rhetorical question: "Won't that be *great?*"
   (b) exclamation: "I can't *wait!*"
Type II: Surprise (extreme reaction to unanticipated event).
   (a) simple: "Oh my *God!*"
   (b) disbelief: "You're kidding!"
Type III: General excitement.
Type IV: Enjoyment/joy.
Expression of delight or pleasure; could be a reminiscence, a story, or the anticipation of an event.

A2.5.6. Anger

This code is fairly wide in scope, but its elements have in common a tendency toward syllabic phrases. The words are abrupt, biting, and often with a key word or syllable highly stressed.

Type I: Direct.
Type II: Accusing.
Type III: Offensive or abrasive.
Sudden release of built-up tension, and increase in volume or rate of speech.
Type IV: Controlled anger. This seems like an unsuccessful attempt to remain rational. It often results in lowering of volume and uniformity of syllables in an apparent attempt to smooth the anger out of the voice. Sometimes characterized by enunciation. Definite edge to the voice.

In the SPAFF, the cues listed are purely illustrative, not definite or exhaustive. They are designed to give each observer a common base of information. However, SPAFF presumes that there is a large variety of specific features in any culture that is indicative of a particular emotion, and for this reason the observer is considered a cultural informant.

A2.5.7. Disgust/Scorn/Contempt

In version 2.0 of the SPAFF, disgust and contempt are separated.

Type I: Disgust.
Sounds fed-up, sickened, repulsed, as in "I've had enough," "I'm not going to swallow any more," or "I'm going to throw up." Speaker is expressing the hidden message.

Type II: Scorn/contempt.
Includes derision, disdain, exasperation, mockery, put down, and communicating that the other person is absurd or incompetent.

Type III: Hostile humor, mockery, or sarcasm.
Also communicates derision, put down, or cold hate. There is often a definite sense of distance, coldness, and detachment in this category.

A2.5.8. Whining

Whining is not really an emotion. It is a well-defined behavior that is quite common in marital interaction, and I am studying it separately until I know where to put it in my specific affects list. Whining is heard as a high-pitched, fluid fluctuation of the voice, generally with one syllable stressed toward the end of the sentence. It reflects dissatisfaction in a very childish way. It is often characterized by a thin edge to the voice and an irritating nasal quality. I have noticed that whining almost always has an innocent victim posture behind it. It is as if the whiner is saying, "It's not fair. Why are you picking on me? I didn't do anything wrong. I'm good." See if you can hear this plaintive, "Oh poor me" message behind the whine. Sylvan Tomkins thought that whining was very close to crying, and probably akin to sadness. However, for now I code it separately.

Type I: Demand. "I told you to see a *doctor*."
Type II: Complaint. "You never take me *any*where."
Type III: Direct expression of feeling like an innocent victim. "I feel I'm ganged up on, I don't have a friend in the world."
Type IV: Defensive.
Can be either abrasive or nonabrasive. Includes indignation, self-righteousness, distinguished from offensive anger largely by content.

As these descriptions suggest, whining can be detected in the content of the words, and not just in the voice tone.

A2.5.9. Sadness

Sadness generally is characterized by a low volume of the voice and a slowness of speech.

Type I: Resigned/passive. "I just don't know what to do anymore" (even stress on syllables). Sometimes there is an evenness in the tempo (a kind of monotony) with lowered amplitude. Often in minor (rather than major) musical key.

Type II: Poignant/crying. "I just don't know what to *do* anymore." The affect is more pronounced here.

Type III: Hurt. "I *do,* I try to look *nice* for you." Also, pay attention to the shape of the amplitude of the voice within a statement. Often a good cue for sadness is a dropping amplitude at the end of a statement.

A2.5.10. Fear (Tension/Stress/Worry/Fear)

Type I: Speech disturbances. This code is based, in part, on selecting particular kinds of speech disturbances. Speech disturbances have been studied and two kinds have been distinguished. One kind, called ah-disturbance, is neutral. Words like *ah, er,* and *um* usually are designed to provide the speaker with thinking time; they tend to be a vehicle for keeping the floor (i.e., for the speaker to hold onto his or her turn). The other kind is called non-ah-disturbances. They are sentence change in middle of a sentence, repetition in mid-sentence, stuttering, omissions, sentence incompletion, slips, intruding incoherent sounds, and generally indicative of tension.

The SPAFF codes as fear only those non-ah-speech-disturbances that are negative in tone. Also, any other indications of fear, worry, or anxiety are coded as fear. People also display non-ah-speech-disturbances when excited and happy, so it is important not to code these excitement affects as indicating tension. Also, non-ah-speech-disturbances could be common in some cultural groups and should not be taken as indexes of tension (e.g., people for whom English is a second language).

Type II: Fundamental frequency shifts. When people speak in a relaxed way, their voices tend to be what is called a chest register. They speak at their normal fundamental frequency. However, when they become tense, the fundamental frequency shifts upward as the vocal pillars become tense and the register shifts from a chest to a head register. It is possible to hear this tightness and tension in the voice.

Type III: Other tension. At times it is possible to see tension in the way the body is held, particularly in the neck.

A2.6. Facial Cues

A2.6.1. Beyond Brows

All SPAFF coders are proficient coders using FACS and EMFACS ("Emotion FACS," unpublished). They have passed the posttest in the Human Interaction Laboratory of Ekman and Friesen. Coders use the FACS materials (available from Consulting Psychologists Press, Inc., 577 College Avenue, Palo Alto, CA 94306) to recognize specific facial actions that Ekman and Friesen (1978) identified in an emotion predictions table. It is necessary to supplement the SPAFF manual with the FACS materials.

In the SPAFF manual, there are a few facial expressions to their EMFACS list. Wherever possible, I followed the recommendations of Ekman and Friesen's more rapid coding EMFACS system. I also followed those expressions used in the Ekman et al. (1983) directed facial action task, which produced distinct autonomic profiles. Researchers who read the SPAFF manual should note that SPAFF coders should be trained to be FACS coders and not just to recognize the specific set of facial cues that I have selected that may or may not have emotional significance.

The SPAFF manual calls the coder's attention to a small set of facial expressions that could be indicative of specific emotions. The manual begins by showing the coder a photograph of a neutral face. It is always important to begin by finding a neutral face, so the coder can identify permanent facial features that are not facial expressions. For example, one person can have a permanent vertical brow furrow that becomes deeper during a facial action, whereas another person may not have this feature.

A2.6.1.1. Distress or Sadness

In the manual, the next picture shows distress in the brow area of the face. The central portion of the brow is raised, giving them an oblique shape. (This is due to AU1.) Notice that the brow is furrowed, but only the medial (central) portion of the brow is furrowed. The brows are also drawn together (AU4). This produces inverted-U wrinkles in the brow, also called Darwin's grief muscle. In a complete brow raise (AU1 and AU2), the entire brow is furrowed.

A2.6.1.2. Contempt/Disgust/Disapproval

For disgust, here are two possible indicators. One is the nose wrinkle, produced by AU9. The second disgust indicator is created by raising the upper lip, a result of AU10. For contempt, a possible indicator is the result of AU14, called the dimpler muscle. Another possible contempt indicator is the eye roll.

A2.6.1.3. Sadness

Sadness may look like distress in the upper face. Look for the following cue in the lower face—mouth corners pulled down (AU15). Sadness also is conveyed by the combination of two action units, AU6, which raises the cheeks and creates crows feet in the eye corners, plus AU15 (lip corner depression). Ekman et al. (1983) included in sadness the following action units: 64 (glance down), 17 (chin raise), and 6 + 12 (cheek raise and lip corner pull).

A2.6.1.4. Anger

The lips and chin boss regions of the face provide clues to anger. AU23 rolls the red part of the lips inward, so that they are tight and lips are more narrow; AU23 can affect only one lip. AU24 presses the lips together without pushing the chin boss up. It tightens and narrows the lips. In the next set of photographs, the chin boss is contracted, as well. AU17, called the chin raiser, pushes the chin boss up, wrinkles the chin boss, and gives the mouth a slight inverted-U shape. If it is strong, the lower lip may protrude as in a pout. AU17 can act in combination with AU23 or AU24 to create a stronger potential signal for anger. Sometimes this action unit is involved when someone is trying to control a display of emotion on the face. Sometimes a strong signal for anger may be observed in the upper face. The next photograph shows the action of three muscles, AU4, which pulls the brows down and together (creating a vertical furrow between the brows); AU7, which tightens the lids (particularly straightening the lower lid) without raising the cheeks; and AU5, which raises the upper lid (and makes it seem like the eyeball is protruding). In the face shown below, anger is portrayed by the action units 4 + 5 + 7 + 23.

A2.6.1.5. Fear

Signals of fear may be detected in the mouth, particularly the result of AU20. AU20 may entail an open mouth, which can be open to varying degrees (i.e., lips part, jaws drop, or mouth stretched).

In a 1 + 2 + 4, only the medial portion of the brow is furrowed horizontally. The horizontal lines do not extend all the way across the brow as in a 1 + 2 (full brow raise). The 1 + 2 + 4 is the distress or fear facial expression.

A2.6.2. Conversational Markers

As Ekman (1984) suggested, not all facial expressions are emotional signals. There are at least five: (a) underliners that emphasize words or phrases, (b) expressions that express questioning, (c) punctuation, (d) expressions that accompany a word search (when a person cannot find the right word), and (e) turn taking (giving up or wanting the floor of the conversation).

In particular, the SPAFF manual calls the coder's attention to two conversational markers that might, at times, relate to an inner feeling about what is being said. These two expressions are 4 and 1 + 2.

AU4 pulls the brows down and together and creates a vertical furrow between the brows. Linda Camras (personal communication, 1980) suggested that it usually is used when a person is expressing worry, doubt, or consternation, or when the person is anticipating or discussing something difficult or complex, or asking a question for which the answer is unknown. People tend to lower their pitch when doing an AU4. The reader might like to try it the other way (i.e., try doing an AU4 and raising the pitch of your voice). It is difficult.

People use AU 1 + 2 when they are looking forward to something, having positive expectations about its outcome, or asking a question to which they know the answer. It usually is accompanied by rises in pitch.

A2.6.3. Toward Whom

The SPAFF also detects toward whom the affect is directed—whether this is selp, partner, or other. For example, contempt may be directed toward the self (e.g., "I'm so dumb in those situations"), toward someone else ("Why can't that repairman fix anything right?"), or toward the partner. This distinction may be critical in examining the physiological correlates of emotion. For example, if both partners are angry at a repairman, this actually may be a moment of expressed solidarity and affection, rather than anger. Hence, a particular SPAFF emotion code always has been directed at the partner.

A3. MARITAL PROBLEM SOLVING

A3.1. The Marital Interaction Coding System (MICS)

Weiss and Summers (1983) reviewed the MICS and the 45 studies that had been completed using it up to that date (see also Jacob & Tennennbaum, 1988). My own use of the MICS is considerably limited. I continue to employ the summary categories that were useful in Gottman and Krokoff (1989). These are conflict engagement, stubbornness, defensiveness, and withdrawal, as well as the z-scores of several sequences involving these codes. Reliabilities of MICS scores for the 1983–1987 study present Cronbach alphas for the variables used in the study.

A3.2. Development of the Rapid Couples Interaction Scoring System (RCISS)

Krokoff et al. (1989) reported the results of a validation study that employed a new and rapid observational coding system developed by Gottman for the study of conflictual problem-solving marital interaction. The new system was called the Rapid Couples Interaction Scoring System (RCISS). The system was developed to meet seven research needs. First, there are currently many observational coding systems, and each of them focuses on unique aspects of marital interaction, particularly the speaker's affect and the listener's behaviors (see Markman & Notarius, 1987). It would be helpful to have an observational coding system that employs all aspects of marital interaction that have discriminated happy from unhappy couples. Second, it would be helpful if such a system were reasonably economical in terms of the expense of coding. Third, it would be important to show that such a system was sufficiently general across different types of couples. Because most marital interaction research has been conducted with white-collar couples (Krokoff, 1987), Krokoff et al. (1989) selected the social-class dimension as a generalizability test for this new system. I had hoped to discriminate happily from unhappily married couples independent of social class.

Fourth, even if one is successful in developing such a system, there are some questions one would wish to answer about its characteristics. For example, it is important to demonstrate that a system based on the coding of marital interaction in a more artificial laboratory setting correlates with marital interaction obtained at home without an observer present. Fifth, previous research has demonstrated the importance of the speaker's affect (Gottman & Levenson, 1986). A further test of the RCISS would be its ability to correlate with affect codes based both on videotapes made in the laboratory and audiotapes made at home. Sixth, an additional question was whether such a rapid and global observational system could tap sequential dimensions of the reciprocity of positive and negative affect, which logically can be independent of positive and negative affect frequencies if Allison–Liker z-scores of sequential connection are employed (Allison & Liker, 1982). Finally, they addressed the question of whether such a global coding system would relate primarily to overall negative or positive affect, or perhaps to one specific affect such as anger.

The RCISS was developed for these reasons. In the Krokoff et al. (1989) report, summary codes were analyzed across scales for the husband as a speaker and the wife as a speaker, and for the husband as a listener and the wife as a listener. In contrast to previous observational studies, in which results have been obtained in primarily young, college-educated samples, this study selected a sample that varied systematically in marital satisfaction and social class, and one that also varied widely in age and other demographic characteristics.

A3.3. Method

A3.3.1. Subjects

The RCISS validation study focused on 52 married couples from Champaign-Urbana, Illinois, that were recruited with a multistage procedure. Details of these procedures were provided previously by Krokoff (1987), therefore only a brief description follows. The recruitment method initially employed random telephone interviews to obtain a large sample of married households varying widely in marital satisfaction, socioeconomic status, and other demographic characteristics (i.e., age, marital length, children in various stages of rearing, family size). Next, letters describing the project were sent to obtain a pool of interested couples from the telephone sample. Finally, informational home meetings were conducted to obtain the participation of interested couples ($N = 120$). Krokoff (1987) found little evidence for any differential drop out of couples after the survey along the variables measured in the telephone survey. Furthermore, the resulting sample was more comparable to the U.S. general population of married households than previous observational studies in terms of age, marital length, occupational status, education, and family size (Krokoff, 1987).

For observational coding, we selected a carefully matched set of 52 of the couples to fill four cells of a 2×2 factorial design: Occupational status (blue collar, white collar) by marital satisfaction (happy, unhappy). Demographics of this sample are described in Krokoff et al. (1988, 1989).

A3.3.2. Laboratory Videotapes and Home Audiotapes

Two marital problems were identified by the couple on the Problem Inventory as continuing areas of marital disagreement (Gottman, 1979), and one was assigned randomly to be discussed while being audiotaped in the home without any observers present (for a description of the home taping procedures, see Krokoff et al., 1988), and the second problem was discussed while being videotaped in the laboratory (for a description of the laboratory videotaping procedures, see Gottman & Krokoff, 1989). Each discussion lasted 15 minutes.

The home audiotapes were transcribed verbatim, and then each coding unit ("thought unit") was coded for positive, neutral, or negative affect using a hierarchy of voice cues from the Couple's Interaction Scoring System (CISS; Gottman, 1979; Notarius & Markman, 1981) as previously described in Krokoff et al. (1988). The validity of the CISS as a reliable discriminator of distressed versus nondistressed marital interactions has been demonstrated in a series of studies varying widely in demographic characteristics, settings, and marital adjustment criteria. The coding procedure yielded six codes: husband positive affect (H+), husband neutral affect (Ho), husband negative affect (H−), wife positive affect (W+), wife neutral affect (Wo), and wife negative affect (W−). The codes were treated as event sequential data (i.e., the codes were arranged sequentially so that no code could follow itself), which reduced the problem of lag-one autocontingency in the sequential analysis (Bakeman & Gottman, 1986).

A random segment of each audiotape (i.e., four pages from the transcript) was coded by a reliability checker. The Cohen's kappa coefficient of interobserver agreement, controlling for chance agreements, was equal to .67 for the entire study. Additionally, the Cronbach alpha coefficient of generalizability was completed for every code to meet the stringent criterion of interobserver agreement for sequential analysis (in which data cannot be collapsed over time to assess interobserver agreement); that is, for husband positive affect, alpha $= 0.95$; for husband neutral affect, alpha $= 0.97$; for husband negative affect, alpha $- 0.91$; for wife positive affect, alpha $= 0.95$; for wife neutral affect, alpha $= 0.98$; and for wife negative affect, alpha $= 0.90$.

Within each couple, Bakeman's program ELAG4 was employed to compute the Allison and Liker (1982) z-score of sequential connection. The z-score measured the direction and gain in prediction of the consequent code's occurrence given knowledge that the antecedent code had occurred. The Sackett z-scores were used to assess the reciprocation of six positive, negative, and neutral affects (H+ → W+, W+ → H+, H° → W°, W° → H°, H− → W−, and W− → H−).

The videotapes were coded independently coded by a second team of coders using the Specific Affects Coding System (SPAFF), which dismantled affect into specific positive and negative affects. In this study, the coding unit for the SPAFF coding was the turn at speech; a turn at speech included all utterances until the speaker yielded the floor to vocalizations that were not listener vocal backchannels (such as

"Mmm-hmm"). In particular, each speech unit was classified as affectively neutral or as one of five negative affects (anger, disgust/contempt, sadness, fear, whining) or one of four positive affects (affection/caring, humor, interest/curiosity, joy/enthusiasm). The Kappa coefficient of reliability, controlling for chance agreements, was equal to 0.68 for the entire SPAFF coding. This was comparable to reliabilities obtained by Gottman and Krokoff (1989) with the SPAFF, where kappas ranged from .71 to .74.

A3.3.3. Development of the RCISS

Next, the videotapes were coded independently by a third team of coders for positive and negative problem-solving and listening behaviors using the new system, the Rapid Couples Interaction Scoring System (RCISS). This system was developed in two steps. The first step involved a review of the research literature on the relationship between marital interaction and marital satisfaction using all observational systems in current use (for a review of many of these observational coding systems, see Markman, Notarius, Stephen, & Smith, 1981). From this review, a checklist was created that consisted of 27 negative speaker acts, 23 positive speaker acts, 9 negative listener acts, and 6 positive listener acts. These 65 items were sorted into 14 scales. The scales were either negative or positive acts in the following categories: (a) listener acts; (b) agenda building, presents own views; (c) agenda building, responds to partner; (d) problem solving, presents own views; (e) problem solving, responds to partner; and (f) repair and maintenance of the interaction, either task or emotional. A codebook was constructed for these 65 items. The system was designed to be rapid by relaxing the mutually exclusive and exhaustive criterion of observational coding. In other words, for every coding unit, observers could check any and all items that applied to a coding unit.

The second step involved coding a subset of 25 of the 52 videotapes of couples in the study to be described in this paper with this 65-item checklist. Within each scale, item analyses were conducted to eliminate poor items (i.e., items that had either an internal consistency reliability less than 0.35 or were used on less than 1% of the turn units). On the basis of this item analysis, a set of 22 items was kept (see Table A.2). The data for the entire sample of 52 couples were then coded by a new team of observers, who employed the RCISS with the reduced set of coding categories listed in Table A.2.

The turn at speech was the coding unit. Each spouse received a speaker score along a positive–negative scale by subtracting the number of assigned negative speaker codes from the number of assigned

TABLE A.2
RCISS Codes as a Function of Marital Satisfaction

Variable	Satisfied	Dissatisfied	F(1,48)
WSPK	7.15	−27.08	9.42**
HSPK	17.27	−20.54	13.45***
WLIST	72.12	32.12	10.47**
HLIST	57.04	29.04	4.34*

*$p < .05$. **$p < .01$. ***$p < .001$.

positive speaker codes summed over the entire interaction. A similar procedure was used to compute the listener scores. This procedure yielded four scores for each couple: husband speaker (HSPK), wife speaker (WSPK), husband listener (HLIST), and wife listener (WLIST). Despite that tapes were equal in time, a 2 × 2 analysis of variance (blue/white collar by happily/unhappily married) of the number of speaker turns was performed to assess for the possible confounding of interactional length with RCISS speaker and listener codes. These results showed no significant ($p < .05$) main effects or interaction effects [social class $F (1, 48) = .24$, ns; marital happiness $F (1, 48) = 2.67$, ns; interaction $F (1, 48) = 2.8$, ns]. Thus, I can be confident that any significant effects obtained as a function of the marital satisfaction–social-class factors were not due to differences in interactional length.

Because the RCISS scores were based on a continuous scale, and not categorical data, for this initial study reliability was assessed using the Pearson product-moment correlation coefficient for the coders and reliability checker's ratings. The correlations were .62 for the speaker scores and .75 for the listener scores. Although there is no fixed guideline for what represents a reasonable level of reliability between observers using correlations, these correlations are statistically significant and represent a fair amount of shared variance between observers across subjects.

The RCISS is considerably more rapid than the CISS. Even with a small coding unit (the turn), the RCISS can be completed in approximately 4 times real time (i.e., it takes an hour to code 15 minutes of interaction), whereas the CISS takes about 20 times real time for content and affect codes. Both systems require a verbatim transcript of the interaction.

A3.4. Results

A3.4.1. Relationship of RCISS Codes to Marital Satisfaction Dimension.

To assess the relationship of the RCISS codes to the marital satisfaction construct, Krokoff et al. (1988, 1989) performed a series of 2 × 2

ANOVAS, in which happy/unhappy marriages and blue-collar/white-collar status were the between groups factors, and the four RCISS codes (HSPK, WSPK, HLIST, WLIST) were the dependent variables (see Table A.2). They argued that if no main effects or interaction effects were obtained for the social-class variable of the experimental design, this would indicate the generalizability of the marital satisfaction–marital interaction relationship I obtain. This prediction was supported by the results (see Table A.2). This is, statistically significant main effects were obtained only for marital satisfaction (which involved all of the RCISS variables), but the blue-collar/white-collar factor did not enter into any statistically significant main effects or interaction effects. Husbands and wives in unhappy marriages were more negative (and less positive) speakers and listeners than were their counterparts in happy marriages.

Therefore, these results demonstrated the validity of the RCISS codes in terms of being interpersonal correlates of marital satisfaction, and this discrimination generalized across the social class factor of the design.

A3.4.2. Relationship of RCISS Codes to Home Audiotapes (CISS) and SPAFF Data

RCISS validity also was assessed in terms of its ability to predict marital interaction on audiotapes made in the home (without an observer present) and its concurrent validity with the SPAFF coding system (from the laboratory videotapes see Table A.3). Correlations were obtained between the RCISS codes and the CISS affect voice codes of the home audiotapes and the SPAFF codes of the laboratory videotapes. To allow comparison to the CISS results, the five SPAFF negative

TABLE A.3
Correlations of RCISS Variables with CISS and SPAFF Codes

| | CISS Audiotapes | | | | | |
	$H+$	Ho	$H-$	$W+$	Wo	$W-$
WSPK	.04	.14	−.30*	.04	.08	−.36**
HSPK	.03	.32*	−.52***	−.03	.21	−.35**
WLIST	.27*	.43***	.02	.29*	.35**	−.06
HLIST	.22	.42***	.13	.40**	.39**	.10

| | SPAFF Videotapes | | | | | |
	$H+$	Ho	$H-$	$W+$	Wo	$W-$
WSPK	−.06	.12	−.43***	−.05	.24*	−.52***
HSPK	−.12	.36**	−.40**	−.10	.35**	−.35**
WLIST	.45***	.32*	.16	.45***	.25*	.24*
HLIST	.35**	.19	.12	.32*	.08	.24*

*$p < .05.$ **$p < .01.$ ***$p < .001.$

codes were combined into a single (negative affect) code, and the four positive codes were combined into a single positive code (see Table A.3).

The CISS and SPAFF data converged to reveal two patterns. First, as expected, the RCISS speaker codes varied inversely with the negative affect dimension. Second, as expected, the RCISS listener codes varied directly with the positive and neutral affect dimensions. Thus, the more positively (and less negatively) husbands and wives discussed problems in the laboratory, the less negative affect they displayed in both laboratory and home interactions; and the more positively (and less negatively) they listened to each other, the more positive and neutral affects they displayed in laboratory and home interactions.

Next they assessed the reciprocity of positive and negative affect. They computed the correlations of the RCISS variables with the measures from the sequential analysis (from CISS audiotapes, see Table A.4). These results were consistent with those for the code frequencies. The more positively (and less negatively) couples discussed problems in the laboratory, the less likely they were to reciprocate negative affect (especially by wives) during conflict resolution discussions in their homes; the more positively (and the less negatively) they (especially husbands) listened to each other in the laboratory, the more likely they were to reciprocate positive and neutral affects at home.

A3.4.3. Relationship of RCISS Codes to Specific Positive and Negative Affects

Next, the specific positive and negative codes from the SPAFF system were employed to explore further the relationship between RCISS and the affective structure of conflict resolution (see Table A.5). The results for the SPAFF codes revealed that the RCISS listener codes varied directly with the amount of humor and inversely with the amount of

TABLE A.4
Correlation of RCISS Variables with Sequential Variables

RCISS Code	$Z(H+/W+)$	$Z(W+/H+)$	$Z(Ho/Wo)$	$Z(Wo/Ho)$	$Z(H-/W-)$	$Z(W-/H-)$
WSPK	.13	−.04	−.01	−.06	−.10	−.32*
HSPK	.31*	.16	.00	−.02	−.18	−.35**
WLIST	.12	.14	.11	.46***	.14	.03
HLIST	.27*	.41***	.33*	.44***	.18	.24*

Note. $(H+/W+)$ should be read "the sequential z-score of the sequence in which $W+$ is the antecedent code and $H+$ is the consequent code." It measures the amount of reduction in uncertainty that one gains in predicting $H+$ (over base rates) in knowing that $W+$ preceded $H+$.

*$p < .05$. **$p < .01$. ***$p < .001$.

TABLE A.5
Correlations of the RCISS Variables with Specific Positive and Negative Affects (SPAFF)

SPAFF Codes	HSPK	WSPK	HLIST	WLIST
Positive				
H Humor	− .15	− .08	.35**	.45***
H Affection	.34*	.21	.11	.08
H Interest	− .01	.06	− .06	− .02
H Joy	.07	.01	.11	.10
W Humor	− .13	− .05	.35**	.49***
W Affection	.21	.11	− .08	− .17
W Interest	− .02	− .08	.02	.00
W Joy	− .03	− .14	− .21	− .21
Negative				
H Anger	− .48***	− .35**	.04	− .07
H Contempt	− .45***	− .36**	.11	.20
H Whine	.23*	.20	.20	.11
H Sad	.16	.05	− .08	− .03
H Fear	.10	− .19	.07	.19
W Anger	− .48***	− .38**	.09	− .05
W Contempt	− .25*	− .49***	.22	.20
W Whine	.28*	.12	.24*	.12
W Sad	− .10	− .06	− .24*	− .31*
W Fear	− .12	− .09	.07	.30*

*$p < .05$. **$p < .01$. ***$p < .001$.

sadness, and the RCISS speaker codes varied inversely with anger and disgust/contempt; both husband and wife whining were related directly to the husband's speaker score.

A3.5. Discussion

These results reported by Krokoff et al. (1988, 1989) demonstrated that it is possible to obtain global codes of conflictual marital interaction reasonably rapidly, and that these codes are able to: (a) discriminate satisfied from dissatisfied married couples; (b) discriminate satisfied from dissatisfied couples independent of social class; (c) correlate well with affect codes of the couples interaction at home (CISS) and with positive and negative affect reciprocity; and (d) correlate with more detailed specific affect codes of the laboratory tapes in interpretable ways that implicate humor, anger, disgust-contempt, sadness, whining, and fear.

The results also have implications for understanding the interpersonal correlates of marital distress, particularly with respect to the relative contributions of global and detailed coding systems. The affective dimension of conflict resolution emerged from observational research conducted in the last 14 years as the most important interpersonal correlate of marital distress. In this research, the negative affect dimension has been the most consistent discriminator of distressed versus nondistressed interactions. Krokoff et al. (1988, 1989) found that the RCISS speaker codes were associated primarily with negative affect. Husbands and wives who constructively raised marital issues were less negative and less likely to escalate negative affect (as measured by the negative affect reciprocity variable). Furthermore, the SPAFF coding revealed that husbands and wives who were more constructive speakers were less angry and contemptuous.

The listener codes, which sampled nonverbal aspects of emotional responsiveness (e.g., facial responsiveness), further contributed to my understanding of the structure of specific negative affects. They found that sad wives were worse listeners and had husbands who were worse listeners, whereas wives who whined had husbands who were better listeners. Fearful wives, who may be more vigilant in monitoring their marital interactions, also were better listeners.

Furthermore, the RCISS listener codes contributed to my understanding of the positive affect dimension. Husbands and wives who were better listeners displayed more positive affect, particularly humor. Husbands who were better listeners had wives who were more affectively engaged in the conflict, in terms of reciprocating both positive and negative affects.

References

Achenbach, T. M., & Edelbrock, C. S. (1981). Behavioral problems and competencies reported by parents of normal and disturbed children aged four through sixteen. *Monographs of the Society for Research in Child Development, 16.*

Achenbach, T. M., & Edelbrock, C. S. (1984). Psychopathology of childhood. *Annual Review of Psychology, 35,* 227–256.

Addis, M. E., & Jacobson, N. S. (1991). Integration of cognitive therapy and behavioral marital therapy for depression. *Journal of Psychotherapy Integration, 1,* 249–264.

Aida, Y., & Falbo, T. (1991). Relationships between marital satisfaction, resources and power strategies. *Sex Roles, 24,* 43–56.

Aitken, S. (1977). *Gender preference in infancy.* Unpublished master's thesis, University of Edinburgh, Great Britain.

Albrecht, S. L. (1979). Correlates of marital happiness among the remarried. *Journal of Marriage and the Family, 41,* 857–867.

Allison, P. D., & Liker, J. K. (1982). Analyzing sequential data on dyadic interaction: A comment on Gottman. *Psychological Bulletin, 91,* 393–403.

Altrocchi, J., & Crosby, R. (1989). Clarifying and measuring the concept of traditional versus egalitarian roles in marriage. *Sex Roles, 20,* 639–658.

Andreassi, J. L. (1989). *Psychophysiology: Human behavior and physiological response.* Hillsdale, NJ: Lawrence Erlbaum Associates.

Andrews, G., Tennant, D., Hewson, D. M., & Valliant, G. E. (1978). Life event stress, social support, coping style, and risk of psychological impairment. *Journal of Nervous and Mental Disease, 166,* 307–316.

Appel, M. A., Holroyd, K. A., & Gorkin, L. (1983). Anger and the etiology and progression of physical illness. In L. Temoshok, C. van Dyke, & L. S. Zegans (Eds.), *Emotions in health and illness: Theoretical and research foundations.* New York: Grune & Stratton.

Aries, E. (1976). Interaction patterns and themes of male, female, and mixed groups. *Small Group Behavior, 7,* 7–18.

Arnold, V. I. (1986). *Catstrophe theory.* Berlin: Springer- Verlag.

Azrin, N. H., Naster, B. J., & Jones, R. (1973). Reciprocity counseling: A rapid learning based procedure for marital counseling. *Behavior Research and Therapy, 11,* 365–382.

Ax, A. A. (1964). Goals and methods of psychophysiology. *Psychophysiology, 1,* 8–25.

Baccus, G. K. (1988). Perception of intent in marital communication: An extension of the behavioral marital approach and the measurement of encoding and decoding. *Dissertation Abstracts International, 48(9-B),* 2775.

Bakeman, R. (1978). Untangling streams of behavior: Sequential analysis of observational data. In G. P. Sackett (Eds.), *Observing behavior: Vol. 2. Data collection and analysis methods.* Baltimore: University Park Press.

Bakeman, R., & Gottman, J. (1986). *Observing interaction: An introduction to sequential analysis.* New York: Cambridge University Press.

Barnett, R., & Baruch. G. (1987). Mother's participation in child care: Patterns and consequences. In F. Crosby (Ed.), *Spouse, parent, worker: On gender and multiple roles.* New Haven, CT: Yale University Press.

Barrett, M., & McIntosh, M. (1982). *The anti-social family.* London: Verso.

Baruch, G., & Barnett, R. (1986). Consequence of fathers' participation in family work: Parents' role strain and well-being. *Journal of Personality and Social Psychology, 51,* 983–992.

Bateson, G., Jackson, D. D., Haley, J., & Weakland, J. (1956). Toward a theory of schizophrenia. *Behavioral Science, 1,* 1–264.

Baucom, D. H. (1982). A comparison of behavioral contracting and problem-solving/communication training in behavioral marital therapy. *Behavior Therapy, 13,* 162–174.

Baucom, D., & Aiken, P. (1984). Sex role identity, marital satisfaction, and response to behavioral marital therapy. *Journal of Consulting and Clinical Psychology, 52,* 438–444.

Baucom, D. H., & Hoffman, J. A. (1986). The effectiveness of marital therapy: Current status and application to the clinical setting. In N. Jacobson & A. Gurman (Eds.), *Clinical handbook of marital therapy* (pp. 597–620). New York: Guilford.

Baum, A., Grunberg, N. E., & Singer, J. E. (1982). The use of psychological and neuroendocrinological measurements in the study of stress. *Health Psychology, 1,* 217–236.

Baum, A. S., Lundberg, U., Grunberg, N. E., Singer, J. E. & Gatchel, R. J. (1985). Urinary catecholamines in behavioral research on stress. In C. R. Lake & M. G. Ziegler (Eds.), *The catecholamines in psychiatric and neurologic disorders* (pp. 55–72). London: Butterworths.

Bales, R. F. (1950). *Interaction process analysis.* Cambridge, MA: Addison-Wesley.

Becker, G. (1971). Social rearing effects in the male and female rat on affiliation and autonomic reactivity in the open field. *Developmental Psychology, 5,* 463–468.

Belenky, M., Clinchy, B., Goldberger, N., & Tarule, J. (1986). *Women's ways of knowing: The development of self, voice and mind.* New York: Basic Books.

Bell, R. R. (1975). *Marriage and family interaction.* Homewood, IL: Dorsey Press.

Belsky, J., Spanier, G. B., & Rovine, M. (1983). Stability and change in marriage across the transition to parenthood. *Journal of Marriage and the Family, 45,* 567–577.

Benin, M., & Agostinelli, J. (1988). Husbands' and wives' satisfaction with the division of labor. *Journal of Marriage and the Family, 50,* 349–361.

Bennett, N. G., Blanc, A. K., & Bloom, D. E. (1988). Commitment and the modern union: Assessing the link between premarital cohabitation and subsequent marital stability. *American Sociological Review, 53,* 127–138.

Bentler, P. M., & Newcomb, M. D. (1978). Longitudinal study of marital success and failure. *Journal of Consulting and Clinical Psychology, 46,* 1053–1070.

Berk, S. (1985). *The gender factory: The apportionment of work in American households.* New York: Plenum Press.

Berkman, L. F., & Breslow, L. (1983). *Health and the ways of living: The Alameda County Study.* New York: Oxford University Press.

Berkman, L. F., & Syme, S. L. (1979). Social networks, host resistance, and mortality: A nine-year follow-up study of Alameda County residents. *American Journal of Epidemiology, 109,* 186–204.

Berley, R. A., & Jacobson, N. S. (1984). Causal attributions in intimate realtionships: Toward a model of cognitive behavioral marital therapy. In P. Kendall (Ed.), *Advances in cognitive-behavioral research and therapy* (Vol. 3, pp. 2–90). New York: Academic Press.

Bernard, J. (1982). *The future of marriage.* New Haven CT: Yale University Press.

Berne, R. M., & Levy, M. N. (1981). *Cardiovascular physiology.* St. Louis: C. V. Mosby.

Berscheid, E. (1983). Emotion. In H. H. Kelley, E. Bersheid, A. Christensen, J. H. Harvey, T. L. Huston, G. Levinger, E. McClintock, L. A. Peplau, & D. R. Peterson (Eds.), *Close relationships* (pp. 110–168). New York: W. H. Freeman.

Berscheid, E., & Walster, E. H. (1969). *Interpersonal attraction.* Cambridge, MA: Addison-Wesley.

Billings, A. (1979). Conflict resolutions in distressed and nondistressed married couples. *Journal of Consulting and Clinical Psychology, 47,* 365–376.

Birchler, G., Weiss, R., & Vincent, J. (1975). Multimethod analysis of social reinforcement exchange between maritally distressed and nondistressed spouse and stranger dyads. *Journal of Personality and Social Psychology, 31,* 349–360.

Bishop, Y. M. M., Fienberg, S. E., & Holland, P. W. (1975). *Discrete multivariate analysis: Theory and practice.* Cambridge, MA: MIT Press.

Block, J. H., Block, J., & Gjerde, P. F. (1986). The personality of children prior to divorce: A prospective study. *Child Development, 57,* 827–840.

Block, J. H., Block, J., & Morrison, A. (1981). Parental agreement-disagreement on child-rearing and gender-related personality correlates in children. *Child Development, 52,* 965–974.

Blood, R. O., & Wolfe, D. M. (1960). *Husbands and wives: The dynamics of married living.* New York: Free Press.

Bloom, B., Asher, S., & White, S. (1978). Marital disruption as a stressor: A review and analysis. *Psychological Bulletin, 85,* 867–894.

Bloom, B., Hodges, W. F., Caldwell, R. A., Systra, L., & Cedrone, A. R. Marital separation: A community survey. *Journal of Divorce, 1,* 7–19.

Blumstein, P., & Schwartz, P. (1983). *American couples.* New York: William & Morrow.

Bohannon, P. (1970). The six stations of divorce. In P. Bohannon (Eds.), *Divorce and after* (pp. 29–55). Garden City, NY: Doubleday.

Bohus, B., Koolhaas, J. M., Steffens, A. B., Fokkema, D. S., & Scheurink, A. J. W. (1989). Catecholamines and behavioral physiology of stress. *Advances in Gynecologic Endocrinology, 1,* 125–130.

Booth, A., Johnson, D., & Edwards, J. N. (1983). Measuring marital instability. *Journal of Marriage and the Family, 45,* 387–394.

Booth, A., Johnson, D. R., White L., & Edwards, J. N. (1984). Women, outside employment, and marital instability. *American Journal of Sociology, 90,* 567–583.

Booth, A., & White, L. (1980). Thinking about divorce. *Journal of Marriage and the Family, 42,* 605–616.

Boulding, K. E. (1962). *Conflict and defense: A general theory.* New York: Harper & Row.

Bower, T. G. R. (1989). *The rational infant: Learning in infancy.* New York: W. H. Freeman.

Brandewien, R. A., Brown, C. A., & Fox, E. M. (1974). Women and children last: The social situation of divorced mothers and their families. *Journal of Marriage and the Family, 36,* 498–514.

Bradley, P. B. (1958). The central action of certain drugs in relation to te reticular formation of the brain. In H. H. Jasper, L. D. Proctor, R. S. Knighton, W. C. Noshay, & R. T. Costello (Eds.), *Reticular formation of the brain.* Boston, MA: Little, Brown.

Brinton-Lee, M. C. (1980). *The determinants of group dissolution: A study of divorce rates in contemporary Japan.* Unpublished masters thesis, University of Washington, Seattle, WA.

Broel-Plateris, A. (1961). *Marriage disruption of divorce law.* Chicago, IL: University of Chicago Press.

Brown, G. S., Bhrolchain, M. N., & Harris, T. (1975). Social class and psychiatric disturbance among women in an urban population. *Sociology, 9,* 223–254.

Brown, P. C., & Smith, T. W. (1992). Social influence, marriage, and the heart: Cardiovascular consequences of interperesonal control in husbands and wives. *Health Psychology, 11,* 88–96.

Bruner, J. S., & Tagiuri, R. (1954). The perception of people. In G. Lindzey (Ed.), *Handbook of social psychology* (Vol. 2, pp. 634–654). Reading MA: Addison-Wesley.

Buck, R. (1975). Nonverbal communication of affect in children. *Journal of Personality and Social Psychology, 31,* 644–653.

Buck, R. (1977). Nonverbal communication of affect in preschool children: Relationships with personality and skin conductance. *Journal of Personality and Social Psychology, 35,* 225–236.

Buck, R. (1980) Nonverbal behavior and the theory of emotion: The facial feedback hypothesis. *Journal of Personality and Social Psychology, 30,* 811–824.

Buck, R. W. (1979). Individual differences in non-verbal sending accuracy and electrodermal responding: The externalizing-internalizing dimension. In R.

Rosenthal (Ed.), *Skill in non-verbal communication* (pp. 140–170). Cambridge, MA: Oelgeschlager, Gunn & Hain.

Buehlman, K. (1991). *The oral history coding system.* Unpublished manual, University of Washington, Seattle, WA.

Buehlman, K., Gottman, J. M., & Katz, L. (1992). How a couple views their past predicts their future: Predicting divorce from an oral history interview. *Journal of Family Psychology, 5,* 295–318.

Bugaighis, M. A., Schumm, W. R., Jurich, A. P., & Bollman, S. R. (1985). Factors associated with thoughts of marital separation. *Journal of Divorce, 9,* 49–59.

Burgaff, C., & Sillars, A. (1986). *A critical examination of sex differences in marital communication.* Paper presented at the Speech Communication Association, Chicago.

Burger, A. L., & Jacobson, N. S. (1979). The relationship between sex role characteristics, couple satisfaction, and couple problem-solving skills. *American Journal of Family Therapy, 7,* 52–60.

Burgess, E. W., & Cottrell, L. S. (1939). *Predicting success or failure in marriage.* Englewood Cliffs, NJ: Prentice Hall.

Burgess, E. W., & Locke, H. J. (1945). *The family, from institustion to companionship.* New York: American Book Co.

Burgess, E. W., Locke, H. J., & Thomes, M. M. (1971). *The Family from Institution to Companionship.* New York: American Book

Burgess, E. W., & Wallin, P. (1953). *Engagement and marriage.* Chicago, Illinois: Lippincott.

Burke, R. J., Weier, T., & Harrison, D. (1976). Disclosure of problems and tensions experienced by marital problems. *Psychological Reports, 38,* 531–542.

Burman, B., & Margolin, G. (1992). Analysis of the association between marital relationships and health problems. *Psychological Bulletin, 112,* 39–63.

Cacioppo, J. T., & Petty, R. E. (Eds.). (1983). *Social psychophysiology.* New York: Guilford.

Cacioppo, J. T., & Tassinary, L. G. (Eds.). (1990). *Principles of psychophysiology: Physical, social, and inferential elements.* New York: Cambridge University Press.

Campbell, A., Converse, P. E., & Rodgers, W. L. (1976). *The quality of American life.* New York: Russell Sage Foundation.

Cannon, W. B. (1915). *Bodily changes in pain, hunger, fear and rage.* New York: Appleton.

Cannon, W. B. (1927). The James–Lange theory of emotion: A critical examination and an alternative theory. *American Journal of Psychology, 39,* 106–124.

Cantor, J. R., Zillmann, D., & Bryant, J. (1975). Enhancement of experienced sexual arousal in response to erotic stimuli through misattribution of unrelated residual excitation. *Journal of Personality and Social Psychology, 32,* 69–75.

Chance, M.R.A., & Larsen, R.R. (1976). *The social structure of attention.* New York: Wiley.

Cherlin, A. (1981). *Marriage, divorce, remarriage.* Cambridge, MA: Harvard University Press.

Chester, R., & Kooy, G.A. (1977). *Divorce in Europe.* Leiden: Martinus Nijhoff Social Sciences Division.

Christensen, A. (1988). Dysfunctional interaction patterns in couples. In P. Noller & M. A. Fitzpatrick (Eds.), *Perspectives on marital interaction* (pp. 31-52). Philadelphia, PA: Multilingual Matters.

Christensen, A. (1991). *The demand withdraw pattern in marital interaction*. Paper presented at the annual meeting of the Association for the Advancement of Behavior Therapy, New York.

Christensen, A., & Heavey, C.L. (1990). Situation versus personality in marital conflict. *Journal of Personality and Social Psychology*.

Cleary, P. D. (1987). Gender differences in stress-related disorders. In R. C. Barnett, L. Biener, & G. K. Baruch (Eds.), *Gender and stress* (pp. 39-72). New York: Free Press.

Cohen, J. (1960). A coefficient of agreement for nominal scales. *Education and Psychological Measurement, 20*, 37-46.

Cohen, R. (1971). *Dominance and defiance: A study of marital instability in an Islamic African society*. Washington, DC: American Anthroplological Association.

Cohen, R. S., & Christensen, A. (1980). A further examination of demand characteristics in marital interaction. *Journal of Consulting and Clinical Psychology, 48*, 121-123.

Coles, M. G. H., Jennings, J. R., & Stern, J. A. (Eds.). (1984). *Psychophysiological perspectives: Festschrift for Beatrice and John Lacey*. New York: Van Nostrand Reinhold.

Collins, A., & Frankenhaeuser, M. (1978). Stress responses in male and female engineering students. *Journal of Human Stress, 4*, 43-48.

Constantine, J. A., & Bahr, S. J. (1980). Locus of control and marital stability: A longitudinal study. *Journal of Divorce, 4*, 11-22.

Coser, L. A. (1964). *The functions of social conflict*. Glencoe, IL: Free Press.

Cousins, P.C., & Vincent, J.P. (1983). Supportive and aversive behavior following spousal complaints. *Journal of Marriage and the Family, 45*, 679-682.

Cowan, C. P, Cowan, P. A., Heming, G., & Miller, N. B. (1991). Becoming a family: Marriage, parenting and child development. In P.A. Cowan & M. Hetherington (Eds.), *Family transitions*. Hillsdale, NJ: Lawrence Erlbaum Associates.

Cowan, P. A., & Cowan, C. P. (1987, April). *Couple's relationships, parenting styles and the child's development at three*. Paper presented at the Society for Research in Child Development. Baltimore, MD.

Cowan, P. A., & Cowan, C. P. (1990). Becoming a family: Research and intervention. In I. Sigel & A. Brody (Eds.), *Family research*. Hillsdale, NJ: Lawrence Erlbaum Associates.

Crane, D. R., & Mead, D. E. (1980). The marital status inventory: Some preliminary data on an instrument to measure marital dissolution potential. *American Journal of Family Therapy, 8*, 31-35.

Crosby, F. (1991). *Juggling: The unexpected advantages of balancing career and home for women and their families*. New York: Free Press.

Crouter, A., Perry-Jenkins, Huston, T., & McHale, S. (1987). Processes underlying father involvement in dual-career and single-earner families. *Developmental Psychology, 23*, 431-440.

Cuber, J. F., & Harroff, P. B. (1965). *The significant Americans.* New York: Appleton-Century-Crofts.

Cummings, E. M. (1987). Coping with background anger in early childhood. *Child Development, 58,* 976–984.

Cummings, E. M., Ballard, M., El-Sheikh, M., & Lake, M (1991). Resolution and children's responses to interadult anger. *Developmental Psychology, 27,* 462–470.

Cummings, E. M., Iannotti, R.J., & Zahn-Waxler, C. (1985). Influence of conflict between adults on the emotions and aggression of young children. *Developmental Psychology, 21,* 495–507.

Cummings, E. M., Vogel, D., Cummings, J., & El-Sheikh,M. (1989). Children's responses to different forms of expression of anger between adults. *Child Development, 60,* 1392–1404.

Cummings, E. M., Zahn-Waxler, C., & Radke-Yarrow, M. (1981). Young children's responses to expressions of anger and affection by others in the family. *Child Development, 52,* 1274–1282.

Darwin, C. (1872). *The expression of the emotions in man and animals.* London: John Murray.

Davidson, R. J. (1984a). Affect, cognition, and hemispheric specialization. In C. E. Izard, J. Kagan, & R. B. Zajonc (Eds.), *Emotions, cognition, and behavior* (pp. 320–365). New York: Cambridge University Press.

Davidson, R. J. (1984b). Hemispheric asymmetry and emotion. In K.R. Scherer & P. Ekman (Eds.), *Approaches to emotion.* Hillsdale, NJ: Lawrence Erlbaum Associates.

Deutsch, M. (1969). Conflicts: Productive and destructive. *Journal of Social Issues, 25,* 7–41.

Deaux, K., & Major, B. (1990). A social-psychological model of gender. In D. L. Rhode (Ed.), *Theoretical perspectives on sexual difference.* New Haven, CT: Yale University Press.

Dembroski, T. M., MacDougall, J. M., Eliot, R. S., & Buell, J. C. (1983). Stress, emotions, behavior, and cardiovascular disease. In L. Temoshok, C. van Dyke, & L. S. Zegans (Eds.), *Emotions in health and illness: Theoretical and research foundations.* New York: Grune & Stratton.

Dickstein, S., & Parke, R. D, (1988). Social referencing in infancy: A glance at fathers and marriage. *Child Development, 59,* 506–511.

DiMascio, A., Boyd, R. W., & Greenblatt, M. (1957). Physiological correlates of tension and antagonism during psychotherapy: A study of "interpersonal physiology." *Psychosomatic Medicine, 19,* 99–104.

DiMascio, A., Boyd, R. W., Greenblatt, M., & Solomon, H. C. (1955). The psychiatric interview: A sociophysiologic study. *Diseases of the Nervous System, 16,* 4–9.

Dimsdale, J. E., & Moss, J. (1980a). Plasma catecholamines in stress and exercise. *JAMA, 243,* 340–342.

Dimsdale, J. E., & Moss, J. (1980b). Short-term catecholamine response to psychological stress. *Psychosomatic Medicine, 42,* 493–497.

Dittes, J. E. (1957a). Extinction during psychotherapy of GSR accompanying "embarassing statements." *Journal of Abnormal and Social Psychology, 54,* 187–191.

Dittes, J. E. (1957b). Galvanic skin response as a measure of patient's reaction to therapist's permissiveness. *Journal of Abnormal and Social Psychology, 55*, 295–303.

Duffy, E. (1957). The psychological significance of the concept of "arousal" or "activation." *Psychological Review, 64*, 265–275.

Duncan, S. D. Jr., & Fiske, D.W. (1977). *Face-to-face interaction: Research methods and theory*. Hillsdale, NJ: Lawrence Erlbaum Associates.

Dutton, D.G. (1988). *The domestic assault of women: Psychological and criminal justice perspectives*. Boston, MA: Allyn & Bacon.

Easterbrooks, M. A. (1987, April). *Early family development: Longitudinal impact of marital quality*. Paper presented at the Meeting of the Society for Research in Child Development, Baltimore, MD.

Easterbrooks, M. A. & Emde, R. A. (1988). Marital and parent–child relationships: The role of affect in the family system. In R. A. Hinde & J. Stevenson-Hinde (Eds.), *Relationships within families: Mutual influence*. Oxford: Clarenden Press.

Easterlin, R. A. (1980). *Birth and fortune: The impact of numbers on personal welfare*. New York: Basic Books.

Echols, A. (1984). The taming of the id: Feminist sexual politics: 1968–1983. In C.S.Vance (Ed.), *Pleasure and danger: Exploring female sexuality*. Boston: Routledge & Kegan Paul.

Eibl-Eibesfeldt, I. (1989). *Human ethology*. New York: Aldine de Gruyter.

Eichorn, D. (1970). Physiological development. In P. H. Mussen (Eds.), *Carmichael's manual of child psychology* (Vol. 1). New York: Wiley.

Eisdorfer, C., Doerr, H., & Follette, W. (1977). Age and sex interaction with electrodermal level and response. *Psychophysiology, 15*, 268.

Ekman, P. (1979). About brows: emotional and conversational signals. In Mivon Cranach, K. F, W. Lepenies, & D. Ploog (Eds.), New York: Cambridge University Press *Human ethology* (pp. 169–249).

Ekman, P. (1984). Expression and the nature of emotion. In K. R. Scherer & P. Ekman (Eds.), *Approaches to emotion*. Hillsdale, NJ: Lawrence Erlbaum Associates.

Ekman, P., & Friesen W. V. (1978). *Facial Action Coding System*. Palo Alto, CA: Consulting Psychologist Press.

Ekman, P., & Friesen, W. V. (1982). Felt, false and miserable smiles. *Journal of Nonverbal Behavior, 6*, 238–252.

Ekman, P., Friesen, W. V., & Ellsworth, P. (1972). *Emotion in the human face: Guidelines for research and an integration of findings*. New York: Pergamon Press.

Ekman, P., Friesen, W. V., & Simons, R. C. (1985). Is the startle reaction an emotion? *Journal of Personality and Social Psychology, 49*, 1416–1426.

Ekman, P., Levenson, R. W., & Friesen, W. V. (1983). Autonomic nervous system activity distinguishes among emotions. *Science, 221*, 1208–1210.

Ekman, P., & Scherer, K. (1982). In P. Ekman & K. Scherer (Eds.), *Approaches to emotion*. Hillsdale, NJ: Lawrence Erlbaum Associates.

Elder, G. H., Jr. (1984). *Children of the great depression*. Chicago, IL: University of Chicago Press.

Elliott, R. (1964). Physiological activity and performance: A comparison ofkindergarten children with young adults. *Psychological Monographs, 78.*

Ellis, D., Fisher, B. A., Drecksel, G., Hoch, D., & Werbel, W. (1976). *Relational interaction coding systems.* Unpublished manuscript, Purdue University, Department of Communication, West Lafayette, IN.

Elwood, R. W., & Jacobson, N. S. (1982). Spouses agreement in reporting their behavioral interactions: A clinical replication. *Journal of Consulting and Clinical Psychology, 50* 783–784.

Emde, J. E. (1991). *Marital communication and stress.* Unpublished doctoral dissertation, University of Denver, Denver, CO.

Emery, R. E. (1982). Interparental conflict and the children of discord and divorce. *Psychological Bulletin, 92,* 310–330.

Emery, R. E. (1988). *Marriage, divorce, and children's adjustment.* Newbury Park, CA: Sage.

Emery, R. E., & O'Leary, K. D. (1982). Children's perceptions of marital discord and behavior problems of boys and girls. *Journal of Abnormal Child Psychology, 10,* 11–24.

Ewart, C. K., Taylor, C. B., Kraemer, H. C., & Agras, W. S. (1984). Reducing blood pressure reactivity during interpersonal conflict: Effects of marital communication training. *Behavior Therapy, 15,* 473–484.

Eysenck, M. W. (1982). *Attention and arousal: Cognition and performance.* Berlin: Springer-Verlag.

Falbo, T., & Peplau, L. A. (1980). Power strategies in intimate relationships. *Journal of Personality and Social Psychology, 38,* 618–628.

Fankish, C. J. (1992). Warning! Your marriage may be hazardous to your health: Spouse-pair risk factors and cardiovascular reactivity. *Dissertation Abstracts International, 52,* 5532.

Feld, S. (1982). *Sound and sentiment.* Philadelphia, PA: Pennsylvania Press.

Feree, M. (1976). The view from below: Women's employment and gender equality in working-class families. In B. Hess & M. Sussman (Eds.), *Women and the family: Two decades of change.* New York: Haworth Press.

Ferraro, B., & Markman, H. (1981). *Application of the behavioral model of marriage to deaf marital relationships.* Paper presented at the Midwestern psychological Association, Detroit.

Ferraro, K. F., & Wan, T. T. (1986). Marital contributions to wellbeing in later life: An examination of Bernard's thesis. *American Behavioral Scientist, 29,* 423–437.

Filsinger, E. E., & Thoma, S. J. (1988). Behavioral antecedents of relationship stability: A five-year longitudinal study. *Journal of Marriage and the Family, 50,* 785–795.

Fincham, F. D., Bradbury, T. N. (1987). The assessment of marital quality: A reevaluation. *Journal of Marriage and the Family, 49,* 797–809.

Fincham, F. D., Bradbury, T. N., & Scott, C. K. (1990). Cognition in marriage. In F. D. Fincham & T. N. Bradbury (Eds.), *The psychology of marriage* (pp. 118–149). New York: Guilford.

Fisher, L. E., & Kotses, H. (1974). Experimenter and subject sex effects in the skin conductance response. *Psychophysiology, 11,* 191–196

Fitzpatrick, M. A. (1984). A typological approach to marital interaction: Recent theory and research. *Advances in Experimental Social Psychology, 18,* 1–47.

Fitzpatrick, M. A. (Ed.).(1988). *Between husbands and wives: Communication in marriage.* Beverly Hills, CA: Sage.

Fitzpatrick, M. A., & Kalbfleisch, P. (1988). Problem solving during marital conflict. In M. A. Fitzpatrick (Ed.), *Between husbands and wives: Communication in marriage* (pp. 150–153). Beverly Hills, CA: Sage.

Fivaz, R. (1991). Thermodynamics of complexity. *Systems Research, 9,* 19–32

Fivaz, R. (in press). *Morphodynamics: Ergodicity in complex systems.* Unpublished manuscript, l'Ecole polytechnique federale de Lausanne and l'Universie de Geneve.

Floyd, F. J., & Markman, H. J. (1983). Observational biases in spouse observation: Toward a cognitive/behavioral model of marriage. *Journal of Consulting and Clinical Psychology, 51,* 450–457.

Forehand, R., Brody, G., Long, N., Slotkin, J., & Fauber, R. (1986). Divorce/ divorce potential and interparental conflict: The relationship to early adolescent social and cognitive functioning. *Journal of Adolescent Research, 1,* 389–397.

Forsman, L., & Lindblad, L. E. (1988). Effect of mental stress on baroreceptor-mediated changes in blood pressure and heart rate and on plasma catecholamines and subjective responses in healthy men and women. *Psychosomatic Medicine, 45,* 435–445.

Fowers, B. J., & Olson, D. H. (1986). Predicting marital success with PREPARE: A predictive validity study. *Journal of Marital and Family Therapy, 12,* 403–413.

Frankenhaeuser, M. (1974). Sex differences in reactions to psychosocial stressors and psychoactive drugs. In L. Levi (Ed.), *Society, stress, and disease, Vol.III: Problems specific to the relationship between woman and man, and to family life.* London: Oxford University Press.

Frankenhaeuser, M. (1975). Experimental approaches to the study of catecholamines and emotion. In L. Levi (Eds.), *Emotions: Their parameters and measurement.* New York: Raven Press.

Frankenhaeuser, M. (1976). The role of peripheral catecholamines in adaptation to understimulation and overstimulation. In G. Serban (Eds.), *Psychopathology of human adaptation.* New York: Plenum.

Frankenhaeuser, M. (1978). Psychoneuroendocrine sex differences in adaptation to the psychosocial environment. In L. Carenza, P. Paucheri, & L. Zichella (Eds.), *Clinical psychoneuroendocrinology in reproduction.* New York: Academic Press.

Frankenhaeuser, M. (1982). Challenge-control interaction as reflected in sympathetic-adrenal and pituitary-adrenal activity: Comparison between the sexes. *Scandanavian Journal of Psychology, 71,* 158–164.

Frankenhaeuser, M., Rauste-von Wright, M., Collins, A., von Wrights, J., Sedvall, G., & Swahn, C. (1978). Sex differences in psychoneuroendocrine reactions to examination stress. *Psychosomatic Medicine, 40,* 334–343.

Friedman, S. B., Mason, J. W., & Hamburg, D. A. (1963). Urinary 17-Hydroxycorticosteroid levels in parents of children with neoplastic disease: A study of chronic psychological stress. *Psychosomatic Medicine, 25,* 365–376.

Frodi, A. M., Lamb, M. E., Leavitt, L. A., & Donovan, W. L. (1978). Fathers and mothers' responses to infant smiles and cries. *Infant Behavior and Development*, 1, 187–198.

Frodi, A., Macaulay, J., & Thome, P. R. (1977). Are women always less aggressive than men? A review of experimental literature. *Psychological Bulletin*, 84, 634–660.

Gaelick, L., Bodenhausen, G. V., & Wyer, R. S. Jr. (1985). Emotional communication in close relationships. *Journal of Personality and Social Psychology*, 49, 1246–1265.

Gagne, R. M. (1977). *The conditions of learning*. New York: Holt, Rinehart & Winston. (Original work published 1965)

Gale, A., & Edwards, J. A. (Eds.), (1983a). *Physiological correlates of human behavior, Vol. 1: Basic issues*. London: Academic Press.

Gale, A., & Edwards, J. A. (Eds.) (1983b). *Physiological correlates of human behavior, Vol. 2: Attention and performance*. London: Academic Press.

Gale, A., & Edwards, J. A. (Eds.), (1983c). *Physiological correlates of human behavior, Vol. 3: Individual differences and psychopathology*. London: Academic Press.

Gersten, J. C., Friis, R., & Langner, T. S. (1976). Life dissatisfactions, job dissatisfactions, and illness of married men over time. *American Journal of Epidemiology*, 103, 333–341.

Gilbert, L. (1985). *Men in dual-career families: Current realities and future prospects*. Hillsdale, NJ: Lawrence Erlbaum Associates.

Gilligan, C. (1982). *In a different voice: Psychological theory and women's development*. Cambridge, MA: Harvard University Press.

Ginsberg, D., & Gottman, J. (1986). The conversation of college roommates. In J. Gottman & J. Parker (Eds.), *Conversations of friends: Speculations on affective development*. NY: Cambridge University Press.

Glass, G. V. & Stanley, J. C. (1970). *Statistical methods in education and psychology*. Engelwood Cliffs, NJ: Prentice Hall.

Glenn, N. D., & Kramer, K. B. (1985). The psychological well-being of adult children of divorce. *Journal of Marriage and the Family*, 47, 905–912.

Glenn, N. D., & Shelton, B. A. (1985). Regional differences in divorce in the United States. *Journal of Marriage and the Family*, 47, 641–651.

Glenn, N. D., & Weaver, C. N. (1978). A multivariate, multisurvey study of marital happiness. *Journal of Marriage and the Family*, 40, 269–282.

Glick, P. C. (1984). How American families are changing. *American Demographics*, 6, 20–27.

Goldfried, M. R., & D'Zurilla, T. J. (1969). A behavioral-analytic model for assessing competence. In C. D. Spielberger (Ed.), *Current topics in clinical and community psychology* (Vol. 1, pp. 151–196). New York: Academic Press.

Goodenough, F. L. (1931). *Anger in young children*. Minneapolis, MN: University of Minnesota Press.

Gottman, J. (1981). *Time series analysis: A comprehensive introduction for social scientists*. New York: Cambridge University Press.

Gottman, J., Markman, H., & Notarius, C. (1977). The topography of marital conflict: A study of verbal and nonverbal behavior. *Journal of Marriage and the Family*, 39, 461–477.

Gottman, J., Notarius, C., Gonso, J., & Markman, H. (1976). *A couple's guide to communication*. Champaign, IL: Research Press.

Gottman, J., & Porterfield, A. (1981). Communicative competence in the nonverbal behavior of married couples, *Journal of Marriage and the Family, 43*, 817–824.

Gottman, J. M. (1979). *Marital interaction: Experimental investigations*. New York: Academic Press.

Gottman, J. M. (1980). Consistency of nonverbal affect and affect reciprocity in marital interaction. *Journal of Consulting and Clinical Psychology, 48*, 711–717.

Gottman, J. M. (1982). Temporal form: Toward a new language for describing relationships. *Journal of Marriage and the Family, 44*, 943–962.

Gottman, J. (1986). The world of coordinated play: Same and cross-sex friendship in young children. In J. Gottman & J. Parker (Eds.). *Conversation of friends*. New York: Cambridge University Press.

Gottman, J. M. (1989). *The Specific Affect Coding System*, Version 2.0: Real time coding with the affect wheel. Unpublished manual, University of Washington, Seattle, WA.

Gottman, J. M. (1990). How marriages change. In G. R. Patterson (Ed.) *Depression and aggression in family interaction*. Hillsdale, NJ: Lawrence Erlbaum Associates.

Gottman, J. M. (1993). The roles of conflict engagement, escalation, or avoidance in marital interaction: A longitudinal view of five types of couples. *Journal of Consulting and Clinical Psychology, 61*, 6–15.

Gottman, J. M. (1991). Choas and regulated change in families: A metaphor for the study of transitions. In P. A. Cowan & M. Hetherington (Eds.) *Family transitions*. Hillsdale, NJ: Lawrence Erlbaum Associates.

Gottman, J. M. (1993). The roles of conflict engagement, escalation, or avoidance in marital interaction: A longitudinal view of five types of couples. *Journal of Consulting and Clinical Psychology, 61*, 6–15.

Gottman, J. M., & Katz, L. (1989). Effects of marital discord on young children's peer interaction and health. *Developmental Psychology, 25*, 373–381.

Gottman, J. M., Kiecolt-Glaser, J., Rushe, R., Glaser, R., & Malarkey, W. (1992). *Behavioral endocrinology of positive and negative emotion in newlywed couples*. Unpublished manuscript, University of Washington, Department of Psychology, Seattle, WA.

Gottman, J. M., & Krokoff, L. J. (1989). The relationship between marital interaction and marital satisfaction: A longitudinal view. *Journal of Consulting and Clinical Psychology, 57*, 47–52.

Gottman, J. M., & Levenson, R. W. (1985). A valid procedure for obtaining self-report of affect in marital interaction. *Journal of Consulting and Clinical Psychology, 53*, 151–160.

Gottman, J. M., & Levenson, R. W. (1986). Assessing the role of emotion in marriage. *Behavioral Assessment, 8*, 31–48.

Gottman, J. M., & Levenson, R. W. (1988). The social psychophysiology of marriage. In P. Noller & M. A. Fitzpatrick (Eds.), *Perspectives on marital interaction* (pp. 182–200). Clevedon, England: Multilingual Matters Ltd.

Gottman, J. M., & Levenson, R. W. (1993). Male withdrawal from marital conflict. Unpublished manuscript, University of Washington, Seattle, WA.

Gottman, J. M. & Levenson, R. W. (1992). Marital processes predictive of later dissolution: behavior, physiology, and health, *Journal of Personality and Social Psychology, 63,* 221-233.

Gottman, J. M., Notarius, C., Markman, H., Bank, S., Yoppi, B., & Rubin, M. E. (1976). Behavior exchange theory and marital decision making. *Journal of Personality and Social Psychology, 34,* 14-34.

Gottman, J. M., & Ringland, J. (1981). The analysis of dominance and bidirectionality in social development. *Child Development, 52,* 393-412.

Gottman, J. M., & Roy, A. K. (1990). *Sequential analysis: A guide for behavioral researchers.* New York: Cambridge University Press.

Gove, W. R. (1978). Sex differences in mental illness among adult men and women: An evaluation of four questions raised regarding the evidence on higher rates of women. *Social Science and Medicine, 12,* 187-198.

Gove, W. R., Hughes, M., & Style, C. B. (1983). Does marriage have positive effects on the psychological well being of the individual? *Journal of Health and Social Behavior, 24,* 122-131.

Graham, F. K., & Clifton, R. K. (1966). Heart-rate change as a component of the orienting response. *Psychological Bulletin, 65,* 305-320.

Graham, D. T., Stern, J. A., & Winokur, G. (1960). The concept of a different set of physiologica; changes in each emotion. *Psychiatric Research Reports, 12,* 8-15.

Greenberg, L. S., & Johnson, S. M. (1988). *Emotionally focused therapy for couples.* New York: Guilford.

Greenberg, L. S., & Safran, J. (1984). Hot cognition: Emotion coming in from the cold. A reply to Rachman and Mahoney. *Cognitive therapy and research, 8,* 559-578.

Greenberg, L. S., & Safran, J. (1987). *Emotion in psychotherapy: Affect and cognition in teh process of change.* New York: Guilford Press.

Griffin, W. (1993). Transitions from negative affect during marital interaction. *Journal of Family Psychology, 6,* 239-244.

Grings, W. W., & Dawson, M. E. (1978). *Emotions and bodily responses.* Orlando, FL: Academic Press.

Gross, J. J., & Levenson, R. W. (1990). *Emotional suppression: Physiology, self-report, and expressive behavior.* Paper presented at the meeting of the Society for Psychophysiological Research, Boston, MA.

Grych, J. H., & Fincham, F. D. (1990). Marital conflict and children's adjustment: A cognitive contextual framework. *Psychological Bulletin, 108,* 267-290.

Grych, J. Seid, M., & Fincham, F. (1991, April). *Children's cognitive and affective responses to different forms of interparental conflict.* Paper presented at the biennial meeting of Society for Research in Child Development, Seattle, WA.

Gunn, C. G., Wolf, S., Block, R. T., & Person, R. J. (1972). Psychophysiology of the cardiovascular system. In N. S. Greenfield & R. A. Sternbach (Eds.), *Handbook of psychophysiology* (pp. 457-489). New York: Holt, Rinehart & Winston.

Gunnar, M. (1987). Psychobiological studies of stress and coping: An introduction. *Child Development, 58,* 1403-1407.

Gunnar, M. (1989). Studies of the human infant's adrenocortical response to potentially stressful events. *New Directions for Child Development, 45,* 3–18.

Guttman, L. L. (1950). The basis for scalogram analysis. In S. A. Stouffer, L. L. Guttman, E. A. Suchman, P. F. Lazarsfeld, S. A. Starr, & J. A. Clausen (Eds.), *Measurement and prediction: Studies in Social Psychology in World War II* (Vol. 4). Princeton, NJ: Princeton University Press.

Hagestad, G. O., & Smyer, M. A. (1982). Dissolving long-term relationships: Patterns of divorcing in middle age. In S. Duck (Ed.), *Personal relationships, 4: Dissolving relationships* (pp. 155–188). New York: Academic Press.

Hahlweg, K., & Markman, H. J. (1983). Effectiveness of behavioral marital therapy: Empirical status of behavioral techniques in preventing and alleviating marital distress. *Journal of Consulting and Clinical Psychology, 56,* 440–447.

Hahlweg, K., Revenstorf, D., & Schindler, L. (1982). Treatment of marital distress: Comparing formats and modalities. *Advances in Behavior Research and Therapy, 4,* 411–435.

Hahlweg, K., Revenstorf, D., & Schindler, L. (1983). *The effects of behavioral marital therapy on the couples' communication and problem-solving skills.* Unpublished manuscript, Max Planck Institut fur Psychiatric Munchen BRD.

Hahlweg, K., Revenstorf, D., & Schindler, L. (1984). Effects of behavioral marital therapy on couples' communication and problem-solving skills. *Journal of Consulting and Clinical Psychology, 52,* 553–566.

Haley, J. (1967). Towards a theory of pathological systems. In G. Zuk & I. Nagy (Eds.), *Family therapy and disturbed families.* Palo Alto, CA: Science and Behavior Books.

Halford, K. (1993). Assessment of cognitive self statements during marital problem-solving: A comparison of two methods. Unpublished manuscript, University of Queensland, Australia.

Hall, J. A. (1979). Gender, gender roles, and nonverbal communication skills. 32–67. In R. Rosenthal (Eds.), *Skill in nonverbal communication.* Cambridge, MAss: Oelgeschlager, Gunn, & Hain.

Harper, R. G., Wiens, A. M., & Matarazzo, J. D. (1978). *Nonverbal communication: The state of the art.* New York: Wiley.

Harrell, A. (1986). Do liberated women drive their husbands to drink? The impact of masculine orientation, status inconsistency, and family life satisfaction on male liquor consumption. *International Journal of the Addictions, 21,* 385–391.

Harrell, J., & Guerney, B. G. (1976). Training married couples in conflict resolution skills. In D. H. Olson (Ed.), *Treating relationships* (pp. 151–165). Lake Mills, IA: Graphic Publishing.

Harvey, J. H., Wells, G. L., & Alvarez, M. D. (1978). Attribution in the context of conflict and separation in close relationships. In J. H. Harvey, W. Ickes, & R. F. Kidd (Eds.), *New direction in attribution research.* Hillsdale, NJ: Lawrence Erlbaum Associates.

Hauser, S. T., Powers, S. I., Weiss-Perry, B., Follansbee, D. J., Rajapark, D., & Greene, W. M. (1987). *The constraining and enabling coding system.* Unpublished manuscript.

Haynes, S. N., Follingstad, D. R., & Sullivan, J. C. (1979). Assessment of marital satisfaction and interaction. *Journal of Consulting and Clinical Psychology, 47,* 789–791.

Hawkins, J. L., Weisberg, C., & Ray, D. L. (1977). Marital communication style and social class. *Journal of Marriage and the Family, 39,* 479–490.

Henry, J. P. (1986). Neuroendocrine patterns of emotional response. In R. Plutchik & H. Kellerman (Eds.), *Emotion, theory and research, Vol 3: Biological foundations of emotion* (pp. 37–607). London: Academic Press.

Henry, J., & Meehan, J. (1981). Psychoscial stimuli, physiological specificty, and cardiovascular disease. In A. Weiner, M. Hofer, & A. Stunkard (Eds.), *Brain behavior, and bodily disease* (pp. 131–142). New York: Raven.

Henry, J. P. (1985). Psychosocial factors, disease, and aging. In J. E. Birren & J. Livingston (Eds.), *Cognition, stress, and aging* (pp. 21–46). Engelwood Cliffs, NJ: Prentice Hall.

Henry, J. P., & Stephens, P. M. (1977). *Stress, health, and the social environment.* New York: Springer-Verlag.

Hetherington, E. M. (1988). Coping with family transitions: Winners, losers and survivors. *Child Development, 60,* 1–14.

Hetherington, E. M., & Clingempeel, W. G., (1992). Coping with marital transitions. *Monographs for the Society for Research in Child Development, 57,* N (227), 1–242.

Hetherington, E. M., Cox, M., & Cox, R. (1978). The aftermath of divorce. In J. H. Stevens, Jr. & M. Matthews (Eds.), *Mother-child, father-child relations.* Washington, DC: National Association for the Education of Young Children.

Hetherington, E. M., Cox, M., & Cox, R. (1982). Effects of divorce on parents and children. In M. Lamb (Ed.), *Nontraditional families* (pp. 233–288). Hillsdale, NJ: Lawrence Erlbaum Associates.

Hiller, D., & Philliber, W. (1986). The division of labor in comtemporary marriage: Expectations, perceptions, and performance. *Social Problems, 33,* 191–201.

Hinde, R. A. (1984). Why do the sexes behave differently in close relationships? *Journal of Personal and Social Relationships, 1,* 471–501.

Hochschild, A., & Machung, A. (1989). *The second shift: Working parents and the revolution at home.* New York: Viking.

Holmes, T. H., & Rahe, R. H. (1967). The social readjustment rating scale. *Journal of Psychosomatic Research, 11,* 213–218.

Holtzworth-Munroe, A., & Jacobson, N. S. (1985). Causal attributions of married couples: When do they search for causes? What do they conclude when they do? *Journal of Personality and Social Psychology, 48,* 1398–1412.

Hops, H., Wills, T. A., Patterson, G. R., & Weiss, R. L. (1972). *The marital interaction coding system (MICS).* Unpublished manuscript, University of Oregon, Eugene, OR.

House, J. S. (1981). *Work, stress, and social support.* Reading, MA: Addison-Wesley.

House, J. S., Landis, K. R., & Umberson, D. (1988). Social relationships and health. *Science, 241,* 540–545.

House, J. S., Wells, J. A., Landerman, L. R., McMichael, A. J., & Kaplan, B. H.

(1979). Occupational stress and health among factory workers. *Journal of Health and Social Behavior* , *20*, 139–160.

Howes, P., & Markman, H. J. (1989). Marital quality and child functioning: a longitudinal investigation. *Child Development, 60*, 1044–1051.

Hoyenga, K. B., & Hoyenga, K. T. (1979). *The question of sex differences*. Boston: Little Brown.

Huberty, C. J., & Morris, J. D. (1989). Multivariate analysis versus multiple univariate analysis. *Psychological Bulletin, 105*, 302–308.

Hummel, A. (1991). *The physiologically arousing effects of producing and receiving facial expressions of contempt in a marital interaction*. Unpublished research report, University of Washington, Seattle, WA.

Huston, T. L., & Ashmore, R. D. (1986). Women and men in personal relationships. In R. D. Ashmore, & F. Del Boco (Eds.), *The social psychology of female–male relations* (pp. 167–210). New York: Academic Press.

Huston, T. L., Surra, C. A., Fitzgerald, N. M., & Cate, R. M. (1981). From courtship to marriage: Mate selection as an interpersonal process. In S. Duck & R. Gilmour (Eds.), *Personal relationships 2: Developing personal relationships* (pp. 55–88).

London: Academic Press. Ickes, W., Robertson, E., Tooke, W., & Teng, G. (1986). Naturalistic social cognition: Methodology, assessment and validation. *Journal of Personality and Social Psychology, 51*, 66–82.

Ickes, W., Stinson, L., Bissonnette, V., & Garcia, S. (1990). Naturalistic social cognition: Empathic accuracy in mixed-sex dyads. *Journal of Personality and Social Psychology, 59*, 730–742.

Izard, C. E. (1971). *The face of emotion*. New York: Appleton-Century-Crofts.

Izard, C. E. (Ed.). (1982). *Measuring emotions in infants and children*. New York: Cambridge University Press.

Izard, C. E., Kagan, J. E., & Zajonc, R. B. (1984). *Emotions, cognition, and behavior*. New York: Cambridge University Press.

Jacklin, C. N., & Maccoby, E. E. (1978). Social behavior at 33 months in same-sex and mixed-sex dyads. *Child Development, 49*, 557–569.

Jacob, T. (1975). Family interaction in disturbed and normal families: A methodological and substantive review. *Psychological Bulletin, 82*, 33–65.

Jacobson, N. S. (1977). Problem solving and contingency contracting in the treatment of marital discord. *Journal of Consulting and Clinical Psychology, 45*, 92–100.

Jacobson, N. S. (1978). Specific and nonspecific factors in the effectiveness of a behavioral approach to the treatment of marital discord. *Journal of Consulting and Clinical Psychology, 46*, 442–452.

Jacobson, N. S., & Addis, M. E. (1993). Research on couples and couple therapy: What do we know? Where are we going? *Journal of Consulting and Clinical Psychology, 61*, 85–93.

Jacobson, N. S., Follette, V. M., Follette, W. C., Holtzworth-Munroe, A., Katt, J. L., & Schmaling, K. B. (1985). A component analysis of behavioral marital therapy: 1-year follow-up. *Behavior Research and Therapy, 23*, 549–555.

Jacobson, N. S., Follette, W. C., & McDonald, D. W. (1982). Reactivity to positive and negative behavior in distressed and nondistressed married couples. *Journal of Consulting and Clinical Psychology, 50,* 706–714.

Jacobson, N. S., & Margolin, G. (1979). *Marital therapy.* New York: Brunner-Mazel.

Jacobson, N. S., McDonald, D. W., Follette, W. C., & Berley, R. A. (1985). Attributional processes in distressed and nondistressed married couples. *Congitive Therapy and Research, 9,* 35–50.

Jacobson, N. S., & Moore, D. (1981). Spouses as observers of the events in their relationship. *Journal of Consulting and Clinical Psychology, 49,* 269–277.

Jacobson, N. S., Schmaling, K., & Holtzworth-Munroe, A. (1987). Component analysis of behavioral marital therapy: 2-year follow-up and prediction of relapse. *Journal of Marital and Family Therapy, 13,* 187–195.

Jemmott J. B., III, & Locke, S.E. (1984). Psychosocial factors, immunologic mediation, and human susceptibility to infectious disease: How much do we know *Psychological Bulletin, 95,* 78–108.

Johnson, A. K., & Anderson, E.A. (1990). Stress and arousal. In J. T. Cacioppo & L. G. Tassinary (Eds.), *Principles of psychophysiology (pp. 216–252). New York:* Cambridge University Press.

Jones, W.H. (1982). Loneliness and social behavior. In L. A. Peplau & D. Perlman (Eds.), *Loneliness: A sourcebook of current theory, research and therapy* (pp.238–254). New York: Wiley.

Kahn, M. (1970). Nonverbal communication and marital satisfaction. *Family Process, 9,* 449–456.

Kahneman, D. (1973). *Attention and effort.* Engelwood Cliffs, NJ: Prentice-Hall.

Kahneman, D., Tursky, B., Shapiro, D., & Crider, A. (1969). Pupillary, heart rate and skin resistance changes during a mental task. *Journal of Experimental Psychology, 79,* 164–167.

Kaplan, H. B., & Bloom, S. W. (1960). The use of sociological and social-psychological concepts in physiological research: A review of selected experimental studies. *Journal of Nervous and Mental Disease, 131,* 128–134.

Kaplan, H. B., Burch, N. R., & Bloom, S. W. (1964). Psysiological covariation in small peer groups. In P. H. Leiderman & D. Shapiro (Eds.), *Psychobiological approaches to social behavior.* Stanford, CA: Stanford University Press.

Kaplan, H. B., Burch, N. R., & Bloom, S. W., & Edelberg, R. (1963). Affective orientation and physiological activity (GSR) in small peer groups. *Psychosomatic Medicine, 25,* 245–252.

Katz, L.F. (1990). *Patterns of marital conflict and children's emotions.* Unpublished doctoral dissertation, University of Illinois at Urbana-Champaign, IL.

Katz, L. F. (1991). The Emotion Regulation Questionnaire. Unpublished manuscript, University of Washington, Seattle, WA.

Katz, L. F., & Gottman, J.M. (1991a). Marital discord and child outcomes: A social psychophysiological approach. In K. Dodge & J. Garber (Eds.), *The development of emotion regulation and disregulation.* New York: Cambridge University Press.

Katz, L. F., & Gottman, J. M. (1991b April). *Marital interaction processes and preschool children's peer interactions and emotional development.* Paper presented at the meeting of the Society for Research in Child Development, Seattle, WA.

Katz, L. F., & Gottman, J. M. (1993). *Patterns of marital conflict predict children's internalizing and externalizing behaviors.* Unpublished manuscript.

Katz, L. F., Kramer, L., & Gottman, J. M. (1992). Conflict and emotions in marital, sibling, and peer relationships. In C. U. Shantz & W. W. Hartup (Eds.), *Conflict in child and adolescent development.* New York: Cambridge University Press.

Kelley, H. H., Bersheid, E., Christensen, A., Harvey, J. H., Huston, T. L., Levinger, G., McClintock, E., Peplau, L. A. & Peterson D. R. (Eds.). (1983). *Close relationships.* New York: W. H. Freeman.

Kelley, H. H., Cunningham, J. D., Chrisham, J. A. Lefebvre, L. M., Sink, C. R., & Yablon, G. (1978). Sex differences in comments made during conflict within close heterosexual pairs. *Sex Roles, 4,* 473–492.

Kelly, L. E., & Conley, J. J. (1987). Personality and compatibility: A prospective analysis of marital stability and marital satisfaction. *Journal of Personality and Social Psychology, 52,* 27–40.

Kendon, A. (1967). Some functions of gaze direction in social interaction. *Acta Psychologica, 26,* 22–63.

Kiecolt-Glaser, J. K., Fisher, B. S., Ogrocki, P., Stout, J. C., Speicher, C. E., & Glaser, R. (1987). Marital quality, marital disruption, and immune function. *Psychosomatic Medicine, 49,* 13–33.

Kiecolt-Glaser, J. K., Kennedy, S., Malkoff, S., Fisher, L., Speicher, C. E., & Glaser, R. (1988). Marital discord and immunity in males. *Psychosomatic Medicine, 50,* 213–229.

Kirby, M. W., & Davis, K. E. (1972). Who volunteers for research on marital counseling? *Journal of Marriage and the Family. 34,* 469–473.

Kitson, G., Babri, K., & Roach, M. J. (1985). Who divorces and why. *Journal of Family Issues, 6,* 255–293.

Kitson, G., & Raschke, H. (1981). Divorce research: What we know; what we need to know. *Journal of Divorce, 4,* 1–37.

Kitson, G. C., & Sussman, M. B. (1982). Marital complaints, demographic characteristics, and symptoms of marital distress in divorce. *Journal of Marriage and the Family, 44,* 87–101.

Kleinke, C.L. (1986). Gaze and eye contact: A research review. *Psychological Bulletin, 100,* 78–100.

Knapp, M. (1972). *Nonverbal communication in human interaction.* New York: Holt, Rinehart & Winston.

Komarovsky, M. (1962). *Blue-collar marriage.* New York: Random House.

Komarovsky, M. (1976). *Dilemmas of masculinity.* New York: Norton.

Korn, J. H., & Meyer, K. E. (1968). Effects of set and sex on the electrodermal orienting response. *Psychophysiology, 4,* 453–459.

Korneva, E. A., Klimenko, V. M., & Shkhinek, E. K. (1985). *Neurohumoral maintenance of immune homeostasis.* Chicago: University of Chicago Press.

Krokoff, L. (1987). Anatomy of negative affect in working class marriages. *Dissertation Abstracts International, 45,7A.* (University Microfilms No. 84–22 109).

Krokoff, L. J. (1984). *A telephone version of the Locke–Wallace test of marital adjustment.* Unpublished manuscript, University of Illinois, Champaign, IL.

Krokoff, L. J., Gottman, J.M., & Haas, S. D. (1989). Validation of a rapid couples interaction scoring system. *Behavioral Assessment, 11*, 65–79.

Krokoff, L. J., Gottman, J. M., & Roy, A. K. (1988). Blue-collar marital interaction and communication orientation. *Journal of Personal and Social Relationships, 5*, 201–221.

Kulka, R. A., & Weingarten, H., (1979). The long-term effects of parental divorce on adult adjustment. *Journal of Social Issues, 35*, 50–78.

Kumagai, F. (1983). Changing divorce in Japan. *Journal of Family History, 8*, 85–108.

Kurdek, L.A. (1993). Predicting marital dissolution: A 5-year prospective longitudinal study of newlywed couples. *Journal of Personality and Social Psychology, 64*, 221–242.

Kvanli, J. A., & Jennings, G. (1986). Recoupling: Development and establishment of the spousal subsystem in remarriage. Special issue: The divorce process: A handbook for clinicians. *Journal of Divorce, 10*, 189–203.

Lacey, J. I. (1956). The evaluation of autonomic responses: Toward a general solution. *Annals of New York Academy of Sciences, 67*, 123–164.

Lacey, J. I. (1967). Somatic response patterning and stress: Some revisions of activation theory. In M. H. Appley & R. Trumbull (Eds.), *Psychological stress: Issues in research* (pp. 14–37). New York: Appleton-Century-Crofts.

Lacey, J. I., Kagan, J., Lacey, B. C., & Moss, H. A. (1963). The visceral level: situational determinants and behavioral correlates of autonomic response patterns. In P. H. Knapp (Ed.), *Expression of the emotions in man*. New York: International University Press.

Lanzetta, J. T., Cartwright-Smith, J., & Kleck, R. E. (1976). Effects of nonverbal dissimulation on emotional experience and autonomic arousal. *Journal of Personality and Social Psychology, 33*, 354–370.

Larsen, A. S., & Olson, D. H. (1989). Predicting marital satisfaction using *PREPARE*: A replication study. *Journal of Marriage and Family Therapy, 15*, 311–322.

Lazarus, R. S., Speisman, J. C., & Mordkoff, A. M. (1963). The relationship between autonomic indicators of psychological stress: Heart rate and skin conductance. *Psychosomatic Medicine, 25*, 19–30.

Lederer, W. J., & Jackson, D. D. (1968). *The mirages of marriage*. New York: W. W. Norton.

Levinger, G., & Moles, O. C. (Eds.). (1979). *Divorce and separation: Context, causes, and consequences*. New York: Basic Books.

Levenson, R. W. (1983). Personality research and psychophysiology: General considerations. *Journal of Research in Personality, 17*, 1–21.

Levenson, R. W., Carstensen, L. L., Friesen, W. V., & Ekman, P. (1991). Emotion, physiology and expression in old age. *Psychology and Aging, 6*, 28–35.

Levenson, R. W., Ekman, P., & Friesen, W. V. (1990). Voluntary facial action generates emotion-specific autonomic nervous system activity. *Psychophysiology, 27*, 363–384.

Levenson, R. W., Ekman, P., Heider, K., & Friesen, W. V. (1992). Emotion and autonomic nervous system activity in the Minangkabau of West Sumatra.

Journal of Personality and Social Psychology, 62, 972–988.

Levenson, R. W., & Gottman, J. M. (1983). Marital interaction: Physiological linkage and affective exchange. *Journal of Personality and Social Psychology, 45,* 587–597.

Levenson, R. W., & Gottman, J. M. (1985). Physiological and affective predictors of change in relationship satisfaction. *Journal of Personality of Social Psychology, 49,* 85–94.

Lever, J. (1976). Sex differences in the games children play. *Social Problems, 23,* 478–487.

Levi, L. (1965). The urinary output of adrenaline and noradrenaline during pleasant and unpleasant emotional states. *Psychosomatic Medicine, 27,* 80–85.

Levi, L. (1972). Stress and distress in response to psychological stimuli. *Acta Medica Scandinavica, Suppl. 528,* 1–166.

Levi L. (Ed.). (1975). *Emotions: Their parameters and measurement.* New York: Raven Press.

Levinger, G. (1966). Sources of marital dissatisfaction among applicants for divorce. *American Journal of Osthophychiatry, 36,* 803–807.

Levinger, G., & Moles, O. C. (Eds.). (1979). *Divorce and separation: Context, causes, and consequences.* New York: Basic Books.

Levis, D. J., & Smith, J. E. (1987). Getting individual differences in autonomic reactivity to work for instead of against you: Determining the dominant "psychological" stress channel on the basis of a "biological" stress test. *Psychophysiology, 24,* 346–352.

Levy, M. N. (1983a). Hunting the wild vagus. *The Physiologist, 26,* 115–118.

Levy, M. N. (1983b). Neural control of cardiac rhythm and contraction. In M. R. Rosen & B. F. Hoffman (Eds.), *Cardiac therapy* (pp. 73–94). Boston and The Hague, Netherlands: Martinus Nijh-off.

Levy, M. N., Martin, P. J., & Stuesse, S. L. (1981). Neural regulation of the heartbeat. *Annual Review of Physiology, 43,* 443–453.

Levy, R. (1976). Psychosomatic symptoms and women's protest: Two types of reactions to structural stress in the family. *Journal of Health and Social Behavior, 17,* 122–134.

Lewis, M., & Brooks, J. (1975). Infants' social perception: A constructivist view. In L. B. Cohen & P. Salapatek (Eds.), *Infant perception: From sensation to cognition* (Vol. 2). New York: Academic Press.

Lewis, R. A., & Spanier, G. B. (1982). Marital quality, marital stability, and social exchange. In F. I. Nye (Ed.), *Family relationships, rewards and costs.* Beverly Hills, CA: Sage.

Liberson, C. W., & Liberson, W. T. (1975). Sex differences in autonomic responses to electric shock. *Psychophysiology, 12,* 182–186.

Liederman, P. H., & Shapiro, D. (Eds.). (1964). *Psychological approaches to social behavior* Stanford, CA: Stanford University Press.

Lindahl, K. M., & Markman, H. J. (1990) Communication. Communciation and negative affect regulation in the family. In E. A. Blechman (Ed.), *Emotion and the family,* for better or for worse (pp. 99–115). Hillsdale, NJ: LawrenceErlbaum Associates.

Lindner, M. S., Hagan, M. S., & Brown, J. C., III. (1992). The adjustment of children in nondivorced, divorced, divorced single-mother, and remarried families. *Monographs for the Society for Research in Child Development, 57* (227), 1–242.

Lindsley, D. B. (1952). Psychological phenomena and the *Electroencephalography and clinical neurophysiology, 4,* 443–456.

Locke, H. J. (1951). *Predicting adjustments in marriage: A comparison of a divorced and a happily married group.* New York: Henry Holt.

Locke, H. J., & Wallace, K. M. (1959). Short marital adjustment and prediction tests: Their reliability and validity. *Marriage and Family Living, 21,* 251–255.

Locke, H. J., & Williamson, R. C. (1958). Marital adjustment: A factor analysis study. *American Sociological Review, 23,* 562–569.

Lundberg, U. (1980). Catecholamine and cortisol excretion under psychologically different laboratory conditions. In Usdin/Kvetnansky/Kopin (Eds.) *Caecholamines and stress: Recent advances* (pp. 455–480). Holland: Elsevier. pp. 455–480.

Lundberg, U. (1983). Sex differences in behavior pattern and catecholamine and cortisol excretion in 3–6 year old day-care children. *Biological Psychiatry, 16,* 109–117.

Lundberg, U., de Chateau, P., Winberg, J., & Frankenhaeuser, M. (1981). Catecholamine and cortisol excretion patterns in three-year-old children and their parents. *Journal of Human Stress, 7,* 3–11.

Maccoby, E. E. (1980). *Social development.* New York: Harcourt, Brace & Jovanovitch.

Maccoby, E. E. (1990). Gender and relationships: A developmental account. *American Psychologist, 45,* 513–520.

Maccoby, E. E., & Jacklin, C. N. (1974). *The psychology of sex differences.* Stanford, CA: Stanford University Press.

Malmo, R. B., Boag, T. J., & Smith, A. A. (1957). Physiological study of personal interaction. *Psychosomatic Medicine, 19,* 105–119.

Mandler, G. (1975). *Mind and emotion.* New York: Wiley.

Margolin, G. (1988). Marital conflict is not marital conflict is not marital conflict. In R. DeV. Peters & R. J. MacMahon (Eds.), *Social learning and systems approaches to marriage and the family.* New York: Brunner/Mazel.

Margolin, G., & Wampold, B. E. (1981). Sequential analysis of conflict and accord in distressed and nondistressed marital partners. *Journal of Consulting and Clinical Psychology, 47,* 554–567.

Margolin, G., & Wampold, B. E. (1982). Sequential analysis of conflict and accord in distressed and nondistressed marital partners. *Journal of Consulting and Clinical Psychology, 49, 49,* 554–567.

Markman, H.J. (1979). Application of a behavioral model of marriage in predicting relationship satisfaction of couples planning marriage. *Journal of Consulting and Clinical Psychology, 47,* 743–749.

Markman, H. J. (1981). Prediction of marital distress: A five-year follow-up. *Journal of Consulting and Clinical Psychology, 49,* 760–762.

Markman, H. J. (1984). The longitudinal study of couples' interactions: Implications for understanding and predicting the development of marital distress.

In K. Hahlweg & N. S. Jacobson (Eds.), *Marital interaction: Analysis and modification* (pp. 253–284). New York: Guilford.

Markman, H. J., & Baccus, G. (1982). *The application of a behavioral model of marriage to Black couples.* Unpublished manuscript.

Markman, H. J., & Floyd, F. (1980). Possibilities for the prevention of marital discord: A behavioral perspective. *American Journal of Family Therapy, 8,* 29–48.

Markman, H. J., & Floyd, F., Dickson-Markman, F. (1982). Toward a model for the prediction and primary prevention of marital and family distress and dissolution. In S. Duck (Eds.), *Personal relationships 4: Dissolving personal relationships.* London: Academic Press.

Markman, H. J., Floyd, F. J., Stanley, S. M., & Storaasli, R. D. (1988). Prevention of marital distress: A longitudinal investigation. *Journal of Consulting and Clinical Psychology , 56,* 210–217.

Markman, H. J., & Notarius, C. I. (1987). Coding marital and family in interaction: Current status. In T. Jacob (Ed.) *Family interaction and psychopathology: Theories methods, and findings.* New York: Plenum Press.

Markman, H. J., Notarius, C. I., Stephen, T., & Smith, T. (1981). Behavioral observation systems for couples: The current status. In E. Filsinger & R. Lewis (Eds.), *Assessing marriage: New behavioral approaches.* Beverly Hills CA: Sage.

Markman, H. J., & Poltrock, S. (1982). A computerized system for recording and analysis of couples' interaction. *Behavior Research Methods and Instrumentation, 14,* 186–190.

Markman, H. J., Renick, M. J., Floyd, F. J., Stanley, S. M., & Clements, M. (1993). Preventing marital distress through communication and conflict management training: A four-and-five -year followup. *Journal of Consulting and Clinical Psychology, 61,* 70–77.

Martin, T. C., & Bumpass, L. (1989). Recent trends in marital disruption. *Demography, 26,* 37–51.

Mason, J. W., (1975a). A historical view of the stress field. *Journal of Human Stress, 1,* 6–12.

Mason, J. W. (1975b). Emotions as reflected in patterns of endocrine integration. In L. Levi (Ed.). *Emotions: Their parameters and measurement.* New York: Raven Press.

Masur, J., Schutz, M. T., & Boerngen, R. (1980). Gender. differences in open-field behavior as a function of age. *Developmental Psychology, 13,* 107–110.

Matthews, K. A., Weiss, S.M., Detre, T., Dembroski, T. M., Falkner, B., Manuck, S. B., & Williams, R. B. (1986). *Handbook of stress, reactivity, and cardiovascular disease.* New York: Wiley.

McCrady, B. S., Stout, R., Noel, N., Abrams, D., & Nelson, H. F. (1991). Effectiveness of three types of spouse-involved behavioral alcoholism treatment, *British Journal of Addiction, 86,* 1415–1424.

McDowell, I., & Newell, C. (1987). *Measuring health: A guide to rating scales and questionnaires.* New York: Oxford University Press.

Miller, J. B. (1976) *Toward a new psychology of women.* Boston: Beacon Press.

Minuchin, S. (1974). *Families and family therapy*. Cambridge, MA: Harvard University Press.

Mirowsky, J. (1985). Depression and marital power: An equity model. *American Journal of Sociology, 91*, 557–591.

Mischel, W. (1968). *Personality and assessment*. New York: Wiley.

Murray, J., Cook, J., White, J., Tyson, R., Rushe, R., & Gottman, J. (1993). *The mathematics of conflict*. Unpublished manuscript, University of Washington, Seattle, WA.

Murray, J. D. (1985). *Mathematical biology*. Berlin: Springer-Verlag.

Nakamura, H. (1983). *Divorce in Java: A study of the dissolution of marriage among Javanese Muslims*. Yogyakarta, Indonesia: Gadjah Mada University Press.

Newcomb, M. D., & Bentler, P. M. (1981). Marital breakdown. In S. Duck & R. Gilmour (Eds.), *Personal relationships* (Vol. 3, pp. 57–94). New York: Academic Press.

Newlin, D. B. (1981). Relationships of pulse transmission times to pre-ejaculation period and blood pressure. *Psychophysiology, 18*, 316–321.

Newlin, D. B., & Levenson, R. W. (1979). Pre-ejection period: Measuring beta-adrenergic influences upon the heart. *Psychophysiology, 16*, 546–553.

Newsome, H. H., & Rose, J. C. (1971). The response of human adrenocortico-trophic hormone and growth hormone to surgical stress. *Journal of Clinical Endocrinology and Metabolism, 33*, 481–487.

Noller, P. (1980). Misunderstandings in marital communication: A study of couples' nonverbal communication. *Journal of Personality and Social Psychology, 39*, 1135–1148.

Notarius, C. I, Benson, P. R., Sloane, D., Vanzetti, N. A., & Hornyak, L. M. (1989). Exploring the interface between perception and behavior: An analysis of marital interactions in distressed and nondistressed couples. *Behavioral Assessment, 11*, 39–64.

Notarius, C. I., & Johnson, J. S. (1982). Emotional expression in husbands and wives. *Journal of Marriage and the Family, 44*, 483–489.

Notarius, C. I., & Levenson, R. W. (1979). Expressive tendencies and physiological responses to stress. *Journal of Personality and Social Psychology, 37*, 1204–1210.

Notarius, C., & Markman, H. (1981). Couples interaction scoring system. In E. E. Filsinger & R. A. Lewis (Eds.), *Assessing marriage: New behavioral approaches*. Beverly Hills, CA: Sage.

Notarius, C., & Markman, H. (1989). *Workshop on marital therapy and outcome*. Presented at the Association for the Advancement of Marriage and Family Therapy meeting, San Francisco.

Notarius, C., & Markman, H. (1990). *A program for preventing and predicting marital distress: Couples' analysis*. Paper presented at the American Association for Advancement of Marital and Family Therapy, San Francisco, CA.

Notarius, C. I., Markman, H. J., & Gottman, J. M. (1983). Couples Interaction Scoring System: Clinical implications. In E. E. Filsinger (Eds.), *Marriage and family assessment*. Beverly Hills, CA: Sage.

Notarius, C. I., & Vanzetti, N. A. (1983). The marital agendas protocol. In E. E. Filsinger (Eds.), *Marriage and family assessment*. Beverly Hills, CA: Sage.

Oakley, A. (1975). *The sociology of housework*. New York: Pantheon Books.

Obrist, P. A. (1976). The cardiovascular behavioral interaction—as it appears today. *Psychophysiology, 13,* 95–107.

Obrist, P. A. (1981) *Cardiovascular psychophysiology*. New York: Plenum Press.

Obrist, P. A., Webb, R. A., & Sutterer, J. R. (1969). Heart rate and somatic changes during aversive consditioning and a simple recction time task. *Psychophysiology, 5,* 696–723.

O'Farrell, T. J., Harrison, R. H., & Cutter, H. S. G. (1981). Marital stability among wives of alcoholics: An evaluation of three explanations. *British Journal of Addiction, 76,* 175–189.

O'Leary, A. (1990). Stress, emotion, and human immune function. *Psychological Bulletin, 108,* 363–382.

Olson, D. H. (1981). Family typologies: Bridging family research and family therapy. In E. E. Filsinger & R. A. Lewis (Eds.), *Assessing marriage: New behavioral approaches* (pp. 74–89). Beverly Hills, CA: Sage.

Olson, D. H., & Ryder, R. G. (1970). Inventory of marital conflicts (IMC): An experimental interaction procedure. *Journal of Marriage and the Family, 32,* 443–448.

Olson, D. H., Spengle, D. H., & Russell, C. S. (1979). Circumplex model of marital and family systems I: Cohesion and adaptability dimensions, family types, and clinical applications. *Family Process, 18,* 3–28.

Osgood, C. E. G., Suci, G. J., & Tannenbaum, P. H. (1957). *The measurement of meaning*. Urbana, IL: University of Illinois Press.

Parsons, T., & Bales, R. F. (Eds.). (1955). *Family, socialization, and interaction process*. Glencoe, IL: Free Press.

Patkai, P. (1971). Catecholamine excretion in pleasant and unpleasant situations. *Acta Psychologia, 33,* 352–363.

Patterson, G. R. (1982). *Coercive family process*. Eugene, OR: Castalia.

Peplau, L. A., & Perlman, D. (1982). *Loneliness: A sourcebook of current theory, research and therapy*. New York: Wiley.

Pennebaker, J. W. (1982). *The psychology of physical symptoms*. New York: Springer-Verlag.

Pennebaker, J. W. (1983). Physical symptoms and sensations: Psychological causes and correlates. In J. T. Cacioppo & R. E. Petty (Eds.), *Social psychophysiology*. New York: Guilford.

Peterson, C., Baucom, D., Elliott, M., Farr, P. (1989). The relationship between sex role identity and marital adjustment. *Sex Roles, 21,* 775–787.

Peterson, J. L., & Zill, N. (1986). Marital disruption, parent-child relationships, and behavior problems in children. *Journal of Marriage and the Family, 48,* 295–307.

Phillips, D. W. (1975). *An investigation of marital fighting behavior*. Unpublished bachelor of arts honors thesis, Indiana University, Bloomington, IN.

Pleck, J. (1985). *Working wives/Working husbands*. Beverly Hills, CA: Sage.

Plutchik, R., & Ax, A. R. (1962). A critique of determinants of emotional state by Schachter and Singer. *Psychophysiology, 4,* 79–82.

Polferone, J. M., & Manuck, S. B. (1987). Gender differences in cardiovascular and neuroendocrine response to stressors. In R. C. Barnett, L. Biener, &

G. K. Baruch (Eds.), *Gender and stress* (pp. 13–38). New York: The Free Press.

Pope, H., & Mueller, C. W. (1979). The intergenerational transmission of marital instability: Comparisons by race and sex. In G. Levinger & O. C. Moles (Eds.), *Divorce and separation: Context, causes, and consequences*. New York: Basic Books.

Popp, K., & Baum, A. (1989). Hormones and emotions: Affective correlates of endocrine activity. In H. Wagner & A. Manstead (Eds.), *Handbook of social psychophysiology* (pp. 99–120). Chichester: Wiley.

Porges, S. W. (1972). Heart rate variability and deceleration as indexes of reaction time. *Journal of Experimental Psychology, 982*, 103–110.

Porges, S. W. (1983). Heart rate patterns in neonates: A potential diagnostic window to the brain. In T. Field & A. Sostack (Eds.), *Infants born at risk*. New York: Grune & Statton.

Porges, S. W. (1984). Heart rate oscillation: An index of neural mediation. In M. G. H. Coles, J. R. Jennings, & J. A. Stern (Eds.), *Psychophysiological perspectives: Festschrift for Beatrice and John Lacey*. New York: Van Nostrand Reinhold.

Porges, S. (1985). Spontaneous Oscillations in Heart Rate: A Potential Index of Stress. *Animal Stress American Physiological Society*, 1–15.

Porges, S. W., Bohrer, R. E., Cheung, M. N., Drasgow, F., McCabe, P. M., & Keren, G. (1980). New time series statistic at detecting rhythmic co-occurrence in the frequency domain: The coherence and its application to psychophysiological research. *Psychological Bulletin, 88*, 580–587.

Porter, B., & O'Leary, K. D. (1980). Marital discord and childhood behavior problems. *Journal of Abnormal Child Psychology, 8*, 287–295.

Posner, M. I., & Snyder, C. R. R. (1975a). Facilitation and inhibition in the processing of signals. In P. M. A. Rabbitt & S. Dornic (Eds.), *Attention and performance* (Vol. V). London: Academic Press.

Posner, M. I., & Snyder, C. R. R. (1975b). Attention and cognitive control. In R. L. Solso (Ed.), *Information processing and cognition: The Loyola Symposium*. Hillsdale, NJ: Lawrence Erlbaum Associates.

Powell, B., & Reznikoff, M. (1976). Role conflict and symptoms of psychological stress in college-educated women: The significance of employment. *Journal of Consulting and Clinical Psychology, 44*, 473–479.

Price-Bonham, S., & Balswick, J. (1980). The noninstitutions: Divorce, desertion, and remarriage. *Journal of Marriage and the Family, 42*, 959–972.

Rabin, C., Gottman, J.M., Levenson, R. W., Carstensen, L., Jacobson, N. S., & Rushe, R. (in press). Gender differences in marriage: Recent research on emotions; II:Two perspectives on gender differences in marriage: Cultural feminist and societal viewpoints. *Neuropsy*.

Rabin, C., & Schwartz, P. (in press). *Power and equity in marriage*. New York: Bantam.

Raush, H. L., Barry, W. A., Hertel, R. K., & Swain, M. A. (1974). *Communication, conflict, and marriage*. San Francisco, CA: Jossey-Bass.

Rauste-von Wright, M., von Wright, J., & Frankenhaeuser, M. (1981). Relationships between sex-related psychological characteristics during adolescence and catecholamine excretion during achievement stress. *Psychophysiology, 18,* 362–370.

Rawson, B. (Ed.). (1991). *Marriage, divorce and children in ancient Rome.* Oxford, England: Clarendon Press.

Reid, J. B. (1970). Reliability assessment of observational data: A possible methodological problem. *Child Development, 41,* 1143–1150.

Reite, M., & Field, T. (1985). *The psychobiology of attachment and separation.* Orlando, FL: Academic Press.

Revenstorf, D., Hahlweg, K., & Schindler, L., & Vogel, B. (1984). Interaction analysis of marital conflict. In K. Hahlweg & N. S. Jacobson (Eds.), *Marital interaction: Analysis and modification* (pp. 159–181). New York: Guilford.

Revenstorf, D., Vogel, B., Wegener, R., Hahlweg, K., & Schindler, L. (1980). Escalation phenomena in interaction sequences: An empirical comparison of distressed and nondistressed couples. *Behavior Analysis and Modification, 2,* 97–116.

Rheinstein, M. (1972). *Marriage stability, divorce, and the law.* Chicago, IL: The University of Chicago Press.

Riessman, C. K., & Gerstel, N. (1985). Marital dissolution and health: Do males or females have greater risk? *Social Science and Medicine, 20,* 627–635.

Riskin, J., & Faunce, E. E. (1970). Family interaction scales, III. Discussion of methodology and substantive findings. *Archives of General Psychiatry, 22,* 527–537.

Riskin, J., & Faunce, E. E. (1972). An evaluative review of family interaction research. *Family Process, 11,* 365–455.

Risman, R. (1987). Intimate relationships form a mirostructural perspective: Men who mother. *Gender and Society, 1,* 6–23.

Roberts, T. W., & Price, S. J. (1987). Instant families: Divorced mothers marry never-married men. *Journal of Divorce, 11,* 71–92.

Robinson, B. F., Epstein, S. E., Beiser, G. D., & Braunwald, E. (1966). Control of heart rate by the autonomic nervous system: Studies in man on the interrelation between baroreceptor mechanisms and exercise. *Circulatory Research, 19,* 400–411.

Rogers, L. E., & Farace, R. V. (1975). Relational communication analysis: New measurement procedures. *Human Communication Research, 1,* 222–239.

Rose, R. M. (1980). Endocrine responses to stressful psychological events. *Psychiatric Clinics of North America, 3,* 257–276.

Rose, R. M., & Hurst, M. W. (1975). Plasma cortisol and growth hormone responses to intravenous catheterization. *Journal of Human Stress, 1,* 22–36.

Rowell, L. (1986). *Human circulation: Regulation during physical stress.* New York: Oxford.

Royce, W. S., & Weiss, R. L. (1975). Behavioral cues in the judgment of marital satisfaction: A linear regression analysis. *Journal of Consulting and Clinical Psychology, 43,* 816–824.

Rubin, L. B. (1976). *Worlds of pain.* New York: Basic Books.

Rudd, N. & McKenry, P. (1986). Family influences on the job satisfaction of employed mothers. *Psychology of Women Quarterly, 10,* 363–372.

Russell, G., & Radin, N. (1983). Increased paternal participation: The father's perspective. In M. E. Lamb & A. Sagi (Eds.). *Fatherhood and family policy.* Hillsdale, NJ: Lawrence Erlbaum Associates.

Rutter, M. (1971). Parent-child separation: Psychological effects on the children. *Journal of Child Psychology and Psychiatry, 12,* 233–260.

Rutter, M., Yule, B., Quinton, D., Rowlands, O., Yule, W., & Berger, M. (1974). Attainment and adjustment in two geographic areas: Some factors accounting for area differences. *British Journal of Psychiatry, 126,* 520–533.

Sackett, G. P. (1974). Sex differences in Rhesus monkeys following varied rearing experiences. In R. C. Friedman, R. M. Richart, R. L. Vande Wiele, & L. O. Stern (Eds.), *Sex differences in behavior.* New York: Wiley.

Sanders, J. D., Smith, T. W., & Alexander, J. F. (1991). Type A behavior and marital interaction: Hostile-dominant responses during conflict. *Journal of Behavioral Medicine, 14,* 567–580.

Sapolsky, B. S., Stocking, S. H., & Zillmann, D. (1977). Immediate vs. delayed retaliation in male and female adults. *Psychological Reports, 40,* 197–198.

Satir, V. (1964). *Conjoint family therapy.* Palo Alto: Science and Behavior Books.

Saunders, P. T. (1990). *An introduction to catastrophe theory.* New York: Cambridge University Press.

Schaap, C. (1982). *Communication and adjustment in marriage.* The Netherlands: Swets and Feitlinger.

Schaap, C. (1984). A comparison of the interaction of distressed and nondistressed married couples in a laboratory situation: Literature survey, methodological issues, and an empirical investigation. In K. Hahlweg & N. S. Jacobson (Eds.), *Marital interaction: Analysis and modification* (pp. 133–158). New York: Guilford.

Schaap, C., Buunk, B., & Kerkstra, A. (1988). Marital conflict resolution. In P. Noller & M. A. Fitzpatrick (Eds.), *Perspectives on marital interaction* (pp. 203–244). Philadelphia, PA: Multilingual Matters.

Schachter, S., & Singer, J. E. (1962). Cognitive, social and physiological determinants of emotional state. *Psychological Review, 69,* 379–399.

Schaninger, C. M., & Buss, W. C. (1986). A longitudinal comparison of consumption and finance handling between happily married and divorced couples. *Journal of Marriage and the Family, 48,* 129–136.

Scherer, K., & Ekman, P. (Eds.). (1982). *Handbook of research on nonverbal behavior.* New York: Cambridge University Press.

Scheurink, A. J. W. (1989). *Central nervous control of metabolism.* Groningen: Rijksuniversiteit.

Schmoldt, R. A., Pope, C. R., & Hibbard, J. H. (1989). Marital interaction and the health and well being of spouses. *Women & Health, 15,* 35–56.

Schneider, W., & Schiffrin, R. M. (1977). Controlled and automatic human information processing; I Detection, search and attention. *Psychological Review, 84,* 1–66.

Schwartz, G. E., Weinberger, D. A., & Singer, J. A. (1981). Cardiovascular differentiation of happiness, sadness, anger, and fear following imagery and exercise. *Psychosomatic Medicine, 43,* 343–364.

Schumm, W. R., & Bugaighis, M. A. (1985). Marital quality and marital stability: Resolving a controversy. *Journal of Divorce, 9,* 73–77.

Segraves, R. T. (1990). Theoretical orientations in the treatment of marital discord. In F. D. Fincham & T. N. Bradbury (Eds.), *The psychology of marriage* (pp. 281–298). New York: Guilford.

Sears, R. R. (1977). Sources of life satisfaction of the Terman gifted men. *Journal of Personality, 39* 1135–1148.

Selye, H. (1956). *The stress of life.* New York: McGraw Hill.

Serbin, L. A., Sprafkin, C., Elman, M., & Doyle, A. (1984). The early development of sex differentiated patterns of social influence. *Canadian Journal of Social Science, 14,* 350–363.

Shannon, C. E., & Weaver, W. (1949). *The mathematical theory of communication.* Champaign, IL: University of Illinois Press.

Shaw, D. S., & Emery, R. E. (1987). Parental conflict and other correlates of the adjustment of school-age children whose parents have separated. *Journal of Abnormal Child Psychology, 15,* 269–281.

Shennum, W. A., & Bugental, D. B. (1982). The development of control over affective expressions in nonverbal behavior. In R. S. Feldman (Ed.) *Development of nonverbal behavior in children.* New York: Springer-Verlag.

Shortt, J. W., Bush, L. K., McCabe, J. L. R., Gottman, J. M., & Katz, L. F. (in press). Children's physiological responses while producing facial expressions of emotions. *Merrill-Palmer Quarterly.*

Sillars, A., Pike, G. R., Jones, T. S., & Redman, K. (1983). Communication and conflict in marriage: One style is not satisfying to all. In R. Bostrom (Ed.), *Communication yearbook 7* (pp. 414–431). Beverly Hills, CA: Sage.

Smith, T. W., & Allred, K. D. (1989). Blood-pressure responses during social interaction in high and low cynically hostile males. *Journal of Behavioral Medicine, 12,* 135–143.

Smith, T. W., Allred, K. D., Morrison, C. A., & Carlson, S. D. (1989). Cardiovascular reactivity and interpersonal influence: Active coping in a social context. *Journal of Personality and Social Psychology, 56,* 209–218.

Smith, T. W., & Brown, P. C. (1991). Cynical hostility, attempts to exert social control, and cardiovascular reactivity in married couples. *Journal of Behavioral Medicine, 14,* 581–592.

Smolen, R. C., Spiegel, D. A., & Martin, C. J. (1986). Patterns of marital interaction associated with marital dissatisfaction and depression. *Journal of Behavior Therapy and Experimental Psychiatry, 17,* 261–266.

Sokolov, E. N. (1963). *Perception and the conditioned reflex.* Oxford: Pergamon Press.

Soskin, W. F., & John, V. P. (1963). The study of spontaneous talk. In R. G. Baker (Eds.), *The stream of behavior: Explorations of its structure and content.* New York: Appleton-Century-Crofts.

Spanier, G. B. (1976). A new measure for assessing the quality of marriage and similar dyads. *Journal of Marriage and the Family, 38,* 15–28.

Spanier, G. B., & Margolis, R. L. (1983). Marital separation and extramarital sexual behavior. *Journal of Sexual Behavior, 19,* 23–48.

Staines, G. & Libby, P. (1986). Men and women in role relationships. In R. Ashmore & F. DelBocca (Eds.), *The social psychology of female-male relationships: A critical analysis of central concepts.* New York: Academic Press.

Stellar, J. R., & Stellar, E. (1985). *The neurobiology of motivation and reward.* New York: Springer-Verlag.

Sutton-Smith, B. (1979). *Play and learning.* New York: Gardner Press.

Taggart, P., & Carruthers, M. (1971) Endogenous hyperlipidaemia induced by emotional stress of racing driving. *Lancet, 1,* 363–366.

Terkel, S. (1980). *American dreams lost and found.* New York: Ballantine Books.

Terman, L. M., Buttenweiser, P., Ferguson, L. W., Johnson, W. B., & Wison, D. P. (1938). *Psychological factors in marital happiness.* New York: McGraw-Hill.

Terman, L. M., & Oden, M. H. (1947). *The gifted child grows up: Twenty five-year followup of a superior group.* Stanford, CA: Stanford University Press.

Terman, L. M., & Wallin, P. (1949). The validity of marriage prediction and marital adjustment tests. *American Sociological Review, 14,* 497–504.

Thayer, R.E. (1989). *The biopsychology of mood and arousal.* New York: Oxford University Press.

Thibaut, J. W., & Kelley, H. H. (1959). *The social psychology of groups.* New York: Wiley.

Ting-Toomey, S. (1983). An analysis of communication patterns in high and low marital adjustment groups. *Human Communication Research, 9,* 306–319.

Thompson, J. G. (1988). *The psychobiology of emotions.* New York: Plenum Press.

Thorne, B. (1986). Girls and boys together . . . But mostly apart: Gender arrangements in elementary schools. In W. W. Hartup & Z. Rubin (Eds.), *Relationships and development* (pp. 167–184). Hillsdale, NJ: Lawrence Erlbaum Associates.

Thornes, B., & Collard, J. (1979). *Who divorce?* London: Routledge & Kegan Paul.

Treggiari, S. (1990). Divorce Roman style: How easy and how frequent was it? In B. Rawson (Ed.), *Marriage, divorce and children in ancient Rome* (pp. 31–46). Oxford, England: Clarendon Press.

Trent, K., & South, S. J. (1989). Structural determinants of the divorce rate: A cross-sectional analysis. *Journal of Marriage and the Family, 51,* 391–404.

Triesman, A. M., & Gelade, G. (1980). A feature-integration theory of attention. *Cognitive Psychology, 12,* 97–136.

Valtysson, G., Vinik, A. I., Glaser, B., Zohglin, G. N. & Floyd, J.C., Jr. (1983). Sex difference in the sensitivity of the human pancreatic polypeptide cell to autonomic nervous stimulation in man. *Journal of Clinical Endocrinological Metabolism, 56,* 21–25.

van Doornen, L. J. P. (1985, October). *Sex differences in physiological reactions to real-life stress and their relationship to psychological variables.* Paper presented at the 25th annual meeting of the Society for Psychophysiological, Research, Houston, TX.

Van Dyke, C., & Kaufman, I. C. (1983). Psychobiology of bereavement, In L. Temoshok, C. van Dyke, & L. S. Zegans (Eds.), *Emotions in health and illness: Theoretical and research foundations.* New York: Grune & Stratton.

Vanfossen, B. (1981). Sex differences in the mental health effects of spouse support and equity. *Journal of Health and Social Behavior, 22,* 130–143.

Van Olst, E. H., & ten Kortenaar, T. (1978). Sex differences in autonomic activity during information processing. *Psychophysiology, 15,* 276.

Vaughn, D. (1990). *Uncoupling: Turning points in intimate relationships.* New York:

Vintage (Random House).

Verbrugge, L. M. (1985). Gender and health: An update on hypothses and evidence. *Journal of Health and Social Behavior, 26,* 156–182.

Verbrugge, L. M. (1989). The twain meet: Empirical explanations of sex differences in health and mortality, *Journal of Health and Social Behavior, 30,* 282–304.

Vincent, J. D. (1990). *The biology of emotions.* Cambridge, MA: Basil-Blackwell.

Vincent, J. P., Friedman, L. C., Nugent, J., & Messerly, L. (1979). Demand characteristics in observations of marital interaction. *Journal of Consulting and Clinical Psychology,* 557–566.

Vincent, J. P., & Friedman, L. C. (1979). Demand characteristics in observations of marital interaction. *Journal of Consulting and Clinical Psychology, 47,* 557–566.

Vincent, J. P., Weiss, R. L., & Birchler, G. R. (1975). A behavioral analysis of problem-solving in distressed and nondistressed married and stranger dyads. *Behavior Therapy, 6,* 475–489.

von Frisch, K. (1953). *The dancing bees: An account of the life and senses of the honey bee.* New York: Harcourt, Brace & World.

Wagner, H. L. (1988). *Social psychophysiology and emotion: theory and clinical applications.* Chichester, England: Wiley.

Waid, W. M. (1984). *Sociophysiology.* New York: Springer-Verlag.

Wallerstein, J. S. & Kelly, J. B. (1975). The effects of parental divorce: The experience of the preschool child. *Journal of the American Academy of Child Psychiatry, 14,* 600–616.

Watzlawick, P., Beavin, J. H., & Jackson, D. D. (1967). *Pragmatics of human communication: A study of interactional patterns, pathologies, and paradoxes.* New York: W. W. Norton.

Weinberger, D. A., Schwartz, G. E., & Davidson, R. J. (1979). Low-anxious, high-anxious, and repressive coping styles: Psychometric patterns and behavioral and physiological responses to stress. *Journal of Abnormal Psychology, 88,* 369–380.

Weiss, R. (1987). Men and their wives' work. In F. J. Crosby (Ed.), *Spouse, parent, worker: On gender and multiple roles.* New Haven, CT: Yale University Press.

Weiss, R., & Patterson, G. R. (1974). A behavioral analysis of the determinants of marital satisfaction. *Journal of Consulting and Clinical Psychology, 42,* 802–811.

Weiss, R. L. (1973). *Loneliness: The experience of emotional and social isolation.* Cambridge, MA: MIT press.

Weiss, R. L. (1978). The conceptualization of marriage from a behavioral perspective. In T. J. Paolino Jr. & B. S. McCrady (Eds.), *Marriage and marital therapy: Psychoanalytic, behavioral and systems theory perspectives.* New York: Brunner/Mazel.

Weiss, R. L. (1980). Strategic behavioral and marital therapy: Toward a model for assessment and intervention. In J. P. Vincent (Ed.), *Advances in family intervention, assessment and theory* (Vol. 1, pp. 229–271). Greenwich, CT: JAI Press.

Weiss, R. L., & Cerreto, M. C. (1980). Development of a measure of dissolution potential. *American Journal of Family Therapy, 8,* 80–85.

Weiss, R. L., & Heyman, R. E. (1990). Observation of marital interaction. In F. D. Fincham & T. N. Bradbury (Eds.), *The psychology of marriage* (pp. 87–117). New York: Guilford.

Weiss, R. L., Hops, H., & Patterson, G. R. (1973). A framework for conceptualizing marital conflict, a technique for altering it, some data for evaluating it. In L. A. Hammerlynck, L. C. Handy, & E. J. Mash (Eds.), *Behavior change*. Champaign, IL: Research Press.

Weiss, R. L., & Summers, K. J. (1983). Marital interaction coding system III. In E. E. Filsinger (Ed.), *Marriage and family assessment*. Beverly Hills, CA: Sage.

White, L. K. (1990). Determinants of divorce: A review of research in the Eighties. *Journal of Marriage and the Family, 52,* 904–912.

Whitehead, L. (1979). Sex differences in children's responses to family stress. *Journal of Child Psychology and Psychiatry, 20,* 247–254.

Wiggins, J. S. (1973). *Personality and prediction.* Reading, MA: Addison-Wesley.

Williams, E., & Gottman, J. (1981). *A user's guide to the Gottman–Williams time-series programs for social scientists.* New York: Cambridge University Press.

Wills, T. A., Weiss, R., & Patterson, G. R. (1974). A behavioral analysis of the determinants of marital satisfaction. *Journal of Consulting and Clinical Psychology, 42,* 802–811.

Williams, E., & Gottman, J. (1981). *A user's guide to the Gottman-Williams time-series programs for social scientists.* New York: Cambridge University Press.

Wilson, B., Katz, L. F., & Gottman, J. (1993). *Vagal tone and facial expressiveness in preschool children.* Unpublished manuscript, University of Washington, Seattle, WA.

Wong, A. K., & Kuo, E. C. Y. (1983). *Divorce in Singapore.* Singapore: Graham Brash (Pte) Ltd.

Woodman, D. D., Hinton, J. W., & O'Niell, M. T. (1978). Plasma catecholamines, stress and aggression in maximum security patients, *Biological Psychology, 6,* 147–154.

Woods, N. (1985). Employment, family roles, and mental ill health in young married women. *Nursing Research, 34,* 4–10.

Yang, B., & Lester, D. (1991). Correlates of staewide divorce rates. *Journal of Divorce and Remarriage, 15,* 219–223.

Yerkes, R. M., & Dodson, J. D. (1908). The relation of strength of stimulus intensity to rapidity of habit-formation. *Journal Comparative Neurological Psychology, 18,* 459–482.

Yogev, S. (1986). Relationships between stress and marital satisfaction among dual-earner couples, *Women and Therapy, 5,* 313–330.

Zajonc, R. B. (1980). Feeling and thinking: Preferences need no inferences. *American Psychologist, 35,* 151–175.

Zillmann, D. (1979). *Hostility and aggression.* Hillsdale, NJ: Lawrence Erlbaum Associates.

Author Index

Subject Index